Stedman's
ABBREV.

ABBREVIATIONS,
ACRONYMS & SYMBOLS

SECOND EDITION

D1052100

Stedman's

ABBREV.

ABBREVIATIONS,
ACRONYMS & SYMBOLS

SECOND EDITION

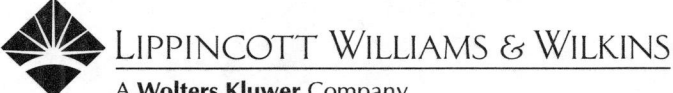

LIPPINCOTT WILLIAMS & WILKINS
A **Wolters Kluwer** Company
Philadelphia • Baltimore • New York • London
Buenos Aires • Hong Kong • Sydney • Tokyo

Series Editor: Maureen Barlow Pugh
Associate Managing Editor: Beverly J. Wolpert
Production Coordinator: Joan D. Scullin
Typesetter: Peirce Graphic Services, Inc.
Printer & Binder: Vicks Lithograph & Printing

First Edition, 1992

Library of Congress Cataloging-in-Publication Data

Stedman's abbreviations, acronyms & symbols. — 2nd ed.
   p. cm.
Rev. ed. of: Stedman's abbrev. c1992.
ISBN 0-683-40459-8
   1. Medicine—Abbreviations. 2. Medicine—Acronyms—Dictionaries.
I. Lippincott Williams & Wilkins. II. Stedman's abbrev. III. Title:
Stedman's abbreviations, acronyms, and symbols IV. Title:
Abbreviations, acronyms, & symbols
  R123 .S69 1999
  610'.148—dc21

          98-31525
          CIP

Contents

Acknowledgments

An important part of our editorial process is the involvement of medical transcriptionists—as advisors, reviewers and/or editors.

Special thanks are due Martha Richards, RRA, for reviewing and proofreading the first edition of *Stedman's Abbreviations, Acronyms & Symbols* (and for doing the necessary research involved with that large task) and to Barbara Werner for updating the appendix symbols sections.

We also extend special thanks to Jeanne Bock, MT, and Sandy Kovacs, CMT, who edited the new abbreviations and expansions added to *Stedman's Abbreviations, Acronyms & Symbols, Second Edition,* as well as reviewing all of the material retained from the first edition. They helped resolve many difficult content and format questions.

Barb Ferretti played an integral role in the process by reviewing the content files for format, updating the database, and providing a final quality check.

As with all our *Stedman's* word references, this resource incorporates the suggestions and expertise of our many contacts in the medical transcriptionist community. Thanks to all our advisory board participants, reviewers, and editors; AAMT meeting attendees; and others who have written us with requests and comments—keep talking, and we'll keep listening.

Publisher's Preface

Stedman's Abbreviations, Acronyms & Symbols, Second Edition offers an authoritative assurance of quality and exactness to the wordsmiths of the healthcare professions—medical transcriptionists, medical editors and copy editors, health information management personnel, court reporters, and the many other users and producers of medical documentation.

Recently, we have received requests for updates to *Stedman's Abbreviations, Acronyms & Symbols, Second Edition*. As the requests continued, we realized that medical language professionals needed a current reference for these dynamic expressions.

This new second edition is a valuable resource for anyone involved in transcribing, recording, copyediting, or reading records, reports, and other documents generated by healthcare professionals. *Stedman's Abbreviations, Acronyms & Symbols, Second Edition*, a compilation of about 70,000 clinically relevant abbreviations, acronyms, and symbols, is the product of expanded, ongoing reviews of medical and allied health professional literature since the publication of the first edition in 1992, including dictionaries, style manuals, "approved lists" from teaching hospitals, nomenclatures, glossaries, and other compendia.

A major focus of this effort, from design specifications to construction of individual entries, involved presenting sought-after information in a format that would facilitate efficient locating, easy reading, and quick comprehension. Novices as well as seasoned professionals are encouraged to read the following descriptions of this reference's organization, format, and style to make the most of its features.

The creation of new abbreviations and usage changes outpace compilation of them. We at Lippincott Williams & Wilkins strive to provide you with the most up-to-date and accurate references available. Your use of this book will prompt new editions, which we will publish as often as new abbreviations and revisions justify. We welcome your suggestions for improvements, changes, corrections, and additions—whatever will make this Stedman's product more useful to you. Please complete the postpaid card at the back of this book, and send your recommendations care of "Stedman's" at Lippincott Williams & Wilkins.

Explanatory Notes

To keep this book within manageable proportions, we had to make some difficult decisions to restrict or exclude certain categories of abbreviations not directly related to the practice of healthcare professionals. Among these categories are professional, specialty, and honorary associations; undergraduate, honorary, and noncertification or nonlicensure degrees; titles of publications; chemical formulas and expressions; and ad hoc coinages.

From institution to institution and from specialty to specialty, an abbreviation and its meaning often vary. "Official" abbreviations issued by nomenclatural groups often are slow to become universally accepted. For these reasons, preferred forms or usages have not been cited. Instead, any variants of form and/or usage are given at each of the variant entries.

Alphabetical Organization

Entries are alphabetized by letter as written or spoken, in the following order: capital letters precede lowercase letters, italics follow nonitalics, and arabic numbers precede roman numerals. Numbers, diacritics, punctuation, spaces, etc. are not considered in alphabetization except when they are the only difference between entries having the same letters. For example:

A	A250
Å	a
A_1	$\bar{a}$
A_2	a
Al	(a)

In some instances, the alphabetical order is arbitrary out of necessity, but such listings are brief and consistent throughout the vocabulary. For example:

AA	A–a
$\overline{AA}$	a–A
A–A	a/A
A/A	aa
A&A	$\overline{aa}$

Entries beginning with a Greek letter are located where the name of the letter would be found alphabetically; thus, A and α are located at "alpha," B and β at "beta," Γ and γ at "gamma." A table of the Greek alphabet follows this section and precedes the beginning of the "A" section.

Greek characters precede Roman characters (α precedes a). Uppercase characters precede lowercase characters (DER precedes DeR, which precedes der). Entries in regular typeface precede those in a different typeface, such as italic or small capitals. Entries with no superscripts or subscripts precede those that do include superscripts or subscripts. Entries with superscripts or subscripts are ordered according to the type of information presented; symbols precede numbers, numbers precede Greek characters, Greek characters precede uppercase letters, and uppercase letters precede lowercase letters, as follows:

Type of information	Example
Symbol	A^+
Number	A^{12}
Greek character	A^α
Uppercase letter	A^A
Lowercase letter	A^a

A superscript of one type precedes a subscript of the same type (A^+ precedes A_+). Entries without punctuation precede those with punctuation (NA precedes N.A.). Entries with all standard alphabetical characters precede those without (A precedes Å).

Special symbols, composed of characters other than letters, cannot be logically alphabetized. Following the "Z" section, the Appendix to this edition includes symbol listings. In a format similar to that of the A-Z abbreviations, these expressions are organized according to similarities of form and construction.

Format and Style

Each entry consists of a boldface abbreviation, acronym, or symbol and its "expansions" or meaning(s) in lightface. When there is more than one expansion, each is indented on a separate line as a subentry under the main entry and listed in alphabetical order. Expansions that "run over" to the next line appear with extra indenting. Bracketed derivations and parenthetical explanatory material or not considered in the alphabetization of expansions.

"*Also*" highlights variant forms of an abbreviation that have the same meaning. For example:

> **CaCC**
> cathodal closure contraction *also* CCC
>
> **CCC**
> cathodal closure contraction *also* CaCC

Periods are used in abbreviations only when parts of the abbreviations could be confused with a word. For example:

add.　　　　　　**addict.**　　　　　　**all.**

Brackets contain derivations of abbreviations originating from a foreign word (etymologies). Each derivation consists of the abbreviation of the originating language (L., Latin; G., Greek; Ger., German; Fr., French; Sp., Spanish; It., Italian) and the foreign word in italics. A derivation immediately follows the expansion of the abbreviation to which it pertains. For example:

> **bid**
> twice a day [L. *bis in die*]
>
> **ad**
> add [L. *adde*]
> axiodistal
> let there be added
> [l. *addetur*] *also* add.
> right ear [L. *aurix dextra*] *also* AD

As shown below, parentheses enclose explanatory material to complete an abbreviated term or phrase:

> **A**
> absolute (temperature)
> (start of) anesthesia

To clarify usage that otherwise might be ambiguous:

> **BEPTI**
> bionomics, environment, *Plasmodium,* treatment, and
> immunity (malaria epidemiology)

xiii

To provide a minidefinition:

Gy
> gray (unit of absorbed dose of ionizing radiation)

Or to identify the generic name of a drug:

CAM
> cyclophosphamide, Adriamycin (doxorubicin), and methotrexate

Greek Alphabet

Name of Greek Letters	Small	Capital	English Transcription
alpha	α	A	A
beta	β	B	B
chi	χ	X	CH
delta	δ	Δ	D
epsilon	ε	E	E
eta	η	H	$\bar{\text{E}}$
gamma	γ	Γ	G
iota	ι	I	I
kappa	κ	K	K, C (Latin)
lambda	λ	Λ	L
mu	μ	M	M
nu	ν	N	N
omega	ω	Ω	$\bar{\text{O}}$
omicron	o	O	O
phi	φ	Φ	PH
pi	π	Π	P
psi	ψ	Ψ	PS
rho	ρ	P	R, RH
sigma	σ	Σ	S
tau	τ	T	T
theta	θ	Θ	TH
upsilon	υ	Y	Y
xi	ξ	Ξ	X
zeta	ζ	Z	Z

Small or lowercase Greek letters are used primarily as symbols. Those used as symbols, along with their meanings, will be found at the alphabetical locations of their spelled-out forms. For example:

A or α at **alpha**   B or β at **beta**   Γ or γ at **gamma**

Greek Alphabet

A

abnormal *also* AB, ABN, Abn, abn, abnor, abnorm
abortion *also* AB, Ab, ab, Abor, ABO
abortus
absolute temperature *also* T
absorbance *also* abs
acceptor
accommodation *also* a, ACC, Acc, acc, accom
acetone
acetum (vinegar)
acid *also* a, AC
acidophil
acidophilic
acromion
actin
activity (radiation)
adenine *also* Ade
adenoma
adenosine
adrenalin (e)
adult
aesthetic
age
akinetic
alanine *also* Ala
albumin (5%, followed by amount in mL) *also* AL, ALB, Alb, alb
alive
allergologist
allergy *also* Al, alg, ALL, all.
alpha (cell) alternate
alpha (first letter of Greek alphabet), uppercase
alveolar
alveolar gas (subscript)
ambulatory *also* AM, AMB, amb, ambul
ampere *also* a
amphetamine
ampicillin *also* AM, AMP
amyloid
anaphylaxis
androsterone
anesthesia *also* AN, ANA, anes, anesth
angioplasty
angle *also* ang
angstrom
Ångström unit *also* Å
anisotropic (band in striated muscle)

annum (Lat.) year
anode *also* a, AN, An
ante (Lat.) before
anterior *also* a, AN, ANT, ant.
antrectomy
apex
apical
apices
aqueous
area *also* a, S
argon
artery [L. *arteria*] *also* a, ART, art.
assessment
asymmetric *also* a, AS
atomic weight
atrium *also* At
atropine *also* ATRO
auricle
auris
auscultation
axial *also* a, ax.
axilla
axillary (temperature) *also* (a)
blood group in the ABO system
ear [L. *auris*]
Helmholtz energy
mass number
(start of) anesthesia
(start of) anesthetic
subspinale (point A. in cephalometrics)
total acidity *also* a
water [L. *aqua*] *also* a, aq.
year [L. *annum*]

AI–III
angiotensin I
angiotensin II
angiotensin III

A250
5% albumin, 250 mL

A1000
5% albumin, 1000 mL

Å
angstrom
Ångström unit *also* A
antinuclear antibody *also* $\overline{A}$, ANA, ANuA
cumulated activity

A.
Actinomyces
Anopheles

A_1
  aortic first sound
  first auditory area

A_2
  aortic second sound
  second auditory area

A_n
  normal atmosphere

$\overline{A}$
  antinuclear antibody *also* Å, ANA,
   ANuA

(a)
  axillary temperature *also* A

a
  absorptivity
  acceleration *also* α, Acc, acc, accel
  accommodation *also* A, ACC, acc,
   accom
  acid *also* A, AC
  acidity *also* AC
  agar
  alpha (first letter of Greek alphabet)
  ampere *also* A
  angular acceleration
  annum
  anode *also* A, AN, An
  anterior *also* A, AN, ANT, ant.
  area *also* A, S
  arterial blood (subscript)
  asymmetric *also* A, AS
  atto-
  auris *also* aur
  axial *also* A, ax.
  thermodynamic activity
  total acidity *also* A

ā
  before [L. *ante*] *also* a.

a.
  artery [L. *arteria*] *also* A, ART, art.
  before [L. *ante*] *also* ā
  water [L. *aqua*] *also* A, aq.

A-A
  atlantoaxial *also* AA

AA
  acetic acid
  active alcoholic
  active-assistive (range of motion) *also*
   AAROM
  active avoidance
  acupuncture analgesia
  acute asthma
  Addicts Anonymous
  adenine arabinoside
  adenylic acid
  adjuvant arthritis
  adrenal androgen
  adrenocortical autoantibody
  aggregated albumin
  agranulocytic angina
  alcohol abuse
  Alcoholics Anonymous
  allergic alveolitis
  alopecia areata
  alveolar-arterial (gradient) *also* A-a
  aminoacetone
  amino acid
  aminoacyl
  amyloid A
  amyloid-associated
  anaplastic astrocytoma
  anesthesiologist's assistant
  antiarrhythmic agent
  anticipatory avoidance
  antigen aerosol
  aortic amplitude
  aortic aneurysm
  aortic arch
  aplastic anemia
  arabinosylcytosine (cytarabine) and
   Adriamycin (doxorubicin)
  arachidonic acid
  arm-ankle (pulse ratio)
  arteries [L. *arteriae*] *also* aa.
  ascaris antigen
  ascending aorta *also* Asc-A
  atlantoaxial *also* A-A
  atomic absorption
  audiologic assessment
  Australia antigen *also* AU, Au Ag
  autoanalyzer
  axonal arborization
  (so much of) each [G. *ana*] *also*
   $\overline{\text{AA}}$, āā, aa., ana

A&A
  aid and attendance
  arthroscopy and arthrotomy
  awake and aware

A/A
  automobile accident

$\overline{\text{AA}}$
  (so much of) each [G. *ana*] *also*
   AA, āā, aa., ana

A-a
  alveolar-arterial (gradient) *also* AA
  aortic artery

aA
abampere
arterial to alveolar [oxygen ratio]
azure A

a/A
arterial to alveolar (oxygen ratio)

aa.
arteries [L. *arteriae*] *also* AA
(so much of) each [G. *ana*] *also*
AA, $\overline{AA}$, $\overline{aa}$, ana

$\overline{aa}$ *also* AA, aa., ana
(so much of) each [G. *ana*] *also*
AA, $\overline{AA}$, aa., ana

AAA
abdominal aortic aneurysm
abdominal aortic aneurysmectomy
acquired aplastic anemia
acute anxiety attack
addiction, autoimmune diseases, and
aging
amalgam *also* aaa
androgenic anabolic
aneurysm of ascending aorta
aromatic amino acid

aaa
amalgam *also* AAA

AAAAA
aphasia, agnosia, apraxia, agraphia,
and alexia

AAAD
aromatic amino acid decarboxylase

AAAE
amino acid-activating enzymes

AAAF
albumin autoagglutinating factor

AA-AMP
amino acid adenylate
(adenomonophosphate)

AAB
action against burns
aminoazobenzene

AABB
American Association of Blood
Banks

AABCC
alertness (consciousness), airway,
breathing, circulation, and cervical
spine

AAC
antibiotic-associated colitis
antimicrobial agent-induced colitis
antimicrobial agents and chemotherapy

AACA
acylaminocephalosporanic acid

AACE
antigen-antibody crossed
electrophoresis

AACG
acute angle-closure glaucoma

AACSH
adrenal androgen corticotropic
stimulating hormone

AAD
acid-ash diet
acute agitated delirium
alloxazine adenine dinucleotide
$alpha_2$-antitrypsin deficiency
antibiotic-associated diarrhea
α-1-antitrypsin deficiency
aromatic acid decarboxylase

$(A\text{-}a)D_{N2}$
difference in nitrogen tension
between mixed alveolar gas and
mixed arterial blood

$(A\text{-}a)D_{O2}$
difference in partial pressures of
oxygen in mixed alveolar gas and
mixed arterial blood

AADC
amino acid decarboxylase

AAdC
anterior adductor of the coxa

AADP
amyloid A-degrading protease

AAE
active assistive exercise *also* A/AEX
acute allergic encephalitis
annuloaortic ectasia

NOTES

AAECS
amino acid-enriched cardioplegic solution

A/AEX
active assistive exercise *also* AAE

AAF
acetic acid-alcohol-formalin (fixative)
acetylaminofluorene
ascorbic acid factor

AAG
α_1-acid glycoprotein *also* AGP
allergic angiitis and granulomatosis
alveolar-arterial gradient
autoantigen

AaG
alveolar arterial gradient

AAGS
adult adrenogenital syndrome

A:AGT
antiglobulin test

AAH
acute alcoholic hepatitis

AAI
acute alveolar injury
arm-ankle indices
atrial inhibited (pacemaker)

AAIA
acquired artery immune augmentation

AAIB
α_1-aminoisobutyrate

AAIN
acute allergic intestinal nephritis

AAK
allo-activated killer

AAL
anterior axillary line

AAM
acute aseptic meningitis
amino acid mixture

AAME
acetylarginine methyl ester

AAMRS
automated ambulatory medical record system

AAMS
acute aseptic meningitis syndrome

AAMT
American Association for Medical Transcription

AAN
AIDS-associated nephropathy
AIDS-associated neutropenia
amino acid nitrogen
α-amino nitrogen
analgesic abuse nephropathy
analgesic-associated nephropathy
attending's admission notes

AAO
amino acid oxidase
awake, alert and oriented

(A-a)O₂
$(A-a)O_2$
alveolar-arterial oxygen gradient

AAOC
antacid of choice

AAOx3
alert, awake, and oriented to time, place, and person

AAP
air at atmospheric pressure
α_1-anti-protease
assessment adjustment pass

A-aP$_{CO2}$
alveolar-arterial carbon dioxide difference

AAPC *also* AAPMC
antibiotic-associated pseudomembranous colitis

AAPF
anti-arteriosclerosis polysaccharide factor

AAPMC *also* AAPC
antibiotic-associated pseudomembranous colitis

AAPSA
age-adjusted prostate-specific antigen

AAR
active avoidance reaction
acute articular rheumatism
antigen-antiglobulin reaction
Australia antigen radioimmunoassay

AAROM
active-assistive range of motion *also* AA

AAS
acid aspiration syndrome
acute abdominal series

A

alcoholic abstinence syndrome
androgenic-anabolic steroid
aneurysm of atrial septum
anthrax antiserum
aortic arch syndrome
atlantoaxial subluxation
atomic absorption spectrophotometry
atypical absence seizure

AASCRN
amino acid screen

Aase
asparaginase *also* ASP, Asp, L-Spar

aa seq
amino acid sequence

AASH
adrenal androgen-stimulating hormone

AASP
acute atrophic spinal paralysis
ascending aorta synchronized pulsation

AAT
Aachen aphasia test
academic aptitude test
activity as tolerated
acute abdominal tympany
alanine aminotransferase
alkylating agent therapy
aminoazotoluene
α-1-antitrypsin *also* A1AT
atrial triggered (pacemaker)
atypical antibody titer
auditory apperception test
automatic atrial tachycardia

A1AT
α-1-antitrypsin *also* AAT

AAU
acute anterior uveitis

AAV
adeno-associated vector
adeno-associated virus

AAVV
accumulated alveolar ventilatory
volume

AAW
anterior aortic wall

AB
abdominal
abnormal *also* A, ABN, Abn, abn,
abnor, abnorm
abortion *also* A, Ab, ab, Abor, ABO
Ace bandage
active bilaterally
aid to the blind
air bleed
Alcian blue
antibiotic
antibody *also* Ab, ab
antigen binding
apex beat
apnea-bradycardia
asbestos body
asthmatic bronchitis
axiobuccal *also* ab
blood group in ABO system

3AB
3-aminobenzamide

A>B
air greater than bone (conduction)

A/B
acid-base ratio
apnea and bradycardia *also* A&B

A&B
apnea and bradycardia *also* A/B

Ab
abortion *also* A, AB, ab, Abor,
ABO
antibody *also* AB, ab

aB
azure B

ab
abortion *also* A, AB, Ab, Abor,
ABO
about
antibody *also* AB, Ab
axiobuccal *also* AB

a-b
air-bone

ABA
abscissic acid
allergic bronchopulmonary aspergillosis
antibacterial activity

NOTES

A [band]
the dark-staining zone of a striated
muscle

AbAP
antibody-against-panel

ABB
Albright-Butler-Bloomberg (syndrome)

ABBQ
Acquired Immunodeficiency Syndrome
Beliefs and Behavior

abbr, abbrev
abbreviated
abbreviation

ABC
abbreviated blood count
absolute band count
absolute basophil count
absolute bone conduction
acalculous biliary colic
acid balance control
aconite-belladonna-chloroform
airway, breathing, and circulation
all but code (resuscitation order)
alternative birth center
aneurysmal bone cyst
antigen-binding capacity
apnea, bradycardia, and cyanosis
applesauce, bananas, and cereal (diet)
artificial beta cells
aspiration biopsy cytology
assessment of basic competency
avidin-biotin complex
axiobuccocervical

A&BC
air and bone conduction

ABC and C&C
airway, breathing, circulation, cervical
spine, and consciousness level

ABCD
amphotericin B colloid dispersion
asymmetry, border, color, and
diameter (of melanoma)

ABCDE
botulism toxin pentavalent

ABCIL
antibody-mediated cell-dependent
immunolympholysis

ABCM
Adriamycin (doxorubicin), bleomycin,
cyclophosphamide, and mitomycin C

ABCX
Adriamycin (doxorubicin), bleomycin,
cisplatin, and radiation therapy

ABD
abdomen
after bronchodilator
aged, blind, and disabled
aggressive behavioral disturbance
average body dose

ABd
(type of) plain gauze dressing

Abd, abd
abdomen *also* abdom
abdominal *also* abdom
abduction *also* abduc
abductor (muscle)

ABDCT
atrial bolus dynamic computer
tomography

Abd hyst
abdominal hysterectomy *also* AH

abdom
abdominal *also* Abd, abd

abd poll
abductor pollicis (muscle)

abduc
abduction *also* Abd

ABDV
Adriamycin (doxorubicin), bleomycin,
vinblastine, and dacarbazine

ABE
acute bacterial endocarditis
adult basic education
botulism equine trivalent antitoxin

ABEP
auditory brainstem-evoked potential

aber
aberrant

ABF
aortobifemoral (bypass)

ABG
air/bone gap
aortoiliac bypass graft
arterial blood gas
axiobuccogingival

abg
addictive behavior group

ABI
ankle-brachial index
atherothrombotic brain infarction

ABID
antibody identification

ABIG
absence of immunoglobulin G

ABK
aphakic bullous keratopathy

ABL
abetalipoproteinemia
African Burkitt lymphoma
Albright-Butler-Lightwood (syndrome)
allograft-bound lymphocyte
angioblastic lymphadenopathy
antigen-binding lymphocyte
axiobuccolingual

ABLB
alternate binaural loudness balance

ABM
adjusted body mass
alveolar basement membrane
artificial basement membrane
autologous bone marrow

ABMA
anti-basement membrane antibody

ABMS
autologous bone marrow support

A/B MS
apnea/bradycardia mild stimulation

ABMT
autologous bone marrow
transplantation

ABN, Abn, abn
abnormal *also* A, AB, abnor, abnorm
abnormality

AbN
antibody nitrogen

ABNC
abnormal curve

ABN F%
abnormal forms percent (sperm
count)

ABNG
AB negative (blood type)

ABNMP
alpha-benzyl-*N*-methyl phenethylamine

abnor, abnorm
abnormal *also* A, AB, ABN, Abn,
abn, ABN

ABO
abortion *also* A, AB, Ab, ab, Abor
absent bed occupancy
blood group system of groups A,
AB, B, and O

ABO-HD
ABO hemolytic disease

Abor
abortion *also* A, AB, Ab, ab, ABO

ABP
Adriamycin (doxorubicin), bleomycin,
and prednisone
ambulatory blood pressure
androgen-binding protein
antigen-binding protein
arterial blood pressure
avidin-biotin peroxidase

ABPA
acute bronchopulmonary asthma
allergic bronchopulmonary aspergillosis

ABPC
antibody-producing cell

ABPE
acute bovine pulmonary edema

ABPM
allergic bronchopulmonary mycosis

ABR
abortus-Bang-ring (test)
absolute bedrest
auditory brainstem response

ABr
agglutination test for brucellosis

Abr
abrasion

Abras, abras
abrasion

NOTES

ABS
abdominal surgery
abnormal brainstem
absent *also* abs
absorbed
absorption *also* Abs, absorb.
Accuchek blood sugar
acrylonitrile-butadiene-styrene
acute brain syndrome
Adaptive Behavior Scale
admitting blood sugar
adult bovine serum
aging brain syndrome
alkylbenzene sulfonate
aloin, belladonna, and strychnine
(laxative)
amniotic band sequence
antibody screen
anti-B serum
Antley-Bixler syndrome
arterial blood supply
at bedside

1:5 ABS
1:5 Absorption-Reiter-Strain
(cerebrospinal fluid test)

Abs
absorption *also* ABS, absorb.

abs
absent *also* ABS
absolute
absorbance *also* A

absc
abscess
abscissa

ABSe
ascending bladder septum

abs. feb.
while fever is absent [L. *absente febre*]

absorb.
absorption *also* ABS, Abs

A/B ss
apnea/bradycardia self-stimulation

abst, abstr
abstract

ABT
aminopyrine breath test

abt
about

ABTX
α-bungarotoxin
alpha-bungarotoxin

ABU
aminobutyrate
asymptomatic bacteriuria

ABV
actinomycin D, bleomycin, and
vincristine
arthropod-borne virus

ABVD
Adriamycin (doxorubicin), bleomycin,
vinblastine, and dacarbazine

ABW
actual body weight

ABx, abx
antibiotics

ABY
acid bismuth yeast (medium)

A-C
adult-versus-child
aortocoronary [bypass]

AC
abdominal circumference
abdominal compression
absorption coefficient
absorptive cell
abuse case
acetate
acetylcholine *also* AcCh, ACH, ACh
acetylcysteine
acid *also* A, a
acidified complement
acidity *also* a
Acinetobacter calcoaceticus
aconitine
acromioclavicular
activated charcoal
acupuncture clinic
acute *also* ac
acute cholecystitis
adenocarcinoma *also* ACA
adenylate cyclase
adherent cell
adrenal cortex
adrenocorticoid
Adriamycin (doxorubicin) and
cyclophosphamide
air chamber
air changes
air conduction
alcoholic cirrhosis

all culture (broth)
alternating current
ambulatory care
ambulatory controls
anchored catheter
anesthesia circuit
angiocellular
anodal closure
ante cibum (Lat.) before meals
antecubital
anterior chamber (of eye) *also* A/C
anterior column
anterior commissure
anterior cruciate
antibiotic concentrate
anticoagulant
anticomplement
antiinflammatory corticoid
antiphlogistic corticoid
aortic closure
aortocoronary
arm circumference
arterial capillary
ascending colon
assist control
atriocarotid
auriculocarotid
axiocervical

A2C
apical two-chamber

5-AC
5-azacytidine

A/C
albumin-coagulin ratio
anterior chamber (of eye) *also* AC
assist/control
assisted control ventilation

Ac
accelerator (globulin)
acetyl *also* ac
actinium

aC
abcoulomb
arabinosylcytosine (cytarabine) *also*
  Ara-C, araC
azure C

a.c.
before meals [L. *ante cibum*]

ac
acetyl *also* Ac
acute *also* AC
antecubital
anterior chamber
assisted control
axiocervical

ACA
abnormal coronary artery
acrodermatitis chronica atrophicans
acute cerebellar ataxia
acyclovir
adenine-cytosine-adenine
adenocarcinoma *also* AC
adenylate cyclase activity
aminocaproic acid
aminocephalosporanic acid
ammonia, copper, and arsenic
amyotrophic choreoacanthocytosis
anomalous coronary artery
anterior cerebral artery
anterior communicating aneurysm
anterior communicating artery
anticanalicular antibody
anticardiolipin antibody
anticentromere antibody
anticollagen autoantibody
anticomplement activity
anticytoplasmic antibody
automatic clinical analyzer

AC/A
accommodation convergence-
  accommodation (ratio)

AcAcOH
acetoacetic acid

ACAD
asymptomatic coronary artery disease

A-CAH
autoimmune chronic active hepatitis

ACAN, ACANTH
acanthrocyte

ACAO
acylcoenzyme A oxidase

ACAT
acylcholesterol acyltransferase
automated computerized axial
  tomography

NOTES

ACB
alveolar-capillary block
antibody-coated bacteria
aortocoronary bypass
arterialized capillary blood
asymptomatic carotid bruit

AC&BC
air conduction and bone conduction

ACBE
air contrast barium enema

ACBG
aortocoronary bypass graft

ACC
acalculous cholecystitits
accident *also* Acc, acc, accid
accommodation *also* A, a, acc, Acc,
 accom
acetylcoenzyme A carboxylase
acinar cell carcinoma
acute care center
adenoid cystic carcinoma *also* Acc
administrative control center
adrenocortical carcinoma
alveolar cell carcinoma
ambulatory care center
amylase creatinine clearance
anodal closure contraction *also* AnCC
antitoxin-containing cell
aplasia cutis congenita
articular chondrocalcinosis
automated cell count

Acc
acceleration *also* a, α, acc, accel
accident *also* ACC, acc, accid
accommodation *also* A, a, ACC, acc,
 accom
adenoid cystic carcinoma *also* ACC

acc
acceleration *also* a, α, Acc, accel
accelerator
accident *also* ACC, Acc, accid
accommodation *also* A, a, ACC,
 Acc, accom
according

accel
acceleration *also* a, α, acc

AcCh
acetylcholine *also* AC, ACH, ACh

AcChR
acetylcholine receptor

AcCHS
acetylcholinesterase *also* AChE

accid
accident *also* ACC, Acc, acc

ACCL, Accl
anodal closure contraction

AcCoA
acetylcoenzyme A *also* acetyl-CoA

accom
accommodation *also* A, a, ACC,
 Acc, acc

ACCR
amylase creatinine clearance ratio

accum
accumulated
accumulation

accur
most carefully

accur.
accurately [L. *accuratissime*]

ACD
absolute cardiac dullness
actinomycin D (dactimomycin)
adult celiac disease
advanced care directive
allergic contact dermatitis
alpha-chain disease
anemia of chronic disease
angiokeratoma corporis diffusum
anterior cervical diskectomy
anterior chamber diameter
anterior chest diameter
anticonvulsant drug *also* AED
area of cardiac disease
area of cardiac dullness
(citric) acid-citrate (trisodium) -
 dextrose (solution)

AcD
alive with disease

AC-DC, ac/dc
alternating current or direct current
bisexual (slang)

ACDF
adult child of dysfunctional family
anterior cervical diskectomy and
 fusion

ACDK
acquired cystic disease of the kidney

ACE
acetonitrile

actinium emanation
acute cerebral encephalopathy
acute coronary event
adrenocortical extract
Adriamycin (doxorubicin),
 cyclophosphamide, and etoposide
aerobic chair exercises
alcohol, chloroform, and ether
 (mixture)
angiotensin-converting enzyme

AICE
 angiotensin I-converting enzyme

ace.
 acentric

ACED
 anhydrotic congenital ectodermal
 dysplasia

ACEDS
 angiotensin-converting enzyme
 dysfunction syndrome

ACEH
 acid cholesterol ester hydrolase

ACEI
 angiotensin-converting enzyme
 inhibitor

AcEst
 acetyl esterase

ACET
 aquatic cardiovascular evaluation and
 testing (system)

acetyl-CoA
 acetylcoenzyme A *also* AcCoA

ACF
 accessory clinical findings
 acute care facility
 advanced communications function
 anterior cervical fusion
 area correction factor

ACFn
 additional cost of false negatives

ACFp
 additional cost of false positives

ACFUCY
 actinomycin D, 5-fluorouracil, and
 cyclophosphamide

ACG
 accelerator globulin (factor V) *also*
 AC-G, AcG, ac-G
 angiocardiogram
 angiocardiography
 aortocoronary graft
 apex cardiogram

AC-G, AcG, ac-G
 accelerator globulin (factor V) *also*
 ACG, AcG

ACH
 acetylcholine *also* AC, AcCh, ACh
 achalasia
 active chronic hepatitis
 adrenocortical hormone
 amyotropic cerebellar hypoplasia
 arm, chest, height
 arm girth, chest depth, and hip
 width (nutritional index)

ACh
 acetylcholine *also* AC, AcCh, ACH

AChA
 anterior choroidal artery

AChE
 acetylcholinesterase *also* AcCHS

ACHOO
 autosomal dominant compelling helio-
 ophthalmic outburst [syndrome]

AChR
 acetylcholine receptor

AChRAb
 acetylcholine receptor antibody

AC&HS
 before meals and at bedtime [L.
 antecibum + *hora somni*]

ACI
 acoustic comfort index
 acute coronary infarction
 acute coronary insufficiency
 adenylate cyclase inhibitor
 adrenocortical insufficiency
 aftercare instructions
 anticlonus index
 average cost of illness

NOTES

ACID
Arithmetic, Coding, Information, and Digit Span

ACIDS
acquired cellular immunodeficiency syndrome

ACIF
anticomplement immunofluorescence

AC IOL
anterior chamber intraocular lens

ACIP
acute canine idiopathic polyneuropathy

ACJ
acromioclavicular joint

ACL
Achievement Check List
acromegaloid features, cutis verticis gyrata, corneal leukoma
anterior cruciate ligament

ACl
aspiryl chloride

aCL
anticardiolipin (antibody)

ACLC
Assessment of Children Language Comprehension

ACLR
anterior cruciate ligament repair

ACLS
advanced cardiac life support

ACM
aclacinomycin (aclarubicin)
acute cerebrospinal meningitis
Adriamycin (doxorubicin), cyclophosphamide, and methotrexate
albumin-calcium-magnesium
alveolar capillary membrane
anticardiac myosin
Arnold-Chiari malformation

ACME
aphakic cystoid macular edema

ACMF
arachnoid cyst of the middle fossa

ACML
atypical chronic myeloid leukemia

ACMP
alveolar-capillary membrane permeability

ACMT
artificial circus movement tachycardia

ACMV
assist-controlled mechanical ventilation

ACN
acute conditioned neurosis

ACO
acute coronary occlusion
alert, cooperative, and oriented

ACOA
adult child of alcoholic

ACoA
anterior communicating artery

ACOAP
Adriamycin (doxorubicin), cyclophosphamide, Oncovin (vincristine), cytosine, arabinoside, and prednisone

A-comm
anterior communicating (artery)

ACOP
Adriamycin (doxorubicin), cyclophosphamide, Oncovin (vincristine), and prednisone

ACOPP
Adriamycin (doxorubicin), cyclophosphamide, Oncovin (vincristine), prednisone, and procarbazine

acous
acoustic
acoustics

ACP
accessory conduction pathway
acid phosphatase *also* AcP, AC-PH, ac phos, AP
acyl carrier protein
anodal closure picture
aspirin-caffeine-phenacetin

AcP
acid phosphatase *also* ACP, AC-PH, ac phos, AP

ACPA
anticytoplasmic antibodies

AC-PH, ac phos
acid phosphatase *also* ACP, AcP, AP

ACPP
adrenocortical polypeptide

ACPP-PF
acid phosphatase prostatic fluid

ACPS
acrocephalopolysyndactyly *also* ACS

acq
acquired
acquisition

ACR
abnormally contracting regions
absolute catabolic rate
acriflavine *also* Acr
adenomatosis of colon and rectum
anterior chamber reformation
anticonstipation regimen
axillary count rate

Acr
acriflavine *also* ACR
acrylic

ACRF
ambulatory care research facility

ACS
acetyl strophanthidin
acrocallosal syndrome
acrocephalosyndactyly *also* ACPS
acute chest syndrome
acute confusional state
acute mountain sickness
ambulatory care services
anodal closure sound
antireticular cytotoxic serum
aperture current setting
arterial cannulation support

ACSL
automatic computerized solvent
litholysis

ACSV
aortocoronary-saphenous vein (graft)

ACSVBG
aortocoronary-saphenous vein bypass
graft

ACT
achievement through counseling and
treatment
actinomycin
activated coagulation time
advanced coronary treatment

allergen challenge test
anterocolic transposition
antichromotrypsin
anticoagulant therapy
antrocolic transposition
anxiety control training
asthma care training
atropine coma therapy
automated computed tomography

act
actinomycin

act.
active
activity *also* activ, α

ACTA
automatic computed transverse axial
(scanning)

ACTC, Act-C
actinomycin C

ACTD, Act-D
actinomycin D (dactinomycin)

ACTe
anodal closure tetanus

Act Ex
active exercise

ACTH
adrenocorticotropic hormone
(corticotropin)

ACTH-RF
adrenocorticotropic hormone-releasing
factor

activ
activity *also* act., α

ACTN
adrenocorticotropin

ACTP
adrenocorticotropic polypeptide

ACTS
acute cervical traumatic sprain or
syndrome
Auditory Comprehension Test for
Sentences

ACTSEB
anterior chamber tube shunt
encircling band

NOTES

13

ACU
acquired cold urticaria
acute care unit
ambulatory care unit

ACUTENS
acupuncture and transcutaneous
electrical nerve stimulation

ACV
acute cardiovascular [disease]
acyclovir
atrial/carotid/ventricular

ACVB
aortocoronary venous bypass

ACVD
acute cardiovascular disease
atherosclerotic cardiovascular disease

ACVRD
arteriosclerotic cardiovascular renal
disease

AC/W
acetone in water

acyl-CoA
acylcoenzyme A

AD
abdominal diameter
accident dispensary
acetate dialysis
achievement drive
active disease
acute dermatomyositis
addict
addiction *also* addict.
adenoid degeneration (agent)
adjuvant disease
admitting diagnosis
adult disease
advanced directive
aerosol deposition
affective disorder
after discharge
alcohol dehydrogenase
Aleutian disease (of mink) *also*
AMD
alveolar duct
Alzheimer dementia
Alzheimer disease
analgesic dose
anodal duration
anterior division
antidepressant
antigenic determinant
appropriate disability

arthritic dose
atopic dermatitis
attentional disturbance
autonomic dysreflexia
autosomal dominant
average day
average deviation
axiodistal
axis deviation

A/D
analog-to-digital (converter)

A&D
admission and discharge
alcohol and drugs
ascending and descending
vitamins A and D

A.D.
right atrium [L. *atrium dextrum*]
right ear [L. *auris dextra*] *also* a.d.

Ad
adenovirus
adipocyte
adrenal
anisotropic disk

a.d.
alternating days (every other day) [L.
alternis dieys]
right ear [L. *auris dextra*] *also* A.D.

ad
adduction *also* ADD, add.
adductor *also* add.
axiodistal

ad.
add [L. *adde*]
let there be added [L. *addetur*] *also*
add.

ADA
adenosine deaminase
anterior descending artery
antideoxyribonucleic acid antibody
approved dietary allowance

ADA #
American Diabetes Association diet
number

ADAM
amniotic deformity, adhesion
mutilation [syndrome]

ADAS
Alzheimer Disease Assessment Scale

ADAS-COG
cognitive portion of the Alzheimer Disease Assessment Scale

ADase
adenosine deaminase

ADAU
adolescent drug abuse unit

ADC
affective disorders clinic
Aid to Dependent Children
AIDS-dementia complex
albumin, dextrose, and catalase (medium)
ambulance design criteria
analog-to-digital converter
anodal duration contraction
antral diverticulum of the colon
anxiety disorder clinic
average daily census
axiodistocervical

AdC
adenylate cyclase
adrenal cortex

ADCC
acute disorder of cerebral circulation
antibody-dependent cell-mediated cytotoxicity

ADCONFU
Adriamycin (doxorubicin), cyclophosphamide, Oncovin (vincristine), and 5-fluorouracil

ADCS
Argonz-del Castillo syndrome

ADD
adduction *also* add., ad
adenosine deaminase
alcohol and drug dependency (unit)
attention deficit disorder
average daily dose

add.
addition
adduction *also* ad, ADD
adductor *also* ad
let there be added [L. *addetur*] *also* ad.

add. c. trit.
add with trituration [L. *adde cum tritu*]

ad def. an.
to the point of fainting [L. *ad defectionem animi*]

ad deliq.
to fainting [L. *ad deliquium*]

addend.
to be added [L. *addendus*]

ADDH, ADD/H, ADD-HA
attention deficit disorder with hyperactivity

addict.
addiction *also* AD
addictive

add poll
adductor pollicis [muscle]

ADDU
alcohol and drug dependence unit

ADE
acute disseminated encephalitis
antibody-dependent enhancement
apparent digestible energy

Ade
adenine *also* A

AdeCbl
adenosyl cobalamin

ADEE
age-dependent epileptic encephalopathy

ad effect.
until effective [L. *ad effectum*]

ADEM
acute disseminated encephalomyelitis
acute disseminating encephalomyelitis

adeq
adequate

ad. feb.
fever being present [L. *adstante febre*]

ADFN
albinism-deafness [syndrome]

NOTES

15

ADFU
agar diffusion for fungus

ADG
atrial diastolic gallop
axiodistogingival

ad gr. acid.
to an agreeable acidity [L. *ad gratum aciditatem*]

ad gr. gust.
to an agreeable taste [L. *ad gratum gustum*]

ADH
adhesion *also* adh
alcohol dehydrogenase
antidiuretic hormone
atypical ductal hyperplasia

adh
adhesion *also* ADH
adhesive

ADHD
attention deficit hyperactivity disorder

adhib.
to be administered [L. *adhibendus*]

ad hoc
temporary
for this (purpose)

ADI
acceptable daily intake
allowable daily intake
antral diverticulum of the ileum
artificial diverticulum of the ileum
atlas-dens interval
autosomal-dominant ichthyosis
axiodistoincisal

ADIC
Adriamycin (doxorubicin) and
dimethyltriazenylimidazole
carboxamide (dacarbazine)

ad int.
meanwhile [L. *ad interium*]

adj
adjacent
adjoining
adjunct
adjuvant

ADK
adenosine kinase

ADKC
atopic dermatitis with
keratoconjunctivitis

ADL
activities of daily living
Amsterdam Depression List

ADLC
antibody-dependent lymphocyte-
mediated cytotoxicity

ad lib.
as desired [L. *ad libitum*]

ADM
abductor digiti minimi [muscle]
administrative medicine
administrator
admission
admit
Adriamycin *also* ADR, ADRIA,
Adria
apparent distribution mass

AdM
adrenal medulla

adm
administration *also* Admin
admission
admove (Lat.) apply

Adm Dr
admitting doctor

ADME
absorption, distribution, metabolism,
and excretion

Admin
administer
administration *also* adm

admov.
let there be applied [L. *admove,
admoveatur*]

Adm Ph
admitting physician

ADMR
average daily metabolic rate

ADMX
adrenal medullectomy

ADN
antideoxyribonuclease *also* ADNase
aortic depressor nerve
Associate Degree in Nursing

adn
adenoid
adenoidectomy

ADNase
antideoxyribonuclease *also* ADN

ad naus.
to the point of producing nausea [L. *ad nauseam*] *also* ad neut.

ADN-B
antideoxyribonuclease B

ad neut.
to neutralization [L. *ad neutralizandum*]
to the point of producing nausea [L. *ad nauseam*] *also* ad naus.

ADO
adolescent medicine
axiodistoocclusal

Ado
adenosine

ADOAP
Adriamycin (doxorubicin), Oncovin (vincristine), arabinosylcytosine, and prednisone

ADOD
arthrodentosteodysplasia

AdoDABA
adenosyl-diaminobutyric acid

ADODM
adult-onset diabetes mellitus

AdoHcy
S-adenosyl-homocysteine

adol
adolescent

AdoMet
S-adenosyl-methionine

Adox
oxidized adenosine

ADP
acute dermatomyositis and polymyositis
adenopathy
adenosine 5'-diphosphate
administrative psychiatry
advanced pancreatitis
ammonium dihydrogen phosphate
approved drug product
area diastolic pressure
arterial demand pacing
automatic data processing

AdP
adductor pollicis

ad part. dolent.
to the painful parts [L. *ad partes dolentes*]

ADPase
adenosine 5'-diphosphatase

ADPKD
autosomal-dominant polycystic kidney disease

ADPL
average daily patient load

ad pond. om.
to the weight of the whole [L. *ad pondus omnium*]

ADPR
adenosine diphosphate ribose

ADPV
anomaly of drainage of pulmonary vein

ADQ
abductor digiti quinti (muscles)
adequate

ADR
acceptable dental remedies
acute dystonic reaction
Adriamycin *also* ADM, ADRIA, Adria
adverse drug reaction
airway dilation reflex
ataxia-deafness-retardation [syndrome]

Adr
adrenaline
Adriamycin

adr
adrenal
adrenalectomy

ad rat.
ad rationem (Lat.) as reasonable

ADRBR
adrenergic beta-receptor

ADRIA, Adria
Adriamycin *also* ADM, ADR

NOTES

ADS
acute death syndrome
acute diarrheal syndrome
Alcohol Dependence Scale
alternative delivery system
anatomical dead space
anonymous donor's sperm
anterior drawer sign
antibody deficiency syndrome
antidiuretic substance

ad sat.
to saturation [L. *ad saturandum*]

adst. feb.
while fever is present [L. *adstante febre*]

ADT
accepted dental therapeutics
adenosine triphosphate
admission, discharge, transfer
agar-gel diffusion test
alternate day therapy
anticipate discharge tomorrow
any desired thing (placebo)
Auditory Discrimination Test
automated dithionite test

ADTe
anodal duration tetanus

ADTP
adolescent day treatment program
alcohol dependence treatment program

ADU
acute duodenal ulcer

ad us.
according to custom [L. *ad usum*]

ad us. ext.
for external application [L. *ad uum externum*]

ADV, Adv
adenovirus
adventitia
Aleutian disease virus

A-DV
arterial-deep venous difference

A/DV
arterio/deep venous

adv
advanced
advice
advise

adv.
against [L. *adversum*]

ad 2 vic.
at two times [L. *ad duas vices*]
for two doses

ADVIRC
autosomal-dominant vitreoretinochoroidopathy

ADW
assault with deadly weapon

A5D5W
5% alcohol and 5% dextrose in water

ADX
adrenalectomized (jargon)

AE
above elbow (amputation)
accident and emergency (department) *also* A&E
acrodermatitis enteropathica
activation energy
acute exacerbation
adrenal epinephrine
adult erythrocyte
aftereffect
agarose electrophoresis
air embolism
air entry
alcoholic embryopathy
androstanediol
anoxic encephalopathy
antiembolitic
antiepileptic
antitoxin unit [Ger. *Antitoxineinhei*]
apoenzyme
aryepiglottic (fold)
atherosclerotic encephalopathy

A&E
accident and emergency (department) *also* AE

AEA
above-elbow amputation
alcohol, ether, and acetone (solution)
antiendomysium antibody

AEB
as evidenced by
atrial ectopic beat
avian erythroblastosis

AEC
ankyloblepharon, ectodermal defects, and cleft lip (syndrome)

aortic ejection click
at earliest convenience

AECB
acute exacerbation of chronic
bronchitis

AECD
allergic eczematous contact dermatitis

AECUS
atypical endocervical cells of
undetermined significance

AED
antiepileptic (anticonvulsant) drug
antihidrotic ectodermal dysplasia
automated external defibrillator

AEDP
automated external defibrillator
pacemaker

AEEU
admission, entrance, and evaluation
unit

AEF
allogenic effect factor
amyloid-enhancing factor
aryepiglottic fold

AEG
air encephalogram
air encephalography
atrial electrogram

aeg.
patient [L. *aeger, aegra*]

AEI
atrial emptying index

AEL
acute erythroleukemia

AEM
ambulatory electrogram monitor
analytical electron microscopy
antiepileptic medication
avian encephalomyelitis

AEN
aseptic epiphyseal necrosis

AEP
acute edematous pancreatitis
appropriateness evaluation protocol
artificial endocrine pancreas

auditory-evoked potential
average-evoked potential

AEq
age equivalent

aeq.
equal [L. *aequales*]

AER
abduction/external rotation
acoustic-evoked response
acute exertional rhabdomyolysis
agranular endoplasmic reticulum
aided equalization response
albumin excretion rate
aldosterone excretion rate
apical ectodermal ridge
auditory-evoked response
average electroencephalic response
average-evoked response

aer
aerosol

AERA
average-evoked response audiometry

AerM
aerosol mask

Aero
Aerobacter

AERP
atrial effective refractory period

AerT
aerosol tent

AES
acetone-extracted serum
anterior aspect esophageal sensor
antiembolic stockings
antieosinophilic sera
antral ethmoidal sphenoidectomy
aortic ejection sound
Auger electron spectroscopy

AEST
aeromedical evacuation support team

AET
absorption-equivalent thickness
atrial ectopic tachycardia

aet.
age [L. *aetas*]

NOTES

aetat.
aged [L. *aetatis*]

AEV
avian erythroblastosis virus

AEVS
automated eligibility verification
system

AF
abnormal frequency
acid-fast
adult female
afebrile *also* AFEB
aflatoxin *also* AFT
albumose-free (tuberculin)
aldehyde fuchsin
amaurosis fugax
aminophylline
amniotic fluid
anchoring fibril
angiogenesis factor
anteflexed
anteflexion
anterior fontanel
anterofrontal
antibody forming
antifibrinogen
aortic flow
aortofemoral
artificially fed
ascitic fluid *also* ascit fl
atrial fibrillation *also* AFib, At Fib,
ATR FIB, atr fib.
atrial flutter *also* AFL
atrial fusion
attenuation factor
attributable fraction
audiofrequency *also* af
auricular fibrillation *also* AUR FIB,
aur fib.

A-F
ankle-foot (orthosis)
antifibrinogen

A/F
air fluid (level)

aF
abfarad

af
audio frequency *also* AF

AFA
advanced first aid
alcohol-formaldehyde-acetic (fixative
or solution)

AFAFP
amniotic fluid alpha-fetoprotein

AFB
acid-fast bacillus
aflatoxin B
air-fluidized bed
aortofemoral bypass
aspirated foreign body

AFBG
aortofemoral bypass graft

AFC
acid-fast culture
adult foster care
air-filled cushions
antibody-forming cell

AFCI
acute focal cerebral ischemia

AFD
accelerated freeze-drying

AFDC
Aid to Families with Dependent
Children

AFE
amniotic fluid embolization

AFEB
afebrile *also* AF

AFF
atrial filling fraction

AF/F
atrial fibrillation and/or flutter

aff
afferent

AFG
aflatoxin G
alpha fetal globulin
amniotic fluid glucose
auditory figure-ground

aFGF
acidic fibroblast growth factor *also*
FGFa

AFH
angiofollicular hyperplasia
anterior facial height

AFI
acute febrile illness
amaurotic familial idiocy
amniotic fluid index

AFib
    atrial fibrillation *also* AF, At Fib, ATR FIB, atr fib.

AFIS
    amniotic fluid infection syndrome

AFL
    air/fluid level
    antifatty liver (factor)
    antifibrinolysin
    artificial limb
    atrial flutter *also* AF

AFLNH
    angiofollicular lymph node hyperplasia

AFLP
    acute fatty liver of pregnancy

AFM
    aflatoxin M

AFN
    afunctional neutrophil

AFND
    acute febrile neutrophilic dermatosis

AFO
    ankle-foot orthosis

AFP
    α-fetoprotein *also* aFP
    anterior faucial pillar
    ascending frontal parietal
    atrial filling pressure
    atypical facial pain

aFP
    α-fetoprotein *also* AFP

AFPP
    acute fibropurulent pneumonia

AFQ
    aflatoxin Q

AFR
    aqueous flare response
    ascorbic free radical

AFRAX
    autism-fragile X [syndrome]

AFRD
    acute febrile respiratory disease

AFRI
    acute febrile respiratory illness

AFS
    acid-fast smear
    acquired or adult Fanconi syndrome
    acromegaloid facial syndrome
    American Fertility Society
    antifibroblast serum

AFSP
    acute fibrinoserous pneumonia

AFT
    aflatoxin *also* AF
    agglutination-flocculation test

AFT$_3$
    absolute free triiodothyronine

AFT$_4$
    absolute free thyroxine

AFTC
    apparent free testosterone concentration

AFTN
    autonomously functioning thyroid nodule

AFV
    amniotic fluid volume

AFVSS
    afebrile, vital signs stable

AFX
    air-fluid exchange
    atypical fibroxanthoma

AG, A:G, A/G
    albumin-globulin (ratio) *also* ALB/GLOB

AG
    abdominal girth
    agarose
    aminoglutethimide *also* AGL
    aminoglycoside
    analytical grade
    anion gap
    antigen *also* Ag, ag, AGN
    antiglobulin
    antigravity
    atrial gallop *also* ag
    attached gingiva
    axiogingival
    azurophilic granule

NOTES

Ag
   antigen *also* AG, ag, AGN
   silver [L. *argentum*] *also* arg.

ag
   antigen *also* AG, Ag, AGN
   atrial gallop *also* AG

AGA
   accelerated growth area
   acetylglutamate
   acute gonococcal arthritis
   allergic granulomatosis and angiitis
   antigliadin antibody
   antiglomerular antibody
   anti-IgA autoantibody
   appropriate for gestational age
   average for gestational age

Ag-Ab
   antigen-antibody complex

AGAG
   acidic glycosaminoglycans

AGAS
   acetylglutamate synthetase

AGC
   absolute granulocyte count
   automatic gain control

AGD
   agar/agarose-gel diffusion (method)

AGDD
   agar-agarose-gel double diffusion
   (method)

AGE
   acrylamide gel electrophoresis
   acute gastroenteritis
   angle of greatest extension

AGED
   automated general experimental device

AGF
   adrenal growth factor
   angle of greatest flexion

ag. feb.
   when the fever is coming on [L.
   aggrediente febre] *also* aggred. feb.

AGG
   agammaglobulinemia

agg
   agglutinate *also* aggl, agglut
   agglutination *also* aggl, agglut
   aggregation *also* aggreg

aggl, agglut
   agglutinate *also* agg
   agglutination *also* agg

aggred. feb.
   when the fever is coming on [L.
   aggrediente febre] *also* ag. feb.

aggreg
   aggregation *also* agg

AGGS
   anti-gas gangrene serum

agit.
   shake [L. *agita*]

agit. ante sum.
   shake before taking [L. *agita ante
   sumendum*]

agit. ante us.
   shake before using [L. *agita ante
   usum*]

agit. bene
   shake well [L. *agita bene*]

agit. vas.
   the vial being shaken [L. *agitato
   vase*]

AGL
   acute granulocytic leukemia
   agglutination
   aminoglutethimide *also* AG

A-GLACTO-LK
   α-galactoside leukocytes

AGLMe
   N-alpha-acetylglycyl-L-lysine

AGMK, AGMk
   African green monkey kidney (cell)

AGML
   acute gastric mucosal lesion

AGN
   acute glomerulonephritis
   agnosia *also* agn
   antigen *also* AG, Ag, ag

agn
   agnosia *also* AGN

AgNOR
   silver-staining nucleolar organizer
   region

AGP
   α₁-acid glycoprotein *also* AAG
   agar-gel precipitation (test) *also*
   AGPT

AGPT
  agar-gel precipitation test *also* AGP

AGR
  aniridia, genitourinary abnormalities, and mental retardation
  anticipatory goal response

AGS
  adrenogenital syndrome
  antiglucagon
  audiogenic seizures

AGT
  abnormal glucose tolerance
  activity group therapy
  acute generalized tuberculosis
  adrenoglomerulotropin *also* AGTr
  antiglobulin test

AGTH
  adrenoglomerulotropic hormone

AGTr
  adrenoglomerulotropin *also* AGT

AGTT
  abnormal glucose tolerance test

AGU
  aspartylglycosaminuria

AGV
  aniline gentian violet

AGVHD
  acute graft-versus-host disease

AH
  abdominal hysterectomy *also* Abd hyst
  absorptive hypercalciuria
  accidental hypothermia
  acetohexamide
  acid hydrolysis
  acute hepatitis
  adrenal hypoplasia
  after-hyperpolarization *also* AHP
  agnathia holoprosencephaly
  alcoholic hepatitis
  amenorrhea and hirsutism
  amenorrhea and hyperprolactinemia
    also A/H
  aminohippurate
  anterior hypothalamus
  antihyaluronidase
  arcuate hypothalamus

arterial hypertension
artificial heart
ascites hepatoma
astigmatic hypermetropia
ataxic hemiparesis
autonomic hyperreflexia
axillary hair

A/H
  amenorrhea and hyperprolactinemia
    also AH

A&H
  accident and health (policy)

A-h
  ampere-hour

aH
  abhenry

ah
  hyperopic astigmatism *also* ASH, AsH

AHA
  acetohydroxamic acid
  acquired hemolytic anemia
  acute hemolytic anemia
  anterior hypothalamic area
  antiheart antibody
  antihistone antibody
  area health authority
  arthritis-hives-angioedema [syndrome]
  aspartylhydroxamic acid
  Australian hepatitis antigen
  autoimmune hemolytic anemia

AHB
  α-hydroxybutyric dehydrogenase

AHBC
  hepatitis B core antibody

AHC
  academic health care
  acute hemorrhagic conjunctivitis
  acute hemorrhagic cystitis
  antihemophilic factor C

AHCy
  S-adenosylhomocysteine

AHD
  acquired hepatocerebral degeneration
  acute heart disease
  antihypertensive drug

NOTES

AHD *(continued)*
arteriohepatic dysplasia
arteriosclerotic heart disease
atherosclerotic heart disease
autoimmune hemolytic disease

AHDMS
automated hospital data management
system

AHDP
azacycloheptane diphosphonate

AHE
acute hemorrhagic encephalomyelitis

AHEC
area health education center

AHES
artificial heart energy system

AHF
acute heart failure
antihemolytic factor (factor VIII)
antihemophilic factor (factor VIII)
Argentinian hemorrhagic fever

AHFS
American Hospital Formulary Service

AHFS-DI
American Hospital Formulary Service-
Drug Information

AHG
aggregated human globulin
antihemolytic globulin
antihemophilic globulin
antihuman globulin

AHGG
aggregated human gamma globulin
antihuman gammaglobulin

AHGS
acute herpetic gingival stomatitis

AHH
α-hydrazine analog of histidine
anosmia and hypogonadotropic
hypogonadism (syndrome)
arylhydrocarbonhydroxylase

AHHD
arteriosclerotic hypertensive heart
disease

AHI
active hostility index
apnea-plus-hypopnea index

AHIP
assisted health insurance plan

AHIS
automated hospital information system

AHJ
artificial hip joint

AHL
apparent half-life

AHLE
acute hemorrhagic leukoencephalitis

AHLG
antihuman lymphocyte globulin

AHLS
antihuman lymphocyte serum

AHM
ambulatory Holter monitor

AHMA
antiheart muscle autoantibody

AHMO
anterior horizontal mandibular
osteotomy

AHN
adenomatous hyperplastic nodule
Army head nurse
assistant head nurse

AHO
Albright hereditary osteodystrophy

AHP
acute hemorrhagic pancreatitis
after-hyperpolarization *also* AH
air at high pressure
Assistant House Physician

AHPO
anterior hypothalamic preoptic (area)

AHR
autonomic hyperreflexia

AHRF
acute hypoxemic respiratory failure

AHS
adaptive hand skills
African horse sickness
allopurinol hypersensitivity syndrome
alveolar hypoventilation syndrome
Assistant House Surgeon

AHSDF
area health service development fund

AHT
aggregation half-time
alternating hypertropia
amiodarone-iodine-induced
thyrotoxicosis

A

antihyaluronidase titer
augmented histamine test
autoantibodies to human thyroglobulin

AHTG
antihuman thymocyte globulin

AHTP
antihuman thymocyte plasma

AHTS
antihuman thymus serum

AHU
acute hemolytic uremic (syndrome)
arginine, hypoxanthine, and uracil

AHuG
aggregated human IgG

AHV
avian herpesvirus

A-I
aortoiliac

AI
accidental injury
accidentally incurred
adiposity index
aggregation index
allergy and immunology *also* A&I
allergy index
angiogenesis inhibitor
anxiety index
aortic incompetence
aortic insufficiency
apical impulse
articulation index
artificial insemination
artificial intelligence
atherogenic index
atrial insufficiency
autoimmune
autoimmunity
axioincisal

A&I
allergy and immunology *also* AI

AIA
acquired artery immune augmentation
allergen-induced asthma
allylisopropylacetamide
amylase inhibitor activity
anti-immunoglobulin antibody

antiinsulin antibody *also* AI-Ab
aspirin-induced asthma
automated image analysis

AI-Ab
antiinsulin antibody *also* AIA

AIB
aminoisobutyric acid *also* AIBA
avian infectious bronchitis

AIBA
aminoisobutyric acid *also* AIB

AIBF
anterior interbody fusion

AIC
aminoimidazole carboxamide

AICA
anterior inferior cerebellar artery
anterior inferior communicating artery
anterior internal cerebral artery

AI-CAH
autoimmune-type chronic active
hepatitis

AICAR
aminoimidazole carboxamide
ribonucleotide

AICC
antiinhibitor coagulant complex

AICD
automatic implantable cardiovascular
defibrillator
automatic implantable cardioverter-
defibrillator

AICF
autoimmune complement fixation

AID
acquired immunodeficiency disease
acute infectious disease
acute ionization detector
antiinflammatory drug
argon ionization detector
artificial insemination donor
autoimmune deficiency
autoimmune disease
automatic implantable defibrillator
average interocular difference

NOTES

AIDH
artificial insemination donor, husband

AIDP
acute inflammatory demyelinating polyradiculopathy

AIDS
acquired immune deficiency syndrome
acquired immunodeficiency syndrome
acute infectious disease series
adult immunodeficiency syndrome
Assessment of Intelligibility of Dysarthric Speech

AIDS-KS
acquired immunodeficiency syndrome with Kaposi sarcoma

AIDSLINE
online information on acquired immunodeficiency syndrome

AIDSTRIALS
clinical trials of acquired immunodeficiency syndrome drugs

AIE
acute inclusion body encephalitis
acute infectious encephalitis
acute infectious endocarditis

AIEP
amount of insulin extractable from pancreas

AIF
anemia-inducing factor
antiinflammatory
antiinvasion factor
aortic-iliac-femoral

AIFD
acute intrapartum fetal distress

AIG
anti-immunoglobulin

AIgA
absence of immunoglobulin A

AIgM
absence of immunoglobulin M

A-IGP
activity-interview group psychotherapy

AIH
artificial insemination, homologous
artificial insemination by husband

AIHA
autoimmune hemolytic anemia

AIHD
acquired immune hemolytic disease

AII
acute intestinal infection

AIIS
anterior inferior iliac spine

AIL
acute infectious lymphocytosis
angiocentric immunoproliferative lesion
angio-immunoblastic lymphadenopathy

AILD
alveolar-interstitial lung disease
angio-immunoblastic lymphadenopathy with dysproteinemia

AILT
amiloride-inhibitable lithium transport

AIM
artificial intelligence in medicine

AIMD
abnormal involuntary movement disorder

AIMS
abnormal involuntary movement scale
arthritis impact measurement scale

AIN
acute interstitial nephritis
anal intraepithelial neoplasia
anterior interosseous nerve

AINS
antiinflammatory nonsteroidal (agent)

A Insuf
aortic insufficiency

AIO
amyloid of immunoglobulin origin

AIOD
aortoiliac occlusive disease

AION
anterior ischemic optic neuropathy

AIP
acute idiopathic pericarditis
acute infectious polyneuritis
acute inflammatory polyneuropathy
acute intermittent porphyria
aldosterone-induced protein
automated immunoprecipitation
average intravascular pressure

AIPC
androgen-independent prostate cancer

AIPE
  acute idiopathic peripheral facial
  nerve palsy

AIR
  accelerated idioventricular rhythm *also*
  AIVR
  aminoimidazole ribonucleotide
  average impairment rating

AIRA
  antiinsulin receptor antibody

AIRF
  alteration in respiratory function

AIRS
  Amphetamine Interview Rating Scale

AIS
  Abbreviated Injury Score
  amniotic infection syndrome
  androgen insensitivity syndrome
  anterior interosseous nerve syndrome
  antiinsulin serum

AISA
  acquired idiopathic sideroblastic
  anemia

AIS/ISS
  Abbreviated Injury Score/Injury
  Severity Score

AIS/MR
  Alternative Intermediate Services for
  the Mentally Retarded

AIT
  acute intensive treatment
  administrator-in-training

AITN
  acute interstititial tubular nephritis

AITP
  autoimmune thrombocytopenia purpura

AITT
  arginine insulin tolerance test
  augmented insulin tolerance test

AIU
  absolute iodine uptake
  antigen-inducing unit

AIVR
  accelerated idioventricular rhythm *also*
  AIR

AIVV
  anterior internal vertebral vein

AJ, A/J
  ankle jerk

AJR
  abnormal jugular reflex

AJS
  acute joint syndrome

AK
  above-knee (amputation) *also* A/K,
  AKA, AK amp
  actinic keratosis
  adenosine kinase
  adenylate kinase
  artificial kidney

A/K
  above-knee (amputation) *also* AK,
  AKA, AK amp

AKA
  above-knee amputation *also* AK,
  A/K, AK amp
  alcoholic ketoacidosis
  all known allergies
  α-allokainic acid
  antikeratin antibody

aka
  also known as

AK amp
  above-knee amputation *also* AK,
  A/K, AKA

AKE
  acrokeratoelastoidosis

A/kg
  amperes per kilogram

AKP
  alkaline phosphatase *also* ALK-P, alk
  phos, alk p'tase, ALP, AlPase, AP,
  KA, P'ase

AKS
  alcoholic Korsakoff syndrome
  arthroscopic knee surgery
  auditory and kinesthetic sensation

AL
  absolute latency
  acinar lumina

NOTES

AL *(continued)*
  acute leukemia
  adaptation level
  albumin (5%, followed by amount in mL) *also* A, ALB, Alb, alb
  alcoholism
  alignment mark
  amyloidosis
  annoyance level
  antihuman lymphocytic (globulin)
  argininosuccinate lysate
  argon laser
  arterial line *also* A-line, art. line
  avian leukosis
  axial length
  axiolingual
  left ear [L. *auris laeva*] *also* a.l., AS, a.s.
  lethal antigen

Al
  allantoic
  allergic *also* all.
  allergy *also* A, alg, ALL, all.
  aluminum

a.l.
  left ear [L. *auris laeva*] *also* AL, AS, a.s.

ALA
  alpha-linolenic acid
  aminolevulinic acid
  anterior lip of the acetabulum
  antilymphocyte antibody
  axiolabial *also* ALa

ALa
  axiolabial *also* ALA

Ala
  alanine *also* A

AL-Ab
  antilymphocyte antibody

ALAC
  antibiotic-loaded acrylic cement

ALAD
  abnormal left axis deviation
  aminolevulinic acid dehydrase *also* ALA-D

ALA-D
  aminolevulinic acid dehydrase *also* ALAD

ALAG, ALaG
  axiolabiogingival

ALAL, ALaL
  axiolabiolingual

ALARA
  as low as reasonably achievable (radiation exposure)

ALARM
  adjustable leg and ankle repositioning mechanism

ALAS
  aminolevulinic acid synthetase

ALAT
  alanine aminotransferase

ALAX
  apical long axis

ALB
  albumin (5%, followed by amount in mL) *also* A, AL, Alb, alb
  avian lymphoblastosis

Alb, alb
  albumin (5%, followed by amount in mL) *also* A, AL, ALB

alb.
  white [L. *albus*]

ALB/GLOB *also* AG
  albumin-globulin (ratio) *also* AG

ALC
  absolute lymphocyte count
  acute lethal catatonia
  alcohol *also* alc
  alcoholic liver cirrhosis
  allogeneic lymphocyte cytoxicity
  alternate level of care
  Alternative Lifestyle Checklist
  approximate lethal concentration
  avian leukosis complex
  axiolinguocervical

alc
  alcohol *also* ALC
  alcoholic
  alcoholism

ALCA
  anomalous left coronary artery

ALCAPA
  anomalous origin of left coronary artery from pulmonary artery

ALCEQ
  Adolescent Life Change Event Questionnaire

ALCL
anaplastic large cell lymphoma

ALCR, AlcR
alcohol rub

AlCr
aluminum crown

ALD
adrenoleukodystrophy
alcoholic liver disease
aldolase *also* Ald
aldosterone *also* Aldo, ALDOST
anterior latissimus dorsi
Appraisal of Language Disturbances

Ald
aldolase *also* ALD

ALDH
aldehyde dehydrogenase

Aldo, ALDOST
aldosterone *also* ALD

ALE
allowable limits of error

ALEC
artificial lung-expanding compound

ALEP
atypical lymphoepithelioid cell
proliferation

ALF
acute liver failure
anterior long fiber

ALFT
abnormal liver function test

ALG
Annapolis lymphoblast globulin
antilymphoblastic globulin
antilymphocytic globulin
axiolinguogingival

alg
allergy *also* A, Al, ALL, all.

ALGOL
algorithm-oriented language

ALH
angiolymphoid hyperplasia
anterior lobe hormone

anterior lobe of hypophysis
atypical lobular hyperplasia

ALHE
angiolymphoid hyperplasia with
eosinophilia

ALI
argon laser iridotomy

A-line
arterial line *also* AL, art. line

ALIP
abnormal localized immature myeloid
precursor

ALK, alk
alkaline
alkylating (agent)
automated lamella keratoplasty

ALK-P
alkaline phosphatase *also* AKP, alk
phos, alk p'tase, ALP, AlPase, AP,
KA, P'ase

alk phos
alkaline phosphatase *also* AKP,
ALK-P, alk p'tase, ALP, AlPase,
AP, KA, P'ase

alk p'tase
alkaline phosphatase *also* AKP,
ALK-P, alk phos, ALP, AlPase, AP,
KA, P'ase

ALL
acute lymphatic leukemia
acute lymphoblastic leukemia
acute lymphocytic leukemia
allergy *also* A, Al, alg, all.
anterior longitudinal ligament

all.
allergic *also* Al
allergy *also* A, Al, alg, ALL

ALLA
acute lymphocytic leukemia antigen

ALLD
athroscopic lumbar laser diskectomy

ALLO
atypical Legionella-like organism

NOTES

ALM
acral lentiginous melanoma
alveolar living material

ALME
acetyl-lysine methyl ester

ALMI
anterior lateral myocardial infarction

ALMV
anterior leaflet of the mitral valve

ALN
anterior lymph node

ALND
axillary lymph node dissection

ALNM
axillary lymph node metastasis

ALO
average lymphocyte output
axiolinguo-occlusal

ALOMAD
Adriamycin (doxorubicin), Leukeran (chlorambucil), Oncovin (vincristine), methotrexate, actinomycin D, and dacarbazine

ALOS
average length of stay

ALP
acute leukemia protocol
acute lupus pericarditis
alkaline phosphatase *also* AKP, ALK-P, alk phos, alk p'tase, AlPase, AP, KA, P'ase
Alupent
anterior lobe of pituitary
antilymphocytic plasma
argon laser photocoagulation

AlPase
alkaline phosphatase *also* AKP, ALK-P, alk phos, alk p'tase, ALP, AP, KA, P'ase

α
acceleration *also* a, Acc, acc, accel
activity *also* activ, act.
alpha (first letter of Greek alphabet), lowercase
alpha particle
Bunsen solubility coefficient
constituent of alpha protein plasma fraction
first in alpha series or group
heavy chain of immunoglobulin A
optical rotation

probability of type I error (statistics)
specific absorption coefficient

$[\alpha]$
specific optical rotation

α_1
antichymotrypsin

α_2-**AP**
alpha$_2$antiplasmin

α_1-**AT**
α_1-proteinase inhibitor

$\alpha_2\beta_1$
alpha-2-beta-1 integrin cell-surface collagen

α-**GLUC**
α-glucosidase

α-**GST**
α-glutathione S-transferase

α-**KG**
α-ketoglutarate

α-**LP**
α-lipoprotein

α_2**M**
α_2-macroglobulin

α-**MSH**
α-melanocyte-stimulating hormone

α_1**PI**
human α_1-proteinase inhibitor
α_1-protease inhibitor

α-**T**
α-tocopherol

ALPI
alkaline phosphatase isoenzymes

ALPS
angiolymphoproliferative syndrome
anterior locking plate system 10000
Aphasia Language Performance Scales

ALPZ
alprazolam

ALRI
acute lower respiratory tract infection
anterolateral rotational instability

ALS
acute lateral sclerosis
advanced life support (system)
afferent loop syndrome
amyotrophic lateral sclerosis
angiotensin-like substance
anticipated lifespan

antilymphocyte serum
antiviral lymphocyte serum

ALSD
Alzheimer-like senile dementia

ALS-PD
amyotrophic lateral sclerosis-
parkinsonism-dementia [complex]

ALT
alanine aminotransferase
argon laser trabeculoplasty *also* Alt,
alt, ALTP
avian laryngotracheitis

Alt, alt
alternate
altitude
argon laser trabeculoplasty *also* ALT,
alt, ALTP

ALT/AST
ratio of serum alanine
aminotransferase to serum aspartate
aminotransferase

ALTB
acute laryngotracheobronchitis

alt. dieb.
every other day [L. *alternis diebus*]

ALTE
acute life threatening event
apparent life-threatening event

ALTEE
acetyl-L-tyrosine ethyl ester

alt. hor.
every other hour [L. *alternis horis*]

alt. noct.
every other night [L. *alternis nocta*]

ALTP
argon laser trabeculoplasty *also* ALT,
Alt, alt

ALTS
acute lumbar traumatic sprain
acute lumbar traumatic syndrome

ALU
arithmetic and logic unit

ALV
Abelson leukemia virus

adeno-like virus
ascending lumbar vein
avian leukosis virus

Alv, alv
alveolar
alveolus

ALVAD
abdominal left ventricular assist
device

alv. adst.
when the bowels are constipated [L.
alvo adstricta]

alv. deject.
discharge from the bowels [L. *alvi
dejectiones*]

ALVM
alveolar mucosa

ALVT
aortic and left ventricular tunnel

alv vent
alveolar ventilation *also* $\dot{V}_A$

Alvx
alveolectomy

ALW
arch-loop-whorl
arch-loop-whorl system

ALWMI
anterolateral wall myocardial infarct

A-LYM
atypical lymphocyte

AM
acrylamide
actomyosin
acute myelofibrosis
adult male
adult monocyte
aerospace medicine
alveolar macrophase
alveolar mucosa
amacrine cell
amalgam *also* AMAL
ambulatory *also* A, AMB, amb,
ambul
amethopterin
ametropia

NOTES

AM *(continued)*
ammeter
amperemeter
ampicillin *also* A, AMP
amplitude modulation *also* A-mode
anovular menstruation
anteromeatal
arithmetic mean
arousal mechanism
arterial mean
articulation manipulation
atrial myxoma
Austin-Moore (prosthesis)
aviation medicine *also* AV, AVM
axiomesial
before noon [L. *ante meridiem*] *also*
  a.m.
meter angle
mixed astigmatism
myopic astigmatism

A 2M
2-microglobulin-origin amyloid deposit

A/m
amperes per meter

Am
americium
amnion
amyl

A-m^2
ampere-square meter

a.m.
before noon [L. *ante meridiem*] *also*
  AM

am.
ametropia
amplitude
meter angle
myopic astigmatism

AMA
actual mechanical advantage
against medical advice
antimitochondrial antibody
antimyosin antibody
antithyroid microsomal antibody

AMAC
adults molested as children

AMAD
morning admission

AMA-DE
American Medical Association Drug
  Evaluation

AMAG
adrenal medullary autograft

AMAL
amalgam *also* AM

AMAP
as much as possible

A-MAT
amorphous material

AMAT
antimalignant antibody test

AMB
ambulate *also* Amb, amb, ambul
ambulatory *also* A, AM, amb, ambul
amphotericin B
anomalous muscle bundle
avian myeloblastosis

Amb
ambulance
ambulate *also* AMB, Amb, ambul
ambulation
ambulatory

amb
ambient
ambiguous *also* ambig
ambulance
ambulate *also* AMB, Amb, ambul
ambulatory *also* A, AM, AMB,
  ambul

AMBER
advanced multiple beam equalization
  radiography

ambig
ambiguous *also* amb

AMBL
acute myeloblastic leukemia *also*
  AML

ambul
ambulate *also* AMB, Amb, amb
ambulation
ambulatory *also* A, AM, AMB, amb

AMC
antibody-mediated cytoxicity
antimalaria campaign
arm muscle circumference
arthrogryposis multiplex congenita
automated mixture control
axiomesiocervical

AMCHA
aminomethylcyclohexane-carboxylic
  acid

A

AMCN
anteromedial caudate nucleus

AM/CR
amylase to creatinine ratio

AMD
acid maltase deficiency
acromandibular dysplasia
actinomycin D
adrenomyelodystrophy
age-related macular degeneration
Aleutian mink disease *also* AD
α-methyldopa
arthroscopic microdiskectomy
axiomesiodistal

AME
anthrax meningoencephalitis
apparent mineralocorticoid excess
(syndrome)
aseptic meningoencephalitis

AMEAE
acute monophasic experimental
autoimmune encephalomyelitis

AMEGL, AMegL
acute megakaryoblastic leukemia

AMet
adenosyl-l-methionine

AMF
antimuscle factor
autocrine motility factor

AMG
acoustic myography
aminoglycoside
amyloglucosidase
amyloglucoside
antimacrophage globulin
axiomesiogingival

A₂MG
alpha$_2$-macroglobulin

AMH
anti-müllerian hormone
automated medical history

Amh
mixed astigmatism with myopia
predominating

AMHT
automated multiphasic health testing

AMI
acquired monosaccharide intolerance
acute myocardial infarction
amitriptyline
anterior myocardial infarction
axiomesio-incisal

AMKL
acute megakaryoblastic leukemia

AML
acute monocytic leukemia *also*
AMOL, mLa
acute mucosal lesion
acute myeloblastic leukemia *also*
AMBL
acute myelogenous leukemia
acute myeloid leukemia
anterior mitral leaflet
automated multitest laboratory

AMLB
alternate monaural loudness balance
(test)

AMLC
adherent macrophage-like cell
autologous mixed lymphocyte culture

AMLR
autologous mixed lymphocyte reaction

AMLS
antimouse lymphocyte serum

AMM
agnogenic myeloid metaplasia
ammonia *also* amm, ammon.
antibody to murine cardiac myosin

amm
ammonia *also* AMM, ammon.

AMML, AMMOL, AMMoL
acute myelomonocytic leukemia

AMMOL
acute myelomonoblastic leukemia

ammon.
ammonia *also* AMM, amm

AMN
adrenomyeloneuropathy

NOTES

AMN *(continued)*
alloxazine mononucleotide
anterior median nucleus

amnio
amniocentesis

AMN SC
amniotic fluid scan

AMO
Assistant Medical Officer
axiomesio-occlusal

A-mode
amplitude mode
amplitude modulation *also* AM

AMOL
acute monoblastic leukemia
acute monocytic leukemia *also* AML,
mLa

AMOR, amor, AMORP, amorp
amorphous (sediment)

AMP
accelerated mental processes
acid mucopolysaccharide
adenosine monophosphate (adenylic
acid)
amphetamine
ampicillin *also* A, AM
ampule *also* amp
amputation *also* amp
average mean pressure

amp
amperage
ampere
ampicillin
amplification
ampule *also* AMP
amputation *also* AMP
amputee

AMP-c
cyclic adenosine monophosphate *also*
cAMP

AMPH
amphetamine

amph
amphoric (respiratory sound)

amp-hr
ampere-hour

ampl.
large [L. *amplus*]

AMPPPE
acute multifocal posterior placoid
pigment epitheliopathy

A-M pr
Austin-Moore prosthesis

AMPS
abnormal mucopolysacchariduria
acid mucopolysaccharide

AMP-S
adenylosuccinic acid

AMPT
α-methyl-*p*-tyrosine (antihypertensive
in pheochromocytoma)

ampul.
ampule [L. *ampulla*]

AMR
acoustic muscle reflex
activity metabolic rate
alternate motion rate
alternating motion reflex

AMRA
American Medical Record Association

AMRI
anteromedial rotatory instability

AMRS
automated medical record system

AMS
acute mountain sickness
aggravated in military service
altered mental status
amylase
antimacrophage serum
aseptic meningitis syndrome
atypical measles syndrome
auditory memory span
automated multiphasic screening
automicrobic system

AMSA
amsacrine

AMSIT
appearance, mood, sensorium,
intelligence, and thought process
(portion of mental status
examination)

AMT
acute miliary tuberculosis
amethopterin
α-methyltyrosine
amitriptyline
amphetamine

amt
  amount

AMTP
  α-methyltryptophan

amu
  atomic mass unit

AmuLV
  Abelson murine leukemia virus
  amphotropic murine leukemia virus

AMV
  alveolar minute ventilation
  assisted mechanical ventilation
  avian myeloblastosis virus

AMVI
  acute mesenteric vascular insufficiency

aMVL
  anterior mitral valve leaflet

AMX
  amoxicillin

AMY
  amylase

AMY-SP
  amylase urine spot (test)

AN
  acanthosis nigricans
  acne neonatorum
  acoustic neuroma
  adult, normal
  aminonucleoside
  amyl nitrate
  anesthesia *also* A, ANA, anes,
   anesth
  aneurysm
  anisometropia *also* An
  anodal *also* An
  anode *also* A, a, An
  anorexia nervosa
  antenatal
  anterior *also* A, a, ANT, ant.
  antineuraminidase
  aseptic necrosis
  atrionodal
  autonomic neuropathy
  avascular necrosis

A/N
  artery and/or nerve
  as needed

An
  actinon
  anatomic
  anatomy response
  aniridia
  anisometropia *also* AN
  anodal *also* AN
  anode *also* A, a, AN

ANA
  acetylneuraminic acid
  anesthesia *also* A, AN, anes, anesth
  anesthetic *also* anes, anesth
  antibody to nuclear antigens
  antinuclear antibody *also* $\overline{A}$, Å,
   ANuA
  aspartyl naphthylamide

ana
  (so much of) each [G. *ana*] *also*
   AA, $\overline{AA}$, aa., $\overline{aa}$

ANAD
  anorexia nervosa and associated
   disorders
  antinicotinamide adenine dinucleotidase

ANA-FL
  antinuclear antibody fluid

ANAG
  acute narrow angle glaucoma

anal
  analgesia
  analgesic
  analysis
  analyst
  analytic

ANAP
  agglutination negative, absorption
   positive (reaction)

ANAS
  anastomosis

anast
  anastomosis

Anat, anat
  anatomical

NOTES

Anat *(continued)*
anatomist
anatomy

ANB
avascular necrosis of bone

ANC
absolute neutrophil count
acid neutralization capacity
antigen-neutralizing capacity

ANCA
antineutrophil cytoplasmic antibodies

AnCC
anodal closure contraction *also* ACC

anch
anchored

ANCOVA
analysis of covariance

AND
administratively necessary days
algoneurodystrophy
anterior nasal discharge

And
androgen

ANDA
Abbreviated New Drug Application

Andro, Andros
androsterone

ANDTE, AnDTe
anodal duration tetanus

anes, anesth
anesthesia *also* A, AN, ANA
anesthesiology
anesthetic *also* ANA

ANESR
apparent norepinephrine secretion rate

AnEx, an ex
anodal excitation

ANF
α-naphthoflavone
antineuritic factor
antinuclear factor
atrial natriuretic factor

ANG
angiogram *also* ang
angiography *also* ang
angiotensin

ang
angiogram *also* ANG
angiography *also* ANG

angle *also* A
angular

Ang GR
angiotensin generation rate

ang pect
angina pectoris

ANH
acute normovolemic hemodilution
artificial nutrition and hydration

anh
anhydrous

ANI
acute nerve irritation

ANIS, ANISO
anisocytosis
Anorexia Nervosa Inventory for Self-
Rating

ANIT
α-naphthyl-isothiocyanate

ank
ankle

ANL, ANLL
acute nonlymphoblastic leukemia
acute nonlymphocytic leukemia

ANLL
acute nonlymphoblastic leukemia
acute nonlymphocytic leukemia
acute nonlymphoid leukemia

ANM
auxiliary nurse midwife

ANN
axillary node negative

Ann
annual

ann fib
annulus fibrosus

annot.
annotation

ANoA
antinucleolar antibody

AnOC
anodal opening contraction *also* AOC

ANOVA
analysis of variance

ANP
acute necrotizing pancreatitis
Adult Nurse Practitioner
Advanced Nurse Practitioner

A-norprogesterone
atrial natriuretic peptide
axillary node positive

A-NPP
absorbed normal pooled plasma

ANRC
American National Red Cross

ANRL
antihypertensive neural renomedullary
lipids

ANS
acanthion
anterior nasal spine
antineutrophilic serum
arterionephrosclerosis
autonomic nervous system

ANSCII
American National Standard Code for
Information Interchange

ANSI
American National Standards Institute

ANT
acoustic noise test
aminoglycoside2′-0-
nucleotidyltransferase
aminonitrothiazole
antimycin *also* ant, AntA

ant.
anterior *also* A, a, AN, ANT
antimycin *also* ANT., AntA

AntA
antimycin *also* ANT

antag
antagonist

ant ax line
anterior axillary line

ante
before [L. *ante*]

anti
antidote

ANTI A:AGT
anti-blood group A antiglobulin test

Anti bx
antibiotic

anticoag
anticoagulant

anti-GMB
antiglomerular basement membrane

anti-HA
antihepatitis antigen

anti-HAA
antibody to hepatitis-associated
antigen

anti-HAV
antibody to hepatitis A virus

anti-HB$_s$
antibody to hepatitis B surface
antigen

anti-HB$_c$
antibody to hepatitis B core antigen

anti-log
antilogarithm

anti-PNM Ab
anti-peripheral nerve myelin antibody

anti-RNP
antiribonucleoprotein

anti-S
anti-sulfanilic acid

anti-Sm
anti-Smith (antibody)

anti-SM/RNP
antibody-smooth
muscle/ribonucleoprotein

ant. jentac.
before breakfast [L. *ante jentaculum*]

ant. pit.
anterior pituitary

ant. prand.
before dinner [L. *ante prandium*]
also AP, a.p.

ANTR
apparent net transfer rate

NOTES

ant. sag D
anterior sagittal diameter

ant. sup. spine
anterior-superior spine

ANuA
antinuclear antibody *also* $\overline{A}$, Å,
ANA

ANUG
acute necrotizing ulcerative gingivitis

ANX, anx
anxiety
anxious

anx neur
anxiety neurosis

anx react
anxiety reaction

A-O
acoustic-optic
atlantooccipital (joint)

AO
abdominal aorta
achievement orientation
acid output
acridine orange (dye or test)
ankle orthosis
anodal opening
anterior oblique
aorta *also* Ao
aortic opening
ascending aorta
atomic orbital
atrioventricular valve opening
auriculoventricular valve opening
average optical density
avoidance of others
axio-occlusal
opening of the atrioventricular valves

A/O
alert and oriented
analog to digital

A&O
alert and oriented

Ao
aorta *also* AO

AOA
abnormal oxygen affinity
average orifice area

AOAA
amino-oxyacetic acid

AOAP
as often as possible

AOB
accessory olfactory bulb
alcohol on breath

AOBS
acute organic brain syndrome

AOC
abridged ocular chart
advanced ovarian cancer
amyloxycarbonyl
anodal opening contraction *also*
AnOC
antacid of choice
aortic opening click
area of concern

AOCD
anemia of chronic disease

AOCl
anodal opening clonus

AOD
adult-onset diabetes mellitus *also*
AODM
alleged onset date
arterial occlusive disease
arterial oxygen desaturation
auriculoosteodysplasia

AODA
alcohol and other drug abuse

AODM
adult-onset diabetes mellitus *also*
AOD

AODP
alcohol and other drug problems

ao-il
aorta-iliac

AOIVM
angiographically occult intracranial
vascular malformation

AOL
acroosteolysis

AOM
acute otitis media
alternatives of management
azoxymethane

AoMP
aortic mean pressure

AOP
anodal opening picture
aortic pressure

AoP
left ventricle to aorta pressure
gradient

AoPW
aortic posterior wall

AOR
auditory oculogyric reflex

Aor
Alvarado Orthopedic Research
[instrument]

aor regurg
aortic regurgitation *also* AR

aort sten
aortic stenosis *also* AS, A sten

AOS
acridine orange staining
anodal opening sound
anterior (o)esophageal sensor
aortic ostial stenosis

AOSC
acute obstructive suppurative
cholangiotomy

AOSD
adult-onset Still disease

AOT
accessory optic tract
antiovotransferrin

AOTe
anodal opening tetanus

AOU
apparent oxygen utilization

AOV
aortic valve

A&Ox3
alert and oriented to person, place,
and time

A&Ox4
alert and oriented to person, place,
time, and date

A-P
abdominoperineal (resection) *also* AP

analytic-psychologic
anterior-posterior

AP
abdominoperineal (resection) *also* A-P
accessory pathway
acid phosphatase *also* ACP, AcP,
AC-PH, ac phos
acinar parenchyma
action potential
active pepsin
acute pancreatitis
acute phase
acute pneumonia
acute proliferative
adenomatous polyposis
adolescent psychiatry
aerosol pentamidine
after parturition
alkaline phosphatase *also* AKP,
ALK-P, alk phos, alk p'tase, ALP,
KA, P'ase
alum-precipitated (vaccine)
amino-peptidase
aminopyrine
angina pectoris
antepartum [L. *ante partum*]
anterior pituitary
anteroposterior
antidromic potential
antiparkinsonian *also* APK
antipyrine
antral peristalsis
aortic pressure
aortic pulmonary
apical pulse
apothecary
appendectomy
appendicitis
appendix
area postrema
arithmetic progression
arterial pressure
artificial pneumothorax
aspiration pneumonitis
assessment and plan *also* A&P
assessment and planning
association period
atherosclerotic plaque
atrial pacing
atrioventricular pathway

NOTES

AP *(continued)*
atrium pace
attending physician
axiopulpal
before dinner [L. *ante prandium*]
  also ant. prand., a.p.
before parturition [L. *ante partum*]

3-AP
3-acetylpyridine (nicotinic antagonist)

4-AP
4-aminopyridine

8AP
eighth nerve action potential

A/P
ascites-plasma (ratio)

A&P
abdominal and perineal
active and present
anatomy and physiology
anterior and posterior
assessment and plan *also* AP
auscultation and palpation
auscultation and percussion

A$_2$P$_2$
aortic second sound, pulmonary
  second sound

A$_2$ < P$_2$
second aortic sound less than second
  pulmonic sound

A$_2$ = P$_2$
second aortic sound equals second
  pulmonic sound

A$_2$ > P$_2$
second aortic sound greater than
  second pulmonic sound

Ap
apex

a.p.
before dinner [L. *ante prandium*]
  also ant. prand., AP
prior to [L. *a priori*]

ap
apothecary

APA
aldosterone-producing adenoma
aminopenicillanic acid
antiparietal antibody
antipernicious anemia (factor)
antiphospholipid antibody

6-APA
6-aminopenicillanic acid

APAA
anterior parietal artery aneurysm

APAB
antiphospholipid antibody

APACHE
acute physiology and chronic health
  evaluation (score, system)

APAD
anterior-posterior abdominal diameter

APAF
antipernicious anemia factor

APB
abductor pollicis brevis (muscle)
atrial premature beat
auricular premature beat

A.P.B.
All-Purpose Boot

APC
absolute phagocyte count
acetylsalicylic acid, phenacetin, and
  caffeine
acute pharyngoconjunctival (fever)
adenoidal-pharyngeal-conjunctival
  (agent or virus) *also* A-P-C
adenomatous polyposis coli
all-purpose capsule (jargon for
  aspirin-phenacetin-caffeine)
alternative patterns of complement
amsacrine, prednisone, and
  chlorambucil
antigen-presenting cell
antiphlogistic corticoid
aperture current
apneustic center (of brain)
aspirin-phenacetin-caffeine
atrial premature complex
atrial premature contraction

A-P-C
adenoidal-pharyngeal-conjunctival *also*
  APC

APCA
antiparietal cell antibody

APCC, APC-C
aspirin-phenacetin-caffeine-codeine

APCD
acquired prothrombin complex
  deficiency [syndrome]
adult polycystic kidney disease *also*
  APKD

A

APCF
acute pharyngo-conjunctival fever

APCG
apex cardiogram

APCKD
adult-type polycystic kidney disease

A-PCR
allele-specific PCR

A-PD *also* APD
anteroposterior diameter *also* APD

APD
action potential duration
acute polycystic disease
adult polycystic disease
afferent pupillary defect
aminohydroxypropylidene diphosphate
anteroposterior diameter *also* A-PD
antipsychotic drug
atrial premature depolarization
autoimmune progesterone dermatitis
automated peritoneal dialysis

APDC
anxiety and panic disorder clinic

APDER
anterior-posterior dual energy
radiography

APDI
Adult Personal Data Inventory

APDT
acellular pertussis vaccine with
diptheria and tetanus toxoid

APE
acetone powder extract
acute polioencephalitis
acute psychotic episode
acute pulmonary edema
airway pressure excursion
aminophylline, phenobarbital, and
ephedrine
anterior pituitary extract
asthma of physical effort
avian pneumoencephalitis

APECED
autoimmune polyendocrinopathy-
candidosis-ectodermal dystrophy

APF
acidulated phosphofluoride
anabolism-promoting factor
animal protein factor
antiperinuclear factor

APG
acid-precipitated globulin
animal pituitary gonadotropin
Apgar (score)

APGAR
adaptability, partnership, growth,
affection, and resolve (family
screening, not Apgar score of
newborn physical status)
American Pediatric Gross Assessment
Record

APGL
alkaline phosphatase activity of
granular leukocytes

APH
adult psychiatric hospital
alcohol-positive history
antepartum hemorrhage
anterior pituitary hormone

aph
aphasia

AP/HC
accreditation program/hospice care

AP/HHC
accreditation program/home health
care

APHP
anti-Pseudomonas human plasma

API
alkaline protease inhibitor
analytical profile index
ankle-arm pressure index
arterial pressure index
Autonomy Preference Index

APIE
assessment plan, implementation, and
evaluation

APIP
additional personal injury protection

NOTES

APIVR
artificial pacemaker-induced ventricular rhythm

APK
antiparkinsonian *also* AP

APKD
adult polycystic kidney disease *also* APCD

APL
abductor pollicis longus (muscle)
accelerated painless labor
acute promyelocytic leukemia
animal placenta lactogen
anterior pituitary-like (hormone)

AP&L, AP&Lat
anteroposterior and lateral (radiologic view)

APLA
antiphospholipid antibody

APLD
automated percutaneous lumbar diskectomy

AP/LTC
accreditation program/long-term care

APM
acid-precipitable material
alternating pressure mattress
anterior papillary muscle
anteroposterior movement
aspartame

APN
acute pyelonephritis
average peak noise

APO
adductor pollicis obliquus (muscle)
Adriamycin (doxorubicin), prednisone, and Oncovin (vincristine)
adverse patient occurrences
aphoxide *also* TEPA
apolipoprotein
apomorphine
apoprotein

Apo
apolipoprotein

apoC
apolipoprotein C

apoE
apolipoprotein E

APOPPS
adjustable postoperative protective prosthetic socket

APORF
acute postoperative renal failure

apoth
apothecary

APP
acute-phase protein
alum-precipitated protein
alum-precipitated pyridine
aminopyrazolopyrimidine
amyloid precursor protein
antiplatelet plasma
appendix *also* App, app, Appx
aqueous procaine penicillin
automated physiologic profile
avian pancreatic polypeptide

App
appendix *also* APP, app, Appx

app
appendix *also* App, APP, Appx
applied
approximate *also* appr, approx

appar
apparatus
apparent

APPG
aqueous procaine penicillin G

appl
appliance
applicable
application
applied

applan.
flattened [L. *applanatus*]

applicand.
to be applied [L. *applicandus*]

appoint.
appointment *also* appt

appr, approx
approximate *also* app
approximately
approximation

appt
appointment *also* appoint.

Appx
appendix *also* APP, App, app

Appy, appy
appendectomy

APR
abdominoperineal resection
absolute proximal reabsorption
accelerator-produced
 radiopharmaceuticals
acute-phase reactant
amebic prevalence rate
anatomic porous replacement
anterior pituitary resection
auropalpebral reflex

aprax
apraxia

APRO
aprobarbital

AProL
acute progranulocytic leukemia
acute promyelocytic leukemia

APRP
acidic proline-rich protein
acute-phase reactant protein

APRT
abdominopelvic radiotherapy
adenine phosphoribosyltransferase

APRV
airway pressure release ventilation

APS
acute physiology score
adenosine phosphosulfate
Adult Protective Services
Adult Psychiatric Service
antiphospholipid syndrome
attending physician's statement
autoimmune polyglandular syndrome
automated patient system

6-APS
6-aminopenicillanic acid

APSAC
anisoylated plasminogen streptokinase
 activator complex

APSD
Alzheimer presenile dementia
aorticopulmonary septal defect

APSGN
acute poststreptococcal
glomerulonephritis

APSQ
Abbreviated Parent Symptom
Questionnaire

APT
alum-precipitated toxoid

APTA
aneurysm of persistent trigeminal
artery

APTD
Aid to Permanently and Totally
Disabled

APTT, aPTT
activated partial thromboplastin time

APTX
acute parathyroidectomy

APUD
amine precursor uptake and
decarboxylation (cell)

APVC
anomalous pulmonary venous
connection

APVD
anomalous pulmonary venous drainage

APVR
aortic pulmonary valve

APW
aortopulmonary window

AQ
achievement quotient
any quantity
aphasia quotient

aq.
aqueous *also* aqu
water [L. *aqua*] *also* A, a

aq. ad
add water [L. *aquam ad*]

aq. astr.
frozen water (ice) [L. *aqua
astrieta*]

aq. bull.
boiling water [L. *aqua bulliens*]

NOTES

43

aq. cal.
hot water [L. *aqua calida*]

aq. com.
common water [L. *aqua communis*]

aq. dest.
distilled water [L. *aqua destillata*]

aq. ferv.
hot water [L. *aqua fervens*]

aq. font.
spring water [L. *aqua fontana*]

aq. frig.
cold water [L. *aqua frigata*]

aq. mar.
sea water [L. *aqua marina*]

aq. pluv.
rain water [L. *aqua pluvialis*]

aq. pur.
pure water [L. *aqua pura*]

AQS
additional qualifying symptoms

aq. tep.
tepid water [L. *aqua tepida*]

aqu
aqueous *also* aq.

AR
abnormal record
achievement ratio
Achilles reflex
acoustic reflex
actinic reticuloid (syndrome)
active resistance
acute rejection
adherence ratio
admitting room
airway resistance *also* R_A, RAW, R_{AW}, R (AW)
alarm reaction
alcohol related
allergic rhinitis
alloy restoration
amplitude ratio
analytical reagent
androgen receptor
ankle reflex
anterior root
aortic regurgitation *also* aor regurg
apical-radial (pulse) *also* A-R, A/R
Argyll Robertson (pupil)
arsphenamine
articulare (craniometric point) *also* Ar
artificially ruptured

artificial respiration
assisted respiration
atrial rate
atrial regurgitation
at risk
atrophic rhinitis
attack rate
aural rehabilitation
autoradiography
autorefractor
autosomal recessive

A-R
apical-radial (pulse) *also* AR, A/R

A&R
adenoidectomy with radium
advised and released

A/R
accounts receivable
apical/radial (pulse) *also* AR, A-R

Ar
argon
articulare (craniometric point) *also* AR

ARA
acetylene reduction activity
adenosine regulating agent
antireticulin antibody
aortic root angiogram

Ara
arabinose

Ara-A, araA
arabinosyladenine (vidarabine)

Ara-C, araC
arabinosylcytosine (cytarabine) *also* aC
cytosine arabinoside *also* CA

araC-Hu
arabinosylcytosine (cytarabine) and hydroxyurea

ARAS
ascending reticular-activating system

ara-U
arabinosyluracil

ARB
adrenergic receptor binder
any reliable brand

arb
arbitrary (unit)

ARBD
alcohol-related birth defects

ARBOR
arthropod-borne (virus)

ARBOW
artificial rupture of bag of waters

ARC
abnormal retinal correspondence
accelerating rate calorimetry
acquired immunodeficiency syndrome-related complex
active renin concentration
AIDS-related complex
alcohol rehabilitation center
American Red Cross
anomalous retinal correspondence
antigen-reactive cell
arcuate nucleus (of brain)
average response computer

ARCA
acquired red-cell aplasia

ARCBS
American Red Cross Blood Services

Arch.
archives

ARCO
antigen-reactive cell opsonization

ARD
absolute reaction of degeneration
acute radiation disease
acute respiratory disease
acute respiratory distress
adult respiratory disease
adult respiratory distress
allergic respiratory disease
anorectal dressing
antibiotic removal device
antimicrobial removal device
aphakic retinal detachment
arthritis and rheumatic diseases
atopic respiratory disease

ARDS
acute respiratory distress syndrome
adult respiratory distress syndrome

ARE
active-resistive exercises
AIDS-related encephalitis

AREDYLD
acrorenal field defect, ectodermal dysplasia, and lipoatrophic diabetes

ARF
acute renal failure
acute respiratory failure
acute rheumatic fever
area resource file

ARFC
active rosette-forming T cell

ARF/CRF
acute renal failure and chronic renal failure

ARG, Arg
alkaline reflux gastritis
arginine *also* R

arg.
silver [L. *argentum*] *also* Ag

ARHL
age-related hearing loss

ARHNC
advanced resected head and neck cancer

ARI
acute renal insufficiency
acute respiratory infection
airway reactivity index
aldose reductase inhibitor
anxiety reaction, intense

ARIA
automated radioimmunoassay

ArKr
argon-krypton [laser]

ARL
average remaining lifetime

ARLD
alcohol-related liver disease

ARM
adrenergic receptor material
aerosol rebreathing method
allergy relief medicine
alternating rate of motion
anorectal manometry
anxiety reaction, mild

NOTES

ARM (continued)
artificial rupture of membranes *also*
AROM
atomic resolution microscopy

ARMD
age-related macular degeneration

ARMS
Adverse Reaction Monitoring System
amplification refractory mutation
system

ARN
acute renal necrosis
acute retinal necrosis
arcuate nucleus

ARNP
Advanced Registered Nurse
Practitioner

AROA
autosomal recessive ocular albinism

AROM
active range of motion
artificial rupture of membranes *also*
ARM

ARP
absolute refractory period
alcohol rehabilitation program
assay reference plasma
assimilation regulatory protein
at-risk period
automaticity recovery phase

ARPES
angular resolved photoelectron
spectroscopy

ARPF
anterior release posterior fusion

ARPKD
autosomal recessive polycystic kidney
disease

ARPKS
autosomal recessive polycystic kidney
disease

ARR
aortic root replacement

arr
arrest
arrested
arrive

ARROM
active resistive range of motion

Arry
arrhythmia

ARS
acquiescent response scale
adult recovery services
adult Reye syndrome
AIDS-related syndrome
alizarin red S (dye)
antirabies serum
arsphenamine
arylsulfatase

Ars
arsphenamine
arylsulfatase

ARS-A, Ars-A
arylsulfatase A *also* ASA, AsA

ARSACS
autosomal recessive spastic ataxia of
Charlevoix-Saguenay

ARS-B, Ars-B
arylsulfatase B *also* AsB

ARS-C, Ars-C
arylsulfatase C *also* AsC

ARSM
acute respiratory system malfunction

ART
absolute retention time
Accredited Record Technician
Achilles (tendon) reflex text
acoustic reflex test
acoustic reflex threshold (s)
algebraic reconstruction technique
arrhythmia research technology
arterial (line)
artery *also* A, a, art.
assisted reproductive technique
autologous reactive T cell
automated reagin test
automaticity recovery time

art.
arterial
artery *also* A, a, ART
articulation
artificial *also* artif

arth.
arthritis
arthrotomy

arthro
arthroscopy

ARTI
acute respiratory tract illness

artif
artificial *also* art.

art. line
arterial line *also* AL, A-line

Art T
art therapy

ARV
AIDS-associated retrovirus
AIDS-related virus
anterior right ventricular (wall)

ARVD
arrhythmogenic right ventricular
dysplasia

ARW
accredited rehabilitation worker

ARWY
airway

AS
above scale
acetylstrophanthidin
acidified serum
acoustic stimulation
active sarcoidosis
active sleep
acute salpingitis
Adams-Stokes (disease or syndrome)
adolescent suicide
aerosol steroid
affective style
alimentary sleep
Alport syndrome
alveolar sac
alveolar space
amphetamine sulfate
amyloid substance
anabolic steroid
anal sphincter
androgen suppression
androsteronesulfate
Angelman syndrome
ankylosing spondylitis *also* ASP
annulospiral
anovulatory syndrome
anterior synechia
antiserum
antisocial
antistreptolysin

antral spasm
anxiety state
aortic sac
aortic sound
aortic stenosis *also* A sten, aort sten
aqueous solution
aqueous suspension
arteriosclerosis *also* asc, ASCL, ATS
artificial sweetener
aseptic meningitis
asthma astrocyte
astigmatism *also* As, AST, Ast
asymmetric *also* A, a
atherosclerosis
atrial sense
atrial septum
atrial stenosis
atropine sulfate
audiogenic seizure
Auto-Suture
left ear [L. *auris sinistra*] *also* AL,
a.l., a.s.
sickle-cell trait (heterozygous
genotype for hemoglobin) *also* A/S

A-S
Adams-Stokes (disease or syndrome)
ascendance-submission

A/S
sickle-cell trait (heterozygous
genotype for hemoglobin) *also* AS

A(s)
asplenia syndrome

As
arsenic
astigmatism *also* AS, AST, Ast
asymptomatic
atmosphere, standard

A·s
ampere-second

aS
absiemens

a.s.
left ear [L. *auris sinistra*] *also* AL,
a.l., AS

ASA
acetylsalicylic acid
active systemic anaphylaxis

NOTES

ASA *(continued)*
Adams-Stokes attack
anterior spinal artery
argininosuccinate
argininosuccinic acid
arylsulfatase A *also* ARS-A, Ars-A,
AsA
aspirin-sensitive asthma
atrial septal aneurysm

ASA I
healthy patient with localized
pathologic process

ASA II
patient with mild to moderate
systemic disease

ASA III
patient with severe systemic disease
limiting activity but not
incapacitating

ASA IV
patient with incapacitating systemic
disease

ASA I–V
American Society of
Anesthesiologists' patient
classifications I to V, followed by
"E" for emergency operations

ASA V
moribund patient not expected to
live

5-ASA
5-aminosalicylic acid

AsA
arylsulfatase A *also* ARS-A, Ars-A,
ASA

Asa
arsenate

ASAA
acquired severe aplastic anemia

ASAC
acidified serum, acidified complement

ASACL
American Society of
Anesthesiologists' classification

ASA-G
guaiacolic acid ester of acetylsalicylic
acid

ASAH
antibiotic-sterilized aortic valve
homograft

ASAI
aortic stenosis and aortic
insufficiency (murmurs)

ASAL
argininosuccinic acid lyase

ASAP
as soon as possible

ASAS
argininosuccinate synthetase

ASAT
aspartate aminotransferase *also* AST

ASB
anencephaly-spinal bifida [syndrome]
anesthesia standby
Anxiety Scale for the Blind
asymptomatic bacteriuria

AsB
arylsulfatase B *also* ARS-B, Ars-B

ASBS
arteriosclerotic brain syndrome

ASC
acetylsulfanilyl chloride
adenosine-coupled spleen cell
altered state of consciousness
ambulatory surgery center
anterior subcapsular cataract
antigen-sensitive cell
antimony-sulfur colloid
ascorbic acid
asthma symptom checklist

AsC
arylsulfatase C *also* ARS-C, Ars-C

asc
anterior subcapsular
arteriosclerosis *also* AS, ASCL, ATS
arteriosclerotic
ascending

Asc-A
ascending aorta *also* AA

ASCAD
arteriosclerotic coronary artery disease
atherosclerotic coronary artery disease

ASCAo
ascending aorta

ASCCC
advanced squamous cell cervical
carcinoma

ASCI
acute spinal cord injury

ASCII
American Standard Code for Information Interchange

ascit fl
ascitic fluid *also* AF

ASCL
arteriosclerosis *also* AS, asc, ATS

ASCR
autologous stem cell rescue

ascr.
ascribed to [L. *ascriptum*]

ASCT
autologous stem-cell transplantation

ASCURD
arteriosclerotic cardiovascular renal disease

ASCUS
atypical squamous cell of undetermined significance

ASCVD
atherosclerotic cardiovascular disease

ASD
aldosterone secretion defect
Alzheimer senile dementia
anterior sagittal diameter
antisiphon device
arthritis syphilitica deformans
atrial septal defect

ASDH
acute subdural hematoma

ASE
acute stress erosion
axilla, shoulder, elbow (bandage)

ASES
Adult Self-Expression Scale

ASF
African swine fever
aniline-sulfur-formaldehyde (resin)
anterior spinal fusion
asialofetium

ASFR
age-specific fertility rate

ASG
advanced stage group

AS/GP
antiserum, guinea pig

ASH
aldosterone-stimulating hormone
ankylosing spinal hyperostosis
antistreptococcal hyaluronidase
asymmetric septal hypertrophy
hypermetropic astigmatism
hyperopic astigmatism *also* ah, AsH

A & Sh
arm and shoulder

AsH
hypermetropic astigmatism
hyperopic astigmatism *also* ah, ASH

ASHCVD
atherosclerotic hypertensive cardiovascular disease

ASHD
arteriosclerotic heart disease
atherosclerotic heart disease
atrial septal heart disease

ASHN
acute sclerosing hyaline necrosis

AS/Ho
antiserum, horse

ASI
active specific immunotherapy
addiction severity index
Anxiety Status Inventory
arthroscopic screw installation

ASIS
anterior superior iliac spine

ASK
antistreptokinase

ASKA
antiskeletal antibody

ASL
American sign language
ankylosing spondylitis, lung
anterolateral sclerosis
antistreptolysin

ASLC
acute self-limited colitis

ASLO, ASL-O
antistreptolysin-O *also* ASO, ASTO

NOTES

ASLT
    antistreptolysin test

ASLV
    avian sarcoma and leukosis virus
    (Rous virus)

ASM
    airway smooth muscle
    anterior scalenus muscle
    myopic astigmatism *also* AsM

AsM
    myopic astigmatism *also* ASM

ASMA
    antismooth muscle antibody

ASMC
    arterial smooth muscle cell

ASMD
    atonic sclerotic muscle dystrophy

ASMI
    anteroseptal myocardial infarction

As/Mk
    antiserum, monkey

ASMR
    age-standardized mortality ratio

asmt
    assessment

ASN
    alkali-soluble nitrogen
    arteriosclerotic nephritis
    asparagine *also* Asn, N

Asn
    asparagine *also* ASN, N

ASO
    aldicarb sulfoxide
    antistreptolysin-O *also* ASLO, ASL-O,
    ASTO
    arteriosclerosis obliterans
    automatic stop order

ASOR
    asialo-orosomucoid

ASOT
    antistreptolysin-O titer

ASP
    abnormal spinal posture
    acute suppurative parotitis
    acute symmetric polyarthritis
    African swine pox
    aged substrate plasma
    alkali-stable pepsin

ankylosing spondylitis *also* AS
antisocial personality
aortic systolic pressure
area systolic pressure
asparaginase *also* Aase, Asp, L-Spar
aspartic acid *also* Asp, asp
aspiration *also* asp

Asp
    asparaginase *also* Aase, ASP, L-Spar
    aspartic acid *also* ASP, asp

asp
    aspartate
    aspartic acid *also* ASP, Asp
    aspirate
    aspiration *also* ASP

ASPAT
    antistreptococcal polysaccharide A test

Asper
    aspergillosis

ASPG
    antispleen globulin

ASPS
    atherosclerotic peripheral vascular
    disease

ASPVD
    arteriosclerotic peripheral vascular
    disease

ASQ
    abbreviated symptom questionnaire
    anxiety scale questionnaire

ASR
    aldosterone secretion rate
    atrial-septal resection

AS/Rab
    antiserum, rabbit

ASS
    acute serum sickness
    acute spinal stenosis
    anterior-superior spine
    argininosuccinate synthetase

ASSC
    acute splenic sequestration crisis

AS-SCORE
    assessing severity: age of patient,
    systems involved, stage of disease,
    complications, response to therapy

Assn, assn
    association *also* Assoc

Assoc, assoc
associate *also* Assn, assn
association *also* Assn, assn

assocd
associated (with)

ASSR
adult situation stress reaction

asst
assistant

AST
angiotensin sensitivity test
anterior spinothalamic tract
antistreoptolysin titer
aspartate aminotransferase *also* ASAT
astemizole
astigmatism *also* AS, As, Ast
atrial overdrive stimulation rate
audiometry sweep test

Ast
astigmatism *also* AS, As, AST

ASTA
anti-α-staphylolysin

A sten
aortic stenosis *also* AS, aort sten

Asth
asthenopia

ASTI
acute soft tissue injury
antispasticity index

ASTO
antistreptolysin-O *also* ASLO, ASL-O,
ASO

AS TOL, as tol
as tolerated

ASTZ
antistreptozyme (test)

ASU
acute stroke unit
ambulatory surgical unit

ASV, AS-V, A/SV
anodic stripping voltametry
antisiphon valve
antisnake venom
arteriosuperficial venous (difference)
avian sarcoma virus

ASVD
arteriosclerotic vascular disease
arteriosclerotic vessel disease

ASVIP
atrial-synchronous ventricular-inhibited
pacemaker

ASW
artificial seawater

asw
artificially sweetened

Asx
amino acid that gives aspartic acid
after hydrolysis
asymptomatic

ASYM, asym
asymmetric
asymmetry

AT
abdominal tympany
Achard-Thiers [syndrome]
achievement test
Achilles tendon
activity therapy
adaptive thermogenesis
adipose tissue
adjunctive therapy
adjuvant therapy
air temperature
air trapping
allergy treatment
aminotransferase
aminotriazole
amitriptyline
anaerobic threshold
anaphylatoxin
anionic trypsinogen
anterior tibia
antithrombin
antitrypsin
antral transplantation
applanation tonometry
ataxia-telangiectasia *also* A-T
atraumatic
atresia, tricuspid
atrial tachycardia
atropine
attenuate
attenuation

NOTES

AT *(continued)*
autoimmune thrombocytopenia
axonal terminal
old tuberculin [Ger. *alt Tuberkulin*]

AT I
angiotensin I

ATIII, AT III
antithrombin III *also* AT III

AT$_7$
hexachlorophene

AT$_{10}$
dihydrotachysterol

At
astatine
atrial *also* ATR
atrium *also* A

a.t.
air tight
ampere turn

at.
atom
atomic

A-T
ataxia-telangiectasia *also* AT

ATA
alimentary toxic aleukia
aminotriazole
antithymic activity
antithyroglobulin antibody
antithyroid antibody
anti-*Toxoplasma* antibody
atmosphere absolute *also* ata
aurin tricarboxylic acid

ata
atmosphere absolute *also* ATA

ATB
antibiotic
atrial tachycardia with block
atypical tuberculosis

ATC
activated thymus cell
aerosol treatment chamber
alcoholism therapy classes
antituberulous chemoprophylaxis
around the clock

ATCS
active trabecular calcification surface
anterior tibial compartment syndrome

ATD
Alzheimer-type dementia

androstatrienedione
anthropomorphic test dummy
antithyroid drugs
aqueous tear deficiency
asphyxiating thoracic dystrophy
autoimmune thyroid disease

A-TDA
aminothiadiazole

ATE
acute toxic encephalopathy
adipose tissue extract
autologous tumor extract

ATEE, ATEe
N-acetyl-l-tyrosine ethyl ester

ATEM
analytic transmission electron
microscope

ATEN
atenolol

A tetra P
adenosine tetraphosphate

ATF
ascites tumor fluid

ATFC
alternative temporal forced choice

At Fib, at. fib.
atrial fibrillation *also* AF, AFib,
ATR FIB, atr fib.

ATFL
anterior talofibular ligament

AT III FUN
antithrombin III functional

ATG
adenine-thymine-guanine
antihuman thymocyte globulin
antithrombocyte globulin
antithymocyte globulin
antithymocyte globulin
antithyroglobulin

ATGAM
antithymocyte gamma globulin

Atgam
lymphocyte immunoglobulin

AT/GC
adenine-thymine/guanine-cytosine
(ratio)

ATH
acetyltyrosine hydrazide
anthropometric total hip

ATh
Associate in Therapy

ATHC
allotetrahydrocortisol

ATHR
angina threshold heart rate

Athsc
atherosclerosis

ATI
abdominal trauma index

ATL
Achilles tendon lengthening
adult T-cell leukemia *also* ATLL
adult T-cell lymphoma *also* ATLL
anterior tricuspid leaflet
antitension line
atypical lymphocytes

ATLA
adult T-cell leukemia antigen

ATLL
adult T-cell leukemia *also* ATL
adult T-cell lymphoma *also* ATL

ATLS
acute tumor lysis syndrome
advanced trauma life support

ATLV
adult T-cell leukemia virus

ATM
abnormal tubular myelin
acute transverse myelitis
acute transverse myelopathy

atm
(standard) atmosphere

ATMA
antithyroid plasma membrane antibody

At ma
atrial milliampere

atmos
atmospheric

ATN
acute tubular necrosis
augmented transition network
tyrosinase-negative oculocutaneous
albinism

ATNC, AT/NC
atraumatic normocephalic

aTNM
(at) autopsy tumor, nodes, and
metastases (staging of cancer)

at. no.
atomic number

ATNR
asymmetric tonic neck reflex

ATON
adductor tenotomy and obturator
neurectomy

ATP
addiction treatment program
adenosine triphosphate
adenosine 5'-triphosphate
ambient temperature and pressure
antitachycardia pacemaker
autoimmune thrombocytopenic purpura

AT-P
antitrypsin-Pittsburgh

A-TP
absorbed test plasma

AtP
attending physician

AT-PAS
aldehyde-thionine-periodic acid-Schiff
(test)

ATPase
adenosine triphosphatase

ATPD
ambient temperature and pressure,
dry

ATP-2Na
adenosine triphosphate disodium

ATPO
Association of Technical Personnel in
Ophthalmology

ATPS
ambient temperature and pressure,
saturated (with water vapor)

ATPTX
acute thyroparathyroidectomy

NOTES

ATR
Achilles tendon reflex
Achilles tendon rupture
atrial *also* At
attenuated total reflection

atr
atrophy

ATRA
all-trans-retinoic acid

ATR FIB, atr fib.
atrial fibrillation *also* AF, AFib, At
Fib

ATRO
atropine *also* A

ATS
Achard-Thiers syndrome
acid test solution
adjustable thigh antiembolism
stockings
American Thoracic Society
anti-rat thymocyte serum
antitetanic serum
antitetanus serum
antithymocyte serum
anxiety tension state
arteriosclerosis *also* AS, asc, ASCL
atherosclerosis
autotransfusion

ATT
arginine tolerance test
aspirin tolerance time

att
attending

ATTR
attached report

ATU
alcohol treatment unit
allylthiourea

ATV
arterioventricular
avian tumor virus

AtV
arteriovenous *also* AV, A-V
assisted ventilation *also* AV
atrioventricular *also* AV, A-V

at. vol
atomic volume

at. wt
atomic weight *also* AW

ATx
adult thymectomy

atyp
atypical

ATZ
anal transitional zone
atypical transformation zone

AU
according to custom [L. *ad usum*]
allergenic unit
allergy unit
Ångström unit
antitoxin unit
arbitrary unit
atomic unit
Australia antigen *also* AA, Au Ag
azauridine *also* AZU, AZUR, AzUr
both ears together [L. *aures unitas*]
also a.u.
each ear [L. *auris uterque*] *also* a.u.

Au
gold [L. *aurum*]

^{198}Au
colloidal gold
radioactive gold

^{198}Au
gold-198

a.u.
both ears together [L. *aures unitas*]
also AU
each ear [L. *auris uterque*] *also* AU

AUA
American Urological Association

Au Ag
Australia antigen *also* AA, AU

AUB
abnormal uterine bleeding

AUC
area under the curve

AUD, aud
arthritis of unknown diagnosis
auditory

AUDIT
Alcohol Use Disorders Identification
Test

aud-vis
audiovisual *also* AV

AUFS
absorbance units, full scale

AUG
  acute ulcerative gingivitis
  adenine, uracil, guanine
  adenine, uridine, guanosine

aug.
  increase [L. *augere*]

AUGH
  acute upper gastrointestinal
  hemorrhage

AUGIB
  acute upper gastrointestinal bleeding

AUHAA
  Australia hepatitis-associated antigen

AUI
  alcohol use inventory

AUL
  acute undifferentiated leukemia

AUM
  asymmetric unit membrane

Å unit
  Ångström unit

AUO
  amyloid of unknown origin

AuP
  Australia antigen protein

AUR
  acute urinary retention

aur, auric
  auricle
  auricular
  auris *also* a

AUR FIB, aur fib.
  auricular fibrillation *also* AF

AUS
  acute urethral syndrome
  artificial urinary sphincter
  auscultation *also* aus, ausc, auscul

aus, ausc, auscul
  auscultation *also* AUS

AuSH
  Australia serum hepatitis (antigen)

AutoAB
  autoantibody

Auto-PEEP
  self-controlled positive end-expiratory
  pressure

aux
  auxiliary

A-V
  arteriovenous *also* AtV, AV
  atrioventricular *also* AtV, AV
  auriculoventricular *also* AV

AV
  Adriamycin (doxorubicin) and
  vincristine
  allergic vasculitis
  alveolar duct
  anteroventral
  anteversion *also* Av, av
  anteverted *also* Av, av
  anticipatory vomiting
  antivirin
  aortic valve
  arteriovenous *also* AtV, A-V
  artificial ventilation
  assisted ventilation *also* AtV
  atrioventricular *also* AtV, A-V
  audiovisual *also* aud-vis
  auditory-visual
  augmented vector
  auriculoventricular *also* A-V
  average *also* Av, av, avg
  aviation medicine *also* AM, AVM
  avoirdupois *also* Av, av, AVDP,
  avdp

A/V
  ampere/volt
  arterial/venous
  atrial/ventricular
  auricular/ventricular

A:V
  arterial-venous (ratio in fundi)

Av, av
  anteversion *also* AV
  anteverted *also* AV
  average *also* AV, avg
  avoirdupois *also* AV, AVDP, avdp

aV
  abvolt

NOTES

AVA
antiviral antibody
aortic valve area
aortic valve atresia
arteriovenous anastomosis
availability

AVAD
acute ventricular assist device

AV/AF
anteverted and anteflexed
anteverted/anteflexed

AVB
atrioventricular block

AVBR
automated ventricular brain ratio

AVC
aberrant ventricular conduction
acrylic veneer crown
allantoin vaginal cream
associative visual cortex
atrioventricular canal
atrioventricular conduction
automatic volume control

AVCD
arterioventricular canal defect

AvCDO₂
arteriovenous oxygen content
difference *also* AVDO₂

AVCS
atrioventricular conduction system

AVD
aortic valvular disease
apparent volume of distribution
arteriosclerotic vascular disease
arteriovenous difference
atrioventricular dissociation

AVDO₂
arteriovenous oxygen content
difference *also* AvCDO₂

AVDP, avdp
asparaginase, vincristine, daunorubicin,
and prednisone
average diastolic pressure
avoirdupois *also* AV, Av, av

AvDP
average diastolic pressure

AVE
aortic valve echocardiogram
atrioventricular extrasystole

aver
average

AVF
antiviral factor
arteriovenous fistula

aVF
augmented voltage unipolar left foot
lead (electrocardiography)

AVFM
arteriovenous fistulous malformation

AVG
ambulatory visit groups (patient
classification)
aortic valve gradient
peak transaortic valve gradient

avg
average *also* AV, Av, av

AVGS
autologous vein graft stent

AVH
acute viral hepatitis

AVHB
atrioventricular heart block

AVHD
acquired valvular heart disease

AVI
air velocity index

A-V IMA
arteriovenous internal mammary
(fistula)

AVJR
atrioventricular junctional rhythm

AVJRe
arterioventricular junctional reentrant

AVJT
atrioventricular functional tachycardia

AVL
anterior vein of the leg

aVL
augmented voltage unipolar left arm
lead (electrocardiography)

AVLINE
audiovisuals on-line

AVM
Adriamycin (doxorubicin), vinblastine,
and methotrexate
arteriovenous malformation
arterioventricular malfunction

atrioventricular malformation
aviation medicine *also* AM, AV

AVN
acute vasomotor nephropathy
arbitrary valve unit
arteriovenous nicking
atrioventricular nodal (conduction)
atrioventricular node
avascular necrosis

AVND
arterioventricular node dysfunction

AVNFH
avascular necrosis of the femoral
head

AVNFRP
atrioventricular node functional
refractory period

AVNR
atrioventricular nodal reentry

AVNRT
atrioventricular nodal reentrant
tachycardia

AVNT
atrioventricular nodal tachycardia

AVO
atrioventricular opening

A-VO$_2$
arteriovenous oxygen difference

AVP
Adriamycin (doxorubicin), vincristine,
and procarbazine
ambulatory venous pressure
antiviral protein
aqueous vasopressin
arginine vasopressin
arteriovenous passage [time]

AVPR2
antidiuretic arginine vasopressin V2
receptor

AVR
accelerated ventricular rhythm
aortic valve replacement

AVr
antiviral regulator

aVR
augmented voltage unipolar right arm
lead (electrocardiography)

AVRB
added viscous resistance to breathing

AVRI
acute viral respiratory infection

AVRP
atrioventricular refractory period

AVRT
atrial ventricular reciprocating
tachycardia
atrioventricular reentrant tachycardia

AVS
aneurysm of membranous ventricular
septum
aortic valve stenosis
arteriovenous shunt
auditory vocal sequencing

AVSC
aortic valve cusp separation

AVSD
atrioventricular septal defect

AVSS
afebrile, vital signs stable

AVSV
aortic valve stroke volume

AVT
Allen vision test
area ventralis of Tsai
arginine oxytocin
arginine vasotocin
atrioventricular tachycardia
atypical ventricular tachycardia

AVTB
absolute volume of trabecular bone

Av3V
anteroventral third ventricle

AVZ
avascular zone

AW
abdominal wall
abnormal wave
above waist
abrupt withdrawal

NOTES

AW *(continued)*
alcohol withdrawal
aluminum wafer
alveolar wall
alveolar wash
anterior wall
atomic warfare
atomic weight *also* at. wt

A3W
crystalline amino-acid solution

A&W
alive and well

A/W
able to work

aw
airway

AWA
as well as
away without authorization

AWBM
alveolar wall basement membrane

AWF
adrenal weight factor

AWG
American wire gauge

AWI
anterior wall infarction
authorized walk-in (patient)

AWMI
anterior wall myocardial infarction

AWO
airway obstruction

AWOL
absent without leave

AWP
airway pressure

AWRS
antiwhole rabbit serum

AWRU
active wrist rotation unit

AWS
alcohol withdrawal syndrome

AWTA
aniridia-Wilms tumor association

awu
atomic weight unit

AX
alloxan

Ax
axilla *also* ax.
axillary *also* ax.

ax
axis

ax.
axial *also* A, a
axilla *also* Ax
axillary *also* Ax
axis
axon

AXB
axillary block

AXC
aortic crossclamp

AXF
advanced x-ray facility

AXG
adult-type xanthogranuloma

ax. grad
axial gradient

AX-HSA
amoxicilloyl-human serum albumin

AXL
axillary lymphoscintigraphy

AXM
acetoxycycloheximide

AXR
abdominal x-ray

Axs
ampere per second

AXT
alternating exotropia

AYA
acute yellow atrophy

AYF
antiyeast factor

AYP
autolyzed yeast protein

AZ
acetazolamide
Aschheim-Zondek (test) *also* A-Z
azathioprine *also* AZA, Aza

A-Z
Aschheim-Zondek (test) *also* AZ

Az
nitrogen [Fr. *azote*]

AZA
azathioprine *also* AZ, Aza

5-AZA
5-azacytidine

Aza
azathioprine *also* AZ, AZA

AzBF
azygos blood flow

AzC
azacytosine

AZG, azg
azaguanine

AZH
assisted zonal hatching

AZO, azo
indicates presence of the group N:N

AZQ
aziridinylbenzoquinone
diaziquone

AZR
alizarin

AZS
automatic zero set

AZT
Aschheim-Zondek test
3′-azido-3′deoxythymidine zidovudine (azidothymidine)
azidothymidine (zidovudine)

AZU, AZUR, AzUr
azauridine *also* AU

AZUR
6-azauridine

NOTES

B

bacillus
bacitracin
bacterium
bands
barometric *also* BAR, bar.
base (chemistry, of a prism) *also* b
baseline
basophil *also* ba, bas, baso
basophilic
bath [L. *balneum*] *also* BAL, bal.
Baumé scale
behavior
bel
Benoist scale
benzoate
beta (second letter of Greek
  alphabet), uppercase
bicuspid
bilateral *also* BIL, bil, bilat
black *also* Bl, blk
blood *also* b, BL, bl, bld
bloody
blue *also* bl
body
boils at *also* b
Bolton point *also* bb, BO, Bo, BP
bone
bone marrow-derived (cell or
  lymphocyte)
born *also* b, n.
boron
both
bound *also* BD
bovine
bregma
bronchial
bronchus
brother *also* br, BRO, bro
bruit
buccal
Bucky (film in cassette in Potter-
  Bucky diaphragm)
bursa cells
corticosterone (compound B)
gauss (unit of magnetic induction)
magnetic flux density
magnetic induction
supramentale (craniometric point) *also*
  b
tomogram with oscillating Bucky
twice [L. *bis*] *also* b., bis.
whole blood *also* QB, WB, W Bld

B1
bifurcation of root

B2
bromobenzene

BI
Billroth I (operation)

BII
Billroth II (operation)

b
barn (unit of area for atomic nuclei)
base *also* B
bis
blood *also* B, BL, bl, bld
boils at *also* B
born *also* B, n.
brain *also* BRA
supramentale (craniometric point) *also*
  B

b.
twice [L. *bis*] *also* B, bis.

B_0
constant magnetic field in nuclear
  magnetic resonance

B_1
radiofrequency magnetic field in
  nuclear magnetic resonance
thiamin

B_2
riboflavin

B_6
pyridoxine

B_7
biotin

B_8
adenosine phosphate

B_{12}
cyanocobalamin

BA
backache *also* B/A
background activity
bacterial agglutination
basilar artery
basion *also* Ba, ba
basket axon
benzanthracene
benzyladenine
benzyl alcohol
benzylamine

BA *(continued)*
best amplitude
betamethasone acetate
bilateral asymmetric
bile acid
biliary atresia
biologic activity
blocking antibody
blood agar
blood alcohol
bone age
boric acid
Bourns assist
bovine albumin
brachial artery (pressure)
breathing apparatus
bronchial asthma
bronchoalveolar
buccoaxial
buffered acetone
butyric acid

B < A
bone conduction less than air
conduction *also* BC < AC

B > A
bone conduction greater than air
conduction *also* BC > AC

B&A
before and after
brisk and active

B/A
backache *also* BA

Ba
barium
barium (enema)
basion *also* BA, ba

b.a.
sand bath [L. *baleum arenae*] *also*
bal. are.

ba
basion *also* BA, Ba
basophil *also* B, bas, baso

BAA
benzoylarginine amide
branched-chain amino acid

BAB
blood agar base

Bab
Babinski (reflex, sign)

BabK
baboon kidney

BAC
bacteria
bacterial adherent colony
bacterial antigen complex
BCNU, ara-C, cyclophosphamide
benzalkonium chloride
blood alcohol concentration
bronchioloalveolar carcinoma
bronchoalveolar cells
buccoaxiocervical

Bac, bac.
bacillary [L. *Bacillus*]
Bacillus

BACCT
base activated clotting time

BaClr
barium chloride

BACO
bleomycin, Adriamycin (doxorubicin),
CCNU (lomustine), and Oncovin
(vincristine)

BACON
bleomycin, Adriamycin (doxorubicin),
CCNU (lomustine), Oncovin
(vincristine), and nitrogen mustard
(mechlorethamine)

BACOP
bleomycin, Adriamycin (doxorubicin),
cyclophosphamide, Oncovin
(vincristine), and prednisone

BACT
BCNU, ara-C, cyclophosphamide, 6-
thioguanine
bischloroethyl-nitrosourea, arabinosylcytosine, Cytoxan
(cyclophosphamide), and 6-
thioguanine
bleomycin, Adriamycin (doxorubicin),
Cytoxan (cyclophosphamide), and
tamoxifen citrate

Bact, bact
bacteriologist
bacteriology

bact
bacteria
bacterial
bacteriologist
bacteriology

BAD
benign anorectal disease

biologic aerosol detection
bipolar affective disorder

BADGE
Bekesy Ascending-Descending Gap Evaluation

BADL
basic activities of daily living

BAE
bovine aortic endothelium
bronchial artery embolization

BaE
barium enema *also* BaEn, BE

BAEE
benzoylarginine ethyl ester

BaEn
barium enema *also* BaE, BE

BAEP
brainstem auditory-evoked potential

BAER
brainstem auditory-evoked response

BAG
buccoaxiogingival

BAGF
brachioaxillary bridge graft fistula

BAGG
buffered azide glucose glycerol

BAI
basilar artery insufficiency

BAIB
β-aminoisobutyric (acid)

BAIF
bile acid independent flow
bile acid independent fraction

BAIT
bacterial automated identification technique

BAL
balance *also* bal
bath [L. *balneum*] *also* B, bal.
blood alcohol level
British antilewisite
bronchoalveolar lavage

bal
balance *also* BAL
balsam *also* bals

bal.
bath [L. *balneum*] *also* B, BAL

bal. are.
sand bath [L. *balneum arenae*] *also* b.a.

BALB
binaural alternate loudness balance

bal. cal.
hot bath [L. *balneum calidum*]

bal. coen.
mud bath [L. *balneum coenosum*]

BALF
bronchoalveolar lavage fluid

bal. frig.
cold bath [L. *balneum frigidum*]

B ALL
B-cell acute lymphoblastic leukemia

bal. lact.
milk bath [L. *balneum lacteum*]

bal. mar.
salt-water or sea-water bath [L. *balneum maris*] *also* b.m.

bal. pneu.
air bath [L. *balneum pneumaticum*]

bals
balsam *also* bal

BALT
bronchus-associated lymphoid tissue

bal. tep.
warm bath [L. *balneum tepidum*]

bal. vap.
steam or vapor bath [L. *balneum vapor*]

BAM
bile acid malabsorption
brachial artery mean (pressure)
bronchoalveolar macrophage

BAm
mean brachial artery (pressure)

NOTES

BaM
barium meal

Bam
benzamide

BAME
benzoylarginine methyl ester

BAN
British approved name

BAND
band neutrophil (stab)

BANS
back, arm, neck, and scalp

BAO
Bachelor of the Art of Obstetrics
basal acid output
brachial artery output

BAO/MAO
ratio of basal acid output to
maximal acid output

BAP
bacterial alkaline phosphatase
basic adaptive process
Behavior Activity Profile
Behavioral Assessment of Pain
bleomycin, Adriamycin (doxorubicin),
and prednisone
blood agar plate
bovine albumin in phosphate buffer
brachial artery pressure

BaP
benzoapyrene

BAPI
barley alkaline protease inhibitor

BAPN
β-aminoproprionitrile fumarate

BAPS
Biomechanical Ankle Platform System
bovine albumin phosphate saline

BAPV
bovine alimentary papillomavirus

BAQ
brain-age quotient

BAR, bar.
bariatrics
barometer
barometric *also* B
beta adrenergic receptor
biofragmentable anastomotic ring

BARACCO
balloon angioplasty versus rotational
angioplasty in chronic coronary
occlusion

Barb, barb
barbiturate

BARI
Bypass Angioplasty Revascularization
Investigation

BARN
bilateral acute retinal necrosis

BART
blood-activated recalcification time

BAS
balloon atrial septostomy
benzyl antiserotonin
bioanalytical systems
boric acid solution

BaS
barium swallow *also* BS

bas
basilar
basophil *also* B, ba, baso
basophilic

BASE
b27-arthritis-sacroiliitis-extraarticular
features (syndrome)

BASH
body acceleration synchronous with
heart rate

BASK
basket cell *also* BC

baso
basophil *also* B, ba, bas

BASO STIP
basophilic stippling

BAT
Basic Aid Training
basic assurance test
benzilic acid 3α-tropanyl ester
best available technology
brain adjacent tumor
Brightness Acuity Test
brown adipose tissue

batt
battery

BAV
balloon aortic valvotomy

balloon aortic valvuloplasty *also*
BAVP
bicommissural aortic valve
bicuspid aortic valve

BAVCP
bilateral abductor vocal cord paralysis

BAVFO
bradycardia after arteriovenous fistula
occlusion

BAVIP
bleomycin, Adriamycin (doxorubicin),
vinblastine, imidazole carboxamide
(dacarbazine), and prednisone

BAVP
balloon aortic valvuloplasty *also*
BAV

BAW
bronchoalveolar washing

BB
baby boy
backboard
bad breath
bath blanket
bed bath
bed board
beta blockade
beta blocker
BioBreeding (rat)
blanket bath
blood bank *also* BLBK
blood buffer (base)
blow bottle
blue bloater (emphysema)
body belts
both bones (fractures)
bowel and bladder (function) *also*
B&B
breakthrough bleeding *also* BTB
breast biopsy *also* B Bx, br bx
brush border
buffer base
bundle branch
isoenzyme of creatine kinase
containing two B subunits

B/B
backward bending

B&B
bowel and bladder *also* BB

Bb
Borrelia burgdorferi

bb
Bolton point *also* B, BO, Bo, BP
both bones

BBA
born before arrival

BBB
blood-brain barrier
blood buffer base
bundle-branch block

BBBB
bilateral bundle-branch block

BBC
bromobenzylcyanide
Brow-Buerger cytoscope

BBD
baby born dead
before bronchodilator
benign breast disease

BBE
Bacteroides bile esculin (agar)

BBEP
brush-border endopeptidase

BBF
bronchial blood flow

BBFD
blood and body fluid precaution

BBG
big big gastrin

BBHB
bundle branch heart block

BBI
Bowman-Birk soybean inhibitor

BBM
banked breast milk
brush-border membrane

BB to MM
belly button to medial malleolus

BBMV
brush-border membrane vesicle

NOTES

BBN
broad-band noise

BBOT
2,5-bis(5-t-butylbenzoxazol-2-yl)thiophene

BBOW
bulging bag of water

BBP
butylbenzyl phthalate

BBPRL
big big prolactin

BBR
bibasilar rale

BBRS
Burks Behavior Rating Scale

BBS
Bardet-Biedl syndrome
bashful bladder syndrome
benign breast syndrome
bilateral breath sounds
bombesin
brown bowel syndrome

BBs
both bones

BBT
basal body temperature

BB/W
BioBreeding/Worcester (rat)

B Bx
breast biopsy *also* BB, br bx

BC
back care *also* bc
backcross
background counts
bactericidal concentration
basal cell
basket cell *also* BASK
battle casualty
bed and chair *also* B&C
beta carotene
bicarbonate *also* Bicarb, bicarb, HCO₃
biliary colic
biotin carboxylase
bipolar cell
birth control
bladder cancer
blastic crisis
blood cardioplegia
blood center
blood count

blood culture *also* BlC, BL CULT, bl cult
Blue Cross (plan) *also* BX
board certified
bone conduction
Bourn control
Bowman capsule
brachiocephalic
bronchial carcinoma
buccal cartilage
buccal cusp
buccocervical
buffalo cap (cap for IV line)
buffy coat
bulbus chordae

B/C
because
blood urea nitrogen/creatinine (ratio)

B&C
bed and chair *also* BC
biopsy and curettage
board and care
breathed and cried

bc
back care *also* BC

b/c
benefit/cost (ratio)

BCA
balloon catheter angioplasty
basal cell atypia
bidirectional cavopulmonary anastomosis
blood color analyzer
Blue Cross Association
brachiocephalic artery
branchial cleft anomaly
breast cancer antigen

BCAA
branched-chain amino acid

BCAC
Breast Cancer Advisory Center

BC < AC
bone conduction less than air conduction *also* B < A

BC > AC
bone conduction greater than air conduction *also* B > A

BCAP
BCNU, cyclophosphamide, Adriamycin, prednisone

BCAT
brachiocephalic arterial trunk

B-CAVe
bleomycin, CCNU (lomustine), Adriamycin (doxorubicin), and Velban (vinblastine)

BCB
blood-cerebrospinal fluid barrier
brilliant cresyl blue (stain)

BCBR
bilateral carotid body resection

BC/BS
Blue Cross/Blue Shield (plan) *also* BX/BS, BX BS

BCC
basal cell carcinoma *also* BCCa
biliary cholesterol concentration
birth control clinic
Bushey compression clamp

bcc
body-centered-cubic

BCCa
basal cell carcinoma *also* BCC

BCCG
British Cooperative Clinical Group

BCCP
biotin carboxyl carrier protein

BCD
basal cell dysplasia
binary-coded decimal
bleomycin, cyclophosphamide, and dactinomycin
borderline of cardiac dullness

BCDDP
Breast Cancer Detection Demonstration Project

BCDF
B-cell differentiation factor

BCDH
bilateral congenital dislocated hip

BCDSP
Boston Collaborative Drug Surveillance Program

BCE
basal cell epithelioma
B-cell enriched
benign childhood epilepsy
bubble chamber equipment

BCF
basophil chemotactic factor
bioconcentration factor
breast cyst fluid

BCFP
breast cyst fluid protein

BCG
bacille Calmette-Guérin (vaccine)
ballistocardiogram
ballistocardiograph
ballistocardiography
bicolor guaiac (test)
bilateral cystogram
bromcresol green
bronchocentric granulomatosis

BCGF
B-cell growth factor

BCH
basal cell hyperplasia
basal cell hypoplasia
benign coital headache

BCHA
bone conduction hearing aid

BChD
Bachelor of Dental Surgery *also* BDS

bChl, Bchl
bacterial chlorophyll

BCHS
Bureau of Community Health Services

BCIC
Birth Control Investigation Committee

BCKA
branched-chain keto acid

BCKD
branched-chain alpha keto acid dehydrogenase

BCL
basic cycle length

NOTES

BCL *(continued)*
B-cell lymphoma
Bekesy comfortable loudness

BCLL
B-cell chronic lymphocytic leukemia

BCLP
bilateral cleft of lip and palate

BCLS
basic cardiac life support (system)

BCM
below costal margin
birth control medication
blood-clotting mechanism (effects)
body cell mass

BCME
bischloromethyl ether

BCN
basal cell nevus
bilateral cortical necrosis

BCNP
board-certified nuclear pharmacist

BCNS
basal cell nevus syndrome

BCNU
bischloroethylnitrosourea (carmustine)

BCO
biliary cholesterol output

BCOC
bowel care of choice

BCP
basic calcium phosphate
biochemical profile
birth control pill
bischloroethylnitrosourea (carmustine),
 cyclophosphamide, and prednisone
blood cell profile
Blue Cross Plan
bromcresol purple

BCPAP
Broun continuous positive airway
 pressure

BCP-D
bromcresol purple desoxycholate
 (agar)

BCPS
battery-charging power supply

BCPV
bovine cutaneous papillomavirus

BCQ
breast central quadrantectomy

BCR
B-cell reactivity
birth control regimen
bromocriptine *also* Brc, BRO
buccal cervical ridge
bulbocavernosus reflex

bcr
breakpoint cluster region

BCRP
Breast Cancer Research Program

BCRT
breast conservation followed by
 radiation therapy

BCRx
birth control drug

BCS
battered-child syndrome
blood cell separator
breast conserving surgery
Budd-Chiari syndrome

BCSI
breast cancer screening indicator

BCSS
bone cell stimulating substance

BCT
brachiocephalic trunk
breast conserving therapy

BCTF
Breast Cancer Task Force

BCtg
bovine chymotrypsinogen

BCtr
bovine chymotrypsin

BCU
burn care unit

BCUG
bilateral cystourethrogram

BCVPP
BCNU, cyclophosphamide, vinblastine,
 procarbazine, prednisone
bleomycin, cyclophosphamide,
 vincristine, procarbazine, prednisone

BCW
biologic and chemical warfare

BCYE
buffered charcoal yeast extract

BD
band neutrophil
barbital-dependent
barbiturate dependence
base deficit
base (of prism) down
basophilic degeneration
Batten disease
beclomethasone dipropionate
Becton Dickinson (catheter, guidewire, spinal needle)
behavioral disorder
behavior disorder
Behçet disease
belladonna
below diaphragm
benzidine
benzodiazepine
bicarbonate dialysis
bile duct
binocular deprivation
birth date
birth defect
black death
block design (test)
blood donor
blue diaper (syndrome)
board *also* Bd
borderline dull
bound *also* B
brain death
brain dysfunction
Briquet disorder
bronchial drainage
bronchodilator
buccodistal
Byler disease
twice a day [L. *bis die*] *also* b.d., BID, b.i.d.

B-D
Becton Dickinson (catheter, guidewire, spinal needle)

B&D
bondage and discipline

Bd
board *also* BD

b.d.
twice a day [L. *bis die*] *also* BD, BID, b.i.d.

bd
band
bundle

BDA
balloon dilation angioplasty
bile duct adenoma
British Dental Association

BDAC
Bureau of Drug Abuse Control

BDAE
Boston Diagnostic Aphasia Examination

BDB
bis-diazotized-benzidine

BDBS
Bonnet-Dechaume-Blanc syndrome

BDC
burn dressing change

BDE
bile duct examination
bile duct exploration

BDentSci
Bachelor of Dental Science *also* BDSc

BDF
bilateral distal femoral
black divorced female

BDG
bilirubin diglucuronide
buccal developmental groove
buffered desoxycholate glucose

BDI
Beck Depression Index
burn depth indicator

BDIBS
Boston Diagnostic Inventory of Basic Skills

BDID
bystander dominates initial dominant (psychology)

BDI SF
Beck Depression Index-Short Form

NOTES

BDL
  below detectable limits
  bile duct ligation

BDLS
  Brachmann-de Lange syndrome

BDM
  Becker muscular dystrophy
  benzphetamine demethylase
  black divorced male
  border detection method

BDMP
  Birth Defects Monitoring Program

bDNA
  branched chain DNA

B-DOPA
  bleomycin, dacarbazine, Oncovin
  (vincristine), prednisone, and
  Adriamycin (doxorubicin)

BDP
  beclomethasone dipropionate
  benzodiazepine
  bilateral diaphragm paralysis
  bronchopulmonary dysplasia

BDR
  background diabetic retinopathy

BDS
  Bachelor of Dental Surgery *also*
  BChD
  biologic detection system
  Blessed Dementia Scale

b.d.s.
  to be taken twice a day [L. *bid in
  die summendus*]

BDSc
  Bachelor of Dental Science *also*
  BDentSci

BDTVMI
  Beery Developmental Test of Visual-
  Motor Integration

BDUR
  bromodeoxyuridine

BDV
  balloon dilation valvuloplasty
  Borna disease virus

BDW
  buffered distilled water

BE
  bacillary emulsion (tuberculin)
  bacterial endocarditis *also* BEC

  barium enema *also* BaE, BaEn
  Barrett esophagus
  base excess
  below-elbow (amputation) *also* B/E
  bile esculin (test)
  board eligible
  bovine enteritis
  brain edema
  bread equivalent
  breast examination
  bronchoesophagology

B↓E
  both lower extremities

B&E
  brisk and equal

B/E
  below-elbow (amputation) *also* BE

B↑E
  both upper extremities

Be
  Baumé (scale)
  beryllium

BEA
  below-elbow amputation
  bromoethylamine

BEAC
  BCNU, etoposide, ara-C,
  cyclophosphamide

BEAM
  BCNU, etoposide, ara-C, melphalan
  brain electrical activity mapping
  brain electrical activity monitoring

BEAP
  bronchiectasis, eosinophilia, asthma,
  pneumonia

BEAR
  Biologic Effects of Atomic Radiation
  (Committee)
  Bourn electronic adult respirator
  brainstem-evoked auditory response

BEB
  blind esophageal brushing

BEC
  bacterial endocarditis *also* BE
  blood ethanol content
  bromoergocryptine

BECF
  blood extracellular fluid

BEE
  basal energy expenditure

BEEP
both end-expiratory pressures

BEF
bronchoesophageal fistula

bef
before

beg.
begin
beginning

BEH
benign essential hypertension

beh
behavior
behavioral

Beh Sp
behavior specialist

BEI
back-scattered electron imaging
Biological Exposure Indexes
butanol-extractable iodine

BEIR
biologic effects of ionizing radiation

BEK
bovine embryonic kidney (cell)

BEL
blood ethanol level
bovine embryonic lung

BELB
below-elbow

BELD
bleomycin, Eldisine, lomustine,
dacarbazine

ben.
well [L. *bene*]

BENAR
blood eosinophilic nonallergic rhinitis

Benz
benzidine
benzoate

BEP
bleomycin, etoposide, and Platinol
(cisplatin)
brain-evoked potential
brainstem-evoked potential

BEPI
β-endorphin immunoreactivity

BEPTI
bionomics, environment, *Plasmodium*,
treatment, and immunity (malaria
epidemiology)

BER
basic electrical rhythm
benign early repolarization

BERA
brainstem electric response audiometry

BES
balanced electrolyte solution

BESM
bovine embryo skeletal muscle

BESP
Bipolar EndoStasis probe
bovine embryonic spleen (cells)

BET
benign epithelial tumor
bleeding esophageal varix
Brunauer-Emmet-Teller (method)

bet.
between

β
anomer of carbohydrate
beta (second letter of Greek
alphabet), lowercase
buffer capacity
carbon separated from carboxyl by
one other carbon in aliphatic
compounds
constituent of plasma protein fraction
probability of type II error
second in series or group
substituent group of steroid that
projects above plane of ring

β⁺
positron

β-HCG
human chorionic gonadotropin beta-
subunit

betaLP
beta lipoprotein

NOTES

B

β₂m
β₂-microglobulin

β-T
β-tocopherol

BETS
benign epileptiform transients of
sleep

BEV
baboon endogenous virus
billion electron volts *also* BeV, Bev,
bev
bleeding esophageal varices

BeV, Bev, bev
billion electron volts *also* BEV

Bex
base excess

BF
bentonite flocculation (test)
bile flow
black female *also* B/F
blastogenic factor
blister fluid
blocking factor
blood flow *also* Q_B
body fat
Bolivian hemorrhagic fever
bone fragment
bouillon filtrate (tuberculin) *also* bf
boyfriend
breakfast fed
breast fed
buccofacial
buffered
burning feet (syndrome)
butter fat

B/F
black female *also* BF
bound/free (antigen ratio)

bf
bouillon filtrate (tuberculin) *also* BF

BFA
baby for adoption
bifemoral arteriogram

BFB
biologic feedback
bronchial foreign body

BFC
benign febrile convulsion

BFD
bias flow down

BFDI
bronchodilation following deep
inspiration

BFDT
Bekesy Functionality Detection Test

BFEC
benign focal epilepsy of childhood

bFGF
basic fibroblast growth factor

BFH
benign familial hematuria

BFL
bird fancier's lung
breast firm and lactating

BFLS
Börjeson-Forssman-Lehmann syndrome

BFM
bendroflumethiazide
black married female

BFNC
benign familial neonatal convulsions

BFO
balanced forearm orthesis
ball-bearing forearm orthesis
blood-forming organ
buccofacial obturator

BFP
biologic false-positive

BFPR
biologic false-positive reaction

BFPSTS
biologic false-positive serological test
for syphilis

BFR
biologic false-positive reactor
blood filtration rate
blood flow rate
bone formation rate
buffered Ringer (solution) *also* BFR
sol

BFR sol
buffered Ringer solution *also* BFR

BFS
blood fasting sugar

BFT
bentonite flocculation test
biofeedback training
bladder flap tube

B

BFU
   burst-forming unit

BFU-E
   burst-forming unit, erythroid

BG
   baby girl
   background *also* BKg
   basal ganglion
   basic gastrin
   bicolor guaiac (test)
   big gastrin
   blood glucose *also* BGlu
   blood group (system)
   bone graft
   Bordet-Gengou (agar, bacillus,
    phenomenon) *also* B-G
   brilliant green
   buccal groove
   buccogingival
   β-galactosidase
   β-glucuronidase

B-G
   Bender-Gestalt (test) *also* BGT
   Bordet-Gengou (agar, bacillus,
    phenomenon) *also* BG

BGA
   blue-green algae

BGAg
   blood group antigen

B-GALACTO
   β-galactosidase

BGAV
   blue-green algae virus

BGC
   basal ganglion calcification
   blood group class

BGCA
   bronchogenic carcinoma

BGCF
   buccal groove of central fossa

BG-corr
   background corrected

BGCT
   benign glandular cell tumor

BGD
   blood group degrading (enzyme)

BGDC
   Bartholin gland duct cyst

BGDR
   background diabetic retinopathy

BGE
   butyl glycidyl ether

BGG
   bovine gammaglobulin

BGH, bGH
   bovine growth hormone

Bg^J
   beige (mouse)

BGL
   blood glucose level

BGLB
   brilliant green lactose broth

BGlu
   blood glucose *also* BG

BGM
   blood glucose monitoring

BGMV
   bean golden mosaic virus

BGO
   bismuth germinate

BGP
   β-glycerophosphatase
   bone Gla protein

BGRS
   blood glucose reagent strip

BGS
   balance, gait, and station
   blood group substance

BGSA
   blood granulocyte-specific activity

BGT
   basophil granulation test
   Bender-Gestalt test *also* B-G
   bungarotoxin

BGTT
   borderline glucose tolerance test

NOTES

BH
  base hospital
  benzalkonium and heparin
  bill of health
  birth history
  Bishop-Harman (instrument)
  board of health
  Bolton-Hunter (reagent)
  borderline hypertensive
  both hands
  bowel habits
  brain hormone
  Braxton-Hicks (contraction)
  breath holding
  bronchial hyperactivity
  bronchial hyperreactivity
  Bryan high titer
  bundle of His

BH$_4$
  tetrahydrobiopterin

BHA
  benign hilar adenopathy
  bilateral hilar adenopathy
  bound hepatitis antibody
  butylated hydroxyanisole

BHAT
  beta blocker heart attack trial

BHB
  β-hydroxybutyrate

bHb
  bovine hemoglobin

BHBA
  β-hydroxybutyric acid

BHC
  benzene hexachloride

bHCG, bhCG
  beta human chorionic gonadotropin

BHD
  BCNU (carmustine), hydroxyurea, and
  dacarbazine

BHD-V
  BCNU (carmustine), hydroxyurea,
  dacarbazine, and vincristine

B-HEXOS-A-K
  β-hexosaminidase A leukocytes

BHF
  Bolivian hemorrhagic fever

BHI
  beef heart infusion (broth)
  biosynthetic human insulin
  brain heart infusion (broth)
  Bureau of Health Insurance

BHIA
  brain heart infusion agar

BHI-ac
  brain heart infusion broth with
  acetone

BHIB
  brain heart infusion broth

BHIBA
  brain heart infusion blood agar

BHIRS
  brain heart infusion and rabbit serum

BHIS
  beef heart infusion-supplemented
  (broth)

BHK
  baby hamster kidney (cells)
  type B Hong Kong (influenza virus)

BHL
  bilateral hilar lymphadenopathy
  biologic half-life

BHM
  Bureau of Health Manpower

BHN
  bephenium hydroxynaphthoate
  bridging hepatic necrosis
  Brinell hardness number

BHP
  basic health profile
  Bureau of Health Professions

BHR
  basal heart rate
  bronchial hyperresponsiveness

BHS
  Bachelor of Health Science
  breath-holding spell
  β-hemolytic streptococcus

BHT
  breath hydrogen test
  butylated hydroxytoluene
  β-hydroxytheophylline

BHU
  basic health unit

BHV
  bovine herpesvirus

BH/VH
  body hematocrit-venous hematocrit
  (ratio)

BHyg
Bachelor of Hygiene

BI
background interval
bacterial index
bactericidal index
bacteriologic index
Barthel index
base (of prism) in
basilar impression
bifocal *also* BIF, bif
biologic indicator
bodily injury
bone injury
bowel impaction
brain injured
brain injury
burn index

Bi
bismuth

bi
between
bilateral

BIA
bioelectrical impedance analysis

BIB, bib
biliointestinal bypass
brought in by

bib.
drink [L. *bibe*]

biblio
bibliography

BIBPD
brought in by police department

B-IBS
B-immunoblastic sarcoma

BIC
blood isotope clearance
brain injury center

Bic
biceps

BICAO
bilateral internal carotid artery
occlusion

BICAP
Bipolar Circumactive Probe
Bipolar Circumactive Probe B unit
bipolar electrocoagulation therapy

Bicarb, bicarb
bicarbonate *also* BC, HCO_3

BiCNU
carmustine

BICROS
bilateral contralateral routing of
signals

BID
bibliographic information and
documentation
bilateral interfacetal dislocation
brought in dead
twice a day [L. *bis in die*] *also*
BD, b.d., b.i.d.

b.i.d.
twice a day [L. *bis in die*] *also*
BD, b.d., BID

BIDLB
block in posteroinferior division of
left branch

BIDS
bedtime insulin, daytime sulfonylurea
(therapy)
brittle hair, intellectual impairment,
decreased fertility, short stature

BIF, bif
bifocal *also* BI

BIFC
benign infantile familial convulsions

BIGGY
bismuth glycine glucose yeast (agar)

BIH
benign intracranial hypertension
bilateral inguinal hernia

bihor.
during two hours [L. *bihorium*]

Bi Isch, bi isch
between ischial tuberosities

BIL, bil
basal insulin level
biceps interval lesion

NOTES

BIL *(continued)*
bilateral *also* B, bilat
bilirubin *also* bili, bilirub, BR, Bu
brother-in-law

BIL/ALB
bilirubin to albumin (ratio)

bilat
bilateral *also* B, BIL, bil

BILAT SLC
bilateral short leg cane

BILAT SXO, bilat sxo
bilateral salpingo-oophorectomy

bili
bilirubin *also* BIL, bil, bilirub, BR, Bu

bili-c
conjugated bilirubin

bilirub
bilirubin *also* BIL, bil, bili, BR, Bu

BIMA
bilateral internal mammary arteries

BIMAb
I-labeled B-cell-specific anti-CD20 monoclonal antibody

BIN
benign intradermal nevus

b.i.n.
twice a night [L. *bis in noctus*]

biochem
biochemical
biochemistry

BIOD
bony intraorbital distance

BIOETHICSLINE
Bioethical Information On-Line

BIOF
biofeedback

Bi(OH)$_3$
bismuth hydroxide

biol
biologic
biology

bioLH
bioassay of luteinizing hormone

biophys
biophysical
biophysics

BIOSIS
BioScience Information Service

BIP
Background Interference Procedure
bacterial intravenous protein
Bezafibrate Infarction Prevention
biparietal (diameter)
bismuth iodoform paraffin
bleomycin, ifosfamide, Platinol
Blue Cross interim payment
Breast Implant Protector
brief infertile period

BiPAP
bilevel positive airway pressure

BiPD
biparietal diameter (fetal skull)

BIPLED
bilateral, independent, periodic, lateralized epileptiform discharge

BIPM
International Bureau of Weights and Measures [Fr. *Bureau International des Poids et Mesures*]

BIPP
bismuth iodoform paraffin paste
bismuth iodoform petrolatum paste

BIR
backward internal rotation
basic incidence rate

BIS, bis
bone cement implantation syndrome
Brain Information Service
building illness syndrome
sodium bicarbonate in invert sugar

bis.
twice [L.] *also* B, b.

bis-GMA
bisphenol A-glycidyl methacrylate

BISP, BiSP
between ischial spines

Bisp, bisp
bispinous or interspinous (diameter)

BIT, BiT
between greater trochanters

BITU
benzylthiourea

BIU
barrier isolation unit

BIVAD
bilateral ventricular assist device

BIW, biw, bi wk
biweekly

BIZ-PLT
bizarre platelets

BJ
Bence Jones (protein, proteinuria)
biceps jerk
Bielschowsky-Jansky (syndrome)
bones and joints *also* B&J

B&J
bones and joints *also* BJ

BJE
bone and joint examination

BJI
bone and joint infection

BJM
bones, joints, and muscles

BJP
Bence Jones protein
Bence Jones proteinuria

BK
bekanamycin
below-knee (amputation) *also* B/K,
BKA, BK amp
bovine kidney (cells)
bradykinin
bullous keratopathy

B/K
below-knee (amputation) *also* BK,
BKA, BK amp

Bk
berkelium

bk
back

BKA
below-knee amputation *also* BK,
B/K, BK amp

BK-A
basophil kallikrein of anaphylaxis

BK amp
below-knee amputation *also* BK,
B/K, BKA

BKC
blepharokeratoconjunctivitis

bkf, bkfst, bkft
breakfast *also* Brkf

BKg
background *also* BG

bkly
back lying

BKO
below-knee orthosis

BKS
beekeeper serum

BKTT
below-knee-to-toe (cast)

BKU
base up

BKV
BK virus

BKWC
below-knee walking cast

BKWP
below-knee walking plaster

BL
bacterial levan
Baralyme
basal lamina
baseline
baseline (fetal heart rate)
Bessey-Lowry (unit) *also* BLU, B.L.
unit
black light
bland *also* bl
blast cells
bleed
bleeding *also* bl
blind loop
blood *also* B, b, bl, bld
blood level
blood loss
bone marrow lymphocyte
borderline lepromatous
bronchial lavage
buccolingual
Burkitt lymphoma
butyrolactone

B

NOTES

B-L
bursa-equivalent lymphocyte

Bl
black *also* B, blk

bl
black
bland *also* BL
bleeding *also* BL, bldg
blood *also* B, b, BL, bld
blue *also* B

BLa
buccolabial

BLAD
borderline left axis deviation

blad
bladder

BLAT
Blind Learning Aptitude Test

BLB
Bessey-Lowry-Brock (method or unit)
black light bulb
Boothby-Lovelace-Bulbulian (oxygen mask)
bulb (syringe)

BLBK
blood bank *also* BB

BL=BS
bilateral equal breath sounds

BLC
beef liver catalase

BlC
blood culture *also* BC, BL CULT, bl cult

BLCL
Burkitt lymphoma cell line

BL CULT, bl cult
blood culture *also* BC, BlC

BLD
basal-cell liquefactive degeneration
benign lymphoepithelial disease
beryllium lung disease

bld
blood *also* B, b, BL, bl

Bld Bk
blood bank

bld chem
blood chemistry

bldg
bleeding *also* BL, bl

bld tm
bleeding time *also* BT

BLDY
grossly bloody

BLE
both lower extremities

BLEED
bleeding time

BLEL
benign lymphoepithelial lesion

BLEO
bleomycin *also* BLM

BLEO-MOP
bleomycin, mechlorethamine, Oncovin (vincristine), and prednisone

BLEP
Breast Lesion Evaluation Project

bleph
blepharoplasty

BLES
bovine lavage extract surfactant

BLESS
bath, laxative, enema, shampoo, and shower

BLFD
buccolinguofacial dyskinesia

BLFG
bilateral firm (hand) grips

BL-FST
blood fasting (glucose tolerance test)

BLG
β-lactoglobulin

blH
biologically active luteinizing hormone

BLI
bombesin-like immunoreactivity

BLIC
beta lactamase inhibitor combination

BLIP
beta lactamase inhibiting protein

BLIS
breast leakage inhibitor system

blk
black *also* B, Bl

BLL
below lower limit
bilateral lower lobe
brows, lids, and lashes

BLLS
bilateral leg strength

BLM
basolateral membrane
bilayer lipid membrane
bimolecular liquid membrane
black lipid membrane
bleomycin *also* BLEO
buccal-lingual-masticatory

BLN
bronchial lymph node

BlObs
bladder obstruction

BLP
β-lipoprotein

BlP
blood pressure *also* BL PR, bl pr,
BP, B/P

BLPB
β-lactamase-producing bacteria

BLPO
β-lactamase-producing organism

BL PR, bl pr
blood pressure *also* BlP, BP, B/P

BLQ
both lower quadrants

BLRA
β-lactamase-resistant antimicrobial

BLS
bare lymphocyte syndrome
basic life support
blind loop syndrome
blood and lymphatic system
blood sugar
Bloom syndrome *also* BS

BlS
blood sugar *also* BS

BLSD
bovine lumpy skin disease

BLST
Bankson Language Screening Test

BLT, BlT
bilateral lung transplant
bladder tumor
bleeding time
blood-clot lysis time
blood test
blood type
blood typing

BLU, B.L. unit
Bessey-Lowry unit *also* BL

BLV
blood volume *also* BlV, BV
bovine leukemia virus

BlV
blood viscosity
blood volume *also* BLV, BV

BLVR
biliverdin reductase

BM
Bachelor of Medicine
bacterial meningitis
basal medium
basal metabolism
basement membrane
basilar membrane
Bergersen medium
betamethasone
biomedical
black male *also* B/M
blind matching
blood monocyte
body mass
Bohr magneton
bone marrow
bowel movement
breast milk
buccal mass
buccomesial

B/M
black male *also* BM

B2M
beta$_2$-microglobin

b.m.
salt-water bath [L. *balneum maris*]
also bal. mar.

NOTES

79

BMA
basaloid monomorphic adenoma
bismuth subsalicylate, metronidazole, and amoxicillin
bone marrow arrest
bone marrow aspirate

BmA
Brugia malayi adult antigen

BMAP
bone marrow acid phosphatase

BMB
biomedical belt
bone marrow biopsy

BMBL
benign monoclonal B-cell lymphocytosis

BMC
balloon mitral commissurotomy
blood mononuclear cell *also* BMNC
bone marrow cell
bone marrow culture
bone mineral content

BMD
Becker muscular dystrophy
Boehringer Mannheim Diagnostics
bone marrow depression
bone mineral densitometry
bone mineral density
bovine mucosal disease
Bureau of Medical Devices

BMDC
Biomedical Documentation Center

BME
basal medium, Eagle
biundulant meningoencephalitis
brief maximal effort

BMed
Bachelor of Medicine

BMedBiol
Bachelor of Medical Biology

BMedSci
Bachelor of Medical Science

BMET
biomedical equipment technician

BMF
bone marrow failure

BMG
benign monoclonal gammopathy

BMI
bicuculline methiodide
body mass index

BMic
Bachelor of Microbiology

BMJ
bones, muscles, joints

BMK, bmk
birthmark

BML
bone marrow lymphocytosis

BMLM
basement membrane-like material

BMLS
billowing mitral leaflet syndrome

BMM
black married male

BMMM
bone marrow micrometastasis

BMMP
benign mucous membrane pemphigoid
bone marrow myeloid precursor

BMN
bone marrow necrosis

BMNC
blood mononuclear cell *also* BMC

BMNR
bone marrow neutrophil reserve

BMOC
Brinster medium for ovum culture

Bmod
behavior modification

B-mode
brightness modulation

BMP
BCNU, methotrexate, and procarbazine
behavior management plan
bone marrow pressure
bone morphogenetic protein

BMP-2
bone morphogenetic protein type 2

BMPI
bronchial mucous proteinase inhibitor

BMPP
benign mucous membrane pemphigus

BMR
basal metabolic rate
best motor response

BMS
Bachelor of Medical Science
betamethasone
biomedical monitoring system
bleomycin sulfate
burning mouth syndrome

BMST
Bruce maximal stress test

BMT
Bachelor of Medical Technology
Bailliére Medical Transparencies
basement membrane thickness
benign mesenchymal tumor
bilateral myringotomy tubes
bilateral myringotomy and tubes
bismuth, metronidazole, tetracycline
bone marrow transplant
bone marrow transplantation
Buschke Memory Test

BMTN
bone marrow transplant neutropenia

BMTU
bone marrow transplant unit

BMU
basic multicellular unit

BMV
balloon mitral valvotomy
balloon mitral valvuloplasty

BMZ
basement membrane zone

BN
bladder neck
brachial neuritis
branchial neuritis
bronchial nodes
brown Norway (rat)
bucconasal

BNA
Basle Nomina Anatomica

BNB
blood-nerve barrier

BNBAS
Brazelton Neonatal Behavioral
Assessment Scale

BNC
binasal cannula
bladder neck contracture

BNCT
boron neutron capture therapy

BNDD
Bureau of Narcotics and Dangerous
Drugs

BNEd
Bachelor of Nursing Education

BNEG
B negative (blood type)

BNG, BNGase
bromonaphthyl-β-galactosidase

BNGF
β-nerve growth factor

BNIST
National Bureau of Scientific
Information [Fr. *Bureau National
d'Information Scientifique*]

BNL
breast needle location

BNML
BN acute myelocytic leukemia

BNMSE
Brief Neuropsychological Mental
Status Examination

BNO
bladder neck obstruction
bowels not opened

BNP
brain natriuretic peptide

BNPA
binasal pharyngeal airway

BNR
bladder neck resection
bladder neck retraction

BNS
benign nephrosclerosis

B

NOTES

BNSc
Bachelor of Nursing Science

BNT
Boston Naming Test
brain neurotransmitter

BNYVV
beet necrotic yellow vein virus

BO
Bachelor of Osteopathy
base (of prism) out
behavior objective
body odor
Bolton (craniometric point) *also* B, bb, Bo, BP
bowel *also* bo
bowel obstruction
bowels open
buccoocclusal

B&O
belladonna and opium

B/O
because of

Bo
Bolton point *also* B, bb, BO, BP

bo
bowel *also* BO

BOA
behavioral observation audiometry
born on arrival
born out of asepsis

BOAT
Balloon versus Optimal Atherectomy Trial

BOB
ball on back

BOBA
β-oxybutyric acid

BOC
beats of clonus
blood oxygen capacity
butyloxycarbonyl
t-butoxycarbonyl *also* t-BOC, Boc

Boc
t-butoxycarbonyl *also* BOC, t-BOC

BOCG
Brudzinski, Oppenheim, Chaddock, and Gullaird (reflex or sign)

BOD
bilateral orbital decompression
biochemical oxygen demand
biologic oxygen demand
borderline *also* BORD
Bureau of Drugs

Bod units
Bodansky units

BOE
bilateral otitis externa

BOEA
ethyl biscoumacetate

BOFA
β-oncofecal antigen

BOH
Board of Health
bundle of His

BOILER
balloon occlusive intravascular lysis-enhanced recanalization

bol
bolus

bol.
pill [L. *bolus*]

BOLD
bleomycin, Oncovin (vincristine), lomustine, and dacarbazine
blood oxygenation level-dependent

BOM
benign ovarian mass
bilateral otitis media

BOMA
bilateral otitis media, acute

BONG
body oscillation neuromuscular gain

BOO
bladder outlet obstruction

BOOP
bronchiolitis obliterans-organizing pneumonia

BOP
bleomycin, Oncovin (vincristine), and prednisone
bromooxyprogesterone
Buffalo orphan prototype (virus)

BOPAM
bleomycin, Oncovin (vincristine), prednisone, Adriamycin (doxorubicin), and methotrexate

BOR
basal optic root

before time of operation
bowels open regularly
branchio-otorenal (syndrome)

BORD
borderline *also* BOD

BORR
blood oxygen release rate

B-O₂S
blood oxygen saturation

BOSE
bleomycin, Oncovin (vincristine), streptozotocin, etoposide

BOSS
Becker orthopaedic spinal system

BOT
base of tongue
botulinum toxin

bot
botany
bottle

BOU
burning on urination

BOW
bag of waters

bowel prep
bowel preparation

BOWI
bag of waters intact

BOW-R
bag of water-ruptured

BP
Bachelor of Pharmacy
back pressure
barometric pressure
basic protein
bathroom privileges
bed pan
before present
behavior pattern
Bell palsy
benzoyl peroxide
benzpyrene
bioequivalence problem
biotic potential

biparietal
biphenyl
bipolar
birthplace
bladder pressure
blood pressure *also* BlP, BL PR, bl pr, B/P
body part
body plethysmography
boiling point *also* bp, b.p.
Bolton point *also* B, bb, BO, Bo
borderline personality
British Pharmacopoeia *also* PB
bronchopleural
bronchopulmonary
buccopulpal
bullous pemphigoid
bullous pemphigus
bypass

B/P
blood pressure *also* BlP, BL PR, bl pr, BP

BPI
bipolar affective disorder, Type 1

bp
base pair
boiling point *also* BP, b.p.

b.p.
boiling point *also* BP, bp

BPA
Bauhinia purpura agglutinin
blood pressure assembly
bovine plasma albumin
bronchopulmonary aspergillosis
bullous pemphigoid antigen
burst-promoting activity

BPB
biliopancreatic bypass
bromphenol blue

BPC
Behavior Problem Checklist
bile phospholipid concentration
British Pharmaceutical Codex
bronchial provocation challenge

BPCF
bronchopleurocutaneous fistula

NOTES

B-Pco$_2$
blood partial pressure of carbon dioxide

BPD
biparietal diameter
blood pressure decreased
borderline personality disorder
bronchopulmonary dysplasia

BPd
bronchopulmonary dysplasia
diastolic blood pressure

BPD-MA
benzoporphyrin derivative, monoacid ring A

BPE
bacterial phosphatidylethanolamine

BPEC
benign partial epilepsy of childhood
bipolar electrocoagulation

BPEI
blepharophimosis, ptosis, epicanthus inversus

BPES
blepharophimos-ptosis-epicanthus inversus syndrome

BPF
bradykinin potentiating factor
bronchopleural fistula
burst-promoting factor

BPG
benzathine penicillin G
blood pressure gauge
bypass graft

BPH
Bachelor of Public Health
benign prostatic hyperplasia
benign prostatic hypertrophy

BPh
buccopharyngeal

B-pH
blood pH

Bph
bacteriopheophytin

BPharm
Bachelor of Pharmacy

BPHEng
Bachelor of Public Health Engineering

BPHN
Bachelor of Public Health Nursing

BPI
Basic Personality Inventory
beef-pork insulin
blood pressure increased

BPL
benign proliferative lesion
benzylpenicilloyl polylysine *also* BPO
bone phosphate of lime
β-propiolactone

BP lar
blood pressure, left arm

BPLN
bilateral pelvic lymph node

BPLND
bilateral pelvic lymph node dissection

BPM, bpm
beats per minute
bipiperidyl mustard
births per minute
blood perfusion monitor
breaths per minute
brompheniramine maleate

BPMS
blood plasma measuring system

BPN
bacitracin, polymyxin B, and neomycin sulfate
brachial plexus neuropathy

BPO
basal pepsin output
benzylpenicilloyl polylysine *also* BPL
bilateral partial oophorectomy
bile phospholipid output

B-PO$_2$
blood partial pressure of oxygen

BPP
biophysical profile
Bloembergen, Purcell, and Pound (theory)
bovine pancreatic polypeptide
bradykinin potentiating peptide
breast parenchymal pattern

BP&P
blood pressure and pulse

BPPN
benign paroxysmal positioning nystagmus

B

BPPP
bilateral pedal pulses present

BP,P,R,T
blood pressure, pulse, respiration, and temperature

BPPV
benign paroxysmal positional vertigo
bovine paragenital papillomavirus

BPQ
Berne pain questionnaire

BPR
blood per rectum
blood pressure recorder
blood production rate

BP rar
blood pressure, right arm

BPRS
brief psychiatric rating scale
brief psychiatric reacting scale

BPS
beats per second
bilateral partial salpingectomy
biophysical profile scoring
bovine papular stomatitis
brain protein solvent
breaths per second

BPs
blood pressure, systolic

BPSA
bronchopulmonary segmental artery

BPSD
bronchopulmonary segmental drainage

BPT
benign paroxysmal torticollis

BPTI
basic pancreatic trypsin inhibitor
basic polyvalent trypsin inhibitor
brachial plexus traction injury

BPV
balloon pulmonary valvuloplasty
benign paroxysmal vertigo
benign positional vertigo
bioprosthetic valve
bovine papillomavirus

BP(VET)
British Pharmacopoeia (Veterinary)

Bq
becquerel (SI unit of radionuclide activity)

BQA
Bureau of Quality Assurance

BQC sol
2,6-dibromoquinone-4-chlorimide solution

BQCT
bone quantitative CT

BR
barrier-reared (experimental animals)
baseline recovery
bathroom
bedrest
bedside rounds
Benzing retrograde
benzodiazepine receptor
bilirubin *also* BIL, bil, bili, bilirub, Bu
biologic response
blink reflex
bowel rest
brachialis
branchial
breathing rate
breathing reserve
bromine
bronchial
bronchitis *also* Br
bronchus
brown *also* br
Brucella
buccal root

Br
breech
bregma
bridge
bromide
bromine
bronchitis *also* BR
brown
Brucella
brucellosis

NOTES

br
    boiling range
    brachial *also* Brach
    branch
    breath
    broiled
    brother *also* B, BRO, bro
    brown *also* BR

BRA
    beta-resorcylic acid
    bilateral renal agenesis
    bone-resorbing activity
    brain *also* b
    brain-reactive antibody
    β-resorcylic acid

BRAC
    basic rest-activity cycle

Brach
    brachial *also* br

BRADY
    bradycardia

BRAO
    branch retinal-artery occlusion *also*
    BR RAO

BRAP
    burst of rapid atrial pacing

BrAP
    brachial artery pressure

BRAS
    Bard rotary atherectomy system

BRAT
    bananas, rice cereal, applesauce, and
    toast (diet)
    Baylor rapid autologous transfusion

BRATT
    bananas, rice, applesauce, tea, and
    toast (diet)

BRB
    blood-retinal barrier
    bright red blood

BRBC
    bovine red blood cell

BRBN
    blue rubber bleb nevus

BRBNS
    blue rubber bleb nevus syndrome

BRBPR, BRBR
    bright red blood per rectum

br bx
    breast biopsy *also* BB, B Bx

Brc
    bromocriptine *also* BCR, BRO

BRCM
    below right costal margin

BRD
    bladder retraining drill

BrDu, BrdU, BrdUrd
    bromodeoxyuridine

BRET
    bretylium tosylate

BRH
    benign recurrent hematuria
    Bureau of Radiological Health

BRI
    Bio-Research Index

BRIC
    benign recurrent intrahepatic
    cholestasis

Brit
    British

BRJ
    brachial radialis jerk

Brkf
    breakfast *also* bkf, bkfst, bkft

BRM
    biologic response modifier
    biuret-reactive material

BrM
    breast milk

BRMP
    Biological Response Modification
    Program

BRN
    Board of Registered Nursing

BRO
    bromocriptine *also* BCR, Brc
    bronchoscopy *also* bronch
    brother *also* B, br, bro

bro
    brother *also* B, br, BRO

BROM
    back range of motion

brom
    bromide

Bron
  bronchi
  bronchial

bronch
  bronchoscope
  bronchoscopy *also* BRO

BRP
  bathroom privileges
  bilirubin production

Brph
  bronchophony

BRR
  baroreceptor reflex response

BR RAO
  branch retinal-artery occlusion *also*
  BRAO

BR RVO
  branch retinal-vein occlusion *also*
  BRVO

BR S
  breath sounds *also* BS, bs

BRT
  Brook reaction test

brth
  breath

B-RTO
  balloon-occluded retrograde
  transvenous obliteration

BRU
  bromide urine

BrU
  bromouracil

Bruc
  Brucella

BRVO
  branch retinal-vein occlusion *also* BR
  RVO

BRW
  Brown-Roberts-Wells [stereotactic
  system]

BRW-PB
  Brown-Roberts-Wells phantom base

BS
  Bachelor of Science *also* Bsc
  Bachelor of Surgery
  Bacillus subtilis
  barium swallow *also* BaS
  Bartter syndrome
  bedside
  before sleep
  Behçet syndrome
  Bennett seal
  bilateral symmetric
  bile salt
  Binet-Simon [test]
  bismuth subgallate
  bismuth subsalicylate
  blood sugar *also* BlS
  Bloom syndrome *also* BLS
  Blue Shield (plan)
  borderline schizophrenia
  bowel sounds *also* bs
  breaking strength
  breath sounds *also* BR S, bs
  British Standard
  buffered saline
  Bureau of Standards

B-S
  Binet-Simon (test)
  Bjork-Shiley (valve prosthesis)

B&S
  Bartholin and Skene (glands)
  Brown and Sharp (suture)

b.s.
  barium swallow

bs
  bedside
  bowel sounds *also* BS
  breath sounds *also* BR S, BS

BSA
  beef serum albumin
  benzenesulfonic acid
  bismuth-sulfite agar
  bis-trimethylsilylacetamide
  Blue Shield Association
  body surface area *also* bsa
  bovine serum albumin *also* bsa
  bowel sounds active

NOTES

bsa
> body surface area *also* BSA
> bovine serum albumin *also* BSA

BSAB
> Balthazar Scales of Adaptive Behavior

BSAER
> brainstem auditory-evoked response

BSAG
> Bristol Social Adjustment Guides

BSAP
> brief short-action potential
> brief, small, abundant potential

BSAPP
> brief, small, abundant, polyphasic potential

BSB
> bedside bag
> body surface burned

BSBC
> buffer-soluble binding component

BS=BL
> breath sounds equal bilaterally

BSC
> bedside care
> bedside commode
> bench scale calorimeter
> bile salt concentration
> Biological Stain Commission
> burn scar contracture

Bsc
> Bachelor of Science *also* BS

BSCA
> bidirectional superior cavopulmonary anastomosis

BSCIF
> bile salt independent canalicular fraction

BSCP
> bovine spinal cord protein

BSCT
> breast stimulation contraction test

BSD
> baby soft diet
> bedside drainage

BSDLB
> block in anterosuperior division of left branch

BSE
> bacillus species enzyme
> behavior summarized evaluation
> bilateral, symmetrical, and equal
> bovine spongiform encephalopathy
> breast self-examination

BSEP
> brainstem-evoked potential

BSepF
> black separated female

BSepM
> black separated male

BSER
> brainstem-evoked response (audiometry)

BSF
> backscatter factor
> basal skull fracture
> black single female
> B-lymphocyte stimulatory factor
> busulfan

BSFR
> basal secretory flow rate

BSG
> branchioskeletogenital (syndrome)

BSGA
> β-hemolytic streptococcus group A

BSGF
> brachiosubclavian bridge graft fistula

BSH
> boron sulfhydryl

BSI
> Behavior Status Inventory
> blood stream infection
> body substance isolation
> borderline syndrome index
> bound serum iron
> brainstem injury
> Brief Symptom Inventory
> British Standards Institution

BSID
> Bayley Scale of Infant Development

BSIF
> bile salt independent fraction

BSL
> benign symmetric lipomatosis
> blood sugar level

BS L base
> breath sounds diminished, left base

BSLM
body surface Laplacian mapping

BSM
Bachelor of Science in Medicine
Bilingual Syntax Measure

BSN
Bachelor of Science in Nursing
bowel sounds normal

BSNA
bowel sounds normal and active

BSNT
breast soft and nontender

BSO
bilateral sagittal osteotomy
bilateral salpingo-oophorectomy
bilateral serous otitis
buthionine sulfoximine

BSOM
bilateral serous otitis media

BSOT
Bachelor of Science in Occupational
Therapy

BSP
body segment parameter
bromsulfophthalein (liver function)
Bromsulphalein

BSp
bronchospasm

BSPA
bowel sounds present and active

BSPh
Bachelor of Science in Pharmacy

BSPM
body surface potential mapping

BSQ
Behavior Style Questionnaire

BSR
basal skin resistance
blood sedimentation rate
bowel sounds regular
brain stimulation reinforcement

BSRI
Bem Sex Role Inventory

BSS
Bachelor of Sanitary Science
balanced saline solution
balanced salt solution
bedside scale
Bernard-Soulier syndrome *also* B-SS
bismuth subsalicylate
black silk suture
buffered saline solution
buffered salt solution
buffered single substrate

B-SS
Bernard-Soulier syndrome *also* BSS

BSSE
bile salt-stimulated esterase

BSSG
sitogluside

BSSI
Basic School Skills Inventory

BSSL
bile salt-stimulated lipase

BSSO
bilateral sagittal split osteotomy

BSSS
benign sporadic sleep spikes

BST
Bacteriuria Screening Test
bedside testing
biceps semitendinosus
blood serologic test
breast stimulation test
brief stimulus therapy

BSTFA
bis-trimethylsilyltrifluoroacetamide

BSTP
basophilic stippling (on differential)

BSU
Bartholin, Skene, and urethral
(glands)
basic structural unit
British Standard Unit

BSV
Batten-Spielmeyer-Vogt (syndrome)
binocular single vision

B

NOTES

BT
Bacillus thuringiensis
base of tongue
bedtime
bitemporal (diameter of fetal head)
bitrochanteric
bituberous
Blacky test
bladder tremor
bladder tumor
bleeding time *also* bld tm
blood transfusion
blood type
blood typing
blue tetrazolium
blue tongue
body temperature
borderline tuberculoid
bovine turbinate (cells)
brain tumor
breast tumor
bulbotruncal

BTA
bladder tumor-associated analytes
brief tone audiometry
N-benzoyl-1-tyrosine amide

BTB
breakthrough bleeding *also* BB
bromothymol blue

BTBC
Boehm Test of Basic Concepts

BTBL
bromothymol blue lactose

BTBV
beat-to-beat variability

BTC
basal temperature chart
bilateral tubal coagulation
bladder tumor check
blood temperature chart
by the clock

BTDS
benzoylthiamine disulfide

BTE
Baltimore Therapeutic Equipment
(work simulator)
behind-the-ear (hearing aid)
bovine thymus extract

BTEA
Boston Test for Examining Aphasia

BTF
blenderized tube feeding

B$_2$-TFn
B$_2$-transferrin

BTFS
breast tumor frozen section

BTG
β-thromboglobulin

BTg
bovine trypsinogen

BThU
British thermal unit *also* BTU

BTI
biliary tract infection
bitubal interruption

BTL
bilateral tubal ligation

BTLS
basic trauma life support

BTM
benign tertian malaria
bilateral tympanic membranes

BTMD
Botten-Turner muscular dystrophy

BTMSA
bis-trimethylsilacetylene

BTO
bilateral tubal occlusion

BTP
biliary tract pain

BTPD
body temperature, pressure, dry

BTPS
body temperature, ambient pressure,
  and saturated with water vapor (gas)

BTR
Bezold-type reflex
biceps tendon reflex
bladder tumor recheck
bovine trypsin
buccal triangular ridge

BTS
bioptic telescopic spectacle
bithional sulfoxide
Blalock-Taussig shunt
blood transfusion service
blue toe syndrome
bradycardia-tachycardia syndrome

BTSG
Brain Tumor Study Group

BTSH, bTSH
beef thyroid-stimulating hormone
bovine thyroid-stimulating hormone

BTU
British thermal unit *also* BThU

BTV
blue tongue virus

BTX
bactrachotoxin
benzene, toluene, and xylene
brevotoxins
bungarotoxin

BTX-B
brevetoxin-B

BTZ
benzothiazepine
Butazolidin

BTZ alka
Butazolidin alka

BU
base (of prism) up
below the umbilicus
Bethesda unit
biologic unit
blood urea
Bodansky unit
bromouracil
burn unit

Bu
bilirubin *also* BIL, bil, bili, bilirub,
  BR
butyl

BUA
blood uric acid

Buc, bucc
buccal

BUD
budesonide

BUDR, BUdR
5-bromodeoxyuridine

BUDS
bilateral upper dorsal sympathectomy

BUE
both upper extremities
built-up edge

BUEC
balloon uterine elevator cannula

BUF
Buffalo (rat)

BUFA
baby up for adoption

BUG
buccal ganglion

BUI
brain uptake index

BULIT
bulimia test

BULL
buccal or upper lingual of lower

bull.
bulletin
let it boil [L. *bulliat*]

BUMP
Behavioral Regression or Upset in
  Hospitalized Medical Patients (scale)

BUN
blood urea nitrogen
bunion

bun br
bundle branch

BUN/CR
blood urea nitrogen/creatine ratio

BUO
bilateral ureteral occlusion
bilirubin of undetermined origin
bleeding of undetermined origin
bruising of undetermined origin

BUQ
both upper quadrants

BUR
backup rate (ventilator)

Bur
bureau

Burd
Burdick (suction)

NOTES

BUS
Bartholin, urethral, and Skene (glands)
busulfan

Bus
busulfan

BUSEG
Bartholin, urethral, and Skene (glands), and external genitalia

BUT
breakup time

But
butyrate
butyric (acid)

but.
butter [L. *butyrum*]

BV
bacitracin V
bacterial vaginitis
bacterial vaginosis
balloon valvuloplasty
billion volts
biologic value
blood vessel
blood volume *also* BLV, BlV
bronchovesicular
buccoversion
bulboventricular

b.v.
steam bath [L. *balneum vaporis*]

BVA
best-corrected visual acuity
bioimpedance venous analysis

BVAD
biventricular assist device

BVAP
BCNU (carmustine), vincristine, Adriamycin (doxorubicin), and prednisone

BVAT
Binocular Visual Acuity Test

BVC
British Veterinary Codex

BVD
BCNU (carmustine), vincristine, and dacarbazine
bovine viral diarrhea

BVDT
Brief Vestibular Disorientation Test

BVDU
bromvinyldeoxyuridine

BVE
binocular visual efficiency
biventricular enlargement
blood vessel endothelium
blood volume expander
blood volume expansion

BVH
biventricular hypertrophy

BVI
Better Vision Institute
blood vessel invasion

BVL
bilateral vas ligation

BVM
bag-valve-mask *also* B-V-M
bronchovascular markings
Bureau of Veterinary Medicine

B-V-M
bag-valve-mask *also* BVM

BVMGT
Bender Visual-Motor Gestalt Test

BVMOT
Bender Visual-Motor Gestalt Test

BVMS
Bachelor of Veterinary Medicine and Surgery

BVO
branch-vein occlusion
brominated vegetable oil

BVP
blood vessel prosthesis
blood volume pulse
Bonhoeffer van der Pol
burst of ventricular pacing

BVR
baboon virus replication

BVRO
bilateral vertical ramus osteotomy

BVRT-R
Benton Visual Retention Test, Revised

BVS
biventricular support
blanked ventricular sense

BVSc
Bachelor of Veterinary Science

BVT
bilateral ventilation tubes

BVU
bromoisovalerylurea

BVV
bovine vaginitis virus

BVX
bacitracin V and X

BW
bacteriologic warfare
bandwidth
bed wetting
below waist
biologic weapon
birth weight *also* BWt
bite-wing (radiograph)
bladder washout
blood Wassermann
body water
body weight *also* bw

B&W
black and white (milk of magnesia
and cascara extract)

bw
body weight *also* BW

BWA
bedwetter admission

BWCS
bagged white-cell study

BWD
bacillary white diarrhea

BWFI
bacteriostatic water for injection

BWidF
black widowed female

BWidM
black widowed male

BWS
battered-woman syndrome
Beckwith-Wiedemann syndrome

BWST
black widow spider toxin

BWSV
black widow spider venom

BWt
birth weight *also* BW

BWYV
beet western yellow virus

BX
bacitracin X
biopsy *also* Bx
Blue Cross (plan) *also* BC

Bx
biopsy *also* BX

BX/BS, BX BS
Blue Cross and Blue Shield (plan)
also BC/BS

BXM
B-cell crossmatch

BXO
balanitis xerotica obliterans

b x s
brother-sister inbreeding

BYDV
barley yellow dwarf virus

BYE
Barile-Yaguchi-Eveland (agar, culture
medium)

BZ, bz
benzodiazepine *also* BZD, BZDZ
benzoyl *also* Bzl

BZA
benzylamine

BZD, BZDZ
benzodiazepine *also* BZ, bz

Bzl
benzoyl *also* BZ

BZQ
benzquinamide

BZSLL
B-zone small lymphocytic lymphoma

Bz-Ty-PABA
benzoyltyrosyl-*p*-aminobenzoic acid
(test)

B

NOTES

C

ascorbic acid
bruised [L. *contusus*] *also* cont., contus.
calcitonin-forming (cell)
calculus
calorie (large) *also* Cal
canine (tooth) *also* c
capacitance
carbohydrate *also* CARB, carb, carbo, CHO, COH, HCO
carbon
cardiovascular (disease)
carrier
cast
cathodal
cathode *also* CA, Ca, Cath, cath
Catholic
Caucasian *also* Cau, Cauc, cauc
cell
Celsius (temperature scale) *also* CEL, Cel
centigrade *also* CENT, cent.
centigrade temperature scale
central *also* CENT, cent.
central electrode placement in electroencephalography
centromeric or constitutive heterochromatic chromosome (banding)
cerebrospinal (fluid)
certified *also* CRT
cervical (spine)
cesarean (section)
chest (precordial lead in electrocardiography)
chloramphenicol *also* chloro, CMC, CP
cholesterol *also* CH, Ch, CHO, CHOL, chol, chol.
class
clear
clearance rate (renal)
clonus
closure
clubbing
coarse (bacterial colonies)
cocaine
coefficient
colored (guinea pig)
color sense
complement
complete *also* cpl
complex
compliance
component
component of complement
compound [L. *compositus*] *also* CO, comp, compd, CP, cpd
concentration *also* c, conc, concentr
conditioned
conditioning
condyle
constant
consultation
contact *also* c
content
contraction *also* contr, contrx, CTX, CTXN, Cx
control
conventionally reared (experimental animal)
convergence
cornea
cornu
correct
cortex *also* cort
costa
coulomb *also* Q
Coxsackie [virus]
creatinine
crystalline
cubic *also* c, cu
cup *also* c
curie *also* c, Ci, CU, cu
cuspid (secondary dentition)
cuticular
cyanosis
cylinder *also* Cyl, cyl, cyl.
cylindrical lens *also* Cyl, cyl, cyl.
cysteine *also* Cys
cytidine *also* Cyd
cytochrome
cytosine
gallon [L. *congius*]
heat capacity
hundred [L. *centum*] *also* c
large calorie
molar heat capacity
rib [L. *costa*]
velocity of light
velocity of sound of blood
with [L. *cum*] *also* c, c̄

°C

degree Celsius

^{11}C
carbon-11

^{12}C
carbon-12

^{13}C
carbon-13

^{14}C
carbon-14 (isotope)

C$_3$
Collins solution

C6
sixth cervical nerve
sixth cervical vertebra
sixth component of complement

C-6
hexamethonium

C-10
decamethonium

CI

CI–XII
cranial nerves I through XII *also* C1–C12

C-I–C-V
DEA controlled substances schedules I through V

C.
Campylobacter
Candida
Chlamydia
Cimex
Clostridium
Corynebacterium
Cryptococcus
Culex

c
about [L. *circa*] *also* ca
calorie (small) *also* cal
candle *also* ca
canine (tooth) *also* C
capacity *also* cap.
capillary blood (subscript)
carat
centi- (prefix)
centum
circumference
concentration *also* C, conc, concentr
contact *also* C
cubic *also* C, cu
culture [medium]
cup *also* C
curie *also* C, Ci, CU, cu

cuspid (primary dentition)
cycle
cyclic
hundred [L. *centum*] *also* C
meal [L. *cibus*]
molar concentration
specific heat capacity
with [L. *cum*] *also* C, c̄

c′
coefficient of partage pulmonary end-capillary
pulmonary end-capillary (blood phase)

c̄
with [L. *cum*] *also* C, c

CA
anterior commissure [L. *commissura anterior*]
calcium antagonist
California (rabbit)
cancer *also* Ca, Can
cancer antigen
caproic acid
carbohydrate antigen
carbonic anhydrase
carcinoma *also* Ca
cardiac-apnea (monitor)
cardiac arrest
cardiac arrhythmia
carotid artery
cast
catecholamine *also* CAT
catecholaminergic
cathode *also* C, Ca, Cath, cath
Caucasian adult
celiac artery
celiac axis
cellulose acetate
cerebral aqueduct
cerebral atrophy
Certified Acupuncturist
cervicoaxial
Chemical Abstracts (Service)
chemotactic activity *also* CTA
chloroamphetamine
cholic acid
chronic anovulation
chronologic age
chronological age
citric acid
clotting assay
coagglutination (test)
coarctation of the aorta *also* CoA, C of A
Cocaine Anonymous

coefficient of absorption
cold agglutinin
collagen antigen
collagenolytic activity
colloid antigen
commissural associated
common antigen
community acquired
compressed air
conceptional age
conditioned abstinence
conditioned air
coronary angioplasty
coronary arrest
coronary artery
corpora allata
corpora amylacea
corpus albicans
cortisone acetate
cricoid arch
croup-associated (virus)
cytosine arabinoside *also* Ara-C, araC
cytotoxic antibody

C of A
coarctation of aorta *also* CA, CoA

CA125, CA-125
cancer antigen 125 (test) *also* CEA-125

CA 19-9
carbohydrate antigen 19-9

C/A, c/a
Clinitest/Acetest *also* C&A

C&A
Clinitest and Acetest *also* C/A, c/a
conscious and alert

Ca
calcium *also* Cal., Calc
cancer *also* CA, Can
Candida albicans
carcinoma *also* CA
carmustine
carmustine antineoplastic
cathode *also* C, CA, Cath, cath

C3a
C3 anaphylatoxin
plasma-activated complement 3

C4a
plasma-activated complement 4

C5a
plasma-activated complement 5

^{45}Ca
calcium-45 (radioisotope)

^{47}Ca
calcium-47

Ca_{O2}
arterial oxygen concentration

c/a (*var. of* C/A)

ca
about [L. *circa*] *also* c
candle *also* c
carcinoma

CAA
cardiac allograft atherosclerosis
carotid audiofrequency analysis
cerebral amyloid angiopathy
chloracetaldehyde
coloanal anastomosis
computer-aided assessment
computer-assisted assessment
constitutional aplastic anemia
coronary artery aneurysm
crystalline amino acids

CAAS
Cardiovascular Angiography Analysis System

CAAT
computer-assisted axial tomography

CAB
captive air bubble
catheter-associated bacteriuria
cellulose acetate butyrate
coronary artery bypass

CABG
coronary artery bypass graft

CABGS
coronary artery bypass graft surgery

CaBI
calcium bone index

C

NOTES

CABOP, CA-BOP
cyclophosphamide, Adriamycin (doxorubicin), bleomycin, Oncovin (vincristine), and prednisone

CaBP
calcium-binding protein

CABRI
Coronary Angioplasty versus Bypass Revascularization Investigation

CABS
coronary artery bypass surgery

CAC
cancer (malignant) cell
cardiac-accelerator center
cardiac arrest code
carotid artery canal
chronic active cirrhosis
circulating anticoagulant
comprehensive ambulatory care

CACB
calcium carbonate

CaCC
cathodal-closure contraction *also* CCC

CACI
computer-assisted continuous infusion

CaCO₃
calcium carbonate

CACP
cisplatin

CACS
cancer, anorexia, cachexia syndrome

CACT
celite-activated clotting time

CaCV
Calicivirus

CACX
cancer of cervix

CAD
cadaver *also* Cad
cadaveric
chronic airway disease
cold agglutinin disease
compressed-air disease
computer-assisted design
computer-assisted diagnosis
congenital abduction deficiency
coronary artery disease
cyclophosphamide, Adriamycin (doxorubicin), and dacarbazine
cytosine arabinoside and daunorubicin

Cad
cadaver *also* CAD
cadaveric

CAD/CAM
computer-aided design/computer-aided manufacturing
computer-assisted design/controlled-alignment method

CADI
computer-assisted diabetic instruction (system)

CADIC
cyclophosphamide, Adriamycin (doxorubicin), and dacarbazine (DTIC)

CADL
Communicative Abilities in Daily Living

CADs
computer-assisted diagnostics

CaDTe
cathodal-duration tetanus

CAE
caprine arthritis-encephalitis
caprine arthritis-encephalomyelitis
cefuroxime axetil suspension
cellulose acetate electrophoresis
contingent aftereffects
coronary artery embolization
cyclophosphamide, Adriamycin (doxorubicin), and etoposide

CaE
calcium excretion

CAEC
cardiac arrhythmia evaluation center

CaEDTA, CaEdTA
calcium disodium edetate
calcium disodium ethylenediaminetetraacetate
edathamil calcium disodium

CAEP
cortical auditory-evoked potential

CAER
caerulein
cortical auditory-evoked response

CAEV
caprine arthritis-encephalitis virus

CAF
cell adhesion factor
chronic atrial fibrillation

citric acid fermenters
continuous atrial fibrillation
continuous atrial flutter
contract administration fees
controlled atrial fibrillation
controlled atrial flutter
coronary artery fistula
cyclophosphamide, Adriamycin
  (doxorubicin), and fluorouracil

CaF
correction of area factor

Caf
caffeine

CAFF
controlled atrial fibrillation/flutter

CAFP
cyclophosphamide, Adriamycin
  (doxorubicin), fluorouracil, and
  prednisone

CAFT
Clinitron air-fluidized therapy

CAFVP
cyclophosphamide, Adriamycin
  (doxorubicin), fluorouracil, vincristine,
  and prednisone

CAG
cholangiogram
cholangiography
chronic atrophic gastritis
continuous ambulatory gamma
  globulin (infusion)
coronary angiogram
coronary angiography

CaG
calcium gluconate

CAGB
coronary artery graft bypass

CAGE
(need to) cut down (on drinking),
  annoyance, guilt (about drinking),
  (need for) eye-opener

CAGEIN
catheter-guided endoscopic intubation

CAH
central alveolar hypoventilation *also*
  CAHV
chronic active hepatitis
chronic aggressive hepatitis
combined atrial hypertrophy
congenital adrenal hyperplasia
congenital adrenogenital hyperplasia
cyanacetic acid hydrazide

CaHA
calcium hydroxyapatite

CAHB
chronic active hepatitis B

CAHC
chronic active hepatitis with cirrhosis

CAHD
coronary arteriosclerotic heart disease
coronary atherosclerotic heart disease

CAHM
complex atypical
  hyperplasia/metaplasia

CAHS
central alveolar hypoventilation
  syndrome

CAHV
central alveolar hypoventilation *also*
  CAH

CAI
carbonic anhydrase inhibitor
complete androgen insensitivity
computer-assisted instruction

CA ION
calcium, ionized

CAIS
complete androgen insensitivity
  syndrome

CAL
café au lait
calcium (test)
calculated average life
callus
calories
chronic airflow limitation
computer-assisted learning
coracoacromial ligament

NOTES

Cal
   calorie (large) *also* C

Cal.
   calcium *also* Ca, Calc

cal
   caliber
   calorie (small) *also* c

Calb, C$_{alb}$
   albumin clearance

Calc
   calcium *also* Ca, Cal.

calc
   calculate
   calculated

calcif
   calcification

cal ct
   calorie count

CALD
   chronic active liver disease

CALEF, calef.
   make warm [L. *calefac*]
   warmed [L. *calefactus*]

CALGB
   cancer and leukemia group B

CALH
   chronic active lupoid hepatitis

calib
   calibrated

cal/kg/day
   calories per kilogram per day

cALL
   common null cell acute lymphocytic
   leukemia

CALLA, cALLA
   common acute lymphoblastic leukemia
   antigen
   common acute lymphocytic leukemia
   antigen

CALM
   café-au-lait macules

cal/oz
   calories per ounce

CAM
   calf aortic microsome
   carminomycin
   Caucasian adult male
   cell adhesion molecule
   cell-associating molecule
   child-adult-mist
   chorioallantoic membrane
   computer-assisted (or aided)
   myelography
   contralateral axillary metastasis
   cyclophosphamide, Adriamycin
   (doxorubicin), and methotrexate
   cystic adenomatous malformation

C$_{am}$
   amylase clearance

CaM
   calmodulin

CAMAC
   computer-automated measurement and
   control

CAMB
   cyclophosphamide, Adriamycin
   (doxorubicin), methotrexate, and
   bleomycin

CAMBO-VIP
   doxorubicin (Adriamycin),
   cyclophosphamide, etoposide,
   ifosfamide, vincristine (Oncovin),

CAMEO
   cyclophosphamide, Adriamycin
   (doxorubicin), methotrexate, etoposide,
   and Oncovin (vincristine)

CAMF
   cyclophosphamide, Adriamycin
   (doxorubicin), methotrexate, and
   fluorouracil

CAML
   Coarticulation Assessment in
   Meaningful Language

CAMP
   Christie-Atkins-Munch-Petersen
   computer-assisted menu planning
   concentration of adenosine
   monophosphate
   cyclophosphamide, Adriamycin
   (doxorubicin), methotrexate, and
   procarbazine

cAMP
   adenosine 3',5'-cyclic monophosphate
   adenosine 3',5'-cyclic phosphate
   (cyclic AMP)
   cyclic adenosine monophosphate *also*
   AMP-c
   cyclic adenosine 3',5'-monophosphate

c. amplum.
heaping spoonful [L. *cochleare amplum*]

CAMS
computer-assisted monitoring system

CAMU
cardiac ambulatory monitoring unit
coronary arrhythmia monitoring unit

CaMV
cauliflower mosaic virus

CAN
continuous albuterol nebulization
cord (umbilical) around neck

CA/N
child abuse and neglect

Can
cancer *also* CA, Ca

Can
Candida
Cannabis

can.
cannabis

CANA
circulation antineuronal antibody

CANC, canc
cancelled

C-ANCA
antineutrophil cytoplasmic antibody

CANCERLIT
Cancer Literature

CANDID
Candida yeast

C-ANP
C-type atrial natriuretic peptide

CANP
calcium-activated neutral protease

CANS
central auditory nervous system

CAO
chronic airflow obstruction
chronic airway obstruction
coronary artery obstruction

CaOC
cathodal opening contraction *also* COC

CaOCl
cathodal opening clonus *also* COC, COCL

CAOD
coronary artery occlusive disease

CAOM
chronic adhesive otitis media

Ca ox
calcium oxalate (crystal)

CAP
camptodactyly-arthropathy-pericarditis (syndrome)
cancer of prostate
capillary blood
capsule *also* cap., caps.
captopril
carcinoma of prostate
catabolite (gene) activator protein
cell attachment protein
cellular acetate propionate
cellulose acetate phthalate
central apical portion
chloramphenicol
chloroacetophenone
cholesteric analysis profile
chronic alcoholic pancreatitis
College of American Pathologists
community-acquired pneumonia
complement-activated plasma
compound action potential
computerized automated psycho-physiologic (device)
coupled atrial pacing
cyclic AMP-binding protein
cyclophosphamide, Adriamycin (doxorubicin), and prednisone
cyclosphosphamide, Adriamycin (doxorubicin), and Platinol (cisplatin)
cystine aminopeptidase

Ca/P
calcium to phosphorus ratio

cap.
capacity *also* c
capillary

NOTES

cap. *(continued)*
capsule *also* CAP, caps.
let him take [L. *capiat*]

CAPA
caffeine, alcohol, pepper, and aspirin (diet free of)
cancer-associated polypeptide antigen

CAPB
central auditory processing battery

CAP-BOP
cyclophosphamide, Adriamycin (doxorubicin), procarbazine, bleomycin, Oncovin, prednisone

CAPC
calcium phosphate

CAPD
chronic ambulatory peritoneal dialysis
continuous abdominoperitoneal dialysis
continuous ambulatory peritoneal dialysis

CAPERS
Computer-assisted Psychiatric Evaluation and Review System

capiend.
to be taken [L. *capiendus*]

cap. moll.
soft capsule [L. *capsula mollis*]

CAPPS
Current and Past Psychopathology Scales

cap. quant. vult
to be taken as much as one wants to [L. *capiat quantum vult*]

CAPR
calcium pyrophosphate

CAPRCA
chronic, acquired, pure red cell aplasia

CAPRI
Cardiopulmonary Research Institute

CAPS
caffeine, alcohol, pepper, and spicy foods (diet free of)
Cardiac Arrhythmia Pilot Study

caps.
capsule *also* CAP, cap.

CAP test
cholesteric analysis profile test

CAPYA
child and adolescent psychoanalysis

CAQ
Clinical Analysis Questionnaire

CAR
cancer-associated retinopathy
cardiac ambulation routine
chronic articular rheumatism
computer-assisted research
conditioned avoidance response

car.
carotid

CARA
chronic aspecific respiratory ailment

CARB
carbohydrate *also* C, carb, carbo, CHO, COH, HCO
coronary artery bypass (graft)

carb
carbohydrate *also* C, CARB, carbo, CHO, COH, HCO
carbonate

CARBAM
carbamazepine

carbo
carbohydrate *also* C, CARB, carb, CHO, COH, HCO

CARD
cardiac automatic resuscitative device
cardiology *also* Card., Cardiol

Card., Cardiol
cardiology *also* CARD

card
cardiac

CARDYA
Coronary Artery Risk Development in Young Adults

CARE
Cholesterol and Recurrent Events

CARE Act
Comprehensive AIDS Resources Emergency Act

CARES
Cancer Rehabilitation Evaluation System

CARF
Commission on Accreditation of Rehabilitation Facilities

CAROT
carotene

CARPORT
Coronary Artery Restenosis Prevention on Repeated Thromboxane Antagonism

CARS
childhood autism rating scale
Children's Affective Rating Scale

cart
cartilage

CARTOS
computer-assisted reconstruction by tracing of serial sections

CARTT
computer-assisted real-time transcription

CAS
calcarine sulcus
calcific aortic stenosis
Cancer Attitude Survey
carbohydrate-active steroid
cardiac adjustment scale
cardiac surgery
carotid artery stenosis
carotid artery system
casein
Celite-activated normal serum
Cell Analysis system
Center for Alcohol Studies
cerebral arteriosclerosis
cerebral atherosclerosis
Chemical Abstracts Service
chronic anovulation syndrome
cold agglutinin syndrome
congenital alcoholic syndrome
congenital asplenia syndrome
control adjustment strap
coronary artery spasm

Cas
casualty

cas
castrated
castration

CASA
cancer-associated serum antigen
computer-assisted self-assessment

CASANOVA
Carotid Artery Stenosis with Asymptomatic Narrowing: Operation Versus Aspirin Study

CASE
computer-assisted sensory examination

CASH
cancer and steroid hormone
classic abdominal Semm hysterectomy
Commission for Administrative Services in Hospitals
corticoadrenal stimulating hormone
cruciform anterior spinal hyperextension

CASHD
coronary arteriosclerotic heart disease
coronary atherosclerotic heart disease

CASMD
congenital atonic sclerotic muscular dystrophy

CA-SP
calcium urine spot (test)

CAS-REGN
Chemical Abstracts Service Registry Number

CASRT
corrected adjusted sinus (node) recovery time

CASS
computer-aided sleep system
computer-assisted stereotactic surgery
Coronary Artery Surgery Study

C-AST
cytoplasmic aspartate aminotransferase

CAST
Canterbury Alcoholism Screening Test
Cardiac Arrhythmia Suppression Trial
Children of Alcoholism Screening Test

CASTNO
cast number (urinalysis)

CAT
California Achievement Test
capillary agglutination test
catalase *also* CAT'ase

C

NOTES

CAT *(continued)*
    cataract *also* cat.
    catecholamine *also* CA
    cellular atypia
    Children's Apperception Test
    chloramphenicol acetyl transferase
    chlormerodrin accumulation test
    choline acetyltransferase
    chronic abdominal tympany
    classified anaphylatoxin
    Cognitive Abilities Test
    computed abdominal tomography
    computed axial tomography
    computer-assisted tomography
    computer of average transients
    computerized axial tomography
    cytosine arabinoside, Adriamycin
    (doxorubicin), and thioguanine

cat.
    catalyst
    cataract *also* CAT

CAT-A-KIT
    Catecholamine Radioenzymatic Assay
    Kit

CAT'ase
    catalase *also* CAT

CAT-CAM
    contoured adduction trochanteric-
    controlled alignment method

CATCH
    Child and Adolescent Trial of
    Cardiovascular Health
    Community Actions to Control High
    Blood Pressure

cat c̄ IL, cat c̄ IOL
    cataract with intraocular lens

Cath, cath
    cathartic
    catheter
    catheterization
    catheterize
    cathode *also* C, CA, Ca

CATLINE
    Catalog On-Line

CAT-S
    Children's Apperception Test,
    Supplemental

CATS
    Captopril and Thrombolysis Study

CAT scan
    computerized axial tomography scan

CATT
    calcium tolerance test

Cau, Cauc, cauc
    Caucasian *also* C

caud
    caudal

caut
    cauterization

CAV
    cardiac allograft vasculopathy
    computer-assisted ventilation
    congenital absence of vagina
    congenital adrenal virilism
    constant angular velocity
    croup-associated virus
    cyclophosphamide, Adriamycin
    (doxorubicin), and vincristine

cav
    cavity

CAVB
    complete atrioventricular block

CAVC
    common arterioventricular canal

CAVD
    complete atrioventricular dissociation
    completion, arithmetic problems,
    vocabulary, following directions
    (battery)

C(a-VDO$_2$)
    arteriovenous oxygen difference

CAVe
    CCNU (lomustine), Adriamycin
    (doxorubicin), and vinblastine

CAVEAT
    Coronary Angioplasty versus
    Excisional Atherectomy Trial

CAVH
    chronic active viral hepatitis
    continuous arteriovenous hemofiltration

CAVH-B
    chronic active viral hepatitis, type B

CAVHD
    continuous arteriovenous hemodialysis
    continuous arteriovenous hemofiltration
    with dialysis

CAVH-NAB
    chronic active viral hepatitis, non-A,
    non-B

CA virus
croup-associated virus

CAVLT
Children's Auditory Verbal Learning Test

CAVO
common atrioventricular orifice
arteriovenous oxygen content difference

CAVP
cyclophosphamide, Adriamycin (doxorubicin), vincristine, and prednisone

CAV-P-VP
cyclophosphamide, Adriamycin (doxorubicin), vincristine, Platinol (cisplatin), and VP16-213 (etoposide)

CAVU
continuous arteriovenous ultrafiltration

CAW
central airways

C_{AW}, C_{aw}
airway conductance *also* GA, GAW

CAWO
closing abductory wedge osteotomy

CAZ
ceftazidime

C-B, C/B
chest-back *also* CB

CB
calcium blocker
carbenicillin
carbonated beverage
carotid body
catheterized bladder
ceased breathing
cesarean birth
chair and bed *also* C&B
chest-back *also* C-B, C/B
chocolate blood (agar) *also* CB agar
chronic bronchitis
circumflex branch
code blue
color blind
compensated base

conjugated bilirubin
contrast bath
coracobrachial
cytochalasin B

C&B
chair and bed *also* CB
crown and bridge

CB_{ll}
phenadoxone hydrochloride

Cb
columbium

cb
cardboard (or plastic film holder without intensifying screens)

CBA
carcinoma-bearing animal
chronic bronchitis with asthma
competitive-binding assay
cost-benefit analysis

CBAB
complement-binding antibody

CBADAA
Certifying Board of the American Dental Assistants Association

CB agar
chocolate blood agar *also* CB

CBAT
Coulter battery

CBB
Coomassie brilliant blue R-250 (stain)

CBBB
complete bundle branch block

CBC
carbenicillin *also* CBCN
cerebrobuccal connective
child behavior characteristics
complete blood (cell) count *also* cbc

cbc
complete blood (cell) count *also* CBC

CBCL
Child Behavior Checklist

NOTES

CBCL/2-3
Child Behavior Checklist for ages 2-3

CBCME
computer-based continuing medical education

CBCN
carbenicillin *also* CBC

CBD
cannabidiol
carotid body denervation
closed bladder drainage
common bile duct
community-based distribution

CBDC
chronic bullous disease of childhood

CBDE
common bile duct exploration

CBDL
chronic bile duct ligation

CBDS
Carcinogenesis Bioassay Data System

CBF
capillary blood flow
cerebral blood flow
ciliary beat frequency
coronary blood flow
cortical blood flow

CBFS
cerebral blood flow studies

CBFV
cerebral blood flow velocity
coronary blood flow velocity

CBG
capillary blood gas
capillary blood glucose
cord blood gas
coronary bypass graft
corticosteroid-binding globulin
cortisol-binding globulin

CBG-BC
corticosteroid-binding globulin-binding capacity

CBG$_v$
corticosteroid-binding globulin variant

CBH
chronic benign hepatitis
collimated beam handpiece
cutaneous basophilic hypersensitivity

CBI
continuous bladder irrigation
convergent beam irradiation

CBIL
conjugated bilirubin

CBIP
Cancer Background Interference Procedure

CBIPBG
Cancer Background Interference Procedure for Bender Gestalt

CBL
circulating blood lymphocytes
(umbilical) cord blood leukocytes

Cbl
cobalamin

cbl
chronic blood loss

CBM
capillary basement membrane
cryopreserved bone marrow

CBMMP
chronic benign mucous membrane pemphigus

CBMT
capillary basement membrane thickness

CBMW
capillary basement membrane width

CBN
cannibinol
central benign neoplasm
chronic benign neutropenia
Commission on Biological Nomenclature

CBOC
completion bed occupancy care

CBP
calcium-binding protein
carbohydrate-binding protein
cardiac bypass
chlorobiphenyl
chronic benign pain
cobalamin-binding protein
copper-binding protein

CBPA
competitive protein-binding assay

CBPP
contagious bovine pleuropneumonia

CBPPA
cyclophosphamide, bleomycin, procarbazine, prednisone, and Adriamycin (doxorubicin)

CBPS
coronary bypass surgery

CBR
carotid bodies resected
chemical, bacteriologic, and radiologic (warfare)
chemically bound residue
chronic bedrest
complete bed-rest
crude birth rate

C$_{BR}$
bilirubin clearance

CBRAM
controlled partial rebreathing - anesthesia method

CBS
capillary blood sugar
cervicobrachial syndrome
Charles Bonnet syndrome
chronic brain syndrome
colloidal bismuth subcitrate
conjugated bile salts
Cruveilhier-Baumgarten syndrome
culture-bound syndrome
cystathionine beta-synthase

CBT
carotid body tumor
cognitive behavior therapy
computed body tomography

CBTIS
computerized bedside transfusion identification system

CBTP
Cognitive Behavior Therapy Package

CBV
capillary blood (flow) velocity
catheter balloon valvuloplasty
central blood volume
cerebral blood volume
circulating blood volume
corrected blood volume
cortical blood volume
Coxsackie B virus

cyclophosphamide, BCNU (carmustine), and VP16-213 (etoposide)
Cytoxan, BCNU, VP-16

CBVD
cerebrovascular disease

CBW
chemical and biologic warfare
critical bandwidth (range of frequencies)

CBX
computer-based examination

CBZ
carbamazepine

Cbz
carbobenzoxy *also* Z

CC
calcaneocuboid
calcium cyclamate
canal catheterization
cardiac catheterization
cardiac cycle
cardiovascular clinic
carotid-cavernous
case coordinator
caval catheterization
cell culture
cellular compartment
central compartment
cerebral commissure
cerebral concussion
cervical collar
chest circumference *also* cc
chief complaint
cholecalciferol
chondro-calcinosis
choriocarcinoma *also* CCA
chronic complainer
ciliated cell
circulatory collapse
classical conditioning
clean catch (of urine)
clinical course
clomiphene citrate
closing capacity
coefficient of correlation
colony count
colorectal cancer

NOTES

CC *(continued)*
columnar cells
commission-certified (stain)
complications and comorbidities
compound cathartic
computer calculated
concave *also* Cc, cc
congenital cardiopathy
consumptive coagulopathy
continuing care
contractile component
contrast cystogram
coracoclavicular
cord compression
coronary collateral
corpus callosum
costochondral
Coulter counter
craniocaudal
craniocervical
creatinine clearance *also* C_{cr}, CrCl, Crcl
critical care
critical condition
Cronkhite-Canada [syndrome]
crus cerebri
crus communis
cubic centimeter *also* cc, c.c., cm^3, cu cm
cup cell
current complaint
current contents
cytochrome C
with correction (with glasses)

C-C
convexoconcave

C1–C7
cervical vertebrae 1 through 7

C1–C8
cervical nerves 1 through 8

C1–C9
serum complement C.

C-1–C-9
activated components of complement 1 through 9

C1–C12
cranial nerves I through XII *also* CI–XII

C_1–C_{12}
first through twelfth ribs [L. *costa*]

C/C
chief complaint

cholecystectomy and (operative) cholangiogram
complete upper and lower dentures

C&C
cold and clammy
confirmed and compatible

Cc
concave *also* CC, cc

cc
carbon copy
chest circumference *also* CC
concave *also* CC, Cc
condylocephalic
corrected
cubic centimeter *also* CC, c.c., cm^3, cu cm
with correction
with spectacles

$\bar{c}\bar{c}$
with meals

c.c.
cubic centimeter *also* CC, cc, cm^3, cu cm

CCA
calcium channel antagonist
cephalin cholesterol antigen
chick-cell agglutination (unit)
chimpanzee coryza agent
choriocarcinoma *also* CC
chromated copper arsenak
circumflex coronary artery
colitis colon antigen
common carotid artery
concentrated care area
congenital contractural arachnodactyly
constitutional chromosome abnormality

CCAIT
Canadian Coronary Atherosclerosis Intervention Trial

CCAM
congenital cystic adenomatoid malformation

CCAP
capsule cartilage articular preservation

CCAT
Canadian Coronary Atherectomy Trial
conglutinating complement absorption test

CCB
calcium channel blocker

CCBV
central circulating blood volume

CCC
calcium cyanamide (carbimide) citrated
Cancer Care Center
care-cure coordination
cathodal-closure contraction *also* CaCC
central counter adaptive changes
child care clinic
cholangiocellular carcinoma
chronic calculous cholecystitis
chronic catarrhal colitis
citrated calcium carbimide
clear cell carcinoma
comprehensive cancer center
comprehensive care clinic
consecutive case conference
continuing community care
critical care complex
cylindrical confronting cisterna

CC&C
colony count and culture

CCCC
centrifugal counter-current chromatography

CCCF
Candlelighters Childhood Cancer Foundation

CCCL, CCCl
cathodal-closure clonus

CCCP
carbonyl cyanide m-chlorophenylhydrazone

CCCR
closed-chest cardiac resuscitation
closed-chest cardiopulmonary resuscitation

CCCS
condom catheter collecting system

CCCT
closed craniocerebral trauma

CCCU
comprehensive cardiac care unit

CCD
calibration curve data
central core disease
charge-coupled device
childhood celiac disease
cortical collecting duct
countercurrent distribution
cumulative cardiotoxic dose

CCDC
Canadian Communicable Disease Center

CCDN
Central Council for District Nursing

ccDNA
closed circle deoxyribonucleic acid

CCDS
color-coded duplex sonography

CCE
carboline-carboxylic (acid) ester
chamois contagious ecthyma
cholesterol crystal embolization
clear-cell endothelioma
clubbing, cyanosis, and edema
countercurrent electrophoresis

CCEI
Crown-Crisp Experimental Index

CCF
cancer coagulation factor
cardiolipin complement fixation
carotid-cavernous fistula
centrifuged culture fluid
cephalin-cholesterol flocculation
compound comminuted fracture
congestive cardiac failure
critical corresponding frequency
crystal-induced chemotactic factor

CCFA
Crohns and Colitis Foundation of America
cycloserine-cefoxitin-fructose agar

CCFE
cyclophosphamide, cisplatin, fluorouracil, and estramustine

CCG
cationic colloidal gold

NOTES

CCG *(continued)*
chole
cholecystogram

CCGC
capillary column gas chromatography

CCGG
cytosine-cytosine-guanine-guanine

CCH
chronic cholestatic hepatitis

CCh
carbamylcholine

CCHD
cyanotic congenital heart disease

CCHP
Consumer Choice Health Plan

cc/hr
cubic centimeters per hour

CCHS
congenital central hypoventilation
syndrome

CCI
chronic coronary insufficiency
corrected count increment

CCIC
contrast chromoscopy using indigo
carmine

CCJ
costochondral junction

CCK
cholecystokinin

CCK-8
cholecystokinin octapeptide *also* CCK-
OP

CCK-GB
cholecystokinin-gallbladder
(cholecystogram)

cc/kg/d
cubic centimeters per kilogram per
day

CCK-LI
cholecystokinin-like immunoreactivity

CCK-OP
cholecystokinin octapeptide *also* CCK-
8

CCK-PZ
cholecystokinin-pancreozymin

CCL
carcinoma cell line
cardiac catheterization laboratory
certified cell line
critical carbohydrate level
critical condition list

CCL cell
centrocyte-like cell

CCLI
composite clinical and laboratory
index

CCM
cerebrocostomandibular (syndrome)
congestive cardiomyopathy
contralateral competing message
craniocervical malformation
critical care medicine
cyclophosphamide, CCNU (lomustine),
and methotrexate

CC/MCL
centrocytic/mantle-cell lymphoma

CCMS
clean-catch midstream (urine) *also*
CCMSU
clinical care management system

CCMSU
clean-catch midstream urine *also*
CCMS

CCMSUA
clean-catch midstream urinalysis

CCMT
catechol methyltransferase

CCMU
critical care medicine unit

CCN
caudal central nucleus
coronary care nursing
critical care nursing

CCNS
cell-cycle nonspecific (agent)

CCNSC
Cancer Chemotherapy National
Service Center

CCNU
cyclohexylchloroethylnitrosurea
(lomustine)

CcO$_2$
oxygen concentration in pulmonary
capillary blood
pulmonary end-capillary blood oxygen
concentration

CCOF
CCNU, Oncovin (vincristine), and prednisone
chromosomally competent ovarian failure

C-collar
cervical collar

CCP
chronic calcifying pancreatitis
ciliocytophthoria
colitis cystica profunda
Crippled Children's Program
crystalloid cardioplegia
cytidine cyclic phosphate

CCPD
continuous cyclical peritoneal dialysis
continuous cycling peritoneal dialysis
crystalline calcium pyrophosphate dihydrate

CCPDS
Centralized Cancer Patient Data System

CCPQ
Children's Comprehensive Pain Questionnaire

CCPR
cerebral cortex perfusion rate *also* CPR
crypt cell production rate

CCR
cardiac catheterization recovery
complete continuous remission
continuous complete remission

C$_{cr}$
creatinine clearance *also* CC, CrCl, Crcl

CCRC
continuing care residential community

CCRN
Critical Care Registered Nurse

CCRS
carotid chemoreceptor stimulation

CCRT
combined chemoradiotherapy

CCRU
critical care recovery unit

CCS
Canadian Cardiovascular Society
casualty clearing station
cell cycle specific (agent)
cholecystosonography
cloudy-cornea syndrome
concentration-camp syndrome
costoclavicular syndrome
Crippled Children's Services
Critical Care Services

CC&S
cornea, conjunctiva, and sclera

CCSA
central chemosensitive area

CCSCS
central cervical spinal cord syndrome

CCSG
Children's Cancer Study Group

CCSK
clear cell sarcoma of the liver

CCSS
Childhood Cancer Survivor Study

CCT
calcitriol
carotid compression tomography
central conduction time
chocolate-coated tablet
closed cerebral trauma
coated compressed tablet
combined cortical thickness
composite cyclic therapy
congenitally corrected transposition (of the great vessels)
controlled cord traction
coronary care team
cranial computed tomography
crude coal tar
cyclocarbothiamine

cct
circuit

CCTe
cathodal-closure tetanus

NOTES

C

CCTGA
congenitally corrected transposition of the great arteries

CCT in PET
crude coal tar in petroleum

CCTV
closed circuit television

CCU
cardiac care unit
cardiovascular care unit
Cherry-Crandall unit
community care unit
coronary care unit
critical care unit

CCUA
clean-catch urinalysis

CCUP
colpocystourethropexy

CCV
CCNU (lomustine), cyclophosphamide, and vincristine
channel catfish virus
conductivity cell volume

CCVB
CCNU (lomustine), cyclophosphamide, vincristine, and bleomycin

CCVD
chronic cerebrovascular disease

CCVPP
CCNU (lomustine), cyclophosphamide, vinblastine, procarbazine, and prednisone

CCW
childcare worker
counterclockwise

Ccw
chest wall compliance

CCX
complications

CCY
cholecystectomy

CD
cadaver donor
canine distemper
carbohydrate dehydratase
carbon dioxide
cardiac disease
cardiac dullness
cardiac dysrrhythmia
cardiovascular deconditioning

cardiovascular disease *also* CVD
Carrel-Dakin (fluid)
Castleman disease
caudad
caudal
cefaloridine
celiac disease
cell dissociation
central deposition
cervical dystonia
cesarean delivered
cesarean delivery
channel down
character disorder
chemical dependency
chemotactic difference
childhood disease
circular dichroism
civil defense
Clostridium difficile
cluster of differentiation
collecting duct
colloid droplet
combination drug
common duct
communicable disease
communication deviance
communication disorders
completely denatured
complicated delivery
conduct disorder
consanguineous donor
contact dermatitis
contagious disease
continuous drainage
control diet
convulsive disorder
convulsive dose
copying drawings
corneal dystrophy
covert dyskinesia
Crohn disease
crossed diagonal
curative dose
current diagnosis
cutdown
cystic duct
cytarabine and daunorubicin
Czapek-Dox (agar)
diagonal conjugate diameter of the pelvis [L. *conjugata diagonalis*]
with the right hand [L. *colla dextra*]

C-D
Cotrel-Dubousset (rod)

CD2-72
cluster of differentiation 2–72

CD3
cluster of differentiation 3

CD4
cluster of differentiation 4

CD8
cluster of differentiation 8

CD$_{50}$
median curative dose

C&D
curettage and desiccation
cystoscopy and dilation

C/D
cigarettes per day
cup-to-disc (ratio)

Cd
cadmium
caudal *also* cd
coccygeal *also* cd
color denial
condylion

cd
candela
caudal *also* Cd
coccygeal *also* Cd
cord

CDA
Canadian Dental Association
Certified Dental Assistant
chenodeoxycholic acid
ciliary dyskinesia activity
complement-dependent antibody
completely denatured alcohol
congenital dyserythropoietic anemia
(types I–III)

CdA
2-chloro-2′-deoxyadenosine

CDAA
chlorodiallylacetamide (herbicide)

CDAD
Clostridium difficile-associated diarrhea

CDAI
Crohn Disease Activity Index

CDAK
Cordis Dow Artificial Kidney

CDAP
continuous distending airway pressure

CDB, C&DB
cough and deep breath

CDBR
computerized diaphragmatic breathing
retraining

CDC
calculated date of confinement
cancer detection center
capillary diffusion capacity
carboplatin, doxorubicin, and
cyclophosphamide
cardiac diagnostic center
cell division cycle
Centers for Disease Control
chenodeoxycholate
chenodeoxycholic (acid) *also* CDCA
child development clinic
Clostridium difficile colitis
Communicable Disease Center
complement-dependent cytotoxicity
Crohn disease of the colon

CD-C
controlled drinker-control

CDCA
chenodeoxycholic acid *also* CDC
choledochocaval anastomosis

CDCF
Clostridium difficile culture filtrate

CDCR
conjunctivodacryocystorhinostomy

CDD
certificate of disability for discharge
chronic degenerative disease
chronic disabling dermatosis
critical degree of deformation

CDDP
cis-diamminedichloroplatinum *also*
DDP
cisplatin

CD-E
controlled drinker-experimental

C

NOTES

CDE
canine distemper encephalitis
Certified Diabetes Educator
chlordiazepoxide
color Doppler energy
common duct exploration
cystine dimethylester

CDEIS
Crohn Disease Endoscopic Index of Severity

CDF
chondrodystrophia foetalis

CDFR
cumulative duration of the first remission

CDG
central developmental groove

CDGD
constitutional delay in growth and development

CDH
ceramide dihexoside
chronic daily headache
chronic disease hospital
congenital diaphragmatic hernia
congenital dislocation of hip
congenital dysplasia of hip

CDI
cell-directed inhibitor
central diabetes insipidus
Children's Depression Inventory
chronic diabetes insipidus

CDILD
chronic diffuse interstitial lung disease

CDIS
continuous distention-irrigation system

CDK
climatic droplet keratopathy

CDL
chlordeoxylincomycin
Copying Drawings with Landmarks

CDLE
chronic discoid lupus erythematosus

CDLS
Cornelia de Lange syndrome

CDM
chemically defined medium
childhood dermatomyositis
clinical decision making

cDNA
complementary deoxyribonucleic acid (DNA)
human-cloned DNA

CDO
Cotrel-Dubousset orthopaedic

CDP
chlordiazepoxide
chronic destructive periodontitis
collagenase-digestible protein
constant distending pressure
continuous distending pressure
Coronary Drug Project
cytidine diphosphate
cytidine 5′-diphosphate

CDPC
cytidine diphosphate choline

CDP-choline
cytidine diphosphocholine

CDP-glyceride
cytidine diphosphoglyceride

CDPS
common duct pigment stones

CDP-sugar
cytidine diphosphosugar

CDQ
corrected development quotient

CDR
calcium-dependent regulator
chronologic drinking record
computed digital radiography
continuing disability review

CDR(H)
cup-to-disc ratio horizontal

CDRS-R
Children's Depression Rating Scale-Revised

CDR(V)
cup-to-disc ratio vertical

CDS
caudal dysplasia syndrome
Chemical Data System
Christian Dental Society
commercial dialysis solution
cul-de-sac
cumulative duration of survival

cd-sr
candela-steradian

CDSS
  clinical decision support system

CDT
  carbon dioxide therapy
  Certified Dental Technician
  combined diphtheria tetanus

CDTA
  cyclohexenediaminetetraacetic acid

CDTe
  cathode-duration tetanus

CDU
  chemical dependency unit
  cumulative dose unit

CDV
  canine distemper virus

CDX
  chlordiazepoxide *also* CDZ

CDY
  cystoduodenostomy

CDYN, C$_{dyn}$, Cdyn
  dynamic compliance (of lung in pulmonary function test)

CDZ
  chlordiazepoxide *also* CDX

CE
  California encephalitis
  capital epiphysis
  cardiac emergency
  cardiac enlargement
  cardioesophageal (junction) *also* CEJ
  cataract extraction
  cell extract
  center-edge
  central episiotomy
  chemical energy
  chick embryo
  chloroform-ether
  cholera exotoxin
  cholesterol esters
  cholinesterase *also* CEA, CHE, ChE, CHS
  chromatoelectrophoresis
  clinical emphysema
  cocaethylene
  columnar epithelium
  community education

  conjugated estrogens
  constant error
  constant estrus
  continuing education
  contractile element
  contrast echocardiology
  converting enzyme
  crude extract
  cytopathic effect

C-E
  chloroform-ether

C&E
  consultation and examination
  cough and exercise
  curettage and electrodesication

Ce
  cerium

CEA
  carcinoembryonic antigen
  carotid endarterectomy
  cholesterol-esterifying activity
  cholinesterase *also* CE, CHE, ChE, CHS
  cost-effectiveness analysis
  crystalline egg albumin

CEA-125
  carcinoembryonic antigen-125 *also* CA125, CA-125

CEA-DT
  carcinoembryonic antigen doubling time

CEARP
  Continuing Education Approval and Recognition Program

CEB
  calcium entry blocker
  cotton elastic bandage

CEBD
  controlled extrahepatic biliary drainage

CEBV
  chronic Epstein-Barr virus

CEC
  ciliated epithelial cell
  contractile electrical complex

NOTES

C

CECD
congenital endothelial corneal
dystrophy

CECT
contrast enhancement computed
tomography

CED
chondroectodermal dysplasia
chronic enthusiasm disorder
cultural/ethnic diversity
cystoscopy-endoscopy dilation

CEE
Central European encephalitis
chick embryo extract

CEEA
curved end-to-end anastomosis

CEEC
calf esophagus epithelial cell

CEEG
computer-analyzed
electroencephalography

CEEV
Central European encephalitis virus

CEF
centrifugation extractable fluid
chick embryo fibroblast
constant electric field

c7E3 Fab
chimeric 7E3 Fab

CE-FAST
contrast-enhanced fast-acquisition
steady state
contrast-enhanced fast sequence

CEG
chronic erosive gastritis

cEGF
concentration epidermal growth factor

CEH
cholesterol ester hydrolase

CEHC
calf embryonic heart cell

CEI
character education inquiry
continuous extravascular infusion
converting enzyme inhibitor
corneal epithelial involvement

CEID
crossed electroimmunodiffusion

CEJ
cardioesophageal junction *also* CE
cement-enamel junction

CEK
chick embryo kidney

CEL
cardiac exercise laboratory
Celsius *also* C, Cel

Cel
Celsius *also* C, CEL

CELF
Clinical Evaluation of Language
Functions

CELI
Carrow Elicited Language Inventory

Cell
celluloid

CELO
chicken embryo lethal orphan

CELOV
chick embryonal lethal orphan virus

CEM
central extensor mechanism
computerized electroencephalographic
map
conventional transmission electron
microscope
CUSA electrosurgical module

cemf
counterelectromotive force

CEN
Certificate for Emergency Nursing

cen
central
centromere

CENP
centromere protein

CENT, cent.
centigrade *also* C
centimeter *also* cm
central *also* C

CEO
chick embryo origin
Chief Executive Officer
chloroethylene oxide

CEOT
calcifying epithelial odontogenic
tumor

CEP
centromere enumeration probe
chronic eosinophilic pneumonia
chronic erythropoietic porphyria
cognitive evoked potential
congenital erythropoietic porphyria
continuing education program
cortical evoked potential
countercurrent electrophoresis
counterelectrophoresis
cyclophosphamide, etoposide, Platinol

CEPA
chloroethane phosphoric acid

CEPB
Carpentier-Edwards porcine
bioprosthesis

CEPH
cephalic *also* ceph
cephalin *also* ceph
cephalosporin *also* ceph

ceph
cephalic *also* CEPH
cephalin *also* CEPH
cephalosporin *also* CEPH

CEPH FLOC, ceph-floc
cephalin flocculation (test)

CEPT
cyclophosphamide, fluorouracil,
prednisone, and tamoxifen

CEQ
Council on Environmental Quality

CER
capital expenditure review
ceramide
conditioned emotional response
conditioned escape response
control electrical rhythm
cortical evoked response

CE&R
central episiotomy and repair

CERA
cardiac-evoked response audiometry

CERD
chronic end-stage renal disease

CERP
Continuing Education Recognition
Program

Cert, cert
certificate *also* CTF
certified

CERULO
ceruloplasmin

cerv
cervical
cervix

CES
cat's-eye syndrome
cauda equina syndrome
central excitatory state
chronic electrophysiologic study
cognitive environmental stimulation

CESD
cholesterol ester storage disease

CESI
cervical epidural steroid injection

CET
capital expenditure threshold
cephalothin
congenital eyelid tetrad
controlled environment treatment

CETE
Central European tick-borne
encephalitis

CETP
cholesterol ester transfer protein

CEU
congenital ectropion uveae
continuing education unit

CEV
California encephalitis virus
cyclophosphamide, etoposide, and
vincristine

CEZ
cefazolin

CF
calcium leucovorin
calf blood flow
calibration factor
cancer-free

C

NOTES

CF *(continued)*
carbol-fuchsin (stain)
cardiac failure
carotid foramen
carrier-free
cascade filtration
case file
Caucasian female
central fossa
cephalothin
characteristic frequency
chemotactic factor
chest and left leg (lead in electrocardiography)
Chiari-Frommel (syndrome)
chick fibroblast
choroid fissure
Christmas factor
cisplatin and fluorouracil
cisplatin, 5-fluorouracil
citrovorum factor
climbing fiber
clotting factor
colicin factor
collected fluid
colonization factor
colony-forming
color and form
compare [L. *confer*] *also* cf., comp, cp.
complement factor
complement fixation *also* com fix
complement-fixing
completely follicular
computed fluoroscopy
constant frequency
contractile force
coronary flow
cough frequency
count fingers (visual acuity test) *also* C/F, cf
counting fingers
coupling factor
cycling fibroblast
cystic fibrosis *also* C/F

CFII
Cohn fraction II

C′F
complement fixing

C/F
colored female
count fingers (visual acuity test) *also* CF, cf
cystic fibrosis *also* CF

C&F
cell and flare
curettage and fulguration

Cf
californium
iron carrier [L. *ferrum*]

²⁵²Cf
californium-252

cf
bring together
centrifugal force
count fingers (visual acuity test) *also* CF, C/F

cf.
compare [L. *confer*] *also* CF, comp, cp.

CFA
clofibric acid
colonization factor antigen
colony-forming assay
common femoral artery
complement-fixing antibody
complete Freund adjuvant
cryptogenic fibrosing alveolitis

CFAC
complement-fixing antibody consumption

C-factor
cleverness factor

CFB
central fibrous body

CFC
capillary filtration coefficient
cardiofaciocutaneous (syndrome)
chlorofluorocarbon
colony-forming capacity
colony-forming cells
continuous-flow centrifugation

CFCL
continuous-flow centrifugation leukapheresis

CFC-S
colony-forming cells-spleen

CFD
cephalofacial deformity
color-flow Doppler
craniofacial dysostosis

CFDS
craniofacial dysostosis

CFE
colony-forming efficiency

CFF
critical flicker frequency
critical flicker fusion (test) *also* cff
critical fusion frequency *also* cff
cystic fibrosis factor
Cystic Fibrosis Foundation

cff
critical flicker fusion (test) *also* CFF
critical fusion frequency *also* CFF

CFFA
cystic fibrosis factor activity

Cf-Fe
carrier-bound iron [L. *ferrum*]

CFH
Council on Family Health

CFI
cardiac function index
chemotactic-factor inactivator
complement fixation inhibition
confrontation fields intact
contour-facilitating instrument

CFIDS
chronic fatigue and immune
dysfunction syndrome

CFL
calcaneofibular ligament
cisplatin, fluorouracil, and leucovorin
calcium

CFM
chemotactic factor for macrophage
chlorofluoromethane
close-fitting mask
craniofacial microsomia
cyclophosphamide, fluorouracil, and
citoxantrone

cfm
cubic feet per minute

CFND
craniofrontonasal dysostosis

CFNS
chills, fever, and night sweats

CFO
chief financial officer

CFP
chronic false positive
Clinical Fellowship Program
cyclophosphamide, fluorouracil, and
prednisone
cystic fibrosis of pancreas
cystic fibrosis patients
cystic fibrosis protein

CFPD
critical frequency of photic driving

CFR
case-fatality ratio
citrovorum-factor rescue
complement-fixation reaction
coronary flow reserve
cyclic flow reduction

CFS
call for service
cancer family syndrome
Chiari-Frommel syndrome
chronic fatigue syndrome
contoured femoral stem
craniofacial stenosis
crush fracture syndrome
Cystic Fibrosis Society

cfs
cubic feet per second

CFSE
crystal field stabilization energy

CFSTI
Clearinghouse for Federal Scientific
and Technical Information

CFT
cardiolipin flocculation test
clinical full-time
complement fixation test
complement fixing titer
crystal field theory

CFTR
cystic fibrosis transmembrane
regulator

CFU
colony-forming unit
color-forming unit

CFUC, CFU-C
colony-forming unit-culture

NOTES

CFU-E
colony-forming unit–erythrocyte
colony-forming unit–erythroid

CFU$_{EOS}$
colony-forming unit–eosinophil

CFU-F
colony-forming unit–fibroblast
colony-forming unit–fibroblastoid

CFU-GEMM
colony-forming unit–granulocyte,
erythrocyte, megakaryocyte,
macrophage

CFU-GM, CFU$_{GM}$
colony-forming unit–granulocyte-
macrophage

CFU$_L$
colony-forming unit–lymphoid

CFU$_M$, CFU$_{MEG}$
colony-forming unit–megakaryocyte

CFU/mL
colony-forming units/mL

CFU$_{NM}$
colony-forming unit–neutrophil-
monocyte

CFU-S, CFU$_S$
colony-forming unit–spleen
colony-forming unit–stem (cell)

CFW
calcofluor white stain
cancer-free white (mouse) *also*
CFWM
Carworth farm (mouse), Webster
strain

CFWM
cancer-free white mouse *also* CFW

CFX
cefoxitin
circumflex (coronary artery)

CFZ
capillary-free zone

CFZC
continuous-flow zonal centrifugation

CG
calcium gluconate
cardiography
Cardio-Green
center of gravity *also* cg
central gray
choking gas (phosgene)

cholecystogram
cholecystography
choriogenic gynecomastia
chorionic gonadotropin *also* CGT
chronic glomerulonephritis *also* CGN
cingulate gyrus
colloidal gold
contact guarding
control group
cryoglobulin
cystine guanine

cg
center of gravity *also* CG
centigram
chemoglobulin

CGA
catabolite gene activator

CGAS
Children's Global Assessment Scale

CGB
chronic gastrointestinal (tract) bleeding

CGC
Certified Gastrointestinal Clinician

CGCF
central groove of central fossa

CGD
chromosomal gonadal dysgenesis
chronic granulomatous disease

CGDE
contact glow discharge electrolysis

CGFH
congenital fibrous histiocytoma

CGH
chorionic gonadotropic hormone

CGI
chronic granulomatous inflammation
Clinical Global Impression (Scale)

CGIC
Clinical Global Impression of Change

CGL
chronic granulocytic leukemia
correction with glasses *also* c gl

c gl
correction with glasses *also* CGL

CGM
central gray matter (spinal cord)
coffee-grounds material

cgm
centigram

CGMMV
cucumber green mottled mosaic virus

cGMP
cyclic guanosine monophosphate
cyclic guanosine 3,'5'-monophosphate
5'-cyclic guanosine monophosphate

CGN
chronic glomerulonephritis *also* CG
Convalescent Growing Nursery

CGNB
composite ganglioneuroblastoma

CG/OQ
cerebral glucose oxygen quotient

CGP
choline glycerophosphatide
chorionic growth hormone prolactin
circulating granulocyte pool

CGRP
calcitonin gene-related peptide

CGS
cardiogenic shock
catgut suture *also* CS
centimeter-gram-second (system, unit)
also cgs

cgs
centimeter-gram-second (system, unit)
also CGS

CGT
chorionic gonadotropin *also* CG
cyclodextrin glucanotransferase

CGTT
cortisol glucose tolerance test
cortisone glucose tolerance test

c-GVHD
chronic graft-versus-host disease

CGY
cystogastrostomy

cGy
centigray

CH
case history
casein hydrolysate
Chédiak-Higashi (syndrome)
child (children) *also* Ch, ch
Chinese hamster

chloral hydrate
cholesterol *also* C, Ch, CHO,
 CHOL, chol, chol.
Christchurch chromosome *also* Ch,
 Ch^1
chronic hepatitis
chronic hypertension
Clarke-Hadfield (syndrome)
cluster headache
common hepatic (duct)
communicating hydrocele
complete healing
congenital hypothyroidism
Conradi-Hünermann (syndrome)
continuous heparinization
convalescent hospital
crown-heel (length) *also* CHL
cycloheximide
wheelchair

C&H
coarse and harsh (breathing)
cocaine and heroin

CH$_{50}$
(total serum) hemolytic complement

C$_H$
constant domain of H chain

Ch
chest *also* ch
Chido (antibody)
chief *also* ch
child *also* CH, ch
cholesterol *also* C, CH, CHO,
 CHOL, chol, chol.
choline *also* ch
Christchurch (syndrome) *also* Ch, Ch^1
chromosome

Ch^1
Christchurch chromosome *also* CH,
 Ch

cH
hydrogen ion concentration

ch
chest *also* Ch
chief *also* Ch
child *also* CH, Ch
choline *also* Ch
chronic

NOTES

CHA
Catholic Hospital Association
chronic hemolytic anemia
common hepatic artery
compound hypermetropic astigmatism
congenital hypoplasia of adrenal
glands
congenital hypoplastic anemia
continuous heated aerosols
cyclohexyladenosine
cyclohexylamine

ChA
choline acetylase

ChAc, ChAct
choline acetyltransferase

CHAD
cyclophosphamide,
hexamethylmelamine, Adriamycin, and
DDP

CHAI
continuous hepatic artery infusion

CHAID
chi-square automatic interaction
detection

CHAL
chronic haloperidol

CHAM-OCA
cyclophosphamide, hydroxyurea,
actinomycin D (dactinomycin),
methotrexate, Oncovin (vincristine),
citrovorum factor (leucovorin), and
Adriamycin (doxorubicin)

CHAMPUS
Civilian Health and Medical
Programs of Uniformed Services

CHAMPVA
Civilian Health and Medical Program
of Veterans Administration

CHANDS
curly hair-ankyloblepharon-nail
dysplasia syndrome

Chang C
Chang conjunctiva cells

Chang L
Chang liver cells

CHAP
Certified Hospital Admission Program
Child Health Assessment Program

cyclophosphamide,
hexamethylmelamine, Adriamycin
(doxorubicin), and Platinol (cisplatin)

CHAR
continuous hyperfractionated
accelerated radiotherapy

CHARGE
coloboma, heart disease, atresia
choanae, retarded growth and
retarded development and/or CNS
anomalies, genital hypoplasia, and
ear anomalies and/or deafness
(syndrome)

CHAS
Center for Health Administration
Studies

CHAT, ChAT, ChaT
choline acetyltransferase

CHB
chronic hepatitis B
complete heart block
congenital heart block

ChB
Bachelor of Surgery [L. *Chirurgiae
Baccalaureus*]

CHBHA
congenital Heinz body hemolytic
anemia

CHC
Canadian Heart Classification
community health center
community health council
concentric hypertrophic
cardiomyopathy

CHCP
correctional health-care program

CHCT
caffeine and halothane contracture
test

CHD
center hemodialysis
Chédiak-Higashi disease
childhood disease
chronic hemodialysis
common hepatic duct
congenital heart disease
congenital hip disease
congenital hip dislocation
congenital hip dysplasia
congestive heart disease
constitutional hepatic dysfunction

coordinate home care
coronary heart disease
cyanotic heart disease

ChD
Doctor of Surgery [L. *Chirurgiae Doctor*]

CHE
cholesterol ester *also* ChE
cholinesterase *also* CE, CEA, ChE, CHS
chronic hepatic encephalopathy

ChE
cholesterol ester *also* CHE
cholinesterase *also* CE, CEA, CHE, CHS

CHEC
community hypertension evaluation clinic

CHEF
Chinese hamster embryo fibroblast

Chem
chemical
chemistry

CHEMLINE
Chemical Dictionary On-Line

chemo
chemotherapy

CHEP
Cuban/Haitian Entrant Program

CHERSS
continuous high-amplitude electroencephalogram rhythmical synchronous slowing

CHESS
chemical shift selective

CHEST
Chick Embryotoxicity Screening Test

CHF
chick embryo fibroblast
chronic heart failure
congenital hepatic fibrosis
congestive heart failure
Crimean hemorrhagic fever

cyclophosphamide, hexamethylmelamine, and 5-fluorouracil

CHFV
combined high-frequency ventilation

CHG, chg
change
changed

Ch Gn
chronic glomerulonephritis

CHH
cartilage-hair hypoplasia

χ
chi (22nd letter of Greek alphabet), lowercase

χ_2
chi-squared (distribution, test)

χ_e
electric susceptibility

χ_m
magnetic susceptibility

CHI
closed head injury
creatinine height index

CHILD
congenital hemidysplasia with ichthyosiform erythroderma and limb defects (syndrome)

CHIME
coloboma, heart anomaly, ichthyosis, mental retardation, and ear abnormality

CHINA
chronic infectious neuropathic agent
chronic infectious neurotropic agent

CHINS
child in need of service (petition)

CHIP
comprehensive health insurance plan
comprehensive hospital infections project
Coping Health Inventory for Parents

C

NOTES

Chir. Doct.
Doctor of Surgery [L. *Chirurgiae Doctor*]

Chix
chickenpox *also* CHPX, chpx, Cp

CHL
Chinese hamster lung
chlorambucil
chloramphenicol
conductive hearing loss
crown-heel length *also* CH

Chl, chl
chloroform *also* chlor

CHLA
cyclohexyllinoleic acid

Chlb
chlorobutanol

CHLD
chronic hypoxic lung disease

chlor
chloride *also* Cl
chloroform *also* Chl, chl

chloro
chloramphenicol *also* C, CMC, CP

ChlVPP
chlorambucil, vinblastine, procarbazine, prednisone

ChM
Master of Surgery [L. *Chirurgiae Magister*]

CHMD
clinical hyaline membrane disease

CHN
carbon, hydrogen, and nitrogen
central hemorrhagic necrosis
Certified Hemodialysis Nurse
child neurology
Chinese (hamster)
community health network
community health nurse

CHO
carbohydrate *also* C, CARB, carb, carbo, COH, HCO
Chinese hamster ovary
cholesterol *also* C, CH, Ch, CHOL, chol, chol.
chorea
cyclophosphamide, hydroxydaunorubicin, and Oncovin (vincristine)

C$_{H2O}$
water clearance

Cho
choline

choc
chocolate

CHOI
considered characteristic of osteogenesis imperfecta

CHOL, chol, chol.
cholesterol *also* C, CH, Ch, CHO

c̄hold
withhold

Chole
cholecystectomy

chol est
cholesterol esters

CHOP
cyclophosphamide, hydroxydaunomycin, Oncovin (vincristine), and prednisone

CHOP-BLEO
cyclophosphamide, hydroxydaunorubicin, Oncovin, prednisone, and bleomycin

CHOR
cyclophosphamide, hydroxydaunorubicin, Oncovin (vincristine), and radiation

CHP
capillary hydrostatic pressure
charcoal hemoperfusion
child psychiatry
comprehensive health planning
coordinating hospital physician
cutaneous hepatic porphyria

ChP
chest physician

CHPP
continuous hyperthermic peritoneal perfusion

CHPX, chpx
chickenpox *also* Chix, Cp

CHQ
chlorquinol (topical antiinfective)

CHR
cercarien-hullen reaction (test)
cerebrohepatorenal (syndrome)

chr
    chromosome
    chronic *also* chron

c-hr
    curie-hour *also* Ci-hr, ci-hr

c hr
    candle hour

ChrA
    chromogranin A

ChRBC
    chicken red blood cell *also* CRBC

ChrBrSyn
    chronic brain syndrome

CHRIS
    Cancer Hazards Ranking and
    Information System

chron
    chronic *also* chr
    chronological

CHRP
    coagulation and hemostatic resection
    of the prostate

CHRPE
    congenital hypertrophy of the retinal
    pigment epithelium

CHRS
    cerebrohepatorenal syndrome
    congenital hereditary retinoschisis

CHS
    central hypoventilation syndrome
    Chédiak-Higashi syndrome
    cholinesterase *also* CE, CEA, CHE,
    ChE
    chondroitin sulfate
    compression hip screw
    congenital hypoventilation syndrome
    contact hypersensitivity

CHSD
    Children's Health Services Division
    congenital hyperphosphatasemic
    skeletal dysplasia

CHSS
    cooperative health statistics system

CHT
    closed head trauma

    combined hormone therapy
    contralateral head turning

ChTg
    chymotrypsinogen

ChTK
    chicken thymidine kinase

CHU
    closed head unit

CHV
    canine herpesvirus

CI
    cardiac index
    cardiac insufficiency
    cell immunity
    cell inhibition
    cephalic index
    cerebral infarction
    cervical incompetence
    cesium implant
    chain initiating
    chemical ionization
    chemoimmunotherapy
    chemotactic index
    chemotherapeutic index
    chronically infected
    chronic inflammation
    clinical impression
    clinical investigation
    clinical investigator
    clomipramine
    clonus index
    closure index
    cochlear implant
    coefficient of intelligence
    colloidal iron
    colony inhibition
    color index
    Colour Index
    complete iridectomy
    confidence interval
    contamination index
    continuous infusion
    coronary insufficiency
    corrected count increment
    crystalline insulin
    cytotoxic index

Ci
    curie *also* C, c, CU, cu

NOTES

C

CIA
    canine inherited ataxia
    chemiluminescent immunoassay
    chronic idiopathic anhidrosis
    chymotrypsin inhibitor activity
    colony-inhibiting activity

CIAA
    competitive insulin autoantibodies

CIAED
    collagen-induced autoimmune ear
    disease

CIB, cib
    crying-induced bronchospasm
    cytomegalic inclusion bodies

cib.
    food [L. *cibus*]

CIBD
    chronic inflammatory bowel disease

CIBHA
    congenital inclusion-body hemolytic
    anemia

CIBP
    chronic intractable benign pain

CIBPS
    chronic intractable benign pain
    syndrome

CIC
    cardioinhibitor center
    Certified Infection Control
    chronic inactive cirrhosis
    circulating immune complex
    clean intermittent catheterization
    complex instability of carpus
    constant initial concentration
    coronary intensive care
    crisis intervention center

CICA
    cervical internal carotid artery

CICE
    combined intracapsular cataract
    extraction

CICU
    cardiac intensive care unit
    cardiovascular inpatient care unit
    coronary intensive care unit

CID
    Central Institute for the Deaf
    central integrative deficit
    cervical immobilization device
    chick infective dose

    chronic intestinal dysmotility
    combined immunodeficiency disease
    cytomegalic inclusion disease *also*
    CMID

CIDEP
    chemically-induced dynamic electron
    polarization

CIDP
    chronic idiopathic polyradiculopathy
    chronic inflammatory demyelinating
    polyneuropathy
    chronic inflammatory demyelinating
    polyradioneuropathy

CIDS
    cellular immunity deficiency syndrome
    cellular immunodeficiency syndrome
    continuous insulin delivery system

CIE
    chemotherapy induced emesis
    congenital ichthyosiform erythroderma
    countercurrent immunoelectrophoresis
    counterimmunoelectrophoresis *also*
    CIEP
    crossed immunoelectrophoresis *also*
    CIEP

CIEA
    continuous infusion epidural analgesia

CIE-C
    counter
    immunoelectrophoresis–colorimetric

CIE-D
    counter
    immunoelectrophoresis–densitometric

CIEP
    counterimmunoelectrophoresis *also*
    CIE
    crossed immunoelectrophoresis *also*
    CIE

CIF
    cartilage induction factor
    claims inquiry form
    clone-inhibiting factor
    cloning inhibitory factor

CIG, cigs
    cigarettes
    cold-insoluble globulin

CIg
    intracytoplasmic immunoglobulin

cIgM
    cytoplasmic immunoglobulin M

cigs (*var. of* CIG)

CIH
carbohydrate-induced hyperglyceridemia
Certificate in Industrial Health
children in hospital

CIHD
chronic ischemic heart disease

Ci-hr, ci-hr
curie-hour *also* c-hr

CIHS
chronic infantile hypotonic syndrome

CII
Carnegie Interest Inventory

CIIA
common internal iliac artery

CIIP
chronic idiopathic intestinal
pseudoobstruction

CIIPS
chronic idiopathic intestinal pseudo-
obstruction syndrome

CIIS
Cattell Infant Intelligence Scale

CIL
Center for Independent Living

CIM
cimetidine
cortical induction of movement
cortically induced movement
Cumulated Index Medicus

Ci/mL
curies per milliliter

CIMS
chemical ionization mass spectrometry
clinical information scale
Conflict in Marriage Scale

CIN
cerebriform intradermal nevus
cervical intraepithelial neoplasia
chemotherapy induced neutropenia
chronic interstitial nephritis
cinoxacin

CIN 1, CIN I
cervical intraepithelial neoplasia, grade 1

CIN 2, CIN II
cervical intraepithelial neoplasia, grade 2

CIN 3, CIN III
cervical intraepithelial neoplasia, grade 3

C_{IN}, C_{in}
inulin clearance

CINCA
chronic infantile neurological
cutaneous and auricular (syndrome)

CINE
chemotherapy-induced nausea and
emesis
cineangiogram

cine MRI
cine magnetic resonance imaging

CIOP
chromosomally incompetent ovarian
failure

CIP
Carcinogen Information Program
Cardiac Injury Panel
cellular immunocompetence profile
chronic idiopathic
polyradiculoneuropathy
chronic inflammatory polyneuropathy
also CIPN

CIPD
chronic inflammatory
polyradiculoneuropathy, demyelinating
chronic intermittent peritoneal dialysis

CIPF
clinical illness promotion factor

CIPN
chronic inflammatory polyneuropathy
also CIP

CIPSO
chronic intestinal pseudo-obstruction

cir
circuit

NOTES

cir *(continued)*
circular
circumference *also* Circ, circ

Circ, circ
circulation
circumcision *also* circum
circumference *also* cir

circ & sen
circulation and sensation

circum
circumcision *also* Circ, circ

CIRF
cocaine-induced respiratory failure

CIRR
cirrhosis

CIS
carcinoma in situ
catheter-induced spasm
central inhibitory state
Chemical Information Service
clinical information system

CI-S
calculus index, simplified

CiS
cingulate sulcus

CISCA
cisplatin, cyclophosphamide, and
Adriamycin (doxorubicin)

***cis*-DDP**
cis-diamminedichloroplatinum
(cisplatin)

CISP
chronic intractable shoulder pain

CIT
citrate *also* cit
cold ischemia time
combined intermittent therapy
conjugated-immunoglobulin technique
conventional immunosuppressive
therapy
conventional insulin therapy

cit
citrate *also* CIT

cit. disp.
dispense quickly [L. *cito dispensetur*]

CITP
capillary isotachophoresis

CIU
chronic idiopathic urticaria

CIV
Chilo iridescent virus
common iliac vein
continuous intravenous (infusion)

CIVII
continuous intravenous insulin
infusion

CIXU
constant infusion excretory urogram

CJ
conjunctivitis

CJD
Creutzfeldt-Jakob disease

CJR
centric jaw relationship

CJS
Creutzfeldt-Jakob syndrome

CK
calf kidney
chicken kidney
cholecystokinin
choline kinase
contralateral knee *also* ck
creatine kinase
cyanogen chloride

CK_1, CK_2, CK_3
isoenzymes of creatine kinase

ck
check (ed)
contralateral knee *also* CK

CK-BB
creatine kinase-BB band
creatine kinase-BB isoenzyme
isoenzyme of creatine kinase with
brain subunits

CKC
closed kinetic chain
cold-knife conization

CKG
cardiokymograph
cardiokymography

CK-ISO
creatine kinase isoenzyme

CK-MB
isoenzyme of creatine kinase with
muscle and brain subunits
myocardial muscle creatine kinase
isoenzyme

CK-MM
  isoenzyme of creatine kinase with muscle subunits

CK-PZ
  cholecystokinin-pancreozymin

CKS
  classic form of Kaposi sarcoma
  Continuum knee system (implant)

CKW
  clockwise

CL
  capacity of the lung
  capillary lumen
  cardinal ligament
  cardiolipin
  cell line
  center line
  centralis lateralis
  cervical line
  chemiluminescence
  chest and left arm (lead in electrocardiography)
  cholelithiasis
  cholesterol-lecithin
  chronic leukemia
  cirrhosis of liver
  clamp lamp
  clear liquid
  cleft lip
  clinical laboratory
  cloudy *also* cl, cldy
  complex loading
  compliance of the lung *also* C_L
  composite lymphoma
  confidence level
  contact lens
  continence line
  corpus luteum *also* cl
  cricoid lamina
  criterion level
  critical list
  current liabilities
  cutis laxa
  cycle length
  cytotoxic lymphocyte

CL286558
  zeniplatin

CL287110
  enloplatin

C-L
  consultation-liaison (psychiatry)

2C-L
  two-chamber longitudinal

C_L
  compliance of the lung *also* CL
  constant domain of L chain

Cl
  chloride *also* chlor
  chlorine
  clavicle
  clear
  clinic *also* cl
  clonus
  closure *also* cl
  colistin

cL
  centiliter *also* cl

cl
  centiliter *also* cL
  clavicle
  cleft
  clinic *also* Cl
  closure *also* Cl
  cloudy *also* CL, cldy
  corpus luteum *also* CL

CL1-CL5
  Papanicolaou class 1 through 5

CLA
  Certified Laboratory Assistant
  cervicolinguoaxial
  community living arrangements
  contralateral local anesthesia
  cyclic lysine anhydride

CLA(ASCP)
  Clinical Laboratory Assistant (American Society of Clinical Pathologists)

CLAH
  congenital lipoid adrenal hyperplasia

C lam
  cervical laminectomy

NOTES

CLAP
contact laser ablation of prostate

CLAS
Cholesterol Lowering Atherosclerosis Study
congenital localized absence of skin

class.
classification

CLAV, clav
clavicle

CLB
chlorambucil
curvilinear body

CLBBB
complete left bundle branch block

CLBP
chronic low back pain

CLC
Charcot-Leyden crystal
Clerc-Levy-Critesco (syndrome)
cork, leather, and celastic (orthotic)

CL/CP
cleft lip and cleft palate

CLD
central language disorder
chronic liver disease
chronic lung disease
congenital limb deficiency
crystal ligand field

cld
cleared
colored

CLDH
choline dehydrogenase

CLDM
clindamycin

cldy
cloudy *also* CL, cl

CLE
centrilobular emphysema
continuous lumbar epidural (anesthesia)

CLED
cystine-lactose electrolyte-deficient (agar)

cler
clear

CLF
cardiolipin fluorescence (antibody)
cholesterol-lecithin flocculation

CLH
chronic lobular hepatitis
corpus luteum hormone
cutaneous lymphoid hyperplasia

CLI
corpus luteum insufficiency

CLi
lithium clearance

CLIA
Clinical Laboratories Improvement Act

CLIF
cloning inhibitory factor
Crithidia luciliae immunofluorescence

Clin, clin
clinic

Clin Path
clinical pathology

Clin Proc
clinical procedure

CLINPROT
Clinical Cancer Protocols

ClinSeg
clinoidal segment

CLIP
cerebral lipidosis (without visceral involvement and with onset of disease past infancy)
corticotropin-like intermediate lobe peptide

CLL
cholesterol-lowering lipid
chronic lymphatic leukemia
chronic lymphocytic leukemia
cow lung lavage

CLLE
columnar-lined lower esophagus

cl liq
clear liquid

CLMA
Clinical Laboratory Management Association

CLML
Current List of Medical Literature

CLMN
complete lower motor neuron (lesion)

clmp
clumped

CLMV
cauliflower mosaic virus

CLN
computer liaison nurse

CLO
Campylobacter-like organism
cod liver oil

CLOF
clofibrate

C-loop
anatomical position (shape) of
duodenum

CLOtest
Campylobacter-like organism test
Clostridium difficile test

CLOT R
clot retraction

CLP
chymotrypsin-like protein
cleft lip with cleft palate *also* CL&P
cycle length, paced

CL&P
cleft lip and palate *also* CLP

ClP
clinical pathology

Clpal
cleft palate *also* CP

CLQ
cognitive laterality quotient

CLRO
community leave for reorientation

CLS
cisplatinum-Lipiodol-Spongel
Clinical Laboratory Scientist
Coffin-Lowry syndrome
Cornelia de Lange syndrome

CLSE
calf lung surfactant extract

CLSH
corpus luteum stimulating hormone

CLSL
chronic lymphosarcoma (cell)
leukemia

CLSM
confocal laser scan microscopy

CLSP
clinical laboratory specialist

CLT
Certified Laboratory Technician
chronic lymphocytic thyroiditis
clinical laboratory technician
clinical laboratory technologist
clot lysis time
clotting time

CLT(NCA)
Laboratory Technician Certified by
the National Certification Agency for
Medical

CLV
constant linear velocity

CL VOID
clean voided specimen (urine)

ClVPP
chlorambucil, vinblastine, procarbazine,
and prednisone

CLX
cloxacillin

CM
California mastitis (test)
calmodulin
capreomycin
carboxymethyl cellulose *also* CMC
cardiac monitor
cardiac muscle
cardiomyopathy *also* CMP
carpometacarpal
Caucasian male
cell membrane
center of mass
centrum medianum
cerebral malaria
cerebral mantle
cervical mucosa
cervical mucus
chemotactic migration
Chick-Martin (coefficient)
chloroquine-mepacrine

NOTES

C

CM *(continued)*
chondromalacia
chopped meat (medium)
chylomicron
circular muscle
circulating monocyte
clinical medicine
coccidioidal meningitis
cochlear microphonic
combined mechanical
common migraine
community meeting
competing message
complete medium
complications *also* cm
conditioned medium
congenital malformation
congestive myocardiopathy
continuous murmur
contrast medium
copulatory mechanism
costal margin
cow's milk
culture medium
cystic mesothelioma
cytometry
cytoplasmic membrane
Master in Surgery [L. *Chirurgiae Magister*]
narrow-diameter endosseous screw implant
tomorrow morning [L. *cras mane*] [Fr. *crête manche*] *also* c.m.

C/M
counts per minute *also* CPM, cpm

C&M
cocaine and morphine

C$_m$
maximal clearance *also* Cm

Cm
curium
maximal clearance *also* C$_m$

cM
centimorgan *also* cMO, cMo

c.m.
tomorrow morning [L. *cras mane*] [Fr. *crête manche*] *also* CM

cm
centime
centimeter *also* CENT, cent.
complications *also* CM
costal margin

cm^2
square centimeter

cm^3
cubic centimeter *also* CC, cc, c.c., cu cm

CMA
Candida metabolic antigen
Certified Medical Assistant
chronic metabolic acidosis
compound myopic astigmatism
cow's milk allergy
cultured macrophages

CMAF
centrifuged microaggregate filter

c. magnum.
tablespoonful [L. *cochleare magnum*]
tablespoon [L. *cochleare magnum*]

CMAmg
corticomedial amygdaloid (nucleus)

CMAP
compound motor action potential
compound muscle action potential

C$_{max}$
maximal drug concentration

CMB
carbolic methylene blue
Central Midwives' Board
chloromercuribenzoate

CMBBT
cervical mucous basal body temperature

CMC
carboxymethylcellulose *also* CM
care management continuity
carpometacarpal joint
cell-mediated cytolysis
cell-mediated cytotoxicity
chloramphenicol *also* C, chloro, CP Chloromycetin
chronic mucocutaneous candidiasis *also* CMCC
critical micellar concentration *also* cmc
cyclophosphamide, methotrexate, and CCNU (lomustine)

cmc
critical micellar concentration *also* CMC

CMCC
chronic mucocutaneous candidiasis *also* CMC

CM-cellulose
carboxymethyl cellulose

CMCP
camphorated mono-parachlorophenol

CMCt
care management continuity (across settings)

CMD
childhood muscular dystrophy
congenital muscular dystrophy
corticomedullary differentiation
count median diameter (of particles)
cystoid macular degeneration
cytomegalic disease

CME
cervical mediastinal exploration
cervical mucous extract
continuing medical education
crude marijuana extract
cystic macular edema
cystoid macular edema

CMED
cyclophosphamide, methotrexate, etoposide, and dexamethasone

CMER
current medical evidence of record

CMF
calcium-magnesium free
catabolite modular factor
chondromyxoid fibroma
cortical magnification factor
craniomandibulofacial
cyclophosphamide, methotrexate, and 5-fluorouracil

CMFE
calcium and magnesium free plus ethylenediaminetetraacetic acid

CMFH
cyclophosphamide, methotrexate, fluorouracil, and hydroxyurea

CMFP
cyclophosphamide, methotrexate, 5-fluorouracil, and prednisone

CMFPTH
cyclophosphamide, methotrexate, 5-fluorouracil, prednisone, tamoxifen, and Halotestin

CMF-TAM
cyclophosphamide, methotrexate, fluorouracil, and tamoxifen

CMFV
cyclophosphamide, methotrexate, fluorouracil, and vincristine

CMFVP
cyclophosphamide, methotrexate, fluorouracil, vincristine, and prednisone
cyclophosphamide, methotrexate, 5-fluorouracil, vincristine, prednisone

CMG
canine myasthenia gravis
chopped meat glucose (medium)
congenital myasthenia gravis
cyanmethemoglobin
cystometrogram
cystometrography

CMGN
chronic membranous glomerulonephritis

CMGS
chopped meat-glucose-starch (medium)

CMGT
chromosome-mediated gene transfer

CMH
congenital malformation of heart

CMHC
community mental health center

CMHN
Community Mental Health Nurse

cm H$_2$O
centimeters of water (cuff pressure)

CMI
carbohydrate metabolism index
care management integration
cell-mediated immunity
cell multiplication inhibition
chronically mentally ill
chronic mesenteric ischemia

NOTES

C

CMI *(continued)*
circulating microemboli index
computer-managed instruction
Cornell Medical Index

CMID
cytomegalic inclusion disease *also*
CID

c/min
cycles per minute *also* cpm

CMIR
cell-mediated immune response

CMIT
Current Medical Information and
Terminology

CMJ
carpometacarpal joint

CMK
chloromethyl ketone
congenital multicystic kidney

CML
cell-mediated lymphocytotoxicity
cell-mediated lympholysis
cell-mediated lysis
chronic myelocytic leukemia
chronic myelogenous leukemia
chronic myeloid leukemia
count median length
cross midline

CMM
cell-mediated mutagenesis
cutaneous malignant melanoma

cmm
cubic millimeter *also* cu mm, mm^3

cm/m²
centimeters per square meter

CMME
chloromethyl methyl ether (carcinogen
at technical grade)

CMML
chronic myelomacrocytic leukemia
chronic myelomonocytic leukemia
also CMMoL

CMMoL
chronic myelomonocytic leukemia
also CMML

CMMS
Columbia Mental Maturity Scale

CMMT
Columbia Mental Maturity Test

CMN
caudal mediastinal node
cystic medial necrosis

CMN-AA
cystic medial necrosis of ascending
aorta

CMO
calculated mean organism
cardiac minute output
card made out
Chief Medical Officer
comfort measures only
corticosterone methyl oxidase

cMO, cMo
centimorgan *also* cM, cMo

CMoL
chronic monoblastic leukemia
chronic monocytic leukemia

CMOMC
cell meeting our morphologic criteria

C-MOPP
cyclophosphamide, mechlorethamine,
Oncovin (vincristine), procarbazine,
and prednisone

CMOR
craniomandibular orthopedic
repositioning device

CMOS
complementary metal-oxide
semiconductor (logic)

CMP
cardiomyopathy *also* CM
cervical mucus penetration
chondromalacia patellae
competitive medical plans
comprehensive medical plan
cow's milk protein
cytidine monophosphate

CMP-FX
complement fixation

CMPGN
chronic membranoproliferative
glomerulonephritis

CMP-NANA
cystidine monophospho-N-
acetylneuraminic acid

cmps
centimeters per second *also* cm/s

CMPT
cervical mucus penetration test

CMR
cerebral metabolic rate
chief medical resident
common mode rejection
crude mortality ratio

CMRG
cerebral metabolic rate of glucose

CMRL
cerebral metabolic rate of lactate

CMRNG
chromosomally mediated resistant *Neisseria gonorrhoeae*

CMRO, CMRO₂
cerebral metabolic rate of oxygen

CMRR
common mode rejection ratio (of amplifiers)

CMS
to be taken tomorrow morning [L. *cras mane sumendus*] *also* c.m.s.
cardiomediastinal silhouette
central material section
central material supply
cervical mucous solution
Christian Medical Society
chromosome modification site
chronic myelodysplastic syndrome
circulation motion sensation
circulation, muscle sensation
clean, midstream (urine)
click-murmur syndrome
clofibrate-induced muscular syndrome
Clyde Mood Scale
council of medical staffs

c.m.s.
to be taken tomorrow morning [L. *cras mane sumendus*] *also* CMS

cm/s
centimeters per second *also* cmps

CMSS
circulation, motor (ability), sensation, and swelling

CMSUA
clean, midstream urinalysis

CMT
California mastitis test

cancer multistep therapy
catechol methyltransferase
Certified Medical Transcriptionist
cervical motion tenderness
Charcot-Marie-Tooth (disease/syndrome)
chronic motor tic
circus movement tachycardia
continuous memory test
Current Medical Terminology

CMT1A
Charcot-Marie-Tooth disease type 1A

CMTC
cutis marmorata telangiectatica congenita

CMTD
Charcot-Marie-Tooth disease

CMTS
Charcot-Marie-Tooth syndrome

CMU
cardiac monitoring unit
chlorophenyldimethylurea
complex motor unit

CMUA
continuous motor unit activity

CMV
cisplatin, methotrexate and Velban
cisplatin, methotrexate, and vinblastine
continuous mechanical ventilation
controlled mechanical ventilation
conventional mechanical ventilation
cool mist vaporizer
cucumber mosaic virus
cytomegalic (inclusion) virus
cytomegalovirus (infection)

CMVIG
cytomegalovirus immunoglobulin

CMV-MN
cytomegaloviral mononucleosis

CMVS
culture midvoid specimen

CN
caudate nucleus
cellulose nitrate
charge nurse
child nutrition

NOTES

CN *(continued)*
clinical nursing
cochlear nucleus
congenital nephrosis
congenital nystagmus
cranial nerve
Crigler-Najjar (syndrome)
cyanogen
cyanosis neonatorum
tomorrow night [L. *cras nocte*] *also*
c.n.

C/N
carbon to nitrogen (ratio)
carrier to noise (ratio)
contrast to noise (ratio)

Cn
color naming
cyanide

c.n.
tomorrow night [L. *cras nocte*] *also*
CN

CNA
calcium nutrient agar
chart not available

CNAF
chronic nonvalvular atrial fibrillation

CNAG
chronic narrow angle glaucoma

CNAP
cochlear nucleus action potential
continuous negative airway pressure

CNB
cutting needle biopsy

CNBr
cyanogen bromide (poisonous vapor)

CNC
clear, no creamy (layer)

CNCbl
cyanocobalamin

CND
canned
cannot determine

CNDC
chronic nonspecific diarrhea of
childhood
chronic nonsuppurative destructive
cholangitis

CNDI
congenital nephrogenic diabetes
insipidus

CNE
chronic nervous exhaustion
concentric needle electrode
could not establish

CNEMG
concentric needle electromyography

CNES
chronic nervous exhaustion syndrome

CNF
chronic nodular fibrositis
congenital nephrotic (syndrome),
Finnish
cyclophosphamide, Novantrone
(mitoxantrone), and fluorouracil

CNH
central neurogenic hyperpnea
central neurogenic hyperventilation
community nursing home
contract nursing home

CNHC
chronodermatitis nodularis helicis
chronicus

CNHD
congenital nonspherocytic hemolytic
disease

CNK
cortical necrosis of kidneys

CNL
cardiolipin natural lecithin
chronic neutrophilic leukemia

CNM
Certified Nurse-Midwife
computerized nuclear morphometry

CNMT
Certified Nuclear Medicine
Technologist

CNN
congenital nevocytic nevus

CNNA
culture-negative neutrocytic ascites

CNOR
Certified Nurse, Operating Room

CNP
community nurse practitioner
continuous negative pressure
cranial nerve palsy
C-type natriuretic peptide
cyclic nucleotide phosphodiesterase

CNPase
cyclic nucleotide phosphohydrolase

CNPS
cardiac nuclear probe scan

CNPV
continuous negative-pressure
ventilation

CNRN
Certified Neuroscience Registered
Nurse

CNRS
citrated normal rabbit serum

CNRT
corrected sinus nodal recovery time

CNS
central nervous system
Chief, Nursing Services
clinical nurse specialist
coagulase-negative staphylococcus
computerized notation system
congenital nephrotic syndrome
Congress of Neurological Surgeons
cyanide sulfonate (sulfocyanate)

c.n.s.
to be taken tomorrow night [L. *cras
nocte sumendus*]

CNSD
chronic nonspecific diarrhea

CNSHA
congenital nonspherocytic hemolytic
anemia

CNS-L
central nervous system leukemia

CNSLD
chronic nonspecific lung disease

CNSN
Certified Nutrition Support Nurse

CNT
could not test
current night terrors

CNU
chloroethylnitrosourea

CNV
choroidal neovascularization

colistimethate, nystatin, and
vancomycin
contingent negative variation
cutaneous necrotizing vasculitis

CO
candidal onychomycosis
carbon monoxide
cardiac output *also* Q, QT
castor oil
casualty officer
centric occlusion
Certified Orthotist
cervical orthosis
choline oxidase
coenzyme *also* Co
community organization
compound *also* C, comp, compd,
CP, cpd
control
corneal opacity
crossover

Co
cobalt
coenzyme *also* CO

Co I
coenzyme I

Co II
coenzyme II

co
cutoff

C/O, c/o
in care of
check out
complains of
complaints
under care of

CO$_2$
carbon dioxide

C$_v$O$_2$
mixed venous oxygen content

57Co, Co 57
cobalt isotope

60Co, Co 60
cobalt isotope

^{57}Co
cobalt-57

NOTES

58Co
cobalt-58

60Co
cobalt-60

c/o (*var. of* C/O)

COA
calculated opening area
cervicooculoacusticus (syndrome)
condition on admission

CoA
coarctation of the aorta *also* CA, C
of A
coenzyme A

COAD
chronic obstructive airway disease
chronic obstructive arterial disease

COAG, coag
chronic open angle glaucoma
coagulated
coagulation

COAG PD
coagulation profile–diagnosis

COAG PP
coagulation profile–presurgery

COAGSC
coagulation screen

COAP
cyclophosphamide, Oncovin
(vincristine), arabinosylcytosine, and
prednisone

coarc
coarctation (of aorta)

CoASH
uncombined coenzyme A

CoA-SPC
coenzyme A-synthesizing protein
complex

COAT
Children's Orientation and Amnesia
Test

COB
chronic obstructive bronchitis
cisplatin, Oncovin (vincristine), and
bleomycin
coordination of benefits

coban
cohesive bandage

COBE
chronic obstructive bullous
emphysema

COBOL
common business-oriented language

COBRA
Consolidated Omnibus Budget
Reconciliation Act

COBS
cesarean (section)-obtained barrier-
sustained (animals)
chronic organic brain syndrome

COBT
chronic obstruction of biliary tract

COC
calcifying odotogenic cyst
cathodal-opening clonus *also* CaOCl,
COCL, COCl
cathodal-opening contraction *also*
CaOC
coccygeal *also* Coc, coc
combination oral contraceptive

Coc, coc
coccygeal *also* COC

Cocci
coccidioidomycosis

coch., cochl.
spoonful [L. *cochleare*]

cochl. amp.
heaping spoonful [L. *cochleare
amplum*]

cochl. mag.
dessert spoonful [L. *cochleare
magnum*]

cochl. parv.
teaspoonful [L. *cochleare parvum*]
also c. parvum

COCI
Consortium on Chemical Information

CO/CI
cardiac output/cardiac index

COCL, COCl
cathodal-opening clonus *also* COC

COCM
congestive cardiomyopathy

Co-Cr-Mo
cobalt-chromium-molybdenum

Co-Cr-W-Ni
cobalt-chromium-tungsten-nickel

coct.
boiling [L. *coctio*]

COD
cause of death
chemical oxygen demand
codeine *also* cod.
condition on discharge

cod.
codeine *also* COD

CODATA
Committee on Data for Science and
Technology

COD-MD
cerebroocular dysplasia-muscular
dystrophy

COE
court-ordered examination

coeff
coefficient

COEPS
cortical originating extrapyramidal
system

COF
cementoossifying fibroma
cutoff frequency

CoF
cobra (venom) factor
cofactor

COFS
cerebrooculofacial-skeletal (syndrome)

COG
center of gravity
Central Oncology Group
clinical obstetrics and gynecology
cognitive (function tests)

COGN
cognition

COGTT
cortisone-primed oral glucose
tolerance test

COH
carbohydrate *also* C, CARB, carb,
carbo, CHO, HCO

COHB, CoHb
carboxyhemoglobin *also* HbCO

COHSE
Confederation of Health Service
Employees

COI
Central Obesity Index
combination of isotonics

COIF
congenital onychodysplasia of the
index finger

COL, col
colicin
colony
color
colored
column
cost of living

col.
strain [L. *cola*]

COLAT., colat.
strained [L. *colatus*]

COLD
chronic obstructive lung disease

COLD A, cold agg
cold agglutinin (titer)

colet.
let it be strained [L. *coletur*]

COLL, coll
collect
collection
collective
colloidal

coll.
eyewash [L. *collyrium*] *also*
COLLYR, collyr.

collat
collateral

collun
nose wash [L. *collunarium*]

COLLUT, collut.
mouthwash [L. *collutorium*]

coll vol
collective volume

NOTES

C

COLLYR, collyr.
eyewash [L. *collyrium*] *also* coll.

col/mL
colonies per milliliter

color
colorimetry, including
spectrophotometry and photometry
let it be colored [L. *coloretur*]

colp, colpo
colporrhaphy
colposcopy

COM
chronic otitis media
computer output on microfilm
cyclophosphamide, Oncovin
(vincristine), and methotrexate
cyclophosphamide, Oncovin
(vincristine), and methyl-CCNU
(semustine)

com
commitment

COMA
Certified Ophthalmic Medical
Assistant
cyclophosphamide, Oncovin
(vincristine), methotrexate, and
arabinosylcytosine

COMB
cyclophosphamide, Oncovin
(vincristine), methyl-CCNU
(semustine), and bleomycin

comb.
combination
combine

COMF, comf
comfortable

com fix
complement fixation *also* CF

COMLA
cyclophosphamide, Oncovin
(vincristine), methotrexate, leucovorin,
and arabinosylcytosine

comm
commission
commissioner
committee
communicable *also* commun

commun
communicable *also* comm

commun dis
communicable disease

COMP
complication
cyclophosphamide, Oncovin
(vincristine), methotrexate, and
prednisone

comp
comparable
comparative
compare *also* CF, cf., cp.
compensated
compensation
complaint
composition *also* compn
compound *also* C, CO, compd, CP,
cpd
compounded *also* compd
compress
compression
computer

compd
compound *also* C, CO, comp, CP,
cpd
compounded *also* comp

compet
competition

compl
completed *also* cpl
completion *also* cpl
complicated *also* complic
complication *also* complic

complic
complicated *also* compl
complication *also* compl

compn
composition *also* comp

COMS
chronic organic mental syndrome

COMT
catechol methyltransferase

COMTRAC
computer-based (case) tracing

CON
certificate of need

Con
concanavalin

con.
against [L. *contra*] *also* cont.

Con A, conA, con A
concanavalin A

Con A-HRP
concanavalin A-horseradish peroxidase

conc, concentr
concentrated
concentration *also* C, c

concis.
cut [L. *concisus*]

cond
condensation
condensed
condition
conditional
conditioned
conductivity *also* σ

cond ref
conditioned reflex *also* CR

cond resp
conditioned response *also* CR

conf.
confection [L. *confectio*]
conference

cong.
congenital *also* congen
gallon [L. *congius*]

congen
congenital *also* cong.

congr
congruent

coniz
conization (of cervix)

conj
conjunctiva
conjunctival

conjug
conjugated
conjugation

CONPADRI I
cyclophosphamide, Oncovin
(vincristine), L-phenylalanine mustard,
and Adriamycin (doxorubicin)

CONPADRI II
CONPADRI I plus high dose
methotrexate

CONPADRI III
CONPADRI II plus intensified
doxorubicin

CONS
consultation *also* cons

cons
conservation
conservative
conserve
consultant
consultation *also* CONS

cons.
keep [L. *conserva*]

CONSENSUS
Cooperative North Scandinavian
Enalapril Survival Study

consperg
dust, sprinkle [L. *consperge*]

const
constant

constit
constituent

cont
containing
contains
contents
continuation
continue
contusions

cont.
against [L. *contra*] *also* con.
bruised [L. *contusus*] *also* C, contus.

contag
contagion
contagious

conter.
rub together [L. *contere*]

contin.
let it be continued [L. *continuetur*]
also pt.

NOTES

contr
contraction *also* C, contrx, CTX, CTXN, Cx

contra
contraindicated

contralat
contralateral

cont, rem.
let the medicine be continued [L. *continuetur remedium*]

contrib
contributory

contrit.
broken down [L. *contritus*]

contrx
contraction *also* C, contr, CTX, CTXN, Cx

contus.
bruised [L. *contusus*] *also* C, cont.

conv
convalescence
convalescent
convalescing
conventional (rat)
convergence
convergent

CONV HOSP
convalescent hospital

conv strab
convergent strabismus

COOD
chronic obstructive outflow disease

coord
coordinated
coordination

COP
capillary osmotic pressure
change of plaster
cicatricial ocular pemphigoid
circumoval precipitin
coefficient of performance
colloid oncotic pressure
colloid osmotic pressure
cyclophosphamide, Oncovin (vincristine), and prednisone

COPA
cyclophosphamide, Oncovin (vincristine), prednisone, and Adriamycin (doxorubicin)

COP-BLAM
cyclophosphamide, Oncovin (vincristine), prednisone, bleomycin, Adriamycin (doxorubicin), and Matulane (procarbazine)

COP-BLEO
cyclophosphamide, Oncovin, prednisone, and bleomycin

COPC
community-oriented primary care

COPD
chronic obstructive pulmonary disease

COPE
chronic obstructive pulmonary emphysema

COPI
California Occupational Preference Inventory

COP$_i$
colloid osmotic pressure in interstitial fluid

COPP
cyclophosphamide, Oncovin (vincristine), procarbazine, and prednisone

COP$_p$
colloid osmotic pressure in plasma

COPRO
coproporphyria
coproporphyrin

COPS
calcinosis cutis, osteoma cutis, poikiloderma, and skeletal abnormalities

CoQ
coenzyme Q (ubiquinone) *also* Q

coq.
boil [L. *coque*]

coq. in s. a.
boil in sufficient water [L. *coque in sufficiente aqua*]

coq. s. a.
boil properly [L. *coque secundum artem*]

coq. simul.
boil together [L. *coque simul*]

COR
body [L. *corpus*]
cardiac output recorder

comprehensive outpatient rehabilitation
(facility)
conditioned orientation reflex
(audiometry)
coroner
corrosion
corrosive
cortisone

Cor
Congo red *also* CR

cor
coronary
corrected *also* corr
correction

CORA
conditioned orientation reflex
audiometry

CORD
chronic obstructive respiratory disease
Commissioned Officer Residency
Deferment

corr
corrected *also* cor
correspondence

CORT
Certified Operating Room Technician

cort
cortex *also* C
cortical

CORTIS
cortisol

COS
cheirooral syndrome
Chief of Staff
clinically observed seizure

cos
change of shift

COSMIS
Computer System for Medical
Information Systems

COSTAR
Computer-stored Ambulatory Record

COSTEP
Commissioned Officer Student
Training and Extern Program

COT
colony overlay test
content of thought
continuous oxygen therapy
contralateral optic tectum
critical off-time

CO_2T
total carbon dioxide content

COTA
Certified Occupational Therapy
Assistant

COTD
cardiac output by thermodilution

COTe
cathodal-opening tetanus

COTH
Council of Teaching Hospitals

COTRANS
Coordinated Transfer Application
System

COTX
cast off, to x-ray *also* CRTX

COU
cardiac observation unit

coul
coulomb

COV
crossover value

COVESDEM
costovertebral segmentation defect
with mesomelia (syndrome)

CoVF
cobra venom factor

COWAT
Controlled Oral Word Association
Test

COWS
cold-opposite, warm-same
cold to opposite and warm to same
side (Hallpike caloric stimulation
response)

COX
cast-off x-ray

NOTES

C

COX *(continued)*
    coxsackie virus *also* CV
    cyclooxygenase

COX-1
    cyclooxygenase-1

COX-2
    cyclooxygenase-2

CP
    candle-power *also* cp
    capillary pressure
    carbamoyl phosphate
    cardiac pacing
    cardiac performance
    cardiac pool
    cardiopulmonary *also* C/P
    cardiopulmonary performance
    Carr-Purcell (sequence)
    cell passaged
    central pit
    centric position
    cerebellopontine
    cerebral palsy
    certified prosthetist
    ceruloplasmin
    cervical probe
    chemically pure *also* cp
    chest pain
    child psychiatry
    child psychology
    chloramphenicol *also* C, chloro, CMC
    chloropurine
    chloroquine-primaquine
    chondrodysplasia punctata
    chondromalacia patellae
    chronic pain
    chronic pancreatitis
    chronic polyarthritis
    chronic pyelonephritis
    cicatricial pemphoid
    circular polarization
    cisplatin
    cleft palate *also* Clpal
    clinical pathology
    closing pressure
    clottable protein
    cochlear potential
    code of practice
    cold pressor
    color perception
    combination product
    combining power
    complete physical
    compound *also* C, CO, comp, compd
    compressed

    congenital porphyria
    constant pressure
    coproporphyria
    coproporphyrin
    coracoid process
    cor pulmonale
    cortical plate
    costal plaque
    C peptide
    creatine phosphate
    creatine phosphokinase
    cross-linked protein
    crude protein
    current practice
    cyclophosphamide *also* CPA, CPM, CTX, CY, Cy, CYC, CYCLO, CYT
    cyclophosphamide and Platinol
    cyclophosphamide and prednisone
    cystosarcoma phyllodes
    cytosol protein

C/P
    cardiopulmonary *also* CP
    cholesterol-phospholipid (ratio)

C&P
    compensation and pension
    complete and pain-free (range of motion)
    cystoscopy and pyelography

C_p
    constant pressure
    phosphate clearance *also* Cp

Cp
    ceruloplasmin
    chickenpox *also* Chix, CHPX, chpx
    peak concentration
    phosphate clearance *also* C_p

cP
    centipoise *also* cp

cp
    candle-power *also* CP
    centipoise *also* cP
    chemically pure *also* CP

cp.
    compare [L. *confer*] *also* CF, cf., comp

CPA
    carboxypeptidase A
    cardiophrenic angle
    cardiopulmonary arrest
    carotid phonoangiography
    carotid photoangiography
    cerebellopontine angle

chlorophenylalanine
chronic pyrophosphate arthropathy
circulating platelet aggregate
costophrenic angle
cyclophosphamide *also* CP, CPM,
CTX, CY, Cy, CYC, CYCLO, CYT
cyproterone acetate

C3PA
complement 3 proactivator
(convertase)

C-PAC
Clinical Probes of Articulation
Consistency

CPAF
chlorpropamide-alcohol flushing

Cpah
p-aminohippuric acid clearance

CPAI
central principal axis of inertia

CPAN
Certified Post-Anesthesia Nurse

CPA/OPG
carotid
phonoangiography/oculoplethys-
mography

CPAP
continuous positive airway pressure

c. parvum
teaspoonful [L. *cochleare parvum*]
also cochl. parv.

CPB
cardiopulmonary bypass
competitive protein binding
cyclophosphamide, Platinol, and
BCNU

CPBA
competitive protein-binding analysis
competitive protein-binding assay

CPBS
cardiopulmonary bypass surgery

CPBV
cardiopulmonary blood volume

CPC
central posterior curve

cerebellar Purkinje cell
cerebral palsy clinic
cetylpyridinium chloride
chronic passive congestion
circumferential pneumatic compression
clinicopathologic conference
committed progenitor cell

CPCL
congenital pulmonary cystic
lymphangiectasia

CPCN
capitated primary care network

CPCP
chronic progressive coccidioidal
pneumonitis

CPCR
cardiopulmonary-cerebral resuscitation

CPCS
circumferential pneumatic compression
suit
clinical pharmacokinetics consulting
service

CPD
calcium pyrophosphate deposition
calcium pyrophosphate dihydrate
cephalopelvic disproportion
childhood polycystic disease
chorioretinopathy and pituitary
dysfunction
chronic peritoneal dialysis
citrate-phosphate-dextrose
congenital penile deviation
congenital polycystic disease
contact potential difference
contagious pustular dermatitis
critical point drying
cyclopentadiene

cpd
compound *also* C, CO, comp,
compd, CP
cycles per degree

CPDA, CPD-A
citrate-phosphate-dextrose-adenine

CPDD
calcium pyrophosphate deposition
disease

NOTES

145

CPDD *(continued)*
calcium pyrophosphate dihydrate deposition disease *also* CPPD
cis-platinum diamminedichloride

CPDL
cumulative population doubling level

CPE
cardiac pulmonary edema
cardiogenic pulmonary edema
chronic pulmonary emphysema
compensation, pension, and education
complete physical examination *also* CPX
complex partial epilepsy
corona-penetrating enzyme
cytopathic effect
cytopathogenic effect

Cped
Certified Pedorthist

CPEHS
Consumer Protection and Environmental Health Service

CPEO
chronic progressive external ophthalmoplegia

CPET
cardiopulmonary exercise test *also* CPX test

CPF
clot-promoting factor
contraction peak force

CP&FD
cephalopelvic disproportion and fetal distress

CPG
capillary blood gases
cardiopneumographic (recording)
carotid phonoangiogram

CPGN
chronic progressive glomerulonephritis
chronic proliferative glomerulonephritis

CPH
Certificate in Public Health
chronic paroxysmal hemicrania
chronic persistent hepatitis
chronic primary headache

CPHA
Commission on Professional and Hospital Activities

CPI
California Personality Inventory
Cancer Potential Index
Cardiac Pacemaker, Inc.
chronic pneumonitis of infancy
congenital palatopharyngeal incompetence
constitutional psychopathic inferiority
coronary prognostic index
cysteine proteinase inhibitor

CPIB
chlorophenoxyisobutyrate

CPID
chronic pelvic inflammatory disease

CPIP
chronic pulmonary insufficiency of prematurity
common peak developed isovolumetric pressure

CPK
creatine phosphokinase

CPKD
childhood polycystic kidney disease

CPKI, CPKISO
creatinine phosphokinase isoenzyme(s)

CPK-MB
myocardial band enzymes of CPK

CPL
caprine placental lactogen
conditioned pitch level
congenital pulmonary lymphangiectasia

C/PL
cholesterol to phospholipid ratio

cpl
complete *also* C
completed *also* compl

CPLM
cysteine-peptone-liver (infusion) medium

CPM
CCNU, procarbazine, methotrexate
central pontine myelinolysis
central pontine myelinosis
chloroethyl cyclohexylnitrosourea (lomustine), procarbazine, and methotrexate
chlorpheniramine maleate
Clinical Practice Model
cognitive-perceptual-motor
Colored Progressive Matrices
continue present management

continuous passive motion (device)
counts per minute *also* C/M, cpm
cyclophosphamide *also* CP, CPA,
CTX, CY, Cy, CYC, CYCLO, CYT

cpm
counts per minute *also* C/M, CPM
cycles per minute *also* c/min

CPmax
peak (maximum) serum concentration

CPMDI
computerized pharmacokinetic model-
driven (drug) infusion

CPMG
Carr-Purcell-Meiboom-Gill (sequence,
spin-echo technique)

CPMI
central principal moments of inertia

CP min
trough (minimum) serum
concentration

CPMM
constant passive-motion machine

CPMP
computer-patient management
problems

CPMS
chronic progressive multiple sclerosis

CPMV
cowpox mosaic virus

CPN
carboxypeptidase N
chronic polyneuropathy
chronic pyelonephritis
cisplatin nephropathy

CPNM
corrected perinatal mortality

CPNP/A
Certified Pediatric Nurse
Practitioner/Associate

CPO
Certified Prosthetist and Orthotist

CPP
cancer proneness phenotype
canine pancreatic polypeptide

cerebral perfusion pressure
chronic pelvic pain
chronic pigmental purpura
cryoprecipitate

CPPB
continuous positive-pressure breathing

CPPD
calcium pyrophosphate deposition
(disease) *also* CPPDD
calcium pyrophosphate dihydrate
calcium pyrophosphate dihydrate
deposition (disease) *also* CPDD
chest percussion and postural
drainage *also* CP&PD

CP&PD
chest percussion and postural
drainage *also* CPPD

CPPDD
calcium pyrophosphate deposition
disease *also* CPPD

CPPT
Coronary Primary Prevention Trial

CPPTS
complete pacemaker patient testing
system

CPPV
continuous positive-pressure ventilation

CPR
cardiac and pulmonary rehabilitation
cardiac pulmonary reserve
cardiopulmonary resuscitation
centripetal rub
chlorophenyl red
clinical partial response
cochleopalpebral reflex
computerized patient record
cortisol production rate
cumulative potency rate
customary, prevailing, and reasonable

CPRAM
controlled partial rebreathing
anesthesia method

CPRS
Children's Psychiatric Rating Scale
Comprehensive Psychiatric Rating
Scale

C

NOTES

CPRS *(continued)*
Comprehensive Psychopathological Rating Scale

CPS
carbamyl phosphate synthetase
cardioplegic perfusion solution
cardiopulmonary support
central patient station
characters per second
Child Personality Scale
Child Protective Services
chloroquine, pyrimethamine, and sulfisoxazole
clinical performance score
clinical pharmacokinetic service
coagulase-positive staphylococci
complex partial seizure
constitutional psychopathic state
contagious pustular stomatitis
C-polysaccharide
cumulative probability of success
current population survey
cycles per second *also* cps, C/S, c/s, c/sec

cps
counts per second
cycles per second *also* CPS, C/S, c/s, c/sec

CPSC
congenital paucity of secondary synaptic clefts (syndrome)
Consumer Product Safety Commission

CPT
carnitine palmityltransferase
carotid pulse tracing
chest physiotherapy
child protection team
choline phosphotransferase
chromopertubation
ciliary particle transport
clinical pharmacokinetics team
cold pressor test
cold pressure test
combining power test
concentration performance test
continuous performance task
continuous performance test
continuous primary test
current perception threshold
Current Procedural Terminology

CPTH
chronic posttraumatic headache
C-terminal parathyroid hormone

CPTN
culture-positive toxin-negative

CPTP
culture-positive toxin-positive

CPTR
cyproterone

CPTX
chronic parathyroidectomy

CPU
caudate putamen
central processing unit

CPUE
chest pain of unknown etiology

CPV
canine parvovirus
cyclophosphamide, Platinol (cisplatin), and VP-16
cytoplasmic polyhidrosis virus

CPVD
congenital polyvalvular disease

CPX
complete physical examination *also* CPE

CPX test
cardiopulmonary exercise test *also* CPET

CPZ
cefoperazone
chlorpromazine
Compazine (prochlorperazine dimaleate)

CQ
chloroquine
chloroquine-quinine
circadian quotient
conceptual quotient

CQA
concurrent quality assurance

CQM
chloroquine mustard

CR
calcification rate
calculus removal
calculus removed
calorie restricted
cardiac rehabilitation
cardiac resuscitation
cardiac rhythm
cardiorespiratory
cardiorrhexis

caries resistant
cartilage residue
case report
cathode ray
central ray
centric relation
chest and right arm (lead in electrocardiography)
chest roentgenogram
chest roentgenography
chief resident
child-resistant (bottle top)
choice reaction
chromium *also* Cr
chronic rejection
clinical record
clinical research
closed reduction
clot retraction
coefficient (of fat) retention
colon resection
colony-reared (animal)
colorectal
complement receptor
complete remission
complete responders
complete response
conditioned reflex *also* cond ref
conditioned response *also* cond ref, cond resp
congenital rubella
Congo red *also* Cor
contact record
continuous reinforcement
controlled release
controlled respiration
controlled response
conversion rate
cooling rate
correct response
corticoresistant
creamed
creatinine *also* Cr, Cre, creat
cremaster ratio
cresyl red
critical ratio
crown
crown-rump (length) *also* CRL

CR0–10
0 to 10 category ratio

CR(1–4)
complement receptor (1–4)

C/R
chorioretinal

C&R
cardiac and respiratory
convalescence and rehabilitation
cystocopy and retrograde

Cr
chromium *also* CR
cranial *also* CR, cran
cranium *also* cran
creatinine *also* CR, Cre, creat
crown

^{51}Cr, Cr 51
chromium isotope

cr.
tomorrow [L. *cras*]

CRA
central retinal artery
Chinese restaurant asthma
chronic rheumatoid arthritis
colorectal adenocarcinoma
colorectal anastomosis
coronary rotational atherectomy

13-CRA
13-*cis*-retinoic acid

CRABP
cellular retinoic acid-binding protein

CRAC
Contract Relax Agonist Contract

CRAG
cerebral radionuclide angiography

CRAMS
circulation, respiration, abdomen, motor, and speech

cran
cranial *also* CR, Cr
cranium *also* Cr

CRAO
central retinal artery occlusion

crast.
for tomorrow [L. *crastinus*]

NOTES

CRB
chemical, radiological, and biological

CRBBB
complete right bundle branch block

CRBC
chicken red blood cell *also* ChRBC

CRBP
cellular retinol-binding protein

Cr&Br
crown and bridge

CRC
cardiovascular reflex conditioning
child-resistant container
clinical research center
colorectal cancer
colorectal carcinoma
concentrated red (blood) cell
Crisis Resolution Center
cross-reacting cannabinoids

CR&C
closed reduction and cast

CrCl, Crcl
creatinine clearance *also* CC, C$_{cr}$

CRCS
cardiovascular reflex conditioning
system

CRD
childhood rheumatic disease
child-restraint device
chorioretinal degeneration
chronic renal disease
chronic respiratory disease
completely randomized design
complete reaction of degeneration
cone-rod dystrophy
congenital rubella deafness
crown-rump distance (fetal
measurement)

CR-DIP
chronic relapsing demyelinating
inflammatory polyneuropathy

CRDS
curdlan sulfate

CRE
cumulative radiation effect

Cre, creat
creatinine *also* CR, Cr

CREA-S
creatinine urine spot (test)

^{51}Cr-EDTA
51-chromium-labeled
ethylenediaminetetraacetate

CRENA
crenated (red blood cells)

CREOG
Council on Resident Education in
Obstetrics and Gynecology

crep.
crepitation [L. *crepitus*]

CREST
calcinosis cutis, Raynaud
phenomenon, esophageal motility
disorder, sclerodactyly, and
telangiectasia (syndrome)

CRF
case report form
chronic renal failure
chronic respiratory failure
citrovorum rescue factor
coagulase-reacting factor
continuous reinforcement
corticotropin-releasing factor

CRFK
Crandell feline kidney (cells)

CRG, CR-gram
cardiorespirogram

CRH
corticotropin-releasing hormone

CRHL
Collaborative Radiological Health
Laboratory

CRHV
cottontail rabbit herpesvirus

CRI
Cardiac Risk Index
catheter-related infection
chronic renal insufficiency
chronic respiratory insufficiency
Composite Risk Index
concentrated rust inhibitor
congenital rubella infection
cross-reactive idiotype

CRIE
crossed radioimmunoelectrophoresis

CRIS
controlled release infusion syndrome

Crit, crit
critical

hematocrit *also* H'crit, HCT, Hct,
hemat, HMT

CRL
cell repository line
Certified Record Librarian
complement receptor location
complement receptor lymphocyte
crown-rump length *also* CR

CRM
certified raw milk
Certified Reference Materials
contralateral remote masking
cross-reacting material
crown-rump measurement

CRMO
chronic recurrent multifocal
osteomyelitis

CRNA
Certified Registered Nurse Anesthetist

cRNA
chromosomal ribonucleic acid

CRNF
chronic rheumatoid nodular fibrositis

CRNI
Certified Registered Nurse Intravenous

cr nn
cranial nerves *also* crns, cr ns

CRNP
Certified Registered Nurse Practitioner

crns, cr ns
cranial nerves *also* cr nn

CRO
cathode ray oscillograph
cathode ray oscilloscope
centric relation occlusion

CROM
cervical range of motion

CROP
compliance, rate, oxygenation, and
pressure
cyclophosphamide, rubidazone,
Oncovin (vincristine), and prednisone

CROS
contralateral routing of signal
contralateral routing of sound

CR/OV
colorectal/ovarian

CRP
cAMP receptor protein
chronic relapsing pancreatitis
confluent, reticulate papillomatosis
corneal-retinal potential
coronary rehabilitation program
C-reactive protein
cross-reactive protein
cyclic adenosine monophosphate
receptor protein

CrP
creatine phosphate
phosphocreatine

CRPA
C-reactive protein antiserum

CRPD
chronic restrictive pulmonary disease

CRPF
chloroquine-resistant *Plasmodium
falciparum*
contralateral renal plasma flow

CRR
canal resonance response

CRRT
Certified Respiratory Therapy
Technician
continuous renal replacement therapy

CRS
catheter-related sepsis
caudal regression syndrome
central supply room
cherry-red spot
Chinese restaurant syndrome
colorectal surgery
compliance of the respiratory system
congenital rubella syndrome
counter rotation system

CRSM
cherry red spot myoclonus

CRSP
comprehensive renal scintillation
procedure

CrSp
craniospinal

NOTES

C

CRST
calcinosis cutis, Raynaud phenomenon, sclerodactyly, and telangiectasia (syndrome)

CRT
cadaver renal transplant
cardiac resuscitation team
cathode ray tube
central reaction time
certified *also* C
Certified Record Technique
choice reaction time
chromium release test
complex reaction time
computed renal tomography
copper reduction test
corrected retention time
cortisone resistant thymocyte
cranial radiation therapy

CRTP
Consciousness Research and Training Project

CrTr
crutch training *also* CT

CRTT
Certified Respiratory Therapy Technician

CRTX
cast removed, take x-ray *also* COTX

CRU
cardiac rehabilitation unit
clinical research unit

CRV
central retinal vein

CRVF
congestive right ventricular failure

CRVO
central retinal vein occlusion

CRW
Cosman-Roberts-Wells

CRY-AB
cryptococcal antibody

CRY-AG
cryptococcal antigen

cryo
cryoglobulin
cryoprecipitate
cryosurgery
cryotherapy

crys, cryst
crystal
crystalline
crystallinized

CRYST
crystal examination screen

CS
calf serum
camptomelic syndrome
carcinoid syndrome
cardiogenic shock
caries susceptible
carotid sheath
carotid sinus
catgut suture *also* CGS
cat scratch (disease) *also* CSD
celiac sprue
central service
central supply
cerebrospinal
cervical spine *also* C-S, C-spine
cervical stimulation
cesarean section *also* C/S, C-section, C sect
chemical sympathectomy
chest strap
chief of staff
cholesterol stone
chondroitin sulfate
chorionic somatomammotropin
chronic schizophrenia
cigarette smoker
cigarette smoke (solution)
citrate synthase
climacteric syndrome
clinical (laboratory) scientist
clinical stage
clinical state
close supervision
Cockayne syndrome
colistin
Collet-Sicard (syndrome)
completed stroke
completed suicide
compression syndrome
concentrated strength (of solution)
conditioned stimulus
congenital syphilis
conjunctival secretion
conjunctiva-sclera
conscious *also* cs
consciousness *also* Cs, cs
constant spring
consultation service
contact sensitivity

continue same (treatment)
continuing smoker
continuous stripping
control serum
convalescence
convalescent
convalescent status
coronary sclerosis
coronary sinus
corpus striatum
cortical spoking
corticoid sensitive
corticosteroid (therapy)
crush syndrome
current smoker
current strength
Cursdmann-Steinert (syndrome)
Cushing syndrome
cycloserine
cyclosporin *also* CSP
with the left hand [L. *colla sinistra*]

C4S
chondroitin 4-sulfate

C-S
cervical spine *also* CS, C-spine

C/S
cesarean section *also* CS, C-section, C sect
Cost-Stirling (antibody)
culture and sensitivity *also* C&S
cycles per second *also* CPS, cps, c/s, c/sec

C&S
conjunctiva and sclera
cough and sneeze
culture and sensitivity *also* C/S
culture and susceptibility

C$_s$
standard clearance *also* Cs
static (lung) compliance *also* CST, Cst

Cs
case *also* cs
cell surface antigen
cesium
consciousness *also* CS, cs
standard clearance *also* C$_s$

^{132}Cs
radioactive cesium

^{137}Cs
cesium-137

cS
centistoke *also* cSt

c/s
cycles per second *also* CPS, cps, C/S, c/sec

cs
case *also* Cs
conscious *also* CS
consciousness *also* CS, Cs

CSA
canavaninosuccinic acid
chondroitin sulfate A
colon-specific antigen
colony-stimulating activity
compressed spectral assay
controlled substance analog
corticosteroid sensitive asthma
cross-sectional area
cyclosporin A *also* CsA, CyA

CsA
cyclosporin A *also* CSA, CyA

CSAD
cysteine sulfinic acid decarboxylase

CSAP
colon-specific antigen protein

CSAS
central sleep apnea syndrome

CSAVP
cerebral subarachnoid venous pressure

CSB
caffeine sodium benzoate
Cheyne-Stokes breathing
contaminated small bowel

CSB I&II
Chemistry Screening Batteries I and II

CSBF
coronary sinus blood flow

CSBO
complete small bowel obstruction

NOTES

C

CSBS
contaminated small bowel syndrome

CSC
blow on blow (administration of small doses of drugs at short intervals) [Fr. *coup sur coup*]
central serous choroidopathy
cigarette smoke condensate
collagen sponge contraceptive
cornea, sclera, and conjunctiva
cryogenic storage container
cryopreserved stem cell

C/S & CC
culture and sensitivity and colony count

CSCD
Center for Sickle Cell Disease

CSCI
continuous subcutaneous infusion

CSCR
central serous chorioretinopathy

C1s–C3s
control proteins C1s–C3s

CSCT
central somatosensory conduction time
comprehensive support care team

CSD
carotid sinus denervation
cat-scratch disease *also* CS
combined system disease
conditionally streptomycin dependent
conduction system disease
cortically spreading depression
craniospinal defect
critical stimulus duration

CS&D
cleaned, sutured, and dressed

CS/DS
chondroitin sulfate/dermatan sulfate

CSE
clinical-symptom/self-evaluation (questionnaire)
combined spinal/epidural (anesthesia)
complete surgical exploration
conventional silicone elastomer
cross-sectional echocardiography

c/sec
cycles per second *also* CPS, cps, C/S, c/s

C-section, C sect
cesarean section *also* CS, C/S

CSEP
cortical somatosensory evoked potential

CSER
cortical somatosensory-evoked response

CSF
cancer family syndrome
cerebrospinal fluid
circumferential shortening fraction
colony-stimulating factor
coronary sinus flow

CSF-1
colony-stimulating factor-1

CSF-FTA-ABS
colony-stimulating factor fluorescent treponemal antibody-absorption (test)

CSFH
cerebrospinal fluid hypotension

CSFI
Cholesterol-Saturated Fat Index

CSF-MHA-TP
colony-stimulating factor microhemagglutination-*Treponema pallidum* (test)

CSFP
cerebrospinal fluid pressure

CSFV
cerebrospinal fluid volume

CSF-VDRL
colony-stimulating factor-developed by Venereal Disease Research Laboratory

CSF-WR
cerebrospinal fluid–Wassermann reaction

CSG
chronic superficial gastritis

CSGBM
collagenase soluble glomerular basement membrane

CSH
capsular synovial-like hyperplasia
carotid sinus hypersensitivity
chronic subdural hematoma
cortical stromal hyperplasia

C-Sh
chair shower

CSHH
congenital self-healing histiocytosis

CSI
calculus surface index
cancer serum index
cavernous sinus infiltration
chemical shift imaging
cholesterol saturation index
continuous subcutaneous infusion

CSICU
cardiac surgery intensive care unit

CSII
continuous subcutaneous insulin
infusion

CSIIP
continuous subcutaneous insulin
infusion pump

CSIN
Chemical Substances Information
Network

CSIS
clinical supplies and inventory system

CSL
cardiolipin synthetic lecithin

CSLM
confocal scanning microscopy

CSLU
chronic stasis leg ulcer

CSM
carotid sinus massage
cerebrospinal meningitis
cervical spondylotic myelopathy
circulation, sensation, mobility
Committee on Safety of Medicines
Consolidated Standards Manual
cornmeal, soybean, milk

CSMA
chemical shift misregistration artifact
chronic spinal muscular atrophy

CSMB
Center for Study of Multiple Births

CSME
cotton-spot macular edema

CSMMG
Chartered Society of Massage and
Medical Gymnastics

CSMN
chronic sensorimotor neuropathy

CSN
cardiac sympathetic nerve
carotid sinus nerve
cystic suppurative necrosis

CS(NCA)
Clinical (Laboratory) Scientist
Certified by the National
Certification Agency (for Medical
Laboratory Personnel)

CSNG
congenital stationary night blindness

CSNRT, cSNRT
corrected sinus node recovery time
also CSRT

CSNS
carotid sinus nerve stimulation

CSO
common source outbreak
copied standing orders

CSOM
chronic serous otitis media
chronic suppurative otitis media

CSOP
coronary sinus occlusion pressure

CSP
Cancer Surveillance Program
carotid sinus pressure
cavum septi pellucidi
cavum septum pellucidum
cell surface protein
cellulose sodium phosphate
chemistry screening profile
Cooperative Statistical Program
criminal sexual psychopath
cyclosporin *also* CS

C-spine
cervical spine *also* CS, C-S

CSPS
continual skin peeling syndrome

NOTES

CSR
central serous retinopathy
central supply room
Cheyne-Stokes respiration
continued stay review
corrected sedimentation rate
corrected survival rate
corrective septorhinoplasty
cortisol secretion rate
cumulative survival rate

CSRT
corrected sinus (node) recovery time
also CSNRT, cSNRT

CSS
Cancer Surveillance System
carotid sinus stimulation
carotid sinus syndrome
chewing, sucking, swallowing
chronic subclinical scurvy
Churg-Strauss syndrome
coronary sinus stimulation
cranial sector scan

CSSD
central sterile supply department

CSSRD
Cooperative Systematic Studies of the
Rheumatic Disease

CST
cardiac stress test
cavernous sinus thrombosis
Certified Surgical Technician
Christ-Siemens-Touraine (syndrome)
Completing Sentence Test
Compton scatter tomography
contraction stress test
convulsive shock therapy
corticospinal tract
cosyntropin stimulation test
static (lung) compliance *also* C$_s$, Cst

Cst
static (lung) compliance *also* C$_s$,
CST

cSt
centistoke *also* cS

CSTI
Clearinghouse for Scientific and
Technical Information

CSTT
cold-stimulation time test

CSU
cardiac surgery unit
cardiac surveillance unit
cardiovascular surgery unit
casualty staging unit
catheter specimen of urine
Central Statistical Unit (of Venereal
Disease Research Laboratory)
clinical specialty unit

CSUF
continuous slow ultrafiltration

CSV
chick syncytial virus

CSVT
central splanchnic venous thrombosis

CSW
Certified Social Worker
current sleepwalker

CT
calcitonin
calf testis
cardiac tamponade
cardiothoracic (ratio) *also* CTR
Cardiovascular Technologist
carotid tracing
carpal tunnel
cationic trypsinogen
cell therapy
cellular therapy
center thickness
cerebral thrombosis
cerebral tumor
cervical traction *also* CXTX
chemotaxis *also* CTX
chemotherapy
chest tube
chloramine T
chlorothiazide
cholera toxin
chordae tendineae
chronic thyroiditis
chymotrypsin
circulation time
classic technique
closed thoracotomy
clotting time
coagulation time
coated tablet
cobra toxin
cognitive therapy
coil test
collecting tubule
combined tumor
compressed tablet
computed tomography

computerized tomography
connective tissue
continue treatment
continuous-flow tub
contraction time
controlled temperature
Coombs test
corneal thickness
corneal transplant
coronary thrombosis
corrected transposition
corrective therapy
cortical thickness
cough threshold
cover test
crest time
crutch training *also* CrTr
cystine-tellurite (medium)
cytarabine, 6-thioguanine
cytotechnologist
cytotoxic therapy

4C-T
four-chamber transverse

5C-T
five-chamber transverse

C&T
color and temperature

C/T
compression to traction ratio
crossmatch to transfusion ratio

Ct
carboxyl terminal *also* C-terminal

C$_{T-1824}$
T-1824 (Evans blue) clearance

CTA
chemotactic activity *also* CA
chromotropic acid
clear to auscultation
computed tomoangiography
computed tomographic angiography
congenital trigeminal anesthesia
cyproterone acetate
cystine trypticase agar
cytoplasmic tubular aggregate
cytotoxic assay
menses [L. *catamenia*] *also* Cta

Cta
menses [L. *catamenia*] *also* CTA

CTAB
cetyltrimethylammonium bromide *also* CTBM

C-TAB
cyanide tablet

CTAC
Cancer Treatment Advisory Committee
Carrow Test for Auditory Comprehension
cetyltrimethylammonium chloride

CTAL
cortical thick ascending limb

c. tant.
with the same amount [L. *cum tanto*]

CTAP
clear to auscultation and percussion
computed tomography angiographic portography
computed tomography during arterial portography
connective tissue-activating peptide

CTAS
colonic transabdominal sonography

CT(ASCP)
Cytotechnologist (American Society of Clinical Pathologists)

CTAT
computed transaxial tomography

CTB
calciotraumatic band
ceased to breathe

CTBA
cetrimonium bromide

CTBM
cetyltrimethyl-ammonium bromide *also* CTAB

CTC
Child-Turcotte classification
chlortetracycline
circular tear capsulotomy

C

NOTES

157

CTC *(continued)*
computer-aided tomographic
cisternography
cultured T cell

CTCL
cutaneous T-cell leukemia
cutaneous T-cell lymphoma

ctCO₂
concentration of total carbon dioxide

CTD
carpal tunnel decompression
chest tube drainage
congenital thymic dysplasia
connective tissue disease
Corrective Therapy Department
cumulative trauma disorder

CT&DB
cough, turn, and deep breathe

CTDTADA
The Council on Dental Therapeutics
of the American Dental Association

CTDW
continues to do well

CTE
calf thymus extract
cultured thymic epithelium

CTEM
conventional transmission electron
microscopy

CTEPH
chronic thromboembolic pulmonary
hypertension

C-terminal
carboxyl terminal *also* Ct

CTF
cancer therapy facility
certificate *also* Cert, cert
Colorado tick fever
cytotoxic factor

CTG
cardiotocography
cervicothoracic ganglion
chymotrypsinogen

C/TG
cholesterol-triglyceride (ratio)

CTGA
complete transposition of great
arteries

CTH
ceramide trihexoside
chronic tension headache
clot to hold

CTI
certification of terminal illness

CTIU
cardiac-thoracic intensive care unit
also CTU

CTL
cervical, thoracic, and lumbar
cytologic T lymphocyte
cytolytic T lymphocyte
cytotoxic T lymphocyte

ctl
contact lens

CTLD
chlorthalidone (diuretic and
antihypertensive agent)

CTLL
cytotoxic T-lymphocyte line

CTLSO
cervicothoracolumbosacral orthosis

CTM
cardiotachometer
Carlo Traverso maneuver
Chlamydia transport media
Chlor-Trimeton (antihistaminic)
computed tomographic myelography
connective tissue massage
continuous tone masking
cricothyroid muscle

CTMM
computed tomographic metrizamide
myelography

CTMM-SE
California Test of Mental
Maturity–Short Form

CT/MPR
computed tomography with
multiplanar reconstructions

CTN
calcitonin
computed tomography number

C&TN BLE
color and temperature normal, both
lower extremities

cTNM
  clinical (staging) of tumors, nodes, and metastases (etc.) as determined by noninvasive examination

CTP
  California Test of Personality
  carboxyl terminal peptide
  comprehensive treatment plan
  cytidine triphosphate
  cytidine 5'-triphosphate
  cytosine triphosphate

ICTP
  type I collagen telopeptide

C-TPN
  cyclic total parenteral nutrition

CTPP
  cerebral tissue perfusion pressure

CTPV
  cavernous transformation of the portal vein
  coal tar pitch volatiles

CTPVO
  chronic thrombotic pulmonary vascular obstruction

CTR
  cardiothoracic ratio *also* CT
  carpal tunnel release
  carpal tunnel repair

ctr
  center

CT-RT
  chemo-radiotherapy

CTS
  cardiothoracic surgery
  carpal tunnel syndrome
  composite treatment score
  computed tomographic scan
  computed tomographic scanner
  computed topographic scan
  computed topographic scanner
  contralateral threshold shift
  corticosteroid

CT scan
  computed tomography scan

CTSNFR
  corrected time of sinoatrial node function recovery

CTSP
  called to see patient

CTT
  cefotetan
  central tegmental tract
  compressed tablet triturate
  computed transaxial tomography

CTU
  cardiac-thoracic unit *also* CTIU
  centigrade thermal unit
  constitutive transcription unit

CTUWSD
  chest tube under water-seal drainage

CTV
  cervical and thoracic vertebrae

CTW
  central terminal of Wilson
  combined testicular weight

CTX
  cefotaxime *also* TAX
  cerebrotendinous xanthomatosis
  chemotaxis *also* CT
  chemotoxins
  contraction *also* C, contr, contrx, CTXN, Cx
  cyclophosphamide *also* CP, CPA, CPM, CY, Cy, CYC, CYCLO, CYT
  Cytoxan (cyclophosphamide) *also* ctx

CTx
  cardiac transplantation

ctx
  Cytoxan (cyclophosphamide) *also* CTX

CTXN
  contraction *also* C, contr, contrx, CTX, Cx

CTZ
  chemoreceptor trigger zone
  chlorothiazide

CU
  cardiac unit
  casein unit

NOTES

CU *(continued)*
cause unknown
chymotrypsin unit
clinical unit
color unit
contact urticaria
control unit
convalescent unit
copper [L. *cuprum*] *also* Cu
curie *also* C, c, Ci, cu
cusp

C$_u$
urea clearance

Cu
copper [L. *cuprum*] *also* CU

cu
cubic *also* C, c
curie *also* C, c, Ci, CU

^{62}CU
copper-62

^{64}Cu
copper-64

^{67}Cu
copper-67

Cu-7
Copper-7 (intrauterine contraceptive device)

CuB
copper band

CUC
chronic ulcerative colitis

cu cm
cubic centimeter *also* CC, cc, c.c., cm^3

CUD
cause undetermined
congenital urinary (tract) deformities

CUE
cumulative urinary excretion

cu ft
cubic foot

CUG
cystidine, uridine, and guanidine
cystourethrogram
cystourethrography

CuHVL
copper half-value layer

CUI
Cox-Uphoff International (tissue expander)

cu in
cubic inch

cuj.
of which [L. *cujus*]

cuj. lib.
of whatever you please [L. *cujus libet*]

cult
culture

CUM
cumulative report

cu m
cubic meter *also* m^3

cum
cubic micrometer *also* μm^3

CUMITECH
Cumulative Techniques and Procedures in Clinical Microbiology

cu mm
cubic millimeter *also* cmm, mm^3

cUMP
cyclic uridine 3,'5'-monophosphate

CUPS
carcinoma of unknown primary site

CUR
curettage
cystourethrorectal

cur
curative
cure
current

curat.
dressing [L. *curatio*]

CURN
Conduct and Utilization of Research in Nursing

CUS
carotid ultrasound examination
catheterized urine specimen
chronic undifferentiated schizophrenia
compression ultrasound
contact urticaria syndrome

CUSA
Cavitron Ultrasonic Surgical Aspirator

CUSALap
Cavitron Ultrasonic Surgical Aspirator for laparoscopy

cusp.
cuspid

CUT
chronic undifferentiated type (schizophrenia)

CuTS
cubital tunnel syndrome

CUX
check-up x-ray

cu yd
cubic yard

CV
cardiac volume
cardiovascular
carotenoid vesicle
cell volume
central venous
cerebrovascular
cervical vertebra
chikungunya virus
cisplatin and Vepesid (etoposide)
closed vitrectomy
closing volume
coefficient of variation
collecting vein
color vision
concentrated volume
conducting vein
conduction velocity
consonant vowel (syllable)
contrast ventriculography
conventional ventilation
conversational voice
corpuscular volume
costovertebral
Coxsackie virus *also* COX
cresyl violet
critical value
crystal violet
curriculum vitae
cutaneous vasculitis
tomorrow evening [L. *cras vespere*] *also* c.v.
true conjugate (diameter of pelvic inlet) [L. *conjugata vera*]

C/V
cervical/vaginal
coulomb per volt

Cv, C$_v$
specific heat at constant volume

c.v.
tomorrow evening [L. *cras vespere*] *also* CV

CVA
cardiovascular accident
cerebrovascular accident
cervicovaginal antibody
chronic villous arthritis
costovertebral angle
cresyl violet acetate
cyclophosphamide, vincristine, and Adriamycin (doxorubicin)

CVA-BMP
cyclophosphamide, vincristine (Oncovin), Adriamycin (doxorubicin), BCNU (carmustine), methotrexate, and procarbazine

CVAH
congenital virilizing adrenal hyperplasia

C-Vasc
cerebral vascular (profile study)

CVAT
costovertebral angle tenderness

CVB
CCNU (lomustine), vinblastine, and bleomycin
chorionic villus biopsy
group B coxsackievirus

CVC
central venous catheter (CV cath)
consonant vowel consonant (syllable)

CV cath
central venous catheter
central venous catheter

CVCT
cardiovascular computed tomography

CVD
cardiovascular disease *also* CD
cerebrovascular disease

NOTES

CVD *(continued)*
cerebrovascular disorder
collagen vascular disease
color vision deviant

cvd
curved

CVE
cerebrovascular evaluation

CVEB
cisplatin, vinblastine, etoposide, and bleomycin

CVF
cardiovascular failure
central visual field
cervicovaginal fluid
cobra venom factor

CVG
contrast ventriculography
coronary vein graft
coronary venous graft

CVH
cerebroventricular hemorrhage
cervicovaginal hood
combined ventricular hypertrophy
common variable hypogammaglobulinemia

CVHD
chronic valvular heart disease

CVI
cardiovascular incident
cardiovascular insufficiency
cavum veli interpositi
cerebrovascular incident
cerebrovascular insufficiency
Children's Vaccine Initiative
chronic venous insufficiency
common variable immunodeficiency *also* CVID
continuous venous infusion

CVID
common variable immunodeficiency *also* CVI

C virus
Coxsackie virus A, B (virus titer) *also* CV

CVL
central venous line
clinical vascular laboratory

CVLT
California Verbal Learning Center

CVM
cardiovascular monitor
cerebral venous malformation
cyclophosphamide, vincristine, and methotrexate

CVN
central venous nutrient
cochleovestibular neurectomy

CVO
central vein occlusion
central venous oxygen
Chief Veterinary Officer
circumventricular organs
obstetric conjugate (of pelvic inlet) [L. *conjugata vera obstetrica*]

CVOD
cerebrovascular obstructive disease

CVOR
cardiovascular operating room

CVP
cardiac valve procedure
cardioventricular pacing
cell volume profile
central venous pressure (catheter)
cerebrovascular profile
cyclophosphamide, vincristine, and prednisone

CVPP
cyclophosphamide, vincristine, prednisone, and procarbazine

CVR
cardiovascular renal (disease) *also* CVRD
cardiovascular resistance
cardiovascular-respiratory
cardiovascular review
cephalic vasomotor response
cerebrovascular resistance

CVRD
cardiovascular renal disease *also* CVR

CVRI
cardiovascular resistance index

CVRR
cardiovascular recovery room

CVS
cardiovascular surgery
cardiovascular system
cerebral vasospasm
challenge virus strain
chorionic villus sampling

clean voided specimen
current vital signs

CVSF
conduction velocity of slower fibers

CVSU
cardiovascular specialty unit

CVT
central venous temperature
congenital vertical talus

CVT-ICU
cardiovascular-thoracic intensive care unit

CVTP-ICU
cardiovascular-thoracic intensive care unit

CVTR
charcoal viral transport medium

CVTS
cardiovascular-thoracic surgery

CVUG
cystoscopy and voiding urethrogram

CVVH
continuous venovenous hemofiltration

CW
cardiac work
careful watch
case work
case worker
cell wall
chemical warfare
chemical weapon
chest wall
children's ward
clockwise *also* cw
clustered waves
compare with
continuous wave *also* cw
cotton-wool (spots) *also* C-W, CWS
crutch walking *also* c/w

C-W
cotton-wool (spots) *also* CW

C/W
compatible with *also* c/w
consistent with *also* c/w

cw
clockwise *also* CW
continuous wave *also* CW

c/w
compatible with *also* CW
consistent with *also* CW
crutch walking *also* CW

CWBTS
capillary whole blood true sugar

CWD
cell wall defective
continuous-wave Doppler

CWDF
cell wall-deficient form (bacteria)

CWE
cotton-wool exudates

CWF
Cornell Word Form

CWH
cardiomyopathy and wooly hair-coat (syndrome)

CWI
cardiac work index

CWL
cutaneous water loss

CWMS
color, warmth, movement sensation

CWOP
childbirth without pain *also* CWP

CWP
centimeters of water pressure
childbirth without pain *also* CWOP
coal worker's pneumoconiosis

CWS
cell wall skeleton
chest wall stimulation
Child Welfare Service
circumferential wall stress
cold water soluble
comfortable walking speed
cotton-wool spots *also* CW, C-W

CWT
cold water treatment

NOTES

C

Cwt, cwt
hundredweight

CX
cancel *also* Cx
cerebral cortex
cervix *also* Cx
chest x-ray (film) *also* Cx, CXR
circumflex
circumflex artery
cloxacillin
controlled expansion
critical experiment
culture
cylinder axis
phosgene oxime

Cx
cancel *also* CX
cervix *also* CX
chest x-ray (film) *also* CX, CXR
circumflex
clearance
complex
complication
contraction *also* C, contr, contrx,
CTX, CTXN
convex

CxBx
cervical biopsy

CXM
cefuroxime
cyclohexamide

CxMT
cervical motion tenderness

CXR
chest x-ray (film) *also* CX, Cx

C x T
concentration times time

CXTX
cervical traction *also* CT

CY
calendar year
cyanogen *also* Cy
cyclophosphamide *also* CP, CPA,
CPM, CTX, Cy, CYC, CYCLO,
CYT

Cy
cyanogen *also* CY
cyclophosphamide *also* CP, CPA,
CPM, CTX, CY, CYC, CYCLO,
CYT

cyst
cytarabine

cy
copy

CyA
cyclosporin A *also* CSA, CsA

CyADIC
cyclophosphamide, Adriamycin
(doxorubicin), and DIC (dacarbazine)

cyath.
a glassful [L. *cyathus*]

CYC
cyclophosphamide *also* CP, CPA,
CPM, CTX, CY, Cy, CYCLO, CYT

cyc
cyclazocine
cycle
cyclotron

CYCLO, CyClo
cyclophosphamide *also* CP, CPA,
CPM, CTX, CY, Cy, CYC, CYT
cyclopropane

Cyclo C
cyclocytidine hydrochloride

Cyd
cytidine *also* C

CYE
charcoal yeast extract (medium)

CyHOP
cyclophosphamide, Halotestin,
Oncovin, and prednisone

CYL
casein yeast lactate (medium)

Cyl
cylinder *also* C
cylindrical lens *also* C

cyl, cyl.

CYN
cyanide

CYNAP
cytotoxicity negative, absorption
positive

CYP
cyproheptadine

CYS
cystoscopy

Cys
cyclosporin
cysteine *also* C

CYSTO, cysto
cystogram
cystoscopy

CYT
cyclophosphamide *also* CP, CPA,
 CPM, CTX, CY, Cy, CYC, CYCLO
cytochrome

Cyt
cytosine

cyt
cytologic *also* cytol
cytology *also* cytol
cytoplasm
cytoplasmic

cytol
cytologic *also* cyt
cytology *also* cyt

CYTOMG
cytomegalovirus

Cyt Ox
cytochrome oxidase

cyt sys
cytochrome system

CY-VA-DIC
cyclophosphamide, vincristine
 (Oncovin), Adriamycin (doxorubicin),
 and DTIC (dacarbazine)

CZ
cefazolin

Cz
central midline placement of
 electrodes in electroencephalography

CZD
cefazedone

CZE
capillary zone electrophoresis

CZI
crystalline zinc insulin

CZP
clonazepam

C

NOTES

D

cholecalciferol
coefficient of diffusion
dacryon *also* dac
date *also* d
daughter *also* da, dau
day *also* d, da
dead *also* d
dead air space
debye
deceased *also* d, DEC, dec, decd,
 dec'd
deciduous *also* DEC, dec
decimal reduction time
decrease *also* d, DC, D/C, DEC,
 dec, DECR, decr
degree *also* d, DEG, Deg, deg
density *also* d
dental
dentin
dermatologic
dermatologist
dermatology
detail response
deuterium *also* d
deuteron *also* d
development(al) *also* dev
deviation *also* DEV, dev
dexter
dextro- *also* d
dextrorotatory
dextrose
diagnosis *also* DG, Dg, Diag, diag,
 Dx, dx
diagonal *also* Diag, diag
diameter *also* d, Dia, dia, diam
diarrhea *also* d
diastole *also* dias
diathermy
didymium (praseodymium)
died *also* d
difference *also* DIFF, Diff, diff
diffusing
diffusion *also* DIFF, diff
dihydrouridine *also* hU, hu
diopter *also* d, diopt, Dptr
diplomate *also* Dip
disease *also* dis, DZ, Dz
distal *also* d, dist
diuresis
diurnal *also* d
diverticulum
divorced *also* d, div

dominant *also* DOM, dom
donor
dorsal
dose [L. *dosis*] *also* d, dos
drive
drug
dual
duodenal
duodenum
duration *also* d
dwarf
(electric) displacement
give [L. *da*] *also* d., DA
let it be given [L. *detur*] *also* d.,
 DD, dd, dent., det.
right [L. *dexter*] *also* d., dex.
unit of vitamin D. potency

2-D (*var. of* 2D)

D-

 stereochemical structure

D̄

 mean dose

1-D

 one-dimensional

2D, 2-D

 two-dimensional

2,4-D

 (2,4-dichlorophenoxy) acetic acid
 2,4-dichlorophenoxyacetic acid

3-D

 delayed double diffusion (test)
 three-dimensional *also* 3D

3D

 three-dimensional *also* 3-D

D/3

 distal third

ᴅ/₃

 distal third

1/D

 diffusion resistance

1/d

 daily, one per day

2/d

 twice a day

d

 atomic orbital with angular
  momentum quantum number 2

d *(continued)*
   date *also* D
   day [L. *dies*] *also* D, da
   dead *also* D
   deceased *also* D, DEC, dec, dec'd, decd
   deci-
   decigram
   decrease *also* D, DC, D/C, DEC, dec, DECR, decr
   degree *also* D, DEG, Deg, deg
   density *also* D
   deoxyribose
   deuterium *also* D
   deuteron *also* D
   dextro- (right, clockwise) *also* D
   diameter *also* D, Dia, diam
   diarrhea *also* D
   died *also* D
   diopter *also* D, diopt, Dptr
   distal *also* D, dist
   diurnal *also* D
   divorced *also* D, div
   dorsal
   dose *also* D, dos
   doubtful
   duration *also* D
   dyne
   relative to rotation of a beam of polarized light

d.
   give [L. *da*] *also* D, DA
   let it be given [L. *detur*] *also* D, DD, dd, dent., det.
   right [L. *dexter*] *also* D, dex.

d-
   dextrorotatary

D-A
   donor-acceptor

DA
   dark agouti (rat)
   daunomycin and cytosine
   decubitus angina
   degenerative arthritis
   delayed action
   delivery awareness
   Dental Assistant
   developmental age
   diabetic acidosis
   diagnostic arthroscopy
   differentiation antigen
   diphenylchlorarsine
   Diploma in Anesthetics

direct admission
direct agglutination
disability assistance
disaggregated
dispense as directed *also* DAD
dopamine
drug addict
drug addiction
drug aerosol
ductus arteriosus
give [L. *da*] *also* D, d.

D/A
   date of accident
   date of admission
   digital-to-analog (converter)
   discharge and advise

D&A
   dilatation and aspiration

Da
   dalton

dA
   day of admission
   deoxyadenosine *also* dAdo

da
   daughter *also* D, dau
   day *also* D, d
   deca-

DAA
   dehydroacetic acid

DA/A
   drug/alcohol addiction

DAB
   days after birth
   diaminobenzidine
   3,3'-diaminobenzidine tetrahydrochloride dihydrate
   3,3-diaminobenzidine tetrahydrochloride solution
   diaminobutyric acid
   dimethylaminoazobenzene
   dysrhythmic aggressive behavior

DAC
   deoxyazacytidine
   diazocholesterol
   digital-to-analog converter
   disabled adult child
   disaster assistance center
   Division of Ambulatory Care

dac
   dacryon *also* D

DACA
dissecting aneurysm of the coronary artery

DACE
dexamethasone, ara-C, carboplatin, and etoposide

DACL
Depression Adjective Check List

DACT
dactinomycin (actinomycin D)

DAD
diffuse alveolar damage
dispense as directed *also* DA
drug administration device

DADA
dichloroacetic acid
diisopropylammonium salt

DADAG
1,2:5,6-diacetyldianhydrogalactitol

DADDS
diacetyldiaminodiphenyl sulfone

dAdo
deoxyadenosine *also* dA

dADP
deoxyadenosine diphosphate

DADPS
diphenylsulfone

DAE
diphenylanthracene endoperoxide
diving air embolism

DAF
decay-accelerating factor
delayed auditory feedback
Draw-A-Family (test)

DAFT
Draw-A-Family test

DAG
diacylglycerol
dianhydrogalactitol
diffuse antral gastritis
dimeric acidic glycoprotein

DAGT
direct antiglobulin test

DAH
diffuse alveolar hemorrhage
disordered action of heart

DAHEA
Department of Allied Health Education and Accreditation

DAHM
Division of Allied Health Manpower

DAI
diffuse axonal injury

DAL
drug analysis laboratory

daL, dal
decaliter

DALA
δ-aminolevulinic acid

DALE
Drug Abuse Law Enforcement

DALM
dysplasia-associated lesion or mass

DAM
degraded amyloid
diacetylmonoxime
diacetylmorphine
discriminant analytic model

dam
decameter

DAMA
discharge against medical advice

dAMP
deoxyadenosine monophosphate
deoxyadenylic acid

DANA
designed after natural anatomy
drug-induced antinuclear antibodies

dand.
to be given [L. *dandus*]

DANS
1-dimethylaminoaphthalene-5 sulfonic acid

DAO
diamine oxidase
duly authorized officer

D

NOTES

DAo, Dao
descending aorta

DAP
dapsone
data acquisition processor
delayed after polarization
depolarizing afterpotential
diabetes-associated peptide
dianhydrogalactital, Adriamycin
(doxorubicin), and Platinol (cisplatin)
diastolic aortic pressure
diastolic augmentation pressure
dihydroxyacetone phosphate
dipeptidyl amino peptidase *also* DAT
direct (latex) agglutination pregnancy
(test) *also* DAPT
distending airway pressure
dose area product
Draw-A-Person (test)
dynamic aortic patch

DAP&E
Diploma of Applied Parasitology and
Entomology

DAPI
46′-diamidino-2-phenylindole-2 HCl

DAPRE
Daily Adjusted Progressive Resistance
Exercise

DAPRU
Drug Abuse Prevention Resource
Unit

DAPS
Differentiation of Auditory Perception
Skill

DAPST
Denver Auditory Phoneme Sequencing
Test

DAPT
diaminophenyl thiazole
direct (latex) agglutination pregnancy
test *also* DAP

DAQ
Diagnostic Assessment Questionnaire

DAR
daily affective rhythm
dual asthmatic reaction

DARF
direct antiglobulin rosette-forming

DARP
drug abuse rehabilitation program

DARTS
Drug and Alcohol Rehabilitation
Testing System

DAS
dead air space
death anxiety scale
delayed anovulatory syndrome
developmental apraxia of speech
dextroamphetamine sulfate
Dialys-Aids Systems
died at scene

DASA
distal articular set angle

DASE
Denver Articulation Screening
Examination
dobutamine-atropine stress
echocardiography

DASH
Distress Alarm for the Severely
Handicapped

DASI
Developmental Activities Screening
Inventory
Duke Activity Status Index

DASP
double antibody solid phase

DAT
daunorubicin, arabinosylcytosine, and
thioguanine
daunorubicin, ara-C (cytarabine), and
thioguanine
delayed-action tablet
dementia of the Alzheimer type
dental aptitude test
Developmental Articulation Test
diet as tolerated
differential agglutination test
differential agglutination titer
Differential Aptitude Test
dipeptidyl amino peptidase *also* DAP
diphtheria antitoxin
direct agglutination test
direct antiglobulin (Coombs) test
Disaster Action Team (of Red Cross)

DATATOP
Deprenyl and tocopherol antioxidative
therapy of Parkinsonism

DATE
dental auxiliary teacher education

dATP
deoxyadenosine triphosphate

DATTA
Diagnostic and Therapeutic Technology Assessment

DATVP
daunomycin, ara-C, thioguanine, vincristine, and prednisone

DAU
Dental Auxiliary Utilization

dau
daughter *also* D, da

DAUNO
daunorubicin *also* DRB

DAV
daunorubicin, ara-C, and VP-16
duck adenovirus

DAVA
desacetyl vinblastine amide

DAVH
dibromodulcitol, Adriamycin, vincristine, and Halotestin

DAVM
dural arteriovenous malformation

DAVTH
dibromodulcitol, Adriamycin (doxorubicin), vincristine, tamoxifen, and Halotestin

DAW
dispense as written

DAWG
demucosalized augmentation with gastric segment

DB
Baudelocque diameter
database
date of birth *also* D/B, DOB
deep breath
dense body
dermabrasion
dextran blue
diabetic *also* Dia, dia, diab
diagonal band
diaphragmatic breathing
diet beverage
direct bilirubin
disability *also* dis
distobuccal
double-blind (study)
dry bulb
duodenal bulb
Dutch belted (rabbit)

D/B
date of birth *also* DB, DOB

dB
decibel *also* db

db
decibel *also* dB
diabetes *also* Dia, dia, diab

DBA
Diamond-Blackfan anemia
dibenzanthracene
Dolichos biflorus agglutinin

DBAE
dihydroxyborylaminoethyl

DBC
dibencozide
distance between centers
distobuccal cusp
dye-binding capacity

DB&C
deep breathing and coughing

DBCL
dilute blood clot lysis (method)

DBCP
dibromochloropropane

DBCR
distobuccal cusp ridge

DBD
definite brain damage
dibromodulcitol

DBDG
distobuccal developmental groove

DBE
deep breathing exercise
dibromoethane

DBED
dibenzylethylenediamine dipenicillin (penicillin G benzathine)

D

NOTES

DBF
disturbed bowel function

DBH
dacarbazine, carmustine, and hydroxyurea
dopamine β-hydroxylase

DBI
development-at-birth index

DBIL, D bili
direct bilirubin

DBIOC
database input/output control

DBIP
Discrimination by Identification of Pictures

DBIR
Director of Biotechnology Information Resources

dBk
decibels above 1 kilowatt

DBL
distance between nasal lines

dbl
double

DBM
database management
decarboxylasebase Moeller
demineralized bone matrix
diabetic management
dibromomannitol
dobutamine

dBm
decibels above 1 milliwatt

DBMC
dystrophica bullosa Mendes da Costa

DBMG
mandelonitrile β-glucuronide

DBMS
database management systems

DBMT
displacement bone marrow transplantation

DBO
distobuccoocclusal

db/ob
diabetic obese (mouse)

DBP
demineralized bone powder
diastolic blood pressure
di-*tert*-butyl peroxide *also* DTBP
dibutyl phthalate
distobuccopulpal
Döhle body panmyelopathy
vitamin D-binding protein

DBPC
dual balloon perfusion catheter

DBQ
debrisoquin

DBR
direct bilirubin
disordered breathing rate
distobuccal root

DBS
deep brain stimulation
Denis Browne splint
despeciated bovine serum
Diamond-Blackfan syndrome
dibromosalicil
diminished breath sounds
direct bonding system
direct brain stimulation
Division of Biological Standards

DBT
disordered breathing time
dry bulb temperature

DBW
desirable body weight
dry body weight

dBW
decibels above 1 watt

DBZ
dibenzamine

DC
daily census
data communication
daunorubicin and cytarabine
decarboxylase
decrease *also* D, d, D/C, DEC, dec, DECR, decr
deep compartment
degenerating cell
Dental Corps
deoxycholate
descending colon
dextran charcoal
diagnostic center
diagnostic code
diagonal conjugate (diameter)
differentiated carcinoma
differentiated cell

diffuse cortical
digit copying
dilatation and curettage
dilation catheter
dilation and curettage *also* D&C
diphenylcyanar-sine
direct and consensual *also* D&C
direct Coombs (test)
direct current *also* dc
Direction Circular
discharge *also* D/C
discharged
discontinue *also* D/C, d/c, dc
discontinued
distal colon
distal cusp
distocervical
Doctor of Chiropractic
donor cells
dorsal column
dressing change
dual chamber
duodenal cap
Dupuytren contracture
dynamic compression
dyskeratosis congenita

D&C, D and C
dilatation and curettage
dilation and curettage *also* DC
direct and consensual *also* DC
drugs and cosmetics

D/C
decrease *also* D, d, DC, DEC, dec, DECR, decr
diarrhea/constipation
discharge *also* DC
discontinue *also* DC, d/c, dc

dC
deoxycytidine

dc
direct current *also* DC
discontinue *also* DC, D/C, d/c

d/c
discharge (vaginal)
discontinue *also* DC, D/C, dc

DC65
Darvon compound 65

DCA
deoxycholate-citrate agar
deoxycholic acid
desoxycorticosterone acetate
dicarboxylic acid
dichloroacetate
directional coronary atherectomy
double cup arthroplasty

DCAG
double coronary artery graft

DCB
dichlorobenzidine
dilutional cardiopulmonary bypass

DC&B
dilation, curettage, and biopsy

DCBE
double contrast barium enema

DCBF
dynamic cardiac blood flow

DCBGS
direct-current bone growth stimulator

DCC
day care center
detected in colon cancer
dextran-coated charcoal
dicyclohexylcarbodiimide *also* DCCD
Disaster Control Center
dorsal cell column
double concave *also* DCc, DDc

DCc
double concave *also* DCC, DDc

DCCD
dicyclohexylcarbodiimide *also* DCC

DCCF
dural carotid-cavernous fistula

DCCMP
daunomycin, cyclocytidine, 6-mercaptopurine, and prednisolone

DC$_{CO2}$
diffusing capacity for carbon dioxide

DCD
Dennis Test of Child Development

D/C'd
discontinued

D

NOTES

DCDA
deuterium with cesium dihydrogen arsenate

DCE
delayed contrast enhancement
demosterol-to-cholesterol enzyme
designated compensable event

DCF
2′-deoxycoformycin
direct centrifugal flotation
dopachrome conversion factor

DCFM
Doppler color flow mapping

DCG
dacryocystography
desoxycorticosterone glucoside
disodium cromoglycate
dynamic electrocardiogram

DCH
delayed cutaneous hypersensitivity
Diploma in Child Health

DCh
Doctor of Surgery [L. *Doctor Chirurgiae*]

DCHA
dicyclohexylamine

DCHFB
dichlorohexafluorobutane

DCHN
dicyclohexylamine nitrate
dicyclohexylamine nitrite

DchO
Doctor of Ophthalmic Surgery

DCI
dichloroisoprenaline
dichloroisoproterenol

DCIA
deep circumflex iliac artery (flap)

DCIS
ductal carcinoma in situ

DCL
dicloxacillin
diffuse cutaneous leishmaniasis
digital counter/locator
disseminated cutaneous leishmaniasis

DCLS
deoxycholate citrate lactose saccharose (agar)

DCM
dichloromethane
dichloromethotrexate
dilated cardiomyopathy
Doctor of Comparative Medicine
dyssynergia cerebellaris myoclonica

DCML
dorsal column medial lemniscus

DCMO
dihydrocarboxanilidomethyloxathin

DCMP
daunorubicin, cytarabine, 6-mercaptopurine, prednisone

dCMP
deoxycytidine monophosphate
deoxycytidylic acid

DCMX
dichloro-*m*-xylenol

DCMXT
dichloromethotrexate

DCN
Data Collection Network (medical records)
delayed conditioned necrosis
dorsal column nucleus
dorsal cutaneous nerve

DCNU
chloroethylnitrosoglucosyl urea (chlorozotocin)

DCO
Diploma of the College of Optics

D$_{CO}$
diffusing capacity for carbon monoxide *also* DLCO, D$_{LCO}$, DL$_{CO}$

DCP
calcium phosphate, dibasic
des-γ-carboxy prothrombin
dicalcium phosphate
dichlorophene
Diploma in Clinical Pathology
Diploma in Clinical Psychology
discharge planner
District Community Physician
dynamic compression plate

DCPC
dichlorodiphenylmethyl carbinol

DCPM
daunorubicin, cytarabine, prednisolone, and mercaptopurine

DCPN
direction-changing positional nystagmus

DCPU
dorsal caudate putamen

DCR
dacryocystorhinostomy
delayed cutaneous reaction
direct cortical response
distal cusp ridge

DCS
decompression sickness
dense canalicular system
diffuse cortical sclerosis
disease control serum
dorsal column stimulation
dorsal column stimulator
dorsal cord stimulation
Dynamic condylar screw
dyskinetic cilia syndrome

DCSA
double-contrast shoulder arthrography

DCSU
day care surgical unit

DCT
daunorubicin, cytarabine, and thioguanine
deep chest therapy
direct Coombs test
distal convoluted tubule
diurnal cortisol test
dynamic computed tomography

3D-CTA
three-dimensional computed tomographic angiography

DCTM
delay computer tomographic myelography

DCTMA
desoxycorticosterone trimethylacetate

dCTP
deoxycytidine triphosphate

DCTPA
desoxycorticosterone triphenylacetate

DCU
dichloral urea

DCUS
duplex color ultrasonography

DCV
dacarbazine, CCNU (lomustine), and vincristine

DCX
double-charge exchange

DCx
double convex

DCYS
Department of Children and Youth Services

DD
daily [L. *de die*] *also* d.d.
dangerous drug
day of delivery
degenerative disease
delusional disorder
dependent drainage
Descemet detachment
detrusor dyssynergia
developmental disability
dialysis dementia
diaper dermatitis
died of the disease
differential diagnosis *also* D/D, DDX, DDx, DIAGNO, diff diag
digestive disease
Di Guglielmo disease
discharged dead
discharge diagnosis
disk diameter
Distortion of Dots
double diffusion
double dose
down drain
drug dependence
dry dressing
dual disorder
Duchenne dystrophy
Dupuytren disease
let it be given to [L. *detur ad*] *also* d.d.

NOTES

D1–D12
first through twelfth dorsal vertebrae
also D_1–D_{12}

D_1–D_{12}
first through twelfth dorsal nerve
first through twelfth dorsal vertebrae
also D1–D12

D→D
discharge to duty

D/D
differential diagnosis also DD, DDX,
DDx, DIAGNO, diff diag

D&D
debridement and dressing
diarrhea and dehydration
drilling and drainage

Dd
unusual detail response

dD
confabulated detail response

d.d.
daily [L. de die] also DD
let it be given to [L. detur ad]
also DD

dd
disc diameter

DDA
Dangerous Drugs Act
dideoxyadenosine
digital differential analyzer
digital display alarm

DDAVP, dDAVP
deamino-8-D-arginine vasopressin
(desmopressin acetate)
deamino-D-arginine-vasopressin
desmopressin
desmopressin acetate

DDC
dangerous drug cabinet
dideoxycytidine (zalcitabine) also
ddC, ddc
diethyldithiocarbamate
(diethyldithiocarbamic acid)
dihydrocollidine
dihydroxyphenylalanine decarboxylase
direct display console
diverticular disease of colon

DDc
double concave also DCC, DCc

ddC, ddc
dideoxycytidine (zalcitabine) also
DDC

DDD
AV universal (pacemaker)
defined daily dose
degenerative disk disease
dense deposit disease
Denver dialysis disease
dichlorodiphenyldichloroethane
dihydroxydinaphthyl disulfide
Dowling Degos disease
dual-mode, dual-pacing, dual-sensing
(pacemaker)

d.d. in d.
from day to day [L. de die in
diem]

DDD CT
double-dose–delay computed
tomography

DDE
dichlorodiphenyldichloroethylene
direct data entry

DDFS
distant-disease-free survival

DDG
deoxy-D-glucose

DDGB
double-dose gallbladder
(cholecystogram)

DDH
developmental dysplasia of the hip
Diploma in Dental Health
dissociated double hypertropia

DDHT
double dissociated hypertropia

DDI
dideoxyinosine also DDL
dressing dry and intact

ddI, ddi
didanosine

DDIB
Disease Detection Information Bureau

DDL
dideoxyinosine also DDI

DDM
Diploma in Dermatological Medicine
Doctor of Dental Medicine
Dyke Davidoff-Masson (syndrome)

DDMS
degenerative dense microsphere

dDNA
denatured DNA

DDNC
Digestive Disease National Coalition

DDO
Diploma in Dental Orthopaedics

DDP
cis-diamminedichloroplatinum *also* CDDP
density-dependent phosphoprotein
diamminedichloroplatinum (cisplatin)
difficult-denture patient
distributed data processing

DDPA
Delta Dental Plans Association

DDR
diastolic descent rate
Diploma in Diagnostic Radiology
discharged during referral

DDS
damaged disk syndrome
dapsone
Demon Dropout Scale
dendrodendritic synaptosome
dental distress syndrome
depressed DNA synthesis
dialysis disequilibrium syndrome
diaminodiphenylsulfone (dapsone) *also* DDSO
directional Doppler sonography
Director of Dental Services
disease disability scale
Doctor of Dental Surgery
dodecyl sulfate
double decidual sac
dystrophy-dystocia syndrome
dystrophy-dystonia syndrome

Dds
detail response to small white space

DDSc
Doctor of Dental Science

DDSO
diaminodiphenylsulfone (dapsone) *also* DDS

DDST
Denver Developmental Screening Test

DDT
dichlorodiphenyltrichloroethane (chlorophenothane)
ductus deferens tumor
dye disappearance test

DDTP
drug dependence treatment program

ddTTP
dideoxythymidine triphosphate

DDU
dermodistortive urticaria

d. in dup.
give twice as much [L. *detur in duplo*]

DDVP
dimethyldichlorovinyl phosphate (dichlorvos)

DDW
double distilled water

D 5% DW
5% dextrose in distilled water

D/DW
dextrose in distilled water

DdW
detail response elaborating the whole

DDX, DDx
differential diagnosis *also* DD, D/D, DIAGNO, diff diag

DE
dendritic expansion
deprived eye
diagnostic error
dialysis encephalopathy
digestive energy
dobutamine echocardiography
dose equivalent
dream elements
drug evaluation
duodenal exclusion
duration of ejection

2DE
two-dimensional echocardiography

D

NOTES

3DE
three-dimensional echocardiography

D&E
diet and elimination
dilatation and evacuation
dilation and evacuation

D₅E₄₈
5% dextrose and electrolyte 48% (solution)

de
edge detail

DEA
dehydroepiandrosterone *also* DHA, DHEA
diethanolamine
diethylamine
Drug Enforcement Agency

DEA #
Drug Enforcement Agency number (physicians' federal narcotic number)

DEA-D, DEAE-D
diethylaminoethyl dextran

DEAE
diethylaminoethanol
diethylaminoethyl (cellulose)

DEB
diepoxybutane
diethylbutanediol
dystrophic epidermolysis bullosa

deb
debridement

DEBA
diethylbarbituric acid

debil
debility

DEBS
dominant epidermolysis bullosa simplex

deb spis
of proper consistency [L. *debita spissutudine*]

DEC
deceased *also* D, d, dec, decd, dec'd
deciduous *also* D, dec
decimal
decimeter
decrease *also* D, d, DC, D/C, dec, DECR, decr
deoxycholate citrate
diethylcarbamazine

dynamic environmental conditioning (cycle)
pour off [L. *decanta*]

Dec
decant *also* dec

dec
decant *also* Dec
deceased *also* D, d, DEC, decd, dec'd
deciduous *also* D, DEC
decompose
decomposition
decrease *also* D, d, DC, DEC, DECR, decr

decd, dec'd
deceased *also* D, d, DEC, dec

DECEL, decel
deceleration

DECO
decreasing consumption of oxygen

decoct
decoction

decomp
decompose
decomposition

decon
decontamination

DECR, decr
decrease *also* D, d, DC, D/C, DEC, dec

dec (R)
decrease, relative

DECUB, decub.
lying down [L. *decubitus*]

decub
decubitus position

DED
date of expected delivery
defined exposure dose
delayed erythema dose

de d. in d.
from day to day [L. *de die in diem*]

DEEG
depth electroencephalogram
depth electroencephalography
depth electrography

DEET
diethyltoluamide

DEF
decayed, extracted, and filled *also* def
decayed, extracted, or filled (permanent teeth)
defecation *also* def
deficiency *also* def, defic
duck embryo fibroblast

def
decayed, extracted, and filled (deciduous teeth) *also* DEF
defecation *also* DEF
deficiency *also* DEF, defic
deficient *also* defic
definite, definition

defib
defibrillate
defibrillation

defic
deficiency *also* DEF, def
deficient *also* def

deform.
deformed
deformity

DEFT
driven equilibrium Fourier transform

DEG, Deg, deg
degeneration *also* degen
degenerative *also* degen
degree *also* D, d

degen
degeneration *also* DEG, Deg, deg
degenerative *also* DEG, Deg, deg

deglut.
let it be swallowed [L. *deglutiatur*]

DEH
dysplasia epiphysealis hemimelica

DEHFT
developmental hand function test

DEHS
Division of Emergency Health Services

dehyd
dehydrated
dehydration

DEJ, dej
dentoenamel junction

del
deletion
delivery
delusion

deliq
deliquescence
deliquescent

δ
delta (fourth letter of Greek alphabet), lowercase
fourth in a series or group
heavy chain of immunoglobulin D

Δ
absence of heat in a reaction
delta (fourth letter of Greek alphabet), uppercase
delta gap
difference (mathematics)
double bond

DEM, Dem
Demerol (meperidine)
department of emergency medicine

DEN
dengue
dermatitis exfoliativa neonatorum
diethylnitrosamine

denat
denatured

denom
denominator

DENS
direct electrical nerve stimulation

DENT
Dental Exposure Normalization Technique

Dent, dent
dental
dentist
dentistry
dentition

dent.
let it be given [L. *dentur*] *also* D, d., DD, dd, det.

NOTES

D

dent. tal. dos.
give of such doses [L. *dentur tales doses*]

DEP
diethylpropanediol
diethyl pyrocarbonate
dilution end point

dep
dependent
deposit

dep.
purified [L. *depuratus*]

DEPA
diethylenephosphoramide

DEPC
diethylpyrocarbonate

depr
depressed
depression

DEPS
distal effective potassium secretion

DEP ST SEG
depressed ST segment

Dept, dept
department

DEQ
Depression Experiences Questionnaire

DER
disulfiramethanol reaction
dual-energy radiograph

DeR
degeneration reaction
reaction of degeneration

der
derivative chromosome
derive

deriv
derivative
derived

DERM, Derm, derm
dermatologic
dermatologist
dermatology

DES
dermal-epidermal separation
dialysis encephalopathy syndrome
diethylstilbestrol
diffuse esophageal spasm

disequilibrium syndrome
doctor's emergency service

DESAD
National Collaborative
Diethylstilbestrol Adenosis Project

DESAT, desat
desaturated

desc
descendant
descending
descent

DESD
detrusor external sphincter dyssynergia

DESI
drug efficacy study implementation

DEST
Denver Eye Screening Test
dichotic environmental sounds test

destil., dest.
distilled [L. *destilla, destillatus*]
distill [L. *destilla, destillatus*]

DET
diethyltryptamine

Det-6
detroid-6 (human sternum marrow
cells)

det
determine

det.
let it be given [L. *detur*] *also* D,
d., DD, dd, dent.

det. in dup., det. in 2 plo.
let twice as much be given [L.
detur in duplo]

determ, determin
determination
determined

detn
detention

detox
detoxification

det. in 2 plo. (*var. of* det. in dup.)

d. et s.
let it be given and labeled [L. *detur
et signetur*]

DEUC
direct electronic urethrocystometry

DEV
deviant
deviation *also* D
duck embryo vaccine
duck embryo virus

dev
develop
development(al) *also* D
deviate
deviation *also* D

devel
development

DevPd
developmental pediatrics

DEVR
dominant exudative vitreoretinopathy

DEX
dexamethasone

dex
Dextrosti

dex.
right [L. *dexter*] *also* D, d.

DEXA
dual-energy x-ray absorptiometry
(scan) *also* DXA

DF
decapacitation factor (sperm)
decayed and filled (permanent teeth)
decontamination factor
deferoxamine
deficiency factor
defined flora (animal)
degree of freedom
dengue fever
desferrioxamine
diabetic father
diaphragmatic function
diastolic filling
dietary fiber
digital fluoroscopy
discriminant function
disseminated foci
distal fossa
distribution factor
dome fragment
dorsiflexion

drug free
dry (gas) fractional (concentration)
dye free

df
decayed and filled (deciduous teeth)
degrees of freedom

DFA
delayed feedback audiometry
diet for age
difficulty falling asleep
direct fluorescent antibody (test)
direct fluorescent antigen (test)
direct fluorescent assay
dorsiflexion assist

DFB
dinitrofluorobenzene
dysfunctional (uterine) bleeding

DFC
deletion of final consonants
dry-filled capsule

DFCI
Dana-Farber Cancer Institute

DFD
defined formula diet
degenerative facet disease
diisopropylphosphorofluoridate

DFDCB
decalcified freeze-dried cortical bone

DFDD
difluorodiphenyldichloroethane

DFDT
difluorodiphenyltrichloroethane

DFE
diffuse fasciitis with eosinophilia
dilated fundus examination
distal femoral epiphysis

DFECT
dense fibroelastic connective tissue

DFG
direct forward gaze

DFI
disease-free interval

DFM
decreased fetal movement

D

NOTES

DFMC
daily fetal movement count

DFMO
difluoromethylornithine
dl-alpha-difluoromethylornithine

DFMR
daily fetal movement record

DFO, DFOM
deferoxamine

DFP
diastolic filling period
diastolic filling pressure
diisopropyl fluorophosphate
diisopropylfluorophosphonate

DF^{32}P
radiolabeled diisopropyl
  fluorophosphonate

DFPP
double filtration plasmapheresis

DFR
diabetic floor routine
dialysate filtration rate

2DFr
two-dimensional Fourier imaging

3DFr
three-dimensional Fourier imaging

DFRC
deglycerolized frozen red cells

DFS
disease-free survival
Doppler flow study
dynamic flow study

DFSP
dermatofibrosarcoma protuberans

DFT
defibrillation threshold *also* XDT
discrete Fourier transform
Doppler flow test

2DFT
two-dimensional Fourier transform

3DFT
three-dimensional Fourier transform

DFT$_4$
dialyzable free thyroxine

DFU
dead fetus in utero
dideoxyfluorouridine

5′-DFUR
5′-deoxy-5-fluorouridine

DFV
diarrhea with fever and vomiting

DFX
desferrioxamine

DG
dark ground
dentate gyrus
deoxyglucose *also* 2DG
diagnosis *also* D, Dg, Diag, diag,
  Dx, dx
diastolic gallop
diglyceride
distogingival
Duchenne-Griesinger (disease)

2DG
2-deoxy-D-glucose *also* DG

Dg
diagnosis *also* D, DG, Diag, diag,
  Dx, dx

dg
decigram *also* dgm

DGCI
delayed gamma camera image

DGE
delayed gastric emptying
density gradient electrophoresis

DGER
duodenogastroesophageal reflux

DGF
digoxin-like factor

DGGE
denaturing gradient gel electrophoresis

DGI
disseminated gonococcal infection

DGL
deglycyrrhizined liquorice

DG-L
deep gastric-longitudinal

DGM
ductal glandular mastectomy

dgm
decigram *also* dg

dGMP
deoxyguanosine monophosphate
deoxyguanylic acid

DGMS
Division of General Medical Services

DGN
diffuse glomerulonephritis

DGO
Diploma in Gynaecology and Obstetrics

DGP
deoxyglucose phosphate

DGR
Degranol (mannomustine)
duodenogastric reflux

DGS
developmental Gerstmann syndrome
diabetic glomerulosclerosis
Di George syndrome

DG-T
deep gastric-transverse

dGTP
deoxyguanosine triphosphate
2-deoxyguanosine-5′-triphosphate

DGV
dextrose, gelatin, Veronal (solution)

DGVB
dextrose-gelatin-Veronal buffer

DH
daily habits
day hospital
dehydrocholic acid
dehydrogenase
delayed hypersensitivity
dental habits
dental hygienist
dermatitis herpetiformis
developmental history
diaphragmatic hernia
diffuse histiocytic (lymphoma)
disseminated histoplasmosis
dominant hand
dorsal horn
drug hypersensitivity
ductal hyperplasia
Dunkin-Hartley (guinea pig)

D/H
deuterium/hydrogen (ratio)

DHA
dehydroascorbic acid
dehydroepiandrosterone *also* DEA, DHEA
dihydroacetic acid
dihydroxyacetone
district health authority

DHAD
dihydroxybis (hydroxyethylaminoethyl) amino-anthraquinone dihydrochloride (mitoxantrone hydrochloride)

DHAP
dihydroxyacetone phosphate

DHAS
dehydroepiandrosterone sulfate *also* DHEAS, DS

DHB
dihydroxybenzoic acid
duck hepatitis B

DHBS
dihydrobiopterin synthetase

DHBV
duck hepatic B virus

DHC
dehydrocholate
dehydrocholesterol

DHCA
deep hypothermia and circulatory arrest
deep hypothermia circulatory arrest

DHCC
dihydroxycholecalciferol

DHD
dissociated horizontal deviation
district health department

DHE
dihematoporphyrin ether
dihydroergocryptine *also* DHEC, DHK
dihydroergotamine

DHEA
dehydroepiandrosterone *also* DEA, DHA

DHEAS
dehydroepiandrosterone sulfate *also* DHAS, DS

D

NOTES

DHEC
dihydroergocryptine *also* DHE, DHK

DHES
Division of Health Examination
Statistics

DHEW
Department of Health, Education, and
Welfare (now Department of Health
and Human Services)

DHF
dengue hemorrhagic fever
dorsihyperflexion

DHF/DSS
dengue hemorrhagic fever/dengue
shock syndrome

DHFK
Dow Hollow Fiber kidney

DHFR
dihydrofolate reductase

DHFS
dengue hemorrhagic fever shock
(syndrome)

DHg
Doctor of Hygiene

DHHS
Department of Health and Human
Services

DHI
Dental Health International
dihydroisocodeine
dihydroxyindole

DHIA
dehydroisoandrosterol
dehydroisoandrosterone

DHIC
detrusor hyperactivity with impaired
contractility

DHK
dihydroergocryptine *also* DHE, DHEC

DHL
diffuse histiocytic lymphoma

DHM
dihydromorphine

DHMA
dihydroxymandelic acid *also* DOMA

DHMSA
Diploma of History of Medicine,
Society of Apothecaries

DHO
deuterium hydrogen oxide
dihydroergocornine *also* DHO 180

DHO 180
dihydroergocornine *also* DHO

DHODH
dihydroorotate dehydrogenase

DHP
dehydrogenated polymer
dihydroprogesterone
dihydroxyacetone phosphate

DHPc
dorsal hippocampus

DHPG
dihydroxyphenylethylene glycol
dihydroxyphenylglycol
dihydroxyproproxymethylguanine
(ganciclovir)

DHPR
dihydropteridine reductase

dhPRL
decidual prolactin

DHR
delayed hypersensitivity reaction

DHS
delayed hypersensitivity
dihydrostreptomycin *also* DHSM
duration of hospital stay
dynamic hip screw

D-5-HS
dextrose 5% in Harman solution

DHSM
dihydrostreptomycin *also* DHS

DHSS
dihydrostreptomycin sulfate

DHST
delayed hypersensitivity test

DHT
dehydrotestosterone
dihydroergotoxine
dihydrotachysterol
dihydrotestosterone
dihydrothymine
dihydroxypropyltheophylline
dissociated hypertropia

DHTP
dihydrotestosterone propionate

DHy, DHyg
Doctor of Hygiene

DHZ
  dihydralazine

DI
  (Beck) Depression Inventory
  date of injury
  Debrix Index
  defective interfering
  degradation index
  dental index
  dentinogenesis imperfecta
  deoxyribonucleic acid index
  depression inventory
  desorption ionization
  deterioration index
  detrusor instability
  diabetes insipidus
  diagnostic imaging
  diaphragm *also* diaph, DPH
  diaphragmatic *also* diaph, DPH
  disability insurance
  dispensing information
  distal intestine
  distoincisal
  dorsal interosseous
  dorsoiliacus
  dose intensity
  double indemnity
  drug information
  drug interactions
  dyskaryosis index
  dyspnea index

DI-S
  Debris Index-Simplified

D&I
  debridement and irrigation
  dry and intact

D$_I$
  insulin dialysance

Di
  didymium
  Diego (blood group)

di
  inside detail

DIA
  depolarization-induced automaticity
  diabetes *also* db, Dia, dia, diab
  drug-induced agranulocytosis

DiA
  Diego antigen

Dia
  diabetes *also* db, DIA, diab
  diabetic *also* DB, dia, diab
  diameter *also* D, d, diam
  diathermy *also* diath

dia, diab
  diabetes *also* db, DIA
  diabetic *also* DB, Dia

DIAC
  diiodothyroacetic acid

Diag, diag
  diagnosis *also* D, DG, Dg, Dx, dx
  diagonal *also* D
  diagram

DIAGNO
  differential diagnosis *also* DD, D/D,
    DDX, DDx, diff diag

diam
  diameter *also* D, d, Dia

diaph
  diaphragm *also* DI, DPH
  diaphragmatic *also* DI, DPH

DIAR
  dextran-induced anaphylactoid reaction

dias
  diastole *also* D
  diastolic

DIAS BP
  diastolic blood pressure

diath
  diathermy *also* Dia, dia

DIATH SW
  diathermy short wave

DIAZ
  diazepam

DIB
  Diagnostic Interview for Borderlines
  disability insurance benefits
  dot immunobinding
  duodenoileal bypass

NOTES

D

DIC
differential interference contrast
(microscopy)
diffuse intravascular clotting
diffuse intravascular coagulation
diffuse intravascular coagulopathy
dimethyltriazenoimidazole carboxamide
(dacarbazine)
disseminated intravascular coagulation
disseminated intravascular
coagulopathy
drip infusion cholangiography
drug information center

dic
dicentric

DICD
dispersion-induced circular dichroism

diclox
dicloxacillin

DID
dead of intercurrent disease
delayed ischemia deficit
double immunodiffusion (technique)
dystonia-improvement-dystonia

DIDD
dense intramembranous deposit
disease

di-di
dichorionic-diamniotic

DIDMOA
diabetes insipidus, diabetes mellitus,
and optic atrophy (syndrome)

DIDMOAD
diabetes insipidus, diabetes mellitus,
optic atrophy, and deafness
(syndrome) *also* DIMOAD

DIDOX
dihydroxybenzohydroxamic acid

DIE
died in emergency (room)

dieb. alt.
on alternate days [L. *diebus alternis*]

dieb. secund.
every second day [L. *diebus
secundis*]

dieb. tert.
every third day [L. *diebus tertiis*]

DIEDA
diethyliminodiacetic acid

Diet. Tech.
Dietetic Technician

DIF
diffuse interstitial fibrosis
diflunisal
direct immunofluorescence (test)
dose increase factor

dif
differential (blood count) *also* DIFF,
Diff, diff

DIFF, diff
difference *also* D, Diff
differential (blood count) *also* dif,
Diff
diffusion *also* D

Diff
difference *also* D, DIFF, diff
different
differential (blood count) *also* dif,
DIFF, diff

diff diag
differential diagnosis *also* DD, D/D,
DDX, DDx, DIAGNO

DIFP
diffuse interstitial fibrosing
pneumonitis
diisopropyl fluorophosphonate

DIG
digitalis *also* dig.
digitoxin
digoxin

dig
drug-induced galactorrhea

dig.
digitalis *also* DIG
let it be digested [L. *digeretur*]

DIGAMI
Diabetes Mellitus Insulin Glucose
Infusion in Acute Myocardial
Infarction

dig. tox
digitalis toxicity

DIH
died in hospital

DIHE
drug-induced hepatic encephalopathy

DIHPPA
diiodohydroxyphenylpyruvic acid

DIJOA
dominantly inherited juvenile optic atrophy

DIL
dilute *also* dil, dilut
diluted *also* dil, dilut
dilution *also* dil, diln, dilut
drug-induced lupus
drug information log

Dil
Dilantin
dilation *also* dil

dil
dilatation *also* dilat
dilute *also* DIL, dilut
diluted *also* DIL, dilut
dilution *also* DIL, diln, dilut

dilat
dilatation *also* dil

DILD
diffuse infiltrative lung disease
diffuse interstitial lung disease
drug-induced liver disease

DILE
drug-induced lupus erythematosus

diln
dilution *also* DIL, dil, dilut

Diluc., diluc.
at daybreak [L. *diluculo*]

dilut
dilute *also* DIL, dil
diluted *also* DIL, dil
dilution *also* DIL, dil, diln

DIM
diminish *also* dim.
divalent ion metabolism

dim.
diminish *also* DIM
one-half [L. *dimidus*]

DIMOAD
diabetes insipidus, diabetes mellitus, optic atrophy, and deafness (syndrome) *also* DIDMOAD

dIMP
deoxyinosine monophosphate (deoxyinosinate)

DIMS
disorders of initiating and maintaining sleep

DIMSA
disseminated intravascular multiple systems activation

DIMT
Dutch Ibopamine Multicenter Trial

DIND
delayed ischemic neurologic deficit

3α-diol-G
5α-androstane-3α,17β-diol glucuronide

diopt
diopter

DIOS
distal intestinal obstruction syndrome

DIP
desquamative interstitial pneumonia
desquamative interstitial pneumonitis
dichlorophenolindophenol
diisopropyl phosphate
distal interphalangeal (joint) *also* DIPJ
drip-infusion pyelogram
drug-induced parkinsonism
dual-in-line package (integrated circuits)

Dip
diplomate *also* D

dip
diploid

DIPA
diisopropylamine

DipBact
Diploma in Bacteriology

DIPC
diffuse interstitial pulmonary calcification

DipChem
Diploma in Chemistry

D

NOTES

DipClinPath
Diploma in Clinical Pathology

DIPD
daily intermittent peritoneal dialysis

DIPF
diisopropylphosphofluoridate

diph
diphtheria

diph-tet
diphtheria-tetanus (toxoid)

diph-tox
diphtheria toxoid

diph-tox AP
alum-precipitated diphtheria toxoid

DIPJ
distal interphalangeal joint *also* DIP

DipMicrobiol
Diploma in Microbiology

DipSocMed
Diploma in Social Medicine

DIR
director
double isomorphous replacement

Dir, dir
direct
director

dir.
direction [L. *directione*]

DIRD
drug-induced renal disease

dir. prop.
with proper direction [L. *directione propria*]

DIS
Diagnostic Interview Schedule
digital imaging spectrophotometer
dislocation *also* dis, Disl, disloc

dis
disability *also* DB
disabled *also* DSBL
disease *also* D, DZ, Dz
dislocation *also* DIS, Disl, disloc
distance
distribution *also* dist

DISC
Diagnostic Interview Schedule for Children
dynamic integrated stabilization chair

disc
discontinue

disch
discharge

DISH
diffuse idiopathic sclerosing hyperostosis
diffuse idiopathic skeletal hyperostosis
disseminated idiopathic skeletal hyperostosis

DISI
distal intercalated segment instability
dorsal intercalary segment instability
dorsal intercalated segment instability
dorsiflexed intercalated segment instability *also* DISMAL

DISIDA
diisopropyl iminodiacetic acid

disinfect.
disinfection

Disl
dislocation *also* DIS, dis, disloc

disloc
dislocated
dislocation *also* DIS, dis, Disl

DISMAL
dorsiflexed intercalated segment instability *also* DISI

disod
disodium

D₅ISOM
dextrose 5% in Isolyte M

disp
dispensary
dispense

dispo
disposition

diss
dissolve(d)

dissem
disseminated
dissemination

dist
distal *also* D, d
distillation *also* distill.
distill(ed)
distribute *also* dis
distribution *also* dis
district

dist fr
distinguished from

distill.
distillation *also* dist

DIT
diet-induced thermogenesis
diiodotyrosine
drug-induced thrombocytopenia

dITP
deoxyinosine triphosphate

DIU
death in utero

DIV
double-inlet ventricle

div
divergence
divergent
divide(d)
division
divorced *also* D, d
double-inlet ventricle

div.
divide [L. *dividetur*]

DIVA
digital intravenous angiography

DIVBC
disseminated intravascular blood
coagulation

DIVC
disseminated intravascular coagulation

div. in par. aeq.
divide into equal parts [L. *dividetur
in partes aequales*]

DJD
degenerative joint disease

DJOA
dominant juvenile optic atrophy

DJS
Dubin-Johnson syndrome

DK
dark *also* dk
de
decay
degeneration of keratinocytes

Déjérine-Klumpke (syndrome)
diabetic ketoacidosis *also* DKA
diet kitchen
diseased kidney
dog kidney (cells)

dk
dark *also* DK

DKA
diabetic ketoacidosis *also* DK
did not keep appointment

DKB
deep knee bends
dideoxykanamycin B

DKDP
deuterium with potassium dihydrogen
phosphate

dkg
decagram

dkL, dkl
decaliter

dkm
decameter

DKP
dibasic potassium phosphate
dikalium phosphate
diketopiperazine

DKS
Damus-Kaye-Stancel (procedure)

DKTC
dog kidney tissue culture

DKV
deer kidney virus

DL
danger list
dansyl lysine
deep lobe
developmental level
diagnostic laparoscopy
difference limen (threshold)
diffuse lymphoma
diffusing capacity of lung
directed listening
direct laryngoscopy
disabled list
distolingual

D

NOTES

DL *(continued)*
Donath-Landsteiner (antibody) *also* D-L
double lumen
drug level
lethal dose [L. *dosis letalis*]

D-L
Donath-Landsteiner (antibody) *also* DL

D$_L$
diffusing capacity of lung *also* DL

DL-
equal quantities of D and L enantiomorphs (formerly dl-)

dL, dl
deciliter

DLA, DLa
distolabial

D-L Ab
Donath-Landsteiner antibody

DLAI, DLaI
distolabioincisal

DLAP, DLaP
distolabiopulpal

DLB
diffuse and lymphoblastic
direct laryngoscopy and bronchoscopy

DL&B
direct laryngoscopy and bronchoscopy

DLBD
diffuse Lewy body disease

DLC
Dental Laboratory Conference
differential leukocyte count
distolingual cusp
double-lumen catheter

DLCL
diffuse large cell lymphoma

DLCO, DL$_{CO}$, D$_{LCO}$
diffusing capacity of lung for carbon monoxide *also* D$_{CO}$

DLCO$_2$, D$_{LCO2}$
carbon dioxide diffusing capacity of the lungs

D$_{LCO}$SB
single-breath carbon monoxide diffusing capacity of lungs

D$_{LCO}$SS
steady-state carbon monoxide diffusing capacity of lungs

DLCR
distolingual cusp ridge

DLE
delayed light emission
dialyzable leukocyte extract
discoid lupus erythematosus
disseminated lupus erythematosus

D$_1$LE
diagonal 1 lower extremity

D$_2$LE
diagonal 2 lower extremity

DLF
digitalis-like factor
digoxin-like factor
distolingual fossa
dorsolateral funiculus

DLG
distolingual groove

DLI
distolinguoincisal
double label index

DLIF
digoxin-like immunoreactive factor

DLIS
digoxin-like immunoreactive substance

DLLI
dulcitol lysine lactose iron (agar)

DLMP
date of last menstrual period

DLNMP
date of last normal menstrual period

DLO
Diploma in Laryngology and Otology
distolinguo-occlusal

DLP
delipidized serum protein
developmental learning problems
direct linear plotting
dislocation of patella
distolinguopulpal
dysharmonic luteal phase

D$_5$LR
dextrose 5% in lactated Ringer (solution)

DLS
daily living skills

DLSC
double lumen subclavian catheter

DLT
dihydroepiandrosterone loading test
dose-limiting toxicity
double lung transplant

DLU
diffused lung uptake

DLV
defective leukemia virus

DLWD
diffuse lymphocytic, well
differentiated

DM
adamsite
dermatologist
dermatology
dermatomyositis
Descemet membrane
dextromaltose
dextromethorphan
diabetes mellitus
diabetic mother
diastolic murmur
diffuse mixed
diphenylaminechlorarsine
distant metastases
Doctor of Medicine [L. *Doctor
Medicinae*] *also* M.D.
dopamine
dorsomedial
dose modification
double membrane
double minute (chromosome)
dry matter
duodenal mucosa
membrane diffusing capacity

D$_M$
membrane component of diffusion

dM
decimorgan

dm
decimeter

dm$_2$
square decimeter

dm$_3$
cubic decimeter

DMA
dimethoxyamphetamine
dimethyladenosine
dimethylamine
dimethylaniline
dimethylarginine
direct memory access (computers)

DMAARD
delayed-mechanism-of-action
antirheumatic drug

DMAB
dimethylaminoazobenzene
dimethylaminobenzaldehyde (Ehrlich
reagent) *also* DMABA

DMABA
dimethylaminobenzaldehyde (Ehrlich
reagent) *also* DMAB

DMAC
dimethylacetamide

DMAD
disease-modifying antirheumatic drug
also DMARD

DMAE
dimethylaminoethanol

DMARD
disease-modifying antirheumatic drug
also DMAD

DMAS
dimethylamine sulfate

DMC
dactinomycin, methotrexate, and
cyclophosphamide
demeclocycline
dichlorodiphenylmethylcarbinol
dimethylcysteine
direct microscopic count
p,p′-dichlorodiphenyl methyl carbinol

DMCC
direct microscopic clump count

DMCM
dimethoxyethylcarboline carboxylate

DMCT, DMCTC
dimethylchlortetracycline

NOTES

D

DMD
desmethyldiazepam *also* DMDZ
disciform macular degeneration
disease-modifying drug
Doctor of Dental Medicine
Duchenne muscular dystrophy
dystonia musculorum deformans

DMDS
dimethyl disulfide

DMDT
dimethoxydiphenyltrichloroethane

DMDZ
desmethyldiazepam *also* DMD

DME
degenerative myoclonus epilepsy
dimethyl diester
dimethyl ether
diphasic meningoencephalitis
director of medical education
dropping mercury electrode
drug-metabolizing enzyme
Dulbecco modified Eagle (medium)
also DMEM
durable medical equipment

DMEM
Dulbecco modified Eagle medium
also DME

DMF
decayed, missing, and filled
(permanent teeth)
dimethylformamide *also* DMFA
diphasic milk fever

dmf
decayed, missing, and filled
(deciduous teeth)

DMFA
dimethylformamide *also* DMF

DMFO
eflornithine

DMFS
decayed, missing, or filled surface
(permanent teeth)

dmfs
decayed, missing, or filled surface
(deciduous teeth)

DMG
dimethylglycine

DMGBL
dimethyl-γ-butyrolactone

DMGG
dimethylguanylguanidine

DMH
Department of Mental Health
Department of Mental Hygiene
diffuse mesangial hypercellularity
dimethylhydrazine

DMI
defense mechanism inventory
desipramine
desmethylimipramine
diabetic muscle infarction
Diagnostic Mathematics Inventory
(psychologic testing)
diaphragmatic myocardial infarct
direct migration inhibition

DMJ
Diploma in Medical Jurisprudence

DMKA
diabetes mellitus ketoacidosis

DML
diffuse mixed lymphoma
distal motor latency

DMM
diffuse malignant mesothelioma
dimethylmyleran
disproportionate micromelia

DMN
dimethylnitrosamine *also* DMNA
dorsal motor nucleus (of vagus)

DMNA
dimethylnitrosamine *also* DMN

DMNL
dorsomedial hypothalamic nucleus
lesion

DMO
dimethyloxazolindinedione

DMOOC
diabetes mellitus out of control

DMP
diffuse mesangial proliferation
dimethylphosphate
dimethylphthalate
dura mater prosthesis

DMPA
demedroxyprogesterone acetate
depomedroxyprogesterone acetate

DMPE
dimethoxyphenylethylamine

DMPP
dimethylphenylpiperazinium
dimethyl-4-phenylpiperazinium

DMPS
dysmyelopoietic syndrome

DMR
Diploma in Medical Radiology
Directorate of Medical Research
distal marginal ridge

DMRE
Diploma in Medical Radiology and
Electrology

DMRF
dorsal medullary reticular formation

DMS
delayed microembolism syndrome
delayed muscle soreness
demarcation membrane system
dense microsphere
Department of Medicine and Surgery
dermatomyositis
diagnostic medical sonography
diffuse mesangial sclerosis
dimethyl sulfate
dimethyl sulfoxide *also* DMSO
Doctor of Medical Science
dysmyelopoietic syndrome

dms
double minute sphere

DMSA
2,3-dimercaptosuccinic acid
dimercaptosuccinic acid (scintigraphy)
disodium monomethanearsonate
Tc-dimercaptosuccinic acid

DMSLT
daytime multiple sleep latency test

DMSO
dimethyl sulfoxide *also* DMS

DMT
dermatophytosis
dimethyltryptamine
Doctor of Medical Technology
N,N-dimethyltryptamine

DMTU
dimethylthiourea

DMU
dimethanolurea

DMV
Doctor of Veterinary Medicine

DMVA
direct mechanical ventricular actuation

D,M,V,P
disk, macula, vessels, periphery

DMWP
distal mean wave pressure

DMX
diathermy, massage, and exercise

DN
Deiters nucleus
dextrose-nitrogen (ratio)
diabetic neuropathy
dibucaine number
dicrotic notch
Diploma in Nursing
Diploma in Nutrition
District Nurse
Doctor of Nursing
down
dysplastic nevus

D&N
distance and near (vision)

D/N
dextrose/nitrogen (ratio)

Dn
dekanem

dn
decinem

DNA
deoxyribonucleic acid
did not answer
did not attend
does not apply

DNAP
deoxyribonucleic acid polymerase

DNA-P
deoxyribonucleic acid phosphorus

DNAse, DNase
deoxyribonuclease

D

NOTES

DNB
dinitrobenzene
Diplomate of the National Board of
Medical Examiners
dorsal noradrenergic bundle

DNBP
dinitrobutylphenol

DNBT
dinitroblue

DNC
did not come
dinitrocarbanilide

DNCB
dinitrochlorobenzene

DND
died a natural death

DNE
Director of Nursing Education
Doctor of Nursing Education

DNFB
dinitrofluorobenzene (Sanger reagent)

DNH
diffuse nodular hyperplasia

DNI
do not intubate

DNKA
did not keep appointment

DNL
diffuse nodular lymphoma
disseminated necrotizing
leukoencephalopathy

DNLL
dorsal nucleus of lateral lemniscus

DNM
daunomycin
descending necrotizing mediastinitis

DNO
District Nursing Officer

DNOC
dinitroorthocresol

DNOCHP
dinitro-*o*-cyclohexyphenol

DNP
deoxyribonucleoprotein *also* Dnp
dinitrophenol
2,4-dinitrophenol *also* Dnp
dynamic nuclear polarization

Dnp
deoxyribonucleoprotein *also* DNP
2,4-dinitrophenol *also* DNP

DNPH
dinitrophenylhydrazine

DNPM
dinitrophenolmorphine

DNPT
diethylnitrophenyl thiophosphate
(parathion) *also* DNTP

DNR
daunorubicin
did not respond
do not report
do not resuscitate
dorsal nerve root

DNS
dansyl *also* Dns
de novo synthesis
deviated nasal septum
diaphragmatic nerve stimulation
did not show
(doctor) did not see (patient)
Doctor of Nursing Services
do not show
do not substitute
dysplastic nevus syndrome

D₅NS, D₅NSS
dextrose 5% in normal saline
solution

Dns
dansyl *also* DNS

DNT
did not test

DNTM
disseminated nontuberculous
mycobacterial (infection)

DNTP
diethylnitrophenyl thiophosphate
(parathion) *also* DNPT

DNUA
distillable nonurea adductable

DNV
dorsal nucleus of vagus

DO
diamine oxidase (histaminase)
diet order
digoxin
Diploma in Ophthalmology
Diploma in Osteopathy

dissolved oxygen
distoocclusal
Doctor of Ophthalmology
Doctor of Osteopathy
doctor's orders
doxycycline
drugs only

D-O
directive-organic

D/O
disorder

D$_1$O$_2$
diffusing capacity of lungs for oxygen

D$_o$
oxygen diffusion

d/o
died of

do.
the same, as before [L. *dicto*]

DOA
date of admission
date of arrival
dead on arrival
diagnostic and operative arthroscopy
dominant optic atrophy
duration of action

DOAC
Dubois oleic albumin complex

DOA-DRA
dead on arrival despite resuscitative attempts

DOAP
daunorubicin, Oncovin (vincristine), araC (cytarabine), and prednisone

DOB
date of birth *also* DB, D/B
delta over baseline
dobutamine
doctor's order book

DOC
date of conception
deoxycholate
deoxycorticosterone

diabetes out of control *also* doc, DOOC
died of other causes
diet of choice
disorder of cornification
drug of choice

doc
diabetes out of control *also* DOC, DOOC
doctor *also* DR, Dr
document
documentation

DOCA
deoxycorticosterone acetate

DOCG
deoxycorticosterone glucoside

DOCLINE
Documents On-Line

DOCS, DOCs
deoxycorticoids

DOcSc
Doctor of Ocular Science

DOC-SR
deoxycorticosterone secretion rate

DOD
date of death
date of discharge
dead of disease
dementia (syndrome) of depression
died of disease
dissolved oxygen deficit

DOE
date of examination
desoxyephedrine
direct observation evaluation
dyspnea on exercise
dyspnea on exertion

DOES
disorders of excessive sleepiness

DOET
dimethoxyethylamphetamine

DOF
degrees of freedom

D

NOTES

DOFOS
disturbance of function occlusion syndrome

DOG
distal oblique groove

DOH
Department of Health

DOHb
Döhle bodies

DOHyg
Diploma in Occupational Hygiene

DOI
date of injury
depth of insertion
died of injuries

DOL
day of life
day of life (followed by number)

dol
dolorimetric unit (of pain intensity)

DOLLS
(Lee) double-loop locking suture

DOLV
double-outlet left ventricle

DOM
deaminated *O*-methyl metabolite
Department of Medicine
dimethoxy-methylamphetamine
2,5-dimethoxy-4-methylamphetamine
dissolved organic matter
dominance *also* D, dom
dominant *also* D, dom

dom
domestic
dominance *also* D, DOM
dominant *also* D, DOM

DOMA
dihydroxymandelic acid *also* DHMA

DOMS
delayed-onset muscle soreness
Diploma in Ophthalmic Medicine and Surgery
Doctor of Orthopedic Medicine and Surgery

DON
diazooxonorleucine
Director of Nursing

don.
until [L. *donec*]

donec alv. sol. fuerit
until bowels are opened (until a bowel movement takes place) [L. *donec alvus soluta fuerit*]

DOOC
diabetes out of control *also* DOC, doc

DOOR
deafness, onychoosteodystrophy, and mental retardation (syndrome)

DOPA
dihydroxyphenylalanine *also* Dopa, dopa
3,4-dihydroxyphenylalanine *also* dopa

Dopa
dihydroxyphenylalanine *also* DOPA, dopa

dopa
dihydroxyphenylalanine *also* Dopa, DOPA
3,4-dihydroxyphenylalanine *also* DOPA, Dopa

DOPAC
dihydrophenylacetic acid

dopase
dihydroxyphenylalanine *also* Dopa, dopa

DOPC
determined osteogenic precursor cell

DOPE
disease-oriented physician education

Doph
Doctor of Ophthalmology

DOPP
dihydroxyphenylpyruvate

DOPS
diffuse obstructive pulmonary syndrome
dihydroxyphenylserine

DORC
Dutch Ophthalmic Research Center

Dors
dorsal

Dorth
Diploma in Orthodontics
Diploma in Orthoptics

DORV
double-outlet right ventricle

DoRx
> date of treatment

DOS
> day of surgery
> deoxystreptamine
> disk operating system
> Doctor of Ocular Science
> Doctor of Optical Science

dos
> dosage *also* D, d
> dose *also* D, d

DOSC
> Dubois oleic serum complex

DOSS
> Department of Social Services
> dioctyl sodium sulfosuccinate
> (docusate sodium)
> distal over-shoulder strap

DOST
> direct oocyte sperm transfer

DOT
> date of transcription
> date of transfer
> died on (operating) table
> directly observed therapy
> direct oocyte transfer
> Doppler ophthalmic test

DOTA
> tetraazacyclododecanetetraacetic acid

DOTC
> Dameshek oval target cell

DOTP
> tetraazacyclododecanetetraacetic
> tetramethylene phosphonate

DOU
> direct observation unit

DOV
> discharged on visit

DOX, Dox
> doxorubicin

Doxy
> D. 100

D-P
> dialysis to plasma (urea ratio)

DP
> data processing
> debonding pliers
> deep pulse
> definitive procedure
> degradation product
> degree of polymerization
> deltopectoral
> dementia praecox
> dementia pugillistica
> dense plate
> dental prosthesis
> dental prosthodontics
> developed pressure
> dexamethasone pretreatment
> diaphragmatic plaque
> diastolic pressure
> diffuse precipitation
> diffusion pressure
> digestible protein
> diphosgene
> diphosphate
> dipropionate
> directional preponderance
> disability pension
> discharge planning
> discriminating power
> disopyramide phosphate
> displaced person
> distal pancreatectomy
> distal phalanx
> distal pit
> distopulpal
> Doctor of Pharmacy
> Doctor of Podiatry
> donor's plasma
> dorsalis pedis
> driving pressure
> dyspnea *also* Dp, dysp
> D-penicillamine *also* DPA, d-pen
> with proper direction [L. *directione*
> *propria*] *also* d.p.

Dp
> dyspnea *also* DP, dysp

d.p.
> with proper direction [L. *directione*
> *propria*] *also* DP

DPA
> Department of Public Assistance

NOTES

D

DPA *(continued)*
Designed Plan Agencies (medical records)
dextroposition of aorta
diphenolic acid
diphenylalanine
diphenylamine
dipicolinic acid
dipropylacetate
dual photon absorptiometry *also* DPX
dynamic physical activity
D-penicillamine *also* DP, d-pen

d. in p. aeq.
divide into equal parts [L. *dividetur in partes aequales*]

DPB
days postburn
diffuse panbronchiolitis

DPC
delayed primary closure
desaturated phosphatidylcholine
direct patient care
discharge planning coordinator
distal palmar crease

DPCRT
double-blind placebo-controlled randomized clinical trial

DPD
depression pure disease
desoxypyridoxine hydrochloride
diffuse pulmonary disease
diphenamid
Diploma in Public Dentistry
dual photon densitometry

DPDA
phosphorodiamidic anhydride

DPDL
diffuse poorly differentiated lymphoma

DPDT, dpdt
double-pole double-throw (switch)

dP/dt
upstroke pattern on apex cardiogram

DPE
Death Personification Exercise (psychology)
dipiperidinoethane

DPEG
dual percutaneous endoscopic gastrostomy

d-pen
D-penicillamine *also* DP, DPA

DPF
Dental Practitioners' Formulary

DPFR
diastolic pressure-flow relationship

DPG
diphosphoglycerate
displacement placentogram

DPGN
diffuse proliferative glomerulonephritis

DPGP
diphosphoglycerate phosphatase

DPH
Department of Public Health
diaphragm *also* DI, diaph
diaphragmatic *also* DI, diaph
diphenhydramine
diphenylhexatriene
diphenylhydantoin
Diploma in Public Health
Doctor of Public Health/Hygiene *also* DrPH

DPharm
Doctor of Pharmacy

DPhC
Doctor of Pharmaceutical Chemistry

DPhc
Doctor of Pharmacology

DPHN
Doctor of Public Health Nursing

Dphys
Diploma in Physiotherapy

DphysMed
Diploma in Physical Medicine

DPI
daily permissible intake
daily protein intake
days postinoculation
dietary protein intake
diphtheria-pertussis immunization
drug-prescribing index
Dynamic Personality Inventory

DPIF
Drug Product Information File

DPJ
dementia paralytica juvenilis

DPL
diagnostic peritoneal lavage

dipalmitoyl lecithin
distopulpolingual

DPLa
distopulpolabial

DPM
digital phase mapping
Diploma in Psychological Medicine
dipyridamole
disabling pansclerotic morphea
discontinue previous medication
disintegrations per minute *also* dpm
Doctor of Physical Medicine
Doctor of Podiatric Medicine
Doctor of Preventative Medicine
Doctor of Psychiatric Medicine
dopamine
drops per minute

dpm
disintegrations per minute *also* DPM

DPN
dermatosis papalosa nigra
diabetic peripheral neuropathy
diabetic polyneuropathy
diphosphopyridine nucleotide *also*
DPNase, DPNH
disabling pansclerotic morphea

DPNase
diphosphopyridine nucleotidase *also*
DPN, DPNH

DPNB
dorsal penile nerve block

DPNH
diphosphopyridine nucleotide
(nicotinamide adenine dinucleotide,
reduced) *also* DPN, DPNase

DPP
differential pulse polarography
dimethoxyphenylpenicillin
dorsalis pedal pulse

DPPC
dipalmitoylphosphatidylcholine

DPR
doctor/population ratio

DPS
dimethylpolysiloxane (simethicone-
antiflatulent)
dysesthetic pain syndrome

dps
disintegrations per second

DPSS
Department of Public Social Service

DPST, dpst
double-pole single-throw (switch)

DPT
Demerol, Phenergan, and Thorazine
department
dichotic pitch (discrimination) test
diphosphothiamine
diphtheria, pertussis, and tetanus
(vaccine)
diphtheric pseudotabes
dipropyltryptamine
dumping provocation test

DPTA
diethylenetriamine pentaacetic acid
also DTPA

^{99mTc}-DPTA
technetium-99m diethylenetriamine
pentaacetic acid

DPTI
diastolic pressure-time index

DPTP
diphtheria, pertussis, tetanus, and
poliomyelitis (vaccine)

DPTPM
diphtheria, pertussis, tetanus,
poliomyelitis, and measles (vaccine)

Dptr
diopter *also* D, d, diopt

DPU
delayed pressure urticaria

DPUD
duodenal peptic ulcer disease

DPV
disabling positional vertigo

DPVNS
diffuse pigmented villonodular
synovitis

D

NOTES

DPW
distal phalangeal width

DPX
dextropropoxyphene
dual photon absorptiometry *also* DPA

DQ
development quotient

Dq
curvilinear threshold shoulder

DR
degeneration reaction
Déjérine-Roussey (syndrome)
delivery room
deoxyribose
diabetic retinopathy *also* dr
diagnostic radiology
diffuse redness
disposable/reusable
distal root
distribution ratio
diurnal rhythm
doctor *also* doc, Dr
donor-related
dorsal raphe
dorsal root *also* dr
dose ratio
drug receptor
dual-chamber rate-responsive
reaction of degeneration (muscle
  fibers) *also* DeR

Dr
doctor *also* doc, DR
rare detail response

dr
diabetic retinopathy *also* DR
dorsal root *also* DR
drachm
drain
dram
dressing *also* DRSG, drsg, dsg
(unusual rare) detail response

DRA
despite resuscitation attempts
dextran-reactive antibody
disease-resistant antigen
drug-related admissions

DRAM
deepithelialized rectus abdominis
  muscle (graft)
dynamic random access memory

dr ap
dram, apothecaries' (weight)

DRAT
differential rheumatoid agglutination
  test

DRB
daunorubicin *also* DAUNO

DRBC
denatured red blood cell
dog red blood cell *also* DRC
donkey red blood cell

DRC
damage risk criteria
dendritic reticulum cell
digitorenocerebral (syndrome)
dog red (blood) cell *also* DRBC
dorsal root, cervical

dRCA
distal right coronary artery

DRD
dorsal root dilator

DRE
digital rectal examination

DREF
dose reduction effectiveness factor

D reg.
diseased region

DRESS
depth-resolved surface (coil)
  spectroscopy

DREZ
dorsal root entry zone

DRF
daily replacement factor (of
  lymphocytes)
dose-reduction factor

DRG
diagnosis-related group
dorsal respiratory group
dorsal root ganglion
duodenal-gastric reflux gastropathy

drg, DRGE
drainage *also* drng
draining *also* drng

DrHyg
Doctor of Hygiene

DRI
Discharge Readiness Inventory

dRib
deoxyribose

DRID
double radial immunodiffusion
double radioisotope derivative

DRL, DRl
differential reinforcement of low
(response rates)
dorsal root, lumbar
dorsoradial ligament
drug-related lupus

D5RL
5% dextrose in Ringer lactate
(solution)

DRM
drug-related morbidity

DRME
Division of Research in Medical
Education

Dr Med
Doctor of Medicine *also* M.D.

DRMS
drug reaction-monitoring system

DrMT
Doctor of Mechanotherapy

DRN
dorsal raphe nucleus
drug-related neutropenia

drng
drainage *also* drg, DRGE
draining *also* drg, DRGE

DRnt
diagnostic roentgenology

DRO
differential reinforcement of other
(behavior)

DRP
digoxin reduction product
dorsal root potential

DrPH
Doctor of Public Health/Hygiene *also*
DPH

DRQ
discomfort relief quotient

DRR
dorsal root reflex

DRS, DRs
descending rectal septum
dorsal root, sacral
drowsiness
Duane retraction syndrome
dynamic renal scintigraphy
Dyskinesia Rating Scale

DRSG, drsg
dressing *also* dr, dsg

DRSP
drug-resistant *Streptococcus
pneumoniae*

DRT, DRT
dorsal root, thoracic
drug-related thrombocytopenia

dRTA
distal renal-tubular acidosis

DRUB
drug (screen) blood

DRUJ
distal radioulnar joint

DRVVT
dilute Russell viper venom test

DS
dead (air) space
Debré-Semelaigne (syndrome)
deep sedative
deep sleep
defined substrate
dehydroepiandrosterone sulfate *also*
DHAS, DHEAS
Déjérine-Sottas (syndrome)
delayed sensitivity
dendritic spine
density (optical) standard
dental surgery
deprivation syndrome
dermatan sulfate
dermatology and syphilology *also*
D&S
desynchronized sleep
Devic syndrome
dextran sulfate
dextrose-saline
dextrose stick
diaphragm stimulation
diastolic murmur

D

NOTES

DS *(continued)*
difference spectroscopy
diffuse scleroderma
digit span
dihydrostreptomycin
dilute strength
dioptric strength
Disaster Services (of Red Cross)
discharge summary
discrimination score
discriminative stimulus
disoriented
disseminated sclerosis
dissolved solids
Doctor of Science
donor's serum
Doppler sonography
double-stranded
double strength
double subordinance
Down syndrome
driving signal
drug store
dry swallow
dumping syndrome
duration of systole

D-S
Doerfler-Stewart (test)

D-5-S
5% dextrose in saline solution
dextrose 5% in saline (solution)

D/S
day of surgery
dextrose/saline
dextrose and sodium chloride

D&S
dermatology and syphilology *also* DS
diagnostic and surgical
dilation and suction

Ds
associative detail response to white
space

ds
double-stranded (DNA, RNA)

DSA
digital subtraction angiography
digital subtraction arteriography
disease-susceptible antigen

DSACT, D-SACT
direct sinoatrial conduction time

DSAP
disseminated superficial actinic
porokeratosis

DSAS
discrete subaortic stenosis

DSB
detachable silicone balloon

Dsb
single-breath diffusing (capacity)

DSBB
double-sheath bronchial brushing

DSBL
disabled *also* dis

DSBT
donor-specific blood transfusion

DSC
decussation of superior cerebellar
(peduncles)
De Sanctis-Cacchione (syndrome)
differential scanning colorimeter
disodium chromoglycate *also* DSCG
disodium cromoglycate
dobutamine stress echocardiography
also DSE
Doctor of Surgical Chiropody
Down syndrome child

DSc
Doctor of Science

DSCF
Doppler-shifted constant frequency

DSCG
disodium cromoglycate *also* DSC

DSCT
dorsal spinocerebellar tract

DSD
depressed spectrum disease
depression sine depression
detrusor sphincter dyssynergia
discharge summary dictated
dry sterile dressing

DSDB
direct self-destructive behavior

DSDDT
double-sampling dye dilution
technique

dsDNA
double-stranded deoxyribonucleic acid

DSDS
daughter sites of dimer strands

DSE
digital subtraction echocardiogram
digital subtraction echocardiography
dobutamine stress echocardiography
also DSC
Doctor of Sanitary Engineering

d. seq.
on the following day [L. *die sequente*]

DSF
disulfiram
dry sterile fluff

DSG
deoxyspergualin *also* DSP
dry sterile gauze

dsg
dressing *also* dr, DRSG, drsg

DSH
deliberate self-harm
dexamethasone-suppressible
  hyperaldosteronism

DSHR
delayed skin hypersensitivity reaction

DSI
deep shock insulin
Depression Status Inventory
digital subtraction imaging
drug-seeking index

DSIAR
double-stapled ileoanal reservoir

DSIM
Doctor of Science in Industrial
  Medicine

DSIP
delta sleep-inducing peptide

DSL
distal sensory latency

DSL M-U
distal sensory latency–median-ulnar

dslv
dissolve

DSM
degradable starch microspheres
dextrose solution mixture

Diagnostic and Statistical Manual (of
  Mental Disorders)
dihydrostreptomycin
Diploma in Social Medicine
dried skim milk

DSO
distal subungual onychomycosis

DSP
decreased sensory perception
delayed sleep phase
deoxyspergualin *also* DSG
dexamethasone sodium phosphate
dibasic sodium phosphate
digital signal processor
digital subtraction phlebography

DSp
digit span

DSPC
disaturated phosphatidylcholine

D-spine
dorsal spine

DSPN
distal sensory polyneuropathy
distal symmetrical polyneuropathy

DSR
dental stain remover
distal splenorenal
double simultaneous recording
dynamic spatial reconstructor

DSRCT
desmoplastic small round-cell tumor

DSRF
drainage subretinal fluid

dsRNA
double-stranded ribonucleic acid

DSRS
distal splenorenal shunt

DSS
dengue shock syndrome
Developmental Sentence Scoring
dioctyl sodium sulfosuccinate
disability status scale
docusate sodium

DSSc
Diploma in Sanitary Science

D

NOTES

DSSEP
dermatomal somatosensory-evoked potential

DSST
digit symbol substitutional test

DST
desensitization test
desensitization time
dexamethasone suppression test
dihydrostrepto-mycin
disproportionate septal thickening
donor-specific transfusion
duodenal secretin test

D-stix
Dextrostix

DSU
day surgery unit
double setup

DSUH
directed suggestion under hypnosis

DSur
Doctor of Surgery

DSV
digital subtraction ventriculography

DSVP
downstream venous pressure

DSWI
deep surgical wound infection

DSX
Dextrostix

DSy
digit symbol

DT
Déjérine-Thomas (syndrome)
delirium tremens *also* DTs
dental technician
depression of transmission
dietetic technician
differently tested
digitoxin
diphtheria-tetanus (immunization)
diphtheria toxoid
discharge tomorrow
dispensing tablet
distal tubule
distance test (hearing)
dorsalis tibialis
double tachycardia
doubling time (of tumor size)
duration tetany

duration of tetany *also* Dt
dye test

D/T
date of treatment
deaths/total (ratio)

D&T
diagnosis and treatment
dictated and typed

Dt
duration of tetany *also* DT

dT
deoxythymidine

d4T
didehydrodeoxythymidine
Zerit

DTA
differential thermoanalysis

DTB
dedicated time block

DTBC
D-tubocurarine *also* DTC, dTc

DTBN
di-*tert*-butyl nitroxide

DTBP
di-*tert*-butyl peroxide *also* DBP

DTC, dTc
day treatment center
differentiated thyroid carcinoma
D-tubocurarine *also* DTBC

DTCD
Diploma in Tuberculosis and Chest Diseases

DTD, dtd
delivered total dose

d.t.d.
daily therapeutic dose [L. *dosis therapeutica die*]
give such a dose [L. *detur talis dosis*]

dTDP
deoxythymidine diphosphate
thymidine diphosphate
thymidine 5′-diphosphate

DTE
desiccated thyroid extract

2-D TEE
two-dimensional transesophageal echocardiography

DTF
> detector transfer function
> distal triangular fossa

D-TGA, d-TGA
> dextro-transposition of great arteries
> D-transposition of great arteries

DTH
> delayed-type hypersensitivity (reaction)

dThd
> thymidine

DTIC
> dacarbazine
> dimethyltriazenoimidazolecarboxamide

DTICH
> delayed traumatic intracerebral
> hemorrhage

D time
> dream time

DTLA
> Detroit Tests of Learning Aptitude

DTM
> dermatophyte test medium

DTMA
> deoxycorticosterone trimethylacetate

DTMC
> ditrichloromethylcarbinol

DTMP, dTMP
> de novo thymidylate (synthesis)
> deoxythmidine monophosphate
> deoxythymidylic acid
> thymidine 5′-monophosphate

DTMVmax
> diastolic transmembrane voltage,
> maximum

DTN
> diphtheria toxin, normal

DTO
> deodorized tincture of opium

DTP
> diphtheria, tetanus, and pertussis
> (vaccine)
> distal tingling on percussion (Tinel
> sign)

DTPA
> diethylenetriamine pentaacetic acid
> *also* DPTA

DTPT
> dithiopropylthiamine

DTR
> deep tendon reflex

DTRTT
> digital temperature recovery time test

DTS
> dense tubular system
> diphtheria toxin sensitivity
> discrete time sample
> donor transfusion, specific

DTs
> delirium tremens *also* DT

DTT
> device for transverse traction
> diagnostic and therapeutic team
> diphtheria-tetanus toxoid
> direct transverse reaction
> dithiothreitol

dTTP
> deoxythymidine triphosphate
> thymidine 5′-triphosphate

DTUS
> diathermy, traction, and ultrasound

DTV
> due to void

DT-VAC
> diphtheria-tetanus vaccine

DTVMI
> Developmental Test of Visual Motor
> Integration

DTVP
> Developmental Test of Visual
> Perception

DTX
> detoxification

DTZ
> diatrizoate

DU
> decubitus ulcer
> density (optical) unknown

D

NOTES

DU *(continued)*
  deoxyuridine
  dermal ulcer
  diabetic urine
  diagnosis undetermined
  dialytic ultrafiltration
  diazouracil
  diffuse and undifferentiated
  dog unit
  dose unit
  duodenal ulcer
  duroxide uptake
  Dutch (rabbit)

D$_U$
  urea dialysance

dU
  deoxyuridine

du
  dial unit

DUA
  dorsal uterine artery

DUB
  Dubowitz (score)
  dysfunctional uterine bleeding

DUCCS
  Duke University Clinical Cardiology
  Study

dUDP
  deoxyuridine diphosphate

D$_1$UE
  diagonal 1 upper extremity

D$_2$UE
  diagonal 2 upper extremity

DUF
  Doppler ultrasonic flowmeter

DUI
  driving under the influence

DUID
  driving under the influence of drugs

DUL
  diffuse undifferentiated lymphoma

dulc.
  sweet [L. *dulcis*]

DUM
  dorsal unpaired median (axon,
  neuron)

dUMP
  deoxyuridine monophosphate

DUNHL
  diffuse undifferentiated non-Hodgkins
  lymphoma

duod
  duodenal
  duodenum

dup
  duplicate
  duplication

DUR
  Drug Usage Review
  duration *also* D, d, dur

dur
  duration *also* D, d, DUR
  hard [L. *duris*]

dur. dol., dur. dolor.
  while pain lasts [L. *durante dolore*]

DUS
  distal urethral stenosis
  Doppler ultrasound stethoscope

DUSN
  diffuse unilateral subacute
  neuroretinitis ("wipe-out" syndrome)

DUV
  damaging ultraviolet

DV
  dependent variable
  dilute volume (of solution)
  distance vision
  distemper virus
  domiciliary visit
  dorsoventral
  double vibrations (unit of frequency
  of sound waves) *also* dv
  double vision *also* dv

D&V
  diarrhea and vomiting
  discs and vessels (ophthalmology)
  ductions and versions

dv
  double vibrations (unit of frequency
  of sound waves) *also* DV
  double vision *also* DV

DVA
  desacetylvinblastine amide (vindesine)
  developmental venous anomaly
  distance visual acuity
  duration of voluntary apnea (test)

D/VA
  diffusion per unit of alveolar volume

D value
decimal reduction time

DVB
cis-diamminedichloroplatinum, vindesine, and bleomycin
divinylbenzene

DVC
direct visualization of vocal cords
divanillalcyclohexanone

DVCC
Disease Vector Control Center

DVD
dissociated vertical deviation
dissociated vertical divergence
double-vessel disease

DV&D
Diploma in Venereology and Dermatology

DVDALV
double-vessel disease with abnormal left ventricle

DVE
duck virus enteritis

DVH
Division for the Visually Handicapped

DVI
atrioventricular sequential pacing
deep venous insufficiency
digital vascular imaging (system) *also* DVIS
Doppler (systolic) velocity index

DVIS
digital vascular imaging system *also* DVI

DVIU
direct vision internal urethrotomy

DVL
deep vastus lateralis

DVLP
daunomycin, vincristine, L-asparaginase, and prednisone

DVM
digital voltmeter
Doctor of Veterinary Medicine

DVMS
Doctor of Veterinary Medicine and Surgery

DVN
dorsal vagal nucleus

DVPA
daunorubicin, vincristine, prednisone, and L-asparaginase *also* DVPL-ASP

DVPL-ASP
daunorubicin, vincristine, prednisone, and L-asparaginase *also* DVPA

DVR
derotational varus osteotomy
digital vascular reactivity
Diploma in Vocational Rehabilitation
Doctor of Veterinary Radiology
double valve replacement
double vein graft
double ventricular response

DVS
direct vesicoureteral scintigraphy
Doctor of Veterinary Science *also* DVSc
Doctor of Veterinary Surgery

DVSA
digital venous subtraction angiography

DVSc
Doctor of Veterinary Science *also* DVS

DVT
deep vein thrombosis
deep venous thrombosis

DVTS
deep venous thromboscintigram

DVXI
direct vision times one

DW
daily weight
deionized water
dextrose in water *also* D/W
distilled water
doing well *also* D/W
dry weight
whole response to detail

NOTES

D5W, D₅W
dextrose 5% in water (solution)

D10W
10% aqueous dextrose solution

D/W
dextrose in water (percent) *also* DW
doing well *also* DW
dry to wet

D₅W (*var. of* D5W)
5% dextrose in water

dw
dwarf (mouse)

DWA
died from wounds

DWD
died with disease

DWDL
diffuse well-differentiated lymphocytic (lymphoma)

DWI
driving while impaired
driving while intoxicated

DWMI
deep white-matter infarct

DWRT
delayed work recall test

DWS
Dandy-Walker syndrome
Disaster Warning System

DWT
Dichotic Word Test

dwt
pennyweight

DX
Dextran
dicloxacillin

Dx
diagnosis *also* D, DG, Dg, Diag, diag, dx
diagnostic therapy

dx
diagnosis *also* D, DG, Dg, Diag, diag, Dx

DXA
dual-energy x-ray absorptiometry *also* DEXA

DXD, Dxd
discontinued

DXM
dexamethasone (suppression test)

DXR
deep x-ray
delayed xenograft rejection
doxorubicin

DXRT
deep x-ray therapy *also* DXT

DXT
deep x-ray therapy *also* DXRT
dextrose

dXTP
deoxyxanthine triphosphate

D-XYL
d-xylose (in urine)

DY
dense parenchyma
Dyke-Young (syndrome)

Dy
dysprosium

dy
dystrophia muscularis

dyn
dynamics
dynamometer
dyne

DYNAFLUVE
dynamic fluorescence video endoscopy

dysp
dyspnea *also* DP, Dp

DZ
diazepam *also* DZP
disease *also* D, dis, Dz
dizygotic
dizygous
dizziness

Dz, dz
disease *also* DZ

DZAPO
daunorubicin, azacytidine, araC (cytarabine), prednisone, and Oncovin (vincristine)

DZP
diazepam *also* DZ

DZT
dizygotic twins

E

air dose
cortisone (compound E)
edema *also* ed
einstein (unit of energy)
elastance
electric affinity *also* EA
electric charge *also* e
electric field vector
electrode potential
electromagnetic force
electron *also* e
embryo *also* Emb
emmetropia
enamel
encephalitis
endangered (animal)
endogenous
endoplasm
enema *also* En, en, enem
energy
engorged
enterococcus
entgegen
enzyme
eosinophil
epicondyle
epinephrine *also* EPI, epineph
epsilon (fifth letter of Greek
  alphabet), uppercase
error
erythrocyte *also* Er, er, ERY, Ery,
  eryth
erythroid
erythromycin *also* EM, ETM
esophagus *also* ES, ESO, eso, esoph
esophoria (for distance)
ester *also* est
estradiol *also* E-diol
ethanol *also* ET, ETH, ETOH
ethmoid (sinus)
ethyl *also* ET, Et
etiocholanolone
etiology
exa-
examiner
exercise *also* Ex, ex, exer
expectancy (wave)
expected frequency in a cell of a
  contingency table
experiment(al) *also* exp, exper, exptl
expired (air)
expired (died) *also* exp

expired (gas)
extension *also* EXT
extinction (coefficient)
extraction fraction
extraction ratio
extralymphatic
eye
glutamic acid *also* Glu
glutamyl *also* Glu
internal energy
kinetic energy of a particle
mathematical expectation
opposite (stereo descriptor to indicate
  configuration at a double bond)
  [Ger. *entgegen*]
redox potential
vectorcardiography electrode
  (midsternal)
vitamin E

E′

esophoria (for near)

E°

standard electrode potential

E*

lesion on erythrocyte cell membrane
  at the site of complement fixation

E+

positron (positive electron)

E⁻, e⁻

negative electron

E₁

estrone

E₂

estradiol
17-β-estradiol

E₃

estriol *also* Es

E₄

estetrol

e

base of natural logarithms
early
egg transfer
electric charge *also* E
electron *also* E
elementary charge
erg
from [L. *ex*]

e⁻ (*var. of* E⁻)

4E
four plus edema

EA
early amniocentesis
early antigen
educational age
egg albumin
elbow aspiration
electric affinity *also* E, E₀
electroacupuncture *also* EAC
electroanesthesia
electrophysiologic abnormality
embryonic antibody
embryonic antigen
emergency area
endocardiographic amplifier
enteral alimentation
enteroanastomosis
enzymatic active
epiandrosterone
epidural anesthesia
erythrocyte antibody
erythrocyte antisera
esophageal atresia
esterase activity
estivoautumnal (malaria)
ethacrynic acid

E&A
evaluate and advise

E/A
E wave to A wave

E→A
"E to A" (in pulmonary
consolidation, all vowels including
"e" heard as "a" through
stethoscope)

ea
each

EAA
electroacupuncture analgesia
electrothermal atomic absorption
essential amino acid
extrinsic allergic alveolitis

EAB
elective abortion
Ethics Advisory Board
extraanatomic bypass

EABV
effective arterial blood volume

EAC
Ehrlich ascites carcinoma
electroacupuncture *also* EA
epithelioma adenoides cysticum
erythema action (spectrum)
erythema annulare centrifugum
erythrocyte, antibody, and complement
expandable access catheter
external auditory canal

EACA
ε-aminocaproic acid

EACD
eczematous allergic contact dermatitis

EACS
exertional anterior compartment
syndrome

EAD
early after depolarization
extracranial arterial disease

ead.
the same [L. *eadem*]

E-ADD
epileptic attention deficit disorder

EAE
effective arterial elastance
experimental allergic encephalitis
experimental allergic encephalomyelitis
experimental autoimmune encephalitis
experimental autoimmune
encephalomyelitis

EAEC
enteroadherent *Escherichia coli*

EAF
emergency assistance to families

EAG
electroantennogram
electroarteriography
electroatriogram

EAHF
eczema, asthma, and hay fever
(complex)

EAHLG
equine antihuman lymphoblast
globulin

EAHLS
equine antihuman lymphoblast serum

EAI
Employment and Adaptation Index
erythrocyte antibody inhibition

EAL
electronic artificial larynx
endoscopic aspiration lumpectomy

EAM
external acoustic meatus
external auditory meatus

EAMG
experimental autoimmune myasthenia
gravis

EAN
experimental allergic neuritis

EANG
epidemic acute nonbacterial
gastroenteritis

EAO
experimental allergic orchitis

EAP
electroacupuncture
epiallopregnanolone
erythrocyte acid phosphatase
etoposide, Adriamycin, and Platinol
evoked action potential

EAQ
eudismic affinity quotient

e-aq
aqueous electron

EAR
electroencephalographic audiometry
(expired air) resuscitation

Ea R
reaction of degeneration [Ger.
Entartungs-Reaktion]

EARLY
ergonomic assessment of risk and
liability

ear ox
ear oximetry

EARR
extended aortic root replacement

EAS
external anal sphincter

EASIC
Evaluating Acquired Skills in
Communication

EAST
elevated-arm stress test
Emory Angioplasty versus Surgery
Trial
external rotation, abduction, stress
test

EAT
Eating Attitudes Test
ectopic atrial tachycardia
Edinburgh Articulation Test
Education Apperception Test
Ehrlich ascites tumor
electroaerosol therapy
experimental autoimmune thymitis
experimental autoimmune thyroiditis

EATC
Ehrlich ascites tumor cell

EAU
experimental autoimmune uveitis

EAV
equine abortion virus
extraalveolar vessel

EAVC
enhanced atrioventricular conduction

EAVM
extramedullary arteriovenous
malformation

EAVN
enhanced arterioventricular nodal
(conduction)

EB
elbow bearing
elementary body
endometrial biopsy
epidermolysis bullosa
Epstein-Barr (virus) *also* E-B
esophageal body
estradiol benzoate *also* E_2B
ethidium bromide
Evans blue (dye)

E-B
Epstein-Barr (virus) *also* EB

E_2B
estradiol benzoate *also* EB

EBA
epidermolysis bullosa acquisita

E

NOTES

EBA *(continued)*
epidermolysis bullosa atrophicans
extrahepatic biliary atresia

EBAB
equal breath sounds bilaterally *also*
EBSB

EBC
esophageal balloon catheter

EBCDIC
extended binary-coded decimal
interchange code

EBCT
electron beam computed tomography

EBD
epidermolysis bullosa dystrophica

EBDA
effective balloon-dilated area

EBDD
epidermolysis bullosa dystrophica,
dominant

EBDR
epidermolysis bullosa dystrophica,
recessive

EBEA
Epstein-Barr (virus) early antigen
also EBVEA

EBER
Epstein-Barr early region (protein)

EBF
erythroblastosis fetalis *also* EF

EBG
electroblepharogram
electroblepharography

EBI
electronic bone stimulation
emetine and bismuth iodide
erythroblastic island
estradiol-binding index

EBK
embryonic bovine kidney

EBL
erythroblastic leukemia
estimated blood loss

eBL
endemic Burkitt lymphoma

EBL/S
estimated blood loss/surgery

EBM
electrophysiologic behavior
modification
expressed breast milk

EBNA
Epstein-Barr (virus) nuclear antigen
also EBVNA

EBNe
Epstein-Barr nasopharyngeal carcinoma

EBNS
endoscopic bladder neck suspension

E/BOD
electrolyte biochemical oxygen
demand

EBP
epidural blood patch
estradiol-binding protein

EBRT
electron beam radiation therapy
electron beam radiotherapy

EBS
elastic back strap
electrical brain stimulation
electrical brain stimulator
epidermolysis bullosa simplex
estrogen binding site

EBSB
equal breath sounds bilaterally *also*
EBAB

EBSS
Earle balanced salt solution

EBT
early bedtime
ethylsulfonylbenzaldehyde
thiosemicarbazone (subathizone)
external beam (photon) therapy

EBV
effective blood volume
epirubicin, bleomycin, vinblastine
Epstein-Barr virus

EB-VCA
Epstein-Barr viral capsid antigen

EBVDNA
Epstein-Barr virus-determinated nuclear
antigen

EBVEA
Epstein-Barr virus, early antigen *also*
EBEA

EBVNA
Epstein-Barr virus, nuclear antigen
also EBNA

EBZ
epidermal basement zone

EC
econazole
effect of closing (of eyes in electroencephalography)
effective concentration
ejection click
electrochemical
electron capture
Ellis-van Creveld (syndrome) *also* EVC
embryonal carcinoma
emetic center
endometrial carcinoma
endothelial cell
enteric-coated (tablet) *also* ECA, ECT
entering complaint
enterochromaffin
enterochromaffin-cell (hyperplasia)
entorhinal cortex
entrance complaint
environmental complexity
Enzyme Commission (of International Union of Biochemistry)
enzyme-treated cell
epidermal cell
epithelial cell
equalization-cancellation
Erb-Charcot (syndrome)
Escherichia coli
esophageal candidiasis
esophageal carcinoma
ether-chloroform (mixture) *also* E-C
excitation-contraction *also* E-C
excitatory center
experimental control
external carotid
external conjugate
extracellular
extracellular compartment
extracellular concentration
extracranial
extruded cell

eye care
eyes closed

E-C
ether-chloroform (mixture) *also* EC
excitation-contraction *also* EC

E/C
endoscopy/cystoscopy
estriol/creatinine (ratio)
estrogen/creatinine (ratio)

EC$_{50}$
median effective concentration

ECA
electric control activity
electrocardioanalyzer
enteric-coated aspirin (tablet) *also* EC, ECT
enterobacterial common antigen
epidemiologic catchment area
ethacrynic acid (diuretic)
ethylcarboxylate adenosine
external carotid artery

E-CABG
endarterectomy and coronary artery bypass grafting

ECAD
extracranial carotid arterial disease

ECAO
enterocytopathogenic avian orphan (virus)

ECASA
enteric-coated acetylsalicylic acid

ECAT
emission computed axial tomography

ECB
electric cabinet bath

ECBD
exploration of common bile duct

ECBI
Eyberg Child Behavior Inventory

ECBO
enterocytopathogenic bovine orphan (virus)

ECBV
effective circulating blood volume

E

NOTES

ECC
edema, clubbing, and cyanosis
electrocorticogram
embryonal cell carcinoma
emergency cardiac care
endocervical cone
endocervical curettage
estimated creatinine clearance
external cardiac compression
extracorporeal circulation
extrusion of cell cytoplasm

ECCE
extracapsular cataract extraction *also* XCCE

ECCO
enterocytopathogenic cat orphan (virus)

ECCO₂R
extracorporeal carbon dioxide removal

ECD
electrochemical detection
electrochemical detector
electron capture detector
endocardial cushion defect
enzymatic cell dispersion
external cardioverter-defibrillator
extracranial cardiac disease

ECDB
encourage to cough and deep breathe

ECDEU
early clinical drug evaluation unit

ECDO
enterocytopathogenic dog orphan (virus)

ECE
early childhood education
endocervical ecchymosis
equine conjugated estrogen
extracapsular extension

ECEMG
evoked compound electromyography

ECEO
enterocytopathogenic equine orphan (virus)

ECF
East Coast fever
effective capillary flow
eosinophilic chemotactic factor
erythroid colony formation
Escherichia coli filtrate

extended care facility
extracellular fluid

ECFA, ECF-A
eosinophilic chemotactic factor of anaphylaxis

ECF-C
eosinophilic chemotactic factor-complement

ECFMG
Educational Commission on Foreign Medical Graduates

ECFMS
Educational Council for Foreign Medical Students

ECFV
extracellular fluid volume *also* EFV

ECG
electrocardiogram *also* EKG
electrocardiograph
electrocardiography

ECGF
endothelial cell growth factor

ECGS
endothelial cell growth supplement

ECH
epichlorohydrin
extended care hospital

ECHINO
echinocyte

ECHO
echocardiogram *also* Echo
echocardiography *also* Echo
echoencephalogram
echoencephalography
echogram
enteric cytopathogenic human orphan (virus)
enterocytopathogenic human orphan (virus) *also* EcHO
etoposide, cyclophosphamide, hydroxydaunomycin (Adriamycin), and Oncovin (vincristine)

EcHO
enterocytopathogenic human orphan (virus) *also* ECHO

Echo
echocardiogram *also* ECHO
echocardiography *also* ECHO
echoencephalogram *also* Echo EG
echoencephalography *also* Echo EG

echo
echocardiogram

Echo EG
echoencephalogram *also* Echo
echoencephalography *also* Echo

Echo-VM
echoventriculometry

ECI
electrocerebral inactivity
eosinophilic cytoplasmic inclusion
extracorporeal irradiation (of blood)
also ECIB

ECIB
extracorporeal irradiation of blood
also ECI

EC-IC
extracranial-intracranial

ECIL
extracorporeal irradiation of lymph

ECIS
endometrial carcinoma in situ

ECK
extracellular kalium (potassium)

ECL
electrogenerated chemiluminescence
emitter-coupled logic
enterochromaffin-like (type)
euglobulin clot lysis
extent of cerebral lesion
extracapillary lesion

eclec
eclectic

ECLP
extracorporeal liver perfusion

ECLS
extracorporeal life support

ECLT
euglobulin clot lysis time

ECM
embryonic chick muscle
erythema chronicum migrans
external cardiac massage
external chemical messenger
extracellular material
extracellular matrix

ECMO
enterocytopathogenic monkey orphan
(virus)
extracorporeal membrane oxygenation
extracorporeal membrane oxygenator

ECMP
enterocoated microspheres of
pancrelipase

ECN
extended-care nursery

EC No.
Enzyme Commission Number

ECochG
electrocochleography *also* ECoG

ECOG
Eastern Cooperative Oncology Group

ECoG
electrocochleography *also* ECochG
electrocorticogram
electrocorticography

E. coli
Escherichia coli also EC

ECOR
extracorporeal CO_2 removal

ECP
ectrodactyly-cleft palate (syndrome)
effector cell precursor
electronic claims processing
endocardial potential
eosinophil cationic protein
erythrocyte coproporphyrin
erythroid committed precursor
Escherichia coli polypeptide
estradiol cyclopentanepropionate
external cardiac pressure
external counterpulsation
extracorporeal photochemotherapy
free cytoporphyrin in erythrocytes

ECPD
external counterpressure device

ECPL
endocavitary pelvic lymphadenectomy

ECPO
enterocytopathogenic porcine orphan
(virus)

E

NOTES

ECPOG
electrochemical potential gradient

ECPR
external cardiopulmonary resuscitation

ECR
electrocardiographic response
emergency chemical restraint
extensor carpi radialis

ECRB
extensor carpi radialis brevis

ECRL
extensor carpi radialis longus

ECRO
enterocytopathogenic rodent orphan
(virus)

ECS
elective cosmetic surgery
electrocerebral silence
electroconvulsive shock
electronic claims submission
extracellular-like, calcium-free solution
extracellular space

E2CS
Edinburgh 2 Coma Scale

ECSO
enterocytopathogenic swine orphan
(virus)

ECSP
epidermal cell surface protein

ECST
European Carotid Surgery Trial

ECT
ectomesenchymal chondromyxoid
tumor
electroconvulsive therapy
emission computed tomography
enhanced computed tomography
enteric-coated tablet *also* EC, ECA
euglobulin clot test
European compression technique
(bone screw and internal fixation)
extracellular tissue

ECTA
Everyman Contingency Table Analysis

ECTEOLA
epichlorohydrin and triethanolamine

ECTR
endoscopic carpal tunnel release

ECU
environmental control unit
extended care unit
extensor carpi ulnaris
extracorporeal ultrafiltration

ECV
external cephalic version
extracellular volume
extracorporeal volume

ECVD
extracellular volume of distribution

ECVE
extracellular volume expansion

ECW
extracellular water

ED
early differentiation
ectodermal dysplasia
ectopic depolarization
effective dose
Ehlers-Danlos (syndrome)
elbow disarticulation
electrodiagnosis *also* EDX, EDx, EI
Dx
electrodialysis
electron diffraction
elemental diet
embryonic death
emergency department
emotional disorder
emotional disturbance
emotionally disturbed
end diastole
entering diagnosis
Entner-Doudoroff (metabolic pathway)
enzyme deficiency
epidural
epileptiform discharge
equilibrium dialysis
equine dermis (cells)
equivalent dose
erectile dysfunction
erythema dose
ethyldichloroarsine
ethylenediamine
ethynodiol
evidence of disease
exertional dyspnea
extensive disease
extensor digitorum
external diameter
external dyspnea
extra-low dispersion

E-D
 ego-defense

ED$_{50}$
 median effective dose

E$_d$
 depth dose

ed
 edema *also* E

EDA
 electrodermal activity
 electrodermal audiometry
 electrolyte-deficient agar
 electron donor-acceptor (interaction)
 end-diastolic (cross-sectional) area

EDA+
 extradomain A positive

EDAM
 electron-dense amorphous material

10-EDAM
 10-ethyl-10-diazaaminopterin

EDAP
 Emergency Department Approval for
  Pediatrics

EDAS
 encephaloduroarteriosynangiosis

EDAX
 energy dispersive x-ray analysis

EDB
 early dry breakfast
 ethylene dibromide
 extensor digitorum brevis

EDBP
 erect diastolic blood pressure

EDC
 effective dynamic compliance
 electrodesiccation and curettage *also*
  ED&C
 emergency decontamination center
 end-diastolic count
 estimated date of conception
 estimated date of confinement
 expected date of confinement
 expected delivery, cesarean
 extensor digitorum communis

ED&C
 electrodesiccation and curettage *also*
  EDC

EDCI
 energetic dynamic cardiac
  insufficiency

E-DCIS
 endocrine ductal carcinoma in situ

EDCP
 eccentric dynamic compression plate

EDCS
 end-diastolic chamber stiffness
 end-diastolic circumferential stress

EDCT
 early distal proximal tubule

EDD
 effective drug duration
 end-diastolic diameter
 end-diastolic dimension
 enzyme-digested delta (endotoxin)
 esophageal detection device
 estimated discharge date
 estimated due date
 expected date of delivery

EDDA
 expanded duty dental auxiliary

edent
 edentulous

EDF
 end-diastolic flow
 extradural fluid

EDG
 electrodermography
 electrodynogram

EdGr
 Edmondson grading

EDH
 epidural hematoma
 extradural hematoma

EDHF
 endothelium-derived hyperpolarizing
  factor

EDICP
 electron-dense iron-containing particle

E

NOTES

EDIM
epidemic disease of infant mice
epizootic diarrhea of infant mice

E-diol
estradiol *also* E

EDit
electric differential therapy

EDL
end-diastolic load
end-diastolic (segment) length
estimated date of labor
extensor digitorum longus

ED/LD
emotionally disturbed and learning disabled

EDM
early diastolic murmur
extensor digiti minimi
extramucosal duodenal myotomy

EDMA
ethylene glycol dimethacrylate

EDMD
Emery-Dreifuss muscular dystrophy

EDN
electrodesiccation
eosinophil-derived neurotoxin

EDNO
endothelium-derived nitric oxide

EDOC
estimated date of confinement

EDP
electron-dense particle
electronic data processing
emergency department physician
end-diastolic pressure

EDPA
ethyldiphenylpropenylamine

EDPCS
exertional deep posterior compartment syndrome

EDQ
extensor digiti quinti

EDR
early diastolic relaxation
edrophonium
effective direct radiation
electrodermal response
electrodialysis with reversed (polarity)

EDRA
electrodermal response test audiometry

EDRF
endothelium-derived relaxing factor

EDS
edema disease of swine
egg drop syndrome
Ego Development Scale
Ehlers-Danlos syndrome
energy-dispersive spectrometer
epigastric distress syndrome
excessive daytime sleepiness
extended data stream
extradimensional shift

EDT
end-diastolic (cardiac wall) thickness

EDTA
ethylenediaminetetraacetic acid (edathamil, edetic acid)

EDTAC
ethylenediaminetetraacetic acid Cetavlon

EdU
eating disorder unit

EDV
end-diastolic volume

EDVI
end-diastolic volume index

EDW
estimated dry weight

EDWGT
emergency drinking water germicidal tablet

EDWTH
end-diastolic wall thickness

EDX, EDx
electrodiagnosis *also* ED, El Dx

EDXA
energy-dispersive x-ray analysis

E-E
end-to-end (anastomosis) *also* EE
erythema-edema (reaction)

EE
embryo extract
end-expiration
end-to-end (anastomosis) *also* E-E
end-to-end (bite, occlusion)
energy expenditure
Enterobacteriaceae enrichment (broth)

equine encephalitis
ethynyl estradiol
expressed emotion
external ear
eyes and ears *also* E&E

E&E
eyes and ears *also* EE

EEA
electroencephalic audiometry
elemental enteral alimentation
end-to-end anastomosis

EEC
ectrodactyly-ectodermal dysplasia-
clefting (syndrome)
enteropathogenic *Escherichia coli*

EECD
endothelial-epithelial corneal dystrophy

EECG
electroencephalogram *also* EEG
electroencephalography *also* EEG

EECP
enhanced external counterpulsation

EEDQ
ethoxycarbonylethoxydihydroquinoline

EEE
eastern equine encephalomyelitis
edema, erythema, and exudate
experimental enterococcal endocarditis
external eye examination

EEEP
end-expiratory esophageal pressure

EEEV
eastern equine encephalomyelitis virus

EEG
electroencephalogram
electroencephalograph
electroencephalography

EEGA
electroencephalographic audiometry

EEGF
esophageal epidermal growth factor

EEG T
Electroencephalographic Technologist

EEJ
electroejaculation

EELS
electron energy loss spectroscopy

EELV
end-expiratory lung volume

EEM
ectodermal dysplasia-ectrodactyly-
macular dystrophy (syndrome)
erythema exudativum multiforme
Test for Examining Expressive
Morphology

EEME
ethynylestradiol methyl ether

EEMG
evoked electromyogram
evoked electromyography

EENT
eye, ear, nose, and throat

EEP
end-expiratory phase
end-expiratory pressure
equivalent effective photon

EEPI
extraretinal eye position information

EEPLND
extraperitoneal endoscopic pelvic
lymph node dissection

EER
electroencephalographic response

EERP
extended endocardial resection
procedure

EES
erythromycin ethylsuccinate
ethyl ethanesulfate
expandable esophageal stent

EESG
evoked electrospinogram

EEV
encircling endocardial ventriculotomy

EF
ectopic focus
edema factor

E

NOTES

EF *(continued)*
ejection factor
ejection fraction
elastic fiber
elastic fibril
electric field
elongation factor
embryo fetal
embryo fibroblast
emergency facility
emotional factor
encephalitogenic factor
endothoracic fascia
endurance factor
eosinophilic fasciitis
epithelial focus
equivalent focus
erythroblastosis fetalis *also* EBF
erythrocytic fragmentation
essential findings
exophthalmic factor
exposure factor
extended field (radiation therapy)
extrafine
extra food
extrinsic factor

EFA
essential fatty acid
extrafamily adoptee

EFAD
essential fatty acid deficiency

EFAS
embryofetal alcohol syndrome

EFBW
estimated fetal body weight

EFC
elastin fragment concentration
endogenous fecal calcium

EFDA
expanded function dental assistant

EFE
endocardial fibroelastosis

eff
effect
efferent *also* effer
efficient
effusion

effect.
effective

effer
efferent *also* eff

EFFU
epithelial focus-forming unit

EF-G
elongation factor G

EFH
explosive follicular hyperplasia

EFHBM
eosinophilic fibrohistiocytic (lesion of
bone marrow

EFL
effective focal length
external fluid loss

EFM
elderly fibromyalgia
electronic fetal monitoring
external fetal monitoring

EFP
effective filtration pressure
endoneural fluid pressure
etoposide, 5-fluorouracil, and Platinol

EFPS
epicardial fat pad sign

EFR
effective filtration rate

E FRAG
erythrocyte (red blood cell) fragility
(test)

EFS
electric field stimulation

EFT
Embedded Figures Test

EFV
extracellular fluid volume *also* ECFV

EFVC
expiratory flow-volume curve

EFW
estimated fetal weight

EF/WM
ejection fraction/wall motion

EG
enteroglucagon
Erb-Goldflam (syndrome)
esophagogastrectomy
esophagogastric
external genitalia

e.g.
for example [L. *exempli gratia*]

EGA
estimated gestational age

EGAT
Educational Goal Attainment Test

EGBPS
equilibrium-gated blood pool study

EGBT
esophagogastric balloon tamponade

EGBUS, EG/BUS
external genitalia, Bartholin, urethral, and Skene (glands) *also* EXGBUS

EGC
early gastric cancer
endocrine granule constituent
epithelioid-globoid cell

EGD
esophagogastroduodenoscopy

EGDF
embryonic growth and development factor

EGE
eosinophilic gastroenteritis

EGF
epidermal growth factor

EGFR
epidermal growth factor receptor

EGG
electrogastrogram
electrogastrography

EGH
equine growth hormone

EGI
endogenous GAD inhibitor

EGJ
esophagogastric junction

EGL
eosinophilic granuloma of lung

EGLT
euglobulin lysis time

EGM
electrogram
extracellular granular material

EGN
experimental glomerulonephritis

EGOT
erythrocytic glutamic oxaloacetic transaminase

EGR
erythrocyte glutathione reductase

EGRA
equilibrium-gated radionuclide angiography

EGS
electrogalvanic stimulation
ethylene glycol succinate
extragonadal seminoma

EGT
ethanol gelation test

EGTA
esophageal gastric tube airway
ethyleneglycoltetraacetic acid

EH
early healed
educationally handicapped
emotionally handicapped
endometrial hyperplasia
enlarged heart
enteral hyperalimentation
environment and heredity *also* E&H
epidermolytic hyperkeratosis
epoxide hydratase
essential hypertension
extramedullary hematopoiesis

E&H
environment and heredity *also* EH

E_h, eH
oxidation-reduction potential *also* ORP

EHA
Environmental Health Agency

EHAA
epidemic hepatitis-associated antigen

EHB
elevate head of bed

EHBA
extrahepatic biliary atresia

EHBD
extrahepatic bile duct

E

NOTES

EHBF
estimated hepatic blood flow
exercise hyperemia blood flow
extrahepatic blood flow (clearance)

EHC
enterohepatic circulation
enterohepatic clearance
essential hypercholesterolemia
extended health care
extrahepatic cholestasis

EH-CF
Entamoeba histolytica-complement
fixation

EHD
electrohemodynamic
epizootic hemorrhagic disease

EHDA, EHDP
ethanehydroxydiphosphonic acid
(etidronate sodium)

EHDV
epizootic hemorrhagic disease virus

EHE
epithelioid hemangioendothelioma

EHEC
enterohemorrhagic *Escherichia coli*

EHF
electrohydraulic fragmentation
epidemic hemorrhagic fever
exophthalmos-hyperthyroid factor
extremely high factor
extremely high frequency

EHH
esophageal hiatal hernia

EHL
effective half-life (of radioactive
substance)
electrohydraulic lithotripsy
endogenous hyperlipidemia
Environmental Health Laboratory
essential hyperlipidemia
extensor hallucis longus

EHM
extrahepatic metastasis

EHME
Employee Health Maintenance
Examination

EHMS
electrohydrodynamic ionization mass
spectrometry

EHO
extrahepatic obstruction

EHP
Environmental Health Perspectives
excessive heat production
extra high potency

EHPAC
Emergency Health Preparedness
Advisory Committee

EHPH
extrahepatic portal hypertension

EHPT
Eddy hot plate test

EHPVO
extrahepatic portal vein obstruction

EHSDS
Experimental Health Services Delivery
System

EHT
electrohydrothermal
essential hypertension

EHV
equine herpesvirus

EI
electrolyte imbalance
electron impact
electron ionization
emotionally impaired
enzyme inhibitor
eosinophilic index
erythema infectiosum
excretory index
external ilium
external intervention

E/I
expiration/inspiration (ratio)

E&I
endocrine and infertility

EIA
electroimmunoassay
enzyme immunoassay
enzyme-linked immunoassay *also*
ELISA
enzyme-linked immunosorbent assay
also ELISA
equine infectious anemia
exercise-induced asthma

EIA-2
second-generation enzyme
immunoassay

EIAB
  extracranial-intracranial arterial bypass

EIB
  electrophoretic immunoblotting
  exercise-induced bronchoconstriction
  exercise-induced bronchospasm

EIC
  elastase inhibition capacity
  enzyme inhibition complex
  extensive intraductal component

EICDT
  Ego-Ideal and Conscience
  Development Test

EICT
  external isovolumic contraction time

EID
  egg-infectious dose
  electroimmunodiffusion
  electronic induction desorption
  electronic infusion device
  emergency infusion device

EIEC
  enteroinvasive *Escherichia coli*

EIEE
  early infantile epileptic
  encephalopathy

EIF, eIF
  erythrocyte initiation factor
  eukaryotic initiation factor

EIFT
  embryo intrafallopian transfer

EIM
  excitability-inducing material

EIMS
  electron ionization mass spectrometry

EIN
  endometrial intraepithelial neoplasia

EIP
  elective interruption of pregnancy
  end-inspiratory pause
  end-inspiratory pressure
  extensor indicis proprius

EIPS
  endogenous inhibitor of prostaglandin
  synthase

EIRnv
  extra-incidence rate in nonvaccinated
  (groups)

EIRP
  effective isotropic radiated power

EIRv
  extraincidence rate in vaccinated
  (groups)

EIS
  endoscopic injection scleropathy
  endoscopic injection sclerotherapy
  Environmental Impact Statement
  Epidemic Intelligence Service

EISA
  electroencephalogram interval spectrum
  analysis

EIT
  erythroid iron turnover

EIV
  external iliac vein

EJ
  ejection (fraction)
  elbow jerk
  external jugular

EJB
  ectopic junctional beat

EJP
  excitation junction potential
  excitatory junction potential

ejusd
  of the same [L. *ejusdem*]

EJV
  external jugular vein

EK
  enterokinase
  erythrokinase

EKC
  epidemic keratoconjunctivitis

EKG
  electrocardiogram *also* ECG
  electrocardiography *also* ECG

EKV
  erythrokeratodermia variabilis

E

NOTES

EKY
electrokymogram
electrokymography

E-L
Eaton-Lambert (syndrome) *also* EL
external lids

EL
early latent
Eaton-Lambert (syndrome) *also* E-L
egg lecithin
elastic limit
electroluminescence
elixir *also* el, Elix, Elx
erythroleukemia
exercise limit
external lamina

El
elastase

el
elbow *also* ELB, elb
elixir *also* EL, Elix, Elx

ELA
endotoxin-like activity

ELAD
extracorporeal liver assist device

ELAFF
extended lateral arm free flap

E-LAM
endothelial-leukocyte adhesion
molecule

ELAM-1
endothelial-leukocyte adhesion
molecule-1

ELAS
extended lymphadenopathy syndrome

ELAT
enzyme-linked antiglobulin test

ELB
early light breakfast
elbow *also* el, elb

elb
elbow *also* ELB, el

ELBF
estimated liver blood flow

ELBNS
extraperitoneal laparoscopic bladder
neck suspension

ELBW
extremely low birth weight

ELCA
excimer laser coronary angioplasty

ELD
egg lethal dose

El Dx
electrodiagnosis *also* ED, EDX, EDx

elec, elect.
electric
electricity
electuary (confection)

elem
elementary

elev
elevated
elevation
elevator

ELF
elective low forceps (delivery)
epithelial lining fluid

ELG
eligible

ELH
egg-laying hormone
endolymphatic hydrops

ELI
endomyocardial lymphocytic infiltrates
Environmental Language Inventory
exercise lability index

ELIA
enzyme-labeled immunoassay

ELICT
enzyme-linked immunocytochemical
technique

ELIEDA
enzyme-linked immunoelectrodiffusion
assay

ELISA
enzyme-linked immunoassay *also* EIA
enzyme-linked immunosorbent assay
also EIA

ELISA-I
enzyme-linked immunosorbent assay I

ELISA-II
enzyme-linked immunosorbent assay
II

Elix, elix
elixir *also* EL, el, Elx

ELLIP, ELLP
ellipotocyte

ELM
>Early Language Milestone (Scale)
external limiting membrane
extravascular lung mass

ELMT
>elements (on urinalysis)

ELND
>elective lymph node dissection

ELOP
>estimated length of program

ELOS
>estimated length of stay
extralymphatic organ site

ELP
>early labeled peak
elastase-like protein
electrophoresis
endogenous limbic potential
Estimated Learning Potential

ELPS
>excessive lateral pressure syndrome

ELR
>Equal Listener Response (scale)

ELS
>Eaton-Lambert syndrome
electron loss spectroscopy
extracorporeal life support
extralobar sequestration

ELSS
>emergency life support system

ELT
>endless loop tachycardia
euglobulin lysis test
euglobulin lysis time

ELU
>extended length of utterance

ELUS
>endoluminal rectal ultrasonography

ELV
>erythroid leukemia virus

Elx
>elixir *also* EL, el, Elix

elytes
>electrolytes *also* LYTES, lytes

EM
>early memory
effective masking
ejection murmur
electromagnetic *also* em
electromechanical
electron micrograph
electron microscope
electron microscopy *also* E/M, EMC, E-MICR
electrophoretic mobility
Embden-Meyerhof (glycolytic pathway) *also* E-M
emergency medicine
emmetropia (normal vision) *also* Em
emotional (disorder)
emotionally (disturbed)
emphysema *also* emph
ergonovine maleate
erythema migrans
erythema multiforme
erythrocyte mass
erythromycin *also* E, ETM
esophageal manometry
esophageal motility
excreted mass
extensive metabolizers
external monitor

E-M
>Embden-Meyerhof (glycolytic pathway) *also* EM

E of M
>error of measurement

E/M
>electron microscope *also* EM, EMC, E-MICR
electron microscopy *also* EM, E-MICR

E&M
>endocrine and metabolic

Em
>emmetropia *also* EM

e/m
>ratio of (electron) charge to mass

em
>electromagnetic *also* EM

E

NOTES

EMA
electronic microanalyzer
emergency assistance
emergency assistant
emergency medical attendant
endomysial antibody
epithelial membrane antigen

E-Mac
English MacIntosh

EMA-CO
etoposide, methotrexate, actinomycin D (dactinomycin), and citrovorum factor (leucovorin)
etoposide, methotrexate-leucovorin, actinomycin D, cyclophosphamide, and Oncovin

EMAD
equivalent mean age at death

EMAP
evoked muscle action potential

Emax
maximum ventricular elastance

EMB
embryology
endometrial biopsy
endomyocardial biopsy
engineering in medicine and biology
eosin-methylene blue (agar)
ethambutol
explosive mental behavior
explosive motor behavior

Emb, emb
embolus
embryo *also* E
embryology *also* embryol

EMBASE
Excerpta Medica Database

embryol
embryology *also* Emb, emb

EMC
electron microscopy *also* EM, E-MICR
emergency medical care
encephalomyocarditis
endometrial curettage
essential mixed cryoglobulinemia

EMC&R
emergency medical care and rescue

EMCRO
Experimental Medical Care Review Organization

EMCV
encephalomyocarditis virus

EMD
electromechanical dissociation
Emery-Dreifuss muscular dystrophy
esophageal mobility disorder

EME
epithelial-myoepithelial (carcinoma)

EMEM
Eagle minimal essential medium

EMER
electromagnetic molecular electronic resonance

emer, emerg
emergency *also* EMG

EMF
electromagnetic flowmeter
electromotive force *also* emf
endomyocardial fibrosis
erythrocyte maturation factor
evaporated milk formula

emf
electromotive force *also* EMF

EMG
electromyelogram
electromyelography
electromyogram
electromyograph
electromyography
emergency *also* emer, emerg
essential monoclonal gammopathy
exomphalos, macroglossia, and gigantism (syndrome)
eye movement gauge

EMGN
extramembranous glomerulonephritis

EMGORS
electromyogram sensors

EMH
educationally mentally handicapped

EMI
electromagnetic interference
electromechanical impactor
emergency medical information

EMIC
emergency maternal and infant care

E-MICR
electron microscopy *also* EM, E/M, EMC

EMIP
European Myocardial Infarction
Project

EMI/RFI
electromagnetic
interference/radiofrequency interference

EMIT
enzyme-multiplied immunoassay
technique
enzyme-multiplied immunoassay test

EMJH
Ellinghausen-McCullough-Johnson-
Harris (medium)

EML
effective mandibular length

EMLA
eutectic mixture of local anesthetics

EMLB
erythromycin lactobionate

EMLD
external muscle layer damaged

EMM
erythema multiforme major

EMMA
eye movement measuring apparatus

EMMM
epidermotropic metastatic malignant
melanoma

EMMV
extended mandatory minute ventilation

EMO
Epstein-Macintosh-Oxford (inhaler)
exophthalmos, myxedema
circumscriptum praetibiale, and
osteoarthropathia hypertrophicans
(syndrome)

emot
emotion
emotional

EMP
electrical membrane property
electromagnetic pulse
Embden-Meyerhof pathway
epimacular proliferation

external membrane protein
extramedullary plasmacytoma

e.m.p.
as directed [L. *ex modo praescripto*]
also m.d., m. dict., MP, u.d., ut dict.

emp
plaster [L. *emplastrum*]

EMPD
extramammary Paget disease

EMPEP
electrophoretic pattern
erythrocyte membrane protein

emph
emphysema *also* EM

EMPP
ethylmethylpiperidinopropiophenone

emp. vesic.
blistering plaster [L. *emplastrum
vesicatorium*]

EMR
educable mentally retarded
electromagnetic radiation
emergency mechanical restraint
empty, measure, and record
endoscopic mucosal resection
essential metabolism ratio
ethanol metabolic rate
eye movement recording

EMS
early morning specimen
early morning stiffness
electrical muscle stimulation
Emergency Medical Services
emergency medical system
endometriosis
eosinophilia-myalgia syndrome
esophageal manometric sequence
ethyl methanesulfonate
extramedullary site

EMT
emergency medical tag
emergency medical team
Emergency Medical Technician
emergency medical treatment

E

NOTES

EMT-A
Emergency Medical Technician-Ambulance

EMT-I
Emergency Medical Technician-Intermediate

EMT-M
Emergency Medical Technician-Military

EMT-P
Emergency Medical Technician-Paramedic

EMU
early morning urine
electromagnetic unit *also* emu

emu
electromagnetic unit *also* EMU

emul
emulsion

EMV
eye, motor, voice (Glasgow coma scale)
eyes, motor, verbal

EMVC
early mitral valve closure

EMW
electromagnetic waves

EN
electronarcosis
endocardial *also* ENDO
enrolled nurse
enteral nutrition
erythema nodosum

E 50% N
extension 50% of normal

En, en
enema *also* E, enem

ENA
extractable nuclear antibodies
extractable nuclear antigen

ENANB
enterically transmitted non-A, non-B (hepatitis)

END
early neonatal death
elective node dissection
endocrinology
endorphin
enhancement Newcastle disease

end, end.
endoreduplication

ENDO
endocardial *also* EN
endodontics *also* Endo
endoscopy
endotracheal *also* Endo, ET

Endo
endocardial
endocardium
endocrine
endocrinology
endodontics *also* ENDO
endotracheal *also* ENDO, ET

endocr
endocrine
endocrinology

ENDOR
electron nuclear double resonance

endos
endosteal

ENE
ethylnorepinephrine

ENeG
electroneurography

enem
enema *also* E, En, en

ENF
Enfamil

ENG
electroneurography
electronystagmogram
electronystagmograph
electronystagmography
engorged

ENI
elective neck irradiation

ENK
enkephalin

1-ENK
leucine-enkephalin

ENL
erythema nodosum leprosum
erythema nodosum leproticum

enl
enlarged
enlargement

ENMG
electroneuromyography

ENNS
Early Neonatal Neurobehavior Scale

Eno
enolase

ENog
electroneurogram
electroneuronography

ENP
extractable nucleoprotein

ENR
eosinophilic nonallergic rhinitis
extrathyroidal neck radioactivity

ENS
enteral nutritional support
enteric nervous system
ethylnorsuprarenin

ENT
ear, nose and throat
enzootic nasal tumor
extranodular tissue

ENTOM
entomology

ENV
ethylnitrosourea

env
envelope (of cell)

environ
environment
environmental

enz, enz.
enzymatic
enzyme

EO
effect of opening (eyes)
elbow orthosis
embolic occlusion
eosinophil *also* eo, EOS, eos, eosin
eosinophilia
ethylene oxide *also* ETOX
eyes open

E_o
electric affinity *also* E, EA
skin (epidermis) dose (radiation) *also* E, EA

E_o+, E^o
oxidation-reduction potential *also* E_h, eH, ORP

eo
eosinophil *also* EO, EOS, eos, eosin

EOA
effective orifice area
erosive osteoarthritis
esophageal obturator airway
examination, opinion, and advice
external oblique aponeurosis

EOAE
evoked otoacoustic emissions

EOB
emergency observation bed

EOC
enema of choice
epithelial ovarian cancer

EO CT
eosinophil count

EOD
electrical organ discharge
entry on duty
every other day *also* eod

eod
every other day *also* EOD

EOE
ethiodized oil emulsion

EOF
end of field
end of file

EOG
electrooculogram
electrooculograph
electrooculography
electroolfactogram
electroolfactography

EOJ
extrahepatic obstructive jaundice

EOL
end of life

EOM
end of message
equal ocular movement
error of measurement

E

NOTES

EOM *(continued)*
external otitis media
extraocular movement
extraocular muscle

EOMA
emergency oxygen mask assembly

EOM F & Conj
extraocular movements full and
conjugate

EOMI
extraocular movements intact
extraocular muscles intact

EOM NL
extraocular eye movements normal

EOMS
extraocular movements
extraocular muscles

EOO
external oculomotor ophthalmoplegia

EOP
emergency outpatient
endogenous opioid peptide
equivalent oxygen performance

EOR
emergency operating room
exclusive OR (binary logic)

EORA
elderly onset rheumatoid arthritis

EORTC
European Organization for Research
and Treatment of Cancer

EORTC QLQ-C30
European Organization for Research
and Treatment of Cancer Core
Quality of Life

EOS
eligibility on-site
eosinophil *also* EO, eo, eos, eosin
European Orthodontic Society

eos, eosin
eosinophil *also* EO, eo, EOS

EOT
effective oxygen transport

EOU
epidemic observation unit

EOWPVT
Expressive One-Word Picture
Vocabulary Test

EP
ectopic pregnancy
edible portion
electrophore
electrophoresis
electrophysiologic
electrophysiology
electroprecipitin
elopement precaution
emergency physician
emergency procedure
endogenous pyrogen
endoperoxide
endorphin
end point
enteropeptidase
environmental protection
enzyme product
eosinophilic pneumonia
ependymal (cell)
epicardial
epithelial *also* EPI, EPITH
epithelium *also* EPI, EPITH
erythrocyte protoporphyrin
erythrophagocytosis
erythropoietic porphyria
erythropoietin *also* Ep, EPO
esophageal pressure
esophoria
etoposide *also* EP, VP, VP-16
evoked potential
extreme pressure

E&P
estrogen and progesterone

Ep
erythropoietin *also* EP, EPO

EPA
eicosapentaenoic acid
Environmental Protection Agency
erect posterior-anterior (projection)
ethylphenacemide
exophthalmos-producing activity
extrinsic plasminogen activator

EPAP
expiratory positive airway pressure

EPAQ
Extended Personal Attributes
Questionnaire

EPA/RCRA
Environmental Protection Agency
Resource Conservation and Recovery
Act

EPB
Environmental Pre-Language Battery
extensor pollicis brevis

EPC
electronic pain control
end-plate current
epilepsia partialis continua
external pneumatic calf compression
external pneumatic compression

EPCA
external pressure circulatory assistance

EPCG
endoscopic pancreatocholangiography

EPD
effective pressor dose
endoscopic papillary balloon dilation

EPDML
epidemiologic
epidemiology

EpDRF
epithelium-derived relaxation factor

EPE
erythropoietin-producing enzyme

EPEA
expense-per-equivalent admission

EPEC
enteropathogenic *Escherichia coli*

EPEG
etoposide *also* EP, VP, VP-16

EPF
early pregnancy factor
endocarditis parietalis fibroplastica
endothelial proliferating factor
Enfamil premature formula
exophthalmos-producing factor

EPG
eggs per gram
electropneumogram
electropneumography
ethanolamine phosphoglyceride

EPH
edema-proteinuria-hypertension
extensor proprius hallucis

EpHM
intraesophageal pH monitoring

EPI
echo planar imaging
Emotions Profile Index
epileptic *also* epil
epinephrine *also* E, epineph
epithelial *also* EP, EPITH
epithelium *also* EP, EPITH
epitheloid cell
epitympanic
evoked-potential index
exocrine pancreatic insufficiency
extrapyramidal involvement
Eysenck Personality Inventory

Epi
epicardium
epiglottis

epid
epidemic

epig
epigastric

epil
epilepsy
epileptic *also* EPI

epineph
epinephrine *also* E, EPI

EPIS, epis
episiotomy
episode
epistaxis

epistom
stopper (on mouth of bottle) [L.
epistomium]

EPITH, epith
epithelial *also* EP, EPI
epithelium *also* EP, EPI

EPK
early prenatal karyotype

EPL
effective patient life
essential phospholipid
extensor pollicis longus
external plexiform layer
extracorporeal piezoelectric lithotripsy

EPM
electronic pacemaker
electron-probe microanalysis

E

NOTES

EPM *(continued)*
electrophoretic mobility
energy-protein malnutrition

EPO
erythropoiesis
erythropoietin *also* EP, Ep
exclusive provider organization
expiratory port occlusion

Epo
erythropoietin

EPP
endplate potential
equal pressure point
erythropoietic protoporphyria

EPPB
end positive-pressure breathing

EPPS
Edwards Personal Preference Schedule

EPQ
Eysenck Personality Questionnaire

EPR
early progressive resistance
electron paramagnetic resonance
electrophrenic respiration
emergency physical restraint
estradiol production rate
extraparenchymal resistance

EPROM
erasable programmable read-only
memory

EPS
elastosis perforans serpiginosa
electrophysiologic study
endoscopic pancreatic stenting
enzymatic pancreatic secretion
exophthalmos-producing substance
expressed prostatic secretion
extrapyramidal side effect
extrapyramidal symptom
extrapyramidal syndrome

EPSD
E-point to septal distance

EPSDT
Early and Periodic Screening,
Diagnosis, and Treatment program

EPSE
extrapyramidal side effects

EPSEM
equal probability of selection method

ε
chain of hemoglobin
dielectric constant
epsilon (fifth letter of Greek
alphabet), lowercase
extinction coefficient
fifth in a series or group
heavy chain of immunoglobulin E
molar absorption coefficient
molar absorptivity
molar extinction coefficient
permittivity
specific absorptivity

EPSP
excitatory postsynaptic potential

EPSS
E-point to septal separation

EPT
early pregnancy test
Eidetic Parents Test
endoscopic papillotomy

EPTE
existed prior to enlistment

EPTFE, E-PTFE, e-PTFE
expanded polytetrafluoroethylene

EPTS
existed prior to service

EPWF
epidural pressure waveform

EPXMA
electron probe x-ray microanalyzer

EQ
educational quotient
encephalization quotient
energy quotient
equal to
equilibrium *also* eq

Eq
equation *also* eqn
equivalency *also* eq, equiv
equivalent *also* eq, equiv

eq
equal
equilibrium *also* EQ
equivalency *also* Eq, equiv
equivalent *also* Eq

EQA
external quality assessment

eqn
equation *also* Eq

equip
equipment

equiv
equivalency *also* Eq, eq
equivalent *also* Eq, eq
equivocal

ER
early reticulocyte
efficacy ratio
ejection rate
electroresection
emergency room
endoplasmic reticulum *also* er
enhanced reactivation
enhancement ratio
environmental resistance
epigastric region
equine rhinopneumonia
equivalent roentgen (unit)
erythrocyte receptor
esophageal rupture
estradiol receptor
estrogen receptor
evoked response
expiratory reserve
extended release (tablet)
extended resistance
external reduction
external resistance
external rotation
extraction ratio
eye research

ER–
decreased estrogen receptor

ER+
estrogen receptor-positive
increased estrogen receptor

E&R
equal and reactive
examination and report

Er
erbium
erythrocyte *also* E, er, ERY, Ery,
eryth

er
endoplasmic reticulum *also* ER

erythrocyte *also* E, Er, ERY, Ery,
eryth

ERA
electrical response activity
electrical response audiometry
electroencephalic response audiometry
estradiol receptor assay
estrogen receptor assay
evoked-response audiometry

ERB
ethnic relational behavior

ERBD
endoscopic retrograde biliary drainage

ERBF
effective renal blood flow

ERC
endoscopic retrograde cholangiography
enterocytopathogenic human orphan-
rhino-coryza (virus)
erythropoietin-responsive cell
(pupils) equal, reactive, and
contracting

ERCCE
endoscopic retrograde
cholecystoendoprosthesis

ERCP
endoscopic retrograde cannulation of
pancreatic (duct)
endoscopic retrograde
cholangiopancreatography
endoscopic retrograde
choledochopancreatography

ERD
early retirement with disability
evoked-response detector

ERDA
Energy Research and Development
Administration

ERE
external rotation in extension

ERF
esophagorespiratory fistula
external rotation in flexion

erf
error function

E

NOTES

ERFC, E-RFC
erythrocyte rosette-forming cell

ERG
electrolyte replacement with glucose
electron radiography
electroretinogram
electroretinograph
electroretinography

erg
energy unit

ERH
egg-laying release hormone

ERHD
exposure-related hypothermia death

ERI
Environmental Response Inventory
erythrocyte rosette inhibitor

ERIA
electroradioimmunoassay

ER/IR
external/internal rotation

ERL
effective refractory length

ERM
electrochemical relaxation method
extended radical mastectomy

ERNA
equilibrium radionuclide angiography

ERP
early receptor potential
effective refractory period
emergency room physician
endocardial resection procedure
endoscopic retrograde pancreatogram
endoscopic retrograde pancreatography
endoscopic retrograde
 parenchymography
equine rhinopneumonitis
estrogen-receptor protein
event-related (brain) potential

ERPF
effective renal plasma flow

ERPLV
effective refractory period of the left
 ventricle

ERPM
early receptor potential mottling

ERPP
endoscopic retrograde
parenchymography of pancreas

ER/PR
estrogen receptor/progesterone receptor

ERR, err.
error

ERRT
extrarenal rhabdoid tumor

ERS
endoscopic retrograde sphincterotomy

ERSNA
efferent renal sympathetic nerve
 activity

ERSP
event-related slow-brain potential

ERT
esophageal radionuclide transit
estrogen replacement therapy
external radiation therapy

ERUS
endorectal ultrasound

ERV
equine rhinopneumonitis virus
expiratory reserve volume
expiratory residual volume

ERY
erysipelas
erythrocyte *also* E, Er, er, Ery, eryth

Ery
erythrocyte *also* E, Er, er, ERY,
 eryth

eryth
erythema
erythrocyte *also* E, Er, er, ERY, Ery

ES
Ego Strength (test)
ejection sound
elastic suspensor
electrical stimulation *also* Es
electrical stimulation *also* Es
electroshock
electrotherapy system
elopement status (psychology)
emergency service
emission spectrometry
endometritis-salpingitis
endoscopic sclerosis
endoscopic sphincterotomy
end stage

end systole
end-to-side (anastomosis) *also* E-S, ETS
environmental stimulation
enzyme substrate
epileptic syndrome
esophageal scintigraphy
esophagus *also* E, ESO, eso, esoph
esophoria
esterase *also* EST
Ewing sarcoma
exfoliation syndrome
Expectation Score
experimental study
ex-smoker
exterior surface
extrasystole
soap enema [L. *enema saponis*] *also* e.s.

E-S
end-to-side (anastomosis) *also* ES, ETS

Es
einsteinium
electrical stimulation *also* ES
estriol *also* E_3

^{255}Es
einsteinium-255

e.s.
soap enema [L. *enema saponis*] *also* ES

ESA
end-to-side anastomosis
epididymal sperm aspiration
ethmoid sinus adenocarcinoma

ESAP
evoked sensory (nerve) action potention

ESAT
extrasystolic atrial tachycardia

ESB
electrical stimulation of brain

ESC
electromechanical slope computer
end-systolic count
erythropoietin-sensitive stem cell

ESCA
electron spectroscopy for chemical analysis

ESCC
electrolyte steroid cardiopathy by calcification
epidural spinal cord compression

ESCH
electrolyte steroid-produced cardiopathy (characterized by) hyalinization

Esch.
Escherichia

ESCN
electrolyte and steroid cardiopathy with necrosis

ESCS
Early Social Communication Scale

ESD
electronic summation device
electron-stimulated desorption
emission spectrometric detector
end-systolic diameter
end-systolic dimension
environmental sex determination
esophagus, stomach, and duodenum
esterase D
exoskeletal device

ESE
electrostatic unit [Ger. *electrostatische Einheit*]

ESEP
elbow sensory potential
extreme somatosensory evoked potential

ESF
electrosurgical filter
erythropoiesis-stimulating factor
external skeletal fixation

ESFL
end-systolic force-length (relationship)

ESG
electrospinogram
estrogen
exfoliation syndrome glaucoma

E

NOTES

ESI
Ego State Inventory
enamel surface index
enzyme substrate inhibitor
epidural steroid injection
extent of skin involvement

ES-IMV
expiration-synchronized intermittent
mandatory ventilation

ESIN
elastic stable intramedullary nailing

ESL
end-systolic (segment) length
English as a second language
extracorporeal shockwave lithotripsy

ESLD
end-stage liver disease
end-stage lung disease

ESLF
end-stage liver failure

ESM
ejection systolic murmur
endolymphatic stromal myosis
endothelial specular microscope
ethosuximide

ESMIS
Emergency Medical Services
Management Information System

ESN
educationally subnormal
estrogen-stimulated neurophysin

ESN(M)
educationally subnormal-moderate

ESN(S)
educationally subnormal-severe

ESO
electrospinal orthosis
esophagoscopy *also* eso, esoph
esophagus *also* E, ES, eso, esoph

eso, esoph
esophagoscopy *also* ESO
esophagus *also* E, ES, ESO

esoph steth
esophageal stethoscope

ESP
early systolic paradox
effective sensory projection
effective systolic pressure
electrosensitive point
electrosurgical pencil

endometritis-salpingitis-peritonitis
end-systolic pressure
eosinophil stimulation promoter
epidermal soluble protein
especially *also* esp
evoked synaptic potential
extramedullary solitary plasmacytoma
extrasensory perception

esp
especially *also* ESP

ESPA
electrical stimulation-produced
analgesia

ESPLR
end-systolic pressure-length
relationship

ESPQ
Early School Personality
Questionnaire

ESR
electric skin resistance
electron spin resonance *also* esr
erythrocyte sedimentation rate

esr
electron spin resonance *also* ESR

ESRD
end-stage renal disease

ESRF
end-stage renal failure

ESRS
extrapyramidal symptom rating scale

ESS
empty sella (turcica) syndrome
endometrial stromal sarcoma
endoscopic sinus surgery
endostreptosin
erythrocyte-sensitizing substance
euthyroid sick syndrome
excited skin syndrome

ess
essence
essential

ESSF
external spinal skeletal fixator

ess neg
essentially negative

EST
electric shock threshold
electroshock therapy
electroshock threshold

endodermal sinus tumor
esterase *also* ES
exercise stress test

est

ester *also* E
estimated
estimation

esth

esthetic

ESTN

epithelioid soft-tissue neoplasm

ESU, esu

electrostatic unit
electrosurgical unit

E-sub

excitor substance

ESV

end-systolic (ventricular) volume
esophageal valve

ESVEM

Electrophysiology Study versus
 Electrocardiographic Monitoring

ESVI

end-systolic volume index

ESVS

epiurethral suprapubic vaginal
 suspension

ESWL

electrohydraulic shock-wave lithotripsy
extracorporeal shock-wave lithotripsy

ESWS

end-systolic wall stress

ESWT

end-systolic wall thickness

ET

Ebbinghaus Test
edge thickness
educational therapy
effective temperature
ejection time
electroneurodiagnostic technologist
embryo transfer
endothelin
endotoxin
endotracheal *also* ENDO, Endo

endotracheal tube *also* ETT
end-tidal
endurance time
enterostomal therapist
enterostomal therapy
epithelial tumor
esotropia
esotropic
essential thrombocythemia
essential tremor
ethanol *also* E, ETH, ETOH, EtOH
ethyl *also* E, Et
etiocholanolone test
etiology *also* et, etio, etiol
eustachian tube
exchange transfusion
exercise test
exercise treadmill
expiration time
extracellular tachyzoite

ET′

near esotropia

ET−

esotropia for near

E/T

effector to target ratio

E(T)

intermittent esotropia

ET$_1$

esotropia at near

ET$_3$

erythrocyte triiodothyronine

ET$_4$

effective thyroxine (test)

Et

ethyl *also* E, ET

et

etiology *also* ET, etio, etiol

η

absolute viscosity
eta (seventh letter of Greek
 alphabet), lowercase

ETA

eicosatetraenoic acid
electron-transfer agent
endotracheal airway

E

NOTES

ETA *(continued)*
endotracheal aspirate
estimated time of arrival
ethionamide

EtA
endothelin A

ETAB
extrathoracic-assisted breathing

et al.
and elsewhere [L. *et alibi*]
and others [L. *et alii*]

E₂TBG
estradiol-testosterone-binding globulin

ETC
estimated time of conception

ETc
corrected ejection time

etc.
and so forth [L. *et cetera*]

ETCD
endoscopic transpapillary cyst
drainage
External Tachyarrhythmia Control
Device

ETCG
endoscopic transpapillary
catheterization of gallbladder

ETCL
enteropathy-associated T-cell
lymphoma

E_TCO₂
end-tidal carbon dioxide
(concentration)

ETD
eustachian tube dysfunction

ETDRS
Early Treatment Diabetic Retinopathy
Study

ETE
end-to-end (anastomosis)

ETEC
enterotoxigenic *Escherichia coli*

ETF
electron-transferring flavoprotein
eustachian tube function

ETH
elixir terpin hydrate
ethanol *also* E, ET, ETOH

ethionamide Ethrane (enflurane)
ethmoid

eth
ether *also* Et₂O

ETHC, ETH/C
elixir terpin hydrate with codeine

ETI
ejective time index

ETIO
etiocholanolone

etio, etiol
etiology *also* ET, et

ETK
erythrocyte transketolase

ETKTM
every test known to mankind

ETL
expiratory threshold load

ETM
erythromycin *also* E, EM

ETN
ethanol-induced tumor necrosis

Et₃N
triethylamine

ET-NANBH
enterically transmitted non-A, non-B
hepatitis

ETO
estimated time of ovulation
ethylene oxide (gas)
eustachian tube obstruction

EtO
ethylene oxide

Et₂O
ether *also* eth

ETOH, EtOH
ethanol *also* E, ET, ETH
ethyl alcohol (consumption,
dependency)

ETOP
elective termination of pregnancy
also ETP

ETOX
ethylene oxide *also* EO

ETP
elective termination of pregnancy
also ETOP
electron transfer particle

electron transport particle
entire treatment period
ephedrine, theophylline, and
  phenobarbital
eustachian tube pressure

ETR
effective thyroxine ratio
epitympanic recess
estimated thyroid ratio

ETS
Educational Testing Service
electrical transcranial stimulation
endoscopic transthoracic
  symphathectomy
endotracheal suction
end-to-side (anastomosis) *also* ES, E-
  S
erythromycin topical solution

ETT
endotracheal tube *also* ET
epinephrine tolerance test
esophageal transit time
exercise tolerance test
exercise treadmill test
extrapyramidal thyroxine
extrathyroidal thyroxine

ETTN
ethyltrimethyloltrimethane trinitrate

ETU
emergency and trauma unit
emergency treatment unit

ETV
educational television
extravascular thermal volume

ETX
ethosuximide

ETYA
eicosatetroenoic acid

EU
Ehrlich unit
emergency unit
endotoxin unit
entropy unit
enzyme unit
esophageal ulcer
esterase unit
etiology unknown

excretory urography *also* EXU
expected utility

Eu
europium
euryon

EUA
examination under anesthesia

EUCD
emotionally unstable character
  disorder

EUG
extrauterine gestation

EUL
expected upper limit

EUM
external urethral meatus

EUP
extrauterine pregnancy

EURONET
European On-Line Network

EUROTOX
European Committee on Chronic
  Toxicity Hazards

EUS
echoendoscopy
endoscopic ultrasonography
external urethral sphincter

eust
eustachian

EUV
extreme ultraviolet (laser)

EV
emergency vehicle
enterovirus
epidermodysplasia verruciformis
esophageal varices
estradiol valerate
eversion *also* ev, ever.
evoked (response)
excessive ventilation
expected value
extravascular

eV
electron volt *also* ev

E

NOTES

ev
electron volt *also* eV
eversion *also* EV, ever.

EVA
ethylene vinyl acetate
ethyl violet azide (broth)
etoposide, vinblastine, Adriamycin

EVAC, evac
evacuate
evacuated
evacuation

eval
evaluate
evaluated
evaluation

EVAN
ergonomic vascular access needle

evap
evaporated
evaporation

EVB
esophageal variceal bleeding

EVC
Ellis-van Creveld (syndrome) *also* EC

EVCI
expected value of clinical information

EVD
external ventricular drainage
extravascular (lung) density

eve
evening

ever.
eversion *also* EV, ev
everted

EVF
ethanol volume fraction

EVG
electroventriculogram
electroventriculography
endovascular grafting

EVI
endocardial, vascular, interstitial

EVL
endoscopic variceal ligation

EVLW
extravascular lung water

EVM
electronic voltmeter
extravascular mass

evol
evolution

EVP
evoked visual potential

EVR
endocardial viability ratio
evoked visual response

EVRS
early ventricular repolarization
syndrome

EVS
endoscopic variceal sclerosis

EVSD
Eisenmenger ventricular septal defect

EVTV
extravascular thermal volume

EW
Edinger-Westphal (nucleus)
emergency ward

ew
elsewhere

EWB
estrogen withdrawal bleeding

EWCL
extended-wear contact lens

EWHO
elbow-wrist-hand orthosis

EWI
Experiential World Inventory

EWL
egg white lysozyme
evaporation water loss

EWSCL
extended-wear soft contact lens

EWT
erupted wisdom teeth
esophageal wall thickness

E(X)
expected value of the random
variable X

Ex, ex
exacerbation
exaggerated *also* exag
examination *also* exam.
examined *also* exam.
example
excision *also* exc
exercise *also* E, exer
exophthalmos

exposure
external movement
extraction *also* EXT

ex aff.
of affinity [L. *ex affinis*]

EXAFS
extended x-ray absorption fine
structure (spectroscopy)

exag
exaggerated *also* Ex, ex

exam.
examination *also* Ex, ex
examine
examined *also* Ex, ex

ex aq.
out of water [L. *ex aqua*]

EXBF
exercise hyperemia blood flow

exc
except
excision *also* Ex, ex

EXCEL
Expanded Clinical Evaluation of
Lovastatin Study

EXD
ethylxanthic disulfide

exec
executive

Ex-ECG
exercise stress electrocardiography

Ex-Echo
exercise stress echocardiography

ExEF
ejection fraction during exercise

EXELFS
extended electron-loss line fine
structure

exer
exercise *also* E, Ex, ex

EXGBUS
external genitalia, Bartholin, urethral,
and Skene (glands) *also* EGBUS

ex gr.
of the group of [L. *ex grupa*]

exhib.
let it be displayed [L. *exhibeatur*]

exist.
existing

ex lap
exploratory laparotomy *also* exp lap

EXO
exonuclease
exophoria

EXP
experienced
exploration
expose

Exp
expectorant *also* exp, expec, expect
expiration *also* expir
expiratory *also* expir
expire *also* expir

exp
expected
expectorant *also* Exp, expec, expect
experiment(al) *also* E, exper, exptl
expired *also* E
exploration
exploratory
exponent
exponential (function)
exposed
exposure

expec, expect.
expectorant *also* Exp, exp, expect

expect
expectorant *also* Exp, exp, expec

exper
experiment(al) *also* E, exptl

ExPGN
extracapillary proliferative
glomerulonephritis

expir
expiration *also* Exp
expiratory *also* Exp
expired *also* Exp

NOTES

E

exp lap
exploratory laparotomy *also* ex lap

expn
expression

exptl
experimental *also* E, exp, exper

EXREM
external radiation-emission-man
(radiation dose)

EXS
externally supported
extrinsically supported

exsicc.
dried out [L. *exsiccatus*]

EXT
extension *also* E
external *also* ext
extract *also* Ex
extraction *also* Ex
extremity *also* ext, extr

ext
extension
extensor
exterior
external *also* EXT
extract
extremity *also* EXT, extr

ext aud
external auditory

extd
extended
extracted

ext fd
fluid extract

Ext FHR
external fetal heart rate (monitoring)

extr
extremity *also* EXT, ext

extrap
extrapolate
extrapolation

extrav
extravasation

ext rot
external rotation

EXTUB
extubation

EXU
excretory urogram
excretory urography *also* EU

EY
egg yolk
epidemiology year

EYA
egg yolk agar

EZ
Edmonston-Zagreb (vaccine)

Ez
eczema

F

bioavailability
brother [L. *frater*]
conjugative plasmid in F⁺ bacterial
  cells
degree of fineness of abrasive
  particles
fa
facial
facies
factor *also* Fac
Fahrenheit *also* Fahr
Fahrenheit temperature scale
failure
fair
false
family *also* fam
farad *also* f, far.
Faraday constant
fascia
fasting (test)
fat (dietary)
father *also* FR
fecal
feces
Fellow
female *also* Fe, fe, FEM, fem
fermentative
fermi
fertility (factor)
fetal
fibroblast
fibrous (protein)
Ficol
field of vision
filament *also* fil
filial generation
fine
finger
firm
fissure
flexed
flexion *also* f
flow (of blood)
fluid *also* f, Fl, fl, FLD, fld
fluoride
fluorine
flutter wave
focal length
focus
foil
fontanel
foot *also* f, ft

foramen
force
form *also* f
forma *also* f
formula
formulary
fossa
fractional (composition of gas in gas
  phase)
fracture *also* Fr, frac, fract, Frx, Fx,
  fx, FXR
fragment of antibody
free
free energy
French (gauge, scale) *also* FR, Fr
frequency *also* f, freq
frontal
frontal electrode placement in
  electroencephalography
full (diet)
function *also* fn, FXN
fundus
fusion beat
gilbert (unit of magnetomotive force)
Helmholz free energy
hydrocortisone (compound F)
inbreeding coefficient
let it be made [L. *fiat*]
(luminous) flux
make *also* f
phenylalanine *also* Phe
son [L. *filius*]
variance ratio
vectorcardiography electrode (left
  foot)
visual field *also* VF, Vf

F′

hybrid F plasmid
secondary focal point (of lens)

°F

degree Fahrenheit

/F

full lower denture *also* FLD

F/

full upper denture *also* FUD

(F)

final

F⁺

bacterial cell with an F plasmid
good form response

243

F⁻
 bacterial cell lacking an F plasmid
 fluoride
 poor form response

FI–FXIII
 factor I through XIII (blood)

F₁
 first filial generation

F₂
 second filial generation

F₃
 TFT—trifluorothymidine

F344
 Fischer 344 (rat)

f
 atomic orbital with angular
  momentum quantum number 3
 farad *also* F, far.
 femto-
 fingerbreadth *also* FB, fb
 fission
 flexion *also* F
 fluid *also* F, Fl, fl, FLD, fld
 focal
 following *also* ff
 foot *also* F, ft
 form *also* F
 forma *also* F
 formyl
 fostered (experimental animal)
 frequency *also* F, freq
 frequently
 fugacity
 make *also* f
 respiratory frequency

f.
 let them be made [L. *fiant, fiat*]

FA
 false aneurysm
 Families Anonymous
 Fanconi anemia
 far advanced
 fatty acid
 febrile antigen
 femoral artery
 fertilization antigen
 fetal age
 fibrinolytic activity
 fibroadenoma
 fibrosing alveolitis
 field ambulance

 filterable agent
 filterable air
 filtered air
 first aid
 fluorescein angiography
 fluorescent antibody
 fluorescent assay
 fluoroalanine
 folic acid
 follicular area
 foramen
 forearm
 fortified aqueous (solution)
 free acid
 Freund adjuvant
 Friedreich ataxia
 functional activities
 fusaric acid
 fusidic acid

F/A
 fetus active

fa
 fatty (rat)

FAA
 febrile antigen agglutination
 flavone acetic acid
 folic acid antagonist
 formaldehyde, acetic acid, and
  alcohol (solution)

FAAD
 fetal activity acceleration
  determination

FAAP
 family assessment adjustment pass

FAB
 fast atom bombardment
 formalin ammonium bromide
 fragment (of immunoglobulin G
  involved in) antigen binding *also*
  Fab
 French-American-British (leukemia
  classification system)
 functional arm brace

F(ab′)₂
 fragment (of immunoglobulin G) afte
  digestion with the enzyme pepsin

Fab
 fragment antigen binding
 fragment (of immunoglobulin G
  involved in) antigen binding *also*
  FAB

FABER
flexion, abduction, and external rotation

faber
flexion in abduction and external rotation

Fabere
flexion, abduction, external rotation, and extension

FABF
femoral artery blood flow

FAB/MS
fast atom bombardment mass spectrometry

FABP
fatty acid-binding protein
folic acid-binding protein

FABQ
Fear Avoidance Beliefs Quest

FAC
femoral arterial cannulation
ferric ammonium citrate
fetal abdominal circumference
5-fluorouracil, Adriamycin (doxorubicin), and cyclophosphamide
fractional area change
fractional area concentration
free available chlorine

Fac
factor *also* F

FACAI
Fellow of the American College of Allergy and Immunology

FACAL
Fellow of the American College of Allergy

FACAS
Fellow of the American College of Abdominal Surgeons

Facb
fragment, antigen, and complement binding

FACC
Fellow of the American College of Cardiologists

FACCP
Fellow of the American College of Chest Physicians

FACCPC
Fellow of the American College of Pharmacology and Chemotherapy

FACD
Fellow of the American College of Dentists

FACES
(unique) facies, anorexia, cachexia, and eye and skin (syndrome)

FACES-III
Family Adaptability and Cohesion Scale-III

FACFP
Fellow of the American College of Family Physicians

FACFS
Fellow of the American College of Foot Surgeons

FACG
Fellow of the American College of Gastroenterology

FACH
forceps to aftercoming head

FACHA
Fellow of the American College of Hospital Administrators

FAC-LEV
5-fluorouracil, Adriamycin (doxorubicin), cyclophosphamide, and levamisole

FACLM
Fellow of the American College of Legal Medicine

FACMTA
Federal Advisory Council on Medical Training Aids

FACN
Fellow of the American College of Nutrition

FACNHA
Foundation of American College of Nursing Home Administrators

NOTES

F

FACNP
Fellow of the American College of Neuropsychopharmacology

FACO
Fellow of the American College of Otolaryngology

FACO$_2$
fraction of alveolar carbon dioxide

FACOG
Fellow of the American College of Obstetricians and Gynecologists

FACOS
Fellow of the American College of Orthopedic Surgeons

FACOSH
Federal Advisory Committee on Occupational Safety and Health

FACP
Fellow of the American College of Physicians
ftorafur, Adriamycin (doxorubicin), cyclophosphamide, and Platinol (cisplatin)

FACPM
Fellow of the American College of Preventative Medicine

FACR
Fellow of the American College of Radiology

FACS
Fellow of American College of Surgeons
fluorescence-activated cell sorter *also* FACScan
5-fluorouracil, Adriamycin (doxorubicin), cyclophosphamide, and streptozocin

FACScan
fluorescence-activated cell sorter scan *also* FACS

FACSM
Fellow of the American College of Sports Medicine

FACT
Flanagan Aptitude Classification Test
Functional Assessment of Cancer Therapy

factor VIIIR
von Willebrand factor *also* VWF, vWF, vWf

FACWA
familial amyotrophic chorea with acanthocytosis

FAD
familial Alzheimer dementia
familial autonomic dysfunction
Family Assessment Device
fetal abdominal diameter
fetal activity-acceleration determination
flavin adenine dinucleotide *also* FADN

FADF
fluorescent antibody darkfield

FADH$_2$
flavin adenine dinucleotide (reduced form)

fadir
flexion, adduction, internal rotation

fadire
flexion, adduction, internal rotation, and extension

FADN
flavin adenine dinucleotide *also* FAD

FADU
fluorometric analysis of DNA unwinding

FAE
fetal alcohol effect

FAF
fatty acid free
fibroblast-activating factor

FAG
fundic atrophic gastritis

FAGA
full-term appropriate for gestational age

FAH
Federation of American Hospitals

Fahr
Fahrenheit *also* F

FAI
first aid instruction
functional aerobic impairment
functional assessment inventory

FAIDS
feline AIDS

FAJ
fused apophyseal joints

FAL
femoral arterial line
functional and anatomic loading

FALG
fowl antimouse lymphocyte globulin

FALL
fallopian

FALP
fluoro-assisted lumbar puncture

FALS
familial amyotrophic lateral sclerosis

FAM
5-fluorouracil, Adriamycin, and mitomycin

Fam, fam
familial
family *also* F

FAMA
Fellow of the American Medical Association
fluorescent antibody to membrane antigen (test)
fluorescent antimembrane antibody

fam doc
family doctor *also* FD, FMD

FAME
fast acquisition multiple excitation
fatty acid methyl ester

FAMe
5-fluorouracil, Adriamycin, and methyl-CCNU

fam hist
family history *also* FH, FH$_x$

FAMMM
familial atypical mole malignant melanoma
familial atypical multiple mole melanoma (syndrome)

FAMP
fludarabine monophosphate

fam per par
familial periodic paralysis

fam phys
family physician *also* FP

FAM-S
5-fluorouracil, Adriamycin (doxorubicin), mitomycin C, and streptozotocin

FAN
finger tension
fuchsin, amido black, and naphthol yellow

FANA
fluorescent antinuclear antibody

FANCAP
fluids, aeration, nutrition, communication, activity, and pain (nursing)

FANCAS
fluids, aeration, nutrition, communication, activity, and stimulation

FANPT
Freeman Anxiety Neurosis and Psychosomatic Test

FANS
Fellow of the American Neurological Society

FANSS&M
fundus anterior, normal size and shape, and mobile

FAP
familial adenomatous polyposis
familial amyloid polyneuropathy
fatty acid poor
fatty acids polyunsaturated
femoral artery pressure
fibrillating action potential
fixed action pattern
frozen animal procedure

FAPA
Fellow of the American Psychiatric Association

FAPHA
Fellow of the American Public Health Association

FAQ
Family Attitudes Questionnaire

F

NOTES

FAR
flight aptitude rating
fractional albuminuria rate

F^{AR}
immediate good function followed by accelerated rejection

far.
farad *also* F, f
faradic

FARS
Fatal Accident Reporting System

FAS
fatty acid synthetase
femoral access stabilization
fetal alcohol syndrome

FASC
free-standing ambulatory surgical center

fasc
fasciculation
fasciculus
fasicle

FASF
Factor Analyzed Short Form

FAST
Fein Articulation Screening Test
Filtered Audiometer Speech Test
flow-assisted short-term (balloon catheter)
Flowers Auditory Screening Test
fluorescent allergosorbent test
fluorescent antibody staining technique
fluoroallergosorbent test
Fourier-acquired steady-state technique
Frenchay Aphasia Screening Test

FAT
family attitudes test
fast axoplasmic transport
fluorescent antibody technique
fluorescent antibody test
food awareness training

FATG
fat globules

F₁ATPase
F_1 adenosine triphosphatase

FATS
Familial Atherosclerosis Treatment Study
fast adiabatic trajectory in steady state

FATSA
Flowers Auditory Test of Selective Attention

FAV
feline ataxia virus
floppy aortic valve
fowl adenovirus

FAZ
Fanconi-Albertini-Zellweger (syndrome)
foveal avascular zone

FB
factor B
fasting blood (sugar) *also* FBS
feedback
fiberoptic bronchoscopy *also* Fib. bronc, FOB
fingerbreadth *also* f, fb
flexible bronchoscope
foreign body
Fusobacterium

F/B
forward bending

fb
fingerbreadth *also* f, FB

f-b
face-bow

FBA
fecal bile acid

FBC
full blood count
functional bactericidal concentration

FBCOD
foreign body of the cornea, oculus dexter (right eye)

FBCOS
foreign body of the cornea, oculus sinister (left eye)

FBCP
familial benign chronic pemphigus

FBD
fibrocystic breast disease
functional bowel disease
functional bowel disorder
functional bowel distress

FbDP
fibrin degradation product *also* FDP, fdp

FBE
full blood examination

FBEC
fetal bovine endothelial cell

FBF
forearm blood flow

FBG
fasting blood glucose
fibrinogen *also* fbg, FG, FGN, FI,
FIB, fib, fib.
foreign body-type granuloma

fbg
fibrinogen *also* FBG, FG, FGN, FI,
FIB, fib, fib.

FBH
familial benign hypercalcemia

FBHH
familial benign hypocalciuric
hypercalcemia

FBI
flossing, brushing, and irrigation

FBL
fecal blood loss
follicular basal lamina

FBM
fetal breathing movement

FBP
femoral blood pressure
fibrin breakdown product
fibrinogen breakdown product

FBR
fresh-blood reaction [Ger. *Frischblut*]

FBRCM
fingerbreadth below right costal
margin

FBS
failed back syndrome
fasting blood sugar *also* FB
feedback signal
feedback system
fetal bovine serum

FBSS
failed back surgery syndrome

FBU
fingers below umbilicus
(measurement)

FBV
fiber bundle volume

FBW
fasting blood work

FC
family conference
fasciculus cuneatus
fast component (of neuron)
febrile convulsion
fecal coli (broth)
feline conjunctivitis
ferric citrate
fever, chills
fibrocystic
fibrocyte
financial class
finger clubbing
finger counting
flexion contracture
flucytosine *also* 5-FC
Foley catheter *also* F cath
form (response determined by) color
foster care
free cholesterol
frontal cortex
functional capacity
functional class

5-FC
5-fluorocytosine

F&C
flare and cell *also* F/C, F+C
foam and condom

F/C
fever and chills
flare and cell *also* F&C, F+C

F+C
flare and cells *also* F/C

Fc
centroid frequency
foot candle *also* fc, ftc
fragment, crystallizable (of
immunoglobulin)
shade response to black areas

Fc′
fragment crystallized in minute
quantities (immunoglobulin)
shade response to light gray area

F

NOTES

fc
foot candle *also* Fc, ftc

FCA
ferritin-conjugated antibody
fracture, complete, angulated
Freund complete adjuvant

FCAP
Fellow of the College of American
Pathologists

F cath
Foley catheter *also* FC

FCC
familial colonic cancer
femoral cerebral catheter
follicular center cell
fracture complete and compound
fracture compound and comminuted

fcc
face-centered-cubic

f/cc
fibers per cubic centimeter (of air)

FCCC
fracture complete, compound, and
comminuted

FCCL
follicular center cell lymphoma

FCD
feces collection device
fibrocystic disease
fibrocystic dysplasia
focal cytoplasmic degradation
fracture complete and deviated

FCDB
fibrocystic disease of breast

FCE
fibrocartilaginous embolism
5-fluorouracil, cisplatin, and etoposide
functional capacity evaluation

FCF
fetal cardiac frequency
fibroblast chemotactic factor

FCFC
fibroblast colony-forming cells

FCG
fifth cusp groove
French catheter gauge

FCGP
Fellow of the College of General
Practitioners

FCH, FCHL
familial combined hyperlipidemia
fibrosing cholestatic hepatitis

FchS
Fellow of the Society of
Chiropodists

FCI
fixed cell immunofluorescence
food-chemical intolerance

F-CL
5-fluorouracil, calcium, and leucovorin

fcly
face lying (position)

FCM
fetal cardiac motion
flow cytometric
flow cytometry

FCMC
family-centered maternity care

FCMD
Fukuyama-type congenital muscular
dystrophy

FCMN
family-centered maternity nursing

FCMS
Fellow of the College of Medicine
and Surgery
Foix-Chavany-Marie syndrome

FCMW
Foundation for Child Mental Welfare

FCO
Fellow of the College of Osteopathy

FCP
fasting chemistry profile
final common pathway
florid cutaneous papillomatosis
flow cytometric platelet
5-fluorouracil, cyclophosphamide, and
prednisone
Functional Communication Profile (of
aphasic adults)

FCPD
fibrocalculous pancreatic diabetes

FCPS
Fellow of the College of Physicians
and Surgeons

FCR
flexor carpi radialis
fractional catabolic rate

FcR
Fc receptor

FCRA
fecal collection receptacle assembly

FCRB
flexor carpi radialis brevis

FCRC
Frederick Cancer Research Center

FCS
fecal containment system
feedback control system
fetal calf serum
foot compartment syndrome

FCSNVD
fever, chills, sweating, nausea, vomiting, and diarrhea

FCSP
Fellow of the Chartered Society of Physiotherapy

FCST
Fellow of the College of Speech Therapists

FCT
food composition table

FCU
flexor carpi ulnaris

FCV
forced vital capacity

FCVD
fracture complete and varus deformity

FCVDS
Framingham Cardiovascular Disease Survey

FCx
frontal cortex

FD
failure to descend
familial dysautonomia
family doctor *also* fam doc, FMD
fan douche
fatal dose
fetal danger
fetal demise
fetal distress
fibrinogen derivative

field desorption
Filatov-Dukes (disease)
fixed and dilated *also* F&D
fluorescence depolarization
fluphenazine decanoate
focal disease
focal distance
Folin-Denis (assay)
follicular diameter
foot drape
forceps delivery
freedom from distractability
freeze-dried
frequency deviation
full denture

F/D
fracture/dislocation *also* fx-dis

F&D
fixed and dilated *also* FD

FD$_{50}$
median fatal dose

Fd
animo-terminal portion of heavy chain of immunoglobulin
ferredoxin
fundus

FDA
Food and Drug Administration
Frenchay Dysarthria Assessment
right frontal anterior (position of fetus) [L. *frontodextra anterior*]

FDB
flexor digitorum brevis

FDBL
fecal daily blood loss

FDC
follicular dendritic cell
frequency dependence of compliance
perfluorodecalin (blood substitute)

FD&C
Food, Drug, and Cosmetic (Act) *also* FFDCA

FDCA
Federal Food, Drug, and Cosmetic Act *also* FFDCA

F

NOTES

FDCPA
Food, Drug, and Consumer Product Agency

FDCT
Franck Drawing Completion Test

FDD
Food and Drugs Directorate

FDDC
ferric dimethyldithiocarbonate

FDDQ
Freedom from Distractibility Deviation Quotient

FDDS
Family Drawing Depression Scale

FDE
female day equivalent
final drug evaluation

FDF
fast death factor
further differentiated fibroblast

FDFQ
Food/Drink Frequency Questionnaire

FDG
F-18 2-deoxyglucose
feeding *also* fdg
fluorodeoxyglucose
2-fluoro-2-deoxyglucose

fdg
feeding *also* FDG

FDGF
fibroblast-derived growth factor

FDH
familial dysalbuminemic hyperthyroxinemia
focal dermal hypoplasia

FDI
first dorsal interosseus
frequency-duration index

FDICT
frequency-difference interferential current therapy

FDIU
fetal death in utero

FDL
flexor digitorum longus
fluorescein dilaurate

FDLMP
first day of last menstrual period

FDLV
fer-de-lance virus

FDM
fetus of diabetic mother
fibrous dysplasia of the mandible

FDMA
first dorsal metatarsal artery

FDNB
fluoro-2,4-dinitrobenzene
fluorodinitrobenzene (Sanger reagent)

FDNS
familial dysplastic nevus syndrome

FDP
fibrin degradation product *also* FbDP, fdp
fibrinogen degradation product
flexor digitorum profundus
fructose diphosphate
right frontal posterior (position of fetus) [L. *frontodextra posterior*]

fdp
fibrin degradation product *also* FbDP, FDP
fibrinogen degradation product *also* FDP

FDPALD
fructose diphosphate aldolase

FDPase
fructose diphosphatase

FDPCA
fixed-dose patient-controlled analgesia

FDQB
flexor digiti quinti brevis

FDR
fractional disappearance rate
frequency dependence of resistance

FDS
for duration of stay
Fellow in Dental Surgery
fiberduodenoscope
flexor digitorum sublimis
flexor digitorum superficialis

FDT
right frontal transverse (position of fetus) [L. *frontodextra transversa*]

F₃dTMP
trifluorothymidylate

FDTVMP
Frostig Developmental Test of Visual Motor Perception

FDTVP
Frostig Developmental Test of Visual Perception

FdUMP
fluorodeoxyuridylate

5-FdUMP
5-fluorodeoxyuridylate

FDV
Friend disease virus

FDZ
fetal danger zone

FE
fatty ester
fecal emesis
fetal erythroblastosin
fetal erythroblastosis
fluid extract
fluorescing erythrocyte
forced expiratory
formalin and ethanol
freely eating

Fe
female *also* F, fe, fem
iron [L. *ferrum*] *also* Fer

^{52}Fe
iron-52

^{55}Fe
iron-55

^{59}Fe
iron-59

fe
female *also* F, Fe, FEM, fem

feb
febrile

feb.
fever [L. *febris*]

feb. dur.
while the fever lasts [L. *febre durante*]

FEBP
fetal estrogen-binding protein

FEC
fluorouracil, etoposide, and cisplatin
forced expiratory capacity
free erythrocyte coproporphyrin *also* FECP
free-standing emergency center
Friend erythroleukemia cell

FECG
fetal electrocardiogram

$FECO_2$, F_{ECO2}
fraction in expired gas of carbon dioxide

FECP
free erythrocyte coproporphyrin *also* FEC

FECT
fibroelastic connective tissue (factor VIII)

FECV
functional extracellular (fluid) volume

FeD, Fe def
iron (ferrum) deficiency

FEE
forced equilibrating expiration

FEEG
fetal electroencephalogram

Fe-EHPG
Fe-ethylenehydroxyphenylglycine

FEF
Family Evaluation Form
forced expiratory flow

FEF_{50}
forced expiratory flow after 50% of vital capacity has been expelled

FEFEK
fractional excretion of potassium

FEF_{50}/FIF_{50}
ratio of expiratory flow to inspiratory flow at 50% of forced vital capacity

FEFmax
maximal forced expiratory flow

FEFV
forced expiratory flow volume

F

NOTES

FEHBP
Federal Employee Health Benefits Program

FEIBA
factor VIII inhibitor bypassing activity

FEKG
fetal electrocardiogram

FEL
familial erythrophagocytic lymphohistiocytosis

FELC
Friend erythroleukemia cell

FELI
fractional excretion of lithium

FeLV
feline leukemia virus *also* FLV

FEM
femoral *also* fem
femur *also* Fem, fem
finite element method
fluid-electrolyte malnutrition

Fem
femur *also* FEM, fem

fem
female *also* F, Fe, fe
feminine
femoral *also* FEM
femur *also* FEM, Fem

fem. intern.
at inner side of thighs [L. *femoribus internus*]

Fem-pop
femoral-popliteal (bypass)

FEN
fluid, electrolytes, and nutrition

FENa, FE$_{Na}$
fractional excretion of sodium

FENF
fenfluramine

Fe$_3$O$_4$
magnetite

F$_{EO2}$
fractional concentration of oxygen in expired gas

FEOM
full extraocular motion
full extraocular movement

FEP
fluorinated ethylene-propylene (polymer)
free erythrocyte porphyrin
free erythrocyte protoporphyrin *also* FEPP

FEPB
functional electronic peroneal brace

FEPP
free erythrocyte protoporphyrin *also* FEP

FEPP-B
vindesine, etoposide, procarbazine, prednisone, and bleomycin

FER
flexion, extension, and rotation
fractional esterification rate

Fer
iron *also* Fe

fert
fertility
fertilized

ferv.
boiling [L. *fervens*]

FES
Family Environment Scale
fat embolism syndrome
flame emission spectroscopy
forced expiratory spirogram
functional electrical stimulation

FESA
finite element stress analysis

FeSO$_4$
ferrous sulfate

FESS
functional endoscopic sinus surgery

FeSV
feline sarcoma virus

FET
field-effect transistor
Fisher exact test
fixed erythrocyte turnover
forced expiratory time

fet
fetus

FETE
Far Eastern tick-borne encephalitis

FETI
  fluorescence energy transfer immunoassay

Fe/TIBC
  iron saturation of serum transferrin

FETs
  forced expiratory time in seconds

FEUO
  for external use only

FE-UR
  iron in urine

FEV
  familial exudative vitreoretinopathy (FEVR)
  forced expiratory volume

FEV₁
  forced expiratory volume in one second

fev
  fever

FEVB
  frequency ectopic ventricular beat

FEV/FVC
  forced expiratory volume timed to forced vital capacity ratio

FEV₁/FVC
  forced expiratory volume in one second to forced vital capacity ratio

FEVR
  familial exudative vitreoretinopathy
  familial exudative vitreoretinopathy

FEVₜ
  forced expiratory volume timed

FEV₁/VC
  ratio of one-second forced expiratory volume to vital capacity

FEXE
  formalin, ethanol, xylol, and ethanol

FeZ
  iron zone

FF
  degree of fineness of abrasive particles
  fat free

fat-free (diet) *also* FFD
father factor
fear of failure
fecal frequency
fertility factor
fibrillation-flutter
fields of Forel
filtration factor
filtration fraction
fine fiber
fine fraction
finger flexion
finger-to-finger *also* f-f, f→f
fixation fluid
fixing fluid
flat feet
flip-flop (electronic logic circuitry)
fluorescent focus
follicular fluid
force fluids *also* ff
forearm flow
forward flexion
foster father
Fox-Fordyce (disease)
free fraction
fresh frozen
fundus firm *also* ff
further flexion

F&F
  filiform (bougie) and follower
  fixes and follows

fF
  ultrafine fiber
  ultrafine fraction

ff
  following *also* f
  force fluids *also* FF
  fundus firm *also* FF

f-f
  finger-to-finger *also* FF, f→f

f→f
  finger-to-finger *also* FF, ff

FFA
  Fellow of the Faculty of Anaesthetists
  female-female adaptor
  free fatty acid
  fundus fluorescein angiogram

F

NOTES

FFA *(continued)*
(unesterified) free fatty acid *also* UFA

FFAP
free fatty-acid phase

FFB
fast feedback
flexible fiberoptic bronchoscopy

FFC
fixed flexion contracture
free from chlorine

FFCM
Fellow of the Faculty of Community Medicine

FFCS
forearm flexion control strap

FFD
fat-free diet *also* FF
Fellow in the Faculty of Dentistry
focal film distance
focus film distance

FFDCA
Federal Food, Drug, and Cosmetic Act *also* FDCA

FFDW
fat-free dry weight

FFE
fecal fat excretion
free flow electrophoresis

FFEM
freeze fracture electron microscopy

FFF
degree of fineness of abrasive particles
field-flow fractionation
flicker fusion frequency (test)

FFG
free fat graft

FFHom
Fellow of the Faculty of Homeopathy

FFI
fast food intake
free from infection
fundamental frequency indicator

FFIT
fluorescent focus inhibition test

FFL
floral variant of follicular lymphoma

FFM
fat-free mass
five-finger movement

FFOM
Fellow of the Faculty of Occupational Medicine

FFP
flexible fluoropolymer
fresh frozen plasma

FFR
Fellow of the Faculty of Radiologists
fractional flow reserve
frequency-following response

FFr
fast Fourier imaging

FFROM
full, free range of motion

FFS
failure of fixation suppression
fat-free solid
fat-free supper
fee for service
flexible fiberoptic sigmoidoscopy

FFT
fast Fourier transform
flicker fusion test
flicker fusion threshold

FFTP
first full-term pregnancy

FFU
femur-fibula-ulna (syndrome)
focus-forming unit

FFW
fat-free weight

FFWC
fractional free-water clearance

FFWW
fat-free wet weight

FG
fasciculus gracilis
fast-glycolytic (muscle fiber)
fast green
Feeley-Gorman (agar) *also* F-G
fibrin glue
fibrinogen *also* FBG, fbg, FGN, FI, FIB, fib, fib.
field gain
Flemish giant (rabbit)
French gauge

F-G
    Feeley-Gorman (agar) *also* FG

fg
    femtogram

FGAR
    formylglycinamide ribonucleotide
    N-formylglycinamide ribotide

FGB
    fully granulated basophil

FGC
    fibrinogen gel chromatography

FGD
    fatal granulomatous disease

FGDS
    fibrogastroduodenoscopy

FGF
    father's grandfather
    fibroblast growth factor
    fresh gas flow

FGFa
    (acidic) fibroblast growth factor *also*
    aFGF

FGG
    focal global glomerulosclerosis
    fowl γ-globulin
    free gingival groove

FGL
    fasting gastrin level

FGLU
    fasting glucose

FGM
    father's grandmother

FGN
    fibrinogen *also* FBG, fbg, FG
    focal glomerulonephritis

FGP
    fundic gland polyp

FGR
    fetal growth restriction

FGRN
    finely granular

FGS
    fibrogastroscopy
    focal glomerular sclerosis

FGT
    female genital tract
    fluorescent gonorrhea test

FGU
    French gauge, urodynamic

FH
    facial hemihyperplasia
    familial hypercholesterolemia *also*
    FHC
    family history *also* fam hist, FH_x
    Fanconi-Hegglin (syndrome)
    fasting hyperbilirubinemia
    favorable histology
    femoral hypoplasia
    fetal head
    fetal heart
    fibromuscular hyperplasia *also* FMH
    Ficoll-Hypaque (technique)
    floating hospital
    follicular hyperplasia
    Frankfort horizontal (plane of skull)
    fundal height

FH^+
    family history positive
    family history positive *also* FHP

FH^-
    family history negative

FH_4
    folacin
    tetrahydrofolic acid

f.h.
    let a draught be made [L. *fiat
    haustus*]

fh
    fostered by hand (experimental
    animal)

FHA
    familial hypoplastic anemia
    Fellow of the Institute of Hospital
    Administrators
    filamentous hemagglutinin
    filterable hemolytic anemia
    fimbrial hemagglutinin

F

NOTES

FHC
familial hypercholesterolemia *also* FH
family health center
Ficoll-Hypaque centrifugation
Fuchs heterochromic cyclitis

FHCH
fortified hexachlorocyclohexane

FHD
familial histiocytic dermatoarthritis
family history of diabetes

FHF
fetal heart frequency
fulminant hepatic failure

FHH
familial hypocalciuric hypercalcemia
family history of hirsutism
fetal heart heard

FHI
Fuchs heterochromic iridocyclitis

FHIP
family health insurance plan

FHL
femoral head line
flexor hallucis longus
functional hearing loss

FHLDL
familial hypercholesterolemia, low-
density lipoprotein

FH-M
fumarate hydratase, mitochondrial

FHM
fat head minnow (cells)
fetal heart motion

FHMI
family history of mental illness

FHN
family history negative

FHNH
fetal heart not heard

FHP
family history positive (FH⁺) *also*
FH⁺

FHR
familial hypophosphatemic rickets
fetal heart rate
fetal heart rhythm

FHRDC
family history, research diagnostic
criteria

FHR-NST
fetal heart rate nonstress test

FHS
fetal heart sound
fetal hydantoin syndrome

FH-S
fumarate hydratase, soluble

FHT
fetal heart tone

FHTG
familial hypertriglyceridemia

FH-UFS
femoral hypoplasia-unusual facies
syndrome

FHVP
free hepatic venous pressure

FH$_x$
family history *also* fam hist, FH

FI
fasciculus interfascicularis
fever caused by infection
fibrinogen *also* FBG, fbg, FG, FGN,
FIB, fib, fib.
fiscal intermediary
fixateur interne
fixator interne
fixed interval (schedule)
flame ionization
forced inspiration
frontoiliacus
functional inquiry

FIA
feline infectious anemia
fluorescent immunoassay
fluoroimmunoassay
focal immunoassay
Freund incomplete adjuvant

FIAC
Fellow of the International Academy
of Cytology

FIB
Fellow of the Institute of Biology
fibrin
fibrinogen *also* FBG, fbg, FG, FGN,
FI, fib, fib.
fibrositis
fibula

fib
fibrinogen *also* FBG, fbg, FG, FGN, FI, FIB, fib.

fib.
fiber
fibrillation *also* fibrill
fibrinogen *also* FBG, fbg, FG, FGN, FI, FIB, fib

Fib. bronc
fiberoptic bronchoscopy *also* FB, FOB

fibrill
fibrillation *also* fib.

FIC
fasting intestinal contents
Fellow of the Institute of Chemistry
forced inspiratory capacity
functional inhibitory concentration

FICA
Federal Insurance Contributions Act
food immune complex assay

FICD
Fellow of the International College of Dentists

FIco$_2$, FI$_{CO2}$
fractional concentration of carbon dioxide in inspired gas

FICS
Fellow of the International College of Surgeons

FICSIT
Frailty and Injuries: Cooperative Studies of Interventional Techniques

FICU
fetal intensive care unit

FID
father in delivery
flame ionization detector
free induction decay
fungal immunodiffusion

FIF
feedback inhibition factor
forced inspiratory flow
formaldehyde-induced fluorescence
(human) fibroblast interferon *also* FIFN

FIFN
(human) fibroflast interferon *also* FIF

FIFR
fasting intestinal flow rate

fig.
figure

FIGD
familial idiopathic gonadotropin deficiency

FIGE
Field inversion gel electrophoresis

FIGLU
formiminoglutamic acid (test)

FIGO
Federation International de Gynecologie et Obstetrique
International Federation of Gynecology and Obstetrics
(classification of tumor staging)

FIH
familial isolated hypoparathyroidism
fat-induced hyperglycemia

FIL
father-in-law

fil
filament *also* F

FILAR
filariasin

filt
filter
filtration

FIM
field ion microscopy
functional independence measure

FIME
5-fluorouracil, ICRF-159 (razoxane), and methyl-CCNU (semustine)

FIMLT
Fellow of the Institute of Medical Laboratory Technology

FIN
fine intestinal needle
flexible intramedullary nail

FINCC
familial idiopathic nonarteriosclerotic cerebral calcification

F

NOTES

F-insulin
fibrous insulin

FIO$_2$, FiO$_2$
fraction of inspired oxygen

FIP
feline infectious peritonitis

FIPT
periarteriolar transudate

FIQ
full scale intelligence quotient

FIR
far infrared
fold increase in resistance

FIRDA
frontal irregular rhythmic delta
activity (electroencephalography)

FIRO-B
Fundamental Interpersonal Relations
Orientation-Behavior

FIRO-F
Fundamental Interpersonal Relations
Orientation-Feelings

FIS
fiberoptic injection sclerotherapy
forced inspiratory spirogram

FISH
fluorescent in situ hybridization

FISP
fast imaging with steady-state
precision

FISS
Flint Infant Security Scale

Fiss, fiss
fissure

fist.
fistula

FIT
Flanagan Industrial Test
fluorescein isothiocyanate *also* FITC
fusion-inferred threshold (test)

FITC
fluorescein isothiocyanate *also* FIT
fluorescein isothiocyanate, conjugated

FITT
frequency, intensity, time, and type
(exercise)

FIUO
for internal use only

FIV
feline immunodeficiency virus
forced inspiratory volume

FIV$_1$
forced inspiratory volume in one
second

FIVB
5-fluorouracil, imidazole (dacarbazine),
vincristine, and BCNU (carmustine)

FIVC
forced inspiratory vital capacity

F-J
Fisher-John (melting point method)

FJD
facet joint disease

FJN
familial juvenile nephrophthisis

FJN-MCD
familial juvenile nephrophthisis-
medullary cystic disease

FJP
familial juvenile polyp

FJRM, FJROM
full joint range of motion
full joint range of movement

FJS
finger joint size

FK
Feil-Klippel (syndrome)
feline kidney
Foster Kennedy (syndrome)
functioning kasai (Belgian Congo
anemia)

FKE
full knee extension

FL
factor level
fatty liver
feline leukemia
femoral length
femur length
fetal length
fibers of Luschka
fibroblast-like
filtered load *also* Fl, fl
filtrationleukapheresis
flavomycin
fluorescein
flutamide andleuprolide acetate
focal length

Friend leukemia (cell) *also* FLC
frontal lobe
full liquids (diet)
functional length
functioning kasai

FL-2
feline lung (cell)

Fl
filtered load *also* FL, fl
florentium *also* fl
fluid *also* F, f, fl, FLD, fld
fluorescence *also* fl, fluores
follicle lysis *also* fl

fL
femtoliter *also* fl

fl
femtoliter *also* fL
filtered load *also* FL, Fl
flank
flexible
flexion
florentium *also* Fl
fluid *also* F, f, Fl, FLD, fld
fluorescence *also* Fl, fluores
flutter
follicle lysis *also* Fl

FLA
fluorescent-labeled antibody
left frontal anterior (position of
fetus) [L. *frontolaeva anterior*]

f.l.a.
let it be done according to rule of
the art [L. *fiat lege artis*]

flac
flaccid
flaccidity

FLAG-ida
fludarabine, ara-C, G-CSF, and
idarubicin

FLAIR
fluid-attenuated inversion recovery

FLAK
flow artifact killer

Fl Ang
fluorescein angiography

FLASH
fast low-angle shot
flat low-angle shot

flav.
yellow [L. *flavus*]

FLC
fatty liver cell
fetal liver cell
Friend leukemia cell *also* FL

FLD
fatty liver disease
fibrotic lung disease
fluid *also* F, f, Fl, fl, fld
flutamide and leuprolide acetate depot
full lower denture *also* /F

fld
field
fluid *also* F, f, Fl, fl, FLD

fld ext
fluid extract *also* fldxt

fl dr
fluid dram

fld rest.
fluid restriction

fl drs
fluff dressing

fldxt
fluid extract *also* fld ext

FLEP
5-FU, leucovorin, Platinol

FLES
Fairview Language Evaluation Scale

FLEX
Federation Licensing Examination

flex.
flexion
flexor

flex sig
flexible sigmoidoscopy

FLGA
full-term, large for gestational age

FL-HCC
fibrolamellar hepatocellular carcinoma

F

NOTES

FLI
fluorescent light intensity

FLIC
Functional Living Index-Cancer

FLK
funny-looking kid (syndrome) (jargon)

FLKS
fatty liver and kidney syndrome

FLM
fasciculus longitudinalis medialis
fetal lung maturity

floc, flocc
flocculation

flor.
flowers (mineral substance in
powdery state after sublimation) [L.
flores]

fl oz
fluid ounce

FLP
left frontal posterior (position of
fetus) [L. *frontolaeva posterior*]

FLPD
flashlamp-pumped pulsed-dye laser
also FPDL

FLPR
flurbiprofen

FLR
funny looking rash

FLS
fatty liver syndrome
fibrous long-spacing (collagen)
flashing lights and/or scotoma
flow-limiting segment
Functional Life Scale

FLSA
follicular lymphosarcoma

FLSP
fluorescein-labeled serum protein

FLT
left frontal transverse (position of
fetus) [L. *frontolaeva transversa*]

FLTA
Fullerton Language Test for
Adolescents

FLTAC
Fisher-Logemann Test of Articulation
Competence

FLU
fluphenazine *also* FPZ

flu
influenza

FLU A
influenza A virus

FLUENT
Fluvastatin Long-Term Extension Trial

fluores
fluorescence *also* Fl, fl
fluorescent

fluoro
fluoroscopy

fl up
flareup
follow up

FLUT
flutamide

FLV
feline leukemia virus *also* FeLV
Friend leukemia virus

FLW
fasting laboratory work

FLZ
flurazepam

FM
face mask
facilities management
fathom
fat mass
feedback mechanism
fetal movement
fibromuscular
fibromyalgia
filtered mass
flavin mononucleotide
flowmeter
fluid movement
fluorescent microscopy
foramen magnum
forensic medicine
formerly married
foster mother
frequence modulation
frequency modulation
Friend-Moloney (antigen)
functional movement
fusobacteria microorganisms
make a mixture [L. *fiat mistura*]
also f.m.

F&M
 firm and midline (uterus)

Fm
 fermium

^{255}Fm
 fermium-255

f.m.
 make a mixture [L. *fiat mistura*]
 also FM

fm
 femtometer
 from *also* fr

FMA
 Frankfort mandibular (plane) angle

FMAC
 fetal movement acceleration test

FMB
 full maternal behavior

FMC
 family medicine center
 fetal movement count
 flight medicine clinic
 focal macular choroidopathy

FMCA
 Forensic Medicine Consultant Advisor

FMD
 family medical doctor *also* fam doc,
 FD
 fibromuscular dysplasia
 foot-and-mouth disease
 frontometaphyseal dysplasia

FMDV
 foot-and-mouth disease virus

FME
 full-mouth extraction

FMEL
 Friend murine erythroleukemia

FMEN
 familial multiple endocrine neoplasia

FMET, F-met, fMet
 formylmethionine

FMF
 familial Mediterranean fever
 fetal movement felt

flow microfluorometry
forced midexpiratory flow

FMFD1
 familial multiple factor deficiency 1

FMG
 fine mesh gauze
 foreign medical graduate

FMGEMS
 Foreign Medical Graduate
 Examination in Medical Sciences

FMH
 family medical history
 fat-mobilizing hormone
 fetomaternal hemorrhage
 fibromuscular hyperplasia *also* FH

FMI
 Foods and Moods Inventory

FMIA
 Frankfort mandibular incisor angle

FMISO
 F-misonidazole

FMIV
 forced mandatory intermittent
 ventilation

FML
 flail mitral leaflet
 fluorometholone (anti-inflammatory)

FMLP
 N-formyl-1-methionyl-1-leucyl-1-
 phenylalamine

FMN
 first malignant neoplasm
 flavin mononucleotide
 frontomaxillonasal (suture)

FMNH, FMNH$_2$
 reduced form of flavin
 mononucleotide

fmol
 femtomole

FMP
 fasting metabolic panel
 first menstrual period

FMR
 fetal movement record

F

NOTES

FMR *(continued)*
Friend-Moloney-Rauscher (antigen)
functional magnetic resonance
(imaging)

FMS
fat-mobilizing substance
fatty meal sonogram
Fellow of the Medical Society
fibromyalgia syndrome
5-fluorouracil, mitomycin, and
streptozocin
full-mouth series (dental x-ray films)

FMSTB
Frostig Movement Skills Test Battery

FMU
first morning urine

FMULC
free monoclonal urinary light chain

FMV
floppy mitral valve
fluorouracil, methyl-CCNU
(semustine), and vincristine

FMX
full-mouth x-ray

F-N, F→N
finger-to-nose (coordination test) *also*
FN, FTN

FN
facial nerve
false negative *also* Fneg
fastigial nucleus
fibronectin
final nitrogen
finger-to-nose (coordination test) *also*
F-N, F→N, FTN
fluoride number

fn
function *also* F, FXN

FNA
fine-needle aspiration

FNa
filtered sodium

FNAB
fine-needle aspiration biopsy

FNAC
fine-needle aspiration cytology

FNC
fatty nutritional cirrhosis

FNCJ
fine-needle catheter jejunostomy

FND
febrile neutrophilic dermatosis
frontonasal dysplasia
functional neck dissection

Fneg
false negative *also* FN

FNF
false-negative fraction
femoral neck fracture
finger-nose-finger (coordination test)

FNH
focal nodular hyperplasia

FNP
Family Nurse Practitioner

fn p
fusion point

FNR
false-negative rate

FNS
food and nutrition services
functional neuromuscular stimulation

FNT
false neurochemical transmitter
finger-to-nose test

FNTC
fine-needle transhepatic
cholangiography

FO
fast oxidative
fiberoptic
focus out
foot orthosis
foramen ovale
forced oscillation
foreign object
frontooccipital (fetal position)

Fo
fomentation
fomenting

FOA
Federation of Orthodontic
Associations

FOAVF
failure of all vital forces

FOB
father of baby
fecal occult blood

feet out of bed
fiberoptic bronchoscope
fiberoptic bronchoscopy *also* FB
foot of bed
foreign object/body

FOBT
fecal occult blood test

FOC
father of child
fluid of choice
frequency of contact scale
frontooccipital circumference

FOCAL
formula calculation (computer
language)

FOCMA
feline oncornavirus-associated cell
membrane antigen

FOD
free of disease

FOE
Fecal Odor Eliminator

FOEB
feet over edge of bed

FOG
fast-oxidative-glycolytic (fiber)
Fluothane, oxygen, and gas (nitrous
oxide)
full-on gain

FOH
family ocular history

FOI
flight of ideas

FOL
fiberoptic light

fol
following

FOM
figure of merit (measure of
diagnostic value per radionuclide
radiation dose)
floor of mouth

FOMI
5-fluorouracil, Oncovin (vincristine),
and mitomycin C

FOOB
fell out of bed

FOOSH
fell on outstretched hand

FOP
fibrodysplasia ossificans progressiva
forensic pathology

FOPR
full outpatient rate

FOPS
fiberoptic proctosigmoidoscopy

FOR, For
forensic

for.
foreign
formula *also* form.

form.
formula *also* for.

fort.
strong [L. *fortis*]

FORTRAN
formula translation (computer
language)

FOS
fiberoptic sigmoidoscope
fiberoptic sigmoidoscopy
fissura orbitalis superior
fractional osteoid surface
full of stool

FOT
forced oscillation technique
frontal outflow tract

found.
foundation

FOV
field of view

FOVI
field of vision intact

FOW
fenestration open window
fenestration of oval window

F-P
femoral popliteal

F

NOTES

FP
false positive
family physician *also* fam phys
family planning
family practice
family practitioner
Fanconi-Petrassi (syndrome)
fibrinolytic potential
fibrinopeptide
filling pressure
filter paper
final pressure
first pass
fixation protein
flat plate
flavin phosphate
flavoprotein
flexor profundus
fluid pressure
fluorescence polarization
food poisoning
foot process
forearm pronated *also* fp
freezing point *also* fp
frontoparietal
frozen plasma
full period
fundal pressure
fundus photos
fusion point

F-6-P
fructose-6-phosphate

F/P
fluid-plasma (ratio)
fluorescein to protein (ratio)

Fp
filtered phosphate
frontal polar electrode placement in
electroencephalography

f.p.
let a potion be made [L. *fiat potio*]
let a powder be made [L. *fiat
pulvis*]

fp
flexor pollicis
foot-pound
forearm pronated *also* FP
freezing point

FPA
fibrinopeptide A *also* fpA
filter paper activity
fluorophenylalanine

fpA
fibrinopeptide A *also* FPA

fpa
far point of accommodation

FPAL
full-term (deliveries), premature
(deliveries), abortion(s), living
(children)

FPB
femoral-popliteal bypass
fibrinopeptide B
flexor pollicis brevis

FPC
familial polyposis coli
family planning clinic
family practice center
fish protein concentrate
forced pair copulation
frozen packed cells

FPCL
fibroblast-populated collagen lattice

FPD
fetopelvic disproportion
fixed partial denture
flame photometric detector

FPDD
familial pure depressive disease

FPDL
flashlamp-pumped pulsed-dye laser
also FLPD

FPDVP
Frostig Program for the Development
of Visual Perception

FPE
first-pass effect

FPF
false-positive fraction
fibroblast pneumocyte factor

FPG
fasting plasma glucose
fluorescence plus Giemsa (stain)
focal proliferative glomerulonephritis
also FPGN

FPGN
focal proliferative glomerulonephritis
also FPG

FPH$_2$
flavin phosphate, reduced

FPHA
family planning health assistant

FPHE
formaldehyde-treated pyruvaldehyde-stabilized human erythrocytes
formalin-treated pyruvaldehyde-stabilized human erythrocytes

FPHx
family psychiatric history

FPI
femoral pulsatility index
formula protein intolerance
Freiburger Personality Inventory

FPIA
fluorescence-polarization immunoassay

f. pil.
let pills be made [L. *fiant pilulae*]

FPK
fructose-6-phosphokinase

FPL
fasting plasma lipid
flexor pollicis longus

FPLA
fibrin plate lysis area

FPM
filter paper microscopic (test)
full passive movements

fpm
feet per minute

FPN
ferric chloride, perchloric acid, and nitric acid (solution)

FPNA
first-pass nuclear angiocardiography

FPO
Federation of Prosthodontic Organizations
freezing point osmometer

FPP
familial paroxysmal polyserositis
ferriprotoporphyrin
free portal pressure

FPPH
familial primary pulmonary hypertension

FPR
fluorescence photobleaching recovery
fractional proximal resorption

FPRA
first-pass radionuclide angiogram

FPS
Fellow of the Pathological Society
Fellow of the Pharmaceutical Society
fetal PCB (polychlorinated biphenyl) syndrome
footpad swelling
foot-pound-second (system, unit) *also* fps

fps
feet per second
foot-pound-second (system, unit) *also* FPS
frames per second

FPSLT
Fluharty Preschool Speech and Language Screening Test

FPT
fixed parenchymal turnover

FPU
Family Participation Unit

FPV
feline panleukopenia virus
fowl plague virus

FPVB
femoral-popliteal vein bypass

FPZ
fluphenazine *also* FLU

FPZ-D
fluphenazine decanoate

FR
failure rate (contraception)
father *also* F
Favre-Racouchot (disease)
feedback regulation
fibrinogen related
Fischer-Race (notation)
Fisher-Race notation

NOTES

F

FR *(continued)*
    fixed ratio
    flocculation reaction
    flow rate
    fluid restriction
    fluid retention
    free radical
    French (gauge, scale) *also* F, Fr
    frequency of respiration
    frequent relapses
    Friend (virus) *also* FV
    full range
    functional residual (capacity)
    reticular formation [L. *formatio reticularis*]

Fr
    fracture *also* F, frac, fract, Frx, Fx, fx, FXR
    francium
    franklin (unit charge)
    French (gauge, scale) *also* F, FR

fr
    fried
    from *also* fm

FRA
    fibrinogen-related antigen
    fluorescent rabies antibody

fra
    fragile site (chromosome in cytogenetics)

frac
    fracture *also* F, Fr, fract, Frx, Fx, fx, FXR

FRACON
    framycetin, colistin, and nystatin

fract
    fraction *also* FX
    fracture *also* F, Fr, frac, Frx, Fx, fx, FXR

fract. dos.
    in divided doses [L. *fracta dosi*]

FRACTS
    fractional urines

frag
    fragile
    fragility
    fragment

FRAP
    fluorescence recovery after photobleaching

FRAT
    free radical assay technique

fra(X)
    fragile X (chromosome, syndrome)

FRBB, Fr BB
    fracture of both bones *also* Fx BB

FRBS
    fast red B salt

FRC
    feedback reduction circuit
    frozen red cell
    functional reserve capacity (of lungs)
    functional residual capacity (of lungs)

FRCD
    fixed ratio combination drugs

FRD
    flexion-rotation-drawer

FRE
    Fischer rat embryo
    flow-related enhancement

FRED
    fog reduction elimination device

FREIR
    Federal Research on Biological and Health Effects of Ionizing Radiation

frem.
    vocal fremitus [L. *fremitus vocalis*]

freq
    frequency *also* F, f

FRF
    fasciculus retroflexus
    filtration replacement fluid
    follicle-stimulating hormone-releasing factor *also* FSH-RF

FRFC
    functional renal failure of cirrhosis

FRH
    follicle-stimulating hormone-releasing hormone *also* FSH-RH

FRHS
    fast-repeating high sequence

frict
    friction (rub)

Fried
    Friedman (test for pregnancy)

frig.
    cold [L. *frigidus*]

FRJM
full range joint motion
full range joint movement

FRM
full range of motion *also* FROM

FRN
fully resonant nucleus

FRNS
frequently relapsing nephrotic syndrome

FROM
full range of motion *also* FRM

FROS
front routing of signal

FRP
follicle regulatory protein
functional refractory period

FRPS
functional resting position splint

FR r, fr r
friction rub

FRS
ferredoxin-reducing substance
first rank symptom
furosemide *also* FSM, FUR

FRT
Family Relations Test
full recovery time

Fru, fru
fructose

frust.
in small pieces [L. *frustillatim*]

FRV
functional residual volume

Frx
fracture *also* F, Fr, frac, fract, Fx, fx, FXR

FS
factor of safety
Fanconi syndrome
Felty syndrome
fetoscope
fibromyalgia syndrome
fibrous synovium

field stimulation
fine structure
fingerstick
fire setter (psychology)
Fisher syndrome
flexible sigmoidoscopy
food service
forearm supination
Fourier series
fracture, simple
fracture site
fragile site
Freeman-Sheldon (syndrome) *also* FSS
Friesinger score
frozen section *also* FZ
full-scale (IQ)
full and soft (diet) *also* F&S
full strength
functional shortening
function study
(human) foreskin (cells)
for skin

F/S
female, spayed (animal)

F&S
full and soft (diet) *also* FS

FSA
fetal sulfoglycoprotein antigen

f.s.a.
let it be made skillfully [L. *fiat secundum artem*] *also* f.s.a.r.

f.s.a.r.
let it be made according to the rules of the art [L. *fiat secundum artem reglas*] *also* f.s.a.

FSB
fetal scalp blood
Fokes sentence builder
full spine board

FSBG
fingerstick blood gas
fingerstick blood glucose

FSBM
full-strength breast milk

FSBP
finger systolic blood pressure

F

NOTES

FSBT
Fowler single breath test

FSC
Forer Sentence Completion (Test)
fracture simple and comminuted
fracture simple and complete
free secretory component
free-standing clinic

FSCC
fracture simple, complete, and comminuted

FSD
focus-skin distance
fracture simple and depressed
full-scale deflection

FSDQ
Frost Self-Description Questionnaire

FSE
fetal scalp electrode
filtered smoke exposure

FSF
fibrin-stabilizing factor (factor XIII)

FSG
fasting serum glucose
focal sclerosing glomerulonephritis
also FSGN
focal segmental glomerulosclerosis

FSGA
full-term, small for gestational age

FSGHS
focal segmental glomerular hyalinosis
and sclerosis

FSGN
focal sclerosing glomerulonephritis
also FSG

FSGO
floating spherical gaussian orbital

FSGS
focal segmental glomerulosclerosis

FSH
fascioscapulohumeral
focal and segmental hyalinosis
follicle-stimulating hormone

FSHD
facioscapulohumeral dystrophy

FSH/LR-RH
follicle-stimulating hormone and
luteinizing hormone-releasing hormone

FSHMD
facioscapulohumeral muscular
dystrophy

FSH-RF
follicle-stimulating hormone-releasing
factor *also* FRF

FSH-RH
follicle-stimulating hormone-releasing
hormone *also* FRH

FSI
foam stability index
Food Sanitation Institute
Function Status Index

FSIA
foot shock-induced analgesia

FSIQ
Full-Scale Intelligence Quotient

FSL
fasting serum level
fixed slit light

FSM
furosemide *also* FRS, FUR

F-SM/C
fungus, smear, and culture

FSME
Frühsommer meningoencephalitis

F-SP
special form (taxonomy) [L. *forma
specialis*]

FSP
familial spastic paraplegia
fibrinogen split product
fibrinolytic split product
fibrin split product
fine suspended particulate
free secretory piece

FSR
Fellow of the Society of
Radiographers
film screen radiography
fragmented sarcoplasmic reticulum
fusiform skin revision

FSS
Familiar Sensory Stimulation
Fear Survey Schedule
focal segmental sclerosis
Freeman-Sheldon syndrome *also* FS
French steel sound
front support strap

full-scale score
functional systems scale

FSST
Full-Scale Score Total

FST
foam stability test

FSU
family service unit
functional spinal unit

FSUM
focused, segmented, ultrasound
  machine

FSV
feline fibrosarcoma virus

FSW
field service worker
flexible spiral wire

FT
false transmitter
family therapy
fast twitch
feeding tube
ferritin *also* F$_t$
ferromagnetic tamponade
fetal tonsil
fibrous tissue
filling time
finger tapping
fingertip
followthrough (after barium meal)
formol toxoid
Fourier transform
free thyroxine
full term
function test

FT$_3$
free triiodothyronine
free triiodothyroxine

FT$_4$
free thyroxine
free (unbound) thyroxine

F$_t$
ferritin *also* FT

Ft
ftorafur

ft
feet
foot *also* F, f
foot/feet *also* F, f
let there be made [L. *fiat or fiant*]

FTA
fluorescein treponema antibody (test)
fluorescent titer antibody

FTA-ABS, FTA-Abs
fluorescent treponemal antibody
  absorption (test)

F-TAG
fast-binding target-attaching globulin

FTAT
fluorescent treponemal antibody test

FTB
fingertip blood

FTBD
fit to be detained
full term, born dead

FTBE
focal tick-borne encephalitis

FTBS
Family Therapist Behavioral Scale

FTC
frames to come (optometry)
frequency threshold curve
full to confrontation

ftc
foot candle *also* Fc, fc

ft. catapl.
let a poultice be made [L. *fiat
  cataplasma*]

ft. cerat.
let a poultice be made [L. *fiat
  ceratum*]

ft. collyr.
let an eyewash be made [L. *fiat
  collyrium*]

FTD
failure to descend
femoral total density

FTE
full-time equivalent (resident)

F

NOTES

ft. emuls.
let an emulsion be made [L. *fiat emulsio*]

ft. enem.
let an enema be made [L. *fiat enema*]

FTF
finger-to-finger (test)

FTFTN
finger-to-finger-to-nose (test)

FTG
full-thickness graft

ft. garg.
let a gargle be made [L. *fiat gargarisma*]

FTI
free thyroxine index

FT₃I
free triiodothyronine index

ft. infus.
let an infusion be made [L. *fiat infusum*]

ft. injec.
let an injection be made [L. *fiat injectio*]

FTIR
Fourier transform infrared (spectroscopy)
functional terminal innervation ratio

FTIUP
full-term intrauterine pregnancy

FTKA
failed to keep appointment

FTLB
full-term live birth

ft lb
foot pound

FTLFC
full-term living female child

ft. linim.
let a liniment be made [L. *fiat linimentum*]

FTLMC
full-term living male child

FTM
fluid thioglycolate medium
fractional test meal

ft. mas.
let a mass be made [L. *fiat massa*]

ft. mas. div. in pil.
let a mass be made and divided into pills [L. *fiat massa dividenda in pilulae*]

ft. mist.
let a mixture be made [L. *fiat mistura*]

FTN
finger-to-nose (coordination test) *also* FN, F-N, F→N
full-term nursery

FTNB
full-term newborn

FTND
full-term normal delivery

FTNS
functional transcutaneous nerve stimulation

FTNSD
full-term, normal, spontaneous delivery

FTO
fructose-terminated oligosaccharide
fulltime occlusion (eye patch)

FTP
failure to progress (in labor)

FTPA
perfluorotripropylamine (blood substitute)

ft. pil.
let pills be made [L. *fiant pilulae*]

ft. pulv.
let a powder be made [L. *fiat pulvis*]

FTR
force translation
fractional turnover rate
for the record

FTRAM
free transverse rectus abdominis myocutaneous (flap)

FTS
Family Tracking System
feminizing testis syndrome
fetal tobacco syndrome
fingertips
fissured tongue syndrome

serum thymic factor [Fr. *facteur thymique sérique*]

FTSD
full-term spontaneous delivery

FTSG
full-thickness skin graft

ft. solut.
let a solution be made [L. *fiat solutio*]

ft. suppos.
let a suppository be made [L. *fiat suppositorium*]

FTT
failure to thrive
fat tolerance test
fraternal twins raised together
fructose tolerance test

ft. troch.
let lozenges be made [L. *fiat trochisci*]

FTU
fluorescence thiourea

ft. ung.
let an ointment be made [L. *fiat unguentum*]

FTX
field training exercise

FU
fecal urobilinogen
Finsen unit *also* Fu
fluorouracil
followup *also* F/U
fractional urinalysis
fundus (at umbilicus) *also* F/U

F↓U
fingers below umbilicus
(measurement)

F↑U
fingers above umbilicus
(measurement)

F/U
followup *also* FU
fundus at umbilicus *also* FU

F&U
flanks and upper quadrants

5-FU
5-fluorouracil

FU-I
first set of followup data

FU-II
second set of followup data

Fu
Finsen unit *also* FU

FUB
found under bridge
functional uterine bleeding

FUC
fucosidase

Fuc
fucose

FU$_{CO}$
functional uptake of carbon monoxide

FUD
full upper denture *also* F/

FUDR
floxuridine *also* 5-FUdR
fluorodeoxyuridine *also* FUdR

FUdR
circadian-modified floxuridine
fluorodeoxyuridine *also* FUDR
5-fluoro-2-deoxyuridine

5-FUdR
floxuridine *also* FUDR

FUE
fever of unknown etiology

FUFA
free volatile fatty acid

fulg
fulguration

FUM
5-fluorouracil and methotrexate
fumarase
fumarate
fumigation

FUMIR
5-fluorouracil, mitomycin C, and radiation

F

NOTES

FUMP
fluorouridine monophosphate

FUN
followup note

func, funct
function
functional

FUNG-C
fungus culture

FUNG-S
fungus smear

FUO
fever of undetermined origin
fever of unknown origin

FUOV
followup office visit

fu p
fusion point

FUR
fluorouracil riboside
fluorouridine
furosemide *also* FRS, FSM

FURAM
ftorafur, Adriamycin (doxorubicin),
and mitomycin C

FUS
feline urologic syndrome
first-use syndrome
fusion

FUT
fibrinogen uptake test

FUTP
fluorouridine triphosphate

FV
Fahr-Volhard (disease)
femoral vein
flow volume
fluid volume
formaldehyde vapors
Friend virus *also* FR

FVA
Friend virus anemia

FVC
false vocal cord
filled voiding flow rate *also* FVFR
forced vital capacity

FVCA
forced vital capacity analysis

FVD
fibrovascular tissue on disk

FVE
fibrovascular tissue elsewhere
forced volume, expiratory

FVFR
filled voiding flow rate *also* FVC

FVH
focal vascular headache
fulminant viral hepatitis

FVL
femoral vein ligation
flexible video laparoscope
flow-volume loop
force, velocity, length

FVM
familial visceral myopathy

FVOP
finger venous opening pressure

FVP
Friend virus polycythemia

FVR
feline viral rhinotracheitis
forearm vascular resistance

FVS
fetal varicella syndrome

f.v.s.
let there be a cutting of a vein [L.
fiat venae sectio]

FW
Falconer-Weddell (syndrome)
Felix-Weil (reaction) *also* FWR
Folin-Wu (method, reaction) *also*
FWM, FWR
forced whisper
fracturing wall
fragment wound

Fw
F wave (fibrillatory wave, flutter
wave)

fw
fresh water

FWB
full weightbearing

FWHM
full width (of line-spread function)
half maximal height

full width (of photopeak measured at) half maximal (count) (tomography)

FWM
Folin-Wu method *also* FW

FWPCA
Federal Water Pollution Control Administration

FWR
Felix-Weil reaction *also* FW
Folin-Wu reaction *also* FW

FWW
front wheel walker

FX
factor X
fluoroscopy
fornix
fractional *also* F, fract, fx

Fx
fractional urine
fracture *also* F, Fr, frac, fract, Frx, fx, FXR
friction

fx
fractional *also* F, fract, FX
fracture *also* F, Fr, frac, fract, Frx, Fx, FXR

Fx BB
fracture of both bones *also* FRBB

fx-dis
fracture-dislocation *also* F/D

FXN
function *also* F, fn

FXR
fracture *also* F, Fr, frac, fract, Frx, Fx, fx

FXS
fragile X syndrome

FY
fiber year
fiscal year
framycetin
full year

FYA
Duffy A positive (blood type)

FYAN
Duffy A negative (blood type)

FYB
Duffy B positive (blood type)

FYBN
Duffy B negative (blood type)

FYI
for your information

F-Y test
fibrinogen qualitative test

FZ
focal zone
frozen section *also* FS
furazolidone

Fz
frontal midline placement of electrodes in electroencephalography

FZRC
frozen section red (blood) cell

NOTES

F

G

acceleration (force)
conductance
d-glucose *also* Glc
force (pull of gravity) *also* g
gallop (heart sound)
ganglion
gap (in cell cycle)
gas *also* g
gastrin
gauge (of needle) *also* g, ga
gauss *also* Gs
gender *also* g, GEN
geometric efficiency
Gibbs free energy *also* G
Giemsa (banding stain)
giga-
gingiva
gingival
glabella
globular (protein)
globulin
glucose *also* Glc, GLU, gluc
glycine *also* GLY, Gly
glycogen
gold inlay
gonidial (bacterial colony)
good
goose
grade *also* gr
Grafenberg spot
gram *also* g, gm
Gram (stain)
gravida (pregnant)
gravitational constant
gravitational units
gravity (unit)
Greek
green *also* GRN, Grn
Gross (leukemia antigen)
guaiac
guanidine
guanine *also* Gua
guanosine *also* Guo
gynecology
immunoglobulin G.
Newtonian constant of gravitation
unit of force of acceleration

G⁺

gram-positive *also* GM+, GP, gr⁺, GrP

G⁻

gram-negative *also* GM–, GN, gr⁻, GrN

G°

standard free energy

GΩ

gigaohm (one billion ohms)

G₀

gap_0
quiescent phase of cells leaving the mitotic cycle

G1

first pregnancy *also* grav 1
gap 1
gap_1
grid 1 (in electroencephalography)

G1–G4

grade 1-4 (heart murmur)

GI

primigravida *also* grav 1, grav I

GII

secundigravida *also* grav 2, grav II

G$_{II}$, G-II

hexachlorophene

GIII

tertigravida *also* grav 3, grav III

G₁

presynthetic gap (phase of cells prior to DNA synthesis)

G2

gap 2
gap_2
grid 2 (in electroencephalography)
second pregnancy *also* grav 2

G₂

postsynthetic gap (phase of cells following DNA synthesis)

G3

third pregnancy *also* grav 3

G₄

dichlorophen

G

Gibbs free energy *also* G

g

gas *also* G
gauge (of needle) *also* G, ga

g *(continued)*
gender *also* G, GEN
grain *also* GR, gr
gram *also* gm, G
gravity *also* gr, grav
group *also* GP, gp, grp
ratio of magnetic moment of a particle to Bohr magneton
standard acceleration due to gravity, 9.80665 m/s^2

g%
gram percent (per deciliter) *also* gm%, g/dL, g/dl

g
relative centrifugal force

GA
airway conductance *also* C_{AW}, C_{aw}, GAW, Gaw
Gamblers Anonymous
gastric analysis
gastric antrum
general anesthesia *also* gen-an
general appearance
gentisic acid
gestational age
Getting Along (psychologic test)
ginger ale *also* G'ale
gingivoaxial
glucoamylase
glucose/acetone
glucuronic acid
Golgi apparatus
gramicidin A
granulocyte adherence
granuloma annulare
guessed average
gut-associated
gyrate atrophy

G/A
globulin/albumin (ratio)

Ga
gallium
granulocyte agglutination

^{67}Ga
gallium-67

^{68}Ga
gallium-68

ga
gauge (of needle) *also* G, g

GAA
gossypol acetic acid

GAAS
Goldberg Anorectic Attituder S

GABA
γ-aminobutyric acid *also* γ-Abu

GABA-T
γ-aminobutyric acid transaminase

GABHS
group A beta hemolytic streptococcus *also* GABS

GABI
German Angioplasty Bypass Surgery Investigation

GABOA
γ-amino-β-hydroxybutyric acid

GABOB
γ-amino-β-hydroxybutyric

GABS
group A beta hemolytic streptococcus *also* GABHS

GAD
generalized anxiety disorder
glutamate decarboxylase
glutamic acid decarboxylase

GADH
gastric alcohol dehydrogenase

GADS
gonococcal arthritis/dermatitis syndrome

GAEL
Grammatical Analysis of Elicited Language

GAF
giant axon formation
global assessment of functioning

GAG
glycosaminoglycan

GAGUA
glycosaminoglycans uronate

GAHS
galactorrhea-amenorrhea-hyperprolactinemia syndrome

GAI
guided affective imagery

GAIPAS
General Audit Inpatient Psychiatric Assessment Scale

GAL
galactosemia

galactosyl
gallus adenolike (virus)
glucuronic acid lactone

Gal, gal.
galactose
gallon

G-ALB
globulin-albumin

G'ale
ginger ale *also* GA

GALK
galactokinase

gal/min
gallons per minute

GalN
galactosamine

GalNAc
N-acetyl-D-galactosamine

gal-1-P
galactose-1-phosphate

GALT
galactose-1-phosphate uridyltransferase
gastrointestinal-associated lymphoid
tissue
gut-associated lymphoid tissue

GAL TT
galactose tolerance test

GALV
gibbon ape leukemia virus

GaLV
gibbon ape lymphosarcoma virus

Galv, galv
galvanic
galvanism
galvanized

GAMG
goat antimouse immunoglobulin G

Γ
gamma (third letter of Greek
alphabet), uppercase

γ
carbon separated from the carboxyl
group by two other carbon atoms

chain of fetal hemoglobin
constituent of gamma protein plasma
fraction
gamma (third letter of Greek
alphabet), lowercase
10^{-4} gauss
heavy chain of immunoglobulin G
monomer in fetal hemoglobin
photon (gamma ray) *also* hν
plasma protein (globulin)

γ-Abu
γ-aminobutyric acid *also* GABA

γ-BHC
γ-benzene hexachloride (lindane) *also*
GBH

γG
immunoglobulin G

γ-HCD
γ-heavy chain disease

γ-HCH
hexachlorocyclohexane (lindane) *also*
HCC, HCH

γ-T
γ-tocopherol

GAN
giant axonal neuropathy

gang, gangl
ganglion
ganglionic

GANS
granulomatosus angiitis of the
nervous system

GAP
Gardner Analysis of Personality
(Survey)
glyceraldehyde phosphate
gonadotropin releasing hormone-
associated peptide

GAPD, GAPDH
glyceraldehyde phosphate
dehydrogenase
glyceraldehyde-3-phosphate
dehydrogenase

NOTES

GAPO
growth retardation, alopecia, pseudoanodontia, and optic atrophy (syndrome)

GAR
genitoanorectal (syndrome)
goat antirabbit (gamma globulin) *also* GARGG
gonococcal antibody reaction

Garg, garg
gargle

GARGG
goat antirabbit gamma globulin *also* GAR

GAS
galactorrhea-amenorrhea syndrome
gastric acid secretion
gastroenterology
general adaptation syndrome
generalized arteriosclerosis
Glasgow Assessment Schedule
Global Assessment Scale
group A streptococcus

GASA
growth-adjusted sonographic age

Gas Anal F&T
gastric analysis, free and total

GASP
gastric augment and single pedicle tube

GAST, gastroc
gastrocnemius (muscle)

Gastro, gastro
gastroenterology
gastrointestinal

GAT
gas antitoxin
gelatin agglutination test
Gerontological Apperception Test
group adjustment therapy

GATase
6-alkyl guanine alkyl transferase

GATB
General Aptitude Test Battery

GAU
geriatric assessment unit

gav
gavage

GAVE
gastric antral vascular ectasia

GAW, Gaw
airway conductance *also* C_{AW}, C_{aw}, GA

GAX
glutaraldehyde cross-linked collagen

GAZT
glucuronide derivative of azidothymidine

GB
gallbladder
Gilbert-Behçet (syndrome)
glass bead
glial bundle
goofball (barbiturate pill)
Gougerot-Blum (syndrome)
Guillain-Barré (syndrome) *also* GBS

G&B
good and bad (days)

GBA
ganglionic-blocking agent
gingivobuccoaxial

GBBHS
group B beta hemolytic streptococcus *also* GBBS

GBBS
group B beta hemolytic streptococcus *also* GBBHS

GBCE
Grassi Basic Cognitive Evaluation

GBD
gallbladder disease
gender behavior disorder
glassblower's disease
granulomatous bowel disease

GBE
Ginkgo biloba extract

GBEF
gallbladder ejection fraction

GBER
gallbladder ejection rate

GBG
glycine-rich β-glycoprotein
gonadal steroid-binding globulin

GBH
γ-benzene hexachloride (lindane) *also* γ-BHC
graphite, benzalkonium, heparin

GBI
globulin-bound insulin

GBIA
Guthrie bacterial inhibition assay

GBL
γ-butyrolactone
glomerular basal lamina

GBM
glioblastoma multiforme
glomerular basement membrane

GBMI
guilty but mentally ill

GBO
gastric bacterial overgrowth

GBP
galactose-binding protein
gastric bypass
gated blood pool

GBPS
gallbladder pigment stones
gated blood-pool study

GBq
gigabequerel

GBS
gallbladder series
gastric bypass surgery
glycerine-buffered saline
group B (β-hemolytic) streptococcus
   also GBBS
Guillain-Barré syndrome *also* GB

GBSS
Grey balanced saline solution
Guillain-Barré-Strohl syndrome

GBT
gastric bleeding time

GC
ganglion cell
gas chromatography
gel chromatography
general circulation
general closure
general condition
geriatric care
geriatric chair
gingival crevice

glucocorticoid
glycocholate
goblet cell
Golgi complex
gonococcal (infection)
gonococcus *also* GN
gonorrhea culture
good condition
Gougerot-Carteaud (syndrome)
graham cracker
granular cast
granular cyst
granule cell
granulocyte cytotoxic
granulomatous colitis
granulosa cell
group-specific component
guanine cytosine
guanylcyclase

G–C
gram-negative cocci *also* GMC

G+C
gram-positive cocci *also* GPC

Gc
gigacycle
group-specific component

GCA
gastric cancerous area
giant cell arteritis

g-cal
gram calorie (small calorie) *also* gm
cal

GCB
gonococcal base

GCBM
glomerular capillary basement

GCDFP
gross cystic disease fluid protein

GCDP
gross cystic disease protein

GCF
giant cell fibroblastoma
greatest common factor

GCFT
gonococcal complement-fixation test
gonorrhea complement-fixation test

NOTES

G-CFU
granulocyte colony-forming unit

GCH
giant cell hepatitis

GCI
General Cognitive Index
gestational carbohydrate intolerance

GCII
glucose-controlled insulin infusion

GCIIS
glucose-controlled insulin infusion system

GCIS
isolated gland carcinoma in situ

GCM
good control maintained

g-cm
gram-centimeter

GC-MS, GC/MS
gas chromatography-mass spectrometry

GCN
giant cerebral neuron

GCR
gastrocolonic response
glucocorticoid receptor
Group Conformity Rating

GCRC
General Clinical Research Centers

GCRS
gynecological chylous reflux syndrome

GCS
general clinical service
Generalized Contentment Scale
Gianotti-Crosti syndrome
Glasgow Coma Score
glucocorticosteroid
glutamylcysteine synthetase
graduated compression stockings

Gc/s
gigacycles per second

GCSA
Gross cell surface antigen

GCSF, G-CSF
granulocyte colony-stimulating factor

GCT
general care and treatment
germ cell tumor
giant cell thyroiditis
giant cell transformation
giant cell tumor
granular cell tumor
granulosa cell tumor

GCTTS
giant cell tumor of tendon sheath

GCU
gonococcal urethritis

GCV
great cardiac vein

GCVF
great cardiac vein flow

GCW
glomerular capillary wall

GCWM
General Conference on Weights and Measures

GCY
gastroscopy

GD
gastroduodenal
general diagnostics
general dispensary
general duties
gestational day
gestational diabetets
Gianotti disease
gonadal dysgenesis
Graves disease
growth and development *also* G and D, G&D

G and D, G&D
growth and development *also* GD

Gd
gadolinium

gd
good

GDA
gastroduodenal artery
germine diacetate

GDB
gas-density balance
guide dogs for the blind

GDC
General Dental Council
giant dopamine-containing cell
Guglielmi detachable coil

Gd-CDTA
gadolinium
cyclohexanediaminetetraacetic acid

GDD
gay disaster disease

Gd-DOTA
gadolinium
tetraazacyclododecanetetraacetic acid

Gd-DTPA
gadolinium-diethylenetriamine
pentaacetic acid
gadopentetate dimeglumine

Gd-DTPA-BMA
gadolinium-diethylenetriamine
pentaacetic acid-bismethylamide

Gd-EDTA
gadolinium ethylenediaminetetraacetic
acid

GDH
glucose dehydrogenase
glutamate dehydrogenase
glutamic acid dehydrogenase
glycerophosphate dehydrogenase
gonadotropic hormone
growth and differentiation hormone
(in insects)

Gd-HP-DO3A
gadoteridol

GDID
genetically determined
immunodeficiency disease

g/dL, g/dl
grams per deciliter *also* g%, gm%

GDM
gestational diabetes mellitus

GDMO
General Duties Medical Officer

gdn
guardian

GDP
gastroduodenal pylorus
gel diffusion precipitin
guanosine diphosphate
guanosine 5′-diphosphate

GDS
Gesell Developmental Schedules
Global Deterioration Scale
gradual dosage schedule

GDT
gel development time

GDW
glass-distilled water

GDXY
gonadal dysgenesis, XY

GE
gainfully employed
Gänsslen-Erb (syndrome)
gastric emptying
gastroemotional
gastroenteritis
gastroenterology
gastroenterostomy
gastroesophageal
gastrointestinal endoscopy
gel electrophoresis
generalized epilepsy
generator of excitation
gentamicin *also* GENT, GM
glandular epithelium
Gsell-Erdheim (syndrome)

G/E
granulocyte/erythroid (ratio)

Ge
Gerbich red cell antigen
germanium

GEA
gastroepiploic artery

GEC
galactose elimination capacity
glomerular epithelial cell

GED
General Education Development
graduated electronic decelerator

GEE
glycine ethyl ester
graft enteric erosion

GEF
gastroesophageal fundoplication
glossoepiglottic fold

NOTES

G

GEF *(continued)*
gonadotropin-enhancing factor
graft enteric fistula

GEFT
Group Embedded Figures Test

GEG
Garren-Edwards gastric

GEH
glycerol ester hydrolase

GEJ
gastroesophageal junction

gel.
gelatin

gel. quav.
in any kind of jelly [L. *gelatina quavis*]

GEM
gemcitabine

GEMS
good emergency mother substitute

GEN
gender *also* G, g
generation
genetics *also* Gen, genet
genital *also* gen, genit

Gen
genetics *also* GEN, genet
genus *also* gen

gen
general *also* gen'l
genital *also* GEN, genit
genus *also* Gen

gen-an
general anesthesia *also* GA

GEN/ENDO
general anesthesia with endotracheal intubation

genet
genetic
genetics *also* GEN, Gen

gen. et sp. nov.
new genus and species [L. *genus et species nova*]

genit
genital *also* GEN, gen
genitalia

gen'l
general *also* gen

gen. nov.
new genus [L. *genus novum*]

gen proc
general procedure

GENPS
genital neoplasm-papilloma syndrome

GENT, gent
gentamicin *also* GE, GM

GENTA/P
gentamicin peak (level)

GENTA/T
gentamicin trough (level)

GEP
gastric-emptying procedure
gastroenteropancreatic

GEPG
gastroesophageal pressure gradient

GER
gastroesophageal reflux
geriatrics *also* geriat
granular endoplasmic reticulum

Ger
German

GERD
gastroesophageal reflux disease

geriat
geriatric
geriatrics *also* GER

GERL
Golgi-associated endoplasmic reticulum lysosome

Geront
gerontologic
gerontologist
gerontology

GES
glucose-electrolyte solution
Group Encounter Survey
Group Environment Scale

GEST, gest
gestation

GET
gastric-emptying time
graded (treadmill) exercise test

GET½
gastric emptying half-time

GETA
general endotracheal anesthesia

GEU
gestation, extrauterine

Gev, GeV
gigaelectron volt

GEX
gas exchange

G-F
globular-fibrous (protein)

GF
gastric fistula
gastric fluid
germ-free
glass factor (tissue culture)
globule fibril
glomerular filtrate
glomerular filtration
gluten-free
grandfather *also* GR-FR
griseofulvin
growth factor
growth failure
growth fraction

gf
gram-force

GFA
glial fibrillary acidic (protein)
global force applicator

G factor
general factor (single variance common to different intelligence tests)

GFAP
glial fibrillary acidic protein

GFD
gluten-free diet
Goodenough Figure Drawing

GFFS
glycogen- and fat-free solid

GFH
glucose-free Hanks (solution)

GFI
glucagon-free insulin
ground-fault interrupter

GFL
giant follicular lymphoma

GFM
good fetal movement

G force
acceleration force

GFP
γ-fetoprotein
gel-filtered platelet
glomerular-filtered phosphate

GFPM
gastric first-pass metabolism of ethanol

GFR
glomerular filtration rate
grunting, flaring, and retracting (neonate)

GFS
global focal sclerosis

GFTA
Goldman-Fristoe Test of Articulation

G-F-W Battery
Goldman-Fristoe-Woodcock Auditory Skills Test Battery

GG
gamma globulin
genioglossus
glyceryl guaiacholate
glycylglycine
guar gum

G=G
grips equal and good

GGA
general gonadotropic activity

GGCT
ground glass clotting time

GGE
generalized glandular enlargement
gradient gel electrophoresis

ggELISA
glycoprotein-based enzyme-linked immunosorbent assay

GGFC
gamma globulin-free calf (serum)

G

NOTES

GGG
gambodium
glycine-rich gamma-glycoprotein

g.g.g.
gamboge [L. *gummi guttae gambiae*]

GGM
glucose-galactose malabsorption

GGPNA
γ-glutamyl-*p*-nitroanilide

GGS, GG or S
glands, goiter, or stiffness (of neck)

GGT
γ-glutamyltransferase
γ-glutamyl transpeptidase *also* GGTP

GGTP
γ-glutamyl transpeptidase *also* GGT

GGVB
gelatin, glucose, and veronal buffer

GH
Gee-Herter (disease)
general health
general hospital
genetically hypertensive (rat)
genetic hemochromatosis
genetic hypertension
geniohyoid
Gilford-Hutchinson (syndrome)
gingival hyperplasia
glenohumeral
good health
growth hormone

GHAA
Group Health Association of America

GHAG
general high altitude questionnaire

GHB
γ-hydroxybutyrate
γ-hydroxybutyric acid *also* GHBA

GHb
glycosylated hemoglobin *also*
GLYCOS Hb

GHBA
γ-hydroxybutyric acid *also* GHB

GHD
growth hormone deficiency

GHDT
Goodenough-Harris Drawing Test

GHK
Goldman-Hodgkin-Katz (equation)

GHL
glenohumeral ligament

GHPP
Genetically Handicapped Persons
Program

GHPQ
General Health Perception
Questionnaire

GHQ
General Health Questionnaire

GHR
granulomatous hypersensitivity reaction

GHRF, GH-RF
growth hormone-releasing factor *also*
GRF

GHRH, GH-RH
growth hormone-releasing hormone
also GRH

GHRIF, GH-RIF
growth hormone release-inhibiting
factor *also* GRIF

GHRIH, GH-RIH
growth hormone release-inhibiting
hormone

GHST
growth hormone stimulation test

GHV
goose hepatitis virus

GHz
gigahertz

GI
gastrointestinal
gelatin infusion (medium)
gingival index
globin insulin
glomerular index
glucose intolerance
granuloma inguinale
growth inhibiting
growth inhibition

Gi
good impression (California
Psychological Inventory)

gi
gill (¼ pint) *also* gl

GIA
gastrointestinal assistant

GIB
gastric-leal bypass
gastrointestinal bleeding

GIBF
gastrointestinal bacterial flora

GIC
gastric interdigestive contraction
general immunocompetence

GICA
gastrointestinal cancer antigen

GID
gastrointestinal distress
gender identity disorder

GIDA
Gastrointestinal Diagnostic Area

GIF
gonadotropin-inhibitory factor
 (somatostatin)
growth hormone-inhibiting factor

GIFT
gamete intrafallopian transfer
granulocyte immunofluorescence test

GIGO
garbage in, garbage out (computers)

GIH
gastric-inhibitory hormone
gastrointestinal hemorrhage
gastrointestinal hormone
growth hormone inhibiting hormone
growth-inhibiting hormone

G-II (*var. of* G_{II})

GII
gastrointestinal infection

GIK
glucose-insulin-potassium (solution)

GIL
gastrointestinal (tract) lymphoma

GILCU
gradual increase in length and
 complexity of utterance

GIM
gonadotropin-inhibiting material

Ging, ging
gingiva
gingival

g-ion
gram-ion

GIP
gastric-inhibitory peptide
gastric-inhibitory polypeptide
giant (cell) interstitial pneumonia
giant (cell) interstitial pneumonitis
glucose-dependent insulin-releasing
 peptide
glucose insulinotropic peptide
gonorrheal invasive peritonitis

GIR
global improvement rating

GIS
gas in stomach
gastrointestinal series
gastrointestinal symptom
gastrointestinal system
Gender Identity Service

GISSI
Gruppo Italiano Per lo Studio Della
 Streptokinase Nell'Infarto Miocardio

GIST
gastrointestinal stromal tumor

GIT
gastrointestinal tract
glutathione-insulin transhydrogenase

GITS
gastrointestinal therapeutic system
gut-derived infectious toxic shock

GITSG
Gastrointestinal Tumor Study Group

GITT
gastrointestinal transit time
glucose insulin tolerance test

GIV
gastrointestinal virus

GiV
giga (electron) volts

giv
give
given

G

NOTES

GIWU
gastrointestinal workup

GJ
gap junction
gastric juice
gastrojejunostomy

GJT
gastrojejunostomy tube

GK
galactokinase
Gasser-Karrer (syndrome)
glomerulocystic kidney
glycerol kinase

GKA
guinea pig keratocyte

GKMDT
Graham-Kendall Memory for Designs
Test

GKN
glucose-potassium-sodium

GL
gastric lavage
Gilbert-Lereboullet (syndrome)
gland *also* gl
glomerular layer
glucagon
glycolipid
glycosphingolipoid
granular layer
greatest length (fetus)
gustatory lacrimation

Gl
beryllium
glabella

g/L, g/l
grams per liter *also* gm/L, gm/l

gl
gill (¼ pint) *also* gi
gland *also* GL
glandular *also* gland.

GLA
α-galactosidase
γ-linolenic acid
gene-linkage analysis
giant left atrium
gingivolinguoaxial
D-glucaric acid

Gla
4-carboxyglutamic acid

glac
glacial

GLAD
gold-labeled antigen detection
(technique)

gland.
glandular *also* gl

GLAT
glutamic acid, lysine, alanine, and
tyrosine

glau
glaucoma *also* glc

GLC
gas-liquid chromatography

Glc
d-glucose *also* G
glucose *also* G, GLU, gluc

glc
glaucoma *also* glau

GlcA
gluconic acid

GLC/MS
gas-liquid chromatography/mass
spectrometry

GlcN
glucosamine

GlcNAc
N-acetylglucosamine

GlcUA
glucuronic acid

GLD
globoid leukodystrophy
glutamate dehydrogenase *also* GLDH

GLDH
glutamate dehydrogenase *also* GLD

GLH
germinal layer hemorrhage
giant lymph node hyperplasia

GLI
glicentin
glucagon-like immunoreactivity

GLIM
generalized linear interactive model
generalized linear interactive modeling

glio
glioma

GLL
glabellolambda line (craniometric point)

GLM
general linear model

GlN
glutamine

Gln
glucagon
glutamine *also* Q
glutaminyl *also* Q

GLNH
giant lymph node hyperplasia

GLNS
gay lymph node syndrome

GLO, Glo
glyoxalase

GLO1
glyoxalase 1

Glob, glob
globular
globulin

glob.
globulin

GLP
Gambro Liendia Plate
glucose-L-phosphate
glycolipoprotein
good laboratory practice
group-living program

Glp
5-oxoproline

GLPC
gas-liquid phase chromatography

GLPP, GL-PP
glucose, postprandial

GLPT
glutamate pyruvate transaminase

GLR
graphic level recorder
gravity lumbar reduction

GLS
gait lock splint

generalized lymphadenopathy syndrome
guinea (pig) lung strip

GLTN
glomerulotubulonephritis

GLTT
glucose-lactate tolerance test

GLU, glu
glucose *also* G, Glc, gluc
glucuronidase
glutamic acid
glutamine

GLU-5
five-hour glucose tolerance test

Glu
glutamic acid *also* E
glutamyl *also* E

glu (*var. of* GLU)

GluA
glucuronic acid

GLUC
glucosidase

Gluc, gluc
glucose *also* G, Glc, GLU

GLUC-S
urine glucose spot (test)

glucur
glucuronide

glu ox.
glucose oxidase

GLUT
glucose transporter

GLV
Gross leukemia virus

Glx
glutamic acid
glutamine
glutaminyl and/or glutamyl (indicates uncertainty between Glu and Gln)

GLY, gly
glycerite
glycerol *also* glyc
glycine *also* G, Gly
glycyl *also* Gly

G

NOTES

Gly
glycine *also* G
glycyl *also* GLY, gly

glyc
glyceride
glycerin
glycerite
glycerol *also* GLY

GLYCOS Hb
glycosylated hemoglobin *also* GHb

GM
gastric mucosa
Geiger-Müller (counter) *also* G-M
general medical
general medicine
genetic manipulation
gentamicin *also* GE, GENT
geometric mean
giant melanosome
gingival margin
grand mal
grandmother *also* GR-MO
grand multiparity
granulocyte-macrophage
granulocyte-monocyte
growth medium
monosialoganglioside (genetic marker)

G-M
Geiger-Müller (counter) *also* GM

GM+
gram-positive *also* G⁺, GP, gr⁻, GrP

GM−
gram-negative *also* G⁻, GN, gr⁻, GrN

Gm
gamma (allotype marker on heavy
chains of immunoglobins)

gm
gram *also* g, G

g/m
gallons per minute

gm%
gram percent (per deciliter) *also* g%,
g/dL, g/dl

g-m
gram-meter *also* gm-m

GMA
glyceral methacrylate
glycol methacrylate
gross motor activity

GMB
gastric mucosal barrier
glioblastoma multiforme
granulomembranous body

GMBF
gastric mucosal blood flow

GMC
general medical clinic
geometric mean concentration
grivet monkey cell

gm cal
gram calorie (small calorie) *also* g-
cal

gm/cc
grams per cubic centimeter

GMCD
grand mal convulsive disorder

GM-CFU
granulocyte-macrophage colony-forming
unit

GM-CSA
granulocyte-macrophage colony-
stimulating activity

GM-CSF
granulocyte-macrophage colony-
stimulating factor

GMCU
gracilis myocutaneous unit

GMD
geometric mean diameter
glycopeptide moiety (modified)
derivative

GME
graduate medical education

GMENAC
Graduate Medical Education National
Advisory Committee

GMEPP
giant miniature endplate potential

GMER
gastric mucosal ectopia in rectum

GMFM
Gross Motor Function Measure

GMH
germinal matrix hemorrhage

GMK
green monkey kidney (cells)

GML
glabellomeatal line
gut mucosal lymphocyte

g/mL, g/ml
grams per milliliter

gm/L, gm/l
grams per liter *also* g/L, gl

GMM
Goldberg-Maxwell-Morris (syndrome)

gm-m
gram-meter *also* g-m

GMN
gradient moment nulling

GMO
general medical officer

g-mol
gram-molecule

GMP
guanosine monophosphate
guanosine 5'-monophosphate
guanylic acid (reductase, synthetase)

G-MP
G-myeloma protein

3',5'-GMP
guanosine 3',5'-cyclic phosphate

GMR
gallops, murmurs, or rubs
gradient moment reduction
gradient moment rephasing

GMS
General Medical Service
Gilbert-Meulengracht syndrome
glyceryl monostearate
Gomori methenamine silver (stain)

GM&S
general medicine and surgery

GMT
geometric mean (antibody) titer
gingival margin trimmer
Greenwich Mean Time

GMV
gram-molecular volume

GMW
gram-molecular weight

GN
Gandy-Nanta (disease)
ganglioneuroma
gaze nystagmus
glomerulonephritis
glucagon
glucose nitrogen (ratio in water)
gnotobiote
gonococcus *also* GC
graduate nurse
gram-negative *also* G⁻, GM−, gr⁻,
  GrN

G/N
glucose/nitrogen (ratio in urine) *also*
  GN, G/Nr

Gn
gnathion
gonadotropin

GNA
general nursing assistance

GNB
ganglioneuroblastoma
gram-negative bacillus

GNBL
ganglioneuroblastoma

GNBM
gram-negative bacillary meningitis

GNC
general nursing care
General Nursing Council
glandular neck cell
gram-negative cocci *also* G–C

GNCA
gastric noncancerous area

GND
gram-negative diplococcus

gnd
ground

GNID
gram-negative intracellular diplococcus

GNP
Gerontologic Nurse Practitioner

GNR
gram-negative rod *also* G-R

G

NOTES

G/Nr
glucose/nitrogen ratio (in urine) *also* GN, G/N

GNRF
guanine nucleotide-releasing factor

GnRF
gonadotropin-releasing factor *also* GRF

GnRH
gonadotropin-releasing hormone *also* GRH

GNS
gerontologic nurse specialist

G/NS
glucose in normal saline

GNTP
Graduate Nurse Transition Program

GO
glucose oxidase *also* GOD
gonorrhea
Gordon-Overstreet (syndrome)

G&O
gas and oxygen

Go
Golgi
gonion

GOAT
Galveston Orientation and Amnesia Test

GOBAB
γ-hydroxy-β-aminobutyric acid

GOD
generation of diversity
glucose oxidase *also* GO

GOD/POD
glucose oxidase-perioxidase (method)

GOE
gas, oxygen, and ether (anesthesia)

GOG
Gynecologic Oncology Group (of National Cancer Institute)

GOH
geroderma osteodysplastica hereditaria

GOL
glabelloopisthion line

GON
gonococcal ophthalmia neonatorum
greater occipital neuritis

GOND
glaucomatous optic nerve damage

Gonio
gonioscopy

GOO
gastric outlet obstruction

GOQ
glucose oxidation quotient

GOR
gastroesophageal reflux
general operating room

GORT
Gilmore Oral Reading Test
Gray Oral Reading Test

GOS
Glasgow Outcome Scale

GOT
glucose oxidase test
glutamic-oxaloacetic transaminase (aspartate aminotransferase)
goals of treatment

GOTM, GOT-M
glutamic-oxaloacetic transaminase, mitochondrial

GOT-S
glutamic-oxaloacetic transaminase, soluble

govt
government

GP
gastroplasty
general paralysis
general paresis
general practice
general practitioner
general proprioception
general purpose
genetic prediabetes
geometric progression
globus pallidus
glucose phosphate
glucose production
glutathione peroxidase
glycerophosphate
glycopeptide
glycoprotein
Goodpasture (syndrome) *also* GPS
gram-positive *also* G⁺, GM+, gr⁺, GrP
group *also* g, gp, grp

guinea pig
gutta-percha

G/P
gravida/para

G-1,6-P
glucose-1,6-phosphate

G3P, G-3-P
glyceraldehyde 3-phosphate

gp
gene product
glycoprotein
group *also* g, GP, grp

GPA
glutaraldehyde, picric acid, acetic
acid
grade point average
gravida, para, abortus (subscript
numbers after each category) *also*
GrPAB
guinea pig albumin

GPAIS
guinea pig antiinsulin serum

G6PASE, G-6-Pase
glucose-6-phosphatase

GPB
glossopharyngeal breathing

GPBP
guinea pig myelin-basic protein

GPC
gastric parietal cell
gel permeation chromatography
giant papillary conjunctivitis
glycerophosphorylcholine
gram-positive cocci *also* G+C
granular progenitor cell
guinea pig complement

GPC/TP
glycerophosphorylcholine to total
phosphate (ratio)

GPD
glucose-6-phosphate dehydrogenase
also G-6-PD
glycerophosphate dehydrogenase
guinea pig dander

G6PD, G-6-PD
glucose-6-phosphate dehydrogenase

G6PDA
glucose-6-phosphate dehydrogenase,
varient A

GPE
glycerylphosphorylethanolamine
guinea pig embryo

GPF
glomerular plasma flow
granulocytosis-promoting factor

GPGG
guinea pig gamma globulin

GPH
giant papillary hypertrophy

Gph
Graduate in Pharmacy *also* Phar G,
PhG

GPHLV
guinea pig herpes-like virus

GPHN
giant pigmented hairy nevus

GPHV
guinea pig herpesvirus

GPI
general paralysis of insane
general paresis of insane
Gingival-Periodontal Index
glucose phosphate isomerase
Gordon Personal Inventory
gram-positive identification
guinea pig ileum

GPIMH
guinea pig intestinal mucosal
homogenate

GPIPID
guinea pig intraperitoneal infectious
dose

GPK
guinea pig kidney (antigen)

GPKA
guinea pig kidney absorption (test)

G-PLT
giant platelets

G

NOTES

GPLV
 guinea pig leukemia virus

Gply
 gingivoplasty

GPM
 general preventive medicine
 giant pigment melanosome

GPMAL
 gravida, para, multiple births,
 abortions, live births

GPN
 Graduate Practical Nurse

GPO
 group purchasing organization

GPP
 Gordon Personal Profile

GPPQ
 General Purpose Psychiatric
 Questionnaire

GPR
 good partial response
 gram-positive rod *also* G+R

GPRBC
 guinea-pig red blood cell

GPS
 Goodpasture syndrome *also* GP
 gray platelet syndrome
 guinea pig serum
 guinea pig spleen

GPT
 glutamic-pyruvic transaminase
 guinea pig trachea

GpTh
 group therapy *also* GT

GPTSM
 guinea pig tracheal smooth muscle

GPU
 guinea pig unit

GPUT
 galactose phosphate uridyl transferase

GPx
 glutathione peroxidase

GQAP
 general question-asking program

G-R
 gram-negative rod *also* GNR

GR
 gamma roentgen *also* gr

 gastric resection
 generalized rash
 general relief
 general research
 glucocorticoid receptor
 glucose response
 gluthathione reductase *also* GSR,
 GSSG-R
 good recovery
 grain *also* g, gr
 granulocyte
 gravid *also* gr, Grav
 γ-ray

G+R
 gram-positive rod *also* GPR

Gr
 Greek

gr
 gamma roentgen *also* GR
 grade *also* G
 graft
 grain *also* g, GR
 gravid *also* GR, Grav
 gravity *also* g, grav
 gray
 great
 gross *also* GRS

gr⁻
 gram-negative *also* G⁻, GM–, GN,
 GrN

gr⁺
 gram-positive *also* G⁺, GM+, GP,
 GrP

GRA
 gated radionuclide angiography
 Gombarts reducing agent
 gonadotropin-releasing agent

GRA⁺
 Gombarts reducing agent-positive

GRABS
 group A beta hemolytic streptococcal
 (pharyngitis)

Grad, grad.
 by degrees [L. *gradatim*]

grad.
 gradient
 gradually
 graduate

GRAE
 generally regarded as effective

GRAN
Gombarts reducing agent-negative

gran
granulated
granule

GRAS
generally recognized as safe

GRASS
gradient recalled acquisition in a
steady state
gradient refocused acquisition in a
steady state

Grav, grav
gravid *also* GR, gr
gravity *also* G, gr

grav 1
first pregnancy *also* G1
pregnant once
primigravida *also* GI, grav I

grav 2
pregnant twice
second pregnancy *also* G2
secundigravida *also* GII, grav II

grav 3
tertigravida *also* GIII, grav III
third pregnancy *also* G3

grav I
primigravida *also* GI, grav 1

grav II
secundigravida *also* GII, grav 2

grav III
tertigravida *also* GIII, grav 3

GRD
gastroesophageal reflux disease
gender role definition
β-glucuronidase *also* GRS, GUSB

grd
ground

GRE
gradient-echo
Graduate Record Examination

GREAT
Graduate Record Examination
Aptitude Test

Grampian Region Early Anistreplase
Trial

GRF
gonadotropin-releasing factor *also*
GnRF
growth hormone-releasing factor *also*
GHRF, GH-RF

GR-FeSV
Gardner-Rasheed feline sarcoma virus

GR-FR
grandfather *also* GF

GRG
glycine-rich glycoprotein

GRH
gonadotropin-releasing hormone *also*
GnRH
growth hormone-releasing hormone
also GHRH, GH-RH

GRID
gay-related immunodeficiency disease

GRIF
growth hormone release-inhibiting
factor *also* GHRIF, GH-RIF

GRL
granular layer

GR-MO
grandmother *also* GM

gr. m. p.
ground in a coarse way [L. *grosso
modo pulverisatum*]

GRN
granules
green *also* G, Grn

GrN
gram-negative *also* G⁻, GM–, GN,
gr⁻

Grn
glycerone
green *also* G, GRN

gros
coarse [L. *grossus*]

GRP
gastrin-releasing peptide

G

NOTES

GrP
gram-positive *also* G⁺, GM+, GP, gr⁺

grp
group *also* g, GP, gp

GrPAB
gravida, para, abortus (subscript numbers after each category) *also* GPA

GRPS
glucose-Ringer-phosphate solution

GRS
β-glucuronidase *also* GRD, GUSB
Graphic Rating Scale
gross *also* gr

GRS&MIC
gross and microscopic

GRT
gastric residence time
glandular replacement therapy
Graduate Respiratory Therapist

GrTr
graphite treatment

GRW
giant ragweed (test)

gr wt
gross weight

GS
gallstone
Gardner syndrome
gastric shield
gastrocnemius soleus
generalized seizure
general surgery
Gilbert syndrome
Glanzmann-Saland (syndrome)
glomerular sclerosis
glucagon secretion
glutamine synthetase
goat serum
Goldenhar syndrome
Goodpasture syndrome
graft survival
Gram stain
granulocyte substance
grip strength
group section
group specific *also* gs
Guérin-Stern (syndrome)

G/S
glucose and saline

Gs
gauss *also* G

gs
group specific *also* GS

g/s
gallons per second

GSA
general somatic afferent (nerve)
Gross (sarcoma) virus antigen
group-specific antigen
guanidinosuccinic acid

GSB
graduated spinal block
Gschwind-Scheier-Bahler

GSBG
gonadal steroid-binding globulin

G-SC
guanosine-coupled spleen cell

GSC
gas-solid chromatography
gravity settling culture (plate)

GSCN
giant serotonin-containing neuron

GSD
genetically significant dose (of mutagenic radiation)
Gerstmann-Sträussler disease
glutathione synthetase deficiency
glycogen storage disease

GSE
general somatic efferent (nerve)
genital self-examination
gluten-sensitive enteropathy
grips strong and equal

GSF
galactosemic fibroblast
genital skin fibroblast

GSH
glomerulus-stimulating hormone
glutathione
golden Syrian hamster
growth-stimulating hormone
reduced glutathione

GSHP
reduced glutathione peroxidase

GSI
genuine stress incontinence

GSK
glycogen synthetase kinase

GSN
giant serotonin-containing neuron

GSP
galvanic skin potential
general survey panel
glycogen synthetase phosphatase
glycosylated serum protein

GSPN
greater superficial petrosal neurectomy

GSR
galvanic skin resistance
galvanic skin response
generalized Shwartzman reaction
glutathione reductase *also* GR,
GSSG-R

GSRA
galvanic skin response audiometry

GSS
gamete-shedding substance
Gerstmann-Sträussler-Schenker
(syndrome)
Gerstmann-Sträussler syndrome

GSSG
oxidized gluthathione

GSSG-R
glutathione reductase *also* GR, GSR

GSSI
Global Sexual Satisfaction Index

GSSR
generalized Sanarelli-Shwartzman
reaction

GST
glutathione-*S*-transferase
gold salt therapy
gold sodium thiomalate *also* GSTM
graphic stress telethermometry
graphic stress thermography
group striction

GSTM
gold sodium thiomalate *also* GST

GSUI
genuine stress urinary incontinence

GSW
gunshot wound

GSWA
gunshot wound to abdomen *also*
GWA

GT
gait
gait training
galactosyl transferase
Gamow-Teller
gastrostomy
gastrostomy tube *also* G-tube
Gee-Thaysen (disease)
generation time *also* Tg
genetic therapy
gingiva treatment
Glanzmann thrombasthenia *also* GTA
glucagon test
glucose tolerance
glucose transport
glucuronyl transferase
γ-glutamyl transferase
glutamyl transpeptidase
glycityrosine
grand total
granulation tissue *also* g/t
greater trochanter
great toe
group tension
group therapy *also* GpTh

GT1-GT10
glycogen storage disease, types 1 to
10

G&T
gowns and towels

gt.
gutta (drop)

g/t
granulation time
granulation tissue *also* GT

GTA
Glanzmann thrombasthenia *also* GT

GTB
gastrointestinal tract bleeding

GTCS
generalized tonic-clonic seizure

GTD
gestational trophoblastic disease

G

NOTES

GTF
gastrostomy tube feeding
glucose tolerance factor
glucosyltransferase

GTG
gold thioglucose

GTH
gonadotropic hormone

GTL
glomerular tip lesion

GTM
grade, location, (lymph node involvement), and metastases (surgical staging system for bone sarcomas)

GTN
gestational trophoblastic neoplasia
gestational trophoblastic neoplasm
glomerulotubulonephritis
glyceryl trinitrate (nitroglycerin)

GTO
Golgi tendon organ

GTP
glutamyl transpeptidase
guanosine triphosphate
guanosine 5′-triphosphate

GTR
galvanic tetanus ratio
generalized time reflex
granulocyte turnover rate

GTS
Gilles de la Tourette syndrome
glucose transport system

GTSTD
Grid Test of Schizophrenic Thought Disorder

GTT
gelatin-tellurite-taurocholate (agar)
glucose tolerance test

gtt.
drops [L. *guttae*]

GTT3H
glucose tolerance test 3 hours (oral)

G-tube
gastrostomy tube *also* GT

GU
gastric ulcer
genitourinary
glucose uptake

glycogenic unit
gonococcal urethritis
gravitational ulcer

[G]u
concentration of glucose in urine

GUA
group of units of analysis

Gua
guanine *also* G

guid
guidance

GUK
guanylate kinase

GULHEMP
general physique, upper extremity, lower extremity, hearing, eyesight, mentality, and personality

Guo
guanosine *also* G

GUS
genitourinary sphincter
genitourinary system

GUSB
β-glucuronidase *also* GRD, GRS

GUSTO
Global Utilization of Streptokinase and t-PA for Occluded Coronary Arteries

gutt.
to the throat [L. *gutturi*]

guttat.
drop by drop [L. *guttatim*]

gutt. quibusd.
with a few drops [L. *guttis quibusdam*]

GV
gastric volume
gentian violet
germinal vesicle
granulosis virus
griseoviridin
Gross virus (nodule)

GVA
general visceral afferent (nerve)

GVB
gelatin-veronal buffer

GVBD
germinal vesicle breakdown

GVE
general visceral efferent (nerve)

GVF
Goldman visual fields
good visual fields

GVH, GvH
graft-versus-host

GVHD, GvHD
graft-versus-host disease

GVHR, GvHR
graft-versus-host reaction

GVL
graft-versus-leukemia (effect)

GVS
gastric vertical stapling

GVTY
gingivectomy

GW
germ warfare
gigawatt
glycerin in water
gradual withdrawal
Gray-Wheelwright
group work

G&W
glycerin and water

G/W
glucose in water

GWA
gunshot wound to abdomen *also*
GSWA

GWBS
global ward behavior scale

GWE
glycerin and water enema

GWG
generalized Wegener granulomatosis

GWT
gunshot wound to throat

GXD EKG
graded exercise electrocardiogram

GXP
graded exercise program

GXT
graded exercise test

GY
gynecologic disease

Gy
gray (unit of absorbed dose of
ionizing radiation)

GYN, gyn
gynecologic
gynecologist
gynecology

GYS
guaranteed yield strength

GZ
Guilford-Zimmerman (personality test)

GZAS
Guilford-Zimmerman Aptitude Survey

GZTS
Guilford-Zimmerman Temperament
Survey

NOTES

G

H

bacterial antigen in serologic classification of bacteria [Ger. *Hauch* film]

deflection in His bundle in electrogram (spike)

draft, drink [L. *haustus*] *also* h., haust., ht.

electrically induced spinal reflex

enthalpy (physics)

eta (seventh letter of Greek alphabet), uppercase

fucosal transferase-producing gene

Hancock

Hartnup (disease)

Hauch (motile microorganism)

he

head *also* h.d., he

heart *also* He, HT, ht

heavy

heelstick

height *also* h, *h*, Hgt, HT, ht

hemagglutination

hemisphere

hemolysis *also* HEM

hemolytic *also* HEM

henry

heparin *also* HEP, HP

hernia *also* her., hern

herniated *also* her., hern

herniation *also* her., hern

heroin

hetacillin

high

histidine *also* HI, Hi, HIS, His, Hist

history *also* Hist, hist, Hx, Hy

Hoffmann (reflex)

Holzknecht (unit)

homosexual *also* HOMO, homo

horizontal *also* h, hor, horiz

hormone

horse *also* Ho

hospital *also* Hosp, hosp, HX

hospitalization *also* Hosp, hosp, HX

hot

Hounsfield (unit) *also* HU

hour *also* h, HR, hr

human *also* h, hu

husband *also* husb

hydrogen

hydrolysis

hygiene *also* Hyg, hyg

hygienic *also* Hyg, hyg

hygienist *also* Hyg, hyg

hyoscine (scopolamine)

hypermetropia *also* h, Hy

hyperopia *also* h, Hy

hyperopic *also* h, Hy

hyperphoria

hyperplasia

hypodermic (injection) *also* (H), h, hypo

hypothalamus *also* HT, Ht, Hth, Hyp

magnetic field strength

magnetization

mustard gas

oersted

per hypodermic

region of sarcomere containing only myosin filaments [Ger. *heller* lighter]

vectorcardiography electrode (neck)

(H)

hip

hypodermic *also* H, h, hypo

H⁺

hydrogen ion

[H⁺]

hydrogen ion concentration

H₀

null hypothesis

H1, ¹H, H¹

protium (light hydrogen)

¹H

hydrogen-1

H₁

alternative hypothesis

histamine receptor type 1

H2, ²H, H²

deuterium (heavy hydrogen)

²H

hydrogen-2

H²

hiatal hernia

H₂

histamine 2

H3, ³H, H³

tritium

³H

hydrogen-3

H

H₃
procaine hydrochloride

³H (*var. of* H3)

h
coefficient of heat transfer
hand-rearing (of experimental animals)
hecto
height *also* H, *h*, Hgt, HT, ht
henry
heteromorphic (region)
high
horizontal *also* H, hor, horiz
hour *also* H, HR, hr
human *also* H, hu
human response
hundred
hypermetropia *also* H, Hy
hyperopia *also* H, Hy
hyperopic *also* H, Hy
hypodermic *also* H, (H), hypo
negatively staining region of
chromosome
Planck constant *also* h
specific enthalpy

hν
photon *also* γ

h.
at bedtime [L. *hora decubitus*] *also*
h.d., hor. decub., hor. som., HS, h.s.,
h. som.
draft, drink [L. *haustas*] *also* H,
haust., ht.

h
height *also* H, h, Hgt, HT, ht
Planck constant *also* h

HA
Hakim-Adams (syndrome)
hallux abductus
halothane anesthesia
H antigen
Hartley (guinea pig)
headache
hearing aid
heated
heated aerosol *also* ht aer
height age
hemadsorbent
hemadsorption (test)
hemagglutinating activity
hemagglutinating antibody

hemagglutinating antigen
hemagglutination
hemolytic anemia
hemophiliac with adenopathy
hepatic adenoma
hepatic artery
hepatitis A
hepatitis-associated (virus)
herpangina
heterophil antibody
Heyden antibiotic
high anxiety
hippuric acid
histamine
histidine ammonialyase
histocompatibility antigen
Horton arteritis
hospital acquired
hospital administration *also* HAD,
HAd
hospital admission
hospital apprentice
household activity
hyaluronic acid
hydroxyanisole
hydroxyapatite
hyperalimentation
hyperandrogenism
hypermetropic astigmatism
hyperopia, absolute
hypersensitivity alveolitis
hypothalmic amenorrhea

H/A
headache
head-to-abdomen (ratio)

HA1
hemadsorption (virus, type 1)

HA2
hemadsorption (virus, type 2)

Ha
absolute hypermetropia
hahnium
hamster

H/a
home with advice

HAA
hearing aid amplifier
hemolytic anemia antigen
hepatitis A antibody *also* HAAb
hepatitis A antigen *also* HAAg

hepatitis-associated antigen
hospital activity analysis

HAAb
hepatitis A antibody *also* HAA

HAAg
hepatitis A antigen *also* HAA

HABA
hydroxybenzeneazobenzoic acid

HABF
hepatic artery blood flow

HAb/HAd
horizontal abduction/adduction

habt.
let the patient have [L. *habeatur*]

HAC
hexamethylmelamine, Adriamycin
(doxorubicin), and cyclophosphamide

HAc
acetic acid

HACE
hepatic artery chemoembolization

HACEK
*Haemophilus aphrophilus,
Actinobacillus actinomycetemcomitans,
Cardiobacterium hominis, Eikenella
corrodens,* and *Kingella kingae*

HAChT
high-affinity choline transport

HACR
hereditary adenomatosis of colon and
rectum

HACS
hyperactive child syndrome

HAD
hearing aid dispenser
hemadsorption *also* HAd
hexamethylmelamine, Adriamycin
(doxorubicin), and cis-diammine-
dichloroplatinum (cisplatin)
hospital administration *also* HA, HAd
hospital administrator
human adjuvant disease
hypophysectomized alloxan diabetic

HAd
hemadsorption *also* HAD
hospital administration *also* HA,
HAD

HADD
hydroxyapatite deposition disease

HAd-I
hemadsorption inhibition

HAE
health appraisal examination
hearing aid evaluation
hepatic artery embolization
hereditary angioedema
hereditary angioneurotic edema

HAEC
Hirschsprung-associated enterocolitis
human aortic endothelial cell

HAF
hepatic arterial flow

HaF
Hageman factor

HAFP
human α-fetoprotein

HAG
heat-aggregated globulin

HAGG
hyperimmune antivariola gamma
globulin

HAGL
humeral avulsion of the glenohumeral
ligament

HAHTG
horse antihuman thymus globulin

HAI
hemagglutination inhibition (titer) *also*
HI
hepatic arterial infusion
histological activity index

HAIC
Hearing Aid Industry Conference
hepatic arterial infusional
chemotherapy

HAIR-AN
hyperandrogenism, insulin resistance,
and acanthosis nigricans (syndrome)

NOTES

H

HaK
hamster kidney

HAL
haloperidol
halothane *also* hal, HALO
hepatic artery ligation
hyperalimentation
hypoplastic acute leukemia

Hal
halogen

hal
halothane *also* HAL, HALO

halluc
hallucination

HALO
halothane *also* HAL, hal
hemorrhage, abruption, labor, placenta previa with mild bleeding

HALP
hyperalphalipoproteinemia

HALT
Heroin Antagonist and Learning Therapy

HaLV
hamster leukemia virus

HAM
hearing aid microphone
helical axis of motion
hexamethylmelamine, Adriamycin (doxorubicin), and melphalan
hexazomacrocycles
human albumin microsphere
human alveolar macrophage
human T-cell lymphotropic virus type 1-associated myelopathy
hypoparathyroidism, Addison disease, and mucocutaneous candidiasis (syndrome)

HAM-56
human alveolar macrophage-56

HAMA
Hamilton Anxiety (Scale)
human antimouse antibody

HAMD
Hamilton Depression (Scale)

HAMM
human albumin minimicrosphere

Hams
hamstrings *also* HS

HaMSV
Harvey murine sarcoma virus

HAN
heroin-associated nephropathy
hyperplastic alveolar nodule

HANA
hemagglutinin neuraminidase

H and E
hematoxylin and eosin (stain) *also* H&E

Handicp
handicapped

HANE
hereditary angioneurotic edema

HANES
health and nutrition examination survey

hANP
human atrial natriuretic peptide

H antigens
flagella antigens of motile bacteria [Ger. *Hauch*]

HAP
Handicapped Aid Program
held after positioning
heredopathia atactica polyneuritiformis
high-amplitude peristalsis
histamine acid phosphate
hospital-acquired pneumonia
humoral antibody production
hydrolyzed animal protein
hydroxyapatite (fractionation procedure)

HAPA
hemagglutinating antipenicillin antibody

HAPC
high-amplitude contraction
hospital-acquired penetration contact

HAPD
home-automated peritoneal dialysis

HAPE
high-altitude pulmonary edema

HAPO
high-altitude pulmonary (o)edema

HAPS
hepatic arterial perfusion scintigraphy

HAPTO
haptoglobin *also* HP, Hp, hp, Hpt

HAQ
Headache Assessment Questionnaire

HAR
high-altitude retinopathy

Har
homoarginine

HARD
hydrocephalus, agyria, retinal
dysplasia

HAREM
heparin assay rapid easy method

HARH
high-altitude retinal hemorrhage

HARM
heparin assay rapid method

harm.
harmonic

HARP
Harvard Atherosclerosis Reversibility
Project

HARPPS
heat, absence of use, redness, pain,
pus, swelling (symptoms of
infection)

HARS
Hamilton Anxiety Rating Scale

HART
Heparin Aspirin Reperfusion Trial

HARTS
heat-activated recoverable temporary
stent

HAS
Hamilton Anxiety Scale
health advisory service
high-amplitude sucking (technique)
highest asymptomatic (dose)
hospital administrative service
hospital advisory service
hyperalimentation solution
hypertensive arteriosclerotic

HASCHD
hypertensive arteriosclerotic heart
disease *also* HASHD

HASCVD
hypertensive arteriosclerotic
cardiovascular disease

HASHD
hypertensive arteriosclerotic heart
disease *also* HASCHD

HASP
Hospital Admissions and Surveillance
Program

HAsP
health aspects of pesticides

HAST
high-altitude simulation test

HAT
Halstead Aphasia Test
harmonic attenuation table
harmonic attenuation test
head, arms, and trunk
heparin-associated thrombocytopenia
heterophil antibody titer
hospital arrival time
hypoxanthine, aminopterin, and
thymidine
hypoxanthine, azaserine, and
thymidine

HATG
horse antihuman thymocyte globulin

HATH
Heterosexual Attitudes Toward
Homosexuality (scale)

HATT
hemagglutination treponemal test
heparin-associated thrombocytopenia
and thrombosis

HATTS
hemagglutination treponemal test for
syphilis

HAU
hemagglutinating unit

haust.
draft, drink [L. *haustus*] *also* H, h.,
ht.

HAV
hallux abducto valgus

NOTES

H

HAV *(continued)*
hemadsorption virus
hepatitis A virus

HAVAB
hepatitis A virus antibody

HAWIC
Hamburg-Wechsler Intelligence Test for Children

HB
head backward
health board
heart block *also* hb
heel to buttock
held backward
hemoglobin *also* Hb, Hbg, hemo, HG, Hg, hg, HGB, Hgb
hemolysis blocking
hepatitis B
His bundle
hold breakfast
hospital bed
housebound
Hutchinson-Boeck (disease)
hybridoma bank
hyoid body

HB1°
first-degree heart block

HB2°
second-degree heart block

HB3°
third-degree heart block

Hb
hemoglobin *also* HB, Hbg, hemo, HG, Hg, hg, HGB, Hgb

hb
heart block *also* HB

HbA
adult hemoglobin
hemoglobin A
hemoglobin α-chain

HbA°
hemoglobin determination

HbA$_1$
major component of adult hemoglobin

HbA$_2$
minor fraction of adult hemoglobin

HBAb, HBAB
hepatitis B antibody

HBAC
hyperdynamic β-adrenergic circulatory

HbA1C
glycosylated hemoglobin

HBAg, HbAg
hepatitis B antigen

HbAS
heterozygosity for hemoglobin A and hemoglobin S (sickle-cell trait)

HBB
hemoglobin b (chain)
hospital blood bank
hydroxybenzylbenzimidazole

HbBC
hemoglobin-binding capacity

HBBW
hold breakfast for blood work

HB$_c$
hepatitis B core (antibody, antigen)

HbC
hemoglobin C

HB$_c$Ab, HBCAB, HB$_{cAb}$, HBcAb
hepatitis B core antibody

HB$_c$Ag, HBCAG, HB$_{cAg}$, HBcAg
hepatitis B core antigen *also* HBcAg, HB$_{cAg}$, HB$_c$Ab

HBCG
heat-aggregated bacille Calmette-Guérin

Hb$_{Chesapeake}$
hemoglobin Chesapeake

HbCO
carbon monoxide hemoglobin
carboxyhemoglobin *also* COHB

HB core
hepatitis B core (antigen)

HbCS
hemoglobin Constant Spring

HBD
has been drinking
hemoglobin δ chain
hydroxybutyric dehydrogenase *also* HBDH
hypophosphatemic bone disease

HbD
hemoglobin D

HBDH
hydroxybutyrate dehydrogenase *also* HBD

HBDT
human basophil degranulation test

HBE
hemoglobin ε chain
His bundle electrogram

HBE₁
His bundle electrogram, distal

HBE₂
His bundle electrogram, proximal

HBₑ
hepatitis Bₑ

HBe
hepatitis Bₑ antigen

HbE
hemoglobin E

HBₑAb, HBₑAb, HBeAb
hepatitis B early antibody

HBₑAg, HBEAG, HBeAg
hepatitis B e antigen *also* HBeAg, HBₑAb, HBe
hepatitis B early antigen

HB-EGF
heparin-binding epidermal growth factor

HBF
fetal hemoglobin *also* HbF
hand blood flow
hemispheric blood flow
hemoglobinuric bilious fever
hepatic blood flow
hypothalamic blood flow

HbF
fetal hemoglobin *also* HBF
hemoglobin F

HBG1
hemoglobin γ chain A

HBG2
hemoglobin γ chain G

Hbg
hemoglobin *also* HB, Hb, hemo, HG, Hg, hg, HGB, Hgb

HBGA
had it before, got it again

HBGF
heparin binding growth factor

HBGF-1
heparin binding growth factor-1

HBGM
home blood glucose monitoring

HbH
hemoglobin H

HBHC
home-based hospital care

Hb-Hp
hemoglobin-haptoglobin (complex)

HBI
hemibody irradiation
hepatobiliary imaging
high (serum)-bound iron

HBID
hereditary benign intraepithelial dyskeratosis

HBIG, H-BIG, HBIg
hepatitis B immunoglobulin

Hb_Kansas
mutant hemoglobin with low affinity for oxygen

HBL
hepatoblastoma

HBLA
human B-lymphocyte antigen

Hb_Lepore
hemoglobin Lepore

HBLLSB
heard best at left lower sternal border

HBLUSB
heard best at left upper sternal border

HBLV
human B-lymphotropic virus

HBM
Health Belief Model
hypertonic buffered medium

NOTES

HbM
hemoglobin M

HbMet
methemoglobin *also* HiHb

HBO
hyperbaric oxygen
hyperbaric oxygenation
hyperbaric oxygen (therapy) *also* HBOT
oxygenated hemoglobin *also* HbO_2

HbO_2
hyperbaric oxygen
oxygenated hemoglobin *also* HBO
oxyhemoglobin

HBOT
hyperbaric oxygen therapy *also* HBO

HBP
hepatic binding protein
high blood pressure

HbP
primitive (fetal) hemoglobin

HBPM
home blood pressure monitoring

HBr
hydrobromic acid

HbR
methemoglobin reductase

HBS
Health Behavior Scale
hepatitis B surface
hyperkinetic behavior syndrome

HB_S
hepatitis B surface (antibody, antigen)

HbS
hemoglobin S
sickle cell hemoglobin
sulfhemoglobin *also* SHB, SHb, SULFHB

HB_SA
hepatitis B surface associated

HB_sAb, HB_{sAb}, HBsAb
hepatitis B surface antibody

HB_sAg, HB_{sAg}, HBsAg
hepatitis B surface antigen *also* HBsAg, HB_{sAg}

HBsAg/adr
hepatitis B surface antigen manifesting group-specific determinant

a and subtype-specific determinants
d and *r*

HBSC
hemopoietic blood stem cell

HbSC, HbsC
sickle cell hemoglobin C

HBSS
Hanks balanced salt solution

HbSS
homozygosity for hemoglobin S

HBSSG
Hanks balanced salt solution plus glucose

HbS-Thal
sickle thalassemia

HBT
human brain thromboplastin
human breast tumor

HBV
hepatitis B vaccine
hepatitis B virus
honey-bee venom

HBV DNA
hepatitis B DNA detection

HBVV
hepatitis B virus vaccine

HBW
high birth weight

H/BW
heart-to-body weight (ratio)
height-to-body weight (ratio)

HbZ
hemoglobin ξ chain
hemoglobin Z
hemoglobin Zürich

HC
hair cell
hairy cell
handicapped *also* HCAP, HCP
head check
head circumference
head compression
healthy control
heart cycle
heat conservation
heavy chain
heel cord
hemochromatosis
hemoglobin concentration
hemorrhage, cerebral

heparin cofactor
hepatic catalase
hepatitis C
hepatocellular cancer
hereditary coproporphyria *also* HCP
Hickman catheter
high calorie *also* hg-cal
hippocampus
histamine challenge
histochemistry
home call
home care
homocystinuria
Hospital Corps
hospital course
hospitalized controls
house call
Huntington chorea
hyaline cast
hydranencephaly
hydraulic concussion
hydrocarbon
hydrocodone
hydrocortisone *also* HCT, Hyd
hydroxycorticoid *also* HOC
hyoid cornu
hypercholesterolemia
hypertropic cardiomyopathy

4-HC
4-hydroperoxycyclophosphamide

H&C
hot and cold

Hc
hydrocolloid

HCA
health-care aide
heart cell aggregate
heel cord advancement
hepatocellular adenoma
home-care aide
Hospital Corporation of America
hydrocortisone acetate

HCAP
handicapped *also* HC, HCP

H-CAP
hexamethylmelamine,
cyclophosphamide, Adriamycin
(doxorubicin), and Platinol (cisplatin)

HCB
hexachlorobenzene

HCC
heat conservation center
hepatitis contagiosa canis (virus)
hepatocellular carcinoma
hepatoma carcinoma cell
hexachlorocyclohexane (lindane) *also*
HCH, γ-HCH
history of chief complaint
25-hydroxycholecalciferol (vitamin D)

25-HCC
25-hydroxycholecalciferol

HCCC
hyalinizing clear cell carcinoma

HCD
health care delivery
heavy chain disease (protein)
herniated cervical disk
high caloric density
high carbohydrate diet *also* HICHO
homologous canine distemper
(antiserum)
hydrocolloid dressing

HCE
hypoglossal carotid entrapment

HCF
hereditary capillary fragility
high carbohydrate, high fiber (diet)
highest common factor
hypocaloric carbohydrate feeding

HCFA
Health Care Financing Administration

HCFSH
human chorionic follicle-stimulating
hormone

HCFU
hexylcarbamoylfluorouracil (carmofur-
antineoplastic)

HCG, hCG
human chorionic gonadotropin

HCGN
hypocomplementemic
glomerulonephritis

NOTES

H

HCH
    hexachlorocyclohexane (lindane) *also*
    HCC, γ-HCH
    Hygroscopic Condenser Humidifier

Hch
    hemochromatosis

HCHO
    formaldehyde

HCHWA
    hereditary cerebral hemorrhage with
    amyloidosis

HcImp
    hydrocolloid impression

HCIS
    Health Care Information System

HCL
    hairy cell leukemia
    hard contact lens
    hemacytology index
    human cultured lymphoblasts

HCl
    hydrochloric (acid)
    hydrochloride

HCLF
    high carbohydrate, low fiber (diet)

HCM
    health care maintenance
    health care management
    hypertrophic cardiomyopathy

HCMM
    hereditary cutaneous malignant
    melanoma

HCMV
    human cytomegalovirus

HCN
    hereditary chronic nephritis
    high calorie and nitrogen
    hydrocyanic acid
    hydrogen cyanide

HCO
    carbohydrate *also* C, CARB, carb,
    carbo, CHO, COH

HCO₃
    bicarbonate *also* BC, Bicarb, bicarb

HCP
    handicapped *also* HC, HCAP
    hepatocatalase peroxidase
    hereditary coproporphyria *also* HC

    hexachlorophene
    high cell passage

H&CP
    hospital and community psychiatry

HCQ
    hydroxychloroquine

HCR
    heme-controlled repressor
    host-cell reactivation
    human-controlled repressor
    hydrochloric acid
    hysterical conversion reaction

HCr
    hemoglobin content of reticulocytes

HCRE
    Homeopathic Council for Research
    and Education

hCRH
    human corticotropin-releasing hormone

H'crit
    hematocrit *also* Crit, crit, HCT, Hct,
    hemat, HMT

HCS
    Hajdu-Cheney syndrome
    health care support
    hematocystic spot
    hourglass contraction of stomach
    human chorionic somatomammotropin
    (human placental lactogen) *also* hCS,
    hcs, HCSM, hCSM
    human chorionic somatotropin
    human cord serum
    hydroxycorticosteroid *also* OH, OHCS

hCS, hcs
    human chorionic somatomammotropin
    (human placental lactogen) *also*
    HCS, HCSM, hCSM

HCSD
    Health Care Studies Division

HCSM, hCSM
    human chorionic somatomammotropin
    (human placental lactogen) *also*
    HCS, hCS, hcs

HCSS
    hypersensitive carotid sinus syndrome

HCT
    Health Check Test
    heart-circulation training
    hematocrit *also* Crit, crit, H'crit, Hct,
    hemat, HMT

histamine challenge test
historic control trial
homocytotrophic
human calcitonin *also* hCT
hydrochlorothiazide *also* HCTZ
hydrocortisone *also* HC, Hyd
hydroxycortisone

Hct
hematocrit *also* Crit, crit, H'crit,
HCT, hemat, HMT

hCT
human calcitonin *also* HCT
human chorionic thyrotropin *also*
HCT

hct
hundred count

HCTC
Health Care Technology Center

HCTD
hepatic computed tomographic density
high cholesterol and tocopherol
deficient

HCTS
high cholesterol and tocopherol
supplemented

HCTU
home cervical traction unit

HCTZ
hydrochlorothiazide *also* HCT

HCTZ-TA
hydrochlorothiazide-triamterene

HCU
homocystinuria
hyperplasia cystica uteri

HCV
hepatitis C virus
human coronary virus

HCVD
hypertensive cardiovascular disease
also HTCVD

HCV EIA 20 test
hepatitis C virus enzyme
immunoassay

HCVR
hypercapnic ventilatory response

HCV RNA
hepatitis C RNA detection
hepatitis C virus RNA

HCVS
human corona virus sensitivity

Hcy
hemocyanin
homocysteine

HD
Haab-Dimmer (syndrome)
Hajna-Damon (broth)
haloperidol decanoate *also* HLD, HL-
D
Hanganatziu-Deicher
Hansen disease
hard corn [L. *heloma durum*]
Harris design
hearing distance
heart disease
helium dilution
Heller-Dor (procedure)
heloma durum
hemidiaphragm
hemodialysis
hemolysing dose
hemolytic disease
hepatitis D
herniated disc
high density
high dosage
high dose
hip disarticulation
Hirschsprung disease
histidine decarboxylase
Hodgkin disease
hormone dependent
hospital day *also* HOD
house dust
human diploid (cell)
Huntington disease
hydatid disease
hydroxydopamine *also* HDA
hypnotic dosage
mustard gas

H and D, H&D
Hunter and Driffield (curve)

HD#
hospital day number

NOTES

H

HD$_{50}$
hemolyzing dose of complement that lyses 50% of sensitized erythrocytes

h.d.
at bedtime [L. *hora decubitus*] *also* h., hor. decub., hor. som., HS, h.s., h. som.
head *also* H, he

HDA
hydroxydopamine *also* HD

HDAC
high-dose cytarabine (araC) *also* HDARAC, HDARA-C

HDAg
hepatitis D antigen

HDARAC, HDARA-C
high-dose ara-C *also* HDAC

HDBD
hydroxybutyric dehydrogenase

HDBH

HDC
high-dose chemotherapy
histidine decarboxylase
human diploid cell
hypodermoclysis

HDCS
human diploid cell strain
human diploid cell system

HDCV
human diploid cell (rabies) vaccine

HDD
half-dose depth
high-dose depth

HDF
high dry field
host defensive factor
human diploid fibroblast

HDFL
human development and family life

HDFP
Hypertension Detection and Followup Program

HDG
high dose group

HDH
heart disease history
high density humidity
Hostility and Direction of Hostility (questionnaire) *also* HDHQ

HDHQ
Hostility and Direction of Hostility Questionnaire *also* HDH

HDI
hemorrhagic disease of infants

HDL
high-density lipoprotein *also* HDLP

HDL-C
high-density lipoprotein-cholesterol

HDL-c
high-density lipoprotein-cell surface (receptor)

HDLP
high-density lipoprotein *also* HDL

HDLS
hereditary diffuse leukoencephalopathy with spheroids

HDLW
hearing distance, left, watch (distance from which watch ticking is heard by left ear)

HDM
hexadimethrine

HDMEC
human dermal microvascular endothelial cell

HDMP
high-dose methylprednisolone

HDMTX
high-dose methotrexate

HDMTX-CF
high-dose methotrexate and citrovorum factor

HDMTX-LV
high-dose methotrexate and leucovorin

HDN
hemolytic disease of newborn
high-density nebulizer

hDNA
deoxyribonucleic acid, histone

HDP
hexose diphosphate
high definition power
high-density polyethylene
hydroxydimethylpyrimidine

HDPAA
heparin-dependent platelet-associated antibody

HDR
heparin dose response
high-dose rate

HDRA
histoculture drug response assay

HDRB
high dose rate brachytherapy

HDRF
Heart Disease Research Foundation

HDRS
Hamilton Depression Rating Scale

HDRV
human diploid (cell strain) rabies
vaccine

HDRW
hearing distance, right, watch
(distance from which watch ticking
is heard by right ear)

HDS
Hamilton Depression (Rating) Scale
Healthcare Data Systems
Health Data Services
health delivery system
herniated disk syndrome
Hospital Discharge Survey

HDU
head-drop unit (curare standard)
hemodialysis unit

HDV
hepatitis delta virus
hepatitis D virus

HDW
hearing distance (with) watch
reticulocyte hemoglobin distribution
width

HDZ
hydralazine

HE
hard exudate
Hektoen enteric (agar)
hemagglutinating encephalomyelitis
hemoglobin electrophoresis
hepatic encephalopathy
hepatitis E
hereditary elliptocytosis

hollow enzyme
human enteric (virus)
hyperextension
hypogonadotropic eunuchoidism
hypophysectomy *also* hyp
hypoxemic episode

H-E
heat exchanger

H&E
hematoxylin and eosin (stain) *also* H
and E
hemorrhage and exudate
heredity and environment

He
heart *also* H, HT, ht
Hedstrom number
helium

he
head *also* H, h.d.

HEA
hexone-extracted acetone
human erythrocyte antigen

HEADSS
home life, education level, activities,
drug use, sexual activity, suicide
ideation/attempts (adolescent medical
history)

HEAL
Health Education Assistance Loan

HEART
Healing and Early Afterload
Reducing Therapy
Health Evaluation and Risk
Tabulation

HEAT
human erythrocyte agglutination test

HEB
hematoencephalic barrier (blood-brain
barrier)

hebdom.
first week of life [L. *hebdomada*]

HEC
hamster embryo cell
Health Education Council
health evaluation center

NOTES

H

HEC *(continued)*
human endothelial cell
hydroxyergocalciferol

HED
hydrotropic electron donor
skin erythema dose [Ger. *Haut-Erythem-Dosis*]
unit skin dose (of x-rays) [Ger. *Haut-Einheits-Dosis*]

HeD
helper determinant

HEDH
hypohidrotic ectodermal dysplasia with hypothyroidism

HEDSPA
^{99m}Tc-etidronate (bone-imaging agent)

HEENT
head, ears, eyes, nose, and throat

HEEP
health effects of environmental pollutants

HEF
hamster embryo fibroblast
human embryo fibroblast

HEG
hemorrhagic erosive gastritis

h-EGF
human epidermal growth factor

HEHR
highest equivalent heart rate

HEI
high-energy intermediate
homogeneous enzyme immunoassay
human embryonic intestine (cell)

HEIR
health effects of ionizing radiation
high-energy ionizing radiation

HEIS
high-energy ion scattering

HEK
human embryo kidney (cell)

HEL
hen egg-white lysozyme
human embryo lung (cell culture)
human erythroleukemia line

HeLa cells
continuously cultured carcinoma cell line used for tissue cultures (named for patient, Henrietta Lacks)

HELF
human embryoic lung fibroblast

heliox
helium-oxygen mixture

HELLP
hemolysis, elevated liver enzymes, and low platelet (count)

HELM
helmet cell

HELP
Hawaii Early Learning Profile
Health Education Library Program
Health Emergency Loan Program
Health Evaluation and Learning Program
heat escape lessening posture
heparin-induced extracorporeal low-density lipoprotein precipitation
Heroin Emergency Life Project
Hospital Equipment Loan Project

HEM, Hem
hematologist *also* hemat
hematology *also* hemat
hemolysis *also* H
hemolytic *also* H
hemorrhage
hemorrhoid

hem
hematuria

HEMA
hydroxyethylmethacrylate

hemat
hematocrit *also* Crit, crit, H'crit, HCT, Hct, HMT
hematologist *also* HEM, Hem
hematology *also* HEM, Hem

hematem
hematemesis

hemi
hemiparalysis
hemiparesis
hemiplegia
hemisphere

hemo
hemoglobin *also* HB, Hb, Hbg, HG, Hg, hg, HGB, Hgb
hemophilia

hemocyt, hemocyt.
hemocytometer

hemorr
hemorrhage

HEMOSID
hemosiderin

HEMPAS
hereditary erythroblastic multinuclearity with positive acidified serum
hereditary erythrocytic multinuclearity with positive acidified serum

HEMRI
hereditary multifocal relapsing inflammation

HEMS
helicopter emergency medical services

HEN
hemorrhages, exudates, and/or nicking

He-Ne
helium-neon

HEP
hemoglobin electrophoresis
hemolysis end point
heparin *also* H, HP
hepatic
hepatoerythropoietic porphyria
high egg passage (virus)
high-energy phosphate
histamine equivalent prick
human epithelial (cell) *also* HEp

HEp
human epithelial (cell) *also* HEP

HEp-1
human cervical carcinoma cells

HEp-2
human laryngeal tumor cells

hEP
human endorphin

hep
hepatitis

HEPA
hamster egg penetration assay
high-efficiency particulate air (filter)
high-efficiency particulate arresting

HEP-AC
hepatitis battery-acute

Hep/Clav
hepatoclavicular

HEPES
4-(2-hydroxyethyl)-1-piperazineethanesulfonic acid

hep-lock
heparin lock

HEPM
human embryonic palatal mesenchymal (cell)

HER
hemorrhagic encephalopathy of rats

her.
hernia *also* H, hern
herniated *also* H, hern
herniation *also* H, hern

herb. recent.
of fresh herbs [L. *herbarium recentium*]

hered
hereditary
heredity

hern
hernia *also* H, her.
herniated *also* H, her.
herniation *also* H, her.

HERP
human exposure (dose)/rodent potency

HERS
Health Evaluation and Referral Service

HES
(acute) hypereosinophilic syndrome
health examination survey
hemotoxylin-eosin stain
human embryonic skin
human embryonic spleen
hydroxyethyl starch (solution)

HET
Health Education Telecommunications
helium equilibration time

Het
heterophil (antibody)

het
heterozygous

NOTES

H

HETE
hydroxyeicosatetraenoic (acid)

HETF
home enteral tube feeding

HETP
height equivalent to a theoretical plate (gas chromatography)

HEV
health and environment
hemagglutination encephalomyelitis virus
hepatitis E virus
hepatoencephalomyelitis virus
high endothelial venule
human enteric virus

HEVI
hibernal epidemic viral infection

HEW
(Department of) Health, Education, and Welfare

HEX
hexosaminidase

HEx
hard exudate

Hex
hexamethylmelamine *also* HM, HMM, HXM

HEX A
hexosaminidase A (α-subunit)

Hexa-CAF
hexamethylmelamine, cyclophosphamide, amphotericin B, 5-fluorouracil

HEX B
hexosaminidase B (β-subunit)

HF
Hageman factor
half *also* hf, S, s., sem., semi, ss
haplotype frequency
hard feces
hard filled (capsule)
harvest fluid
hayfever
head of fetus
head forward
heart failure
helper factor
hemofiltration
hemorrhagic factor
hemorrhagic fever
hepatocyte function

Hertz frequency
high-fat (diet)
high flow
high frequency *also* hf
hollow filter (dialyzer)
hot fomentation
house formula
human fibroblast
hydrogen fluoride (catalyst)
hyperflexion

H/F
HeLa/fibroblast (hybrid)

Hf
hafnium

hf
half *also* HF, S, s., sem., semi, ss
high frequency *also* HF, Hfr

HFAK
hollow-fiber artificial kidney

HFAS
hereditary flat adenoma syndrome

HFB
high frequency band

HFC
hand-filled capsule
high-frequency current
histamine-forming capacity
hydrofluorocarbon

HFCS
high-fructose corn syrup

HFCWC
high-frequency chest wall compression

HFD
hemorrhagic fever of deer
high-fiber diet
high forceps delivery
hospital field director
Human Figure Drawing

HFDK
human fetal diploid kidney (cell)

HFDL
human fetal diploid lung (cell)

HFEC
human foreskin epithelial cell

HFEE
high-frequency epicardial echocardiography

HFF
human foreskin fibroblast

HFG
hand-foot-genital (syndrome)

HFH
hemifacial hyperplasia

hFH
heterozygous familial hypercholesterolemia

HFHL
high-frequency hearing loss

HFI
half-Fourier imaging
hereditary fructose intolerance
human fibroblast interferon *also* HFIF

HFIF
human fibroblast interferon *also* HFI

HFIP
hexafluoroisopropranolol

HFJ
high-frequency jet

HFJV
high-frequency jet ventilation

HFL
human fetal lung

HFM
hemifacial microsomia *also* HM

HFO
hard food orientation
high-frequency oscillation

HFOV
high-frequency oscillatory ventilation

HFP
hypofibrinogenic plasma

HFPP
high-frequency positive pressure

HFPPV
high-frequency positive-pressure ventilation

HFPV
high-frequency percussive ventilation

HFR
heart frequency
high frequency of recombination *also* Hfr

Hfr
high frequency
high frequency of recombination *also* HFR

Hfr mutant
high-frequency recombination mutant

HFRS
hemorrhagic fever with renal syndrome

HFS
hemifacial spasm
Hospital Financial Support

hfs
hyperfine structure

hFSH, HFSH
human follicle-stimulating hormone

HFST
hearing-for-speech test

HFT
hemofiltration therapy
high-frequency transduction
high-frequency transfer

HFU
hand-foot-uterus (syndrome)

HFUPR
hourly fetal urine production rate

HFV
high-frequency ventilation

HG
hand grip (exercise)
hemoglobin *also* HB, Hb, Hbg, hemo, Hg, hg, HGB, Hgb
herpes genitalis
herpes gestationis
Herter-Gee (syndrome)
Heschl gyrus
high glucose
human gonadotropin
human growth (factor)
Hutchinson-Gilford (syndrome)
hypoglycemia

Hg
hectogram *also* hg
hemoglobin *also* HB, Hb, Hbg, HG, HGB, Hgb

NOTES

H

Hg *(continued)*
mercury [L. *hydrargyrum* silver water] *also* hydrarg.

195mHg
mercury-195m

hg
hectogram *also* Hg
hemoglobin *also* HB, Hb, Hbg, HG, Hg, HGB, Hgb

HGA
homogentisate (homogentisic acid oxidase)

HGB, Hgb
hemoglobin *also* HB, Hb, Hbg, hemo, HG, Hg, hg

hg-cal
high calorie *also* HC

HgCl2
mercury chloride

HGD
high-grade dysplasia

HGE
human granulocytic ehrlichiosis

HGF
hepatocyte growth factor *also* HPG
human growth factor
hyperglycemic-glucogenolytic factor (glucagon)

Hg-F
hemoglobin, fetal

HGG
herpetic geniculate ganglionitis
human gamma globulin *also* hGG

hGG
human gamma globulin *also* HGG

HGH, hGH
high growth hormone
human (pituitary) growth hormone

HGM
hog gastric mucin
human glucose monitoring

HGMCR
human genetic mutant cell repository

HGO
hepatic glucose output
hip guidance orthosis
human glucose output

HGP
hepatic glucose production
hyperglobulinemia purpura

HGPRT, HG-PRTase
hypoxanthine guanine phosphoribosyltransferase

HGSHS
Harvard Group Scale of Hypnotic Susceptibility

HGSIL
high-grade squamous intraepithelial lesion

Hgt
height *also* H, h, *h*, HT, ht

HGV
hepatitis G virus

HH
halothane hepatitis
hard of hearing *also* HOH
Head-Holms (syndrome)
healthy hemophiliac
Henderson and Haggard (inhaler)
hiatal hernia
holistic health
home health
home help
Hunter-Hurler (syndrome)
hydroxyhexamide
hypergastrinemic hyperchlorhydria
hyperhidrosis
hypogonadotropic hypogonadism
hyporeninemic hypoaldosteronism

H/H, H&H
hemoglobin and hematocrit

Hh
hemopoietic histocompatibility

HHA
Health Hazard Appraisal
hereditary hemolytic anemia
Home Health Agency
hypothalamic hypophyseal adrenal (system)

HHAA
hypothalamo-hypophyseo-adrenal axis

HHB, HHb
hypohemoglobinemia
reduced hemoglobin
unionized hemoglobin

HHC
home health care

HHCA
hypothermic hypokalemic cardioplegic arrest

HHCS
high-altitude hypertrophic cardiomyopathy syndrome

HHD
hand-held dynamometer
high heparin dose
home hemodialysis
hypertensive heart disease *also* HTHD

HHE
health hazard evaluation
hemiconvulsion-hemiplegia-epilepsy (syndrome)

HHF-35
muscle-specific actin *also* MSA

HHFM
high-humidity face mask

HHG
hypertrophic hypersecretory gastropathy

HHH
hyperornithinemia, hyperammonemia, and homocitrillinemia (syndrome)

HHHO
hypotonia, hypomentia, hypogonadism, and obesity (syndrome)

HHLL
histocytoid hemangioma-like lesion

HHM
hemohydrometry
humoral hypercalcemia of malignancy

H-Hm
compound hypermetropic astigmatism

HHN
hand-held nebulizer
hyperosmolar hyperglycemic nonketotic (syndrome)

HHNC
hyperosmolar hyperglycemic nonketotic coma

HHNK
hyperglycemic hyperosmolar nonketotic (coma)

HHNKS
hyperglycemic hyperosmolar nonketotic syndrome

HHPC
hyperoxic-hypercapnic

HHRH
hereditary hypophosphatemic rickets with hypercalciuria
hypothalamic hypophysiotropic-releasing hormone

HHS
(Department of) Health and Human Services
Hearing Handicap Scale
hereditary hemolytic syndrome
human hypopituitary serum
hyperkinetic heart syndrome

HHT
head halter traction *also* HHTx
hereditary hemolytic telangiectasia
hereditary hemorrhagic telangiectasia
heterotopic heart transplant
hydroxyheptadecatrienoic (acid)

HHTA
hypothalamohypophyseothyroidal axis

HHTC
high-humidity trach collar

HHTM
high-humidity trach mask

HHTS
high-humidity tracheostomy shield

HHTx
head halter traction *also* HHT

HHV
human herpesvirus

HHV1–7
human herpesvirus 1–7

HI
Haemophilus influenzae
head injury
health insurance
hearing impaired

NOTES

H

HI *(continued)*
heart infusion
heat inactivated
heat input
hemagglutination inhibition (titer) *also* HAI
hepatic insufficiency
hepatobiliary imaging
high impulsiveness
histidine *also* H, Hi, HIS, His, Hist
homoridal ideation
hormone dependent
hormone insensitive
hospital induced
hospital insurance
humoral immunity
hydriodic acid
hydroxyindole
hyperglycemic index
hypomelanosis of Ito
hypothermic ischemia

Hi
histamine
histidine *also* H, HI, HIS, His, Hist

HIA
heat infusion agar
hemagglutination inhibition antibody
hemagglutination inhibition assay

HIAA
hydroxyindoleacetic acid *also* OH-IAA

5-HIAA
5-hydroxyindoleacetic acid

21-HIAA
21-hydroxyindoleacetic acid

HIB
Haemophilus influenzae type b (vaccine) *also* HITB
heart infusion broth
hemolytic immune body

HIBAC
Health Insurance Benefits Advisory Council

HIB-C
Haemophilus influenzae B vaccine conjugate

HIC
Heart Information Center

H-ICD-A
International Classification of Diseases, Adopted Code for Hospitals

HICHO
high carbohydrate (diet) *also* HCD

HiCn
cyanmethemoglobin

HICROS
high-frequency contralateral routing of signals

HID
headache, insomnia, and depression (syndrome)
herniated intervertebral disc
human infectious dose
hyperkinetic impulse disorder

HIDA
hepatic 2,6-dimethyliminodiacetic acid
hepatoiminodiacetic acid

HI-DAC
high-dose cytosine arabinoside

HIE
human intestinal epithelium
hyperimmunoglobulin E
hypoxic-ischemic encephalopathy

HIES
hyperimmunoglobulin E syndrome

HIF
higher integrative function
higher intellectual function
histoplasma (tissue) inhibitory factor
Historical Information Form

HIFBS
heat-inactivated fetal bovine serum

HIFC
hog intrinsic factor concentrate

HIFCS
heat-inactivated fetal calf serum

HIG, HIg, hIG

HIH
hypertensive intracerebral hemorrhage

HIHA
high impulsiveness, high anxiety

HiHb
hemoglobin (methemoglobin) *also* HbMet

HII
Health Industries Institute

Health Insurance Institute
hemagglutination inhibition
  immunoassay
hepatic iron index

HIIC
heated intraoperative intraperitoneal
  chemotherapy

HIL
hypoxic-ischemic lesion

HILA
high impulsiveness, low anxiety

HIM
hemopoietic inductive
  microenvironment
hepatitis-infectious mononucleosis
hexosephosphateisomerase
Hill Interaction Matrix (psychologic
  test)

HIMC
hepatic intramitochondrial crystalloid

HIMP
high-dose intravenous
  methylprednisolone

HIMT
hemagglutination inhibition morphine
  test

Hind II, Hind III
restriction endonucleases from
  Haemophilus influenzae

H inf
hypodermoclysis infusion

HINI
hypoxic-ischemic neuronal injury

H&Ins
health and accident insurance

Hint.
Hinton (flocculation test for syphilis)

HIO
hole-in-one technique
hypoiodism
hypoiodite (salt of hypoiodous acid)

HIOS
high index of suspicion

HIP
health illness profile
health insurance plan
homograft incus prosthesis
hospital insurance program
humoral immunocompetence profile
hydrostatic indifference point

HIPC
hormone independent prostate cancer

HiPIP
high-potential iron protein

HIPO
hemihypertrophy, intestinal web,
  preauricular skin tag, and congenital
  corneal opacity (syndrome)
Hospital Indicator for Physicians
  Orders

HiPro, HiProt
high protein (diet) *also* HP

HIR
head injury routine
high irradiance response

HIRF
histamine inhibitory releasing factor

HIS
Hanover Intensive Score
Haptic Intelligence Scale
health information system
Health Intention Scale
Health Interview Survey
high intermittent suction
histidine *also* H, HI, Hi, His, Hist
hospital information system
hyperimmune serum
hyperimmunized suppressed

His
histidine *also* H, HI, Hi, HIS, Hist

His-
histidyl

-His
histidino

HISG
human immune serum globulin

NOTES

H

321

HISMS
How I See Myself Scale
(psychologic test)

HISS
human immune status survey

HISSG
Hospital Information Systems Sharing
Group

HIST
hospital in-service training

Hist, hist
histidine *also* H, HI, Hi, HIS, His
histidinemia
history *also* H, Hx, Hy

HISTLINE
History of Medicine On-Line

Histo
histology
histoplasmin skin test

histol
histologic
histologist
histology

HIT
hemagglutination inhibition test
heparin-induced thrombocytopenia
Hirudin in Thrombolysis
histamine inhalation test
histamine ion transfer
Holtzman Inkblot Technique
hypertrophic infiltrative tendinitis
hypertrophied inferior turbinate

HITB, HiTb
Haemophilus influenzae type B
(meningitis) *also* HIB

HITES
hydrocortisone, insulin, transferrin,
estradiol, and selenium

HITT
heparin-induced thrombocytopenia with
thrombosis

HITTS
heparin-induced thrombosis-
thrombocytopenia syndrome

HIU
head injury unit
hyperplasia interstitialis uteri

HIV
human immunodeficiency virus

HIV-1
human immunodeficiency virus 1

HIV-2
human immunodeficiency virus 2

HIV-AB
human immunodeficiency virus
antibody

HIVAN
HIV-associated nephropathy

HIVAT
home intravenous antibiotic therapy

HIVD
herniated interverterbral disc

HIVIG
anti-HIV immune serum globulin
HIV immunoglobulin

HiVit
high vitamin

HIV-P
human immunodeficiency virus-
associated periodontitis

HIV-SGD
HIV-associated salivary gland disease

HJ
hepatojugular (reflux) *also* HJR
Howell-Jolly (bodies) *also* HJB

HJB
Howell-Jolly bodies *also* HJ

HJR
hepatojugular reflux *also* HJ

H-K
hand-to-knee (test)
heel-to-knee (test) *also* HK, HTK

HK
heat killed
heel-to-knee (test) *also* H-K, HTK
hexokinase
Hoffa-Kastert (syndrome)
human kidney (cell) *also* HKC

H→K
hand to knee (coordination)

HK1
hexokinase 1

HKAFO
hip-knee-ankle-foot orthosis

HKAO
hip-knee-ankle orthosis

HKC
human kidney cell *also* HK

HKH
hyperkinetic heart syndrome

HKLM
heat-killed *Listeria monocytogenes*

HKO
hip-knee orthosis (splint)

HKS
heel-knee-shin (test)
hyperkinesis syndrome

HL
hairline
half-life (of radioactive element)
hallux limitus
haloperidol
harelip
hearing level
hearing loss
heart and lungs *also* H&L
heavy lifting
hectoliter
hemolysis
heparin lock *also* H/L
hepatic lipase
Hickman line
histiocytic lymphoma
histocompatibility locus
Hodgkin lymphoma
human leukocyte
human lymphocyte
hydrophil/lipophil (number)
hygienic laboratory
hyperlipidemia
hyperlipoproteinemia
hypermetropia, latent
hypertrichosis lanuginosa
latent hypermetropia
latent hyperopia
lateral habenular (nucleus)

H/L
heart disease, low risk
heparin lock *also* HL
hydrophil/lipophil (ratio)
hyperopia, latent *also* Hl

H&L
heart and lungs *also* HL

HL7
health level seven

Hl
hypermetropia, latent
hyperopia, latent *also* H/L

hL, hl
hectoliter

HLA
heart, lungs and abdomen
histocompatibility leukocyte antigen
histocompatibility locus antigen
homologous leukocyte antibody
human leukocyte antigen (system)
human lymphocyte antibody
human lymphocyte antigen
hypoplastic left atrium

HLA-A, HLA-B, HLA-C, HLA-D, HLA-DR
varieties of human leukocyte antigen

HLALD
horse liver alcohol dehydrogenase

HLA-LD
human lymphocyte antigen-lymphocyte defined

HLA-SD
human lymphocyte antigen-serologically defined

HLB
hydrophilic-lipophilic balance
hypotonic lysis buffer

HLBI
human lymphoblastoid interferon

HLC
heat loss center

HLCL
human lymphoblastoid cell line

HLD
haloperidol decanoate *also* HD, HL-D
hepatolenticular degeneration
herniated lumbar disc
high level disinfection
hypersensitivity lung disease
von Hippel-Lindau disease

HL-D
haloperidol decanoate *also* HD, HLD

NOTES

HLDH
heat-stable lactic dehydrogenase

HLE
human leukocyte elastase

HLEG
hydrolysate lactalbumin Earle glucose

HLF
heat-labile factor
human lung field
human lung fluid

HLFCB
horizontal laminar flow clean benches

HLG
hypertrophic lymphocytic gastritis

HLH
helix-loop-helix
hemophagocytic lymphohistiocytosis
human luteinizing hormone *also* hLH
hypoplastic left heart (syndrome) *also*
HLHS

hLH
human luteinizing hormone *also* HLH

HLHS
hypoplastic left heart syndrome *also*
HLH

HLI
hemolysis inhibition
human leukocyte interferon
human lymphocyte interferon

HLK, H-L-K
heart, liver, and kidneys

HLN
hilar lymph node
human Lesch-Nyhan (cell)
hyperplastic liver nodule

H&L OK
heart and lungs normal

HLP
hepatic lipoperoxidation
hind leg paralysis
hyperkeratosis lenticularis perstans
hyperlipoproteinemia

HLR
heart-lung resuscitation
heart-lung resuscitator

HLS
Health Learning System
Hippel-Lindau syndrome

HLT
heart-lung transplant
human lipotropin
human lymphocyte transformation *also*
hLT

hLT
human lymphocyte transformation *also*
HLT

hlth
health

HLV
herpes-like virus
hypoplastic left ventricle

HLVS
hypoplastic left ventricular syndrome

HM
hand motion
hand movement
harmonic mean
health maintenance
heart murmur
heavily muscled
Heine-Medin (disease)
heloma molle (soft corn)
hemifacial microsomia *also* HFM
hepatic metabolism
hexamethylmelamine *also* Hex, HMM,
HXM
Holter monitor
homosexual male
hospital management
human milk
hydatidiform mole
hyperimmune mouse
hyperopia, manifest (hypermetropia)
also Hm
hypoxic-metabolic

Hm
hyperopia, manifest (hypermetropia)
also HM
manifest hyperopia

hm
hectometer

HMA
hemorrhages and microaneurysms

HMAC
Health Manpower Advisory Council

HMAS
hyperimmune mouse ascites (fluid)

HMB, HMB45
homatropine methylbromide

HMBA
hexamethylene bisacetamide

HMC
hand-mirror cell
health maintenance cooperative
heroin, morphine, and cocaine
hospital management committee
hydroxymethyl cytosine
hyoscine-morphine-codeine
hypertelorism-microtia-clefting
  (syndrome)

HMCCMP
human mammary carcinoma cell
  membrane proteinase

HMD
hyaline membrane disease

HMDP
hydroxymethylene diphosphonate

HME
Health Media Education
heat, massage, and exercise *also*
  HMX
heat/moisture exchanger

HMETSC
heavy metal screen

HMF
hydroxymethylfurfural

HM/3ft
hand motion at 3 feet

HMG
high mobility group
human menopausal gonadotropin *also*
  hMG
hydroxymethylglutaric (acid)

hMG
human menopausal gonadotropin *also*
  HMG

HMG CoA, HMG-CoA
hepatic 3-methylglutaryl coenzyme A
  reductase
β-hydroxy-β-methylglutaryl-CoA
hydroxymethylglutaryl coenzyme A
3-hydroxy-3-methylglutaryl coenzyme
  A

HMI
healed myocardial infarction

HMIS
hospital medical information system

HMK
high molecular weight kininogen *also*
  HMWK
homemaking

HML, hML
human milk lysozyme

HM & LP
hand motion and light perception

HMM
heavy meromyosin (of muscle)
hexamethylmelamine *also* Hex, HM,
  HXM

HMMA
4-hydroxy-3-methoxymandelic acid

HMO
health maintenance organization
heart minute output
hypothetical mean organism

HMP
hexose monophosphate (pathway)
hot moist packs
human menopausal
hydromotive pressure

HMPA
hexamethylphosphoramide

HMPAO
hexametazime
hexamethylpropyleneamine oxime

^{99mTc}-HMPAO
^{99mTc}-hexamethylpropyleneamine oxime

HMPG
hydroxymethoxyphenylglycol

HMPS
hexose monophosphate shunt *also*
  HMS

HMPT
hexamethylphosphoric triamide

HMR
histiocytic medullary reticulosis

NOTES

H

H-mRNA
H-chain messenger ribonucleic acid

HMRTE
human milk reverse transcriptase enzyme

HMS
hexose monophosphate shunt *also* HMPS
high methacholinesensitivity
hyperactive malarial splenomegaly
hypermobility syndrome
hypothetical mean strain

HMSAS
hypertrophic muscular subaortic stenosis

HMSN
hereditary motor and sensory neuropathy

HMSS
Hospital Management Systems Society

HMT
hematocrit *also* Crit, crit, H'crit, HCT, Hct, hemat
hexamethylenetetramine (methenamine) *also* HMTA
histamine methyltransferase
hospital management team

hMT
human molar thyrotropin

HMTA
hexamethylenetetramine (methenamine) *also* HMT

HMW
high molecular weight

HMWC
high molecular weight component

HMWGP
high molecular weight glycoprotein

HMWK
high molecular weight kininogen *also* HMK

HMWM
heavily muscled white male

HMWPE
high molecular weight polyethylene

HMX
heat, massage, and exercise *also* HME

H&N
head and neck *also* HN

HN
head and neck *also* H&N
head nurse
Heller-Nelson (syndrome)
hemagglutinin neuraminidase
hematemesis neonatorum
hemorrhage of newborn
hereditary nephritis
high nitrogen
hilar node
histamine-containing neuron
home nursing
hospital man
human nutrition
hypertensive nephrosclerosis
hypertrophic neuropathy

HN2
nitrogen mustard *also* NM

HN$_2$
mechlorethamine (nitrogen mustard)

h.n.
tonight [L. *hoc nocte*]

HNA
heparin-neutralizing activity

HNAC
Heymann nephritis antigenic complex

HNB
human neuroblastoma
hydroxynitrobenzylbromide

HNC
head and neck cancer
human neutrophil collagenase
hypernephroma cell
hyperosmolar nonketotic coma
hyperoxic normocapnic
hypothalamoneurohypophyseal complex

HNKDC
hyperosmolar nonketotic diabetic coma

HNKDS
hyperosmolar nonketotic diabetic state

HNLN
hospitalization no longer necessary

H&N mot
head and neck motion

HNP
hereditary nephritic protein

HNP
herniated nucleus pulposus *also* HPN
human neurophysin

HNPCC
hereditary nonpolyposis colorectal
cancer

HNPP
hereditary neuropathy (with liability
to) pressure palsies

hnRNA
heterogeneous nuclear ribonucleic acid

hnRNP
heterogeneous nuclear
ribonucleoprotein

HNS
head, neck, and shaft (of bone)
head and neck surgery
home nursing supervisor

HNSHA
hereditary nonspherocytic hemolytic
anemia

HNTD
highest nontoxic dose

HNTLA
Hiskey-Nebraska Test of Learning
Aptitude

HNV
has not voided

HO
hand orthosis
Hematology-Oncology
heterotopic ossification
high oxygen
hip orthosis
Holt-Oram (syndrome)
house officer
hyperbaric oxygen
hypertrophic ossification

H/O, h/o
history of

Ho
holmium
horse *also* H

HOA
hip osteoarthritis
hypertrophic osteoarthritis

Ho antigen
low-frequency blood group antigen

HOAP-BLEO
hydroxydaunomycin (doxorubicin),
Oncovin (vincristine), ara-C
(cytarabine), prednisone, and
bleomycin

HoaRhLG
horse anti-Rhesus lymphocyte globulin

HoaTTG
horse antitetanus toxoid globulin

HOB
head of bed

HOB UPSOB
head of bed up for shortness of
breath

HOC
Health Officer Certificate
human ovarian cancer
hydroxycorticoid *also* HC

HOCA
high osmolar contrast agent

HOCM
high-osmolar contrast medium *also*
HOM
hypertrophic obstructive
cardiomyopathy

hoc vesp.
this evening [L. *hoc vespere*]

HOD
hereditary opalescent dentin
Hoffer-Osmond Diagnostic
hospital day *also* HD
hyperbaric oxygen drenching

HOF
hepatic outflow
human oviduct fluid

HofF
height of fundus

Hoff
Hoffman (reflex)

HOG
halothane, oxygen, and gas (nitrous
oxide)

NOTES

H

HOGA
hyperornithinemia with gyrate atrophy

HOH
hard of hearing *also* HH

HOI
hospital onset of infection
hypoiodous acid

HoIg
horse immunoglobulin

HOM
hexamethylmelamine, Oncovin
(vincristine), and methotrexate
high-osmolar (contrast) medium *also*
HOCM

HOME
Home Observation for Measurement
of the Environment
Home-Oriented Maternity Experience

Homeo, Homeop
homeopathy

HOMO
highest occupied molecular orbital
homosexual *also* H, homo

homo
homosexual *also* H, HOMO

homolat
homolateral

HOOD
hereditary osteoonychodysplasia

HOODS
hereditary onychoosteodysplasia
syndrome

HOOI
Hall Occupational Orientation
Inventory

HOP
high oxygen pressure
hydroxydaunomycin (doxorubicin),
Oncovin (vincristine), and prednisone

HOPD
hospital outpatient department

HOPE
Healthcare Options Plan Entitlement
health-oriented physical education
holistic orthogonal parameter
estimation

HOPI
history of present illness *also* HPI

HOPP
hepatic-occluded portal pressure

hor, horiz
horizontal *also* H, h

hor. decub.
at bedtime [L. *hora decubitus*] *also*
h., h.d., hor. som., HS, h.s., h. som.

hor. interm.
at the intermediate hour [L. *hora
intermedia*]

horiz (*var. of* hor)

hor. som.
at bedtime [L. *hora somni*] *also* h.,
h.d., hor. decub., HS, h.s., h. som.

hor. un. spat.
at the end of one hour [L. *horae
unius spatio*]

HOS
Holt-Oram syndrome
human osteosarcoma

HoS
horse serum *also* HS

Hosp, hosp
hospital *also* H, HX
hospitalization *also* H, HX

HOST
hypoosmotic shock treatment

HOT
human old tuberculin
hyperbaric oxygen therapy
hypertension optimal treatment

HOTC
heterozygous ornithine
transcarbamylase

HOTS
hypercalcemia-osteolysis-T-cell
syndrome

HOW
hypothermia oxygen warmer

Ho:YAG
holmium:yttrium-aluminum-garnet

HP
Haemophilus pleuropneumoniae
halogen phosphorus
handicapped person
haptoglobin *also* HAPTO, Hp, Hpt,
hp
Harding-Passey (melanoma)
hard palate

Harvard pump
hastening phenomenon
health professional
heater probe
heat production
heel-to-patella *also* H→P
Helicobacter pylori
hemiparesis
hemipelvectomy
hemiplegia *also* Hp
hemoperfusion
heparin *also* H, HEP
hereditary pancreatitis
highly purified
high potency
high power
high pressure
high protein (diet) *also* HiPro
Hodgen and Pearson (suspension
   traction) *also* H&P
horizontal plane
horsepower
hospital participation
hot pack
hot pad
house physician
human pituitary
hybridoma product
hydrocollator pack
hydrogen peroxide
hydrophilic petrolatum
hydrophobic protein
hydrostatic pressure
hydroxyproline *also* HYP, hyp, hyp,
   hypro
hydroxypyruvate
hyperparathyroidism *also* HPT, HPTH,
   hyperpara
hyperphoria
hyperplastic polyp
hypersensitivity pneumonitis
hypertension plus proteinuria
hypoparathyroidism
hypopharynx

H-P
Hilgenreiner-Perkins

H&P
history and physical (examination)
   also HPE

Hodgen and Pearson (suspension
   traction) *also* HP

H→P
heel-to-patella *also* HP

Hp
haptoglobin *also* HAPTO, HP, hp,
   Hpt
hematoporphyrin
hemiplegia *also* HP

hp
haptoglobin *also* HAPTO, HP, Hp,
   Hpt
heaping
horsepower

HPA
α-haptoglobin
Helix pomatia agglutinin
hemagglutinating penicillin antibody
Hereford Parental Attitude (Survey)
human papillomavirus
human platelet antigen
hypothalamic-pituitary-adrenal (axis)
   also HPAA
hypothalamic-pituitary axis
hypothalmo-pituitary-adrenocortical
   (system) *also* HPAC

HPA-23
antimonium tungstate

HPAA
hydroperoxyarachidonic acid
hydroxyphenylacetic acid
hypothalamic-pituitary-adrenal axis
   also HPA

HPAC
hypothalamic-pituitary-adrenocortical
   (system) *also* HPA

HPAT
home parenteral antibiotic therapy

HPBC
hyperpolarizing bipolar cell

HPBF
hepatotropic portal blood factor

HPBL
human peripheral blood leukocyte

NOTES

H

HPC
hemangiopericytoma
hippocampal pyramidal cell
history of present complaint
hydrophilic-coated (guidewire)
hydroxyphenylcinchoninic (acid)
hydroxypropylcellulose

HPCD
hemostatic puncture closure device

HPD
hearing protection device
hematoporphyrin derivative *also* HpD
highly probably drunk
high-protein diet
home peritoneal dialysis

HP-D
Hough-Powell digitizer

HpD
hematoporphyrin derivative *also* HPD

HPE
hepatic portoenterostomy
high permeability edema
history and physical examination *also*
H&P
hydrostatic pulmonary edema

HPETE
hydroperoxyeicosatetraenoic acid

HPF
heparin-precipitable fraction
hepatic plasma flow
high-pass filter
high-power field (microscope) *also*
hpf
hypocaloric protein feeding

hpf
high-power field (microscope) *also*
HPF

HPFH
hereditary persistence of fetal
hemoglobin

hPFSH, HPFSH
human pituitary follicle-stimulating
hormone

HPG
hepatocyte growth factor *also* HGF
human pituitary gonadotropin
hypothalamic-pituitary-gonadal

hPG
human pituitary gonadotropin *also*
HPG

HPGe
high-purity germanium

HPH
halothane-percent-hour

HPI
hepatic perfusion index
hepatocyte proliferation inhibitor
Heston Personality Inventory (Test)
history of present illness *also* HOPI

HPL
human parotid lysozyme
human peripheral lymphocyte
human placental lactogen *also* hPL
hyperplexia

hPL
human placental lactogen *also* HPL

HPLA
hydroxyphenyllactic acid

HPLAC
high-pressure liquid affinity
chromatography

HPLC
high-performance liquid
chromatography
high-power liquid chromatography
high-pressure liquid chromatography

HPLO
Helicobacter pylori-like organism

HPM
Harding-Passey melanoma
hemiplegic migraine

HPMC
human peripheral mononuclear cell

HPN
home parenteral nutrition
hypertension *also* HT, HTN, hypn

h.p.n.
our own purgative draft [L. *haustus
purgans noster*]

HPNS
high-pressure neurologic syndrome

HPO
high-pressure oxygen
hydroperoxide
hydrophilic ointment
hypertrophic pulmonary osteoarthritis
hypertrophic pulmonary
osteoarthropathy *also* HPOA

HPOA
hypertrophic pulmonary osteoarthropathy *also* HPO

HPP, hPP
hereditary pyropoikilocytosis
history (of) presenting problems
human pancreatic polypeptide
hydroxyphenylpyruvate
hydroxypyrazolopyrimidine

2HPP
two-hour postprandial (blood sugar)

HPPA
hydroxyphenylpyruvic acid

HPPH
hydroxyphenylphenylhydantoin

HPPO
high partial pressure of oxygen
hydroxyphenylpyruvate oxidase

HPR
hospital peer review

HPr, hPr, HPRL
human prolactin

HPRP
human platelet-rich plasma

HPRT
hot plate reaction time
hypoxanthinephospho-ribosyltransferase

HPS
Hantavirus pulmonary syndrome
hematoxylin, phloxine, and saffron
Hermansky-Pudlak syndrome
high-protein supplement
His-Purkinje system
human platelet suspension
hypertrophic pyloric stenosis
hypothalamic pubertal syndrome

HPSEC
high-performance size-exclusion chromatography

HPSL
Health Professions Student Loan

HPT
histamine provocation test
hot plate test
human placental thyrotropin *also* hPT

human proximal tubule
hyperparathyroid
hyperparathyroidism *also* HP, HPTH, hyperpara
hypothalmic-pituitary-thyroid

Hpt
haptoglobin *also* HAPTO, HP, Hp, hp

hPT
human placental thyrotropin *also* HPT

HPTH
hyperparathyroid hormone
hyperparathyroidism *also* HP, HPT, hyperpara

hPTH
human parathyroid hormone I_{34} (teriparatide)

HPTIN
human pancreatic trypsin inhibitor

HPTM
home prothrombin time monitoring

HPU
heater probe unit

HPV
Haemophilus pertussis vaccine
hepatic portal vein
human papillomavirus
human parvovirus
hypoxic pulmonary vasoconstriction

HPV 16
human papillomavirus 16

HPVD
hypertensive pulmonary vascular disease

HPV-DE
high-passage virus-duck embryo (cell)

HPV-DK
high-passage virus-dog kidney (cell)

HPVG
hepatic portal venous gas

HPX
high peroxide-containing (cell)
hypophysectomized *also* HX, hypox
partial hepatectomy

NOTES

H

Hpx
hemopexin (serum protein)

HPZ
high pressure zone

H₂Q
ubiquinol *also* Q-H₂

HQC
hydroquinone cream

HR
hallux rigidus
Halstead-Reitan (battery) *also* HRB
Hamman-Rich (syndrome)
Harrington rod
heart rate *also* HRT
hemirectococcygeus
hemorrhagic retinopathy
heterosexual relations (scale)
higher rate
high resolution
high-risk
hormonal response
hospital record
hospital report
hour *also* H, h, hr
Howship-Romberg (syndrome)
human resources
hydroxyethylrutinosides (treatment of
venous disorders)
hyperimmune reaction
hypoxic responder

H&R
hysterectomy and radiation

2HR
two-hour pregnancy test

hr
hour *also* H, h, HR

HRA
health risk appraisal
heart rate audiometry
high right atrium
histamine-releasing activity
Human Resources Administration

H2RA
histamine₂ receptor antagonist

HRAE
high right atrium electrocardiogram

HRANA
histone-reactive antinuclear antibody

HRB
Halstead-Reitan Battery *also* HR
histamine release from basophils

HRBC
horse red blood cell

HRC
help-rejecting complainer
high-resolution chromatography
horse red cell
human rights committee

HRCT
high-resolution computed tomography

HRD
human retroviral disease

HRE
high-resolution electrocardiography
hormone-receptor enzyme

HREC
hepatic reticuloendothelial cell

HREH
high-renin essential hypertension

HREM
high-resolution electron microscopy

HRES
high-resolution endoluminal
sonography

HRF
Harris return flow
histamine-releasing factor

HRH
hypothalamic-releasing hormone

HRHS
hypoplastic right heart syndrome

HRI
Harrington rod instrumentation

HRIG, HRIg
human rabies immunoglobulin

HRL
head rotation to left

HRLA
human reovirus-like agent

HRLM
high-resolution light microscopy

hRNA
heterogeneous ribonucleic acid

HRNB
Halstead-Reitan Neuropsychological
Battery

HRP
high right parasternal (view)
high-risk pregnancy

histidine-rich protein
horseradish peroxidase

HRPD
Hamburg Rating Scale for Psychiatric
Disorders

HRR
Hardy-Rand-Ritter (color vision test
kit)
head rotation to right
heart rate range
heart rate reserve

HRRI
heart rate retardation index

HRS
Hamilton Rating Scale
Haw River syndrome
hepatorenal syndrome
hormone receptor site
humeroradial synostosis

HRSA
Health Resources and Services
Administration

HRS-D
Hamilton Rating Scale for Depression

HRT
half relaxation time
heart rate *also* HR
hormone replacement therapy

HRTE
human reverse transcriptase enzyme

HRTEM
high-resolution transmission electron
microscopy

HRV
heart rate variability
human rotavirus

HRVL
human reovirus-like

HS
at bedtime [L. *hora somni hour of
sleep*] *also* h., h.d., hor. decub., hor.
som., h.s., h. som.
half strength
Hallervorden-Spatz (syndrome)
hamstrings *also* Hams

hand surgery
Hartmann solution
Haynes-Stellite
head sign
head sling
healthy subject
heart sound
heat stable
heavy smoker
heel spur
heelstick
Hegglin syndrome
heme synthetase
Henoch-Schönlein (syndrome)
heparin sulfate
hereditary spherocytosis
herpes simplex
hidradenitis suppurativa
high school
homologous serum
Hopelessness Scale
horizontally selective (visual cell)
Horner syndrome
horse serum *also* HoS
hospital ship
hospital staff
hospital stay
hour of sleep
house surgeon
human serum
Hurler syndrome
hypereosinophilic syndrome
hyperplastic synovium
hypersensitivity
hypertonic saline
hysterosalpingography *also* HSG, HSP

H/S
helper-suppressor (ratio)

H&S
hearing and speech
hemorrhage and shock
hysterectomy and sterilization

H→S
heel-to-shin (test) *also* HTS

H₂S
Hering law-EOM innervation, both
eyes
Sherrington law-EOM innervation, one
eye

NOTES

H

Hs
hypochondriasis

h.s.
at bedtime [L. *hora somni hour of sleep*] *also* h., h.d., hor. decub., hor. som., HS, h. som.

HSA
Hazardous Substances Act
health service area
Health Services Administration
Health Systems Agency
horse serum albumin
human serum albumin *also* HuSA
hypersomnia-sleep apnea (syndrome)

HSAG
HEPES (hydroxyethylpiperazine ethanesulfonic acid)-saline-albumin-gelatin

HSAP
heat-stable alkaline phosphatase

HSAS
hypertrophic subaortic stenosis *also* HSS

HSBG
heel-stick blood gas

HSC
Hand-Schüller-Christian (disease) *also* HSCD
health sciences center
health screening center
hematopoietic stem cell
horizontal semicircular canal
human skin collagenase

HSCD
Hand-Schüller-Christian disease *also* HSC

HSCL
Hopkins Symptom Checklist

HS-CoA
reduced coenzyme A

HSD
honest significance difference
hydroxysteroid dehydrogenase

3βHSD
3β-hydroxysteroid dehydrogenase

HSDA
high single dose alternate day

HSDI
Health Self-Determination Index

HSE
health and safety executive
hemorrhagic shock and encephalopathy
herpes simplex encephalitis
human serum esterase
hypertonic saline-epinephrine (solution)

Hse
homoserine

HSES
hemorrhagic shock-encephalopathy syndrome

HSF
heated soybean flower
histamine-induced suppressor factor
histamine-sensitizing factor
hypothalamic secretory factor

HSG
herpes simplex genitalis
hysterosalpingogram
hysterosalpingography *also* HS

hSGF
human skeletal growth factor

HSGP
human sialoglycoprotein

HSHC
hemisuccinate of hydrocortisone

HSI
heat stress index
human seminal (plasma) inhibitor

HSK
herpes simplex keratitis

HSL
herpes simplex labialis

H-SLAP
human stromelysis aggregated proteoglycan

HSLC
high-speed liquid chromatography

HSM
hepatosplenomegaly
holosystolic murmur

HSMHA
Health Services and Mental Health Administration

HSMN III
hereditary sensory motor neuropathy, type III

HSN
Hansen-Street nail
hereditary sensory neuropathy
herpes simplex neonatorum

hSOD
human superoxide dismutase

h. som.
at bedtime [L. *hora somni hour of sleep*] *also* h., h.d., hor. decub., hor. som., HS, h.s.

HSP
Health Systems Plan
heat shock protein
hemostatic screening profile
Henoch-Schönlein purpura
human serum prealbumin
human serum protein
hypersensitivity pneumonitis panel
hysterosalpingography *also* HS, HSG

hsp
heat shock protein

HSPG
heparan sulfate proteoglycan

H spike
His bundle electrogram deflection

HSPM
hippocampal synaptic plasma membrane

HSPN
Henoch-Schönlein purpura nephritis

HSPQ
High School Personality Questionnaire

HSQB
Health Standards and Quality Bureau

HSR
Harleco synthetic resin
heated serum reagent
homogeneous staining region (of chromosome)

HSRA
high-speed rotational atherectomy

HSRC
Health Services Research Center
Human Subjects Review Committee

HSRD
hypertension secondary to renal disease

HSRI
Health Systems Research Institute

HSRS
Health-Sickness Rating Scale
Hess School Readiness Scale

HSS
Hallerman-Streiff syndrome
Hallervorden-Spatz syndrome
Henoch-Schönlein syndrome
hepatic stimulatory substance
high-speed supernatant
hyperstimulation syndrome
hypertrophic subaortic stenosis *also* HSAS

HSSCC
hereditary site-specific colon cancer

HSSE
high soapsuds enema

HST
health screening test
Hemoccult slide test
horseshoe tear

HSTF
human serum thymus factor

HSTS
human-specific thyroid stimulator

HSV
herpes simplex virus
highly selective vagotomy
hyperviscosity syndrome

HSV-1–2
herpesvirus type 1–2

HSVE
herpes simplex virus encephalitis

HSVtk
herpes simplex virus thymidine kinase

HSyn
heme synthase

HT
hammertoe
Hand Test (psychologic test)

NOTES

H

HT *(continued)*
Hashimoto thyroiditis
hearing test
hearing threshold
heart *also* H, He, ht
heart test
heart tone *also* ht
heart transplant
heart transplantation
height *also* H, h, *h*, Hgt, ht
hemagglutination titer
high temperature
high tension *also* ht
Histologic Technologist
histotechnology
home treatment
hospital treatment
Hubbard tank
Huhner test
human thrombin
hydrocortisone test
hydrotherapy *also* hydro
5-hydroxytryptamine (serotonin) *also* 5-HT, 5HT, HTA
hyperopia, total (hypermetropia) *also* Ht
hypertension *also* HPN, HTN, hypn
hyperthyroidism
hypertransfusion
hypertropia
hypodermic tablet
hypothalamus *also* H, Ht, Hth, Hyp

3-HT
3-hydroxytyramine (dopamine)

5-HT, 5HT
5-hydroxytryptamine (serotonin) *also* HT, HTA
serotonin

H&T
hospitalization and treatment

H(T)
intermittent hypertropia

Ht
height of heart
heterozygote
hypermetropia, total
hyperopia, total *also* HT
hypothalamus *also* H, HT, Hth, Hyp, hyp

ht
heart *also* H, He, HT
heart tone *also* HT

heat
height *also* H, h, *h*, Hgt, HT
high tension *also* HT

ht.
draft, drink [L. *haustas*] *also* H, h., haust.
draught, drink [L. *haustus*] *also* H, h

HTA
heterophil transplantation antigen
human thymocyte antigen
5-hydroxytryptamine (serotonin) *also* HT, 5-HT, 5HT
hypophysiotropic area (of hypothalamus)

HTACS
human thyroid adenylcyclase stimulator

ht aer
heated aerosol *also* HA

HT(ASCP)
Histologic Technologist certified by Board of Registry of American Society of Clinical Pathologists

HTAT
human tetanus antitoxin

HTB
hot tub bath
house tube (feeding) *also* HTF
human tumor bank

HTC
heated tracheostomy collar
hepatoma cell
hepatoma tissue culture
homozygous typing cell
hypertensive crisis

HTCA
human tumor colony assay

HTCVD
hypertensive cardiovascular disease *also* HCVD

HTD
human therapeutic dose

HTDW
heterosexual development of women

HTF
heterothyrotropic factor
house tube feeding *also* HTB

HTG
hypertriglyceridemia

HTGL
hepatic triglyceride lipase

HTH
helix-turn-helix
homeostatic thymus hormone

Hth
hypothalamus *also* H, HT, Ht, Hyp

HTHD
hypertensive heart disease *also* HHD

HTI
hemisphere thrombotic infarction
human tetanus immunoglobulin

HTIG
homologous tetanus immune globulin

hTIg
human tetanus immunoglobulin

HTK
heel-to-knee (test) *also* HK, H-K

HTL
hamster tumor line
hearing threshold level
histologic technologist
histotechnologist
human T-cell leukemia
human T-cell lymphoma
human thymic leukemia

HTLA
high titer, low acidity
human T-lymphocyte antigen

HTL(ASCP)
Histotechnologist certified by the
Board of Registry of the American
Society of Clinical Pathologists

HTLV
human T-cell leukemia virus
human T-cell lymphoma virus
human T-cell lymphotrophic virus
human T-lymphotrophic retrovirus

HTLV-I
human T-cell leukemia virus type I
human T-cell lymphotrophic virus
type I

HTLV-II
human T-cell leukemia virus type II
human T-cell lymphotrophic virus
type II

HTLV-III
human T-cell leukemia virus type III
human T-cell lymphotrophic virus
type III

HTLV-MA
human T-cell leukemia virus-
associated membrane antigen

HTN
Hantaan(-to like virus)
hypertension *also* HPN, HT, hypn
hypertensive nephropathy

HTO
heterotropic ossification
high tibial osteotomy
hospital transfer order

HTOH
hydroxytryptophol

HTP
House-Tree-Person (Projective
Technique psychologic test)
hydroxytryptophan
hypothromboplastinemia

5-HTP
5-hydroxytryptophan

HTPN
home total parenteral nutrition

HTR
hard tissue replacement
hypermetropia, right

HTR-MFI
hand tissue replacement-malleable
facial implant

HTS
head traumatic syndrome
heel-to-shin (test) *also* H→S
hemangioma-thrombocytopenia
syndrome
human thyroid-stimulating (hormone)
also HTSH, hTSH
human thyroid stimulator

NOTES

H

hTSAb
human thyroid-stimulating antibody

HTSCA
human tumor stem cell assay

HTSH, hTSH
human thyroid-stimulating hormone
also HTS

HTST
high temperature-short time
(pasteurization)

HTT
hand thrust test

HTV
herpes-type virus

HTVD
hypertensive vascular disease *also*
HVD

HTX
hemothorax

HU
head unit
heat unit
hemagglutinating unit
hemagglutinin unit
hemolytic unit
Hounsfield unit *also* H
human urinary
human urine
hydroxyurea *also* HUR, HYD
hyperemia unit

Hu
human *also* H, h

hU, hu
dihydrouridine *also* hu, D

HUC
hypouricemia

HU-CSF
human urinary CSF

HuEPO
human erythropoietin

hu-FSH, HU-FSH
human urinary follicle-stimulating
hormone

HUI
Harris uterine injector
headache unit index

HUIFM
human leukocyte interferon milieu

HuIFN
human interferon

HUIS
high-dose urea in invert sugar

HUK
human urinary kallikrein

HUM
heat (or hot packs), ultrasound, and
massage
hematourimetry
home uterine monitoring

hum.
humerus

HUMARA
X-linked human androgen receptor

HUMI
Harris-Kronner uterine
manipulator/injector

HUP
Hospital Utilization Project

HUR
hydroxyurea *also* HU, HYD

HURA
health in underserved rural areas

HURT
hospital utilization review team

HUS
hemolytic uremic syndrome
hyaluronidase unit for semen

HuSA
human serum albumin *also* HSA

husb
husband *also* H

HUTHAS
human thymus antiserum

HUTTT
head-up tilt-table test

HUV
human umbilical vein

HUVEC
human umbilical vein endothelial cell

HV
hallux valgus
Hantaan virus
has voided
heart volume
Hemovac
hepatic vein

herpes virus
high voltage
high volume
home visit
hospital visit
hyperventilation

H&V
hemigastrectomy and vagotomy

h.v.
this evening [L. *hoc vespere*]

HVA
homovanillic acid

HVc
hyperstriatum ventrale, pars caudale

HVD
hypertensive vascular disease *also*
  HTVD
hypoxic ventilatory drive

HVDO
hypovitaminosis D osteopathy

HVE
hepatic vascular exclusion
hepatic venous effluence
high-voltage electrophoresis
high volume evacuator

HVEM
high voltage electron microscope

HVF
hepatocycle volume fraction

HVFP
hepatic vein free pressure

HVG
hematoxylin and van Gieson (stain)
host-versus-graft (disease, response)

HVGS
high-voltage galvanic stimulation
  (physical therapy)

HVH
Herpesvirus hominis

HVHMA
Herpesvirus hominis membrane
  antigen

HVID
horizontal visible iris diameter

HVI-DHP
hepatic venous isolation by direct
  hemoperfusion

HVJ
hemagglutinating virus of Japan

HVL, hvl
half-value layer

HVLP
high volume, low pressure

HVLT
high-velocity lead therapy

HVM
hypothalamic ventromedial (nucleus)

HVO
hallux valgus orthosis

HVOO
hepatic venous outflow obstruction

HVPE
high-voltage paper electrophoresis

HVPG
hepatic venous pressure gradient

HVPGS
high-voltage pulse galvanic
  stimulation

HVR
hypoxic ventilatory response

HVR1
hypervariable region 1

HVS
herpesvirus of Saimiri
herpesvirus sensitivity
herpesvirus simplex
hyperventilation syndrome
hyperviscosity syndrome

H vs A
home versus (against) advice

HVSD
hydrogen-detected ventricular septal
  defect

HVT
half-value thickness
herpesvirus of turkeys
high-voltage therapy

NOTES

H

HVTEM
high-voltage transmission electron microscopy

HVUS
hypocomplementemic vasculitis urticaria syndrome

HW
Hayem-Widal (syndrome)
healing well
heart weight
hemisphere width
heparin well
Hertwig-Weyers (syndrome)
housewife

HWB, hwb
hot water bottle

HWE
hot water extract

HWOK
heel walking normal (OK)

HWP
hepatic wedge pressure
hot wet pack
Hutchinson-Weber-Pentz (syndrome)

HWRS
Habits of Work and Recreation Survey

HWS
hot water soluble

HWY
hundred woman years (of exposure)

HX
histiocytosis X
hospital *also* H, Hosp, hosp
hospitalization *also* H, Hosp, hosp
hydrogen exchange
hypophysectomized *also* HPX, hypox

Hx
history *also* H, Hist, hist, hx, Hy
hypoxanthine *also* Hyp, hyp

hx
history *also* H, Hist, hist, Hx, Hy

2-HxG
di(hydroxyethyl)glycine

HXIS
hard x-ray imaging spectrometer

HXM
hexamethylmelamine *also* Hex, HM, HMM

HXR
hypoxanthine riboside

HXV
herpes simplex virus

HY
hypophysis *also* hyp

Hy
history *also* H, Hist, hist, Hx, hx
hydraulics
hydrostatics
hypermetropia *also* H, h
hyperopia *also* H, h
hyperopic *also* H, h
hypothenar
hysteria *also* hy, hys, hyst

hy
hysteria *also* Hy, hys, hyst

HYD
hydralazine
hydrated to hydration
hydroxyurea *also* HU, HUR

Hyd
hydrocortisone *also* HC, HCT
hydrostatics

hydr
hydraulic

hydrarg.
mercury [L. *hydrargyrum* silver water] *also* Hg

hydro
hydrotherapy *also* HT

hydrox
hydroxyline

hyd and tur
hydration and turgor

Hyg, hyg
hygiene *also* H
hygienic *also* H
hygienist *also* H

HYL, Hyl
hydroxylysine

5Hyl
5-hydroxylysine

HYLO
hyaline

HYP
hydroxyproline *also* HP, Hyp, hyp, hypro
hypnosis *also* hypno

Hyp, hyp
hydroxyproline *also* HP, HYP, hypro
hyperresonance
hypertrophy
hypothalamus *also* H, HT, Ht, Hth
hypoxanthine *also* Hx

3Hyp
3-hydroxyproline

hyp
hypalgesia
hypophysectomy *also* HE
hypophysis *also* HY

hyperal, hyper-al
hyperalimentation

hyper-IgE
hyperimmunoglobulinemia E

hyperpara
hyperparathyroidism *also* HP, HPT,
HPTH

hyper T&A
hypertrophy of tonsils and adenoids

hypes
hypesthesia

hypn
hypertension *also* HPN, HT, HTN

hypno
hypnosis *also* HYP

hypo
hypochromasia

hypochromia
hypodermic *also* H, (H), h

hypo A
hypoactive

hypox
hypophysectomized *also* HPX, HX

HYPP
hypersegmented neutrophil

HypRF
hypothalamic-releasing factor

hypro
hydroxyproline *also* HP, HYP, Hyp,
hyp

hys, hyst
hysterectomy
hysteria *also* Hy, hy
hysterical

HZ
herpes zoster

Hz
hertz

HZFO
hamster zona-free ovum (test)

HZO
herpes zoster ophthalmicus

HZV
herpes zoster virus

NOTES

H

I

electric current
implantation
impression *also* IMP, imp
inactive *also* inac
incisor (deciduous, permanent)
increased
independent *also* ind
index *also* ind
indicated
induction *also* Ind, ind
inhalation *also* INH, inhal
inhibiting *also* inhib
inhibition *also* inhib
inhibitor
initial
inosine *also* Ino
insoluble *also* insol
inspiration *also* Insp, inspir
inspired (gas)
insulin *also* IN, In, INS
intact (bag of waters)
intake
intensity
intensity of magnetism
intermediate *also* INT, int, Intmd
intestine
iodide
iodine
ionic strength
iota (ninth letter of Greek alphabet),
  uppercase
iris
isochromosome
isoleucine
isotope
isotropic (band, disk)
luminous intensity
moment of inertia
optically inactive (chemical)
radiant intensity
vector cardiography electrode (right
  midaxillary line)

I-123

iodine-123 *also* ^{123}I

^{123}I

iodine-123 *also* I-123
iodine radioisotope

^{125}I

iodine-125
iodine radioisotope

^{127}I

iodine-127

^{131}I

iodine-131
iodine radioisotope

^{132}I

iodine-132
iodine radioisotope

IA

ibotenic acid *also* ibo
image amplification
immune adherence
immunobiologic activity
impedance angle
inactive alcoholic
incidental appendectomy
incurred accidentally
Indian-American (Native American)
indolaminergic-accumulating (cells)
indulin agar
infantile apnea
infantile autism
infected area
inferior angle
inferior apical
inhibitory antigen
internal auditory
intraalveolar
intraamniotic *also* iam
intraaortic
intraarterial
intraarticular
intraatrial
intraauricular
intrinsic activity
isonicotinic acid

I/A, I&A

irrigation and aspiration
irrigation/aspiration

Ia

immune (region)-associated antigen

Ia+

immune-associated antigen-positive
  macrophage

IAA

ileoanal anastomosis
indoleacetic acid
infectious agent, arthritis
interruption of aortic arch
iodoacetic acid

I-3-AA
indole-3-acetic acid

IAAR
imidazoleacetic acid ribonucleotide

IAB
Industrial Accident Board
intraabdominal
intraaortic balloon

IABA
intraaortic balloon assistance

IABC
intraaortic balloon catheter
intraaortic balloon counterpulsation
also IABCP

IABCP
intraaortic balloon counterpulsation
also IABC

IABM
idiopathic aplastic bone marrow

IABP
intraaortic balloon pump *also* IBP

IABPA
intraaortic balloon pumping assistance

IAC
ineffective airway clearance
internal auditory canal
interposed abdominal compression
intraarterial chemotherapy
Inventory of Anger Communications

IACB
intraaortic counterpulsation balloon

IAC-CPR
interposed abdominal compressions-
cardiopulmonary resuscitation

IACD
implantable automatic cardioverter-
defibrillator
intraatrial conduction defect

IACG
intermittent angle closure glaucoma

IACP
intraaortic counterpulsation

IAD
inactivating dose
inhibiting antibiotic dose
internal absorbed dose
intractable atopic dermatitis

IADH
inappropriate antidiuretic hormone

IADHS
inappropriate antidiuretic hormone
syndrome

IADR
International Association for Dental
Research

IAds
immunoadsorption

IADSA
intraarterial digital subtraction
angiography

IAE
intraarterial electrocardiogram
intraatrial electrocardiogram

IAEA
International Atomic Energy Agency

IAFI
infantile amaurotic familial idiocy

IAG
International Academy of Gnathology

IAGT
indirect antiglobulin test *also* IAT,
IDAT

IAH
idiopathic adrenal hyperplasia
implantable artificial heart

IAHA
idiopathic autoimmune hemolytic
anemia
immune adherence hemagglutination

IAHD
idiopathic acquired hemolytic disease

IAHIA
immune adherence immunosorbent
assay *also* IAIA

IAHS
infection-associated hemophagocytic
syndrome

IAI
intraabdominal infection

IAIA
immune adherence immunosorbent
assay *also* IAHIA

IAM
Institute of Aviation Medicine
internal acoustic meatus
internal auditory meatus

iam
intraamniotic *also* IA

IAN
idiopathic aseptic necrosis
intern admission note

IAO
immediately after onset
intermittent aortic occlusion
International Association for
Orthodontics

IAP
immunosuppressive acidic protein
innervated antral pouch
inosinic acid pyrophosphorylase
intermittent acute porphyria
International Academy of Pathology
intraabdominal pressure
islet-activating protein

IAPG
interatrial pressure gradient

IAR
immediate asthmatic reaction
inhibitory anal reflex
iodine-azide reaction

IARF
ischemic acute renal failure

IARSA
idiopathic acquired refractory
sideroblastic anemia

IART
intraartrial reentrant tachycardia

IAS
idiopathic ankylosing spondylitis
immunosuppressive acidic substance
infant apnea syndrome
interatrial septum
interatrial shunting
internal anal sphincter
intraabdominal sepsis
intraamniotic saline (infusion)

IASA
interatrial septal aneurysm

IASD
interatrial septal defect *also* ISD
interauricular septal defect

IASH
isolated asymmetric septal hypertrophy

IASHS
Institute for Advanced Study in
Human Sexuality

IAT
immunoaugmentative therapy
indirect antiglobulin test *also* IAGT,
IDAT
instillation abortion time
invasive activity test
iodine azide test
Iowa Achievement Test

IAV
interactive video
intermittent assisted ventilation
intraarterial vasopressin

IAVM
intramedullary arteriovenous
malformation

I-B
interbody (vertebral)

IB
Ibrahim-Beck (disease)
idiopathic blepharospasm
ileal bypass
immune balance
immune body
inclusion body *also* IncB
index of body build
infectious bronchitis
inferior basal
isolation bed

ib.
in the same place [L. *ibidem*] *also*
ibid.

IBA
isobutyric acid

I band
isotropic band (striated muscle fiber)
also I disk

IBAT
intravascular bronchoalveolar tumor

IBB
intestinal brush border

IBBB
intrablood-brain barrier

NOTES

IBBBB
incomplete bilateral bundle branch block

IBC
Institutional Biosafety Committee
iodine-binding capacity
iron-binding capacity
isobutyl cyanoacrylate *also* IBCA

IBCA
isobutyl cyanoacrylate

IBD
infectious bowel disease
inflammatory bowel disease
irritable bowel disease
ischemic bowel disease

IBED
Inter-African Bureau for Epizootic Diseases

IB-EP
immunoreactive beta endomorphin

IBF
immature brown fat (cell)
immunoglobulin-binding factor
Insall-Burstein-Freeman (total knee instrumentation)

IBG
iliac bone graft
insoluble bone gelatin

IBI
intermittent bladder irrigation
ischemic brain infarction

ibid.
in the same place [L. *ibidem*] *also* ib.

IBIDS
ichthyosis plus BIDS

IBILI
indirect bilirubin

IBK
infectious bovine keratoconjunctivitis

IBL
immunoblastic lymphadenopathy

IBM
inclusion body myositis
isotonic-isometric brief maximum

IBNR
incurred but not reported

ibo
ibotenic acid *also* IA

IBOW
intact bag of waters

IBP
intraaortic balloon pump
iron-binding protein

IBPMS
indirect blood pressure measuring system

IBPS
Insall-Burstein posterior stabilizer

IBQ
Illness Behavior Questionnaire

IBR
immediate breast reconstruction
Infant Behavior Record
infectious bovine rhinotracheitis (virus)

IBRS
Inpatient Behavior Rating Scale

IBRV
infectious bovine rhinotracheitis virus

IBS
imidazole-buffered saline
inflammatory bowel syndrome
inside bathing solution
Interpersonal Behavior Survey
irritable bowel syndrome
isobaric solution

IBSA, iBSA
immunoreactive bovine serum albumin
iodinated bovine serum albumin

IBSN
infantile bilateral striated necrosis

IBT
ink blot test (Rorschach test)

IBTR
ipsilateral breast tumor recurrence

IBU
ibuprofen
international benzoate unit

IBV
infectious bronchitis vaccine
infectious bronchitis virus

IBW
ideal body weight

IC
between meals [L. *inter cibos*] *also* i.c., int. cib.
icteric *also* ICT

ileocecal
iliococcygeal
iliorostral
immune complex
immune cytotoxicity
immunocompromised
immunocytochemistry *also* ICC
impedance cardiogram
incomplete (diagnosis)
indirect calorimetry
indirect Coombs (test)
individual counseling
infection control
inferior colliculus
information content
inhibitory concentration
inner canthal (distance)
inorganic carbon
inspiratory capacity
inspiratory center
institutional care
integrated circuit
integrated concentration
intensive care
intercarpal
intercostal (space) *also* ICS, IS
intermediate care
intermittent catheterization *also* Ic
intermittent claudication
internal capsule
internal carotid
internal cerebral
internal cholecystectomy
internal conjugate (diameter)
International Classification
interstitial cell
interstitial change
intracameral
intracapsular
intracardiac
intracarotid
intracavitary
intracellular (concentration)
intracerebral
intracisternal *also* ICI
intracoronary
intracranial
intracutaneous
intrapleural catheter
irritable colon

islet cell (of pancreas)
isovolumic contraction

I/C
 invalid chair

IC$_{50}$
 concentration that inhibits 50%

Ic
 intermittent catheterization *also* IC

i.c.
 between meals [L. *inter cibos*] *also*
 IC, int. cib.

ICA
 ileocolic anastomosis
 immunocytochemical assay
 Institute of Clinical Analysis
 intercountry adoption
 intermediate care area
 internal carotid artery
 intracranial anatomy
 intracranial aneurysm
 islet cell antibody *also* ICAb

iCa
 ionized calcium

ICAb
 islet cell antibody *also* ICA

ICAF
 internal carotid artery flow

ICAM
 intercellular adhesion module

ICAM-1
 intercellular adhesion molecule-1

ICAO
 internal carotid artery occlusion

ICAP
 intracisternal A particle

ICAS
 intermediate coronary artery syndrome

ICAV
 intracavitary

ICB
 intracranial bleeding

ICBF
 inner cortical blood flow

NOTES

347

ICBG
iliac crest bone graft

ICBP
intercellular binding protein
intracellular binding protein

ICBT
intercostobronchial trunk

ICC
immunocompetent cell
immunocytochemistry *also* IC
Indian childhood cirrhosis
intensive coronary care
interchromosomal crossing-over
intermediate cell column
intermittent clean catheterization
internal conversion coefficient
islet cell carcinoma

ICCE
intracapsular cataract extraction

ICCEc̄PI
intracapsular cataract extraction with
peripheral iridectomy

ICCM
idiopathic congestive cardiomyopathy

ICCU
intensive coronary care unit
intermediate coronary care unit

ICD
I-cell disease
immune complex disease
implantable cardioverter-defibrillator
inclusion cell disease
induced circular dichroism
instantaneous cardiac death
Institute for Crippled and Disabled
intercanthal distance
internal cardioverter-defibrillator
internal cervical device
International Classification of Diseases
(of World Health Organization)
intracervical device
intrauterine contraceptive device *also*
IUCD, IUD
ischemic coronary disease
isocitrate dehydrogenase *also* ICDH
isolated conduction defect

ICDA
International Classification of
Diseases, Adapted (for use in
United States)

ICD-ATP
implantable cardioverter-
defibrillator/atrial tachycardia pacing

ICDC
implantable cardioverter/defibrillator
catheter

ICDCD
International Classification of Diseases
and Causes of Death

ICD-CM
International Classification of
Diseases–Clinical Modification

ICDH
isocitrate dehydrogenase *also* ICD
isocitric acid dehydrogenase *also* IDH

ICD-O
International Classification of Diseases
for Oncology

ICDRG
International Contact Dermatitis
Research Group

ICDS
Integrated Child Development Scheme

ICE
ice, compression, and elevation
ichthyosis-cheek-eyebrow (syndrome)
ifosfamide, carboplatin, and etoposide
individual career exploration
iridocorneal endothelial (syndrome)

ICES
ice, compression, elevation, and
support

ICET
(Forty-Eight) Item Counseling
Evaluation Test

ICEUS
intracaval endovascular
ultrasonography

ICF
indirect centrifugal flotation
intensive care facility
intercellular fluorescence
interciliary fluid
intermediate care facility
intracellular fluid
intravascular coagulation and
fibrinolysis (syndrome)

ICFA
incomplete Freund adjuvant *also* IFA
induced complement-fixing antigen

ICF-MR
intermediate-care facility for mentally retarded

IC fx
intracapsular fracture

ICG
indocyanine green (dye)
isotope cisternography

ICGN, IC-GN
immune complex glomerulonephritis

ICH
idiopathic cortical hyperostosis
immunocompromised host
infectious canine hepatitis
intracerebral hematoma
intracerebral hemorrhage
intracerebral hypertension
intracranial hemorrhage
intracranial hypertension

ICHD
Inter-Society Commission for Heart Disease
ischemic coronary heart disease

ICHPPC
International Classification of Health Problems in Primary Care

ICI
Interpersonal Communication Inventory
intracardiac injection
intracisternal *also* IC

ICIDH
International Classification of Impairments, Disabilities, and Handicaps

ICJ
ileocecal junction

ICL
idiopathic CD4 T-cell lymphocytopenia
intracorneal lens
intracorporeal laser lithotripsy
iris-clip lens

ICLE
intracapsular lens extraction

ICLH
Imperial College, London Hospital

ICM
infracostal margin
inner cell mass
intercostal margin
intracytoplasmic membrane
ion conductance modulator
ipsilateral competing message
isolated cardiovascular malformation

ICMI
Inventory of Childhood Memories and Imaginings

ICN
infection control nurse
intensive care neonatal
intensive care nursery
intermediate care nursery

ICNC
intracerebellar nuclear cell

ICO
idiopathic cyclic oedema
impedance cardiac output

ICP
incubation period *also* IP
inductively coupled plasma
infection-control practitioner
infectious cell protein
inflammatory cloacogenic polyp
intermittent catheterization protocol
intracranial pressure
intracytoplasmic
intrahepatic cholestasis of pregnancy

↑ICP
increased intracranial pressure *also* IICP

ICPC
intracranial pressure catheter

ICPMM
incisors, canines, premolars, and molars (permanent dentition formula)

ICPP
intubated continuous positive-pressure

ICPS
Interpersonal Cognitive Problem Solving

NOTES

ICR
(distance between) iliac crests
Institute for Cancer Research
intermittent catheter routine
international calibrated ratio
intracardiac catheter recording
intracavitary radium
intracranial reinforcement
ion cyclotron resonance

ICRD
Index of Codes for Research Drugs

ICRETT
International Cancer Research
Technology Transfer

ICREW
International Cancer Research
Workshop

ICRF
bispiperazinedione

I-CRF
immunoreactive corticotropin-releasing
factor

ICRP
International Commission on
Radiological Protection

ICRS
Index Chemicus Registry System

ICRU
International Commission on
Radiological Units

ICS
ileocecal sphincter
immotile cilia syndrome
impulse-conducting system
inferior capsular shift
intensive care, surgical
intercellular space *also* IS
intercostal space *also* IC, IS
International compression system
intracellular-like, calcium-bearing
crystalloid solution
intracranial stimulation
irritable colon syndrome

ICSA
islet cell surface antibody

ICSC
idiopathic central serous
chorioretinopathy

ICSH
International Committee for
Standardization in Hematology
interstitial cell-stimulating hormone

ICSI
intracytoplasmic sperm injection

ICSS
intracranial self-stimulation

ICT
icteric *also* IC
icterus *also* Ict, ict
immunoglobulin consumption test
indirect Coombs test
indirect Coombs titer
inflammation of connective tissue
insulin coma therapy
insulin convulsive therapy
intensive conventional therapy
intermittent cervical traction *also*
ICTX
interstitial cell tumor
intracardiac thrombus
intracranial tumor
intradermal cancer test
intraoral cariogenicity test
isolated cortical tubule
isovolumic contraction time *also*
IVCT

Ict, ict
icterus *also* ICT

iCT
immunoreactive calcitonin

ict ind
icterus index *also* II

ICTS
idiopathic carpal tunnel syndrome

ICTX
intermittent cervical traction *also* ICT

ICU
immunologic contact urticaria
infant care unit
intensive care unit
intermediate care unit

ICUS
intracoronary ultrasound

ICV
intracellular volume
intracerebroventricular *also* icv

icv
into cerebral ventricles
intracerebroventricular *also* ICV

I

ICVH
ischemic cerebrovascular headache

ICW
intact canal wall
intensive care ward
intercellular water
intracellular water

ICX
immune complex

ICXA
intermediate circumflex artery

ID
identification
identify
iditol dehydrogenase
ill-defined
immunodeficiency
immunodiffusion (test)
immunoglobulin deficiency
inappropriate disability
inclusion disease
index of discrimination
individual dose
induction delivery
infant death
infectious disease *also* inf dis
infective dose
inhibitory dose
inhomogeneous deposition
initial diagnosis
initial dose
initial dyskinesia
injected dose
inner diameter
inside diameter
insufficient data
interdigitating (cells)
internal diameter
interstitial disease
intradermal *also* i.d.
intraduodenal
isosorbide dinitrate *also* ISD, ISDN

I-D
intensity-duration (curve)

I&D
incision and drainage
irrigation and debridement
irrigation and drainage

ID$_{50}$
median infective dose

Id
idiotypic
infradentale
interdentale

i.d.
during the day [L. *in diem*]
intradermal *also* ID

id.
the same [L. *idem*]

IDA
idiopathic destructive arthritis
image display and analysis
iminodiacetic acid
insulin-degrading activity
iron-deficiency anemia

id. ac
the same as [L. *idem ac*]

IDAMIS
Integrated Dose Abuse Management
Informational Systems

IDARP
Integrated Drug Abuse Reporting
Process

IDAT
indirect antiglobulin test *also* IAGT,
IAT

IDAV
immunodeficiency-associated virus

IDBR
indirect bilirubin

IDBS
infantile diffuse brain sclerosis

IDC
idiopathic dilated cardiomyopathy
infiltrating ductal carcinoma
interdigitating cells
interdigitating dendritic cell
intraductal carcinoma
invasive ductal carcinoma

IDCF
immunodiffusion complement fixation

IDCI
intradiplochromatid interchange

NOTES

351

IDD
insulin-dependent diabetes *also* IDDM
intraluminal duodenal diverticulum

IDDF
investigational drug data form

IDDM
insulin-dependent diabetes mellitus
also IDD

IDDS
implantable drug delivery system
investigational drug data sheet

IDDT
immuno-double diffusion test

IDE
inner dental epithelium
Investigational Device Exemption

ID/ED
internal diameter to external diameter
(cardiac valve replacement ratio)

IDEM
ischemic, drug, electrolyte, metabolic
(effect)

IDFC
immature dead female child

IDG
interdental groove
interdisciplinary group
intermediate dose group

IDH
isocitric acid dehydrogenase *also*
ICDH

IDH1, IDH-S
isocitrate dehydrogenase, soluble

IDH2, IDH-M
isocitrate dehydrogenase, mitochondrial

IDI
immunologically detectable insulin
induction-delivery interval
interdentale inferius *also* IdI

IdI
interdentale inferius *also* IDI

IDIC
Internal Dose Information Center

IDIS
intraoperative digital subtraction

I disk
isotropic disk (striated muscle fiber)
also I band

IDK
internal derangement of knee (joint)

IDL
Index to Dental Literature
intensity difference limen
intermediate density lipoprotein

IDM
idiopathic disease of myocardium
immune defense mechanism
indirect method
infant of diabetic mother
intermediate dose methotrexate

IDMC
immature dead male child
interdigestive motility complex
interdigestive motor complex

IDMEC
interdigestive myoelectric complex
also IMC

ID-MS
isotope dilution-mass spectrometry

IDMTX
intermediate dose methotrexate

iDNA
intercalary deoxyribonucleic acid

idon. vehic.
in a suitable vehicle [L. *idoneo
vehiculo*]

IDP
imidoliphosphonate
immunodiffusion procedure
initial dose period
inosine diphosphate *also* IDPase
inosine 5′-diphosphate
instantaneous diastolic pressure

IDPase
inosine diphosphatase *also* IDP

IDPH
idiopathic pulmonary hemosiderosis
also IPH

IDPN
β-iminodipropionitrile
intradialytic parenteral nutrition

IDR
idarubicin
idiosyncratic drug reaction
intradermal reaction

IDS
immunity deficiency state
infectious disease service

I

inhibitor of DNA synthesis
intraduodenal stimulation
intrinsic sphincter deficiency *also*
ISD
investigational drug service

IdS
interdentale superius

IDSA
Infectious Disease Society of
America
intraoperative digital subtraction
angiography

IDST
intraductal secretin test

IDT
immune diffusion test
instillation delivery time
interdivision time
intradermal typhoid (and paratyphoid
vaccine)

IDU
idoxuridine *also* IDUR, IdUrd, IUDR
iododeoxyuridine *also* IUDR
Ivy dog unit

IdUA
iduronic acid

IDUR, IdUrd
idoxuridine *also* IDU, IUDR

IDUS
intraductal ultrasonography

IDV
intermittent demand ventilation

IDVC
indwelling venous catheter

IDX
4'-iodo-4'-deoxydoxorubicin

Idx
cross-reactive idiotype

IE
immunizing unit [Ger. *immunitäts
Einheit*] *also* IU, ImmU
immunoelectrophoresis *also* IEP
induced emesis
infectious endocarditis
infective endocarditis

inner ear
intake energy (unit of food)
internal ear
internal elastica
international unit (European
abbreviation)
intraepithelial
Introversion-Extroversion (scale)

I/E, I:E
inspiratory/expiratory (ratio)

I&E
internal and external

i.e.
that is [L. *id est*]

IEA
immediate early antigen
immunoelectroadsorption
immunoelectrophoretic analysis
infectious equine anemia
inferior epigastric artery
intravascular erythrocyte aggregation

IEBD
intraesophageal balloon distention

IEC
injection electrode catheter
inpatient exercise center
intraepithelial carcinoma
ion-exchange chromatography

IE Ca cx
intraepithelial carcinoma of cervix

IECRT
intraoperative endoscopic Congo red
test

IED
inherited epidermal dysplasia

IEE
inner enamel epithelium

IEF
isoelectric focusing

IEI
isoelectric interval

IEL
internal elastic lamina
intimal elastic lamina

NOTES

IEL *(continued)*
intraepithelial leukocyte
intraepithelial lymphocyte

IEM
immunoelectron microscopy
inborn error of metabolism
ineffective esophageal motility

IEMG
integrated electromyogram

IEMT
intermediate emergency medical
technician

IEOP
immunoelectroosmophoresis

IEP
immunoelectrophoresis *also* IE
individualized education program
isoelectric point *also* IP, I.P., i.p.,
pH_1, PI, pI, pIs

IER
Institute of Educational Research
(intelligence test)

IES
ingressive-egressive sequence

I-E Scale
internal versus external (control of
reinforcement) scale

IEU
idiopathic esophageal ulcer

IF
idiopathic fibroplasia
ifosfamide *also* Ifex, IFOS, IFX
immersion foot
immunofluorescence *also* IFL
indirect fluorescence
inferior facet
infrared *also* IFR, infra., IR
inhibiting factor
initiation factor
inspiratory force
interferon *also* IFN, INF, ITF
intermaxillary fixation *also* IMF
intermediate filament *also* IMF
intermediate frequency
internal fixation
internal friction
interstitial fluid *also* ISF
intracellular fluid
intrinsic factor
involved field

IFA
idiopathic fibrosing alveolitis
immunofluorescent antibody
immunofluorescent assay
incomplete Freund adjuvant *also*
ICFA
indirect fluorescent antibody
indirect fluorescent assay
silver stain

IF-A
inflammatory factor of anaphylaxis

IFAT
indirect fluorescent antibody test

IFC
inspiratory flow cartridge
intermittent flow centrifugation
intrinsic factor concentrate

IFCC
International Federation of Clinical
Chemistry

IFCL
intermittent flow centrifugation
leukapheresis

IFCS
inactivated fetal calf serum

IFDS
isolated follicle-(stimulating hormone)
deficiency syndrome

IFE
immunofixation electrophoresis
interfollicular epidermis

Ifex
ifosfamide *also* IF, IFOS, IFX

IFF
inner fracture face

IFGS
interstitial fluids and ground
substance

IFI
Institutional Functioning Inventory
(psychologic test)
intrafollicular insemination

IFIX
immunofixation

IFL
immunofluorescence *also* IF

IFLrA
recombinant human leukocyte
interferon A

IFM
internal fetal monitoring
intrafusal muscle

IFN-β
(human fibroblast) interferon
interferon beta

IFN
immunoreactive fibronectin
interferon *also* IF, INF, ITF

IFN-α
(human leukocyte) interferon
interferon alpha

IFN-γ (*var. of* IFN-G)

IFN-C
partially pure human leukocyte
interferon

If nec
if necessary

IFN-G, IFN-γ
interferon gamma

IFOBT
immunological fecal occult blood test

IFOS
ifosfamide *also* IF, Ifex, IFX

IFP
inflammatory fibroid polyp
insulin, Kendall compound F
(hydrocortisone), and prolactin
intermediate filament protein
intrapatellar fat pad

IFR
infrared (light) *also* IF, infra., IR
inspiratory flow rate

IFRA
indirect fluorescent rabies antibody
(test)

IFROS
ipsilateral frontal routing of signals

IFRP
International Fertility Research
Program

IFS
interstitial fluid space

IFT
immunofluorescence technique
immunofluorescence test
International Frequency Tables
inverse Fourier transform

IFU
interferon unit

IFV
interstitial fluid volume *also* ISFV
intracellular fluid volume

IFX
ifosfamide *also* IF, Ifex, IFOS

IG
image guide
immature granule
immunoglobulin *also* Ig
Inspector General
intragastric *also* ig

I-G
insulin-glucagon

Ig
immunoglobulin *also* IG

iG
immunoreactive human gastrin

ig
intragastric *also* IG

IGA
infantile genetic agranulocytosis

IgA
immunoglobulin A

IgA1, IgA2
subclasses of immunoglobulin A

IGC
intragastric cannula

IGD
idiopathic growth hormone deficiency
interglobal distance
isolated gonadotropin deficiency

IgD
immunoglobulin D

IgD1, IgD2
subclasses of immunoglobulin D

IGDE
idiopathic gait disorders of elderly

NOTES

IGDM
infant of mother with gestational diabetes mellitus

IGE
impaired gas exchange

IgE
immunoglobulin E

IgE1
subclass of immunoglobulin E

IGF
insulin-like growth factor *also* ILGF

IGF-1
insulin-like growth factor-1

IGF-2
insulin-like growth factor-2

IgF
immunoglobulin F

IGFBP
insulin-like growth factor-binding protein

IGFBP-1
insulin-like growth factor-binding protein-1

IGFET
insulated gate field effect transistor

IgG
immunoglobulin G *also* IgG1

IgG1, IgG2, IgG3, IgG4, IgG2a
subclasses of immunoglobulin G

IGGNU
intratubular germ cell neoplasia of the unclassified type

IgG RF
immunoglobulin G rheumatoid factor

IGH
idiopathic growth hormone
immunoreactive growth hormone *also* IRGH

IGHD
isolated growth hormone deficiency

IGHL
inferior glenohumeral ligament

IGI
Institutional Goals Inventory

IGIM
immunoglobulin, intramuscular

IGIV
immunoglobulin, intravenous

IgM
immunoglobulin M

IgM1
subclass of immunoglobulin M

IgM RF
immunoglobulin M rheumatoid factor

IGP
intestinal glycoprotein

IgQ
immunoglobulin quantitation

IGR
immediate generalized reaction
integrated gastrin response
intrauterine growth retardation

IGS
inappropriate gonadotropin secretion

IgSC
immunoglobulin-secreting cell

IGT
impaired glucose tolerance
interpersonal group therapy
intragastric titration

IGTT
intravenous glucose tolerance test

IGV
idiopathic genu valgum
intrathoracic gas volume *also* ITGV

IH
in hospital
ichthyosis hystri
idiopathic hirsutism
immediate hypersensitivity
incomplete healing
indirect hemagglutination
industrial hygiene
infantile hydrocephalus
infectious hepatitis
inguinal hernia
inhibiting hormone
inner half
inpatient hospital
intermittent heparinization
intracerebral hematoma
iris hamartoma
iron hematoxylin

IHA
idiopathic hyperaldosteronism
immune hemolytic anemia

indirect hemagglutination antibody
(test)
infusion hepatic arteriography
intrahepatic atresia

IHAS
idiopathic hypertrophic aortic stenosis

IHB
incomplete heart block

IHb
hemoglobin content indices

IHBT
incompatible hemolytic blood
transfusion

IHBTD
incompatible hemolytic blood
transfusion disease

IHC
idiopathic hemochromatosis
idiopathic hypercalciuria
immobilization hypercalcemia
inner hair cell (of cochlea)
intrahepatic cholestasis *also* IHPC

IHCA
isocapnic hyperventilation with cold
air

IHCP
Institute of Hospital and Community
Psychiatry

IHD
in-center hemodialysis
intraheptic duct(ule)
ischemic heart disease

IHES
idiopathic hypereosinophilic syndrome

IHG
ichthyosis hystrix gravior

IHGD
isolated human growth deficiency

IHH
idiopathic hypogonadotropic
hypogonadism
idiopathic hypothalamic hypogonadism
infectious human hepatitis

IHHS
idiopathic hyperkinetic heart syndrome

IHMS
(sodium) isonicotinylhydrazide
methanesulfonate

IHO
idiopathic hypertrophic
osteoarthropathy

IHP
idiopathic hypoparathyroidism
idiopathic hypopituitarism
interhospitalization period
inverted hand position

IHPC
intrahepatic cholestasis *also* IHC

IHPH
intrahepatic portal hypertension

IHPP
Intergovernmental Health Project
Policy

IHR
inguinal hernia repair
intrahepatic resistance
intrinsic heart rate

IHRA
isocapnic hyperventilation with room
air

IHS
Idiopathic Headache Score
idiopathic hypereosinophilic syndrome
inactivated horse serum
Indian Health Service
infrahyoid strap *also* IS
International Headache Society

IHSA
iodinated human serum albumin

IHSC
immunoreactive human skin
collagenase

IHSS
idiopathic hypertrophic subaortic
stenosis

IHT
insulin hypoglycemia test
intravenous histamine test
ipsilateral head turning

NOTES

I5HT
intraplatelet serotonin

IHW
inner heel wedge

I or I
illness or injuries

II
icterus index *also* ict ind
image intensifier
insurance index
irradiated iodine

IIA
internal iliac artery

IIC
integrated ion current

IICP
increased intracranial pressure *also*
↑ICP

IICU
infant intensive care unit

IID
insulin-independent diabetes

IIDM
insulin-independent diabetes mellitus

IIE
idiopathic ineffective erythropoiesis

IIF
immune interferon
indirect immunofluorescence

IIFT
intraoperative intraarterial fibrinolytic
therapy

IIGR
ipsilateral instinctive grasp reaction

IIH
idiopathic infantile hypercalcemia
iodine-induced hyperthyroidism

IIIVC
infrahepatic interruption of inferior
vena cava

IIME
Institute of International Medical
Education

[¹²³I]IMP
iodoamphetamine

IINB
iliohypogastric nerve block
ilioinguinal nerve block

IIP
idiopathic interstitial pneumonia
idiopathic intestinal pseudo-obstruction
indirect immunoperoxidase
Intra- and Interpersonal (Relations
Scale)

IIPF
idiopathic interstitial pulmonary
fibrosis

IIS
intensive immunosuppression
intermittent infusion set
International Institute of Stress

IIT
ineffective iron turnover
integrated isometric tension

IJ
ileojejunal *also* I-J
internal jugular (vein)
intrajejunal

I-J
ileojejunal *also* IJ

IJC
internal jugular catheter

IJD
inflammatory joint disease

IJP
inhibitory junction potential
internal jugular pressure

IJR
idiojunctional rhythm

IJT
idiojunctional tachycardia

IJV
internal jugular vein

IK
immobilized knee
immune body [Ger. *Immunekörper*]
immunoconglutinin
infusoria killing (unit) *also* IKU
interstitial keratitis

IKE
ion kinetic energy

IKI
iodine potassium iodide (Lugol
solution)

IKU
infusoria killing unit *also* IK

IL
ileum
iliolumbar
immature lung
incisolingual
independent laboratory
insensible (weight) loss
inspiratory loading
intensity level
interleukin
intermediary letter
intestinal lymphocyte
intralipid
intralumbar
intraocular lens

IL-1–15
interleukin-1–15

I-L
intensity-latency

Il
illinium (promethium)

il
intralesional

ILA
insulin-like activity

ILa
incisolabial

ILB
infant, low birth (weight) *also* ILBW

ILBBB
incomplete left bundle branch block

ILBW
infant, low birth weight *also* ILB

ILC
ichthyosis linearis circumflex
incipient lethal concentration
infiltrating lobular carcinoma

Ilc
isoleucine *also* ILE, Ile, Ileu, ISL

ILD
interstitial lung disease
ischemic leg disease
ischemic limb disease
isolated lactase deficiency

ILDCSI
Individual Learning Disabilities
Classroom Screening Instrument

ILE, Ile, Ileu
isoleucine *also* Ilc, ISL

ILFC
immature living female child

ILGF
insulin-like growth factor *also* IGF

ILL
intermediate lymphocytic lymphoma

illic. lag. obturat.
let the bottle be closed at once [L.
illico lagena obturatur]

ILM
insulin-like material
internal limiting membrane

ILMC
immature living male child

ILMI
inferolateral myocardial infarct (ion)

ILo
iodine lotion

ILP
inadequate luteal phase
interstitial lymphocytic pneumonia
interstititial laser photocoagulation
isolated limb perfusion

ILR
irreversible loss rate

ILS
idiopathic leucine sensitivity
idiopathic lymphadenopathy syndrome
increase in life span
infrared liver scanner
intralobular sequestration
intraluminal stapler

ILSA
Interpersonal Language Skills and
Assessment

ILSS
integrated life support system
intraluminal somatostatin

NOTES

ILUS
intraluminal ultrasound

ILVEN
inflamed linear verrucous epidermal nevus
inflammatory linear verrucal epidermal nevus

IM
idiopathic myelofibrosis *also* IMF
immunosuppression method
Index Medicus *also* Ind Med
indomethacin *also* IMT, IND, INDO
industrial medicine *also* Ind-Med
infection medium
infectious mononucleosis *also* INFM, inf mono
inner membrane
innocent murmur
inspiratory muscle
intermediate megaloblast
intermetatarsal
intermuscular
internal malleolus
internal mammary (artery)
internal medicine *also* Int Med
internal monitor
intestinal mesenchyme
intramedullary
intramuscular (injection site) *also* I.M., i.m.
invasive mole

I.M., i.m.
intramuscular *also* IM

IMA
inferior mesenteric artery
Interchurch Medical Assistance
internal mammary artery

IMAA
iodinated macroaggregated albumin

IMAB
internal mammary artery bypass

IMAC
ifosfamide, mesna uroprotection, Adriamycin (doxorubicin), and cisplatin

IMAG
internal mammary artery graft

IMAGE
International Multicenter Angina Exercise

IMAI
internal mammary artery implant

IMARD
immunomodulating antirheumatic drug

IMB
intermenstrual bleeding

IMBC
indirect maximal breathing capacity

IMC
immunohistochemical
interdigestive migrating complex
interdigestive migrating contraction
interdigestive myoelectric complex *also* IDMEC
intermittent catheterization
intestinal (mucosal) mast cell
intramedullary catheter

IMCD
inner medullary collecting duct

IMCU
intermediate medical care unit

IMD
immunologically mediated disease
inherited metabolic disorder

ImD$_{50}$
immunizing dose sufficient to protect 50% of subjects

IMDC
intramedullary metatarsal decompression

IMDD
idiopathic midline destructive disease

IME
independent medical examination
independent medical examiner
indirect medical education

IMEM
improved minimal essential medium

IMEM-HS
improved minimal essential medium, hormone supplemented

IMET
isometric endurance time

IMF
idiopathic myelofibrosis *also* IM
ifosfamide, mesna uroprotection, methotrexate, and fluorouracil
immobilization mandibular fracture
inframammary fold

intermaxillary fixation *also* IF
intermediate filament *also* IF

IMG
inferior mesenteric ganglion
internal mammary graft
internal medicine group (practice)

IMGG
intramuscular gamma globulin

IMH
idiopathic myocardial hypertrophy
indirect microhemagglutination (test)
also IMHT

IMHT
indirect microhemagglutination test
also IMH

IMI
imipramine
immunologically measurable insulin
impending myocardial infarction
indirect membrane
immunofluorescence
inferior myocardial infarction
intermeal interval
intramuscular injection

^{131}I-mIB6
monoiodobenzylguanidine

I-123-MIBG
iodine-123 metaiodobenzylguanidine

I-125 MIBG
iodine-125 metaiodobenzylguanidine

IMIC
International Medical Information
Center

IMIG
intramuscular immunoglobulin

IML
internal mammary lymphoscintigraphy

IMLA, IMLAD
intramural left anterior descending
(artery)

IMLC
incomplete mitral leaflet closure

IMLNS
idiopathic minimal lesion nephrotic
syndrome

ImLy
immune lysis

IMM
inhibitor-containing minimal medium
internal medial malleolus

immat
immature
immaturity

IMMC
interdigestive migrating motor
complex

immed
immediately

immobil
immobilization
immobilize

ImmU
immunizing unit *also* IE, IU

immun
immune
immunity
immunization

Immunol
immunology

IMN
internal mammary (lymph) node
intramedullary nailing

IMP
idiopathic myeloid proliferation
impacted *also* imp, Impx
important *also* imp
impression *also* I, imp
improved *also* imp
incomplete male
pseudohermaphroditism
individual Medicaid practitioner
Innovative Medical Products
inosine 5'-monophosphate
inosine monophosphate (inosinic acid)
Inpatient Multidimensional Psychiatric
(scale)
intramembranous particle
intramuscular (compartment) pressure

imp
impacted *also* IMP, Impx
important *also* IMP

NOTES

imp *(continued)*
impression *also* I, IMP
improved *also* IMP

IMPA
incisal mandibular plane angle

IMPAC
Immediate Psychiatric Aid and Referral Center

IMPACT
Integrelin to Manage Platelet Aggregation to Prevent Coronary Thrombosis

imperf
imperfect
imperforate

IMPEX
immediate postexercise

IMPL
impulse

IMPS
Inpatient Multidimensional Psychiatric Scale

impvt
improvement

Impx
impacted *also* IMP, imp

IMR
individual medical record
infant mortality rate
infectious mononucleosis receptor
Institute for Medical Research
institution for the mentally retarded

IMRAD, IMRD
introduction, materials and methods, results, and discussion (formal structure of scientific article)

Imreg-1, Imreg-2
immunomodulator

IMS
incurred in military service
Indian Medical Service
industrial methylated spirit
integrated medical services

IMSS
in-flight medical support system

IMT
indomethacin *also* IM, IND, INDO
induced muscular tension
inflammatory myofibroblastic tumor

inspiratory muscle training
intimal-medial thickness

ImU
international milliunit

IMV
inferior mesenteric vein
intermittent mandatory ventilation
intermittent mechanical ventilation
isophosphamide, methotrexate, and vincristine

IMVC, IMViC, imvic
indole, methyl red, Voges-Proskauer, and citrate (test)

IMVP
idiopathic mitral valve prolapse

IMVP-16
ifosfamide, mesna uroprotection, methotrexate, etoposide

IN
icterus neonatorum
impetigo neonatorum
incidence
incompatibility number
infantile nephrotic (syndrome)
infundibular nucleus
insulin *also* I, In, INS
intermediate nucleus
interneuron
internist *also* INT, int
interstitial nephritis
intranasal

In
indium
inion
insulin *also* I, IN, INS
internal
inulin

^{111}In
indium-111

^{113m}In
indium-113m

in.
inch

in^2
square inch

in^3
cubic inch

INA
infectious nucleic acid
inferior nasal artery

INAA
  instrumental neutron activation
    analysis

inac
  inactive *also* I

INAD
  infantile neuroaxonal dystrophy
  investigational new animal drug

INAH
  isonicotinic acid hydrazide

INB
  ischemic necrosis of bone

inbr
  inbreeding

INC
  incisal
  incision
  incomplete *also* inc
  inconclusive
  incontinent *also* inc
  increase *also* inc, incr
  inside-the-needle catheter
  interstitial nucleus of Cajal

Inc
  including *also* incl
  incorporated

inc
  incisional
  incompatibility
  incomplete *also* INC
  inconclusive
  incontinent *also* INC
  increase *also* INC, incr
  increment *also* incr
  incurred

INCA
  infant nasal cannula assembly

Inc Ab
  incomplete abortion

IncB
  inclusion body *also* IB

INCD
  infantile nuclear cerebral degeneration

incid.
  cut [L. *incide*]

incl
  including *also* Inc

incomp, incompl
  incomplete

incont
  incontinent

incr
  increase *also* INC, inc
  increment *also* inc

inc (R)
  increase (relative)

INCS
  incomplete resolution, scan (to)
    follow

incur
  incurable

IND
  indapamide
  indomethacin *also* IM, IMT, INDO
  induced
  industrial (medicine) *also* indust
  internodal distance
  investigational new drug

Ind
  induction *also* ind

ind
  independent *also* I
  index *also* I
  indicate
  indigent
  indigo
  indirect
  induction *also* I, Ind

in d.
  daily [L. *in dies*]
  in a day [L. *in die*]

INDEP
  independent

indic
  indicated
  indication

indig
  indigestion

INDIV
  individual

NOTES

INDM
infant of nondiabetic mother

Ind Med
Index Medicus *also* IM

Ind-Med
industrial medicine *also* IM

INDO
indomethacin *also* IM, IMT, IND

indust
industrial (medicine) *also* IND

INE
infantile necrotizing
encephalomyelopathy

INEX
inexperienced

in extrem.
in the last (hours of life) [L. *in extremis*]

INF
infant *also* inf
infantile *also* inf
infarction
infected *also* inf, infect., infx
infection *also* inf, infect., infx
infectious (disease)
infective *also* inf, infect.
inferior *also* inf, infer.
infirmary *also* inf
information
infundibulum (of neurohypophysis)
infused
infusion *also* inf
interferon *also* IF, IFN, ITF
pour in [L. *infunde*] *also* inf.

in f
at the end [L. *in fine*]
finally

inf
infancy
infant *also* INF
infantile *also* INF
infarct
infect
infected *also* INF, infect.
infection *also* INF, infect., infx
inferior *also* INF, infer.
infirmary *also* INF
infusion *also* INF

inf.
pour in [L. *infunde*] *also* INF

inf dis
infectious disease *also* ID

infect.
infected *also* INF, inf
infection *also* INF, inf, infx
infective *also* INF, inf

infer.
inferior *also* INF, inf

INFH
ischemic necrosis of femoral head

infl
inflamed
inflammation *also* Inflamm
inflammatory *also* Inflamm
influence
influx

Inflamm
inflammation *also* infl
inflammatory *also* infl

infl proc
inflammatory process

INFM
infectious mononucleosis *also* IM, inf
mono

Inf MI
inferior (wall) myocardial infarction

inf mono
infectious mononucleosis *also* IM,
INFM

info
information

infra.
infrared *also* IF, IFR, IR

infx
infection *also* INF, inf, infect.

ING
inguinal *also* ing
isotope nephrogram

ing
inguinal *also* ING

INH
inhalation *also* I, inhal
isoniazid
isonicotinic acid hydrazide (isoniazid)

Inh
inhaler

inhal
inhalation *also* I, INH

INH-G
isonicotinoylhydrazone of D-glucuronic acid lactone (glyconiazide)

inhib
inhibiting *also* I
inhibition *also* I

INI
intranasal insulin
intranuclear inclusion (agent)

inj
injection *also* inject.
injured
injurious
injury

inject.
injection *also* inj

inj. enem.
let an enema be injected [L. *injiciatur enema*]

INK
injury not known

inl
inlay

INLSD
ichthyosis and neutral lipid storage disease

INN
International Nonproprietary Name

innerv
innervated
innervation

INO
infantile nephrotic (syndrome), other (types)
internuclear ophthalmoplegia

Ino
inosine *also* I

INOC, inoc
inoculate
inoculation

INOP
internodal ophthalmoplegia

inop
inoperable

inorg
inorganic

iNOS
nitric oxide synthase *also* NOS

Inox
inosine, oxidized

INP
idiopathic neutropenia

INPAV
intermittent negative pressure-assisted ventilation *also* INPV

INPEA
isopropylnitrophenylethanolamine (β-adrenergic blocker)

INPH
iproniazid phosphate

INPRCNS, INPRONS
information processing in central nervous system

IN-PT
inpatient

in pulm.
in gruel [L. *in pulmento*]

INPV
intermittent negative pressure-(assisted) ventilation *also* INPAV

INQ
inferior nasal quadrant

INR
international normalized ratio

INREM
internal roentgen equivalent, man (radiation dose)

INS
idiopathic nephrotic syndrome
insulin *also* I, IN, In
insurance *also* ins

ins
insertion
insurance *also* INS
insured

INS Ab
insulin antibody

NOTES

insem
  insemination

insid
  insidious

insol
  insoluble *also* I

Insp
  inspect
  inspection
  inspiration *also* I, inspir

inspir
  inspiration *also* I, Insp

INSS
  International Neuroblastoma Staging
  System
  International Staging System

INST
  instrumental (delivery)

Inst
  institute

inst
  instrument

insuf, insuff
  insufficiency
  insufficient
  insufflation

INT
  intermediate *also* I, int, Intmd
  intermittent *also* int, INTR
  intermittent needle therapy
  intern *also* int
  internal *also* int, intern.
  internist *also* IN, int
  p-iodonitrotetrazolium

int
  intact
  integral
  interest
  intermediate *also* I, INT, Intmd
  intermittent *also* INT, INTR
  intern *also* INT
  internal *also* INT, intern.
  internist *also* IN, INT
  interval
  intestinal *also* Intest

int.
  to the innermost [L. *intime*]

int. cib.
  between meals [L. *inter cibos*] *also*
  IC, i.c.

INTEG
  integument

intern.
  internal *also* INT, int

internat
  international

intertroch
  intertrochanteric

Intest
  intestinal *also* int
  intestine *also* int

Int/Ext
  internal/external (rotation)

INTH
  intrathecal (anesthesia injection) *also*
  IT, ITh, i-thec

int hist
  interval history

Intmd
  intermediate *also* I, INT, int

Int Med
  internal medicine *also* IM

int noct
  during the night [L. *inter noctem*]

int obst
  intestinal obstruction *also* IO

INTOX
  intoxication

INTR
  intermittent *also* INT, int

intracal
  intracalvaria

int-rot
  internal rotation *also* IR

int trx
  intermittent traction *also* IT

INV
  inferior nasal vein

inv
  invalid
  inverse
  inversion *also* inver
  involuntary *also* invol

inver
  inversion *also* inv
  inverted

invest.
investigation

invet
inveterate

Inv/Ev
inversion/eversion

inv ins
inverted insertion

invol
involuntary *also* inv

involv
involved
involvement

involv.
coat [L. *involve*]

INVOS
in vivo optical spectroscopy

IO
incisal opening
inferior oblique
inferior oblique (eye muscle)
inferior olive
initial opening (pressure)
inside-out (vesicle)
intensive observation
internal os (cervix)
intestinal obstruction *also* int obst
intraocular (pressure)
intraoperative

I and O
intake and output

I&O, I/O
input/output
intake and output *also* I and O
in and out

Io
ionium

IOA
inner optic anlage
intact on admission

IOC
intern on call
intraoperative cholangiogram *also* IOCG
in our culture

IOCG
intraoperative cholangiogram *also* IOC

IOD
injured on duty
integrated optical density
interorbital distance

IODM
infant of diabetic mother

IOEBT
intraoperative electron beam therapy

IOF
intraocular fluid
intraoperative fentanyl

IOFB
intraocular foreign body

IOFNA
intraoperative fine-needle aspiration

IOH
idiopathic orthostatic hypotension

IOI
intraosseous infusion

IOL
intraocular lens

IOLI
intraocular lens implantation

IOM
Institute of Medicine
intraocular muscle
intraoperative neurophysiologic
 monitoring

IOML
infraorbitomeatal line

ION
ischemic optic neuropathy

IONIS
indirect optic nerve injury syndrome

IOP
intraocular pressure

IOR
index of response
inferior oblique recession
information outflow rate

NOTES

IORT
intraoperative electron beam radiotherapy
intraoperative radiation therapy

IOS
intraoperative sonography

IOT
intraocular tension
intraocular transfer
ipsilateral optic tectum

ι
iota (ninth letter of Greek alphabet), lowercase

IOTA
information overload testing aid

IOU
intensive (therapy) observation unit
international opacity unit

IOV
initial office visit

IOVP
interesophageal variceal pressure

IP
icterus praecox
iliopsoas (muscle)
immune precipitate
immunoblastic plasma
immunoperoxidase
implantation (test)
inactivated pepsin
incisoproximal
incisopulpal
incontinentia pigmenti
incubation period *also* ICP
individualized plan
induced potential
induction period
industrial population
infection prevention
infundibular process
infundibulopelvic (ligament)
infusion pump
initial pressure
inorganic phosphate
inosine phosphorylase
inpatient
instantaneous pressure
International Pharmacopoeia
interpeduncular (nucleus)
interphalangeal (joint, keratosis) *also* IPH, IPJ
interpharyngeal

interpositus (nucleus)
interpupillary
intestinal pseudoobstruction
intracellular proteolysis
intraperitoneal *also* I.P., i.p.
ionization potential
isoelectric point *also* IEP, I.P., i.p., pH_1, PI, pI, pIs
isoproterenol *also* IPT, IS, ISO, iso, ISP
L'Institut Pasteur
in plaster

IP$_3$
inositol 1,4,5-triphosphate

I/P
iris and pupil

I.P.
intraperitoneal *also* IP, i.p.
isoelectric point *also* i.p., pI

i.p.
intraperitoneal *also* IP, I.P.
isoelectric point *also* I.P., pI

IPA
ifosfamide, Platinol, and Adriamycin
incontinentia pigmenti achromians
independent practice association
indole pyruvic acid
International Phonetic Alphabet
interpleural analgesia
intrapulmonary artery
invasive pulmonary aspergillosis
isopropyl alcohol

IPAA
ileal pouch anal anastomosis

IPAO
insulin-induced peak acid output

IPAP
inspiratory positive airway pressure

IPAR
Institute of Personality Assessment and Research

IPAT
(Cattell's) Institute for Personality and Ability Testing (Anxiety Scale)
Iowa Pressure Articulation Test

IPB
infrapopliteal bypass

IPC
intermediate posterior curve
intermittent pneumatic compression
interpeduncular cistern

intraductal papillary carcinoma
intraperitoneal chemotherapy
ion-pair chromatography
isopropyl chlorophenyl
isopropyl phenylcarbamate (propham)

IPCD
idiopathic paroxysmal cerebral
dysrhythmia
infantile polycystic disease

IPCS
intrauterine progesterone contraceptive
system

IPD
idiopathic Parkinson disease
idiopathic protracted diarrhea
immediate pigment darkening
increase in pupillary diameter
incurable problem drinker
inflammatory pelvic disease
intermittent peritoneal dialysis
intermittent pigment darkening
interpupillary distance
Inventory of Psychosocial
Development

IPE
infectious porcine encephalomyelitis
initial psychiatric development
injury pulmonary edema
interstitial pulmonary emphysema

IPEH
intravascular papillary endothelial
hyperplasia

IPF
idiopathic pulmonary fibrosis
infection-potentiating factor
International Primary Factors (Test
Battery)
interstitial pulmonary fibrosis

IPFD
intrapartum fetal distress

IPG
impedance phlebograph
impedance plethysmography
inspiratory phase gas

iPGE
immunoreactive prostaglandin E

IPH
idiopathic portal hypertension
idiopathic pulmonary hemosiderosis
also IDPH
infant passive hand
inflammatory papillary hyperplasia
interphalangeal (joint) *also* IP, IPJ
intraparenchymal hemorrhage

IPHP
intraperitoneal hyperthermic perfusion

IPHR
inverted polypoid hamartoma of
rectum

IPI
Imagined Process Inventory
interphonemic interval
interpulse interval

IPIA
immunoperoxidase infectivity assay

IPJ
interphalangeal joint *also* IP, IPH

IPK
interphalangeal keratosis
intractable plantar keratosis

IPKD
infantile polycystic kidney disease

IPL
inner plexiform layer
interpupillary line
intrapleural

IPLVAS
implantable left ventricular assist
system

IPM
impulses per minute
inches per minute
infant passive mitt (slang for hand)
intrauterine pressure monitor

IPMI
inferoposterior myocardial infarction

IPN
infantile periarteritis nodosa
interim progress note
interpeduncular nucleus
interpenetrating polymer network

NOTES

IPn
interstitial pneumonitis

IPNA
isopropylnoradrenaline (isoproterenol)

IPNP
intraductal papillary neoplasm of the pancreas

IPO
improved pregnancy outcome
initial planning option

IPOF
immediate postoperative fitting

IPOM
intraperitoneal onlay mesh

IPOP
immediate postoperative prosthesis

IPP
independent practice plan
inferior point of pubic (bone)
inflatable penile prosthesis
inorganic pyrophosphate *also* PPi, PP$_i$
inosine, pyruvate, and (inorganic) phosphate
intermittent positive pressure
intrahepatic portal pressure
intrapleural pressure

IPPA
inspection, palpation, percussion, and auscultation

IPPB
intermittent positive-pressure breathing

IPPB/I
intermittent positive-pressure breathing/inspiratory

IPPB(R,V)
intermittent positive-pressure breathing (respiration, ventilation)

IPPF
immediate postoperative prosthetic fitting

IPPI
interruption of pregnancy for psychiatric indication

IPPO
intermittent positive-pressure (inflation with) oxygen

IPPR
integrated pancreatic polypeptide response

intermittent positive-pressure respiration

IPPT
Inter-Person Perception Test

IPPUAD
immediate postprandial upper abdominal distress

IPPV
intermittent positive-pressure ventilation

IPQ
Intermediate Personality Questionnaire (for Indian Pupils)
intimacy potential quotient

IPR
independent professional review
insulin production rate
interval patency rate
intraparenchymal resistance
iproniazid

i-Pr
isopropyl- (prefix denoting 1-methylethyl group)

IPRL
isolated perfused rabbit lung
isolated perfused rat liver

iPrSGal
isopropylthiogalactoside *also* IPTG

IPRT
interpersonal reaction test

IPS
idiopathic postprandial syndrome
impulse per second
inches per second
infundibular pulmonary stenosis
initial prognostic score
intermittent photic stimulation (electroencephalography)
Interpersonal Perception Scale
intraperitoneal shock
ischiopubic synchondrosis
p-iodophenylsulfonyl (pipsyl)

Ips
pipsyl

ips
inches per second

IPSB
intrapartum stillbirth

IPSC
inhibitory postsynaptic current

IPSC-E
Inventory of Psychic and Somatic Complaints in the Elderly

IPSF
immediate postsurgical fitting (of prosthesis)

IPSID
immunoproliferative small intestinal disease

IPSP
inhibitory postsynaptic potential

IPSS
International Prostate Symptom Score

IPT
immunoperoxidase technique
immunoprecipitation
industrial physical therapist
intermittent pelvic traction *also* IPTX
interpersonal psychotherapy
ipratropium
isoproterenol *also* IP, IS, ISO, iso, ISP

IPTG
isopropylthiogalactoside *also* iPrSGal

iPTH
immunoreactive parathyroid hormone

IPTX
intermittent pelvic traction *also* IPT

IPU
inpatient unit

IPV
inactivated poliomyelitis (virus) vaccine
inactivated poliovirus vaccine
incompetent perforator vein
infectious pustular vaginitis
infectious pustular vulvovaginitis (of cattle)
intrapulmonary vein

IPVC
interpolated premature ventricular contraction

IPVD
index of pulmonary vascular disease

IPW
interphalangeal width

IPZ
insulin-protamine zinc

IQ
intelligence quotient

i.q.
the same as [L. *idem quod*]

IQ&S
iron, quinine, and strychnine

I-R
Ito-Reenstierna (reaction, test)

IR
ileal resection
immune response (genes) *also* Ir
immunization rate
immunologic response
immunoreactive *also* ir
immunoreagent
incisal ridge
index of response
individual reaction
inferior rectus (muscle)
infrared (light) *also* IFR
inside radius
insoluble residue
inspiratory reserve
inspiratory resistance
insulin receptor
insulin requirement
insulin resistance
insulin response
integer ratio
intelligence ratio
internal reduction
internal resistance
internal rotation *also* int-rot
inversion recovery
inverted repeats
ionizing radiation
irritant reaction
isotonic reversal
isovolumetric relaxation

I&R
insertion and removal

NOTES

Ir
immune response (genes) *also* IR
iridium

^{192}Ir
iridium-192

^{194}Ir
iridium-194

ir
immunoreactive *also* IR
intrarectal
intrarenal

IRA
ileorectal anastomosis
immunoradioassay
immunoregulatory α-globulin
inactive renin activity

IR-ACTH
immunoreactive adrenocorticotropic
hormone

IRA-EEA
ileorectal anastomosis with end-to-end
anastomosis

IRB
institutional review board

IRBBB
incomplete right bundle branch block

IRBC
immature red blood cell *also* iRBC
infected red blood cell

iRBC
immature red blood cell *also* IRBC

IRBP
interphotoreceptor retinoid-binding
protein

IRC
indirect radionuclide cystography
infrared coagulator
infrared photocoagulation
inspiratory reserve capacity
instantaneous resonance curve
Instrument Recirculation Center
International Red Cross

IRCA
intravascular red cell aggregation

IRCS
International Research Communications
System

IRCU
intensive respiratory care unit

IRD
immune renal disease
infantile Refsum syndrome
isorhythmic dissociation

IRDM
insulin-resistant diabetes mellitus

IRDS
idiopathic respiratory distress
syndrome
infant respiratory distress syndrome

IRE
internal rotation in extension

IRES
internal ribosome entry site

IRF
idiopathic retroperitoneal fibrosis
internal rotation in flexion

IRG
immunoreactive gastrin
immunoreactive glucagon *also* IRGl
immunoreactive glucose

IRGH
immunoreactive growth hormone *also*
IGH

IRGl
immunoreactive glucagon *also* IRG

IRH
Institute of Religion and Health
Institute for Research in Hypnosis
intraretinal hemorrhage

IRHC
immunoradioassayable human
chorionic (somatomammotropin)

IRhCG
immunoreactive human chorionic
gonadotropin

IRHCS
immunoradioassayable human
chorionic somatomammotropin

IRhCS
immunoreactive human chorionic
somatomammotropin

IRhGH
immunoreactive human growth
hormone

IRhPL
immunoreactive human placental
lactogen

IRI
    immunoreactive insulin
    insulin radioimmunoassay
    insulin resistance index

IRIA
    indirect radioimmunoassay

irid
    iridescent

IRI/G
    immunoreactive insulin to serum or
      plasma glucose (ratio)

IRIg
    insulin-reactive immunoglobulin

IRIS
    intensified radiographic imaging
      system
    interleukin regulation of immune
      system
    International Research Information
      Service

IRM
    innate releasing mechanism

IRMA
    Immediate Response Mobile Analysis
    immunoradiometric assay
    intraretinal microangiopathy
    intraretinal microvascular abnormality

IRME
    immunoreactive methionine-enkephalin

IRMP
    intersegmental range of motion
      palpation

IRMS
    isotope ratio mass spectrometry

iRNA
    immune ribonucleic acid
    informational ribonucleic acid

IROS
    ipsilateral routing of signal

IRP
    idiopathic recurrent pancreatitis
    immunoreactive plasma
    immunoreactive proinsulin
    incus replacement prosthesis
    inhibitor of radical processes

    insulin-releasing polypeptide
    International Reference Preparation
    interstitial radiation pneumonitis

IRPGN
    idiopathic rapidly progressive
      glomerulonephritis

IRR
    infrared refractometry
    intrarenal reflux
    irregular rate and rhythm
    irritation *also* Irr, irr

Irr, irr
    irradiation
    irritation *also* IRR

irreg
    irregular
    irregularity

IRRIG, IRRG
    irrigate
    irrigation

IRS
    immunoreactive secretin
    impaired regeneration syndrome
    infrared spectrophotometry
    insulin receptor species
    Intergroup Rhabdomyosarcoma Study

IRSA
    idiopathic refractory sideroblastic
      anemia
    iodinated rat serum albumin

IRSE
    inversion recovery spin-echo sequence

IRT
    immunoreactive trypsin
    immunoreactive trypsinogen
    instrument retrieval container
    interresponse time
    isometric relaxation time
    item response theory (psychologic
      testing)

IRTO
    immunoreactive trypsin output

IRTU
    integrating regulatory transcription
      unit

NOTES

IRU
industrial rehabilitation unit
interferon reference unit

IRV
inferior radicular vein
inspiratory reserve volume
inverse ratio ventilation

IS
ilial segment
immediate sensitivity
immune serum
immune suppressor
immunosuppression
incentive spirometer
index of saponification
index of sexuality
induced sputum
infant size
information system
infrahyoid strap *also* IHS
initial segment
insertion sequence
insufficient signal
insulin secretion
intercellular space *also* ICS
intercostal space *also* IC, ICS
interictal spike (in
electroencephalography)
internal standard
interspace *also* i.s., ISP
interstitial space
interventricular septum *also* IVS
intracardial shunt
intraspinal
intrasplenic
intrastriatal
invalided from service
inventory of systems
Ionescu-Shiley (artificial cardiac
valve) *also* I-S
ipecac syrup
Irvine syndrome
ischemic score
island *also* is.
isoproterenol *also* IP, IPT, ISO, iso,
ISP
in original place [L. *in situ*]

I-10-S
invert sugar (10%) in saline

I-S
Ionescu-Shiley (artificial cardiac
valve) *also* IS

is.
island *also* IS
islet
isolation

i.s.
interspace *also* IS, ISP
in situ

ISA
ileosigmoid anastomosis
intrinsic stimulating activity
intrinsic sympathomimetic activity
iodinated serum albumin
irregular spiking activity (in
electroencephalography)

ISA₅
internal surface area of lung at
volume of five liters

ISADH
inappropriate secretion of antidiuretic
hormone

ISAM
Intravenous Streptokinase in Acute
Myocardial Infarction Study

ISB
incentive spirometry breathing

ISBP
interscalen brachial plexus

ISC
immunoglobulin-secreting cell
indwelling subclavian catheter
insoluble collagen
intensive supportive care
intermittent straight catheterization
International Statistical Classification
intershift coordination
interstitial cell
intersystem crossing
irreversibly sickled cell
Isolette servo control

ISCCO
intersternocostoclavicular ossification

ISCF
interstitial cell fluid

ISCLT
International Society for Clinical
Laboratory Technology

ISCN
International System for (Human)
Cytogenetic Nomenclature

ISCP
infection surveillance and control program
International Society of Comparative Pathology

ISD
immunosuppressive drug
inhibited sexual desire
initial sleep disturbance
intensity (of service), severity (of illness), discharge (screens)
interatrial septal defect *also* IASD
interventricular septal defect *also* IVSD
intrinsic sphincter deficiency *also* IDS
intrinsic sphincter dysfunction
isosorbide dinitrate *also* ID, ISDN

ISDB
indirect self-destructive behavior

ISDN
isosorbide dinitrate *also* ID, ISD

ISE
inhibited sexual excitement
integrated square error
ion-selective electrode

ISED
Interview Schedule for Events and Difficulties

ISEL
in-situ end labelling

ISF
interstitial fluid *also* IF

ISFET
ion-specific field effect transducer

ISFV
interstitial fluid volume *also* IFV

ISG
immune serum globulin

ISGP
International Society for Gynecologic Pathology

ISH
icteric serum hepatitis
International Society of Hematology
isocapnic hyperventilation
isolated septal hypertrophy
isolated systolic hypertension
in situ hybridization

ISHLT
International Society for Heart and Lung Transplant

ISI
infarct size index
initial slope index
injury severity index
International Sensitivity Index
International Slope Index
interstimulus interval

ISIH
interspike interval histogram

ISIS
integrated shape and imaging system

ISIS-2
Second International Study of Infarct Survival

ISL
interscapular line
interspinous ligament
isoleucine *also* Ilc, ILE, Ile, Ileu

Is of Lang
islets of Langerhans

ISM
International Society of Microbiologists
intersegmental muscle

ISMA
infantile spinal muscular atrophy

IS-5-MN, Is-5-Mn
isosorbide-5-mononitrate

ISO
International Standards Organization
isoproterenol *also* IP, IPT, IS, iso, ISP
isotropic *also* iso

ISO2
oxygen saturation indices

NOTES

Iso, iso
isoproterenol *also* IP, IPT, IS, ISO, ISP
isotropic *also* ISO

Isol
Isolette

isol
isolated
isolation

isom
isometric
isometropic

IsoRAS
isorenin-angiotensin system

isox
isoxsuprine

ISP
distance between iliac spines
immunoreactive substance P
input signal processor
interspace *also* IS, i.s.
interspinal
intraspinal
isoproterenol *also* IP, IPT, IS, ISO, iso

ISPT
interspecies (ovum) penetration test

ISPX
Ionescu-Shiley pericardial xenograft

i.s.q.
unchanged [L. *in status quo*]

ISR
information storage (and) retrieval *also* IS and R
Institute for Sex Research
Institute of Surgical Research
insulin secretion rate

IS and R
information storage and retrieval *also* ISR

ISS
idiopathic short stature
Injury Severity Scale
Injury Severity Score
ion-scattering spectroscopy
ion surface scattering
irritable stomach syndrome

ISSI
interspinous segmental spinal instrumentation (technique)

ISSVD
International Society for the Study of Vulvar Diseases

IST
insulin sensitivity test
insulin shock therapy
interstitiospinal tract
isometric systolic tension

ISTD
insulin standard

I-sub
inhibitor substance

ISW
interstitial water

ISWI
incisional surgical wound infection

ISY
intrasynovial

IT
iliotibial
immunity test
immunologic test
immunotherapy
implantation test
individual therapy
inferior temporal
inferior turbinate
information technology
inhalation test
inhalation therapist
inhalation therapy
inspiratory time *also* I-time
insulin treatment
intact
intensive therapy
intentional tremor
intermittent traction *also* int trx
internal thoracic
interstitial tissue
intertrochanteric
intertuberous (pelvic diameter)
intimal thickening
intolerance and toxicity
intracellular tachyzoite
intradermal test
intratesticular
intrathecal (anesthesia injection) *also* INTH, ITh, i-thec
intrathoracic
intratracheal (tube) *also* ITR
intratumoral *also* i-tumor
ischial tuberosity

isomeric transition (of radioactive isotopes)

I/T
intensity/duration
intensity/time (duration of contractions)

ITA
individual treatment assessment
inferior temporal artery
internal thoracic artery
itaconic acid

ITAG
internal thoracic artery graft

ITB
iliotibial band

ITC
imidazolylthioguanine chemotherapy
incontinence treatment center
Interagency Testing Committee
Interventional Therapeutics Corporation

ITc
International Table calorie

ITCP
idiopathic thrombocytopenic purpura *also* ITP

ITCU
intensive thoracic cardiovascular unit

ITCVD
ischemic thrombotic cerebrovascular disease

ITD
insulin-treated diabetic

ITE
in the ear (hearing aid)
insufficient therapeutic effect
intrapulmonary interstitial emphysema

ITET
isotonic endurance test

ITF
interferon *also* IF, IFN, INF

ITFF
intertrochanteric femoral fracture

ITFS
iliotibial tract friction syndrome

incomplete testicular feminization syndrome

ITGCN
intratubular germ cell neoplasia

ITGP
immunotactoid glomerulopathy

ITGV
intrathoracic gas volume *also* IGV

ITh, i-thec
intrathecal (anesthesia injection) *also* INTH, IT

IthP
intrathyroidal parathyroid

ITI
International Team Implantologists
intertrial interval
intratubal insemination

I-time
inspiratory time *also* IT

ITLC
instant thin-layer chromatography

ITLC-SG
instant thin-layer chromatography-silica gel

ITM
improved Thayer-Martin (medium)
intrathecal methotrexate

ITOU
intensive therapy observation unit

ITP
idiopathic thrombocytopenic purpura *also* ITCP
immune thrombocytopenic purpura
inosine triphosphate
inosine 5'-triphosphate
interim treatment plan
islet-cell tumor of the pancreas

ITPA
Illinois Test of Psycholinguistic Abilities
inosine triphosphatase *also* ITPase

ITPase
inosine triphosphatase *also* ITPA

NOTES

ITQ
Infant Temperament Questionnaire
inferior temporal quadrant

ITR
intraocular tension recorder
intratracheal *also* IT

I tracing
interrupted tracing

ITSC
It Scale for Children (psychologic test)

ITSHD
isolated thyroid stimulating hormone deficiency

ITT
identical twins (raised) together
iliotibial tract
insulin tolerance test
internal tibial torsion
iron tolerance test

ITU
intensive therapy unit

i-tumor
intratumoral *also* IT

ITV
infantile tibia vara
inferior temporal vein

ITVAD
indwelling transcutaneous vascular access device

ITX
intertriginous xanthoma

IU
immunizing unit *also* IE, ImmU
indouracil
International Unit
intrauterine
in utero

[I]U
concentration of insulin in urine

iu
infectious unit

IUA
intrauterine adhesion

IUC
idiopathic ulcerative colitis
intrauterine catheter

IUCD
intrauterine contraceptive device *also* ICD, IUD

IUD
intrauterine (contraceptive) device *also* ICD, IUCD
intrauterine death

IUDR
idoxuridine *also* IDU, IDUR, IdUrd
iododeoxyuridine *also* IDU

IUF
isolated ultrafiltration

IUFB
intrauterine foreign body

IUFD
intrauterine fetal death
intrauterine fetal demise
intrauterine fetal distress

IUFGR
intrauterine fetal growth retardation

IUFT
intrauterine fetal transfusion

IUG
infusion urogram
intrauterine gas
intrauterine gestation
intrauterine growth

IUGR
intrauterine growth rate
intrauterine growth retardation

IUI
intrauterine insemination (catheter)

IU/L
International Unit per liter

IUM
internal urethral meatus
intrauterine (fetally) malnourished
intrauterine malnourishment
intrauterine membrane

IU/min
International Unit per minute

IUP
intrauterine pregnancy
intrauterine pressure

IUPAC
International Union of Pure and Applied Chemistry

IUPC
intrauterine pressure catheter

IUPD
intrauterine pregnancy, delivered

IUPTB
intrauterine pregnancy, term birth

IUP,TBCS
intrauterine pregnancy, term birth,
cesarean section

IUP,TBLC
intrauterine pregnancy, term birth,
living child

IUP,TBLI
intrauterine pregnancy, term birth,
living infant

IUR
intrauterine retardation

IUT
intrauterine transfusion

IUTD
immunizations up to date

IV
ichthyosis vulgaris
interventricular
intervertebral
intravascular
intravenous *also* I.V., i.v.
intraventricular *also* IVT
intravertebral
invasive
iodine value *also* iv
in vitro
in vivo

I-V
intraventricular

I.V., i.v.
intravenous *also* IV

iv
iodine value *also* IV

IVA
intraoperative vascular angiography

IVAC
intravenous accurate control (device)

IVAD
implantable vascular access device

IVag
intravaginal

IVAP
in vitro antibody production (assay)
in vivo adhesive platelet

IVAR
insulin variable

IVB
intraventricular block
intravitreal blood

IVBAT
intravascular bronchioalveolar tumor

IVBC
intravascular blood coagulation

IVC
individually viable cell
inferior vena cava
inferior venacavogram *also* IVCV
inferior venacavography *also* IVCV
inspiratory vital capacity
inspired vital capacity
integrated vector control
intravascular coagulation
intravenous chemotherapy
intravenous cholangiogram *also* IVCh
intravenous cholangiography *also*
IVCh
intraventricular catheter
isovolumic contraction

IVCC
intravascular consumption
coagulopathy

IVCD
intraventricular conduction defect
intraventricular conduction delay

IVCh
intravenous cholangiogram *also* IVC
intravenous cholangiography *also* IVC

IVCP
inferior vena cava pressure

IVCR
inferior vena cava reconstruction

IVCT
inferior vena cava thrombosis

NOTES

IVCT *(continued)*
intravenously (enhanced) computed tomography
isovolumic contraction time *also* ICT

IVCV
inferior venacavogram *also* IVC
inferior venacavography *also* IVC

IVD
intervertebral disk
intravenous drip

IVDA
intravenous drug abuse

IVDSA
intravenous digital subtraction angiography

IVDU
intravenous drug use

IVF
interventricular foramen
intravascular fluid
intravenous fluid
intravenous fluorescein
intravertebral foramen
in vitro fertilization
in vivo fertilization

IVFA
intravenous fluorescein angiography

IVFE
intravenous fat emulsion

IVF-ET
in vitro fertilization-embryo transfer

IVFT
intravenous fetal transfusion

IVG
isotopic ventriculogram

IVGG
intravenous gamma globulin

IVGTT
intravenous glucose tolerance test

IVH
intravenous hyperalimentation
intraventricular hemorrhage (Grade I, II, III, IV)

IVIG
intravenous immune serum globulin
intravenous immunoglobulin

IVIg *also* IVIg
intravenous immunoglobulin *also* IVIG

IVJC
intervertebral joint complex

IVL
intravenous leiomyomatosis
intravenous lock

IVLBW
infant of very low birth weight

IVM
immediate visual memory
intravascular mass

IVMP
intravenous methylprednisolone

IVN
intravenous nutrition

IVNF
intravitreal neovascular frond

IVO
intraoral vertical osteotomy

IVOTTS
Irvine viable organ-tissue transport system

IVOX
intravascular oxygenator

IVP
intravenous push (dose) *also* IVp, IVPU
intravenous pyelogram
intravenous pyelography
intraventricular pressure
intravesical pressure

IVp
intravenous push (dose) *also* IVP, IVPU

IVPB
intravenous piggyback (drug administration)

IVPD
in vitro protein digestibility

IVPF
isovolume pressure flow (curve)

IVPU
intravenous push (dose) *also* IVP, IVp

IVR
idioventricular rhythm
internal visual reference
intravaginal ring
intravenous retrograde
isolated volume responder

isovolumic relaxation (time) *also* IVRT

IVRA
intravenous regional anesthesia

IVRO
intraoral vertical ramus osteotomy

IVRP
isovolumetric relaxation period

IVRT
isovolumic relaxation time *also* IVR

IVS
inappropriate vasopressin secretion
intact ventricular septum
intervening sequence
interventricular septum *also* IS
intervillous space
irritable voiding syndrome

IVSD
interventricular septal defect *also* ISD

IVSE
interventricular septal excursion

IVSO
intraoral vertical segmental osteotomy

IVSS
intravenous Soluset

IVT
idiopathic ventricular tachycardia
index of vertical transmission
intravenous transfusion
intraventricular *also* IV
isovolumic time

IVTTT
intravenous tolbutamide tolerance test

IVU
intravenous urogram
intravenous urography

IVUC
intravenous ultrasound catheter

IVUS
intravascular ultrasound

IVV
influenza virus vaccine
intravenous vasopressin

IW
inner wall

I-5-W
invert sugar 5% in water

IWI
inferior wall infarction
interwave interval

IWL
insensible water loss

IWMI
inferior wall myocardial infarction

IWML
idiopathic white matter lesion

IWS
Index of Work Satisfaction

IWT
ice water test
impacted wisdom teeth

IYS
inverted Y-suspensor

IZ
infarction zone

IZS
insulin zinc suspension

NOTES

J

dynamic movement of inertia
electric current density
Jewish
joint *also* jnt, jt
joule
joule equivalent
journal *also* jour, jrl, jrnl
juice *also* j, jc
juvenile *also* juv
juxtapulmonary-capillary (receptor)
magnetic polarization
polypeptide chain in polymeric
  immunoglobulins
reference point following QRS
  complex, at beginning of ST
  segment
sound intensity

J1–J3

Jaeger test type number 1–3

J

flux (density)

j

jaundice *also* jaund, JD
juice *also* J, jc

JA

juvenile arthritis
juvenile atrophy
juxtaarticular

JAI

juvenile amaurotic idiocy

JAMA

Journal of the American Medical
  Association

JAMG

juvenile autoimmune myasthenia
  gravis

JAS

Jenkins Activity Survey (psychologic
  test)
Job Attitude Scale
joint activated system

jaund

jaundice *also* j, JD

JBC

Jesness Behavior Checklist

JBE

Japanese B encephalitis

JC

Jakob-Creutzfeldt (syndrome)
joint contracture
junior clinician

J/C

joule per coulomb

jc

juice *also* J, j

JCA

juvenile chronic arthritis

JCAH

Joint Commission on Accreditation of
  Hospitals

JCAHO

Joint Commission on Accreditation of
  Healthcare Organizations

JCAHPO

Joint Commission on Allied Health
  Personnel in Ophthalmology

JCE

job capacity evaluation

JCF

juvenile calcaneal fracture

JCL

job control language (computers)

J/cm

joules per centimeter

JCML

juvenile chronic myelocytic leukemia
juvenile chronic myelogenous
  leukemia

JCP

juvenile chronic polyarthritis

JCT

juxtaglomerular cell tumor

jct

junction

JCV

Jamestown Canyon virus
JC virus

JD

Janet disease
jaundice *also* j, jaund
jejunal diverticulitis
jugulodigastric (node)
juvenile delinquent

JD *(continued)*
juvenile-onset diabetes *also* JDM, JOD, JODM

JDM
juvenile-onset diabetes mellitus *also* JD, JOD, JODM

JDMS
juvenile dermatomyositis

JDMS/PM
juvenile dermato/polymyositis

JE
Japanese encephalitis
junctional escape

JEB
junctional epidermolysis bullosa
junctional escape beat

JEE
Japanese equine encephalitis

JEJ, Jej, jej
jejunum

JEMBEC
agar plates for transporting cultures of gonococci

jentac.
breakfast [L. *jentaculum*]

JEPI
Junior Eysenck Personality Inventory

JER
Japanese erection ring
junctional escape rhythm

JET
junctional ectopic tachycardia

JEV
Japanese encephalitis virus

JF
joint fluid
jugular foramen
junctional fold

JFET
junction field-effect transistor

JFS
Jewish Family Service
jugular foramen syndrome

JG
June grass (test)
juxtaglomerular *also* jg, j-g

jg, j-g
juxtaglomerular *also* JG

JGA
juxtaglomerular apparatus

JGC
juxtaglomerular cell

JGCT
juvenile granulosa cell tumor
juxtaglomerular cell tumor

JGI
jejunogastric intussusception
juxtaglomerular granulation index
juxtaglomerular index

JGP
juvenile general paralysis

JH
juvenile hormone (of insects)

j_H
heat transfer factor

JHA
juvenile hormone analog

JHMO
Junior Hospital Medical Officer

JHMV
J. Howard Mueller virus

JHR
Jarisch-Herxheimer reaction

JI
jejunoileal (bypass)
jejunoileitis
jejunoileostomy

JIB
jejunoileal bypass

JIDC
juvenile intervertebral disk calcifications

JIH
joint interval histogram

JIS
juvenile idiopathic scoliosis

JJ
jaw jerk
jejunojejunostomy

J & J
Johnson & Johnson

JKD
Junius-Kuhnt disease

J/kg
joule per kilogram

J

JKST
Johnson-Kenney Screening Test (psychologic test)

JL
Jadassohn-Lewandowski (syndrome)
Jaffe-Lichtenstein (syndrome)
Judkins left

JL4
Judkins left 4

JLP
junvenile laryngeal papillomatosis
juvenile laryngeal papilloma

JM
josamycin
jugomaxillary

j_M
mass transfer factor (in heat transfer)

JMD
juvenile macular degeneration

JMH
John Milton Hagen (antibody)

JMR
Jones-Mote reactivity

JMS
junior medical student

JND
just noticeable difference

jnt
joint *also* J, jt

JNVD
jugular neck vein distention

JOA
Japanese Orthopaedic Association

JOD, JODM
juvenile-onset diabetes *also* JD, JDM

JOMAC
judgment, orientation, memory, abstraction, and calculation

JOMACI
judgment, orientation, memory, abstraction, and calculation intact

JOR
jaw-opening reflex

jour
journal *also* J, jrl, jrnl

JP
Jackson-Pratt (drain)
Jobst pump
joint protection *also* JTP
juvenile periodontitis

JPB
junctional premature beat

JPC
junctional premature contraction

JPD
juvenile plantar dermatosis

JPI
Jackson Personality Inventory

JPS
joint position sense

JR
Jolly reaction
Judkins right
junctional rhythm

JRA
juvenile rheumatoid arthritis

JRAN
junior resident admission note

Jr BF
junior baby food

JRC
joint replacement center

JRCOMP
Joint Review Committee for Ophthalmic Medical Personnel

jrl
journal *also* J, jour, jrnl

jrnl
journal *also* J, jour, jrl

JROM
joint range of motion

JS
jejunal segment
Job syndrome
junctional slowing
Junkman-Schoeller (unit of thyrotropin) *also* JSU, JS unit

NOTES

J/s
joule per second

JSI
Jansky Screening Index (psychologic test)

JSU, JS unit
Junkman-Schoeller unit (of thyrotropin) *also* JS

JSV
Jerry-Slough virus

JT
jejunostomy tube
junctional tachycardia

J/T
joule per tesla

jt
joint *also* J, jnt

jt asp
joint aspiration

JTF
jejunostomy tube feeding

JTP
joint protection *also* JP

JTPS
juvenile tropical pancreatitis syndrome

Ju
jugale

jug.
jugular

jug. comp
jugular compression (test)

junct
junction *also* Jx

juv
juvenile *also* J

juxt.
near [L. *juxta*]

JV
jugular vein
jugular venous (pressure, pulse)

JVC
jugular venous catheter

JVD
jugular venous distention

JVIS
Jackson Vocational Interest Survey

JVP
jugular venous pressure
jugular venous pulse

JVPT
jugular venous pulse tracing

JW
Jehovah's Witness
jump walker

Jx
junction *also* junct

JXG
juvenile xanthogranuloma

K

burst of diphasic slow waves in response to stimuli during sleep (in electroencephalography)
calix [Gr. *kalyx* cup]
capsular antigen [Ger. *Kapsel* capsule]
carrying capacity (genetics)
cathode
coefficient of heat transfer
coefficient of scleral rigidity
cretaceous
dissociation constant *also* K_d
electron capture
electrostatic capacity
equilibrium constant
ionization constant
kalium (potassium)
kallikrein inhibiting unit
kanamycin *also* KM
kappa (10th letter of Greek alphabet), uppercase
Kell blood system
Kell factor
kelvin (SI fundamental unit of temperature)
keratometer
kerma
ketotifen
kidney
killer (cell)
kilo- *also* k
kilopermeability coefficient
kinetic energy *also* KE
knee *also* Kn, kn
Küntscher (nail)
lysine *also* LYS
modulus of compression
motor coordination (in General Aptitude Test Battery)
1024 (number of bytes in kilobyte)
one thousand *also* kilo
phylloquinone *also* K_1
potassium [L. *kalium*] *also* Kal, pot., potass
ratio of curvature of flattest meridian of apical cornea (in fitting of contact lens)
vitamin K.

K-10

gastric tube

17K, 17-K

17-ketosteroid *also* 17-Keto, 17-KS

°K

degree on the Kelvin scale (obsolete, now K)

^{39}K

potassium-39

^{40}K

potassium-40
radioactive potassium isotope

^{42}K

potassium-42
radioactive potassium isotope

^{43}K

potassium-43
radioactive potassium isotope

K_1

phylloquinone *also* K

K_3

menadione

K_4

menadiol sodium diphosphate

k

Boltzmann constant
constant
kilo- *also* K
magnetic susceptibility
rate constants
rate of velocity constant
reaction rate constant
velocity constants

K-A

King-Armstrong (unit) *also* KA, KAU

KA

alkaline phosphatase *also* AKP, ALK-P, alk phos, alk p'tase, ALP, AlPase, AP, P'ase
kainic acid
keratoacanthoma
ketoacid
ketoacidosis
King-Armstrong (unit) *also* K-A, KAU
kynurenic acid

K/A

ketogenic/antiketogenic (ratio)

K$_a$
acid ionization (dissociation) constant

K_a
dissociation constant of an acid *also* K$_d$

Ka
cathode (kathode)
kallikrein
kathodal

kA
kiloampere

KAAD
kerosene, alcohol, acetic acid, and dioxane (mixture)

KAB
knowledge, attitude, and behavior

KABC
Kaufman Assessment Battery for Children

KABINS
knowledge, attitude, behavior, and improvement in nutritional status

KACT
kaolin-activated clotting time

KAF
conglutinogen-activating factor
killer-assisting factor
kinase-activating factor

KAFO
knee-ankle-foot orthosis

KAL
Kallmann (syndrome)

Kal
potassium [L. *kalium*] *also* K, pot., potass

KAO
knee-ankle orthosis

KAP
knowledge, aptitudes, (and) practices (fertility)

κ
kappa (10th letter of Greek alphabet), lowercase
magnetic susceptibility
one of two immunoglobulin light chains

K:A ratio
ketogenic-antiketogenic ratio

KAS
Katz Adjustment Scales (psychologic test)

KASH
knowledge, abilities, skills, (and) habits

KAST
Kindergarten Auditory Screening Test

KAT
kanamycin acetyltransferase
Kinesthetic Ability Trainer

kat
katal (enzyme unit of measurement)

kat/L
katal per liter

KAU
King-Armstrong unit *also* KA, K-A

KB
human oral epidermoid carcinoma cells
Kashin-Bek (disease)
ketone body
kilobyte
knee-bearing
knee brace
knuckle-bender (splint)

K-B
Kleihauer-Betke (test)

K/B
knee-bearing (prosthesis)

K$_b$
base ionization constant
dissociation constant of a base

K_b
dissociation constant of a base

kb
kilobase

kbp
kilobase pair (nucleic acid molecules)

kBq
kilobecquerel

KBR
ketone body ratio

KBr
potassium bromide

KBS
Klüver-Bucy syndrome

KC
cathodal (kathodal) closing
keratoconjunctivitis
keratoconus
keratoma climacterium
knees to chest
knuckle cracking
Kupffer cell

kC
kilocoulomb

kc
kilocycle

K Cal, Kcal
kilocalorie *also* kcal

kcal
kilocalorie *also* K Cal
kilogram calorie

k$_{cat}$
turnover number

KCC
cathodal (kathodal) closing contraction
[Ger. *Kathodenschlie βungs-
Kontraktion*] *also* KSK
Kulchitzky cell carcinoma

KCCT
kaolin-cephalin clotting time

K cell
killer cell

KCG
kinetocardiogram

kCi
kilocurie

KCl
potassium chloride

K complex
slow waves related to sleep arousal
(in electroencephalography)

kcps
kilocycle per second *also* kc/sec,
kc/s

KCS
keratoconjunctivitis sicca

kc/sec, kc/s
kilocycle per second *also* kcps

KCT, KCTe
cathodal (kathodal) closing tetanus
also KST

KCZ
ketoconazole

KD
cathodal (kathodal) duration
Kawasaki disease
Keto-Diasti
kidney donor
killed
knee disarticulation
knitted Dacron

K$_d$
dissociation constant *also* K
dissociation constant of an acid *also*
K_a
distribution coefficient
partition coefficient

kD, kd
kilodalton *also* kdal

KDA
known drug allergies

kdal
kilodalton *also* kD, kd

KDC
cathodal (kathodal) duration
contraction

KDO
ketodeoxyoctonic (acid)

KDP
potassium dihydrogen phosphate

KDS
Kaufman Development Scale
Kocher-Debré-Sémélaigne (syndrome)

KDSM
keratinizing desquamative squamous
metaplasia

KDSS
Kurtzke Disability Status Scale

KDT, KDTe
cathodal (kathodal) duration tetanus

kdyn
kilodyne

K

NOTES

KE
Kendall compound E (cortisone)
kinetic energy *also* K

K_e
exchangeable body potassium

KED
Kendrick extrication device

Kemo Tx
chemical therapy (chemotherapy)

K_eq
equilibrium constant

Kera
keratitis

KERV
Kentucky equine respiratory virus

KET
ketoconazole

17-Keto
17-ketosteroid *also* 17K, 17-K, 17-KS

kev, keV
kiloelectron volt

KF
Kayser-Fleischer (ring)
Kenner-fecal (medium)
kidney function
Klippel-Feil (syndrome)

kf
flocculation rate in antigen-antibody
reaction

KFA
kinetic fibrinogen assay

KFAB, KFAb
kidney-fixing antibody

K factor
γ-ray dose (roentgens per hour at 1
cm from 1-mCi point source of
radiation)

KFAO
knee-foot-ankle orthosis

KFD
Kinetic Family Drawing
Kyasanur forest disease

KFR
Kayser-Fleischer ring

KFS
Klippel-Feil syndrome

KG
ketoglutarate

KG-1
Koeffler Golde-1 (cell line)

kG
kilogauss

kg
kilogram *also* kilo

KGC
Keflin (cephalothin), gentamicin, and
carbenicillin

kg-cal
kilogram-calorie

kg/cm²
kilogram per square centimeter

KGDH
ketoglutarate dehydrogenase

KGDHC
ketoglutarate dehydrogenase complex

kgf
kilogram-force

KGHT
kidney Goldblatt hypertension

kg/L
kilogram per liter

KGM
ketoglutaramate

kg-m
kilogram-meter

kg/m²
kilogram per meter squared

kg-m/s²
kilogram-meter per second squared

Kgn
kininogen

kgps (*var. of* kg/s)

KGS
ketogenic steroid

17-KGS
17-ketogenic steroid

kg/s, kgps
kilogram per second

KH
Krebs-Henseleit (cycle)

K24H
potassium in 24-hour (urine)

KHB
Krebs-Henseleit bicarbonate (buffer)

KHb
potassium hemoglobinate *also* K hgb

KHC
kinetic hemolysis curve

KHD
kinky hair disease

KHF
Korean hemorrhagic fever

K hgb
potassium hemoglobinate *also* KHb

KHM
keratoderma hereditaria mutilans

KHN
Knoop hardness number (of solids)

KHS
kinky hair syndrome
Krebs-Henseleit solution

kHz
kilohertz

KI
karyopyknotic index *also* KPI
knee immobilizer
Krönig isthmus

K$_I$
dissociation of enzyme-inhibitor
 complex
inhibition constant

KIA
Kligler iron agar (medium)

KIC
ketoisocaproic (acid)

KICB
killed intracellular bacteria

KID
keratitis-ichthyosis-deafness
keratitis, ichthyosis, and deafness
 (syndrome)

KIDS
Kent Infant Development Scale

kilo
kilogram *also* kg
kilometer *also* km
one thousand *also* K

KIMSA, KIMSV, KI-MSV
Kirsten murine sarcoma virus

KIP
key intermediary protein

KIS
Krankenhaus Information System

KISS
key integrative social system
kidney internal splint/stent
potassium iodide, saturated solution

KIT
Kahn intelligence test

KIU
kallikrein inactivation unit
kallikrein-inhibiting unit

KJ, kj
knee jerk

kJ
kilojoule

KK
kallikrein-kinin
knee kick

kkat
kilokatal

KL
kidney lobe
Klebs-Löffler (bacillus)
Kleine-Levin (syndrome)

kL
kiloliter *also* kl

kl
kiloliter *also* kL
musical overtone (ringing, in
 acoustics) [Ger. *Klang*]

KL-BET
Kleihauer-Betke (test) *also* K-B

K level
lowest level (of x-rays)

KLH
keyhole-limpet hemocyanin

KLS
kidneys, liver, and spleen
Kreuzbein lipomatous syndrome

K

NOTES

KLST
Kindergarten Language Screening Test

KM
κ-immunoglobulin (light chain)
kanamycin *also* K
Kraepelin-Morel (disease)

K_m
Michaelis-Menten constant

Km, K_m
Michaelis constant (in enzyme assays)
Michaelis-Menten dissociation constant

km
kilometer *also* kilo

km^2
square kilometer

kMc
kilomegacycle

K-MCM
potassium-containing minimal capacitation medium

kMc/s, kMcps
kilomegacycle per second

KMDAT
Key Math Diagnostic Arithmetic Test

KMEF
keratin, myosin, epidermin, and fibrin (class of proteins)

kmps, km/s
kilometer per second

KMS
kwashiorkor-marasmus syndrome

KMV
killed measles virus (vaccine)

Kn
knee *also* K, kn
Knudsen number (low-pressure gas flow)

kN
kilonewton

kn
knee *also* K, Kn

KNF model
Koshland-Némethy-Filmer model

KNO
keep needle open

knork
knife and fork (physiatry)

KNRK
Kirsten sarcoma virus in normal rat kidney (cell)

KO
keep on (continue) *also* K/O
keep open *also* K/O
killed organism
knee orthosis
knocked out *also* KO'd

K/O
keep on (continue) *also* KO
keep open *also* KO

KOC
cathodal (kathodal-obsolete) opening contraction

KO'd
knocked out *also* KO

KOH
potassium chloride (stain)
potassium hydroxide

KOIS
Kuder Occupational Interest Survey

KOT
Knowledge of Occupations Test

KP
Kaufmann-Peterson (base)
keratic precipitate
keratitic precipitate
keratitis punctata
keratoprecipitate
keratotic patch
kidney protein
kidney punch (trauma)
killed parenteral (vaccine)
kilopond

K-P
Kaiser-Permanente (diet)

kPa
kilopascal

kPas/L
kilopascal-second per liter

KPB
kalium (potassium) phosphate buffer
ketophenylbutazone (kebuzone)

KPE
Kelman phacoemulsification

KPI
karyopyknotic index *also* KI

KPM
kilopond meters

KPR
key pulse rate
Kuder Preference Record

KPR-V
Kuder Preference Record—Vocational

KPS
Karnofsky performance score

KPT
kidney punch test (physical exam)
Kuder Performance Test

KPTI
Kunitz pancreatic trypsin inhibitor

KPTT
kaolin partial thromboplastin time

KPV
killed parenteral vaccine
killed polio vaccine

KR
knowledge of results
Kopper Reppart (medium)

Kr
krypton

^{81m}Kr
krypton-81m

kR
kiloroentgen

KRA
Klinefelter-Reifenstein-Albright
(syndrome)

KRB
Krebs-Ringer bicarbonate (buffer) *also*
KRBB

KRBB
Krebs-Ringer bicarbonate buffer *also*
KRB

KRBG
Krebs-Ringer bicarbonate (buffer) with
glucose

KRBS
Krebs-Ringer bicarbonate solution

KRD
kinetic rehab device

KRP
Kolmer (test with) Reiter protein
(antigen)
Krebs-Ringer phosphate

KRPS
Krebs-Ringer phosphate (buffer)
solution

KRRS
kinetic resonance Raman spectroscopy

KS
Kallmann syndrome
Kaposi sarcoma
Kartagener syndrome
Kawasaki syndrome
keratan sulfate
ketosteroid
Klinefelter syndrome
Kochleffel syndrome
Korsakoff syndrome
Kugel-Stoloff (syndrome)
Kveim-Siltzbach (test)

17-KS
17-ketosteroid *also* 17K, 17-K, 17-
Keto

ks
kilosecond

KSA
knowledge, skills, and abilities

KSHV
Kaposi sarcoma-associated herpesvirus

KSK
cathodal closing contraction [Ger.
Kathodenschließungs-Kontraktion] *also*
KCC

KS/OI
Kaposi sarcoma and opportunistic
infections

KSP
Karolinska Scale of Personality
kidney-specific protein

K$_{sp}$
potassium solubility product

K

NOTES

KSS
Kearns-Sayre-Shy (syndrome)
Kearns-Sayre syndrome

KST
cathodal-closing tetanus *also* KCT, KCTe

KSU
Kent State University (Speech Discrimination Test)

KT
kidney transplant
kidney transplantation
kidney treatment
kinesiotherapy
Klippel-Trenaunay (syndrome)
Kuder test

KTI
kallikrein-trypsin inhibitor

KTP
potassium-titanyl-phosphate

KTS
kethoxal thiosemicarbazone

KTSA
Kahn Test of Symbol Arrangement

KTVS
Keystone Telebinocular Visual Survey

KTWS
Klippel-Trenaunay-Weber syndrome

KU
kallikrein unit
Karmen unit

Ku
kurchatovium

KUB
kidneys, ureters, bladder
kidneys and urinary bladder

KUS
kidneys, ureters, and spleen

KV
kanamycin-vancomycin
killed vaccine

kV, kv
kilovolt
kilovoltage

kVA, kVa
kilovolt-ampere

KVBA
kanamycin-vancomycin blood agar

kVcp, kvcp
kilovolt constant potential

KVE
Kaposi varicelliform eruption

KVLBA
kanamycin-vancomycin laked blood agar

KVO
keep vein open (IV lines)

KVO C D5W
keep vein open with 5% dextrose in water

kVp, kvp
kilovoltage peak
kilovoltage potential

KW
Keith-Wagener (classification of eye ground findings) *also* KWB
kidney weight
Kimmelstiel-Wilson (disease, syndrome)
Kugelberg-Welander (disease)

K_w
dissociation constant of water

kW, kw
kilohm
kilowatt

KWB
Keith-Wagener-Barker (classification of eye ground findings) *also* KW

kWh, kW-hr, kw-hr
kilowatt-hour

KWIC
keyword in context (computers)

K wire, K-wire
Kirschner wire *also* K-wire

KWOC
keyword out of context (computers)

kyph
kyphosis

KZ
Kaplan-Zuelzer (syndrome)

L

angular momentum
Avogadro constant/number *also* Λ, N, Na, N_A
boundary *also* LIM
coefficient of induction
diffusion length
inductance
lambert (unit of luminance) *also* La
latent (heat)
latex *also* LX, Lx
Latin *also* Lat
left *also* (L), l, laev., lf, LT, lt
length *also* l
Lente (insulin)
lesser
let
lethal (Erlich's symbol for fatal) *also* l
leucine *also* LEU, Leu
lewisite
licensed (to practice)
lidocaine *also* LIDO
ligament, ligamentum *also* Lgt, lgt, lig
light (chain of protein molecules) *also* LT, lt
light sense
lilac (indicator color)
limes
lincomycin
lingual *also* ling
linking (number)
liquor
liter *also* l
liver *also* LIV
living *also* liv
longitudinal (section)
low *also* LO
lower *also* LO
lowest *also* LO
lumbar
lumen *also* lm
luminance
lung *also* LU, Lu
lymph
lymphocyte
lymphogranuloma
lysosome
pound *also* lb., lib., pnd.
radiance
self-inductance

syphilis
threshold

L1–L5, L_1–L_5
first through fifth lumbar vertebrae or lumbar nerve

L-I, L-II, L-III
stages of lues (syphilis)

(L)
left *also* L, l, laev., lf, LT, lt
lunch

L_+
limes tod (toxin-antitoxin mixture that contains one fatal dose in excess)

L_0
limes zero (neutralized toxin-antitoxin mixture) [L. *limes nul*]

L/3
lower third (of leg bone)

l
left *also* L, (L), laev., lf, LT, lt
length *also* L
lethal *also* L
line
liter *also* L
long
longitudinal
radioactive constant
specific latent heat

l-
levorotatory

L-
sterically related to L-glyceraldehyde

LA
lactic acid
language age
large amount
late abortion
late antigen
lateral apical
latex agglutination
Latin American
left angle
left angulation
left arm
left atrial (pressure)
left atrium (echocardiography image)
left auricle
leucine aminopeptidase *also* LAP
leukemia antigen

L

LA *(continued)*
leukoagglutinating
leuprolide acetate
levator ani (muscle)
lichen amyloidosis
Lightwood-Albright (syndrome)
linguoaxial
linoleic acid
lobuloalveolar
local anesthesia
long-acting (drug)
long arm (cast)
low anxiety
Ludwig angina
lupus anticoagulant
lymphocyte antibody

LA50
total body surface area of burn that will kill 50% of patients (lethal area)

L&A, L+A, l&a
light and accommodation
living and active (family history)

La
labial
lambert *also* L
lanthanum

l.a.
according to the art [L. *lege artis*]

LAA
left atrial abnormality
left atrial appendage
left auricular appendage
leukemia-associated antigen
leukocyte ascorbic acid

LA:A, La:A
left atrial to aortic (ratio)

LAAL
lower anterior axillary line

LAAO
L-amino acid oxidase

LAARD
long-acting antirheumatic drug

LAB
Leisure Activities Blank (psychology)

lab
laboratory *also* LB
rennet ferment coagulating milk [Ger. *Lab* chymosin]

LABA
laser-assisted balloon angioplasty

LABBB
left anterior bundle branch block

LABS
Laboratory Admission Baseline Studies

LABV
left atrial ball valve

LABVT
left atrial ball-valve thrombus

LAC
laceration *also* lac
La Crosse (arbovirus)
lactose
left atrial contraction
linguoaxiocervical
long arm cast
low amplitude contraction
lung adenocarcinoma cell
lupus anticoagulant

LaC
labiocervical

lac
laceration *also* LAC
lactate *also* lact
lactation *also* lact

lac & cont
lacerations and contusions

LACI
lipoprotein-associated coagulation inhibitor

LACN
local area communications network

lacr
lacrimal

LAC T
lactose tolerance

LACT
Lindamood Auditory Conceptualization Test (psychology)

lact
lactate *also* lac
lactating
lactation *also* lac
lactic

LACT-ART
lactate arterial

lact hyd
lactalbumin hydrolysate

LAD
lactic acid dehydrogenase *also* LADH
language acquisition device
left anterior descending (coronary artery) *also* LADA, LADCA
left atrial dimension
left axis deviation
leukocyte adhesion deficiency
ligament augmentation device
linoleic acid depression
lipoamide dehydrogenase
lymphocyte-activating determinant

LADA
laboratory animal dander allergy
left acromiodorsoanterior (position of fetus)
left anterior descending (coronary) artery *also* LAD, LADCA

LADCA
left anterior descending coronary artery *also* LAD, LADA

LADD
lacrimoauriculodentodigital (syndrome)
left anterior descending diagonal (branch of coronary artery)

LADH
lactic acid dehydrogenase *also* LAD
liver alcohol dehydrogenase

LADME
liberation, absorption, distribution, metabolism, and excretion

LAD-MIN
left axis deviation, minimal

LADP
left acromiodorsoposterior (position of fetus)

LADPG
laparoscopically assisted distal partial gastrectomy

LADu
lobuloalveolar-ductal

LAE
left atrial enlargement
long above-elbow (cast)

LAEC
locally advanced esophageal cancer

LAEDV
left atrial end-diastolic volume

LAEI
left atrial emptying index

LAER
late auditory-evoked response

LAESV
left atrial end-systolic volume

laev.
left [L. *laevus*] *also* L, (L), l, lf, LT, lt

LAF
laminar air flow
Latin American female
leukocyte-activating factor
low animal fat
lymphocyte-activating factor

LAF-3
leukocyte antigen factor-3

LAFB
left anterior fascicular block

LAFR
laminar air flow room

LAFU
laminar air flow unit

LAG
labiogingival *also* LaG
linguoaxiogingival
lymphangiogram
lymphangiography

LaG
labiogingival *also* LAG

lag.
flask [L. *lagena*]

LAH
lactalbumin hydrolysate
left anterior hemiblock *also* LAHB
left atrial hypertrophy
lithium-aluminum hydride

LAHB
left anterior hemiblock *also* LAH

LAHV
leukocyte-associated herpesvirus

NOTES

LAI
labioincisal *also* LaI
latex (particle) agglutination inhibition
left atrial involvement
leukocyte adherence inhibition (assay)

LaI
labioincisal *also* LAI

LAIF
leukocyte adherence inhibition factor

LAIT
latex agglutination inhibition test

LAK
lymphokine-activated killer (cell)

LAL
left axillary line
limulus amebocyte lysate
low air loss

LaL
labiolingual

L-Ala
L-alanine

LALI
lymphocyte antibody lymphocytolytic
interaction

LAM
L-asparaginase and methotrexate
lactation amenorrhea method
laminar air flow
laminectomy *also* Lam, lam
late ambulatory monitoring
Latin American male
left anterior measurement
left atrial myxoma
limb accurate measurement
lymphangioleiomyomatosis

LAM-1
leukocyte adhesion molecule-1

Lam, lam
lamina
laminectomy *also* LAM
laminogram

LAMA
laser-assisted microanastomosis

LA–MAX
maximal left atrial (dimension)

LAMB
lentigines, atrial myxoma, and blue
nevi

lentigines, atrial myxoma,
mucocutaneous myxomas, and blue
nevi

L-AmB
liposomal-amphotericin B

Λ
Avogadro number *also* N, N_A, Na,
N, L
lambda (11th letter of Greek
alphabet), uppercase
Ostwald solubility coefficient
radioactive constant
wavelength

λ
craniometric point
decay constant
junction of lambdoid and sagittal
sutures (craniotomy)
lambda (11th letter of Greek
alphabet), lowercase
mean free path
microliter *also* μL, μl
one of two forms of immunoglobulin
light chain
thermal conductivity *also* TC
wavelength *also* WL

lam & fus
laminectomy and fusion

lami
laminotomy

LAMMA
laser microprobe mass analyzer

LAMP-1
lysosomal membrane glycoprotein-1

LAMP-2
lysosomal membrane glycoprotein-2

LAN
local area network
long-acting neuroleptic
lymphadenopathy

LANC
long arm navicular cast

Lang, lang
language

L ANT
left anterior

LANV
left atrial neovascularization

LAO
left anterior oblique
left anterior occipital
left atrial overloading

LAP
laparoscopy *also* lap.
laparotomy *also* lap.
left atrial pressure
leucine aminopeptidase *also* LA
leukocyte alkaline phosphatase (stain)
low atmospheric pressure
lyophilized anterior pituitary (tissue)

lap
laparotomy

lap.
laparoscopy *also* LAP
laparotomy *also* LAP

LAPA
leukocyte alkaline phosphatase activity

LAPF
low-affinity platelet factor

lapid.
stony [L. *lapideum*]

LAPIS
Late Potential Italian Study

LAPMS
long arm posterior-molded splint

LAPOCA
L-asparaginase, prednisone, Oncovin (vincristine), cytarabine, and Adriamycin (doxorubicin)

LAPSE
long-term ambulatory physiological surveillance (vital sign monitor)

LAPW
left atrial posterior wall

LAR
laryngology *also* Laryngol
late asthmatic response
left arm, reclining (blood pressure, pulse measurement)

left arm, recumbent (blood pressure, pulse measurement)
low anterior resection

lar
larynx *also* lx

LARC
leukocyte automatic recognition computer

LARD
lacrimoauriculoradiodental (syndrome)

LARS
Language-Structured Auditory Retention Span (Test)
leucyl-transfer ribonucleic acid synthetase

laryn
laryngeal
laryngitis
laryngoscopy

Laryngol
laryngology *also* LAR

LAS
laboratory automation system
lateral amyotrophic sclerosis
laxative abuse syndrome
left anterior-superior
left arm, sitting (blood pressure, pulse measurement)
leucine acetylsalicylate
linear alkyl sulfonate
local adaptation syndrome
long arm splint
lower abdominal surgery
lymphadenopathy syndrome
lymphangioscintigraphy

LASA
left anterior spinal artery
Lisfranc articular set angle

LASE
laser-assisted spinal endoscopy

LASEC
left atrial spontaneous echo contrast

LASER, laser
Light Activation by Stimulated Emission of Radiation

L

NOTES

399

LASER *(continued)*
light amplification by stimulated emission of radiation

LASFB
left anterior-superior fascicular block

LASH
left anterior-superior hemiblock

LASIK
laser in situ keratomileusis

L-ASP
L-asparaginase

l-**ASP**
l-asparaginase

LASS
labile aggregation stimulating substance
Linguistic Analysis of Speech Samples

LAST
left anterior small thoracotomy
leukocyte-antigen sensitivity testing

LAT
lactic acidosis threshold
latent
lateral *also* lat
latex agglutination test
left anterior thigh
left atrial thrombus

Lat
Latin *also* L

lat
lateral *also* LAT
latissimus (dorsi)
latitude

LAT-A
latrunculin A

lat. admov.
let it be applied to the side [L. *lateri admoveatum*]

LAT-B
latrunculin B

LATCH
literature attached to charts

lat. dol.
to the painful side [L. *lateri dolenti*]

LATE
Late Assessment of Thrombolytic Efficacy

lat & loc
lateralizing and localizing

l·atm
liter-atmosphere

lat men
lateral meniscectomy

LATP
left atrial transmural pressure

LATPT
left atrial transesophageal pacing test

lat Rin
lactated Ringer (solution) *also* LR

LATS
long-acting thyroid-stimulating (hormone)
long-acting transmural stimulator

LATS-P
long-acting thyroid stimulator-protector

LATu
lobuloalveolar tumor

LAUP
laser-assisted uvulopalatoplasty

LAV
lymphadenopathy-associated virus
lymphocyte-associated virus

lav
lavoratory

LAVH
laparoscopic-assisted vaginal hysterectomy
laparoscopic-assisted vaginal hysteroscopy

LAW
left atrial wall

LAX
long axis

lax.
laxative
laxity

LB
laboratory (data) *also* lab
lamellar body
large bowel
lateral basal
lateral bending
Lederer-Brill (syndrome)
left breast
left bundle
left buttock

leiomyoblastoma *also* LMB
lipid body
live birth
liver biopsy
Living Bank
loose body
low back (pain) *also* LBP
low breakage
lung biopsy

L-B
Liebermann-Burchard (test for cholesterol)

L&B
left and below

Lb
pound force *also* lbf

lb.
pound [L. *libra*] *also* L, lib., pnd.

LBA
laser balloon angioplasty
left basal artery

lb. ap.
apothecary pound [L. *libra apothecary*]

lb. av.
avoirdupois pound [L. *libra avoirdupois*]

LBB
left breast biopsy
left bundle branch
low back bend

LBBB
left bundle branch block

LBBsB
left bundle branch system block

LBBX
left breast biopsy examination

LBC
lidocaine blood concentration
lymphadenosis benigna cutis

LBCD
left border of cardiac dullness

LBCF
Laboratory Branch Complement Fixation (test)

LBD
large bile duct
left border dullness (of heart to percussion)
Lewy body dementia

LBDQ
Leader Behavior Description Questionnaire

LBE
long below-elbow (cast)

LBF
Lactobacillus bulgaricus factor (pantetheine)
limb blood flow
liver blood flow

lbf
pound force *also* Lb

lbf-ft
pound force foot

lb-ft
pound-feet

LBH
length, breadth, height

LBI
low serum-bound iron

lb/in²
pounds per square inch *also* PSI

LBL
labeled lymphoblast
lymphoblastic lymphoma *also* LL

LBM
last bowel movement
lean body mass
loose bowel movement
lung basement membrane

LBNP
lower body negative pressure

LBO
large bowel obstruction

LBP
low back pain *also* LB
low blood pressure

LBPQ
Low Back Pain Questionnaire

L

NOTES

LBQC
large base quad cane

LBRF
louse-borne relapsing fever

LBS
lactobacillus selector (agar)
low back syndrome

lbs.
pounds [L. *librae*]

LBSA
lipid-bound sialic acid *also* LSA

LBT
low back tenderness
low back trouble
lupus band test

lb. t.
pound troy [L. *libra troy*] *also* lb. tr.

LBTI
lima bean trypsin inhibitor

lb. tr.
pound troy [L. *libra troy*] *also* lb. t.

LBV
left brachial vein
lung blood volume

LBW
lean body weight
low birth weight

LBWI
low birth weight infant

LBWR
lung-body weight ratio

LC
lactation consultant
Laënnec cirrhosis
lamina cortex
Langerhans cell
laparoscopic cholecystectomy
large chromophobe
large cleaved (cell)
late clamped (umbilical cord)
lateral compression
lateral projection
lecithin cholesterol (acyltrans-ferase)
left circumflex (coronary artery) *also*
 LCCA, LCF, LCX, LCx
left (ear), cold (stimulus)
leisure counseling
lethal concentration
Library of Congress
life care

light chain
light coagulation
lingual cusp
linguocervical
lining cell
lipid cytosome
liquid chromatography
liquid crystal
lithocolic (acid)
live clinic
liver cirrhosis
liver clinic
living children
locus ceruleus
long-chain (triglycerides)
longus capitis
low calorie *also* lo cal
lung cancer
lung cell
lymph capillary
lymphocyte count
lymphocytotoxin *also* LCT, LT
lymphoma culture

l.c.
in the place cited [L. *loco citato*]

LCA
Leber congenital amaurosis
left carotid artery
left circumflex artery
left coronary artery
leukocyte common antigen
light contact assist
lithocolic acid
liver cell adenoma
lymphocyte chemoattractant activity
lymphocytotoxic antibody *also* LCTA

LCA-DCA
lithocolic acid-deoxycholic acid (ratio)

LCAL
large cell anaplastic lymphoma

LCAO
linear combination of atomic orbitals

LCAO-MO
linear combination of atomic orbital-
molecular orbital

LCAR
late cutaneous anaphylactic reaction

LCAT
lecithin-cholesterol acyltransferase

LCB
Laboratory of Cancer Biology

left costal border
lymphomatosis cutis benigna

LCBF
local cerebral blood flow

LCC
lactose coliform count
left coronary cusp
liver cell carcinoma

LCCA
late cortical cerebellar atrophy
left circumflex coronary artery *also*
LC, LCX, LCx
left common carotid artery
leukoclastic angiitis
leukocytoclastic angiitis

LCCP
limited channel-capacity process

LCCS
lower cervical cesarean section

LCCSCT
large cell calcifying Sertoli cell
tumor

LCD
lipochondral degeneration
liquid crystal display
liquor carbonis detergens (coal tar
solution)
localized collagen dystrophy
low-calcium diet

LCDCP
low contact dynamic compression
plate

LCDD
light-chain deposition disease

LCDE
laparoscopic common duct exploration

LCE
laparoscopic cholecystectomy
left carotid endarterectomy

LCED
liquid chromatography with
electrochemical detection

LCF
least common factor

left circumflex (coronary artery) *also*
LC, LCCA, LCX, LCx
left common femoral (artery)
linear correction factor
low-frequency current field
lymphocyte culture fluid

L-CF
leucovorin-citrovorum factor

LCFA
long-chain fatty acid

LCFAO
long-chain fatty acid oxidation

LCFC
linear combination of fragment
configuration

LCFM
left circumflex marginal

LCFU
leukocyte colony-forming unit

LCG
Langerhans cell granule
Langerhans cell granulomatosis
liquid chemical germicide

LCGU
local cerebral glucose utilization

LCH
Langerhans cell histiocytosis
local city hospital

LCHAD
long-chain 3-hydroxyacyl coenzyme A
dehydrogenase

L chain
light chain (polypeptides with low
molecular weight)

LCI
length complexity index
lung clearance index

LCIS
lobular carcinoma in situ

LCL
lateral collateral ligament
Levinthal-Coles-Lillie (cytoplasmic
inclusion body)
lower confidence limit
lymphoblastoid cell line

L

NOTES

LCL *(continued)*
lymphocytic leukemia *also* LL
lymphocytic lymphosarcoma
lymphoid cell line

LCLC
large cell lung carcinoma

LCM
latent cardiomyopathy
left costal margin
leukocyte-conditioned medium
lower costal margin
lowest common multiple
lymphatic choriomeningitis
lymphocytic choriomeningitis

LCMG
long-chain monoglyceride

l/cm H₂O
liters per centimeter of water

LCMV
lymphocytic choriomeningitis virus

LCN
lateral cervical nucleus
left caudate nucleus

LCO
low cardiac output

LCOS
low cardiac output syndrome

LCP
Legg-Calvé-Perthes (disease) *also*
LCPD
long-chain polysaturated (fatty acid)

LCPD
Legg-Calvé-Perthes disease *also* LCP

LCQG
left caudal quarter ganglion

LCR
late cortical response
late cutaneous reaction
leurocristine (vincristine)

LCS
left coronary sinus
Leydig cell stimulation
lichen chronicus simplex
life care service
liquor cerebrospinalis
low constant suction
low continuous suction

LCSG
left cardiac sympathetic
ganglionectomy

LCSW
Licensed Clinical Social Worker

LCT
liquid crystal thermography
liver cell tumor
long-chain triglyceride
low cervical transverse
lung capillary time
Luscher Color Test
lymphocytotoxicity test
lymphocytotoxin *also* LC, LT

LCTA
lymphocytotoxic antibody *also* LCA

LCTCS
low cervical transverse cesarean
section

LCTD
low-calcium test diet

LCU
life change unit

LCV
lecithovitellin
leucovorin *also* LEU, LV, LVR
leukocytoclastic vasculitis
low cervical vertical (incision)

LCX, LCx
left circumflex (coronary artery) *also*
LC, LCCA, LCF

LD
L-dopa
laboratory data
labor and delivery *also* L&D
labyrinthine defect
lactate dehydrogenase *also* LDG,
LDH
lactic (acid) dehydrogenase *also*
LDG, LDH
last dose
L-DOPA
learning disability
learning disabled
learning disorder
left deltoid
Legionnaire disease
Leishman-Donovan (body) *also* L-D
lethal dose
levodopa *also* L-DOPA, L-dopa
light-dark
light difference
light differentiation
light duty
limited disease

linear dichroism
linguodistal
lipodystrophy
lithium diluent
lithium discontinuation
liver disease
living donor
loading dose
Lombard-Dowell (agar)
longitudinal diameter (of heart)
long (time) dialysis
low density
low dose
lung destruction
Lyme disease
lymphocyte-defined
lymphocyte depletion
lymphocytically determined

L-D
Leishman-Donovan (body) *also* LD

L/D
light/dark (ratio)

L&D
labor and delivery *also* LD
light and distance (in ophthalmology)

LD$_1$–LD$_5$
lactate dehydrogenase fraction 1
  through 5 *also* LDH$_1$–LDH$_5$

LD$_{50}$
median lethal dose (lethal for 50%
  of test subjects)

LD$_{50/30}$
dose that is lethal dose for 50% of
  test subjects within 30 days

LD$_{100}$
lethal dose in all exposed subjects

LDA
laser Doppler anemometry
left dorsoanterior (fetal position)
linear discriminant analysis
linear displacement analysis
low density area
lymphocyte-dependent antibody

LDAR
latex direct agglutination reaction

LDB
lamb dysentery bacillus
Legionnaire disease bacillus

LDC
leukocyte differential count
lymphoid dendritic cell

LDCC
lectin-dependent cellular cytotoxicity

LDCI
low-dose continuous infusion

LDCT
late distal cortical tubule

LDD
laser disk decompression
late dedifferentiation
light-dark discrimination
low drain (class) D

LDE
lauric diethamide

LDEA
left deviation of electrical axis

LDER
lateral-view dual-energy radiography

LD-EYA
Lombard-Dowell egg yolk agar

LDF
laser Doppler flowmetry
laser Doppler flux
limit dilution factor
lumbodorsal fascia

LDG
lactate dehydrogenase *also* LD, LDH
lactic (acid) dehydrogenase *also* LD,
  LDH
lingual developmental groove
long-distance group
low-dose group

LDH
lactic (acid) dehydrogenase *also* LD,
  LDG
low-dose heparin

LDH$_1$–LDH$_5$
lactate dehydrogenase fraction 1
  through 5 *also* LD$_1$–LD$_5$

NOTES

LDHA
lactate dehydrogenase A

LDHB
lactate dehydrogenase B

LDHI
lactate dehydrogenase isoenzyme *also* LDISO

LDIH
left direct inguinal hernia

L-dioa (*var. of* L-DOPA)

LDISO
lactate dehydrogenase isoenzyme *also* LDHI

LDL
loudness discomfort level
low-density lipoprotein *also* LDLP
low-density lymphocyte

LDLA
low-density lipoprotein apheresis

LDLC, LDL-C
low-density lipoprotein cholesterol

LDLP
low-density lipoprotein *also* LDL

LDM
lactate dehydrogenase, muscle

LDMF
latissimus dorsi myocutaneous flap

LD-NEYA
Lombard-Dowell neomycin egg yolk agar

L-DOPA, L-dioa, l-dopa, ʟ-dopa
levodopa *also* ʟ-dopa

LDP
left dorsoposterior (fetal position)
lumbodorsal pain

LDR
labor, delivery, and recovery
low-dose rate

LDRP
labor, delivery, recovery, postpartum

LDS
Licentiate in Dental Surgery
ligate-divide-staple
ligating and dividing stapler

LDT
left dorsotransverse (fetal position)

LDU
long double upright (brace) *also* LDUB

LDUB
long double upright brace *also* LDU

LDV
lactic dehydrogenase virus
large dense-cored vesicle
laser Doppler velocimetry
lateral distant view

LE
left eye *also* O.L., O.S.
lens extraction
leukocyte esterase *also* LKESTR
leukoerythrogenetic
leukoerythrogenic
live embryo
Long Evans (rat)
lower extremity *also* L ext, l/ext, LX, Lx, lx
lupus erythematosus (cell)

Le
Leonard (cathode ray unit)
Lewis (number, diffusivity:diffusion coefficient of a fluid)

Le^b
Lewis antibody

Le^a
Lewis antibody

LEA
language experience approach
lower extremity amputation
lower extremity arterial
lumbar epidural anesthesia

LEADS
Leadership Evaluation and Development Scale

LEB
lupus erythematosus body

LEC
leukoencephalitis
low-energy charged (particle)

LECP
low-energy charged particle

LED
light-emitting diode
lowest effective dose
lupus erythematosus disseminatus

LEDC
low energy direct current

LEED
low-energy electron diffraction

LEEDS
low-energy electron diffraction
spectroscopy

LEEP
left end-expiratory pressure
loop electrical excision procedure
loop electrocautery excision procedure
loop electrosurgical excision procedure

LEER
lower extremity equipment related

LEE W
Lee White tritium (clotting time)
also L&W, L/W, LWCT

LEF
leukokinesis-enhancing factor
lupus erythematosus factor

leg.
legal
legislation
legislative

leg com
legal commitment
legally committed

LEHPZ
lower esophageal high-pressure zone

LeIF
leukocyte interferon

leio
leiomyoma

LEIS
low-energy ion scattering

LEJ
ligation of esophagogastric junction

LEL
lowest effect level (of toxicity)

LEM
lateral eye movement
Leibovitz-Emory medium
leukocyte endogenous mediator
light electron microscope

LEMO
lowest empty molecular orbital

LEMS
Lambert-Eaton myasthenic syndrome

LENI
lower extremity noninvasive

lenit
lenitive

lenit.
gently [L. *leniter*]

LEOD
lens extraction, oculus dexter

LEOPARD
lentigines, electrocardiographic
(conduction abnormalities), ocular
(hypertelorism), pulmonary (stenosis),
abnormal (genitalia), retardation (of
growth), and deafness (syndrome)

LEOS
lens extraction, oculus sinister

LEP
lethal effective phase (leptospirosis)
lipoprotein electrophoresis *also* LPE
low egg passage (strain of virus)
lower esophageal pressure

L$_{EPN}$
effective perceived noise level

LE$_{prep}$
lupus erythematosus preparation

LEPT
leptocyte

LEPTOS
leptospirosis agglutinins

Leq
loudness equivalent

LER
lysozymal enzyme release

LERG
local electroretinogram

L-ERX
leukoerythroblastic reaction

LES
Lambert-Eaton syndrome
Lawrence Experimental Station (agar)
Life Experience Survey
local excitatory state

NOTES

407

LES (*continued*)
Locke egg serum (medium)
lower esophageal segment
lower esophageal sphincter
lower esophageal stricture
lupus erythematosus, systemic

les
lesion
low excitatory state

LESA
liposomally entrapped second antibody

LESP
lower esophageal sphincter pressure

LESS
lateral electrical spine stimulation
lateral electrical surface stimulation

LET
language enrichment therapy
leukocyte esterase test
linear energy transfer
liposome-encapsulated tetracaine
low energy transfer

LETD
lowest effective toxic dose

LETS
large external transformation-sensitive
(fibronectin)

LEU
leucine *also* L, Leu
leucovorin *also* LCV, LV, LVR
leukocyte equivalent unit

Leu
leucine *also* L, LEU

leu-CAM
leukocyte cell adhesion molecule

Leu-Dox
N-1-leucyldoxorubicin

leuk, leuko
leukocyte

LEUKAP
leukocyte alkaline phosphatase

LEV
levamisole
lower extremity venous

lev
levator (muscle)

levit.
lightly [L. *leviter*]

LEW
Lewis (rat)

LEX
lactate extraction

L ext, l/ext
lower extremity *also* LE, LX, Lx, lx

LF
labile factor
laryngo-fissure
Lassa fever
latex fixation
lavage fluid
leaflet
left foot
left forearm
leucine flux
ligamentum flavum
limit of flocculation *also* Lf
lingual fossa
low-fat (diet)
low forceps (delivery) *also* LFD
low frequency *also* lf

Lf
limes flocculation (unit, dose of
toxin per mL)
limit of flocculation *also* LF

lf
left *also* L, (L), l, laev., LT, lt
low frequency *also* LF

LFA
left femoral artery
left forearm
left frontoanterior (fetal position)
leukotactic factor activity
low friction arthroplasty
lymphocyte function-associated antigen

LFA-1
leukocyte factor antigen-1
lymphocyte function antigen-1

LFAC
low frequency alternating current

LFB
lingual-facial-buccal
liver, iron, and B complex
low frequency band

LFC
left frontal craniotomy
living female child
low fat and cholesterol (diet)

LFCS
low flap cesarean section

LFD
 lactose-free diet
 large for date
 late fetal death
 lateral facial dysplasia
 least fatal dose
 low-fat diet
 low-fiber diet
 low forceps delivery *also* LF

LFECT
 loose fibroelastic connective tissue

LFER
 linear free-energy relationship

LFH
 left femoral hernia

LFL
 left frontolateral
 leukocyte feeder layer

LFN
 lactoferrin

LFOV
 large field of view

LFP
 left frontoposterior position (fetal)

LFPPV
 low-frequency positive pressure
  ventilation

LFR
 lymphoid follicular reticulosis

LF-RF
 local-regional failure

LFS
 lateral facet syndrome
 Li-Fraumeni syndrome
 limbic forebrain structure
 liver function series

LFT
 latex fixation test
 latex flocculation test
 left frontotransverse (fetal position)
 liver function test
 low-frequency tetanic (stimulation)
 low-frequency tetanus
 low-frequency transduction
 low-frequency transfer

LFTSW
 left foot switch

LFU
 limit flocculation unit
 lipid fluidity unit

LFV
 Lassa fever virus
 low-frequency ventilation

L fx
 linear fracture

LG
 lactoglobulin
 lamellar granule
 large *also* lg, lge
 laryngectomy
 lateral ground
 left gluteal
 left gluteus
 Lennox-Gastaut (syndrome) *also* LGS
 light guide
 lingual groove
 linguogingival
 lipoglycopeptide
 liver graft
 low glucose
 lymph gland
 lymphocytic gastritis

lg
 large *also* LG, lge
 leg
 long

LGA
 large for gestational age
 left gastric artery

LGB
 Landry-Guillain-Barré (syndrome) *also*
  LGBS
 lateral geniculate body

LGBS
 Landry-Guillain-Barré syndrome *also*
  LGB

LGC
 left giant cell

L

NOTES

LGD
Leaderless Group Discussion (situational test)
low-grade dysplasia

LGd
dorsal lateral geniculate (nucleus)

LGE
Langat encephalitis *also* LGT

lge
large *also* LG, lg

LGF
lateral giant fiber

LGH
lactogenic hormone *also* LTH
little growth hormone

LGI
large glucagon immunoreactivity
lower gastrointestinal

LGL
large granular leukocyte
large granular lymphocyte
lobular glomerulonephritis
low grade lymphoma
Lown-Ganong-Levine (syndrome)

LGM
left gluteus medius

LGMD
limb-girdle muscular dystrophy

LGN
lateral geniculate nucleus
lobular glomerulonephritis

LGP
labioglossopharyngeal

LGS
large green soft (stool)
Lennox-Gastaut syndrome *also* LG
limb girdle syndrome

LGSIL
low-grade squamous intraepithelial lesion

LGT
Langat encephalitis *also* LGE
late generalized tuberculosis

Lgt, lgt
ligament, ligamentum *also* L, lig

LGV
large granular vesicle
lymphogranuloma venereum *also* LVG

LGVHD
lethal graft-versus-host disease

LgX
lymphogranulomatosis X

LH
late healed
lateral hypothalamic (syndrome)
lateral hypothalamus
left hand
left hemisphere
left hyperphoria
liver homogenate
loop of Henle
lower half
lues hereditaria (hereditary syphilis)
lung homogenate
luteinizing hormone
luteotropic hormone *also* LTH

L/H
lymphocytic/histiocytic (cell)

LHA
lateral hypothalamic area
left hepatic artery

LHb
lateral habenular

LHBT
lactose hydrogen breath testing

LHBV
left heart blood volume

LHC
Langerhans cell histiocytosis
left heart catheterization
left hypochondrium

LHCG
luteinizing hormone-chorionic gonadotropin (hormone)

LHF
left heart failure
ligament of head of femur

LHFA
lung Hageman factor activator

LH/FSH-RF
luteinizing hormone/follicle-stimulating hormone-releasing factor

LHG
left hand grip
localized hemolysis in gel

LHH
left homonymous hemianopia

LHI
lipid hydrocarbon inclusion

LHL
left hemisphere lesion
left hepatic lobe

LHM
lisuride hydrogen maleate

LHMP
Life Health Monitoring Program

LHN
lateral hypothalamic nucleus

LHP
left hemiparesis
left hemiplegia

LHPC
lipomatous hemangiopericytoma

LHPZ
lower (esophageal) high-pressure zone

LHR
leukocyte histamine release (test)
liquid holding recovery

l-hr
lumen-hour (unit quantity of light)

LH-RF
luteinizing hormone-releasing factor
also LRF

LHRF
luteinizing hormone-releasing factor
luteotropin hormone-releasing factor

LHRH, LH-RH
luteinizing hormone-releasing hormone
also LRH

LHRT
leukocyte histamine release test

LHS
left hand side
left heart strain
left heel strike
lymphatic and hematopoietic system

LHT
left hypertropia

LHV
left hepatic vein

LI
labeling index
lactose intolerance
lamellar ichthyosis
large intestine
laser iridotomy
learning impaired
left injured
left involved
life island
linguoincisal
lithogenic index
loop ileostomy
low impulsiveness

L&I
liver and iron

Li
labrale inferius
lithium

LIA
Laser Institute of America
laser interference acuity
left iliac artery
leukemia-associated inhibitory activity
lock-in amplifier
lymphocyte-induced angiogenesis
lysine-iron agar

LIAC
light-induced absorbance change

LIAF
laser-induced arterial fluorescence
lymphocyte-induced angiogenesis
factor

LIAFI
late infantile amaurotic familial
idiocy

LIB
left in bottle

lib.
pound [L. *libra*] *also* L, lb., pnd.

LIBC
latent iron-binding capacity

LIBR
Librium

LIC
left iliac crest

NOTES

LIC *(continued)*
left internal carotid
leisure-interest class
limiting isorrheic concentration

LICA
left internal carotid artery

LICC
lectin-induced cellular cytotoxicity

LICD
lower intestinal Crohn disease

LICM
left intercostal margin

LICS
left intercostal space *also* LIS

LID
late immunoglobulin deficiency
lymphocytic infiltrative disease

LIDC
low-intensity direct current

LIDO
lidocaine *also* L

LIE
labioincisal edge
linguoincisal edge

LIF
laser-induced fluorescence
left iliac fossa
left index finger
leukemia inhibitory factor
leukocyte infiltration factor
leukocyte inhibitory factor
leukocytosis-inducing factor
liver (migration) inhibitory factor

LIFE
Longitudinal Interval Followup
 Evaluation
lung imaging fluorescence endoscope
lung imaging fluorescent endoscopy

LIFO
last in, first out (re: computer data)

LIFT
lymphocyte immunofluorescence test

lig
ligament, ligamentum *also* L, Lgt,
 lgt
ligate
ligation
ligature *also* ligg

ligg
ligamenta
ligaments
ligature *also* lig

LIH
left inguinal hernia

LIHA
low impulsiveness, high anxiety

LII
Leisure Interest Inventory

LIJ
left internal jugular

LILA
low impulsiveness, low anxiety

LIM
boundary [L. *limes*] *also* L

lim
limit
limitation

LIMA
left internal mammary artery (graft)

LIMIT
Leicester Intravenous Magnesium
Intervention Trial

LIMITS
Liquaemin in Myocardial Infarction
 during Thrombolysis with Saruplase

lin
linear
liniment *also* Linim

LINAC
linear accelerator (system)

LINES
long interspersed elements

ling
lingual *also* L
lingular

Linim
liniment *also* lin

LIO
left inferior oblique (muscle)

LIP
lithium-induced polydipsia
lymphocytic interstitial pneumonia
lymphoid interstitial pneumonia

Lip
lipoate (lipoic acid)

LIPA
lysosomal acid lipase A

LIPB
lysosomal acid lipase B

LIPHE
Life Interpersonal History Enquiry

LIPID
Long-Term Intervention with Pravastatin in Ischemic Disease

lipoMM
lipomyelomeningocele

LIP P
lipid profile

LIPS
Leiter International Performance Scale

LIPT
Leiter International Performance Test

LIPV
left inferior pulmonary vein

LIQ
low inner quadrant

liq.
liquid [L. *liquor*]
liquor [L. *liquor*]

liq dr
liquid dram

liq oz
liquid ounce

liq pt
liquid pint

liq qt
liquid quart

LIR
left iliac region
left inferior rectus

LIRBM
liver, iron, red bone marrow

LIS
laboratory information system
lateral intercellular space
left intercostal space *also* LICS
lithium salicylate
lobular in situ (carcinoma)

locked-in syndrome
low intermittent suction
low ionic strength
lung injury score

LISL
laser-induced intracorporeal shock wave lithotripsy

LISP
List Processing Language

LISS
low ionic strength solution (medium test)

LITA
left internal thoracic artery

litho
lithotripsy

LIV
law of initial value
left innominate vein
liver *also* L

liv
live
living *also* L

LIV-BP
leucine, isoleucine, and valine-binding protein

LIVC
left inferior vena cava

LIVEN
linear inflammatory verrucous epidermal nevus

LIVIM
lethal intestinal virus of infant mice

LIVPRO
liver profile

LIWS
low intermittent wall suction

LJ
Larsen-Johansson (syndrome)
Löwenstein-Jensen (medium) *also* LJM

LJL
lateral joint line

L

NOTES

LJM
limited joint mobility
Löwenstein-Jensen medium *also* LJ

LK
lamellar keratoplasty *also* LKP
Landry-Kussmaul (syndrome)
left kidney *also* LKID
lichenoid keratosis
Löhr-Kindberg (syndrome)

LK⁺
low potassium ion

LKA
Lazare-Klerman-Armour (Personality Inventory)

LKESTR
leukocyte esterase *also* LE

LKID
left kidney *also* LK

LKKS
liver, kidneys, and spleen *also* LKS

LKM
liver-kidney microsome

LKP
lamellar keratoplasty *also* LK

LKPD
Lillehei-Kaster pivoting disk

LKS
Landau-Kleffner syndrome
liver, kidneys, and spleen *also* LKKS

LKSB
liver, kidneys, spleen, and bladder

LKS non. pal.
liver, kidneys, and spleen not palpable

LKV
laked kanamycin vancomycin (agar)
Lengyeh-Kerman-Vargar (rating)

LL
large local
large lymphocyte
lateral lemniscus
left lateral *also* LLAT, L lat, lt lat
left leg
left lower
left lung
lepromatous leprosy
Lewandowski-Lutz (syndrome)
lid lag
lines

lingual lipase
lipoprotein lipase *also* LPL
long leg
loudness level
lower (eye)lid
lower limb
lower lip
lower lobe
lumbar length
lung length
lymphoblastic lymphoma *also* LBL
lymphocytic leukemia *also* LCL
lymphocytic lymphoma
lymphoid leukemia
lysolecithin *also* LLT

L&L
lids and lashes

LLA
lids, lashes, and adnexa
limulus lysate assay
lupus-like anticoagulant

L lam
lumbar laminectomy

LLAT
left lateral *also* LL, L lat, lt lat
lysolecithin acyltransferase
lysolecithin-lecithin acyltransferase

L lat
left lateral *also* LL, LLAT, lt lat

LLB
left lateral bending
left lateral border
left lower border
long leg brace
lower lobe bronchus

LLBCD
left lower border of cardiac dullness

LLBP
long leg brace with pelvic (band)

LLC
labrum-ligament complex
laparoscopic laser cholecystectomy
Lewis lung carcinoma
liquid-liquid chromatography
long leg cast
lower level of care
lymphocytic leukemia, chronic

LLCC
long leg cylinder cast

LLD
Lactobacillus lactis, Dorner (factor)

LLD
left lateral decubitus (muscle)
leg length discrepancy
liquid-liquid distribution
long-lasting depolarization

LLDF
Lactobacillus lactis Dorner factor
(vitamin B$_{12}$)

LLDH
liver lactate dehydrogenase

LLE
left lower extremity *also* LLX

LLETZ
large loop excision of transformation
zone

LLF
Laki-Lorand factor (factor XIII)
left lateral femoral (site of injection)
left lateral flexion

LL-GXT
low-level graded exercise test

LLI
leg length inequality

LLL
left liver lobe
left long leg (brace)
left lower (eye)lid
left lower leg
left lower limb
left lower lobe (of lung)
left lower lung
localized *Leishmania* lymphadenitis

LLLE
lower lid, left eye *also* LLOS

LLLL
lids, lashes, lacrimals, lymphatics

LLLM
low liquid level monitor

LLLNR
left lower lobe, no rales

LLM
localized leukocyte mobilization

LLO
Legionella-like organism
lower limb orthosis

LLOD
lower lid, oculus dexter (right eye)
also LLRE

LLOS
lower lid, oculus sinister (left eye)
also LLLE

LLP
late luteal phase
long-lasting potentiation
long leg plaster (cast)
lower limb prosthesis

LLPMS
long leg posterior molded splint

LLQ
left lower quadrant

LLR
large local reaction
left lateral rectus (eye muscle)
left lumbar region

LLRE
lower lid, right eye *also* LLOD

LLS
lateral loop suspensor
lazy leukocyte syndrome
long leg splint

LLSB
left lower scapular border
left lower sternal border

LLT
left lateral thigh
lysolecithin *also* LL

LLV
lymphatic leukemia virus
lymphoid leukosis virus

LLV-F
lymphatic leukemia virus, Friend
(virus associated)

LLVP
left lateral ventricular pre-excitation

LLW
low-level waste

LLWC
long leg walking cast

NOTES

L

LLX
 left lower extremity *also* LLE

LM
 labiomental
 lactic (acid) mineral (medium)
 lactose malabsorption
 laryngeal muscle
 lateral malleolus
 left main
 left median
 legal medicine
 lemniscus medialis
 Licentiate in Midwifery
 light microscope
 light microscopy
 light minimum
 lincomycin
 lingual margin
 linguomesial
 lipid mobilization
 liquid membrane
 longitudinal muscle
 Looser-Milkman (syndrome)
 lower motor (neuron) *also* LMN

L/M
 liters per minute *also* L/min, l/min,
 Lpm, lpm

lm
 lumen *also* L

LMA
 lactose malabsorption
 laryngeal mask airway
 left mentoanterior (fetal position)
 limbic midbrain area
 liver (cell) membrane autoantibody
 liver membrane antibody

LMB
 Laurence-Moon-Biedl (syndrome) *also*
 LMBS
 left main stem bronchus
 leiomyoblastoma *also* LB

LMBB
 Laurence-Moon-Bardet-Biedl
 (syndrome)

LMBS
 Laurence-Moon-Biedl syndrome *also*
 LMB

LMC
 large motile cell
 lateral motor column
 left main coronary (artery)

 left middle cerebral (artery)
 living male child
 lymphocyte-mediated cytolysis
 lymphocyte-mediated cytotoxicity
 lymphocyte microcytotoxicity
 lymphomyeloid complex

LMCA
 left main coronary artery
 left middle cerebral artery

LMCAD
 left main coronary artery disease

LMCAT
 left middle cerebral artery thrombosis

LMCL
 left midclavicular line
 lower midclavicular line

LMCT
 ligand-to-metal charge transfer

LMD
 left main disease (cardiology)
 lipid-moiety modified derivative
 local medical doctor
 low molecular (weight) dextran *also*
 LMDX, LMWD

LMDF
 lupus miliaris disseminatus faciei

LMDX
 low molecular (weight) dextran *also*
 LMD, LMWD

LME
 left mediolateral episiotomy *also*
 LMLE
 leukocyte migration enhancement

LMEE
 left middle ear exploration

LMF
 left middle finger
 Leukeran (chlorambucil), methotrexate,
 and 5-fluorouracil
 leukocyte mitogenic factor
 lymphocyte mitogenic factor

LMFCC
 licensed marriage family and child
 counselor

LMFT
 licensed marriage and family therapist

lm/ft²
 lumen per square foot

LMG
lethal midline granuloma
low mobility group

LMH
lipid-mobilizing hormone

lm·h
lumen hour

LMI
leukocyte migration inhibition (assay)

LMIF
leukocyte migration inhibition factor

L/min, l/min
liters per minute *also* L/M, LPM,
lpm

L/min/m²
liter per minute per square meter

LMIR
leukocyte migration inhibition reaction

LMIT
leukocyte migration inhibition test

LML
large and medium lymphocytes
left mediolateral (episiotomy)
left middle lobe
lower midline

LMLE
left mediolateral episiotomy *also*
LME

LML scar w/h
lower midline scar with hernia

LMM
Lactobacillus maintenance medium
lentigo maligna melanoma
light molecular (weight) meromyosin

lm/m²
lumen per square meter

LMN
lower motor neuron *also* LM

LMNL
lower motor neuron lesion

LMO
localized molecular orbital

LMP
last menstrual period
left mentoposterior (fetal position)
also MLP
low malignant potential
lumbar puncture *also* LP

LMP-1
latent membrane protein-1
(expression)

LMR
left medial rectus (eye muscle)
linguomandibular reflex
localized magnetic resonance
log magnitude ratio

LMS
lateral medullary syndrome
leiomyosarcoma *also* LS

lm·s
lumen-second

LMSV
left maximal spatial voltage

LMT
left main trunk
left mentotransverse (fetal position)
also MLT
leukocyte migration technique
luteomammotrophic (hormone)

LMTA
Language Modalities Test for
Aphasia

LMV
larva migrans visceralis

LMW
low molecular weight

lm/W
lumen per watt *also* lpw

LMWD
low molecular weight dextran *also*
LMD, LMDX

LMWH
low molecular weight heparin

LN
labionasal
later (onset) nephrotic (syndrome)
Lesch-Nyhan (syndrome)

NOTES

L

417

LN *(continued)*
lipoid nephrosis
lobular neoplasia
lupus nephritis
lymph node

L/N
letter/numerical (system)

LN₂
liquid nitrogen

ln
logarithm, natural

LNa
low sodium *also* LoNa, LS

LNAA
large neutral amino acid

LNaCl
low salt

L-NAME
NG-nitro-L-arginine methyl ester

LNB
lymph node biopsy

LNC
lymph node cell

LND
Lesch-Nyhan disease
light-near dissociation
lymph node dissection

LNE
lymph node enlargement
lymph node excision

LNF
laparoscopic Nissen fundoplication

LNG
liquified natural gas

LNH
large number hypothesis

LNI
logarithm neutralization index

LNKS
low natural killer syndrome

LNL
lower normal limit
lymph node lymphocyte

LNLS
linear-nonlinear least squares

LNM
lymph node metastasis

LNMP
last normal menstrual period

LNNB
Luria-Nebraska Neuropsychological Battery

LNP
large neuronal polypeptide

LNPF
lymph node permeability factor

LNR
lymph node region

LNS
lateral nuclear stratum
Lesch-Nyhan syndrome
lymph node seeking (equivalent)

LO
lateral oblique (x-ray view)
leucine oxidation
linguo-occlusal
low *also* L
lower *also* L
lowest *also* L
lumbar orthosis

LOA
leave of absence
Leber optic atrophy
left occipitoanterior (fetal position)
looseness of associations
lysis of adhesions

LOC
laxative of choice *also* LXC
left main disease
level of care
level of consciousness
liquid organic compound
local *also* loc
locus of control
loss of consciousness
low-molecular-weight dextran

loc
local *also* LOC
localized
location

LoCa
low calcium (diet) *also* lo calc

lo cal
low-calorie (diet) *also* LC

lo calc
low-calcium (diet) *also* LoCa

LOC-C
Locus of Control-Chance

loc. cit.
in the place cited [L. *loco citato*]

loc. dol.
to the painful spot [L. *loco dolenti*]

LOC-E
Locus of Control-External

LoCHO
low carbohydrate

LoChol
low cholesterol

LOC-I
Locus of Control-Internal

LOCM
low-osmolality contrast material
low osmolar contrast medium

LOC-PO
Locus of Control-Powerful Others

LOD
line of duty
logarithm of odds (method of
genetics linkage analysis) *also* lod

lod
logarithm of odds *also* LOD

LOF
leaking of fluid
low outlet forceps

LOFD
low outlet forceps delivery

log.
logarithm

logMAR
logarithmic Minimum Angle of
Resolution

LOH
loop of Henle

LOHF
late onset hepatic failure

LOI
level of incompetence
level of injury

Leyton Obsessive Inventory
limit of impurities

LOIH
left oblique inguinal hernia

LoK
low kalium (potassium)

LOL
left occipitolateral (fetal position)

Lol p
Lolium perenne

LOM
left otitis media
limitation of motion
limitation of movement
loss of motion
loss of movement
low-osmolar (contrast) medium

LOMAC
leucovorin, Oncovin, methotrexate,
Adriamycin, cyclophosphamide

LOMPT
Lincoln-Oseretsky Motor Performance
Test

LOMSA
left otitis media, suppurative, acute

LOMSC, LOMSCH
left otitis media, suppurative, chronic

LoNa
low sodium *also* LNa, LS

long.
longitudinal

LOP
laparoscopic orchiopexy
leave on pass
left occiput posterior (fetal position)

LoPro
low protein *also* LP

LOPS
length of patient stay

LOQ
Leadership Opinion Questionnaire
lower outer quadrant

LOR
lorazepam *also* LRZ

NOTES

LOR *(continued)*
 lorcainide
 loss of righting (reflex)

lord
 lordosis
 lordotic

LORS-1
 Level of Rehabilitation Scale 1

LOS
 length of stay
 loss of site
 low (cardiac) output syndrome
 lower (o)esophageal sphincter
 (pressure)

LOT
 lateral olfactory tract
 left occipitotransverse (fetal position)
 lengthened off time

lot.
 lotion

LOV
 large opaque vesicle
 loss of vision

LOWBI
 low-birth-weight infant

lox.
 liquid oxygen

LOZ
 lozenge

LP
 labile peptide
 labile protein
 laboratory procedure
 lactic peroxidase
 lamina propria
 laryngopharyngeal
 latency period
 latent period
 lateral plantar
 lateral pylorus
 latex particle
 leading pole
 leukocyte poor
 leukocytic pyrogen
 levator palati
 lichen planus
 ligamentum patellae
 lightly padded
 light perception *also* LPerc
 linear programming
 linguopulpal

lipoprotein
lost privileges
low potency
low power (microscopy)
low pressure
low protein *also* LoPro
lumbar puncture *also* LMP
lumboperitoneal
lung parenchyma
lymphocyte predominant
lymphoid plasma
lymphoid predominance
lymphomatoid papulosis
lymphomatous polyposis
(nucleus) lateralis posterior

L/P
 lactate/pyruvate (ratio)
 liver/plasma (concentration ratio)
 lymphocyte/polymorph (ratio)
 lymph/plasma (ratio)

LPA
 larval photoreceptor axon
 latex particle agglutination
 left pulmonary artery

Lp(a)
 lipoprotein(a)

LPAM, L-PAM, *l*-PAM
 L-phenylalanine mustard (melphalan)
 also MEL

LPB
 lipoprotein B
 low-profile bioprosthesis *also* LPBP

LPBP
 low-profile bioprosthesis *also* LPB

LPC
 laser photocoagulation
 late positive component
 leukocyte-poor cell
 lysophosphatidyl choline

LPCM
 low-placed conus medullaris

LPc̄P
 light perception with projection

LPCT
 late proximal cortical tubule

LPD
 leiomyomatosis peritonealis
 disseminata
 low-protein diet
 luteal phase defect
 lymphoproliferative disease

LPDA
left posterior descending artery

LPDF
lipoprotein-deficient fraction

LPE
lipoprotein electrophoresis *also* LEP

LPerc
light perception *also* LP

LPF
leukocytosis-promoting factor
leukopenia factor
lipopolysaccharide factor
liver plasma flow
localized plaque formation
low-power field *also* lpf
lymphocytosis-promoting factor

lpf
low-power field *also* LPF

LPFB
left posterior fascicular block

LPFN
low–pass-filtered noise

LPFS
low–pass-filtered signal

LPG
liquified petroleum gas

LPH
left posterior hemiblock *also* LPHB
lipotropic hormone
lipotropic pituitary hormone
(lipotropin)

LPHB
left posterior hemiblock *also* LPH

LPHD
lymphocyte predominance Hodgkin
disease

LPI
laser peripheral iridectomy
left posterior-inferior
long process of incus
lysinuric protein intolerance

LPICA
left posterior internal carotid artery

LPIFB
left posterior-inferior fascicular block

LPIH
left posterior-inferior hemiblock

LPK
liver pyruvate kinase

LPL
lamina propria lymphocyte
left posterolateral
lichen planus-like lesion
lipoprotein lipase *also* LL

LPLA
lipoprotein lipase activity

LPLND
laparoscopic pelvic lymph node
dissection

LPM
lateral pterygoid muscle
left posterior measurement
liver plasma membrane
localized pretibial myxedema
lymphoproliferative malignancy

Lpm
liters per minute *also* L/M, L/min,
lpm

lpm
lines (printed) per minute
liters per minute *also* L/M, L/min,
Lpm

LPN
Licensed Practical Nurse

LPO
lateral preoptic (area)
left posterior oblique
left posterior occipital
light perception only
lobus parolfactorius

LPOA
lateral preoptic area

L POST
left posterior

LPP
lateral pterygoid plate
leak point pressure

NOTES

LP&P
light perception and projection

LPPH
late postpartum hemorrhage

LPR
lactate-pyruvate ratio
late-phase response

LPRBC
leukocyte-poor red blood cell

LProj
light projection

LPS
last Pap smear
levator palpebrae superioris (muscle)
linear profile scan
lipase
lipopolysaccharide
London Psychogeriatric Scale

lps
liter per second

LPSR
lipopolysaccharide receptor

LPT
Language Proficiency Test
lateral position test
lipotropin

LPV
left portal view
left pulmonary vein
lymphopathia venereum
lymphotropic papovavirus

LPVP
left posterior ventricular pre-excitation

LPW
lateral pharyngeal wall

lpw
lumen per watt *also* lm/W

LPX, Lp-X
lipoprotein-X

LQ
longevity quotient
lordosis quotient
lower quadrant
lowest quadrant

LQTS
long Q-T syndrome

LR
labeled release (experiment)
laboratory reference
laboratory report
labor room
lactated Ringer (solution) *also* lat Rin
large reticulocyte
latency reaction
latency relaxation
lateral rectus (eye muscle)
left rotation
ligand receptor
light reaction
light reflex
limit of reaction
lingual ridge
lingual root
lymphocyte recruitment

L-R, L R, L→R, L/R
left to right

L&R
left and right

Lr
lawrencium *also* Lw
limes reacting (dose of diphtheria
toxin)

LRA
left radial artery
left renal artery
low right atrium

LRC
locomotor-respiratory coupling
lower rib cage

LRD
living related donor
living renal donor

LRDT
living related donor transplant

LRE
lamina rara externa
least restrictive environment
leukemic reticuloendotheliosis
lymphoreticuloendothelial

LREH
low renin essential hypertension

LRF
latex and resorcinol formaldehyde
left rectus femoris
liver residue factor
luteinizing hormone-releasing factor
also LH-RF

LRH
luteinizing hormone-releasing hormone
also LHRH, LH-RH

LRI
lamina rara interna
lower respiratory (tract) illness *also* LRTI
lower respiratory (tract) infection *also* LRTI
lymphocyte reactivity index

LRLT
living-related donor transplantation

LRM
left radical mastectomy

LRMP
last regular menstrual period

LRN
lateral reticular nucleus

LRNA
low renin, normal aldosterone

LRND
left radical neck dissection

LROP
lower radicular obstetrical paralysis

LRP
lichen ruber planus
lipoprotein receptor-related protein
long-range planning

LRQ
lower right quadrant

LRQG
left rostral quarter ganglion

LRR
labyrinthine righting reflex
lymphatic return rate

LRS
lactated Ringer solution
lateral recess stenosis
lateral recess syndrome
lumboradicular syndrome

LRSF
lactating rat serum factor
liver regenerating serum factor

LR-SH
left-right shunt

LRSP
long-range systems planning

LRSS
late respiratory systemic syndrome

LRT
living related transplant
local radiation therapy
lower respiratory tract

LRTI
ligament reconstruction with tendon interposition
living related transplant donor
lower respiratory tract illness *also* LRI
lower respiratory tract infection *also* LRI

LRV
left renal vein

LRZ
lorazepam *also* LOR

LS
lateral septal
lateral suspensor (ligament)
left sacrum
left septum
left side
legally separated
Leigh syndrome
leiomyosarcoma *also* LMS
length of stay
lesser sac
Letterer-Siwe (disease)
Libman-Sacks (disease)
lichen sclerosus et atrophicus
life science
light sensitive
light sensitivity
light sleep
liminal sensation
liminal sensitivity
linear scleroderma
lipid synthesis
liver scan
liver and spleen *also* L&S
lower segment
low-sodium (diet) *also* LNa, LoNa
lumbar spine
lumbosacral *also* L/S
lumbosacral spine

NOTES

L

LS *(continued)*
lung strip
lymphosarcoma *also* LSA, Lyp

L-S
lipid-saccharide

L/S
lactase/sucrase (ratio)
lecithin/sphingomyelin (ratio) *also* l/s
liver/spleen (ratio)
lumbosacral *also* LS

L&S
ligation and stripping
liver and spleen *also* LS

l/s
lecithin/sphingomyelin (ratio) *also* L/S

LSA
Language Sampling Analysis
left sacroanterior (fetal position)
left subclavian artery
leukocyte-specific activity
lichen sclerosis (et) atrophicus *also*
LS&A
lipid-bound sialic acid *also* LBSA
lymphosarcoma *also* LS, Lyp

LS&A
lichen sclerosis et atrophicus *also*
LSA

LSANA
leukocyte-specific antinuclear antibody

LSAR
lymphosarcoma cell

LSA/RCS
lymphosarcoma-reticulum cell sarcoma

LSB
least significant bit (binary numbers)
left scapular border
left sternal border
local standby
long spike burst
lumbar sympathetic block

LSBM
lumbar spine bone mineral density

LS BPS
laparoscopic bilateral partial
salpingectomy

LSC
late systolic click
left-sided colon (cancer)
left subclavian (artery)
lichen simplex chronicus

liquid scintillation counting
liquid-solid chromatography
lower segment cesarean (section) *also*
LSCS

LSCA, LScA
left scapuloanterior (fetal position)
left subclavian artery

LSCL
lymphosarcoma cell leukemia

LSCP, LScP
left scapuloposterior (fetal position)

LSCS
lower segment cesarean section *also*
LSC

LSCV
left subclavian vein

LSD
least significant difference
least significant digit (computers)
low-salt diet
low-sodium diet
lysergic acid diethylamide *also* LSD-
25

LSD-25
lysergic acid diethylamide *also* LSD

LSE
left sternal edge
local side effect

l/sec
liters per second

LSEP
left somatosensory evoked potential

LSF
line spread function
low saturated fat
lymphocyte-stimulating factor

LSG
labial salivary gland

LSH
lutein-stimulating hormone
lymphocyte-stimulating hormone

LSI
large-scale integration
Life Satisfaction Index
light scattering index
lumbar spine index

LSK
liver, spleen, and kidneys

LSKM
liver-spleen-kidney megaly

LSL
left sacrolateral (fetal position)
left short leg (brace)
lymphosarcoma (cell) leukemia

LSM
late systolic murmur
lymphocyte separation medium

LSN
left substantia nigra
left sympathetic nerve

LSO
lateral superior olive (of brain)
left salpingo-oophorectomy
left superior oblique
lumbosacral orthosis

LSP
left sacroposterior (fetal position)
liver-specific membrane lipoprotein
liver-specific protein

LSp
life span

L-Spar
asparaginase (Elspar) *also* Aase, ASP, Asp

L-spine
lumbar spine

LSQ
least square

LSR
lanthanide shift reagent (in magnetic resonance imaging)
left superior rectus

LSRA
low septal right atrium

LSS
Life Span Study
Life Study Sample
life support station
liver-spleen scan
lumbar spinal stenosis
lumbosacral spine

LSSA
lipid-soluble secondary antioxidant

LST
lateral sinus thrombophlebitis
lateral spinothalamic tract
left sacrotransverse (fetal position)

LSTC
laparoscopic tubal cautery
laparoscopic tubal coagulation

LSTL
laparoscopic tubal ligation *also* LTL

Ls & Ts
lines and tubes

LSU
lactose-saccharose-urea (agar)
life support unit

LSV
lateral sacral vein
left subclavian vein

LSVC
left superior vena cava

LSW
left-sided weakness

LSWA
large amplitude, slow wave activity (in electroencephalography)

LT
(heat-)labile toxin
lactate threshold
laminar tomography
left *also* L, (L), l, laev., lf, lt
left thigh
left triceps
less than
lethal time
leukotriene
Levin tube
levothyroxine
light *also* L, lt
light touch
long term
low temperature
low transverse
lues test
lumbar traction
lymphocyte transformation
lymphocyte transitional
lymphocytic thyroiditis

L

NOTES

425

LT *(continued)*
lymphocytotoxin *also* LC, LCT
lymphotoxin

lt
left *also* L, (L), l, laev., lf, LT
light *also* L, LT
low tension

LTA
laryngeal tracheal anesthesia
leukotriene A
lipoate transacetylase
lipotechoic acid
local tracheal anesthesia
lymphocyte-transforming activity

LTAF
local tissue advancement flap

LTAS
lead tetraacetate Schiff
left transatrial septal

LTB
laparoscopic tubal banding
laryngotracheobronchitis
leukotriene B

LTB4
leukotriene B4

LTC
large transformed cell
left to count
leukotriene C
lidocaine tissue concentration
long-term care
low transverse cesarean
lysed tumor cell

LTCBDE
laparoscopic transcystic common bile
duct exploration

LTCF
long-term care facility

LTCP
L-tryptophan-containing product

LTCS
low transverse cervical (cesarean)
section

LTD
largest tumor dimension
Laron-type dwarfism
leukotriene D
limited *also* ltd
long-term disability

ltd
limited *also* LTD

LTDA
limited quantity (test performed on
small specimen)

LTE
laryngotracheoesophageal
leukotriene E

LT-ECG
long-term electrocardiography

LTF
lipotropic factor
lymphocyte-transforming factor

LTG
long-term goal

LTGA
left transposition of great artery

LTH
lactogenic hormone *also* LGH
local tumor hyperthermia
low-temperature holding
(pasteurization)
luteotropic hormone *also* LH

LtH
left-handed

LTI
low temperature isotropic
lupus-type inclusion

LTK
laser thermal keratoplasty

LTL
laparoscopic tubal ligation *also* LSTL

lt lat
left lateral *also* LL, LLAT, L lat

LTM
long-term memory

LTO
laparoscopic total occlusion

LTOT
long-term oxygen therapy

LTP
laryngotracheoplasty
laser trabeculoplasty
leukocyte thromboplastin
long-term potentiation
L-tryptophan

LTPP
lipothiamide pyrophosphate

LTR
long terminal repeat (sequence)
lymphocyte transfer reaction

LTS
laparoscopic tubal sterilization
long-term storage
long-term surviving
long tract sign (neurology)

LTT
lactose tolerance test
leucine tolerance test
limited treadmill test
lymphoblastic transformation test
lymphocyte transformation test

LTUI
low transverse uterine incision

LTV
Lucké tumor virus
lung thermal volume

LTW
Leydig-cell tumor in Wistar (rat)

LTX
lophotoxin

LTx
lung transplant

LU
left uninjured
left uninvolved
left upper (limb)
living unit
loudness unit
lung *also* L, Lu
lytic unit

L&U
lower and upper (extremities)

Lu
lung *also* L, LU
lutetium

^{197}Lu
lutetium-177

LUA
left upper arm

LUC
large unstained cell

luc. prim.
at daybreak [L. *luce prima*]

LUD
left uterine displacement device

LUE
left upper extremity *also* LUX

LUF
luteinized unruptured follicle

LUFS
luteinized unruptured follicle
syndrome

LUIS
low-dose urea in invert sugar

LUL
left upper (eye)lid
left upper limb
left upper lobe (lung)
left upper lung

lum, lumb
lumbar

LUMO
lowest unoccupied molecular orbital

LUNA
laser uterosacral nerve ablation

LUO
left ureteral orifice

LUOB
left upper outer buttock

LUOQ
left upper outer quadrant

LUP
left ureteropelvic (junction)

LUQ
left upper quadrant

LURD
living unrelated donor

LUS
laparoscopic ultrasound
lower uterine segment

LUSB
left upper scapular border
left upper sternal border

L

NOTES

427

LUST
lower uterine segment transverse (cesarean section)

lut.
yellow [L. *luteum*]

LUTT
lower urinary tract tumor

LUV
large unilamellar vesicle

LUX
left upper extremity *also* LUE

LV
Lactobacillus viridescens
lactoovovegetarian
laryngeal vestibule
lateral ventricle
left ventricle
left ventricular (echocardiography images)
leucovorin *also* LCV, LEU, LVR
leukemia virus
live vaccine
live virus
low vertical
low volume
lumbar vertebra
lung volume

lv
leave

LVA
left ventricular aneurysm
left ventricular aneurysmectomy
left vertebral artery
low vision aid

LVAD
left ventricular assist device

L-VAM
leuprolide acetate, vinblastine, Adriamycin (doxorubicin), and mitomycin

LVAS
left ventricular assist system

LVAT
left ventricular activation time

LVBBB
left ventricular bundle branch block

LVBP
left ventricle bypass pump

LVC
laser vision correction
low-viscosity cement

LVCS
low vertical cesarean section

LVD
left ventricular dimension *also* LVDI
left ventricular dysfunction

LV$_D$, LVd
left ventricular (end-)diastolic (pressure)

LVDd
left ventricular dimension (in end)-diastole

LVDI
left ventricular dimension *also* LVD

LVDP
left ventricular diastolic pressure

LVDT
linear variable differential transformer

LVDV
left ventricular diastolic volume

LVE
left ventricular ejection
left ventricular enlargement

LVED
left ventricular end-diastole

LVEDa
left ventricular end-diastolic area

LVEDC
left ventricular end-diastolic circumference

LVEDD
left ventricular end-diastolic diameter
left ventricular end-diastolic dimension

LVEDP
left ventricular end-diastolic pressure *also* LVEP

LVEDV
left ventricular end-diastolic volume

LVEF
left ventricular ejection fraction

LVEndo
left ventricular endocardial (half)

LVEP
left ventricular end-diastolic pressure *also* LVEDP

LVER
liver fraction elevated

LVESa
left ventricular end-systolic area

LVESD
left ventricular end-systolic dimension

LVESV
left ventricular end-systolic volume

LVESVI
left ventricular end-systolic volume index

LVET
left ventricular ejection time

LVETI
left ventricular ejection time index

LVF
left ventricular failure
left ventricular function
left visual field
low-voltage fast
low-voltage foci

LVFP
left ventricular filling pressure

LVFT$_2$
left ventricular slow filling time

LVG
left ventrogluteal
lymphogranuloma venereum *also* LGV

LVH
large vessel hematocrit
left ventricular hypertrophy

LVI
left ventricular insufficiency
left ventricular ischemia

LVID
left ventricular internal diastolic
left ventricular internal dimension

LVIDD
left ventricular internal diastolic diameter

LVIDd
left ventricular internal dimension diastole

LVID(ed)
left ventricular internal diameter (end diastole)

LVID(es)
left ventricular internal diameter (end systole)

LVIDP
left ventricular initial diastolic pressure

LVIDs
left ventricular internal dimension systole

LVIV
left ventricular infarct volume

LVL
left vastus lateralis (muscle)

LVLG
left ventrolateral gluteal (injection site)

LVM
lateral ventromedial (nucleus)
left ventricular mass

LVMF
left ventricular minute flow

LVMM
left ventricular muscle mass

LVN
lateral ventricular nerve
lateral vestibular nucleus
Licensed Visiting Nurse
Licensed Vocational Nurse
limiting viscosity number

LVO
left ventricular outflow
left ventricular overactivity

LVOA
left ventricular overactivity

LVOT
left ventricular outflow tract

LVP
large volume paracentesis
large volume parenteral (infusion)
left ventricular pressure
levator veli palatini (muscle)
lysine-vasopressin

L

NOTES

LVPEP
left ventricular preejection period

LVPFR
left ventricular peak filling rate

LVPSP
left ventricular peak systolic pressure

LVPW
left ventricular posterior wall

LVPWT
left ventricular posterior wall
thickness

LVR
leucovorin *also* LCV, LEU, LV
limb vascular resistance
lung volume reduction

L₁VR
first lumbar ventral (nerve) root

L₂VR
second lumbar ventral (nerve) root

LVRS
lung volume reduction surgery

LVS
lateral venous sinus
left ventricular strain

LVs
(mean) left ventricular systolic
(pressure)

LVSEMI
left ventricular subendocardial
myocardial ischemia

LVSI
left ventricular systolic index
lymphvascular involvement

LVSO
left ventricular systolic output

LVSP
left ventricular systolic pressure

LVST
lateral vestibulospinal tract

LVSV
left ventricular stroke volume

LVSW
left ventricular septal wall
left ventricular stroke work

LVSWI
left ventricular stroke work index

LVT
left ventricular tension
lysine vasotonin

LVT₁
left ventricular fast filling time

LVV
left ventricular volume
LeVeen valve
live varicella vaccine

LVW
lateral vaginal wall
lateral ventricular width
left ventricular wall
left ventricular work

LVW/HW
lateral ventricular width to
hemispheric width

LVWI
left ventricular work index

LVWM
left ventricular wall motion

LVWMA
left ventricular wall motion
abnormality

LVWMI
left ventricular wall motion index

LVWT
left ventricular wall thickness

LW
lacerating wound
lateral wall
Lee-White (blood clotting method)
also L&W, L/W, LWCT
left (ear), warm (stimulus)
Léri-Weill (syndrome)
lung weight
lung width

L-10-W
levulose (10%) in water

L/W, L&W
Lee and White (clotting time) *also*
LW, LWCT

Lw
lawrencium *also* Lr

LWBS
left without being seen

LWC
leave without consent

LWCT
Lachar-Wrobel Critical Items
Lee-White clotting time *also* LW,
L&W, L/W

LWD
living with disease

LWK
large white kidney

LWP
large whirlpool
lateral wall pressure

LX, Lx
latex *also* L
local irradiation
lower extremity *also* LE, L ext, l/ext,
lx
lux *also* lx

lx
larynx *also* lar
lower extremity *also* LE, L ext, l/ext,
LX, Lx
lux *also* LX, Lx

LXC
laxative of choice *also* LOC

LXT
left exotropia

LY
lymphocyte *also* lym, lymph
lyophilization

LYDMA
lymphocyte-detected membrane antigen

LYEL
lost years of expected life

LYG
lymphomatoid granulomatosis

LYM
lymph

lym, lymph
lymphocyte *also* LY
lymphocytic

LYMPH%
percentage of lymphocytes (in
differential count)

LyNeF
lytic nephritic factor

lyo
lyophilized

LYP
lactose, yeast, and peptone (agar)
lower yield point

Lyp
lymphosarcoma *also* LS, LSA

LYS, Lys
lysine *also* K
lysosome

LySLk
lymphoma syndrome leukemia

LYTES, lytes
electrolytes *also* elytes

LZM, lzm
lysozyme

LZT
lead/zirconium/titanium

L

NOTES

M

blood factor in the MNS blood group system
cardiac murmur *also* m, (m)
chin [L. *mentum*] *also* m.
concentration in moles per liter
death [L. *mors*]
dullness (of sound) [L. *mutitas*]
dumbness [L. *mutitas*]
handful [L. *manipulus*] *also* m., man., manip.
macerated [L. *macerare*] *also* m
macerate [L. *macerare*] *also* m.
macroglobulin
magnetization
male
malignant *also* MAL, mal, malig
manual
marital
married
masculine
mass
massage *also* mass, MSS, mss
maternal contribution
matrix
matt (dull, slightly granular, bacterial colonies)
mature *also* MAT, Mat., mat.
maximum
mean *also* m, μ
meatus
media
medial
median *also* m, md
mediator (chemical released in the tissues)
medical
medicine
medium
mega-
megohm
melts at *also* m
membrane
memory (associative)
mental
mesial *also* m, MES
meta-
metabolite
metal
metastasis *also* MET, met, metas
meter
methionine *also* Met
method

methotrexate *also* MTRX, MTX
mexiletine
million
minim
minimum
minute
mitochondria
mitosis
mitral
mix
mixed
mixture
molarity
molar (permanent tooth)
molar (solution)
mole
molecular
molecular weight
moment of force
Monday
monkey
monocyte
month *also* MO, mo, mon
morgan (unit of gene separation)
morphine
mother
motile
mouse
mouth
movement response to human figure
mucoid (colony)
mucous (adjective)
mucus (noun)
multipara
murmur *also* m, (m)
muscle
muscular response to electrical stimulation of motor nerve
mu (12th letter of Greek alphabet), uppercase
myeloma or macroglobulinemia (component)
myopia
myopic
myosin
noon [L. *meridies*] *also* m., N
soften [L. *macerare*] *also* ma., mac
strength of pole
thousand [L. *mille*]

M1

left mastoid

M2
right mastoid
vincristine, carmustine,
cyclophosphamide, melphalan, and
prednisone

M–2
vincristine, carmustine,
cyclophosphamide, melphalan, and
prednisone

M/3
middle third (long bones)

M/10
tenth molar solution

M/100
hundredth molar solution

M^2
square meter (body surface) *also* m^2

M$_1$
mitral first sound (slight dullness)
myeloblast

M$_2$
mitral second sound (marked
dullness)
promyelocyte

M$_3$
mitral third sound (absolute dullness)
myelocyte at third stage of
maturation

M$_4$
myelocyte at fourth stage of
maturation

M$_5$
metamyelocyte

M$_6$
band form in sixth stage of
myelocyte maturation

M$_7$
polymorphonuclear neutrophil *also*
PMN, PMNN

M$_8$
spin quantum number

(m)
by mouth *also* m
murmur *also* M, m

m
by mouth *also* (m), PO, p.o.
electromagnetic moment
electron rest mass
in the morning [L. *mane*]

magnetic moment *also* μ
magnetic quantum number
mass
me
mean *also* M, μ
median *also* M
melts at *also* M
mesial *also* M, MES
meter
milli-
minim
minute
modulus
molality
molar (deciduous tooth)
morphine
motile
mucoid
murmur *also* M, (m)
sample mean

m.
chin [L. *mentum*] *also* M
handful [L. *manipulus*] *also* M
macerate [L. *macerare*] *also* M
mix [L. *misce*]
mixture [L. *mistura*] *also* mist.
noon [L. *meridies*] *also* M, m.
send [L. *mitte*] *also* mit.

m^2
square meter (body surface) *also* M^2

m^3
cubic meter *also* cu m

M/A
male, altered (animal) *also* MALT
mood and/or affect

MA
machine
mafenide acetate
main arteriole
mandelic acid
manifest achievement
Martin-Albright (syndrome)
masseter
maternal aunt
mean arterial
medical abbreviation
medical assistance
medical assistant
medical audit
medical authorization
mega-ampere
megaloblastic anemia
megestrol acetate

membrane antigen
menstrual age
mental age
mentum anterior (fetal position)
metatarsus aductus
meter angle
Mexican-American
microagglutination
microaneurysm
microcytotoxicity assay
microscopic agglutination
Miller-Abbott (tube)
milliampere
mitochondrial antibody
mitogen activation
mitotic apparatus
mixed agglutination
moderately advanced
monoamine
monoarthritis
monoclonal antibody *also* MAB,
 MAb, MCA, MCAB, MoAb
motorcycle accident *also* MCA
multiple action
muscle activity
mutagenic activity
myelinated axon

MA–1
mechanically assisted (Bennett brand
 of respirator)

Ma
mass of atom
masurium (technetium)

mA
meter-angle
milliamperage
milliampere *also* ma

mÅ
milliangstrom

ma
milliampere *also* mA

ma.
soften [L. *macera*] *also* M, mac

MAA
macroaggregated albumin *also* MIAA
Medical Assistance for the Aged
melanoma-associated antigen

monoarticular arthritis
technetium-99m macroaggregated
 albumin *also* ^{99mTc}-MAA

^{99mTc}-MAA
technetium-99m macroaggregated
 albumin *also* MAA

MAAAP
macroaggregated albumin arterial
 perfusion

MAACL
Multiple Affect Adjective Check List

MAAS
Multicenter Anti-Atheroma Study

MAB, MAb
maximal androgen blockade
monoclonal antibody *also* MA, MCA,
 MCAB, MoAb

MABI
Mother's Assessment of the Behavior
 of Her Infant

MABOP
Mustargen (nitrogen mustard),
 Adriamycin (doxorubicin), bleomycin,
 Oncovin (vincristine), and prednisone

MABP
mean arterial blood pressure

MAC
MacConkey (agar)
MacIntosh (blade)
macrocytic erythrocyte
macule
malignancy-associated change
maximal acid concentration
maximal allowable concentration
maximal allowable cost
medical alert center
membrane attack complex
membranolytic attack complex
methotrexate, actinomycin D, and
 chlorambucil
methotrexate, actinomycin D, and
 cyclophosphamide
midarm circumference
minimal anesthetic concentration
minimal antibiotic concentration
minimum alveolar anesthetic
 concentration

M

NOTES

MAC *(continued)*
minimum alveolar concentration
Minimum Auditory Capabilities Test
mitral annular calcium
modulator of adenylate cyclase
monitored anesthesia care
monitored anesthesia control
multiaccess catheter
multidimensional actuarial
classification
Mycobacterium avium complex
Mycobacterium avium-intracellulare
also MAI

1-MAC
1-minimum alveolar concentration

MAC III
methotrexate, actinomycin D, and
cyclophosphamide

Mac
MacIntosh (laryngoscope blade)
macula

mac
maceration *also* macer
soften [L. *macerare*] *also* M, ma.

MAC AWAKE
minimal alveolar (anesthetic)
concentration (patient recovering
from general anesthesia able to
respond to instructions)

MACC
macroovalocyte
methotrexate, Adriamycin
(doxorubicin), cyclophosphamide, and
CCNU (lomustine)
methotrexate, ara-C,
cyclophosphamide, and CCNU

m. accur.
mix very accurately [L. *misce
accuratissime*]

MACDP
Metropolitan Atlanta Congenital
Defects Program

MACE
methylchloroform chloroacetophenone

macer
maceration *also* mac

mAChR
muscarinic acetylcholine receptor

MACOB
methotrexate, Adriamycin
(doxorubicin), cyclophosphamide,
Oncovin (vincristine), bleomycin

MACOP-B
methotrexate-leucovorin, Adriamycin,
cyclophosphamide, Oncovin,
prednisone, bleomycin

MACR
macrocytosin
mean axillary count rate

macro
macrocyte
macrocytic
macroscopic

macro-EMG
macroelectromyography

MACS
magnetically activated cell sorter
Multicenter AIDS Cohort Study

MACs
malignancy-associated changes

MAD
maximal allowable dose
maximum accumulated dose
maximum acid output
methandriol
methylandrostenediol
mind-altering drug
minimal average dose
myoadenylate deaminase

mAD, MADA
muscle adenylate deaminase

MADD
Mothers Against Drunk Drivers
multiple acyl–CoA dehydrogenation
deficiency

MADDOC
mechlorethamine, Adriamycin,
dacarbazine, DDP, Oncovin, and
cyclophosphamide

MADRS
Montgomery-Asberg Depression Rating
Scale

MAE
medical air evacuation
moves all extremities
Multilingual Aphasia Examination

MAEW
moves all extremities well

MAF
macrophage-activating factor
macrophage-agglutinating factor
master apical file
minimal audible field
minimum acceptable field
minimum audible field
mouse amniotic fluid
movement after effect

MAFA
midarm fat area
movement-associated fetal (heart rate)
 accelerations

MAFH
macroaggregated ferrous hydroxide

MAFO
molded ankle foot orthosis

MAFP
maternal alpha fetoprotein

MAG
multifocal atrophic gastritis
myelin-associated glycoprotein

MAG-3
mercaptotriglycylglycine

Mag
magnesium *also* mag, Mg

mag
large [L. *magnus*]
magnesium *also* Mag, Mg
magnification
magnify

mag cit
magnesium citrate

MAGE
mean amplitude of glycerine
 excursion

MAGF
male accessory gland fluid

MAggF
macrophage agglutination factor

MAGIC
microprobe analysis generalized
 intensity correction

MAGP
meatal advancement
 glandulophaleoplasty
microfil-associated glycoprotein

MAGPI
meatal advancement, glanduloplasty,
 penoscrotal junction meatomy
meatal advancement and glansplasty

MAGS
Multidimensional Assessment of Gains
 in School (psychologic test)

mag sulf
magnesium sulfate

mAH
milliampere-hours

MAHA
microangiopathic hemolytic anemia
 also MHA
microangiopathic hemolytic aneurysm

MAHH
malignancy-associated humoral
 hypercalcemia

MAI
maximal aggregation index
microscopic aggregation index
minor acute illness
morbid anxiety inventory
movement assessment of infants
Mycobacterium avium-intracellulare
 also MAC

MAID
mesna, Adriamycin, ifosfamide, and
 dacarbazine
mesna, Adriamycin, interleukin-3, and
 dacarbazine

MAIDS
murine-acquired immunodeficiency
 syndrome

MAII
Milwaukee Academic Interest
 Inventory

MAK-6
monoclonal anticytokeratin

MAKA
major karyotypic abnormality

M

NOTES

MAL
malfunction *also* Mal
malignant *also* M, mal, malig
midaxillary line

Mal
ill [L. *malum*]
malate
malfunction *also* MAL

mal
malignant *also* M, MAL, malig

mal.
by blistering [L. *malanandro*]

MALA
malarial parasites

MALAR
malaria

Mal-BSA
maleated bovine serum albumin

MALG
Minnesota antilymphoblast globulin

malig
malignant *also* M, MAL, mal

MALIMET
Master List of Medical (Indexing) Terms

MALT
male, altered (animal) *also* M/A
mucosa-associated lymphoid tissue

MAM
methylazoxymethanol

M-Am
compound myopic astigmatism

mam
milliampere-minute *also* MA min, ma-min

MAMA
midarm muscle area
monoclonal antimalignin antibody

MAM Ac
methylazoxymethanol acetate

MAMC
mean arm muscle circumference
midarm muscle circumference

MAmg
medial amygdaloid (nucleus)

MA min, ma-min
milliampere-minute *also* mam

mammo
mammography

mAMSA, m-AMSA
amsacrine

MaMT
Maudsley Mentation Test

MAN
magnocellular nucleus (of anterior neostratum)
mannose

man.
handful [L. *manipulus*] *also* M, m., manip.
manipulate
morning [L. *mane*]

mand
mandible
mandibular

manip.
handful [L. *manipulus*] *also* M, m
manipulation

MANOVA
multivariate analysis of variance

man. pr.
first thing in morning [L. *mane primo*]

manu
manufacture

MAO
maximal acid output
medical ankle orthosis
monoamine oxidase

MAOI
monoamine oxidase inhibitor

MAP
malignant atrophic papulosis
maximal aerobic power
mean airway pressure
mean aortic pressure
mean arterial pressure
Medical Audit Program
megaloblastic anemia of pregnancy
mercapturic acid pathway
methyl acceptor protein
methylacetoxyprogesterone
methylaminopurine
microlithiasis alveolarum pulmonum
microtubule-associated protein
minimal audible pressure
minimum audible pressure

mitomycin, Adriamycin (doxorubicin),
and cisplatin
monophasic action potential
mouse antibody production (test)
Multiaxial Assessment of Pain
Muma Assessment Program
muscle-action potential
Musical Aptitude Profile

MAPA
muscle adenosine phosphoric acid

MAPC
migrating action potential complex

MAPD
monophasic action potential duration

MAPE
Multidimensional Assessment of
Philosophy of Education

MAPF
microatomized protein food

MAPI
microbial alkaline protease inhibitor
Millon Adolescent Personality
Inventory

MAPS
Make A Picture Story (test)
Multivessel Angioplasty Prognosis
Study

MAR
Main Admitting Room
marasmus
marrow
maximal aggregation ratio
medication administration record
microanalytical reagent
minimal angle resolution
mixed antiglobulin reaction

mar.
margin *also* marg, MG
marker (chromosome)

MARC
multifocal and recurrent choroidopathy

MARCATOR
Multicenter American Research Trial
with Cilazapril after Angioplasty to
Prevent

marg
margin *also* mar., MG

MARIA
macroaggregated radioiodinated
albumin

MARS
Mathematics Anxiety Rating Scale
Modular Acetabular Revision System
mouse antirat serum

MARSA
methicillin-aminoglycoside-resistant
Staphylococcus aureus

MARTI
mobile advanced real-time image

MAS
macrophage activation syndrome
Management Appraisal Survey
Manifest Anxiety Scale
Maternal Attitude Scale
McCune-Albright syndrome
mean allograft survival
meconium aspiration syndrome
medical advisory service
mesoatrial shunt
milk-alkali syndrome
milliamperage X seconds
milliampere-second *also* Mas, mA-s,
mas
minor axis shortening (of left
ventricle)
mobile arm support
Morgagni-Adams-Stokes (syndrome)
motion analysis system

Mas, mA-s, mas
milliampere-second *also* MAS

masc
masculine
mass concentration *also* massc

MASE
microsurgical extraction of sperm
from epididymis

MASER
microwave amplification by stimulated
emission of radiation

MASF
Melcher acid-soluble fraction

M

NOTES

MASH
Mobile Army Surgical Hospital
multiple automated sample harvester

mas. pil.
pill mass [L. *massa pilularum*]

MASS
mitral valve prolapse, aortic
anomalies, skeletal changes, and skin
changes

mass
massage *also* M, MSS, mss
massive

massc
mass concentration *also* masc

MAST
Michigan Alcoholism Screening Test
military antishock trousers (treatment)
motion artifact suppression technique

mAST
mitochondrial aspartate
aminotransferase

mast
mastectomy
mastoid

MAT
Manipulative Aptitude Test
manual arts therapist
maternal
maternity
mature *also* M, Mat., mat.
mean absorption time
medication administration team
methionineadenosyltransferase
Metropolitan Achievement Tests
microagglutination test
Miller-Abbott tube
Miller Analogies Test
motivation analysis test
multifocal atrial tachycardia
multiple agent therapy

Mat., mat.
material
maternal (origin)
maternity
mature *also* M, MAT

MATE
Maternal Attitudes Evaluation

MATSA
Marek associated tumor-specific
antigen

matut.
in the morning [L. *matutinus*]

MAU
Meyenburg-Altherr-Uehlinger
(syndrome)

MAV
mechanical auxiliary ventricle
minimal apparent viscosity
minute alveolar volume
movement arm vector
multinucleated atypia of the vulva
myeloblastosis-associated virus

MAVA
multiple abstract variance analysis

MAVIS
mobile artery and vein imaging
system

MAVR
mitral and aortic valve replacement

max
maxilla
maxillary
maximum

max EP
maximal esophageal pressure

MB
buccal margin
isoenzyme of creatine kinase
containing M and B subunits
Mallory body
mamillary body
margin, buccal
Marsh-Bendall (factor)
medulloblastoma
megabyte
mercury bougie
mesiobuccal
methyl bromide
methylene blue *also* MBl, MEB,
MeB
microbiologic assay
muscle balance
myocardial band
myocardial bridging

6MB
six-meal bland (diet)

Mb
mandible body
myoglobin *also* MbCO, MbO$_2$

m.b.
mix well [L. *misce bene*]

mb
  millibar *also* mbar

MBA
  methylbenzyl alcohol
  methylbischloroethylamine (nitrogen
    mustard)
  methylbovine albumin

M-BACOD
  methotrexate, bleomycin, Adriamycin
    (doxorubicin), cyclophosphamide,
    Oncovin (vincristine), and
    dexamethasone

m-BACOD
  moderate-dose methotrexate,
    bleomycin, Adriamycin,
    cyclophosphamide, Oncovin, and
    dexamethasone

M-BACOS
  methotrexate, bleomycin, Adriamycin,
    cyclophosphamide, Oncovin, and
    Solu-Medrol

MBAR
  myocardial β-adrenergic receptor

mbar
  millibar *also* mb

MBAS
  methylene blue active substance

MBB
  modified barbital buffer

MBC
  male breast cancer
  maximum bladder capacity
  maximum breathing capacity
  mesiobuccal cusp
  metastatic breast cancer
  methotrexate, bleomycin, and cisplatin
  methylthymol blue complex
  microcrystalline bovine collagen
  minimal bactericidal concentration

MB-CK
  creatinine kinase isoenzyme containing
    M and B subunits

MbCO
  carbon monoxide myoglobin
  myoglobin *also* Mb, MbO₂, MYO,
    MYOGLB

MBCR
  mesiobuccal cusp ridge

MBCU
  metallic bead-chain cystourethrograph

MBD
  main pancreatic duct
  Marchiafava-Bignami disease
  maximal bactericidal dilution
  methotrexate, bleomycin, and
    diamminedichloroplatinum (cisplatin)
  methylene blue dye
  minimal brain damage
  minimal brain dysfunction (syndrome)
  Morquio-Brailsford disease

MBDG
  mesiobuccal developmental groove

MBE
  may be elevated
  medium below elbow (cast)

MBEST
  modulus blipped echo-planar single-
    pulse technique

MBF
  meat base formula
  medullary blood flow
  muscle blood flow
  myocardial blood flow

MBFC
  medial brachial fascial compartment

MBFLB
  monaural bifrequency loudness
    balance

MBG
  mean blood glucose

MBGS
  Morphine-Benzedrine Group Scale

MBH
  maximal benefit from hospitalization
  medial basal hypothalamus

MBH₂
  methylene blue, reduced *also* MBR

MBHI
  Million Behavioral Health Inventory

M

NOTES

MBI
Maslach Burnout Inventory
methylene blue instillation

MBK
methyl butyl ketone

MBL
medium brown loose (stool)
menstrual blood loss
minimal bactericidal level

MBl
methylene blue *also* MB, MEB, MeB

MBLA
methylbenzyl linoleic acid
mouse-specific bone marrow-derived lymphocyte antigen

MBM
mineral basal medium
mother's breast milk

MBNW
multiple-breath nitrogen washout

MBO
mesiobuccoocclusal

MbO₂
myoglobin *also* Mb, MbCO, MYO, MYOGLB
oxymyoglobin

MBP
major basic protein
malignant brachial plexopathy
maltose-binding protein
mean blood pressure
melitensis, bovine, porcine (antigen from *Brucella melitensis*, *B. bovis* and *B. suis*)
mesiobuccopulpal
modified Bagshawe protocol
myelin basic protein

MBPS
multigated (cardiac) blood pool scanning

MBq
megabecquerel

MBR
mesiobuccal root
methylene blue, reduced *also* MBH₂

MBRT
methylene blue reduction time

MBS
Martin-Bell syndrome
modified barium swallow

MBSA
methylated bovine serum albumin

MBSD
maple bark stripper disease

MBT
mercaptobenzothiazole
mixed bacterial toxin

MBTI
Myers-Briggs Type Indicator (psychologic test)

MBV
mitral balloon valvotomy

M-C
Magovern-Cromie (prosthesis)
mineralocorticoid *also* MC

MC
macroglobulinemia
mass casualty
mast cell
maximal concentration
Medical Corps
medium-chain (triglyceride)
medullary cavity
medullary cystic (disease)
megacoulomb
megacurie *also* MCi
megacycle
melanoma cell
meningeal carcinomatosis
Merkel cell
mesangial cell
mesenteric collateral
mesiocervical
mesocaval (shunt)
metacarpal
metatarsocuneiform
methyl cellulose
methylcholanthrene *also* MCA
microcephaly
microciliary clearance
microcirculation
midcapillary
midcarpal
mineralocorticoid *also* M-C
minimal change
Minkowski-Chauffard (syndrome)
mitomycin C *also* MIT-C, Mit-C, MITO-C, MMC, MTC
mitotic cycle
mitoxantrone and cytarabine

mitral commissurotomy
mixed cellularity
mixed cryoglobulinemia
molluscum contagiosum
monkey cell
mononuclear cell
mouth care
mycelial phase (of fungi)
myocarditis

MC-540
merocyanine 540

M&C
morphine and cocaine

M/C
male, castrated (animal)

Mc
mandible coronoid

mC
millicoulomb

mc
millicurie *also* mCi

MCA
major coronary artery
medical care administration
megestrol, cyclophosphamide, and
Adriamycin (doxorubicin)
mesial contact area
metacarpal amputation
methylcholanthrene *also* MC
micrometastases clonogenic assay
middle cerebral aneurysm
middle cerebral artery
middle colic artery
monocarboxylic acid
monoclonal antibody *also* MA, MAB,
MAb, MCAB, MoAb
motorcycle accident *also* MA
mucin-like carcinoma-associated
antigen
multichannel analyzer
multiple congenital abnormalities
multiple congenital anomalies

MCAB, MC-Ab
monoclonal antibody *also* MA, MAB,
MAb, MCA, MoAb

MCAD
medium-chain acyl-CoA
dehydrogenase

MCA/MR
multiple congenital anomalies/mental
retardation (syndrome)

MCAR
mixed cell agglutination reaction

MCAS
middle cerebral artery syndrome

MCAT
Medical College Admission Test
middle cerebral artery thrombosis

m. caute
mix with caution [L. *misce caute*]

MCB
membranous cytoplasmic body
monochlorobenzidine

McB
McBurney (point)

mCBF
mean cerebral blood flow

MCBM
muscle capillary basement membrane

MCBMT
muscle capillary basement membrane
thickening

MCBP
melphalan, cyclophosphamide, BCNU
(bischloroethylnitrosourea), and
prednisone

MCBR
minimal concentration of bilirubin

MCC
marked cocontraction
mean corpuscular (hemoglobin)
concentration *also* MCHbC, MCHC
medial cell column
metacarpal-carpal (joints)
metacerebral cell
metastatic cord compression
microcrystalline collagen
midstream clean catch (urine)
minimal complete-killing concentration
mucocutaneous candidiasis

M

NOTES

MCC *(continued)*
mutated in colon cancer
mutated colorectal carcinoma

McC
McCarthy (panendoscope)
McCoy (antibody)

MCCD
minimal cumulative cardiotoxic dose

MCCNU
methylchlorethyl-cyclahexylnitrosourea
(semustine)

MCCU
mobile coronary care unit

MCD
magnetic circular dichroism
margin crease distance
mast cell degranulation
mean cell diameter
mean of consecutive differences
mean corpuscular diameter
medullary collecting duct
medullary cystic disease
metabolic coronary dilation
metacarpal cortical density
minimal cerebral dysfunction
minimal change disease
multicystic disease
multiple carboxylase deficiency
muscle carnitine deficiency

mcD
millicuries destroyed

MCDI
Minnesota Child Development
Inventory

MCDK
multicystic dysplastic kidney

MCDP
mast cell degranulating peptide

MCDT
mast cell degranulation test
multiple choice discrimination test

MCE
medical care evaluation
Medicare Code Editor
multicystic encephalopathy
multiple cartilaginous exostosis
myocardial contrast echocardiography

MCES
multiple cholesterol emboli syndrome

MCF
macrophage chemotactic factor
macrophage cytotoxicity factor
median cleft face
medium corpuscular fragility
microcomplement fixation
monocyte chemotactic factor
monocyte (leukotactic) factor
mononuclear cell factor
most comfortable frequency
myocardial contractile force

MCFA
medium-chain fatty acid
miniature centrifugal fast analyzer

MCFP
mean circulating filling pressure

MCG
magnetocardiogram
membrane coating granule
mesencephalic central gray
monoclonal gammopathy *also* MG

mcg
microgram *also* μg

MCGC
metacerebral giant cell

MCGF
mast cell growth factor

mcg/kg/min
micrograms per kilogram per minute

MCGN
mesangiocapillary glomerulonephritis
minimal-change glomerulonephritis
mixed cryoglobulinemia with
glomerulonephritis

MCH
Maternal and Child Health
mean cell hemoglobin
mean corpuscular hemoglobin *also*
MCHb, MCHg
methacholine
microfibrillar collagen hemostat
muscle contraction headache

M-CH
mitomycin (adsorbed onto activated)
charcoal

mc-h
millicurie-hour *also* mchr, mCi-hr

MCHA
microsome antibody

MCHb
mean corpuscular hemoglobin *also* MCH, MCHg

MCHbC
mean cell hemoglobin concentration *also* MCHC
mean corpuscular hemoglobin concentration *also* MCHC
mean corpuscular hemoglobin count *also* MCHC

MCHC
maternal and child health care
mean cell hemoglobin concentration *also* MCHbC
mean corpuscular hemoglobin concentration *also* MCHbC, MCC
mean corpuscular hemoglobin count *also* MCHbC

MChD
Master of Dental Surgery

MCHg
mean corpuscular hemoglobin *also* MCH, MCHb

MChOrth
Master of Orthopaedic Surgery

MChOtol
Master of Otology

mchr
millicurie-hour *also* mc-h, mCi-hr

MCHS
Maternal and Child Health Service

MCI
mean cardiac index
methicillin *also* METH
midcarpal instability

MCi
megacurie *also* MC

mCi
millicurie *also* mc

mCid
millicuries destroyed

mCi-hr
millicurie-hour *also* mc-h, mchr

MCINS
minimal change idiopathic nephrotic syndrome

MCK
multicystic kidney

MCKD
multicystic kidney disease

MCL
mantle cell lymphoma
maximal comfort level
maximal containment laboratory
medial collateral ligament
midclavian line
midclavicular line
midcostal line
minimal change lesion
mixed culture, leukocyte
modified chest lead
most comfortable listening (level) *also* MCLL
most comfortable loudness (level) *also* MCLL

MCLD
Mycobacterium chelonei-like organism

MCLL
most comfortable listening level *also* MCL
most comfortable loudness level *also* MCL

MCLNS, MCLS
mucocutaneous lymph node syndrome

MCLR
most comfortable loudness range

MClSci
Master of Clinical Science

MCMAI
Millon Clinical Multiaxial Inventory

MCMI
Millon Clinical Multiaxial Inventory (psychiatric battery)

mcmol
micromole

MCMV
mouse cytomegalovirus
murine cytomegalovirus

M

NOTES

445

MCN
minimal-change nephropathy
mixed cell nodular (lymphoma)

MC-N
mixed cell nodular (lymphoma)

MCNS
minimal-change nephrotic syndrome

MCO
medical care organization

MCommH
Master of Community Health

mcoul
millicoulomb

MCP
maximal closure pressure
mean carotid pressure
melanosis circumscripta precancerosa
melphalan, cyclophosphamide, and
 prednisone
membrane cofactor protein
metacarpal
metacarpophalangeal *also* MCPH, MP
metaclopramide
methyl-accepting chemotaxis protein
mitotic-control protein
mucin clot-prevention (test)
mucopolysaccharidoses

MCP-1
monocyte chemoattractant protein-1
monocyte chemotactic protein-1

MCPH
metacarpophalangeal *also* MP, MCP

MCPJ
metacarpophalangeal joint

MCPS
Missouri Children's Picture Series
 (psychologic test)

Mcps, mcps
megacycles per second

MCQ
multiple choice question

MCR
Medical Corps Reserve
mesial cusp ridge
message competition ratio
metabolic clearance rate
steroid metabolic clearance rate

MCS
malignant carcinoid syndrome

Marlowe-Crown (Social Desirability)
 Scale *also* MCSDS
massage of the carotid sinus
mesocaval shunt
methylcholanthrene(-induced) sarcoma
microculture and sensitivity
moderate constant suction
multiple chemical sensitivity
multiple combined sclerosis
myocardial contractile state

mc/s
megacycles per second

MCSA
minimal cross-sectional area
Moloney cell surface antigen

MCSDS
Marlowe-Crown Social Desirability
 Scale *also* MCS

M-CSF
macrophage colony-stimulating factor

MCSS
multiple chemical sensitivity syndrome

MCT
manual cervical traction
mean cell thickness
mean cell threshold
mean circulation time
mean colonic transit
mean corpuscular thickness
medium-chain triglyceride
medullary carcinoma of thyroid
medullary collecting tubule
monocrotaline
mucociliary transport
multiple compressed tablet

MCTC
metrizamide computed tomographic
 cisternography

MCTD
mixed connective-tissue disease

MCTF
mononuclear cell tissue factor

MCU
malaria control unit
maximal care unit
micturating cystourethrography
motor cortex unit

McU
microunit

MCUG
micturating urogram

MCV
    mean cell volume
    mean clinical value
    mean corpuscular volume
    median cell volume
    melanoma whole-cell vaccine
    molluscum contagiosum virus
    motor conduction velocity

mcv
    microvolt

MCVr
    reticulocyte mean corpuscular volume

MCZ
    miconazole

MD
    macula densa
    macular degeneration
    magnesium deficiency
    main duct
    maintenance dialysis
    maintenance dose
    major depression
    malate dehydrogenase
    malic dehydrogenase
    malrotation of duodenum
    mammary dysplasia
    mandibular
    manic depression
    manic-depressive
    Mantoux diameter
    Marek disease
    maternal deprivation
    maximal dose
    mean deviation
    mean diastolic
    measurable disease
    Meckel diverticulum
    medialis dorsalis (nucleus)
    mediastinal disease
    medical department
    medical doctor
    mediodorsal
    medium dosage
    Ménétrier disease
    mental deficiency
    mental depression
    mesiodistal
    methyldichloroarsine
    Minamata disease

    minimal dosage
    mitral disease
    mixed diet
    moderate disability
    monocular deprivation
    movement disorder
    multiple deficiency
    muscular dystrophy
    myeloproliferative disease
    myocardial damage
    myocardial disease

M.D.
    Doctor of Medicine [L. *Medicinae Doctor*]

Md
    mendelevium *also* Mv

m.d.
    as directed [L. *more dicto*] *also* e.m.p., m. dict., MP, u.d., ut dict.

md
    median *also* M, m

MDA
    malondialdehyde
    manual dilatation of anus
    micrometastases detection assay
    monodehydroascorbate
    motor discriminative acuity
    multivariant discriminant analysis
    right mentoanterior (fetal position) [L. *mento-dextra anterior*]

MDAD
    mineral dust airway disease

MDAP
    Machover Draw-A-Person (Test)

MDBDF
    March of Dimes Birth Defect Foundation

MDBK
    Madin-Darby bovine kidney (cell)

MDBSS
    Mischell-Dutton balanced salt solution

MDC
    major diagnostic category
    medial dorsal cutaneous (nerve)
    metoprolol dilated cardiomyopathy
    minimum detectable concentration

M

NOTES

MDCA
mean distal contraction amplitude

MDCK
Madin-Darby canine kidney (cell)

MDCM
mildly dilated congestive cardiomyopathy

MDD
Doctor of Dental Medicine
major depressive disorder
manic-depressive disorder
mean daily dose
mesial developmental depression

MDDA
Minnesota Differential Diagnosis of Aphasia

MDE
major depressive episode

MDEBP
mean daily erect blood pressure

MDentSc
Master of Dental Science

MDF
mean dominant frequency
myocardial depressant factor

MDG
mean diastolic gradient

MDGF
macrophage-derived growth factor

MDH
malate dehydrogenase
medullary dorsal horn

MDHM
malate dehydrogenase, mitochondrial

MDHR
maximum determined heart rate

MDHS
malate dehydrogenase, soluble

MDHV
Marek disease herpesvirus

MDI
manic-depressive illness
mental development index
metered-dose inhaler
multidirectional instability
multiple daily injection
multiple dosage insulin
Multiscore Depression Inventory

MDIA
Mental Development Index, Adjusted

m. dict.
as directed [L. *moro dicto*] *also* e.m.p., m.d., MP, u.d., ut dict.

MDII
multiple daily insulin injection

MDIT
mean disintegration time

MDL
Master Drug List

MDLO
metoclopramide, dexamethasone, lorazepam, and ondansetron

MDLVP
mean diastolic left ventricular pressure

MDM
middiastolic murmur
minor determinant mix (penicillin)

MDMA
3,4-methylelenedioxy-methamphetamine (ecstasy)

MDMS
methylene dimethane sulfonate

mdn
median

MDNB
mean daily nitrogen balance
metadinitrobenzene
methylene diphosphate

MDNCF
monocyte-derived neutrophil chemotactic factor

MDP
mandibular dysostosis and peromelia
manic-depressive psychosis
methylene diphosphate
methylene diphosphonate
muramyldipeptide
muscular dystrophy, progressive
right mentoposterior (fetal position) [L. *mento-dextra posterior*]

MDPD
maximum dose permissible dose

MDPI
maximal daily permissible intake

MDPIT
Multicenter Diltiazem Post-Infarction Trial

MDQ
memory deviation quotient
Menstrual Distress Questionnaire
minimal detectable quantity

MDR
mammalian diving response
median duration of response
minimal daily requirement
multidrug resistance

MDREF
multidrug resistant enteric fever

MDRH
multidisciplinary rehabilitation hospital

MDRS
Mattis Dementia Rating Scale

MDR-TB
multidrug-resistant tuberculosis

MDS
Master of Dental Surgery
maternal deprivation syndrome
medical data screen
medical data system
membrane-spanning domain
microdilution system
microsurgical drill system
milk drinker's syndrome
Miller-Dieker syndrome
multidimensional scaling
myelodysplastic syndrome
myocardial depressant substance

MDSBP
mean daily supine blood pressure

MDSO
mentally disordered sex offender

MDT
mast (cell) degeneration test
mean dissolution time
median detection threshold
multidisciplinary team
right mentotransverse (fetal position)
[L. *mento-dextra transversa*]

MDTA
McDonald Deep Test of Articulation

MDTP
multidisciplinary treatment plan

MDTR
mean diameter-thickness ratio

MDUO
myocardial disease of unknown origin

MDV
Marek disease virus
mucosal disease virus
multiple dose vial

MDY
month, date, year

Mdyn
megadyne

ME
Mache Einheit
macular edema
magnitude estimation
male equivalent
malic enzyme
manic episode
maximal effort
median eminence
medical education
Medical Examiner
meningoencephalitis
mercaptoethanol
metabolic and electrolyte (disorder)
metabolic energy
metabolism
metabolizable energy
metamyelocyte
methyleugenol
microembolization
middle ear
mouse embryo
mouse epithelial (cell)
muscle examination

M

2ME, 2 ME
2-mercaptoethanol

M/E, M:E ratio
myeloid/erythroid (ratio)

ME$_{50}$
50% maximal effect

NOTES

Me
menton
methyl *also* meth

MEA
mercaptoethylamine
multiple endocrine abnormalities
multiple endocrine adenomatosis

MEA-I
multiple endocrine adenomatosis type I

MEA-I–II
multiple endocrine adenomatosis type I and II

MeAIB
methylaminoisobutyric acid

meas
measurement

MEB, MeB
Medical Evaluation Board
methylene blue *also* MB, MBl
muscle-eye-brain (disease)

MeBSA
methylated bovine serum albumin

MEC
mecillinam
meconium
median effective concentration
middle ear canal
middle ear cell
minimum effective concentration
myoepithelial cell

Mec, mec
meconium

MeCCNU, methyl-CCNU
methylchloroethyl-cyclohexylnitrosourea (semustine)

MECG
maternal electrocardiogram
mixed essential cryoglobulinemia

MeCP
methyl-CCNU, cyclophosphamide, and prednisone

MECT
maximal extrapolated clotting time

MECTA
mobile electroconvulsive therapy apparatus

MECY
methyltrexate and cyclophosphamide

MED
medial *also* Med, med
median erythrocyte diameter
medical *also* Med, med
medication
medicine *also* Med, med
medium *also* Med, med
minimal effective diameter
minimal erythema dose
minimum effective dose
multiple epiphyseal dysplasia

Med, med
medial *also* MED
median
medical *also* MED
medicine *also* MED
medium *also* MED

MEDAC
multiple endocrine deficiency, Addison disease, and candidiasis (syndrome)
multiple endocrine deficiency-autoimmune candidiasis

MED-ART
Medical Automated Records Technology

MEDEX, Medex
extension of physician (physician assistant program using former military medical corpsmen [Fr. *médicin extension*]

medic.
medical corpsman [L. *medicus*]

MEDICO
Medical International Cooperation

MEDICS
Medical Examination and Diagnostic Coding System

MEDIHC
Military Experience Directed into Health Careers

MEDLARS
Medical Literature Analysis and Retrieval System

MEDLINE
MEDLARS On-Line

med men
medial meniscectomy
medial meniscus

MEDPAR
Medical Provider Analysis and Review

MEdREP
Medical Education Reinforcement and Enrichment Program

MEDS
microsurgical extraction of ductal sperm

MEDScD
Doctor of Medical Science

MedSurg
medicine and surgery

Med Tech
Medical Technician
Medical Technologist
Medical Technology

MEE
measured energy expenditure
methylethyl ether
middle ear effusion

MEET
Multistage Exercise Electrocardiographics Test

MEF
maximal expiratory flow
middle ear fluid
midexpiratory flow
migration enhancement factor
mouse embryo fibroblast

MEF$_{50}$
mean maximal expiratory flow

MEFA
methyl-CCNU (semustine), 5-fluorouracil, and Adriamycin (doxorubicin)

MEFR
maximal expiratory flow rate

MEFSR
maximal expiratory flow-static recoil (curve)

MEFV
maximal expiratory flow volume

MEFVC
maximal expiratory flow volume curve
mechanical expiratory flow volume curve

MEG
magnetoencephalogram
magnetoencephalography
megakaryocyte
mercaptoethylguanidine
multifocal eosinophilic granuloma

MEG-CSF
megakaryocyte colony-stimulating factor

MEGD
minimal euthyroid Graves disease

mEGF
mouse epidermal growth factor

MEGX
monoethylglycinexylidide

MEIA
microparticle enzyme immunoassay

MEK
methylethylketone

MEKS
Mediterranean Kaposi sarcoma

MEL
melphalan *also* LPAM, L-PAM, *l*-PAM
metabolic equivalent level
mouse erythroleukemia
murine erythroleukemia

mel
melanoma
melena

MELAN
melanin

MELC
murine erythroleukemia cell

MELDOS
meliodosis

MELI
metenkephalin-like immunoreactivity

M

NOTES

MEM
Eagle minimum essential medium
macrophage electrophoretic mobility
malic enzyme, mitochondrial *also*
MEm
minimum essential medium

MEm
malic enzyme, mitochondrial *also*
MEM

MEMA
methyl methacrylate *also* MMA

memb
membrane

MEMR
multiple exostoses-mental retardation
(syndrome)

MEN
methylethylnitrosamine
multiple endocrine neoplasia, types I,
II, III
multiple endocrine neoplasm

men
meningeal
meninges
meningitis
meniscectomy

MEN 2A
multiple endocrine neoplasia 2A

MEN 2B
multiple endocrine neoplasia 2B

MEND
Medical Education for National
Defense

MENS
microamperage electrical nerve
stimulation
multiple endocrine neoplasia syndrome

menst
menstrual
menstruate
menstruating

MEO
malignant external otitis

MeOH
methyl alcohol

MEOS
microsomal ethanol-oxidizing system

MEP
maximal expiratory pressure
mean effective pressure
meperidine *also* mep
mitomycin C, etoposide, and Platinol
motor end plate
motor-evoked potential
multimodality-evoked potential
myogenic motor-evoked potential

mep
meperidine *also* MEP

MEPC
miniature endplate current

MEPH
mephobarbital

MEPP
miniature endplate potential

MePr
methylprednisolone

mEQ, mEq, meq
milliequivalent

mEq/L
milliequivalent per liter

MER
mean ejection rate
mersalyl (acid)
methanol extraction residue
methanolextraction residue (of bacille
Calmette-Guérin)
methanol-extruded residue
molar esterification rate
motor-evoked response
multimodality-evoked response

M:E ratio (*var. of* M/E)

MERB
Medical Examination and Review
Board
metenkephalin receptor binding

MERCATOR
Multicenter European Research Trial
with Cilazapril after Angioplasty to
Prevent

MERG
macular electroretinogram

MES
maintenance electrolyte solution
maximal electroshock (seizure)
mesial *also* M, m
Metrazol-electroshock seizure
morpholinoethanesulfonic acid

muscle in elongated state
myoelectric signal

Mes
mesencaphalon
mesencephalic

MESA
microsurgical epididymal sperm
aspiration

Mesc
mescaline

MESCH
Multi-Environment Scheme

MESGN
mesangial glomerulonephritis

MeSH
Medical Subject Heading (in
MEDLARS)

mesna
2-mercaptoethane sulphonate sodium

MesPGN
mesangial proliferative
glomerulonephritis

MESS
Mangled Extremity Severity Score

MET
medical emergency treatment
metabolic *also* metab
metabolic equivalents of task
metabolic equivalent test
metamyelocyte
metastasis *also* M, metas, met
metastatic *also* M, metas, met
methionine
metoprolol
midexpiratory time
multistage exercise test

Met
methionine *also* M

met
metallic (chest sounds)
metastasis *also* M, MET, metas
metastasize
metastasizing
metatarsal *also* MT

META
metamyelocyte
methacryloxyethyltrimellitic anhydride

meta
metacarpal
metatarsal

metab
metabolic *also* MET
metabolism

metas
metastasis *also* M, MET, met
metastatic *also* MET

METH
methicillin *also* MCI

Meth
methedrine

meth
methyl *also* Me

Met-Hb, metHb
methemoglobin *also* MHB, MHb

MeTHF
methyltetrahydrofolic acid

methyl-CCNU (*var. of* MeCCNU)

MetMb, metMb
metmyoglobin

m. et n.
morning and night [L. *mane et
nocte*]

METS
metabolic equivalents (multiples of
resting oxygen consumption)
metastases *also* Mets, mets

Mets, mets
metastases *also* METS

m. et sig.
mix and write a label [L. *misce et
signa*]

METT
maximal exercise tolerance test

m. et v.
morning and evening [L. *mane et
vespere*]

M

NOTES

Metz
Metzenbaum

MEV
maximal exercise ventilation
million electron volts
murine erythroblastosis virus

MeV, mev
megaelectron volt
megavolt *also* MV

mev
million electron volts

MEWDS
multiple evanescent white dot
syndrome

MEX
Mexican
mexiletine

MF
masculinity/femininity
mass fragmentography
meat free
medium frequency
megafarad
melamine formaldehyde
merthiolate-formaldehyde (solution)
methanol formaldehyde
methoxyflurane
microfibrile
microfilament
microfilia
microscopic factor
midcavity forceps
mitogenic factor
mitomycin-fluorouracil
mitotic figure
mossy fiber
mucosal fluid
multifactorial
multiplication factor
mutation frequency
mutton fat
mycosis fungoides
myelin figure
myelofibrosis
myocardial fibrosis
myofibrillar

M/F
male to female (ratio)
moment:force ratio

M&F
male and female
mother and father

Mf
maxillofrontal
microfilaria *also* mf

mF
millifarad

mf
microfilaria *also* Mf

MFA
methyl fluoracetate
monofluoroacetate
multifocal functional autonomy
multifunctional acrylic
multiple factor analysis

MFAT
multifocal atrial tachycardia

MFB
medial forebrain bundle
metallic foreign body

MFC
mean frequency of compensation
medial femoral condyle
minimal fungicidal concentration

m-FC
membrane focal coli (broth)

MFCC
marriage, family, and child counselor

MFD
mandibulofacial dysostosis
Memory for Designs
midforceps delivery
milk-free diet
minimal fatal dose

MFEM
maximal forced expiratory maneuver

MFG
manofluorography
modified heat-degraded gelatin

MFH
malignant fibrous histiocytoma
membrane-free hemolysate

MFID
multielectrode flame ionization
detector

m. flac.
flaccid membrane (Shrapnell
membrane) [L. *membrana flaccida*]

MFM
millipore filter method

MFO
mixed function oxidase

MFP
monofluorophosphate
myofascial pain

MFPVC
multifocal premature ventricular
contraction

MFR
mean flow rate
midforceps rotation
mucus flow rate
myofascial release

MFRL
maximal force at rest length

MFS
medical fee schedule
merthiolate formaldehyde solution
Miller-Fisher syndrome
Minnesota Followup Study

MF sol
merthiolate-formaldehyde solution

MFSS
Medical Field Service School

MFST
Medical Field Service Technician

MFT
multifocal atrial tachycardia
muscle function test

m. ft.
let a mixture be made [L. *mistura
fiat*]

MFU
medical followup

MFVD
midforceps vaginal delivery

MFVNS
middle fossa vestibular nerve section

MFVPT
Motor-Free Visual Perception Test
also MVPT

MFVR
minimal forearm vascular resistance

MFW
multiple fragment wounds

M-G
Marcus Gunn (pupil) *also* MG, MGP

MG
Marcus Gunn (pupil) *also* M-G,
MGP
margin *also* mar., marg
medial gastrocnemius (muscle)
membranous glomerulonephritis *also*
MGN
membranous glomerulopathy
menopausal gonadotropin
mesiogingival
methylglucoside
methylguanidine
Michaelis-Gutmann (body)
minigastrin
monoclonal gammopathy *also* MCG
monoglyceride
mucigen granule
mucous granule
muscle group
myasthenia gravis *also* MyG
myoglobin

Mg
magnesium *also* Mag, mag

mg
milligram *also* mgm, mgr

mg%
milligrams percent
milligrams per 100 cubic centimeters
or per 100 grams
milligrams per deciliter
milligrams per 100 milliliters

MGA
malposition of great arteries
medical gas analyzer
melengestrol acetate

MGAB
mucous gland adenoma of bronchus

mγ
micromilligram
milligamma
nanogram

MGB
medial geniculate body

NOTES

Mgb
myoglobulin

MGBG
methylglyoxal-bis-guanylhydrazone

MGC
minimal glomerular change

MgC
magnocellular neuroendocrine cell

MGCE
multifocal giant cell encephalitis

MGCT
malignant glandular cell tumor

MGD
maximal glucose disposal
meibomian gland dysfunction
mixed gonadal dysgenesis

mg/dL
milligram per deciliter

mg-el
milligram-element

MGES
multiple gated equilibrium
  scintigraphy

MGF
macrophage growth factor
maternal grandfather

MGG
May-Grünwald-Giemsa (staining)
molecular and general genetics
mouse gamma globulin

MGGH
methylglyoxal guanylhydrazone

MGH
microglandular hyperplasia
monoglyceride hydrolase

mgh, mg-hr
milligram-hour

MGHL
middle glenohumeral ligament

MGI
macrophage and granulocyte inducer

MGJ
mucogingival junction

mg/kg
milligram per kilogram

MGL
minor glomerular lesion

mg/L
milligram per liter

MGM
maternal grandmother

mgm
milligram *also* mg, mgr

MGN
membranous glomerulonephritis *also*
  MG

MGP
Marcus Gunn pupil *also* MG, M-G
marginal granulocyte pool
marginated granulocyte pool
matrix Gla protein
membranous glomerulonephropathy
methyl green pyronin (dye)
mucinglycoprotein
mucous glycoprotein

MGR
modified gain ratio
multiple gas rebreathing
murmurs, gallops, or rubs

mgr
milligram *also* mg, mgm

MGS
malignant glandular schwannoma
metric gravitational system

MGSA
melanoma growth-stimulating activity

MGSD
mean gestational sac diameter

mgtis
meningitis

MGUS
monoclonal gammopathies of
  undetermined significance

MGW
magnesium sulfate, glycerin, and
  water (enema)

MGXT
multistage graded exercise test

mGy
milligray

MH
maleic hydrazide
malignant histiocytosis
malignant hyperpyrexia
malignant hypertension
malignant hyperthermia

mammotropic hormone
mannoheptulose
marital history
medial hypothalamus
medical history
Medtronic-Hall
melanophore-stimulating hormone *also*
 MSH
menstrual history
mental health
mental hygiene
mesothelial hyperplasia
moist heat
monosymptomatic hypochondriasis
multiple handicapped
murine hepatitis
mutant hybrid
myohyoid

M-H
Mueller-Hinton (agar) *also* MHA

M/H
microcytic hypochromic (anemia)

Mh
mandible head

mH
millihenry

MHA
May-Hegglin anomaly
Mental Health Association
methemalbumin
microangiopathic hemolytic anemia
 also MAHA
microhemagglutination assay
middle hepatic artery
mixed hemadsorption
Mueller-Hinton agar *also* M-H

MHA-TP
microhemagglutination-*Treponema pallidum*

MHA-TPA
microhemagglutination assay-
Treponema pallidum assay

MHB
maximal hospital benefit
mental health (assistance) benefit
methemoglobin *also* Met-Hb, metHb,
MHb

MHb
medial habenular
methemoglobin *also* Met-Hb, metHb,
 MHB
myohemoglobin

MHBSS
modified Hanks balanced salt solution

MHC
major histocompatibility complex
mental health care
mental health center
mental health counselor
multiphasic health checkup

mhcp
mean horizontal candle power

MHCS
Mental Hygiene Consultation Service

m/hct
microhematocrit

MHCU
mental health care unit

MHD
maintenance hemodialysis
maximal human dose
mean hemolytic dose
mental health department
minimal hemolytic dilution
minimal hemolytic dose

M-HEART
Multi-Hospital Eastern Atlantic
 Restenosis Trial

MHI
malignant histiocytosis of intestine
Mental Health Index (information)
Mental Health Institute

MHLC
Multidimensional Health Locus of
 Control

MHLS
metabolic heat load stimulator

MH/MR
mental health and mental retardation

MHN
massive hepatic necrosis

M

NOTES

MHN *(continued)*
Mohs hardness number
morbus haemolyticus neonatorum

MHNTG
multiheteronodular toxic goiter

MHO
microsomal heme oxygenase

mho
reciprocal ohm
siemens unit (ohm spelled backward)

MHP
maternal health program
methoxyhydroxypropane
monosymptomatic hypochondriacal
psychosis

MHPA
mild hyperphenylalaninemia
Minnesota-Hartford Personality Assay

MHPG
methoxyhydroxyphenylglycol

MHR
major histocompatibility region
malignant hyperthermia resistance
maximal heart rate
methemoglobin reductase *also* MR,
MR-E

MHRI
Mental Health Research Institute

MHS
major histocompatibility system
malignant hypothermia susceptibility
multiple health screening

MHSA
microaggregated human serum
albumin

MHST
multiphasic health screen test

MHT
multiphasic health testing

MHTI
minor hypertensive infant

MHTS
Multiphasic Health Testing Services

MHV
magnetic heart vector
middle hepatic vein
minimal height velocity
mouse hepatitis virus

MHVD
Marek herpesvirus disease

MHW
medial heel wedge
mental health worker

MHx
medical history

MHz
megahertz

MI
maturation index
medical inspection
melanophore index
membrane intact
menstruation induction
mental illness
mental institution
mentally impaired
mercaptoimidazole
mesioincisal
metabolic index
metaproterenol inhaler
methyl indole
migration index
migration inhibition
mild irritant
mitotic index
mitral incompetence
mitral insufficiency
mononucleosis infectiosa
morphology index
motility index
myocardial infarct
myocardial infarction
myocardial ischemia
myoinositol

M&I
maternal and infant (care)

Mi
mitomycin *also* MIT

mi
mile

MIA
medically indigent adult
missing in action
multi-institutional arrangement

MIAA
microaggregated albumin *also* MAA

MIAP
modified innervated antral pouch

MIAs
multiple intracranial aneurysms

MIB
Medical Impairment Bureau

MIBG, mIBG
metaiodobenzylguanidine

MIBI
methoxyisobutyl isonitrile

MIBK
methylisobutyl ketone

MIC
maternal and infant care
medical intensive care
Medical Interfraternity Conference
methacholine inhalation challenge
microcytic erythrocyte
microscope
microscopic
minimal inhibitory concentration
minimal isorrheic concentration
mobile intensive care
model immune complex

MiC
minocycline

MICG
macromolecular insoluble cold
globulin

MICN
mobile intensive care nurse

mic. pan.
bread crumb [L. *mica panis*]

MICR
methacholine inhalation challenge
response

micro
microcyte
microcytic
microscopic

microbiol
microbiological
microbiology

MICU
medical intensive care unit
mobile intensive care unit

MID
maximum inhibiting dilution
maximum inhibiting duration
mesioincisodistal
midazolam
minimal infecting dose
minimal infective dose
minimal inhibitory dilution
minimal inhibitory dose
minimal irradiation dose
multiinfarct dementia
multiple ion detection

mid
middle
midposition

mid/3
middle third (of long bone)

MIDAS
Myocardial Infarction Data
Acquisition System

Mid I
middle insomnia

MIDS
Management Information Decision
System

midsag
midsagittal

MIE
meconium ileus equivalent
medical improvement expected
methylisoeugenol

MIF
macrophage-inhibiting factor
melanocyte-inhibiting factor
merthiolate-iodine-formaldehyde
(method)
merthiolate-iodine-formalin (solution)
methylene-iodine-formalin
microimmunofluorescence (test)
midinspiratory flow
migration-inhibiting factor
mixed immunofluorescence
müllerian-inhibiting factor

MIFA
mitomycin-C, 5-fluorouracil, and
Adriamycin (doxorubicin)

M

NOTES

MIFC
merthiolate-iodine-formaldehyde concentration

MIFR
maximal inspiratory flow rate
midinspiratory flow rate

MIFT
merthiolate-iodine-formaldehyde technique

MIG
measles immunoglobulin *also* MIg

MIg
malaria immunoglobulin
measles immunoglobulin *also* MIG
membrane immunoglobulin

MIGET
multiple inert gas elimination technique

MIGW
maximal increment in growth and weight

MIH
melanotropin release-inhibiting hormone
methylhydrazine
methylisopropylbenzamide
migraine with interparoxysmal headache
minimal intermittent (dosage of) heparin
monoiodohistidine

Mik
Mikulicz

MIKA
minor karyotype abnormality

MIKE
mass-analyzed ion kinetic energy

MIL
military
mother-in-law *also* M/L

MILIS
Multicenter Investigation for the Limitation of Infarct Size

MILP
mitogen-induced lymphocyte proliferation

MILS
medication information leaflet for seniors

MIME
mean indices of meal excursions

MIMS
Medical Information Management System
Medical Inventory Management System

MIN
medial interlaminar nucleus
mineral *also* min
minimal *also* min
minimum *also* min
minor *also* min
minute *also* min

min
mineral *also* MIN
minim
minimal *also* MIN
minimum *also* MIN
minor *also* MIN
minute *also* MIN

MINA
monoisonitrosoacetone

MINE
medical improvement not expected
mesna uroprotection, ifosfamide, mitoxantrone, and etoposide

MINIA
monkey intranuclear inclusion agent

mini-lap
minilaparotomy

mini-VAB
vinblastine, actinomycin D, and bleomycin

MIO
minimal identifiable odor

MIP
macrophage inflammatory protein
maximal inspiratory pressure
mean intravascular pressure
medical improvement possible
metacarpointerphalangeal
minimal inspiratory pressure

MIPS
myocardial isotopic perfusion scan

MIR
multiple isomorphous replacement

MIRD
medical internal radiation dose
medical internal radiation dosimetry

MIRF
macrophage immunogenic antigen-recruiting factor

MIRP
myocardial infarction rehabilitation program

MIRU
myocardial infarction research unit

MIS
management information system
Medical Information Service
meiosis-inducing substance
minimally invasive surgery
mitral insufficiency
moderate intermittent suction
müllerian inhibiting substance

Mis Astig
mixed astigmatism

misc
miscarriage
niiscellaneous

MISG
modified immune serum globulin

MISHAP
microcephalus-imperforate anus-syndactyly-hamartoblastoma-abnormal

MISO
misonidazole

MISS
modified injury severity score (scale)

MISSGP
mercury in Silastic strain gauge plethysmography

MIST
Medical Information Service by Telephone
minimally invasive surgical technique

mist.
mixture [L. *mistura*] *also* m.

MIT
Male Impotence Test
marrow iron turnover
mean input time
meconium in trachea
melodic intonation therapy

metabolism inhibition test
migration inhibition test
miracidial immobilization test
mitomycin *also* Mi
monoiodotyrosine

mit
mitral

mit.
send [L. *mitte*] *also* m.

MIT-C, Mit-C
mitomycin C *also* MC, MITO-C, MMC, MTC

Mith
mithramycin

MITI
Myocardial Infarction Triage and Intervention

mit insuf
mitral insufficiency

MITO-C
mitomycin C *also* MC, MIT-C, Mit-C, MMC, MTC

mit. sang.
blood-letting procedure [L. *mitte sanguinem* let go the blood]

mitt. tal.
send such [L. *mitte tales*]

MIU
million international units

mIU
milli-International unit (one-thousandth of an International Unit)

MIV
major injury vector

mix.
mixture *also* mixt

mix. mon
mixed monitor

mixt
mixture *also* mix.

MJ
Machado-Joseph (disease)
marijuana
megajoule

M

NOTES

mJ
millijoule

MJA
mechanical joint apparatus

MJAD
Machado-Joseph Azorean disease

MJD
Machado-Joseph disease

MJL
medial joint line

MJT
Mead Johnson tube
Mowlem-Jackson technique

MK
marked
menaquinone (vitamin K_2)
monkey kidney *also* MkK
myokinase

M-K
McCarey-Kaufman (medium)

MK-6
menaquinone-6
vitamin K_2

MK-7
menaquinone-7

Mk
monkey

MKAB
may keep at bedside

mkat
millikatal

mkat/L
millikatal per liter

MKB
megakaryoblast

MKC
monkey kidney cell

MK-CSF
megakaryocyte colony-stimulating
factor

mkg
meter-kilogram

MKHS
Menkes kinky hair syndrome

MKI
mitosis-karyorrhexis index

MkK
monkey kidney *also* MK

MKP
monobasic potassium phosphate

MKS, mks
meter-kilogram-second

MKSAP
Medical Knowledge Self-Assessment
Program

MKTC
monkey kidney tissue culture

MKV
killed measles vaccine

M-L
Martin-Lewis (medium)

ML
Licentiate in Midwifery *also* LM
malignant lymphoma
marked latency
maximal left
meningeal leukemia
mesiolingual
middle lobe
midline
molecular layer
motor latency
mucolipidosis
multiple lentiginosis
muscular layer
myeloid leukemia

M/L
mediolateral
monocyte/lymphocyte (ratio) *also* M:L
mother-in-law *also* MIL

M:L
maltase to lactase (ratio)
monocyte-lymphocyte ratio *also* M/L

mL
millilambert *also* mLa
milliliter *also* ml

ml
midline
milliliter *also* mL

MLA
left mentoanterior (fetal position)
[L. *mento-laeva anterior*]
Medical Library Association
medium long-acting
mesiolabial *also* MLa
monocytic leukemia, acute
multilanguage aphasia

MLa
mesiolabial *also* MLA

mLa
acute monocytic leukemia *also* AML, AMOL
millilambert *also* mL

MLAB
Multilingual Aphasia Battery

MLAC
minimum local analgesic concentration

MLAI, MLaI
mesiolabioincisal

MLAP
mean left atrial pressure

MLaP
mesiolabiopulpal

MLB
monaural loudness balance (test)

MLb
macrolymphoblast

MLBP
mechanical low back pain

MLBW
moderately low birth weight

MLC
Marginal Line Calculus (Index)
mesiolingual cusp
minimal lethal concentration
mixed leukocyte concentration
mixed leukocyte culture
mixed ligand chelate
mixed lymphocyte concentration
mixed lymphocyte culture
morphine-like compound
multilamellar cytosome
multilevel care
multilumen catheter
myelomonocytic leukemia, chronic

MLCK
myosin light-chain kinase

MLCN
multilocular cystic nephroma

MLCP
myosin light-chain phosphatase

MLCR
mesiolingual cusp ridge
mixed lymphocyte culture reaction

MLCT
metal-to-ligand charge transfer

ML-CVP
multilumen central venous pressure

MLCW
mixed lymphocyte culture, weak

MLD
masking level difference
median lethal dose *also* MLD_{50}
metachromatic leukodystrophy
microlumbar diskectomy
microsurgical lumbar diskectomy
minimal lesion disease
minimal lethal dose *also* mld
minimal luminal diameter

MLD_{50}
median lethal dose *also* MLD

mld
minimal lethal dose *also* MLD

MLDG
mesiolingual developmental groove

mL/dL
milliliter per deciliter

MLE
maximal likelihood estimation

MLEpis
mediolateral episiotomy
midline episiotomy

MLF
medial longitudinal fasciculus
mesiolingual fossa
morphine-like factor

MLG
mesiolingual groove
mitochondria lipid glucogen

MLGN
minimal lesion glomerulonephritis

ML-H
malignant lymphoma, histiocytic

MLI
mesiolinguoincisal

M

NOTES

MLI *(continued)*
mixed lymphocyte interaction
motilin-like immunoreactivity

mL/kg
milliliter per kilogram

MLL
malignant lymphoma, lymphoblastic
(type)

mL/L
milliliters per liter

MLN
manifest latent nystagmus
membranous lupus nephropathy
mesenteric lymph node

MLNS
mucocutaneous lymph node syndrome

MLO
mesiolinguo-occlusal

MLP
left mentoposterior (fetal position)
[L. *mento-laeva posterior*] *also* LMP
mesiolinguopulpal
microsomal lipoprotein
multiple lymphomatous polyposis

ML-PCR
mixed-linker PCR

ML-PDL
malignant lymphoma, poorly
differentiated lymphocytic

MLR
major liver resection
mean length of response
middle latency response
mixed leukocyte reaction
mixed leukocyte response
mixed lymphocyte reaction
mixed lymphocyte response

mlRNA
messenger-like RNA

MLS
mean life span
median life span
median longitudinal section
middle lobe syndrome
mucolipidoses
myelomonocytic leukemia, subacute

MLT
left mentotransverse (fetal position)
[L. *mento-laeva transversa*] *also*
LMT
mean latency time
median lethal time
Medical Laboratory Technician

MLT(AMT)
Medical Laboratory Technician
(American Medical Technologists)

MLT(ASCP)
Medical Laboratory Technician
certified by American Society of
Clinical Pathologists

MLTC
mixed leukocyte-trophoblast culture

MLTI
mixed lymphocyte target interaction

MLU
mean length of utterance

MLV
Moloney leukemogenic virus
monitored live voice
mouse leukemia virus
multilaminar vesicle
murine leukemia virus

MLVDP
maximal left ventricular developed
pressure

mlx
millilux

MM
macromolecule
major medical (insurance)
malignant melanoma
manubrium of malleus
Marshall-Marchetti (procedure for
urinary incontinence)
medial malleolus
megamitochondria
melanoma metastasis
meningococcic meningitis
mercaptopurine and methotrexate
metastatic melanoma
methadone maintenance
middle molecule
milk and molasses *also* M&M
millimeter *also* mm
minimal medium
mismatch
morbidity and mortality *also* M&M
motor meal
mucous membrane
Muller maneuver
multiple myeloma
muscles *also* mm

muscularis mucosae
myeloid metaplasia
myelomeningocele

M&M

milk and molasses *also* MM
morbidity and mortality *also* MM

Mm

mandible mentum

mM

millimolar
millimole *also* mmol

mm

methylmalonyl
millimeter *also* MM
mucous membrane
murmur
muscles *also* MM

mm^2

square millimeter

mm^3

cubic millimeter *also* cmm, cu mm

MMA

mastitis-metritis-agalactia (syndrome)
medical materials account
methylmalonic acid
methylmercuric acetate
methyl methacrylate *also* MEMA
monocyte monolayer assay

MMAA

mini-microaggregated albumin colloid

MMAD

mass median aerodynamic diameter

MMATP

methadone maintenance and aftercare
treatment program

MMC

migrating motor complex
migrating myoelectric complex
minimal medullary concentration
mitomycin C *also* MC, MIT-C, Mit-
C, MITO-C, MTC
mucosal mast cell
murine mesangial cell

MMD

malignant metastatic disease

mass median aerodynamic diameter
mass median diameter (of particles)
mean marrow dose
minimal morbidostatic dose
myotonic muscular dystrophy *also*
MyMD

MMDA

methyoxymethylene dioxyamphetamine

MMDG

mesial marginal developmental groove

MME

M-mode echocardiography
mouse mammary epithelium

MMECT

multiple monitored electroconvulsive
therapy

Mmed

Master of Medicine

MMEF

maximal midexpiratory flow *also*
MMF

MMEFR

maximal midexpiratory flow rate *also*
MMFR

MMF

magnetomotive force
maximal midexpiratory flow *also*
MMEF
mean maximal flow

MMFG

mouse milk fat globule

MMFR

maximal midexpiratory flow rate *also*
MMEFR
maximal midflow rate

MMFV

maximal midexpiratory flow volume

MMG

mean maternal glucose

MMH

monomethylhydrazine

mmH$_2$0

millimeters of water

M

NOTES

mmHg
millimeters of mercury

MMI
macrophage migration index
macrophage migration inhibition
methimazole
methylmercaptoimidazole

MMIH
megacystis, microcolon, intestinal
hypoperistalsis

MMIHS
megacystis-microcolon-intestinal
hypoperistalsis syndrome

MMIS
Medicaid Management Information
System

MMK
Marshall-Marchetti-Krantz
(cystourethropexy)

MML
Moloney murine leukemia (virus)
also MMLV, MMuLV
monomethyllysine
myelomonocytic leukemia

mM/L
millimoles per liter *also* mmol/L

MMLV
Moloney murine leukemia virus *also*
MML, MMuLV

MMM
microsome-mediated mutagenesis
mucous membrane moist
myelofibrosis with myeloid metaplasia
myeloid metaplasia with myelofibrosis
myelosclerosis with myeloid
metaplasia

mmm
micromillimeter
millimicron

MMMF
man-made mineral fiber

MMMT
malignant mixed mesodermal tumor
malignant mixed müllerian tumor
metastatic mixed müllerian tumor

MMN
morbus maculosus neonatorum
multiple mucosal neuroma

MMNC
marrow mononuclear cell

MMO
methane monooxygenase

MMOA
maxillary mandibular odentectomy
alveolectomy

M-mode
motion mode

MMoL
myelomonoblastic leukemia

mmol
millimole *also* mM

mmol/L
millimoles per liter *also* mM/L

MMP
matrix metalloproteinase
multiple medical problems

MMP-2
matrix metalloproteinase-2

MMP-3
matrix metalloproteinase-3

MMP-7
matrix metalloproteinase-7

MMP-8
matrix metalloproteinase-8

MMP-9
matrix metalloproteinase-8 *also* MMP-
8

MMP-10
matrix metalloproteinase-10

MMPI
McGill-Melzack Pain Index
Minnesota Multiphasic Personality
Inventory

MMPI-D
Minnesota Multiphasic Personality
Inventory Depression (Scale)

MMPNC
Medical Maternal Program for
Nuclear Casualties

mmpp
millimeters partial pressure

MMPR
methylmercaptopurine riboside

mm-PTH
mid-molecule parathyroid hormone

MMR
mass miniature radiography
mass miniature roentgenography

maternal mortality rate
measles-mumps-rubella (vaccine)
mesial marginal ridge
midline malignant reticulosis
mild mental retardation
mobile mass x-ray
monomethylolrutin
myocardial metabolic rate

MMS
Maloney murine sarcoma
Master of Medical Science
methyl methanesulfonate
Mini-Mental State (examination) *also*
 MMSE
mixed mesodermal sarcoma

MMSA
Master of Midwifery, Society of
 Apothecaries

MMSc
Master of Medical Science

MMSE
Mini-Mental State Examination *also*
 MMS

mm/sec
millimeters per second

mm st
muscle strength

MMT
malignant mesenchymal tumor
manual muscle test
Mini Mental Test
mouse mammary tumor

MMTA
methylmetatyramine

MMTP
methadone maintenance treatment
 program

MMTV
monomorphic ventricular tachycardia
mouse mammary tumor virus

MMU
medical maintenance unit
mercaptomethyl uracil

mµ
millimicron

mmu
millimass unit

MMUA
macromolecular uronate

mµc
millimicrocurie

mµg
millimicrogram

MMuLV
Moloney murine leukemia virus *also*
 MML, MMLV

mµs
millimicrosecond

MMV
mandatory minute ventilation
mandatory minute volume

MMWR
Morbidity and Mortality Weekly
 Report

MN
blood group in MNS blood group
 system
malignant nephrosclerosis
meganewton *also* mN
melanocytic nevus
melena neonatorum
membranous neuropathy
mesentericnode
metanephrine
midnight *also* M/N, Mn, mn
mononuclear
motor neuron
mucosal neurolysis
multinodular
myoneural

M/N
macrocytic/normochromic (anemia)
microcytic/normochromic (anemia)
midnight *also* MN, Mn, mn

M&N
morning and night

Mn
manganese
midnight *also* MN, M/N, mn

NOTES

mN
meganewton *also* MN
micronewton
millinormal

mn
midnight *also* MN, M/N, Mn

MNA
maximal noise area

MNAP
mixed nerve action potential

MNB
murine neuroblastoma

MNC
monomicrobial necrotizing cellulitis
mononuclear cell
mononuclear leukocyte *also* MNL

MNCV
motor nerve conduction velocity

MND
minimal necrosing dose
minor neurologic dysfunction
modified neck dissection
motor neuron disease

MNF
myelinated nerve fiber

MNG
multinodular goiter

mng
morning

MNJ
myoneural junction

MNL
maximal number of lamellae
mononuclear leukocyte *also* MNC

MNM
mononeuritis multiplex

MN/m²
meganewton per square meter

MNMK
maximal number of microbes killed

MNMS
myonephropathic metabolic syndrome

MNO
minocycline

MNP
mononuclear phagocyte

MNPA
methoxynaphthyl propionic acid

MNR
marrow neutrophil reserve

MNS
blood group system consisting of
groups M, N, and MN
medial nuclear stratum
Melnick-Needles syndrome
microamperage neural stimulation
a minor blood group

MNSER
mean normalized systolic ejection
rate

Mn-SOD
manganese-superoxide dismutase

MnSSEP
median nerve somatosensory evoked
potential

MNTB
medial nucleus of trapezoid body

Mn-TPPS$_4$
manganese tetrasodium-meso-tetra

MNU
methylnitrosourea

MNZ
metronidazole

MO
manually operated
Master of Obstetrics
Master of Osteopathy
medial oblique (x-ray view)
medical officer
mesioocclusal
mineral oil
minute output
mitral orifice
molecular orbital
monooxygenase
month *also* M, mo, mon
months old *also* mo
morbidly obese
mother
no evidence of distant metastases
sulfamethoxine

MO$_2$
myocardial oxygen consumption

Mo
mode
Moloney (strain)
molybdenum
monoclonal

^{99}Mo
   molybdenum-99

mo
   mode
   month *also* M, MO, mon
   months old *also* MO

MOA
   mechanism of action
   medical office assistant

MoAb
   monoclonal antibody *also* MA, MAB,
   MAb, MCA, MCAB

MOAD
   methotrexate, Oncovin (vincristine), L-
   asparaginase, and dexamethasone

MOB
   mechlorethamine, Oncovin
   (vincristine), and bleomycin

mob, mobil
   mobility
   mobilization

MOB-PT
   mitomycin C, Oncovin (vincristine),
   bleomycin, and cisplatin

MOC
   maximal oxygen consumption
   mother of child
   multiple ocular coloboma

MOCA
   methotrexate, Oncovin (vincristine),
   Cytoxan (cyclophosphamide), and
   Adriamycin (doxorubicin)

MoCM
   molybdenum-conditioned medium

MOD
   maturity-onset diabetes *also* MODM
   Medical Officer of the Day
   mesial, occlusal, and distal
   mesiodistocclusal
   mesioocclusodistal
   moderate *also* mod

mod
   moderate *also* MOD
   moderation
   modification

modulation
module

modem
   modulator/demodulator

MODM
   maturity-onset diabetes mellitus *also*
   MOD

mod. praesc.
   in the way directed [L. *modo
   praescripto*]

MODY
   maturity-onset diabetes of youth

MOF
   marine oxidation/fermentation
   methotrexate, Oncovin (vincristine),
   and 5-fluorouracil
   methoxyflurane
   multiple organ failure

MOFS
   multiple-organ failure syndrome

MOH
   Medical Officer of Health

MOI
   maximal oxygen intake
   multiplicity of infection

MOIVC
   membranous obstruction of the
   inferior vena cava

MOJAC
   mood, orientation, judgment, affect,
   and content

MOL
   molecular layer

mol
   mole
   molecular
   molecule

molc
   molar concentration

molfr
   mole fraction

mol/kg
   mole per kilogram

M

NOTES

moll.
soft [L. *mollis*]

mol/L, mol/l
mole per liter

mol/m³
mole per cubic meter

mol/s
mole per second

mol wt
molecular weight *also* MW, MWt

MOM
milk of magnesia
mucoid otitis media

MoM, mom
multiples of the median

MOMA
methoxyhydroxymandelic acid
methylhydroxymandelic acid

MOMS
multiple organ malrotation syndrome

MoMSV
Moloney murine sarcoma virus

MON
mongolian (gerbil)
monitor

mon
monocyte *also* mono
month *also* M, MO, mo

MONO, Mono
mononucleosis *also* mono

Mono
Monospot (test)

mono
monocyte *also* mon
mononucleosis *also* MONO, Mono
monospot

monos
monocytes

MOOW
Medical Officer of the Watch

MOP
major organ profile
medical outpatient
medical outpatient program
methotrexate, Oncovin (vincristine),
and prednisone

5-MOP
5-methoxypsoralen

8-MOP
8-methoxypsoralen

MOP-BAP
Mustargen (mechlorethamine), Oncovin
(vincristine), prednisone, bleomycin,
Adriamycin (doxorubicin), and
procarbazine

MOPP
Mustargen (mechlorethamine), Oncovin
(vincristine), procarbazine, and
prednisone

MOPP/ABV
mechlorethamine, Oncovin,
procarbazine, prednisone, Adriamycin,
bleomycin, vinblastine

MOPV
monovalent oral polio virus vaccine

MOR
Medical Officer Report
morphine *also* morph

MORA
mandibular orthopedic repositioning
appliance

MORC
Medical Officers Reserve Corps

MORD
magnetic optical rotatory dispersion

mor. dict.
in the manner directed [L. *more
dicto*]

morph
morphine *also* MOR
morphological *also* morphol
morphology *also* morphol

morphol
morphological *also* morph
morphology *also* morph

mor. sol.
in the usual way [L. *more solito*]

mortal.
mortality

MOS
medial orbital sulcus
mirror optical system
mitral opening snap
months
myelofibrosis osteosclerosis

mOs
milliosmolal

mos
months

MOSFET
metal oxide semiconductor field
effect transistor

mOsm, MOsm, mOsmol
milliosmole

mOsm/kg, mosm/kg
milliosmoles per kilogram

MOT
mini-object test
motility (examination)
mouse ovarian tumor

MOTT
mycobacteria other than tubercle

MOU
memorandum of understanding

MOUS
multiple occurrence of unexplained
symptoms

MOV
multiple oral vitamin

MOVC
membranous obstruction (of inferior)
vena cava

MOX
moxalactam

MP
as directed [L. *modo prescripto*] *also*
e.m.p., m.d., m. dict., u.d., ut dict.
macrophage
matrix protein
mean pressure
mechanical percussion
mechanical percussor
medial plantar
melphalan and prednisone
melting point *also* mp, T_m
membrane potential
menstrual period
mentoposterior
mentum posterior
mercaptopurine
mesenteric panniculitis
mesial pit

mesiopulpal
metacarpophalangeal *also* MCP,
MCPH
metaphalangeal
metatarsophalangeal (joint) *also* MTP,
MTPJ
methylprednisolone *also* MPS
microfibrillar protein
minimal pigment
modulator protein
moist pack
monophosphate
mouthpiece
mouth pressure
mucopolysaccharide *also* MPS
multiparous
muscle potential
mycoplasmal pneumonia

4MP4
methylpyrazole

6-MP
6-mercaptopurine *also* Shy

m.p.
as directed [L. *ex modo praescripto*]
also e.m.p., m.d., m. dict., MP, u.d.,
ut dict.
early in the morning [L. *mane
primo*]

mp
melting point *also* MP, T_m
millipond

MPA
main pulmonary artery
medial preoptic area
Medical Procurement Agency
medroxyprogesterone acetate
methylprednisolone acetate
microstomia prevention appliance
minor physical anomaly
mycophenolic acid

MPa, mPa
megapascal

MPAG
McGill Pain Assessment Questionnaire

MPAP
mean pulmonary artery pressure

M

NOTES

MPAWP
mean pulmonary artery wedge pressure

MPB
male pattern baldness
meprobamate

MPBNS
modified Peyronie bladder neck suspension

MPC
marine protein concentrate
maximal permissible concentration
meperidine, promethazine, and chlorpromazine
metallophthalocyanine
micropapillary component
minimal mycoplasmacidal concentration
minimal protozoacidal concentration
mucopurulent cervicitis
myeloblast-promyelocyte compartment

MPCD
minimal perceptible color difference

MPCN
microscopically positive, culturally negative

MPCO
micropolycystic ovary (syndrome)

MPCUR
maximal permissible concentration of unidentified radionuclides

MPCWP
mean pulmonary capillary wedge pressure

MPD
main papillary duct
maximal permissible dose
mean population doubling
membrane potential difference
minimal perceptible difference
minimal phototoxic dose
minimal popular dose
minimal port diameter
Minnesota Percepto-Diagnostic (Test)
also MPDT
multiplanar display
multiple personality disorder
myeloproliferative disease
myofascial pain dysfunction

MPDS
mandibular pain dysfunction syndrome
myofascial pain dysfunction syndrome

MPDT
Minnesota Percepto-Diagnostic Test
also MPD

MPDW
mean percentage of desirable weight

MPE
malignant pleural effusion
maximal possible effect
maximal possible error

MPEC
monopolar electrocoagulation

MPED
minimal phototoxic erythema dose

MPEH
methylphenylethylhydantoin

MPF
maturation-promoting factor
mean power frequency
methylparaben free

MPFL
medial patellofemoral ligament

MPFM
mini-Wright peak flow meter

MPG
magnetopneumography

MPGM
monophosphoglycerate mutase

MPGN
membranoproliferative glomerulonephritis, type I and II
mesangioproliferative glomerulonephritis

MPGR
multiple planar gradient-recalled

MPH
male pseudohermaphroditism
Master of Public Health
milk protein hydrolysate

mph
miles per hour

MPHARM
Master in Pharmacy

M phase
phase of mitosis in cell growth cycle

MPHD
methoxyhydroxphenolglycerol
multiple pituitary hormone
deficiencies

MPHR
maximal predicted heart rate

MPI
mannose phosphate isomerase
Maudsley Personality Inventory
maximal permitted intake
maximal point of impulse
Multiphasic Personality Inventory
Multivariate Personality Inventory
myocardial perfusion imaging

MPJ
metacarpophalangeal joint
metaphalangeal joint
metatarsophalangeal joint

mpk
milligram per kilogram

MPL
maximal permissible level
melphalan
mesiopulpolabial *also* MPLA, MPLa
mesiopulpolingual *also* MPLA, MPLa

MP-L
midpapillary longitudinal

MPLA, MPLa
mesiopulpolabial *also* MPL
mesiopulpolingual *also* MPL

MPM
malignant papillary mesothelioma
malignant pleural mesothelioma
medial pterygoid muscle
Mortality Probability Model
multiple primary malignancy
multipurpose meal

MPMT
Murphy punch maneuver test

MPMV
Mason-Pfizer monkey virus

MPN
most probable number

MPO
maximal power output

minimal perceptible odor
myeloperoxidase

MPOA
medial preoptic area

MPOS
myeloperoxidase system

MPP
massive periretinal proliferation
maximal perfusion pressure
maximal print position
medial pterygoid plate
medical personnel pool
mercaptopyrazidepyrimidine
metacarpophalangeal profile

mppcf
millions of particles per cubic foot
(of air)

MPPG
microphotoelectric plethysmography

MPPN
malignant persistent positional
nystagmus

MPPT
methylprednisolone pulse therapy

MPQ
McGill Pain Questionnaire

MPR
mannose-6-phosphate receptors
marrow production rate
massive preretinal retraction
maximal pulse rate
mercaptopurine riboside
myeloproliferative reaction

MP-RAGE
magnitude preparation-rapid acquisition
gradient echo

MPRE
minimal pure radium equivalent

MPRG
Multicenter Postinfarction Research
Group

MPS
methylprednisolone *also* MP
Michigan Picture Stories
microbial profile system

M

NOTES

MPS (*continued*)
mononuclear phagocyte system
Montreal platelet syndrome
movement-produced stimulus
mucopolysaccharide *also* MP
mucopolysaccharidosis
multiphasic screening
myocardial perfusion scintigraphy
myofascial pain syndrome

MPSMT
Merrill-Palmer Scale of Mental Tests

MPSRT
matched pairs signed rank test

MPSS
methylprednisolone sodium succinate

MPSV
myeloproliferative sarcoma virus

MPSYMED
Master of Psychological Medicine

MPT
maximal predicted phonation time
Michigan Picture Test
multiple-parameter telemetry
multiple puncture test

MP-T
midpapillary transverse

MPTAH
Mallory phosphotungstic acid
hemotoxylin

MPTR
motor, pain, touch, reflex (deficit)

MPT-R
Michigan Picture Test, Revised

MPU
Medical Practitioners Union

MPV
mean plasma volume
mean platelet volume
metatarsus primus varus
mitral valve prolapse

mpz
millipièze

MQ
memory quotient
menaquinone

MQC
microbiologic quality control

MR
Maddox rod

magnetic resonance
malar rash
mandibular reflex
manifest refraction
mannose-resistant
maximal right
may repeat
measles-rubella (vaccine)
medial rectus (muscle)
median raphe
medical record
medical rehabilitation
medication responder
medium range
megaroentgen
menstrual regulation
mentally retarded
mental retardation
mesencephalic raphe
metabolic rate
methemoglobin reductase *also* MHR,
MR-E
methyl red
milk ring
milliroentgen *also* mR, mr
mitral reflux
mitral regurgitation
mixed respiratory
moderate resistance
modulation rate
mortality rate
mortality ratio
motivation research
multicentric reticulohistiocytosis
multiplication rate
multiplicity reactivation
muscle receptor
muscle relaxant
myotactic reflex

M&R
measure and record

M$_r$, *M*$_r$
molecular weight ratio
relative molecular mass

Mr
mandible ramus

mR, mr
milliroentgen *also* MR, mr

MRA
magnetic resonance angiography
magnetic resonance arteriography
main renal artery
marrow repopulation activity

medical records administrator
midright atrium
multivariate regression analysis

MRad
Master of Radiology

mrad
millirad

MRAN
medical resident admitting note

MRAP
maximal resting anal pressure
mean right atrial pressure

MRAS
main renal artery stenosis
mean renal artery stenosis

MRBC
monkey red blood cell
mouse red blood cell

MRBF
mean renal blood flow

MRC
maximal recycling capacity
Medical Registration Council
Medical Research Council
Medical Reserve Corps
methylrosaniline chloride (gentian
violet, crystal violet)

MRCA
magnetic resonance coronary
angiography

MRCC
metastatic renal cell carcinoma

MRCL
Medical Research Council
Laboratories

MRCNS
methicillin-resistant coagulase-negative
Staphylococcus

MRD
margin reflex distance
medical records department
method of rapid determination
minimal reacting dose *also* mrd
minimal renal disease
minimal residual disease

mrd
millirutherford
minimal reacting dose *also* MRD

MRDM
malnutrition-related diabetes mellitus

MRE
maximal restrictive exercise
maximal risk estimate

MR-E
methemoglobin reductase *also* MHR,
MR

mrem
millirem
milliroentgen equivalent man

mrep
milliroentgen equivalent physical

MRF
magnetic resonance flowmetry
medical record file
melanocyte-releasing factor
mesencephalic reticular formation
midbrain reticular formation
mitral regurgitant flow
moderate renal failure
monoclonal rheumatoid factor
müllerian regression factor

mRF
monoclonal rheumatoid factor

MRFC
mouse rosette-forming cell

MRFIT
Multiple Risk Factor Intervention
Trial

MRFT
modified rapid fermentation test

MRG
murmurs, rubs, and gallops

MRH
Maddox rod hyperphoria
melanocyte(-stimulating hormone)-
releasing hormone
melanotropin-releasing hormone

MRHA
mannose-resistant hemagglutination

M

NOTES

MRHD
maximal recommended human dose

mrhm
milliroentgens per hour at one meter

MRHT
modified rhyme hearing test

MRI
machine-readable identifier
magnetic resonance imaging
medical records information
Medical Research Institute
moderate renal insufficiency

MRIF
melanocyte release-inhibiting factor

MRIH
melanocyte release-inhibiting hormone

MRK
Mayer-Rokitansky syndrome

MRL
Medical Records Librarian
Medical Research Laboratory
minimal response level

MRM
magnetic resonance mammography
modified radical mastectomy

MRN
malignant renal neoplasm

mRNA
messenger ribonucleic acid
messenger ribonucleoprotein acid

mRNP
messenger ribonucleoprotein

MRO
minimal recognizable odor
muscle receptor organ

MROD
Medical Research and Operations
Directorate

MRP
maximal reimbursement point
mean resting potential
medical reimbursement plan

MRPAH
mixed reverse passive antiglobulin
hemagglutination

MRPN
medical resident progress note

MRR
marrow release rate

maximal relation rate
maximal relaxation rate

MRS
magnetic resonance spectroscopy
mania rating scale
median range score
medical receiving station
Melkersson-Rosenthal syndrome
methicillin-resistant *Stapylococcus
(aureus) also* MRSA

MRSA
methicillin-resistant *Staphylococcus
aureus also* MRS

MRSE
methicillin-resistant *Staphylococcus
epidermidis*

MRSI
magnetic resonance spectroscopic
imaging

MRT
magnetic resonance tomography
major role therapy
mean residence time
mean resistance time
median reaction time
median recognition threshold
median relapse time
Medical Records Technician
milk ring test
modified rhyme test
muscle response test

MRTA
magnetic resonance tomographic
angiography

MRU
mass radiography unit
mean relational utterance
measure of resource use
minimal reproductive unit

MRUS
maximal rate of urea synthesis

MRV
minute respiratory volume
mixed respiratory vaccine

MRVP
mean right ventricular pressure
methyl red, Voges-Proskauer
(medium)

MRx1
may repeat one time

MS
main scale
maladjustment score
mannose-sensitive
mass spectrometry
mass spectrophotometer
mean score
mechanical stimulation
Meckel syndrome
medical services
medical student
medical supply
medical-surgical
medical survey
menopausal syndrome
mental status
metaproterenolsulfate
microscope slide
Mikuliez syndrome
milkshake
minimal support
mitral sound
mitral stenosis
mobile surgical (unit)
modal sensitivity
molar solution
mongolian spot
morning stiffness
morphine sulfate *also* ms
motile sperm
mucosubstance
multilaminated structure
multiple sclerosis
muscle shortening
muscle strength
musculoskeletal *also* Ms, MSK
myasthenic syndrome

MS I, II, III, IV
medical student–first, second, third
and fourth year

MS-222
tricaine methane sulfonate

M&S
microculture and sensitivity

Ms
murmurs
musculoskeletal *also* MS, MSK

ms
manuscript
millisecond *also* msec, σ
morphine sulfate *also* MS

m/s
meters per second *also* m/sec

m/s²
meters per second squared

MSA
major serologic antigen
male specific antigen
mammary serum antigen
mannitol salt agar
Medical Services Administration
membrane stabilizing action
mouse serum albumin
multichannel signed averager
Multidimensional Scalogram Analysis
multiple system atrophy
multiplication-stimulating activity
muscle-specific actin *also* HHF-35
muscle sympathetic activity

MSAA
multiple sclerosis-associated agent

MSAF
meconium-stained amniotic fluid

MSAFP
maternal serum alpha fetoprotein

MSAO
meal-stimulated acid output

MSAP
mean systemic arterial pressure

MSB
mainstem bronchus
Martius scarlet blue
mediastinal shed blood
mid-small bowel
most significant bit

MSBC
maximal specific binding capacity

MSBLA
mouse-specific B-lymphocyte antigen

MSBOS
maximal surgical blood order
schedule

NOTES

MSBP
Münchhausen syndrome by proxy

MSC
Medical Service Corps
multiple sib case

MSCA
McCarthy Scales of Children's
Abilities

MScD
Doctor of Medical Science
Master of Dental Science

MSCE
monitored self-care evaluation

MSCLC
mouse stem cell-like cell

MScMed
Master of Science in Medicine

MScN
Master of Science in Nursing

MSCNS
methicillin-susceptible coagulase-
negative *Staphylococcus*

MSCP, mscp
mean spherical candle power

MSCU
medical special care unit

MSCWP
musculoskeletal chest wall pain

MSD
mean square deviation
metabolic screening disorder
microsurgical discectomy
microsurgical diskectomy
midsleep disturbance
mild sickle (cell) disease
most significant digit
multiple sulfatase deficiency

MSDI
Martin Suicide Depression Inventory

MSDS
material safety data sheet

MSE
medical support equipment
mental status examination
muscle-specific enolase

mse
mean square error

msec
millisecond *also* ms, σ

m/sec
meters per second *also* m/s

MSEL
myasthenic syndrome of Eaton-
Lambert

MSER
mean systolic ejection rate
Mental Status Examination Record

MSES
medical school environmental stress

MSET
multistage exercise test

MSF
macrophage slowing factor
macrophage spreading factor
meconium-stained fluid
Mediterranean spotted fever
megakaryocyte-stimulating factor
migration-stimulating factor
modified sham feeding

MSG
massage
methysergide
monosodium glutamate

MSGV
mouse salivary gland virus

MSH
medical self-help
melanocyte-stimulating hormone
melanophore-stimulating hormone *also*
MH

MSHA
mannose-sensitive hemagglutination

MSH-IF
melanocyte-stimulating hormone-
inhibiting factor

MSHRF
melanocyte-stimulating hormone-
releasing factor

MSHSC
multiple self-healing squamous
carcinoma

MSHyg
Master of Science in Hygiene

MSI
magnetic source imaging
medium-scale integration

MSIR
morphine sulfate immediate-release (tablet)

MSIS
multistate information system

MSK
medullary sponge kidney
musculoskeletal *also* MS, Ms

MSKP
Medical Sciences Knowledge Profile

MSL
mean sentence length
midsternal line
multiple symmetric lipomatosis

MSLA
mouse-specific lymphocyte antigen
multisample Luer adapter

MSLR
mixed skin (cell) leukocyte reaction

MSLT
Multiple Sleep Latency Test

MSM
Master of Medical Science
medial superior olive
mineral salts medium

MSN
Master of Science in Nursing
medial septal nucleus
mildly subnormal

MSNA
muscle sympathetic nerve activity

MSOF
multiple system organ failure
multisystem organ failure

MSP
mouse serum protein
Münchausen syndrome by proxy

MSPGN
mesangial proliferative glomerulonephritis

MSPH
Master of Science in Public Health

MSPhar
Master of Science in Pharmacy

MSPN
medical student progress note

MSPQ
Modified Somatic Perception Questionnaire

MSPS
myocardial stress perfusion scintigraphy

MSPU
medical short procedure unit

MSQ
mental status questionnaire

MSR
mitral stenoregurgitation
monosynaptic reflex
muscle stretch reflex

MS Rad
Master of Science in Radiology

MSRPP
Multidimensional Scale for Rating Psychiatric Patients

MSRT
Minnesota Spatial Relations Test

MSS
Marital Satisfaction Scale
Marshall-Smith syndrome
massage *also* M, mass, mss
Medicare Statistical System
mental status schedule
Metabolic Support Service
minor surgery suite
motion sickness susceptibility
mucus-stimulating substance
multiple sclerosis susceptibility
muscular subaortic stenosis

mss
massage *also* M, mass, MSS

MSSA
methicillin-susceptible *Staphylococcus aureus*

MSSc
Master of Sanitary Science

MSSE
Master of Science in Sanitary Engineering

NOTES

479

MSSG
multiple sclerosis susceptibility gene

MST
maximum stimulation test
mean survival time
mean swell time (botulism test)
median survival time

MSTA
mumps skin test antigen

MSTh
mesothorium

MSTI
multiple soft tissue injuries

MSTS
Musculoskeletal Tumor Society

MSU
maple syrup urine
medical studies unit
midstream urine (specimen)
monosodium urate
myocardial substrate uptake

MSUA
midstream urinalysis

MSUD
maple syrup urine disease

MSUM
monosodium urate monohydrate

MSURG
Master of Surgery

MSV
maximal sustained (level of)
ventilation
mean scale value
Moloney sarcoma virus
murine sarcoma virus

mSv
millisievert (radiation unit)

MSVC
maximal sustained ventilatory capacity

MSVL
maximal spatial vector to left

MSW
Master of Social Welfare
Master of Social Work
Medical Social Worker
multiple stab wounds

MSWYE
modified sea water yeast extract
(agar)

MT
antimetallothionein antibody
empty
malaria therapy
malignant teratoma
mammary tumor
Martin-Thayer (plate, medium)
mastoid tip
maximal therapy
medial thalamus
medial thickening
mediastinal tube
Medical Technologist
Medical Transcriptionist
medical treatment
melatonin
membrana tympani
membrane thickness
mesangial thickening
metatarsal *also* met
metatarsophalangeal *also* MTP
methyltyrosine
microtome
microtubule
midtrachea
minimal threshold
Monroe tidal drainage *also* MTD
more than
Muir-Torre (syndrome)
multiple tics
multitest (plate)
muscle and tendon
muscle test
muscle testing
music therapy
tympanic membrane [L. *membrana
tympani*]

M-T
macroglobulin-trypsin

M/T
masses (of) tenderness
myringotomy (with) tubes

M&T
myringotomy and tubes

Mt
Magadhan

mt
send of such [L. *mitte tabis*]

3-MT
3-methoxytyramine

MT6
mercaptomerin

MTA
    malignant teratoma, anaplastic
    mammary tumor agent
    Medical Technical Assistant
    metatarsus adductus
    myoclonic twitch activity

MTAC
    mass transfer-area coefficient

MTAD
    tympanic membrane of right ear [L.
    membrana tympana auris dextrae]

MTAL
    medullary thick ascending limb

MT(AMT)
    Medical Technologist (American
    Medical Technologists)

MTAS
    tympanic membrane of left ear [L.
    membrana tympana auris sinistrae]

MT(ASCP)
    Medical Technologist certified by
    American Society of Clinical
    Pathologists

MT(ASCP)SBB
    Medical Technologist (American
    Society of Clinical   Pathologists)

MTAU
    tympanic membranes of both ears
    [L. *membranae tympani aures
    unitae*]

MTB
    methylthymol blue
    Mycobacterium tuberculosis

MTBE
    meningeal tick-borne encephalitis
    methyl-*tert*-butyl ether (therapy)

MTBF
    mean time between (or before)
    failures

MTC
    mass transfer coefficient
    maximal tolerated concentration
    medical test cabinet
    medical training center
    medullary thyroid carcinoma

    metoclopramide
    mitomycin C *also* MC, MIT-C, Mit-
    C, MITO-C, MMC
    multilocular thymic cyst

MTD
    maximal tolerated dose
    mean total dose
    metastatic trophoblastic disease
    Monroe tidal drainage *also* MT
    multiple tic disorder
    Mycobacterium tuberculosis direct

m.t.d.
    send such doses [L. *mitte tales
    doses*]

MTDDA
    Minnesota Test for Differential
    Diagnosis of Aphasia

MTDI
    maximal tolerable daily intake

MT-DN
    multitest, dermatophytes, and
    Nocardia (plate)

mtDNA
    mitochondrial deoxyribonucleic acid

MTDT
    modified tone decay test
    Mycobacterium tuberculosis direct test

MTE
    medical toxic environment

MTET
    modified treadmill exercise testing

MTF
    maximal terminal flow
    medical treatment facility
    mesial triangular fossa
    mithramycin
    modulation transfer factor
    modulation transfer function

MTG
    midthigh girth

MTg
    mouse thyroglobulin

MTHF
    methyl tetrahydrofolic acid

NOTES

MTI
malignant teratoma, intermediate
minimal time interval

MTJ
midtarsal joint

MTLP
metabolic toxemia of late pregnancy

MTM
Thayer-Martin, modified (agar)

MT-M
multitest, mycology (plate)

MTMT
maximum tolerated medical therapy

MTO
Medical Transport Officer

MTOC
microtubule organizing center
mitotic organizing center

MTP
master treatment plan
maximal tolerated pressure
medial tibial plateau
medical termination of pregnancy
metatarsophalangeal *also* MT
metatarsophalangeal (joint) *also* MP,
MTPJ
microtubule protein

MTPI
metatarsophalangeal implant

MTPJ
metatarsophalangeal joint *also* MP,
MTP

MTPT
1-methyl-4-phenyl-1,2,3,6-
tetrahydropyridine

MTQ
methaqualone

MTR
mass, tenderness, rebound (abdominal
examination)
Meinicke turbidity reaction
mental treatment rules
metronidazole

MTR-0
no masses, tenderness, or rebound
(abdominal examination)

MTRX
methotrexate *also* M, MTX

MTS
medial tibial syndrome
mesial temporal sclerosis
moderate tactile stimulus
multicellular tumor spheroid

MTSO
medical transcription service
organization

MTSS
medial tibial stress syndrome

MTST
maximal treadmill stress test

MTT
malignant trophoblastic teratoma
maximal treadmill testing
meal tolerance test
mean transit time
monotetrazolium

MTU
malignant teratoma, undifferentiated
medical therapy unit
methylthiouracil

M-TURP
minimal transurethral resection of
prostate

MTV
mammary tumor virus (of mice)
metatarsus varus

MTX
methotrexate *also* M, MTRX

MT-Y
multitest yeast (plate)

MTZ
mitoxantrone

μ
chemical potential
dynamic viscosity
electrophoretic mobility
heavy chain of immunoglobulin M
linear attenuation coefficient
magnetic moment *also* m
mean *also* M, m
micro-
micrometer *also* μm
micron
mutation rate
mu (12th letter of Greek alphabet),
lowercase
permeability
population mean (statistics)

MU
　Mache unit *also* Mu
　maternal uncle
　megaunit
　mescaline unit
　million units
　Montevideo unit
　motor unit
　mouse unit

Mu
　Mache unit *also* MU

mU
　milliunit

mu
　micron *also* μ
　millimicron *also* mμ
　mouse unit *also* MU

μA
　microampere

MUA
　middle uterine artery
　multiple unit activity

MUAC
　middle upper arm circumference

MUAP
　(macro) motor unit action potential

μb
　microbar *also* μbar

μbar
　microbar *also* mb

μβ
　Bohr magneton

μC
　microcoulomb *also* mcoul

MUC
　maximal urinary concentration
　mucosal ulcerative colitis

μc
　microcurie *also* mCi

muc
　mucilage

μch, μ-hr
　microcurie-hour *also* μCi-hr

μCi
　microcurie *also* μc

μCi-hr
　microcurie-hour *also* μch, μ-hr

μcoul
　microcoulomb *also* μC

MUCP
　maximum urethral closure pressure

MUD
　matched unrelated donor
　minimal urticarial dose

μ Eq
　microequivalent

μF, μf
　microfarad

MUG
　MUMPS Massachusetts General
　Hospital Utility Multi-Programming
　System Users' Group

μg
　microgram *also* mcg

MUGA
　multigated angiogram
　multiple gated acquisition (blood pool
　image; scan)

μγ
　microgamma

MUGEx
　multiple (blood pool scan during)
　exercise *also* MUGX

μg/kg
　microgram per kilogram

μg/L, μg/l
　microgram per liter

MUGR
　multigated (blood pool image at) rest

MUGX
　multigated (blood pool image during)
　exercise *also* MUGEx

μGy
　microgray

μH
　microhenry

NOTES

μHg
micrometer of mercury *also* μmHg

μ-hr (*var. of* μch)

μin
microinch

μIU
one-millionth International Unit

μkat
microkatal

μL, μl
microliter *also* λ

MULE
microcomputer upper limb exerciser

mult
multiple
multiplication

multi-CSF
multi-colony-stimulating factor

multip
multiparous

MuLV, MuLv
murine leukemia virus

μM
micromolar

μm
micrometer *also* μ
micromilli-

μm³
cubic micrometer *also* cum

μmg
micromilligram (nanogram)

μmHg
micrometer of mercury *also* μHg

μmm
micromillimeter (nanometer)

μmμ
meson

μmol
micromole

μmol/L
micromolar

MUMPS
Massachusetts General Hospital Utility
Multi-Programming System

MuMTv
murine mammary tumor virus

μμ
micromicro-
micromicron

μμC
micromicrocurie (picocurie)

μμc
micromicrocurie

μμF
micromicrofarad (picofarad)

μμg
micromicrogram (picogram)

MUN(WI)
Munich Wistar (rat)

μₒ
permeability of vacuum

MUO
myocardiopathy of unknown origin

μΩ
microhm

MΩ
megohm

mΩ
milliohm

μOsm
micro-osmolar

MUP
major urinary protein
maximal urethral pressure
motor unit potential
mouse urine protein

μR, μr
microroentgen

Mur
muramic acid

MURC
measurable undesirable respiratory
contaminants

MurNAc
N-acetylmuramate

μs
microsecond *also* μsec

musc
muscle
muscular
musculature

μsec
microsecond *also* μs

mus-lig
  musculoligamentous

MUST
  medical unit, self-contained and transportable

MUU
  mouse uterine unit

μU
  microunit

μV
  microvolt

μW
  microwatt

MUWU
  mouse uterine weight unit

MV
  main venule
  malignant (rabbit fibroma) virus
  maternal venous
  maximal ventilation
  measles virus
  mechanical ventilation
  megavolt *also* MeV
  microvilli
  millivolt
  minute ventilation
  minute volume
  mitoxantrone and VePesid (etoposide)
  mitral valve
  mixed venous
  multivesicular
  multivessel

Mv
  mendelevium *also* Md

mV, mv
  millivolt

m.v.
  veterinary physician [L. *Medicus Veterinarius*]

MVA
  malignant ventricular arrhythmia
  mechanical ventricular assistance
  mevalonic acid
  mitral valve area
  modified vaccine (virus) Ankara
  motor vehicle accident

MV·A
  megavolt-ampere

mV·A
  millivolt-ampere

MVAC, M-VAC
  methotrexate, vinblastine, Adriamycin, and cisplatin

MVB
  mixed venous blood
  multivesicular body

MVC
  maximal vital capacity
  maximal voluntary contraction
  myocardial vascular capacity

MVD
  Doctor of Veterinary Medicine *also* DMV, DVM
  Marburg virus disease
  microvascular decompression
  mitral valve disease
  mouse vas deferens
  multivessel (coronary) disease

MVE
  mitral valve echo
  mitral valve (leaflet) excursion
  Murray Valley encephalitis

MVG, MVgrad
  mitral valve gradient

MVH
  massive variceal hemorrhage
  massive vitreous hemorrhage
  methotrexate, VP-16, and hexamethylonelamine

MVI
  multiple vitamin injection
  multivalvular involvement
  multivitamin infusion

MVI-12
  multivitamin infusion

MVK
  Massachusetts Vision Kit

MVL
  mitral valve leaflet

M

NOTES

MVLS
mandibular vestibulolingual sulcoplasty
Mecham Verbal Language Scale

MVM
microvillose membrane
minute virus of mice

MVMT
movement

MVN
medial ventromedial nucleus

MVO
maximal venous outflow
mean venous outflow

MVO2, MVO$_2$
maximal venous oxygen
  (consumption)
myocardial ventilation, oxygen (rate)
oxygen content of mixed venous
  blood

mVO$_2$
minimal venous oxygen (consumption)

MVOA
mitral valve orifice area

MVOS
mixed venous oxygen saturation

MVP
mean venous pressure
microvascular pressure
mitomycin, vinblastine, and Platinol
mitral valve prolapse

MVPP
mechlorethamine, vinblastine,
  procarbazine, and prednisone
mustine, vinblastine, procarbazine, and
  prednisone

MVPS
mitral valve prolapse syndrome

MVPT
Motor-Free Visual Perception Test
  also MFVPT

MVR
massive vitreous reaction
massive vitreous retractor (blade)
maximal ventilation rate
microvitreoretinal
minimal vascular resistance
mitral valve regurgitation
mitral valve replacement

MVRI
mixed vaccine, respiratory infection
mixed virus respiratory infection

MVS
Massachusetts XII Vitrectomy System
mitral valve stenosis
motor, vascular, and sensory

mV-sec
millivolt-second

MVT
maximal ventilation time

MV-T
mitral valve-transverse

MVTR
moisture vapor transmission rate

MVV
maximal ventilatory volume
maximal voluntary ventilation

MVV$_1$
maximal ventilatory volume

MVVPP
mechlorethamine, vincristine,
  vinblastine, procarbazine, and
  prednisone
Mustargen (nitrogen mustard),
  vincristine, vinblastine, procarbazine,
  and prednisone

MW
mean weight
megawatt
microwave *also* mw
molecular weight *also* mol wt, MWt
Munich Wistar (rat)

M-W
Mallory-Weiss syndrome
men and women

mW
milliwatt

mw
microwave *also* MW

mWb
milliweber

MWC
Monod-Wyman-Changeux (model)

MWCB
manufacturer's working cell bank

MWD
microwave diathermy
molecular weight distribution

MWI
Medical Walk-In (Clinic)

MWLT
Modified Word Learning Test

MWMT
Monotic Word Memory Test

MWP
mean wedge pressure

MWPC
multiwire proportional chamber

MWS
Marden-Walker syndrome
Mickety-Wilson syndrome
Moersch-Woltman syndrome

MWT
malpositioned wisdom teeth
myocardial wall thickness

MWt
molecular weight *also* mol wt, MW

MX
matrix

Mx
mastectomy
maxillary
maxwell
MEDEX (q.v.)
multiple
myringotomy

M$_{xy}$
transverse magnetization

My
myopia
myxedematous

my
mayer (unit of heat capacity)

Mycol
mycologist
mycology

MYD
mydriatic

MyD
myotonic (muscular) dystrophy

MYEL
multiple myeloma

Myel
myelocyte

myel
myelin
myelinated

Myelo
myelogram
myelography

MyG
myasthenia gravis *also* MG

Myg
myriagram

MyL, Myl
myrialiter

Mym
myriameter

MyMD
myotonic muscular dystrophy *also* MMD

MYO
myoglobin *also* Mb, MbCO, MbO$_2$, MYOGLB

myo
myocardial
myocardium

MYOGLB
myoglobin *also* Mb, MbCO, MbO$_2$, MYO

myop
myopia

MYS
myasthenia syndrome

MYTGC
Miller-Yoder Test of Grammatical Comprehension

MZ
mantle zone
mezlocillin
monozygotic

M$_z$
longitudinal magnetization

m/z
mass-to-charge ratio

NOTES

MZA
    monozygotic (twins raised) apart

MZL
    marginal zone lymphocyte

MZT
    monozygotic (twins raised) together

N

antigenic determinant of erythrocytes
asparagine *also* ASN, Asn
Avogadro constant/number *also* Λ, Na, N_A, L
inherited blood factor in MNS blood group
loudness
nasal *also* n, NAS
nasion
nausea
negative *also* neg
negro
neomycin *also* NE, neo, NM
neper (unit for comparing magnitude of two powers)
nerve *also* n
neural
neuraminidase
neurologist *also* neur, neuro, neurol
neurology *also* neur, neuro, neurol
neuropathy
neutron number
neutrophil
newton
nicotinamide
nitrogen *also* N2
no
nodal
node
nodule
none
nonmalignant
Nonne (globulin test)
noon *also* M, m.
nor *also* n
normal *also* n, NL, Nl, nl, NOR, norm, NR
normal concentration
normality (equivalent/liter)
not
noun
NPH insulin
nucleoside *also* Nuc
nucleus
number *also* n, NO, No, no.
number of atoms
number density (number of moles of substance per unit of volume)
number of molecules
number of neutrons in an atomic nucleus

number of observations (in statistics) *also* n
number in sample
numerical aptitude (General Aptitude Test Battery)
nu (13th letter of Greek alphabet), uppercase
population size
radiance
refractive index *also* n
sample size *also* n
spin density
unit of neutron dosage

N-I—N-XII
first through twelfth cranial nerves

N.II
optic nerve

N.III
oculomotor nerve

N.IV
trochlear nerve

N.V
trigeminal nerve

0.02N
fiftieth-normal (solution) *also* N/50

0.1N
tenth-normal (solution) *also* N/10

0.5N
half-normal (solution) *also* N/2

2N
double-normal (solution)

N2
nitrogen *also* N
second nerve

5'-N
5'-nucleotidase

N/2
half-normal (solution) *also* 0.5N
seminormal

N/10
tenth-normal (solution) *also* 0.1N

N/50
fiftieth-normal (solution) *also* 0.02N

^{13}N
nitrogen-13

^{14}N
  nitrogen-14

^{15}N
  nitrogen-15

n *also* N
  amount of substance expressed in
    moles
  haploid chromosome number
  index of refraction
  nano- (prefix)
  nasal *also* N
  nerve *also* N
  neuter *also* neut
  neutron
  neutron dosage (unit of)
  neutron number density
  night
  nor *also* N
  normal *also* N, NL, Nl, nl, NOR,
    norm, NR
  normal concentration
  number *also* N, NO, No, no.
  number of density of molecule
  number of observations *also* N
  principle quantum number
  refractive index *also* RI
  rotational frequency
  sample size *also* N

2n
  diploid chromosome number

3n
  triploid chromosome number

4n
  tetraploid

n̄
  mean value of n for a number of
    observations (in statistics)

n.
  born [L. *natus*]
  nostril [L. *naris*]

n_0
  Loschmidt's number

NA
  nalidixic acid
  Narcotics Anonymous
  Native American
  network administrator
  neuraminidase
  neurologic age
  neutralizing antibody
  neutrophil antibody
  nicotinamide

  nicotinic acid
  nitric acid
  no abnormality
  Nomina Anatomica
  nonadherent
  non-A (hepatitis)
  nonalcoholic
  nonamnionic
  nonmyelinated axon
  noradrenaline
  not admitted
  not antagonized
  not applicable *also* N/A
  not attempted
  not available
  nuclear antibody
  nuclear antigen
  nucleic acid
  nucleus accumbens (septi)
  nucleus ambiguus
  numeric aperture
  nurse anesthetist
  nurse's aid
  nursing action
  nursing assistant

N&A
  normal and active

N/A
  no alternative
  not applicable *also* NA

N_A
  Avogadro number *also* Λ, Na, N, L

Na
  Avogadro number (constant) *also* Λ,
    N, N_A, L
  natrium
  noise rating number (in acoustics)
  sodium [L. *natrium*]

^{23}Na
  sodium-23

^{24}Na
  sodium-24

nA
  nanoampere

na
  nephrogenic adenoma

NAA
  N-acetylaspartate
  naphthalene acetic acid
  neutral amino acid
  neutron activation analysis
  neutrophil aggregation activity

nicotinic acid amide
no apparent abnormalities

NAAC
no apparent anesthetic complication

NAACLS
National Accrediting Agency for Clinical Laboratory Sciences

NAACP
neoplasia, allergy, Addison (disease), collagen (vascular disease), and parasites

NAAP
N-acetyl-4-amino-phenazone

NAB
nonweightbearing ambulation
novarsenobenzene

NABS
normoactive bowel sounds

NAC
accessory nucleus (Monakow nucleus)
N-acetyl-L-cysteine
neoadjuvant chemotherapy
nitrogen mustard, Adriamycin (doxorubicin), and CCNU (lomustine)
nonadherent cell

NACD
not acidified

NACDG
North American Contact Dermatitis Group

NAC-EDTA
N-acetyl-L-cysteine ethylenediamine-tetraacetic acid

n-Ach
achievement need (in psychology)

NACI
National Advisory Committee on Immunization

NACS
Neurologic and Adaptive Capacity Score

NAD
new antigenic determinant
nicotinamide adenine dinucleotide
nicotinic acid dehydrogenase

no abnormal discovery
no abnormality demonstrable
no active disease
no acute disease
no apparent disease
no appreciable disease
normal axis deviation
nothing abnormal detected
nothing abnormal discovered

NAD⁺
oxidized form of nicotinamide adenine dinucleotide

NaD
sodium dialysate

NADA
New Animal Drug Application

NADG
nicotinamide adenine dinucleotide glycohydrolase

NADH
nicotinamide adenine dinucleotide (reduced form)

NADL
National Association of Dental Laboratories

NaDodSO₄
sodium dodecyl sulfate *also* SDS

NADP
nicotinamide adenine dinucleotide phosphate *also* NADPH

NADP⁺
oxidized form of nicotinamide adenine dinucleotide phosphate

NADPH
nicotinamide adenine dinucleotide phosphate *also* NADP

NADSIC
no apparent disease seen in chest

NAE
net acid excretion

Na$_e$
exchangeable body sodium (natrium)

NAEP
National Asthma Education Program

N

NOTES

NAF
nafcillin *also* NF
net acid flux
neutrophil activating factor

NaF
sodium fluorescein

NAG
N-acetyl-β-glucosaminidase
N-acetylglutamate
narrow-angle glaucoma
nonagglutinable (vibrios)
nonagglutinating

NAGO
neuraminidase and galactose oxidase

NAHI
National Athletic Health Institute

NAI
net acid input (urinary)
neuraminidase inhibition *also* NI
no acute inflammation
nonaccidental injury
nonadherence index

NAIR
nonadrenergic inhibitory response

NaI(T)
thallium-activated sodium iodide
(sodium iodide crystal)

NaI(TI)
thallium-activated sodium iodide
crystal (in gamma ray detectors)

Na&K
sodium and potassium (in urine)

NaK ATPase
sodium- and potassium-activated
adenosine triphosphatase

Na&KSP
sodium and potassium spot (urine
test)

NAL
nonadherent leukocyte

NALD
neonatal adrenoleukodystrophy

NALL
null (cell line of) acute lymphocytic
leukemia

NALP
neuroadenolysis of pituitary

NALS
neonatal adjuvant life support

NAM
natural actomyosin

NAMCS
National Ambulatory Medical Care
Survey

NAME
nevi, atrial myxoma, myxoid
neurofibroma, and ephelides
(syndrome)

NAMES
National Association of Medical
Equipment Suppliers

NAMN
nicotinic acid mononucleotide

NAMRU
Navy Medical Reserve Unit

NANB
non-A, non-B (hepatitis)

NANBH
non-A, non-B hepatitis

NANBNCH
non-A, non-B, non-C hepatitis

NANBV
non-A, non-B (hepatitis) virus

NANC
nonadrenergic noncholinergic
noncholinergic (neuron)

NAND
not-and (result is false only if all
arguments are true—otherwise, result
is true)

N ant/post
anterior and posterior "zones" (nerve
cell groups—nuclei of hypothalamus)

NAP
narrative, assessment, and plan
nasion pogonion (angle of convexity
in craniometrics)
nerve action potential
neutrophil-activating protein
neutrophil alkaline phosphatase
nonacute profile
nucleic acid phosphatase

NaP
sodium phosphate-based laxative

NAPA
N-acetyl procainamide

NAPD
no active pulmonary disease

Na Pent
Pentothal Sodium

NaPG
sodium pregnanediol glucuronide

NAPH
naphthyl

NAPI
Neurodevelopmental Assessment Procedure for Preterm Infants

NAPQI
N-acetyl-p-benzoquinoneimine

naqs
number of planar acquisitions per phase-encoding step

NAR
nasal airway resistance
no action required
no adverse reaction
not at risk

NARA
Narcotics Addict Rehabilitation Act

NARC, narc
narcotic *also* narco
narcotics (officer, slang) *also* narco, NO

narc
nucleus arcuatus (nucleus infundibularis)

narco
narcolepsy
narcotic *also* NARC
narcotic addict (slang)
narcotics (hospital, officer, treatment center—slang) *also* NARC, NO

NARMC
Naval Aerospace and Regional Medical Center

NAS
nasal *also* N, n
neonatal abstinence syndrome
neonatal air leak syndrome
neuroallergic syndrome
no added salt
normalized alignment score

NASCET
North American Symptomatic Carotid Endarterectomy Trial

NASDAD
National Association of Seventh-Day Adventist Dentists

NAS-NRC
National Academy of Science-National Research Council

Na-Spt
sodium spot (urine test)

NAT
N-acetyltransferase
natal
neonatal alloimmune thrombocytopenia
no action taken
nonaccidental trauma

Nat
native *also* nat
natural *also* nat

nat
national
native *also* Nat
natural *also* Nat
nature

NATB
Nonreading Aptitude Test Battery

NATM
sodium aurothiomalate

NATP
neonatal autoimmune thrombocytopenic purpura

NATR
National Association of Tumor Registrars

NB
nail bed
needle biopsy
Negri bodies
nervus buccalis
neuroblast
neuroblastoma
neurometric (test) battery
newborn *also* nb
nitrogen balance
nitrous oxide-barbiturate

N

NOTES

NB *(continued)*
non-B (hepatitis)
normoblast
note well [L. *nota bene*] *also* n.b.
novobiocin
nuclear bag (certain intrafusal muscle
fiber nuclei of a neuromuscular
spindle)
nutrient broth

N/B
neopterin to biopterin (ratio)

Nb
niobium

n.b.
note well [L. *nota bene*] *also* NB

nb
newborn *also* NB

NBC
nephroblastomatosis complex
nonbattle casualty
nonbed care
nuclear, biologic, chemical

NBCC
nevoid basal cell carcinoma

NBCCS
nevoid basal cell carcinoma syndrome

NBCIE
nonbullous congenital ichthyosiform
erythroderma

NBD
neurogenic bladder dysfunction
neurologic bladder dysfunction
no brain damage
nucleotide-binding domain

NBE
northern bean extract

NBEI
non–butanol-extractable iodine
(syndrome)

NBF
not breastfed

NBI
neutrophil bactericidal index
no bone injury
nonbattle injury

NBICU
newborn intensive care unit *also* NB
Int, NICU

NBIL
neonatal bilirubin

NB Int
newborn intensive (care unit) *also*
NBICU

nbl
normoblast

NBM
no bowel movement
normal bone marrow
normal bowel movement
nothing by mouth *also* NPO
nucleus basalis of Meynert

nbM
newborn mouse

nbMb
newborn mouse brain

NBME
National Board of Medical Examiners
normal bone marrow extract

NBN
narrow band noise
newborn nursery

NBO
nonbed occupancy

NBP
needle biopsy of prostate
neoplastic brachial plexopathy
nonbacterial prostatitis

NBQC
narrow-base quad cane

NBS
National Bureau of Standards
Neri-Barré syndrome
nevoid basal (cell carcinoma)
syndrome
newborn screen (serum thyroxine &
phenylketonuria)
Nijmegen breakage syndrome
no bacteria seen
normal blood serum
normal bowel sounds
normal brain stem
normal burro serum
nystagmus blockage syndrome

NBT
nitroblue tetrazolium (test)
normal breast tissue

NBTE
nonbacterial thrombotic endocarditis

NBTF
National Biomedical Tracer Facility

NBTG
nitrobenzylthioguanosine

NTNF
newborn, term, normal, female

NTNM
newborn, term, normal, male

NBTS
National Blood Transfusion Service

NBVV
nonbleeding visible vessel

NBW
normal birth weight

NC
nabothian cyst
nasal cannula
nasal clearance
natural cytotoxicity
neck complaint
neonatal cholestasis
nephrocalcin
nerve conduction
neural crest
neurogenic claudication
neurologic check
neurologic control
nevus comedonicus
nitrocellulose
nitrosocarbazole
no casualty
no change *also* N/C
no charge
no complaints *also* N/C
noise criterion
noncirrhotic
noncontributory
normal control
normocephalic
nose clip
nose cone
not classified
not completed
not cultured
nucleocapsid
Nurse Corps
nursing coordination

N:C
nuclear-cytoplasmic (ratio) *also* N/C, NCR

N&C
nerves and circulation *also* N/C

N/C
nerves and circulation *also* N&C
neurocirculatory
no change *also* NC
no complaints *also* NC
nuclear/cytoplasmic (ratio) *also* N:C, N&C, HCR

nC
nanocoulomb

nc
nanocurie *also* nCi

NCA
neurocirculatory asthenia
neutrophil chemotactic activity
no congenital abnormalities
nodulocystic acne
noncontractile area
nonspecific cross-reacting antigen
nuclear cerebral angiogram

NCAM, N-CAM
neural cell adhesion molecule

NCAMLP
National Certification Agency for Medical Laboratory Personnel

NcAMP
nephrogenous cyclic adenosine monophosphate

NCAP
nasal continuous airway pressure

NCAS
neocarzinostatin (zinostatin) *also* NCS

NCAT, NC/AT
normocephalic and traumatic

NCB
no code blue

NCC
no concentrated carbohydrates
noncoronary cusp
nucleus caudalis centralis
nursing care continuity

NCCLS
National Committee for Clinical Laboratory Standards

N

NOTES

NCCS
National Coalition for Cancer
Survivorship

NCCU
newborn convalescent care unit

NCD
neurocirculatory dystonia
nitrogen clearance delay
no congenital deformities
normal childhood diseases
normal childhood disorders
not considered disabling

NCDV
National Communicable Disease
Center
Nebraska calf diarrhea virus

NCE
negative contrast echocardiography
new chemical entity
nonconvulsive epilepsy

NCEP
National Cholesterol Education
Program

NCF
night care facility
no cold fluids
(polymorphonuclear) neutrophil
chemotactic factor

NCF(C)
neutrophil chemotactic factor
(complement)

NCGL
nucleus corporis geniculati lateralis

NCHLS
National Council of Health
Laboratory Services

NCHS
National Center for Health Statistics

NCI
naphthalene creosote and iodoform
National Cancer Institute
nuclear contour index
nucleus colliculi inferioris
nursing care integration

nCi
nanocurie *also* nc

NCJ
needle catheter jejunostomy

NCL
neuronal ceroid lipofuscinosis
nuclear cardiology laboratory

NCLEX-RN
National Council Licensure
Examination for Registered Nurses

NCM
nailfold capillary microscope

N/cm²
newton per square centimeter

NCMC
natural cell-mediated cytotoxicity

NCME
Network for Continuing Medical
Education

NCMHI
National Clearinghouse for Mental
Health Information

NCNC
normochromic normocytic
(erythrocyte)

NCNCA
normochromic normocytic anemia

NCO
no complaints offered

NCP
no caffeine or pepper
nonclonogenic proliferating (cells)
noncollagen protein
nursing care plan

n-CPAP
nasal continuous positive airway
pressure

NCPE
noncardiogenic pulmonary edema

NCPF
noncirrhotic portal fibrosis

NCPR
no cardiopulmonary resuscitation

NCR
neurologic/circulatory/range of motion
neutrophil chemotactic response
nuclear-cytoplasmic ratio *also* N/C,
N:C

NCRC
non–child-resistant container

NCRP
National Council on Radiation
Protection (and Measurements)

CS
neocarzinostatin (zinostatin) *also* NCAS
nerve conduction study
newborn calf serum
no concentrated sweets
noncircumferential stenosis
noncoronary sinus
noncured sarcoidosis
noncurrent serum

CT
nerve conduction test
neural crest tumor
neutron capture therapy
noncontact tonometry
number connection test

CTC
National Cancer Tissue Culture
National Collection of Type Cultures

CV
nerve conduction velocity (study)
no commercial value
noncholera vibrio

CVS
nerve conduction velocity study

CYC
National Collection of Yeast Cultures

D
Doctor of Naturopathy
nasal deformity
nasolacrimal duct
natural death
Naval Dispensary
neonatal death *also* NND
neoplastic disease
nervous debility
neurologic development
neuropsychologic deficit
neurotic depression
neutral density
Newcastle disease
new drug
nifedipine *also* NIF
no data
no date
no disease
nondetectable
nondetermined

nondiabetic
nondisabling
none detectable
normal delivery
normal deposition
normal development
normal dose
Norrie disease
nose drops
not determined
not diagnosed
not done
nothing done
not nondetectable
nucleus of Darkshewitsch
nurse's diagnosis
nutritionally deprived

N&D
nodular and diffuse (lymphoma)

N/D
no defects

N$_D$, n$_D$
refractive index

Nd
neodymium
number of dissimilar (matches)

NDA
National Dental Association
New Drug Application
no data available
no demonstrable antibodies
no detectable activity
no detectable antibody

NDC
National Data Communications
National Drug Code
Naval Dental Clinic
nondifferentiated cell
nuclear dehydrogenating clostridia

NDCD
National Drug Code Directory

NDD
no-dialysis days

NDDG
National Diabetes Data Group

N

NOTES

NKHHC
nonketotic hyperglycmic-hyperosmolar coma

NKHOC
nonketotic hyperosmolar coma

NKHS
nonketotic hyperosmolar syndrome
normal Krebs-Henseleit solution

NKMA
no known medication allergies

NKSF
natural killer cell-stimulating factor

NKTS
natural killer target structure

NL
nasolacrimal
neural lobe
neutral lipid
nodular lymphoma
normal *also* N, n, Nl, nl, NOR, norm, NR
normal libido
normal limits
normolipemic
Nyhan-Lesch (syndrome)

Nl
normal *also* N, n, NL, nl, NOR, norm, NR

nL
nanoliter *also* nl

n.l.
it is not clear [L. *non liquet*]
it is not permitted [L. *non licet*]

nl
nanoliter *also* nL
normal limits
normal (value) *also* n, NL, NOR, norm

NLA
neuroleptanalgesia
neuroleptanesthesia
normal lactase activity

NLAA
naphthoxylactic acid

NLAL
nodule-like alveolar lesion

NLB
needle liver biopsy

NLC&C, NL C/Cl
normal libido, coitus, and climax

NLD
nasolacrimal duct
necrobiosis lipoidica diabeticorum

NLDL
normal low-density lipoprotein

NLE
neonatal lupus erythematosus
nurse's late entry

Nle
norleucine

NLF
nasolabial fold
neonatal lung fibroblast
nonlactose fermentation

NLH
nodular lymphoid hyperplasia

NLM
National Library of Medicine
noise level monitor

NLMC
nocturnal leg muscle cramp

NLN
no longer needed

NLP
neurolinguistic program
nodular liquefying panniculitis
no light perception
normal light perception
normal luteal phase

NLPD
nodular-lymphocytic, poorly differentiated

NLS
neonatal lupus syndrome
nonlinear least squares (method)
normal lymphocyte supernatant

NLSD
normal life span for dogs

N

NOTES

NLT
Names Learning Test
normal lymphocyte transfer (test)
not later than *also* nlt
not less than *also* nlt
nucleus lateralis tuberis

nlt
not later than *also* NLT
not less than *also* NLT

NLX
naloxone *also* Nx

NM
neomycin *also* N, NE, neo
neuromedical
neuromuscular
nictitating membrane [L. *nictitare* to
wink]
night and morning *also* N&M, n.m.
nitrogen mustard *also* HN2
nodular melanoma
nodular mixed (lymphocytic-
histiocystic)
nonmalignant
nonmotile (bacteria)
nonwhite male
normetadrenaline
normetanephrine
not measurable
not measured
not mentioned
not motile
nuclear medicine
nuclear membrane

N/M
newton per meter

N&M
nerves and muscles
night and morning *also* NM, n.m.

N/m²
newton per square meter

Nm
nux moschata (nutmeg) *also* nm

nM
nanomolar

n.m.
night and morning [L. *nocte et
mane*]

nm
nanometer
nonmetallic
nux moschata (nutmeg) *also* Nm

NMA
neurogenic muscular atrophy

NMAC
National Medical Audio-Visual Center

NM(ASCP)
Technologist in Nuclear Medicine
certified by American Society of
Clinical Pathologists

NMATWT
New Mexico Attitude Toward Work
Test

NMB
neuromuscular blockade

NMBA
neuromuscular blocking agent
nitrosomethylbenzylamine

NMC
National Medical Care
neuromuscular control
nodular, mixed cell (lymphoma)
nucleus reticularis magnocellularis
nurse-managed center

NMCD
nephrophthisis-medullary cystic disease

NMCPT
New Mexico Career Planning Test

NMCUES
National Medical Care Utilization and
Expenditure Survey

NMD
neuromuscular disorder
neuromyodysplasia
normal muscle development

NMDA
N-methyl-D-aspartate

NMEP
neurogenic motor-evoked potential

NMES
neuromuscular electrical stimulation
neuromuscular electrical stimulator

NMF
nonmigrating fraction (of
spermatozoa)

NMFI
National Master Facility Inventory

NMG
N-methyl-D-glucamide

NMGTD
nonmetastatic gestational trophoblastic disease

NMH
neurally mediated hypotension

NMI
no mental illness
no middle initial
normal male infant

NMJ
neuromuscular junction

NMJAPT
New Mexico Job Application Procedures Test

NMKOT
New Mexico Knowledge of Occupations Test

NML
National Medical Library
nodular mixed lymphoma

NMM
nodular malignant melanoma
Nonne-Milroy-Meige (syndrome)

NMN
nicotinamide mononucleotide
no middle name
normetanephrine

NMN+
nicotinamide mononucleotide (reduced form)

NMNRU
National Medical Neuropsychiatric Research Unit

NMO
nitrogen mustard oxide

nmol
nanomole

nmol/L
millimicromolar
nanomole per liter

NMOS
N-type metal oxide semiconductor

NMP
neutral metallopeptidase

normal menstrual period
nucleoside 5'-monophosphate

NMPCA
nonmetric principal component analysis

NMR
Neill-Mooser reaction
neonatal mortality rate
nictitating membrane response
nuclear magnetic resonance

NMRDC
Naval Medical Research and Development Command

NMRI
nuclear magnetic resonance imaging

NMRL
Naval Medical Research Laboratory

NMRS
nuclear magnetic resonance spectroscopy

NMRU
Naval Medical Research Unit

NMS
Naval Medical School
neuroleptic malignant syndrome
neuromuscular spindle
normal mouse serum

N·m/s
newton meter per second

NMSE
normalized mean square root

NMSIDS
near-miss sudden infant death syndrome

NMT
nebulized mist treatment
neuromuscular tension
neuromuscular transmission
no more than
nuclear medicine technology

NMTB
neuromuscular transmission blockade

NMTD
nonmetastatic trophoblastic disease

NOTES

N

NMTS
neuromuscular tension state

NMU
neuromuscular unit

NMUT
nitrosomethylurethane

N/N
negative/negative
nurse's notes *also* NN

NN
neonatal
nevocellular nevus
normally nourished
normal nursery
nurse's notes *also* N/N

N-N
nurse to nurse (orders)

N:N
azo group (chemical group with two
nitrogen atoms)

n.n.
new name [L. *nomen novum*] *also*
n. nov., nom. nov., nov. n.

nn
nerves

NNA
normochromic normocytic anemia

NNAS
neonatal narcotic abstinence syndrome

NNBC
node negative breast cancer

NNC
National Nutrition Consortium

NND
neonatal death *also* ND
New and Nonofficial Drugs
nonspecific nonerosive duodenitis

NNDC
National Naval Dental Center

NNE
neonatal necrotizing enterocolitis
nonneuronal enolase

NNG
nonspecific nonerosive gastritis

NNHS
National Nursing Home Survey

NNI
noise and number index

NNL
no new laboratory (test orders)

NNM
neonatal mortality
Nicolle-Novy-MacNeal (medium) *also*
NNN

NNN
nitrosonornicotine

NNO
no new orders

n. nov.
new name [L. *nomen novum*] *also*
n.n., nom. nov., nov. n.

NNP
neonatal nurse practitioner
nerve net pulse

NNR
New and Nonofficial Remedies
not necessary to return

NNS
neonatal screen (hematocrit, total
bilirubin, and total protein)
nonneoplastic syndrome
nonnutritive sucking

NNT
neonatally tolerant
nuclei nervi trigemini

NNU
net nitrogen utilization

NNWI
Neonatal Narcotic Withdrawal Index

NO
narcotics officer *also* NARC, narc,
narco
nasal oxygen
nitric oxide
nitroso-
nitrous oxide *also* nit. ox.
none obtained
nonobese
number *also* N, n, No, no.
nursing office

N₂O
nitrous oxide

No, no.
nobelium
number [L. *numero*] *also* N, n, NO

NOA
nurse obstetric assistant

NOBT
nonoperative biopsy technique

noc, noct
nocturia
nocturnal [L. *noctis* of the night]

NO-CCE
no clubbing, cyanosis, or edema

noc. maneq.
at night and in the morning [L. *nocte maneque*]

noct (*var. of* noc)

NOCTI
National Occupation Competency Testing (Program)

NOD
nodular (melanoma)
nondefinitive (pattern)
nonobese diabetic
notify of death

NOE
nuclear Overhauser effect

NOEL
no observed effect level (of toxin)

no ess abn
no essential abnormalities

NOF
nonossifying fibroma

NOFT
nonorganic failure to thrive

NOGM
no gammopathy (detected)

NOII
nonocclusive intestinal ischemia

NOK
next of kin

NOM
nonsuppurative otitis media
normal extraocular movements

nom. dub.
a doubtful name [L. *nomen dubium*]

NOMI
nonocclusive mesenteric infarction

nom. nov.
new name [L. *nomen novum*] *also* n.n., n. nov., nov. n.

nom. nud.
name without designation [L. *nomen nudum*]

NOND
none detected

NONF
nonfasting

non-MALT
non–ucosa-associated lymphoid tissue (lymphoma)

non pal
not palpable

non reb
nonrebreathing (mask)

nonREM, non-REM
nonrapid eye movement *also* NREM

non rep., non repetat.
do not repeat (norefills) [L. *non repetatur*] *also* NR

NONS
nonspecific

nonsegs
nonsegmented (neutrophils)

nonvis, nonviz
nonvisualized

NOOB
not out of bed

N$_2$O/O$_2$/opioid
nitrous oxide-oxygen-opioid (anesthetic technique)

NOP
national outpatient profile
not otherwise provided (for) *also* NP

NOR
noradrenaline *also* Noradr
normal *also* N, n, NL, Nl, nl, norm, NR
nortriptyline
nucleolar organizing region (cytogenetics)

N

NOTES

Noradr
noradrenaline *also* NOR

NORC
normal curve

NOR-EPI
norepinephrine *also* NE

norleu
norleucine

norm
normal *also* N, n, NL, Nl, nl,
NOR, NR

normet
normetanephrine

NOS
network operating system
nitric oxide synthase *also* iNOS
not on staff
not otherwise specified

nos
numbers

NOSAC
nonsteroidal antiinflammatory
compound

NOSIE
Nurses' Observation Scale for
Inpatient Evaluation

NOSTA
Naval Ophthalmic Support and
Training Activity

NOT
nocturnal oxygen therapy
nucleus of optic tract

NOTT
nocturnal oxygen therapy trial

Nov
novobiocin

nov.
new [L. *novum*]

nov. n.
new name [L. *novum nomen*] *also*
n.n., n. nov., nom. nov.

NOVS
National Office of Vital Statistics

nov. sp.
new species [L. *novum species*]

NOW
negotiable order of withdrawal

NP
nasal prongs
nasopharyngeal
nasopharynx *also* NPhx
near point (ophthalmology)
neonatal-perinatal
nerve palsy
neuritic plaque
neuropathology *also* neuropath
neuropeptide
neurophysin *also* Np
neuropsychiatry
newly presented
new patient
Niemann-Pick (disease)
nitrogen-phosphorus (detector in gas
chromatography)
nitrophenide
nitrophenol
nitroprusside
nodular paragranuloma
nonpalpable
nonpathologic
nonpaying
nonphagocytic
nonpracticing
nonproducer (cell)
no pain
no phone
no progression
normal plasma
normal pressure
nosocomial pneumonia
not (otherwise) provided (for) *also*
NOP
not palpable
not perceptible
not performed
not practiced
not pregnant
not present
nuclear pharmacist
nuclear pharmacy
nucleoplasmic (index)
nucleoprotein
nucleoside phosphorylase
nursed poorly
Nurse Practitioner
nursing practice
nursing procedure
proper name [L. *nomen proprium*]
also n.p.

N-P
need-persistence

Np
    neper (unit for comparing magnitude of two powers, usually electrical or acoustic)
    neptunium
    neurophysin *also* NP

n.p.
    proper name [L. *nomen proprium*] *also* NP

np
    nucleotide pair

NPA
    nasopharyngeal airway
    nasopharyngeal aspirate
    near point of accommodation
    no previous admission
    nucleus of pretectal area

NPa
    nail patella

NPAT
    nonparoxysmal atrial tachycardia

Np-AVP
    neurophysin associated with vasopressin

NPB
    nodal premature beat
    nonprotein bound

NPBF
    nonplacental blood flow

NPC
    nasopharyngeal cancer
    nasopharyngeal carcinoma
    near point of convergence
    nodal premature contractions
    nonparenchymal (liver) cell
    nonpatient contact
    nonproductive cough
    nonprotein calorie
    no prenatal care *also* NPNC
    no previous complaint
    nucleus of posterior commissure

NPCa
    nasopharyngeal carcinoma

NPCPAP
    nasopharyngeal continuous positive airway pressure

NPCR
    normalized protein catabolic rate

NPD
    narcissistic personality disorder
    natriuretic plasma dialysate
    negative pressure device
    Niemann-Pick disease
    nitrogen-phosphorus detector
    nonprescription drugs
    no pathologic diagnosis

NPDL
    nodular poorly differentiated lymphocyte
    nodular poorly differentiated lymphocytic (lymphoma)

NPDR
    nonproliferative diabetic retinopathy

NPE
    neurogenic pulmonary edema
    neuropsychologic examination
    nonpulmonary route of elimination
    no palpable enlargement
    normal pelvic examination

N periv
    nuclei periventriculares

NPEV
    nonpolio enterovirus

NPF
    nasopharyngeal fiberscope
    no predisposing factor

NPFT
    Neurotic Personality Factor Test

NPG
    nonpregnant

NPGS
    neopentyl glycol succinate

NPH
    neutral protamine Hagedorn (insulin)
    no previous history
    normal pressure hydrocephalus
    nucleus pulposus herniation

NPHI
    neutral protamine Hagedorn insulin

NPhx
    nasopharynx *also* NP

N

NOTES

NPI
Narcissistic Personality Inventory
neonatal perception inventory
neuropsychiatric institute
no present illness
nucleoplasmic index

NPIC
neurogenic peripheral intermittent
claudication

NPII
Neonatal Pulmonary Insufficiency
Index

NPJT
nonparoxysmal (atrioventricular)
junctional tachycardia

NPL
neoproteolipid
nodular poorly differentiated
lymphoma

NPM
nothing per mouth

NPN
nonprotein nitrogen

NPNC
no prenatal care *also* NPC

NPO
nothing by mouth [L. *non per os*]
also NBM
nucleus preopticus

NPO/HS
nothing by mouth at bedtime [L.
nulla per os hora somni]

NPOS
nitrite positive

Np-OT
oxytocin-associated neurophysin

NPP
nitrophenylphosphate
normal pool plasma
normal postpartum

NPPB
normal perfusion pressure
breakthrough

NPPNG
non–penicillinase-producing *Neisseria
gonorrheae*

NP polio
nonparalytic poliomyelitis

NPR
net protein ratio
normal pulse rate
nothing per rectum
nucleoside phosphoribosyl

NPRM
notice of proposed rulemaking

Nps
nitrophenylsulfenyl

NPSA
nonphysician surgical assistant
normal pilosebaceous apparatus

NPSG
nocturnal polysomnogram

NPSH
nonprotein sulfhydryl (group)

NPT
neoprecipitin test
nocturnal penile tumescence
normal pressure and temperature

NPU
net protein utilization

NPV
negative predictive value
negative pressure ventilation
nuclear polyhidrosis virus
nucleus paraventricularis

NPY
neuropeptide Y

NQA
nursing quality assurance

NQMI
non–Q-wave myocardial infarction

NQR
nuclear quadruple resonance

NQWMI
non–Q-wave myocardial infarction

NR
do not repeat (no refills) [L. *non
repetatur*] *also* non rep., non repetat.,
n.r.
nerve root
neural retina
neutral red
noise reduction
nonreactive
nonrebreathing
nonreimbursable
no radiation
no reaction

no recurrence
no refill
no rehearsal
no rejection
no report
no response
no return
normal *also* N, n, NL, Nl, nl, NOR, norm
normal range
normal reaction
normal record
normotensive rat *also* NTR
not reached
not readable
not recorded
not reported
not resolved
nurse
nutrition ratio
Reynolds number *also* N_R

N/R
not remarkable

N_R
Reynolds number *also* NR

n.r.
do not repeat [L. *non repetatur*] *also* non rep., NR

nr
near
no refills

NRA
nitrate reductase
nucleus raphe alatus
nucleus retroambigualis

NRAF
nonrheumatic atrial fibrillation

NRB
nonrejoining (DNA strand) break

NRBC
normal red blood cell
nucleated red blood cell (mass) *also* NRbc

NRbc
nucleated red blood cell (mass) *also* NRBC

NRBS
nonrebreathing system

NRC
National Research Council
noise reduction coefficient
normal retinal correspondence
not routine care
Nuclear Regulatory Commission

NRCC
National Registry in Clinical Chemistry

NRCL
nonrenal clearance

NRD
nonrenal death

NREH
normal renin essential hypertension

NREM
nonrapid eye movement (sleep) *also* nonREM, non-REM

NREMS
nonrapid eye movement sleep

NRF
normal renal function

NRFC
non–rosette-forming cell

NRGC
nucleus reticularis gigantocellularis

NRH
nodular regenerative hyperplasia (of liver)

NRI
nerve root involvement
nerve root irritation
neutral regular insulin
nonrespiratory infection

NRK
normal rat kidney

NRL
nucleus reticularis lateralis

NRM
National Registry of Microbiologists
non-rebreathing mask
normal ang (of) motion *also* NROM

NOTES

NRM *(continued)*
normal retinal movement
nucleus raphe magnus
nucleus reticularis magnocellularis

NRMI
National Registry of Myocardial
Infarction

NRMP
National Residency Matching Plan

NRN
no return necessary

nRNA
nuclear ribonucleic acid
nuclear RNA

nRNP
nuclear ribonucleoprotein

NROM
normal range of motion *also* NRM

NRP
nucleus reticularis parvocellularis

NRPAT
net revenue, patient

NRPC
nucleus reticularis pontis caudalis

NRPG
nucleus reticularis paragigantocellularis

NRR
net reproduction rate
Noise Reduction Rating
note, record, report

NRS
nonimmunized rabbit serum
normal rabbit serum
normal reference serum
numerical rating scale
numeric rating scale

NRSCC
National Reference System in
Clinical Chemistry

NRSFPS
National Reporting System for
Family Planning Services

nrsng
nursing *also* NSG, nsg

NRT
neuromuscular reeducation technique

NRTOT
net revenue, total

NRV
nucleus reticularis ventralis

NS
natural science
needle shower
nephrosclerosis
nephrotic syndrome
nervous system
neurologic sign
neurologic surgery
neurologic survey
neurosecretory
neurosurgery *also* neurosurg, NSurg
neurosyphilis
neurotic score
nipple stimulation
nodular sclerosis
nodus sinuatrialis
nonsmoker *also* NSM
nonsnorer
nonspecific
nonstimulation
nonstructural (protein)
nonstutterer
nonsymptomatic
Noonan syndrome
normal saline *also* N/S
normal serum
normal sodium (diet)
normal study
Norwegian scabies
no sample
no sequelae *also* ns
no specimen *also* ns
not seen
not significant *also* ns
not specified *also* NSP
not stated
not sufficient
not symptomatic
nuclear sclerosis
nursing services
nylon suture *also* ns

N/S
normal saline *also* NS

Ns
nasopinale
nerves

ns
nanosecond *also* nsec
no sequelae *also* NS
no specimen *also* NS
not significant *also* NS
nylon suture *also* NS

NSA
    normal serum albumin
    no salt added *also* nsa
    no serious abnormality
    no significant abnormality
    no significant anomaly
    nutritional status assessment

nsa
    no salt added *also* NSA

NSAA
    nonsteroidal antiandrogen

NSABP
    National Surgical Adjuvant Breast
    Project

NSAD
    no signs of acute disease

NSAE
    nonsupported arm exercise

NSAIA
    nonsteroidal antiinflammatory agent

NSAID
    nonsteroidal antiinflammatory drug

NSBGP
    nonspecific bowel gas pattern

NSC
    neurosecretory cell
    non–service-connected (disability) *also*
      NSCD
    nonspecific suppressor cell
    no significant change

NSCC
    nonsmall cell carcinoma

NSCD
    non–service-connected disability *also*
      NSC

NSCLC
    non–small-cell carcinoma
    non–small-cell lung cancer

NSD
    Nairobi sheep disease
    nasal septal deviation
    neonatal staphylococcal disease
    night sleep deprivation
    nitrogen-specific detector
    nominal single dose

    nominal standard dose
    normal single dose
    normal spontaneous delivery
    no significant defect
    no significant deficiency
    no significant deviation
    no significant difference
    no significant disease

NSDA
    non–steroid-dependent asthmatic

NSE
    neuron-specific enolase
    nonspecific esterase
    normal saline enema

NsE
    nausea without emesis [Fr. *sans*]

nsec
    nanosecond *also* ns

NSED
    nonsurgeon, emergency department

NSF
    nodular subepidermal fibrosis
    no significant findings

NSFTD
    normal spontaneous full-term delivery

NSG
    neurosecretory granule
    nursing *also* nrsng, nsg

nsg
    nursing *also* nrsng, NSG

NSGCT
    nonseminomatous germ cell tumor

NSGCTT
    nonseminomatous germ cell testicular
    tumor

NSG STA
    nursing station

NSHD
    nodular sclerosing Hodgkin disease

NSI
    negative self-image
    no sign of infection
    no sign of inflammation

NOTES

NSICU
neurosurgery intensive care unit

NSIDS
near-sudden infant death syndrome

NSILA
nonsuppressible insulin-like activity

NSILP
nonsuppressible insulin-like protein

NSL
nonsalt loser

NSLF
normal sheep lung fibroblast

NSM
neurosecretory material
nonantigenic specific mediator
nonsmoker *also* NS
nutrient sporulation medium

N·s/m²
newton-second per square meter

NSN
nephrotoxic serum nephritis
nicotine-stimulated neurophysin
number of similar negatives

NSND
nonsymptomatic, nondisabling

NSO
Neosporin ointment
nucleus supraopticus

NSol
nerve to soleus

NSP
neck and shoulder pain
neuron-specific protein
not specified *also* NS
number of similar positives

NSPE
no specimen (obtainable)

NSPVT
nonsustained polymorphic ventricular
tachycardia

NSQ
Neuroticism Scale Questionnaire
not sufficient quantity

NSR
nasoseptal reconstruction
nasoseptal repair
nonspecific reaction
nonsystemic reaction

normal sinus rhythm
not seen regularly

nSRBC
normal sheep red blood cell

NSRP
nerve-sparing radical prostatectomy

NSRR
normal sinus rate and rhythm

NSS
neurological signs stable
normal saline solution
normal size and shape
not statistically significant
nutritional support service

NSSC
normal size, shape, and consistency

NSSL
normal size, shape, and location

NSSP
normal size, shape, and position

NSSPAVAF
normal size, shape, and position,
anteverted and anteflexed (uterus)

NSST
nonspecific ST (wave segment
changes on electroencephalogram)
Northwestern Syntax Screening Test

NSSTT
nonspecific ST and T (wave)

NST
neospinothalamic (tract)
nonshivering thermogenesis
nonstress test (fetal monitoring)
normal sphincter tone
not sooner than
nutritional status type
nutritional support team

NSTI
necrotizing soft tissue infection

NSTT
nonseminomatous testicular tumor

NSU
neurosurgical unit
nonspecific urethritis

NSurg
neurosurgeon *also* neurosurg
neurosurgery *also* neurosurg, NS

NSV
nonspecific vaginitis

NSVD
normal spontaneous vaginal delivery

NSVT
nonsustained ventricular tachycardia

NSX
neurosurgical examination

NSY
nursery

NT
nasotracheal
neotetrazolium
neurotensin
neutralization technique
neutralization test
neutralizing *also* Nt
nicotine tartrate
nontypable
normal temperature
normal tissue
normotensive
nortriptyline
no test
not tender
not tested
nourishment taken
nucleation time

N-T, N&T
nose and throat

5'-NT
5'-nucleotidase

Nt
amino terminal
neutralizing *also* NT

NTA
natural thymocytotoxic autoantibody
nitrilotriacetic acid
Nurse Training Act

NTAB
nephrotoxic antibody

N/TBC
nontuberculous

NTBR
not to be resuscitated

NTC
neurotrauma center

NTCS
no tumor cells seen

NTD
negative to date
neural tube defect
nitroblue tetrazolium dye
noise tone difference

NTE
neurotoxic esterase
nontest ear
not to exceed
nuclear track emulsion

NTF
normal throat flora

NTG
nitroglycerin *also* NG, nitro, NTZ
nontoxic goiter
nontreatment group
normal triglyceridemia

NTGO
nitroglycerin ointment

NTHH
nontumorous hypergastrinemic
hyperchlorhydria

NTI
nasotracheal intubation
nonthyroid illness
nonthyroid index
no treatment indicated

NTIS
National Technical Information
Service

NTLI
neurotensin-like immunoreactivity

NTM
Neuman-Tytell medium
nocturnal tumescence monitor
nontuberculous mycobacteria *also*
NTMB

NTMB
nontuberculous mycobacteria *also*
NTM

NTMI
nontransmural myocardial infarction

NOTES

NTMNG
  nontoxic multinodular goiter
NTN
  nephrotoxic nephritis
NTND
  not tender, not distended (abdomen)
NTP
  National Toxicology Program
  nitropaste
  normal temperature and pressure
  nucleoside triphosphate
  sodium nitroprusside
NTPPH
  nucleoside triphosphate
   pyrophosphohydrolase
NTR
  negative therapeutic reaction
  normotensive rat *also* NR
  nutrition
NTS
  nasotracheal suction
  nephrotoxic serum
  nonturning (against) self (psychology)
  nucleus tractus solitarius
NTS-AICD
  nonthoracotomy system antitachycardia
   device
NTT
  nasotracheal tube
  nearly total thyroidectomy
NTV
  nervous tissue vaccine
NTX
  naltrexone
NTZ
  nitazoxanide
  nitroglycerin *also* NG, nitro, NTG
  normal transformation zone
   (colposcopy)
ν
  frequency
  kinematic viscosity *also* υ
  neutrino
  number of degrees of freedom
  nu (13th letter of Greek alphabet),
   lowercase
  stoichiometric number
NU
  name unknown

Nu
  nucleolus
  nucleus
nU
  nanounit *also* nu
nu
  nanounit *also* nU
  neurilemma
  nude (mouse)
NUC
  nuclear *also* nucl
  nuclear medicine
  sodium urate crystal
Nuc
  nucleoside *also* N
nuc
  nucleated
nucl
  nuclear *also* NUC
NUD
  nonulcer dyspepsia
NUG
  necrotizing ulcerative gingivitis
NUI
  number user identification
nullip
  nulliparous
num
  numerator
numc
  number concentration
NUN
  nonurea nitrogen
NURB
  Neville upper reservoir buffer
NURD
  nonuniform rotational defect
NUV
  near-ultraviolet
NV
  naked vision *also* Nv
  nausea and vomiting *also* N/V, N&V
  near vision
  negative variation
  neovascularization
  neurovascular
  new vessel
  next visit
  nonvegetarian

nonveteran
normal value
normal volunteer
norverapamil
not vaccinated
not venereal
not verified
not volatile

N/V, N&V
nausea and vomiting *also* NV

Nv, Nv.
naked vision *also* NV

nv
nonvolatile

NVA
near visual acuity
normal visual acuity

Nva
norvaline

NVAC
National Vaccine Advisory Committee

NVAF
nonvalvular atrial fibrillation

NVB
neurovascular bundle

NVC
nonvalved conduit
normal vital capacity

NVCC
neurovascular cross compression

NVD
nausea, vomiting, and diarrhea
neck vein distention
neovascularization (of optic) disc
neurovesicle dysfunction
Newcastle virus disease
nonvalvular (heart) disease
no venereal disease
no venous distention

NVDC
nausea, vomiting, diarrhea, and
constipation

NVE
native valve endocarditis

neovascularization (of new vessels)
elsewhere
new vessels elsewhere

NVFS
nuclear ventricular function study

NVG
neovascular glaucoma
neoviridogrisein
nonventilated group

NVL
neurovascular laboratory

NVM
nonvolatile matter

NVP
near visual point

NVR
no radiographically visible recurrence

NVS
neurologic vital signs
nonvaccine serotype

NVSS
normal variant short stature

NVWSC
nonvolatile whole-smoke condensate

NW
naked weight
nasal wash
nonwithdrawn
not weighed

NWB
nonweightbearing
no weightbearing

NWC
number of words chosen

NWD
neuroleptic withdrawal

NWF
new working formulation

NWI
notch width index

NWm
nitrogen washout, multiple (breath)

NOTES

NWR
normotensive Wistar rat

NWs
nitrogen washout, single (breath)

NWSM
Nocardia water-soluble nitrogen

NX, Nx
naloxone *also* NLX
nephrectomy
regional lymph nodes cannot be
 addressed

N x m
newton by meter

NY
nystatin

NYC
New York City (medium)

NYD
not yet diagnosed
not yet discovered

NYHA
New York Heart Association
(classification)

NYP
not yet published

nyst
nystagmus

NYU
New York University

NZ
enzyme
neutral zone
normal zone

NZB
New Zealand black (mouse)

NZO
New Zealand obese (mouse)

NZR
New Zealand red (rabbit)

NZW
New Zealand white (mouse)

O, Θ

negative
nil
no
none
nonmotile organism
omicron (15th letter of Greek
  alphabet), uppercase
orotidine *also* Ord
oxygen *also* O2
without *also* ō, S, s̄, WO, w/o, wo

O

absence of sex chromosome
agglutinative reactions
blood type in ABO blood group
eye [L. *oculus*]
nonmotile microorganisms and their
  somatic antigens, antibodies, and
no special preparation necessary (for
  test)
obese *also* OB, ob
objective (findings) *also* Obj
observation *also* OBS, Obs
obstetrics
obvious
occipital *also* Occ, occip
occiput *also* Occ, occip
occlusal
often
old
open *also* o, opg
opening *also* o, opg
operator
operon (genetics)
opium
oral *also* (O)
orally *also* (O)
orange (indicator color)
orbit
orderly *also* ord
Oriental
orthopedic *also* OR, Orth, ortho
osteocyte
other
output
oxidative
oxygen *also* O2, O₂, OXY, oxy
pint [L. *octarius*] *also* Ō, oct.
respirations (on anesthesia chart)

O2, O₂

both eyes *also* O.U.

oxygen (symbol for the diatomic
  gas) *also* O, OXY, oxy

(O)

oral *also* O
orally *also* O

O₃

ozone

¹⁵O

oxygen-15

¹⁶O

oxygen-16

¹⁷O

oxygen-17

¹⁸O

oxygen-18

O₂ (*var. of* O2)

Ō

pint [L. *octarius*] *also* O, oct.

Θ (*var. of* O)

o

omicron (15th letter of Greek
  alphabet), lowercase
opening *also* O, opg

ō

negative
none
without *also* O, S, s̄, WO, w/o, wo

o-

ortho- (chemical symbol)

O-A

Objective-Analytic (Anxiety Battery)

OA

object assembly (psychology)
obstructive apnea
occipital artery
occipitoanterior (fetal position)
occiput anterior
occupationally induced asthma
ocular albinism
old age
oleic acid
opiate analgesia
opsonic activity
optic atrophy
oral airway *also* OAW
oral alimentation
orotic acid *also* Oro

OA *(continued)*
orthopedic assistant
orthophonic acid
osteoarthritis *also* osteo
ovalbumin *also* OVA, OV
overall assessment
Overeaters Anonymous
oxalic acid
oxolinic acid

O&A
observation and assessment
odontectomy and alveoloplasty

O₂a
oxygen availability

OAA
Old Age Assistance
oxaloacetic acid (test)

OAAD
ovarian ascorbic acid depletion (test)

OAB
old age benefits

OABP
organic anion-binding protein

OAC
oral anticoagulant
overaction

OAD
obstructive airway disease
occlusive arterial disease
organic anionic dye

OADC
oleic acid, albumin, dextrose, and
catalase (medium)

OADMT
Oliphant Auditory Discrimination
Memory Test

OAE
otoacoustic emission (test)

OAF
open air factor
osteoclast-activating factor

OAG
open-angle glaucoma

OAH
ovarian androgenic hyperfunction

OAJ
open apophyseal joint

OALF
organic acid-labile fluoride

OALL
ossification of anterior longitudinal
ligament

o. alt. hor.
every other hour [L. *omnibus
alternis horis*]

OAM
outer acrosomal membrane
oxyacetate malonate

OAP
old age pension
old age pesioner
Oncovin (vincristine), araC
(cytarabine), and prednisone
ophthalmic artery pressure
osteoarthropathy
oxygen at atmospheric pressure

OAPs
Occupational Ability Patterns
(psychologic test)

OAR
orientation/alertness remediation
other administrative reasons

OARSA
oxacillin aminoglycoside-resistant
Staphylococcus aureus

OAS
old-age security
oral allergy syndrome
organic anxiety syndrome
osmotically active substance

OASDHI
Old Age, Survivors, Disability, and
Health Insurance

OASDI
Old Age, Survivors, and Disability
Insurance

OASI
Old Age and Survivors Insurance

OASIS
One Action, Stent Introduction
System
Organization to Assess Strategies for
Ischemic Syndromes
osteotomy analysis simulation
software

OASO
overactive superior oblique

OASP
organic acid-soluble phosphorus

OASR
overactive superior rectus

OAST
Oliphant Auditory Synthesizing Test

OAT
ornithine aminotransferase

OAV
oculoauriculovertebral (dysplasia, syndrome)

OAW
oral airway *also* OA

OAWO
opening abductory wedge osteotomy

OB
he died [L. *obiit*] *also* ob.
obese *also* O, ob
objective benefit
obstetrician
obstetrics *also* OBS, Obs, Obst
occult bleeding
occult blood
olfactory bulb *also* OLB
oligoclonal band
osteoblast
osteoblastoma
she died [L. *obiit*] *also* ob.

OB+
occult blood positive

O&B
opium and belladonna

ob
obese *also* O, OB

ob.
he died [L. *obiit*] *also* OB
she died [L. *obiit*] *also* OB

OBA
oral bile acid

OBB
own bed bath

OBD
optimum biologic dose
organic brain disease

OBE
out-of-body experience

OBF
organ blood flow

OBG, ObG
obstetrician-gynecologist *also* OB-GYN, OB/GYN
obstetrics and gynecology *also* OB-GYN, OB/GYN, OG, O&G

OBGS
obstetric and gynecologic surgery

OB-GYN, OB/GYN
obstetrician-gynecologist *also* OBG, ObG
obstetrics and gynecology *also* OBG, ObG, OG, O&G

Obj, obj
objective *also* O

obj
object

obl
oblique

OBLA
onset of blood lactate accumulation

OBN
occult blood-negative

OBP
occult blood-positive
ova, blood, and parasites (stool exam)

OBRR
obstetric recovery room

OBS
observation *also* O, Obs
obstetrical service
obstetrics *also* OB, Obs, Obst
organic brain syndrome

Obs
observation *also* O, OBS
observed *also* obsd
obstetrician *also* OB, OBS, Obst
obstetrics *also* OB, OBS, Obst

obs
obsolete

obsd
observed *also* Obs

O

NOTES

Obst
    obstetrician *also* OB, Obs
    obstetrics *also* OB, OBS, Obs

obst
    obstipation
    obstructed
    obstruction

obstet
    obstetric

obt
    obtained

OB-US
    obstetrical ultrasound

O-C, O&C
    onset and course (of disease)

OC
    obstetrical conjugate
    occlusocervical
    office call
    on call
    only child
    optic chiasm *also* OX
    oral care
    oral cavity
    oral contraceptive
    organ culture
    original claim
    outer canthal (distance)
    ovarian cancer
    oxygen consumed

Oc
    ochre (suppressor)

OCA
    oculocutaneous albinism
    olivopontocerebellar atrophy *also*
      OPCA
    open care area
    operant conditioning audiometry
    oral contraceptive agent

OCAD
    occlusive carotid artery disease

O$_2$ cap.
    oxygen capacity

OCBF
    outer cortical blood flow

Occ
    occasional *also* occ, occas
    occipital *also* O, occip
    occiput *also* O, Occ
    occlusion *also* occl
    occlusive

occ, occas
    occasional *also* Occ
    occasionally
    occupation *also* occup
    occurrence

OCCC
    open-chest cardiac compression

occip
    occipital *also* O, Occ
    occiput

occip F
    occipitofrontal *also* OF

occip-F HA
    occipitofrontal headache *also* OF-HA

occl
    occlusion *also* Occ

OCCM
    open chest cardiac massage

OCCPR
    open-chest cardiopulmonary
      resuscitation

OccTh
    occupational therapist *also* OT
    occupational therapy *also* Occup Rx,
      OT

occup
    occupation *also* occ
    occupational
    occupies
    occupying

Occup Rx
    occupational therapy *also* OccTh, OT

OCD
    obsessive-compulsive disorder
    Office of Child Development
    Office of Civil Defense
    osteochondritis dissecans
    ovarian cholesterol depletion (test)

OCG
    omnicardiogram
    oral cholecystogram
    oral cholecystography

OCH
    oral contraceptive hormone

OCHS
    Office of Cooperative Health
      Statistics

Ochs
    Ochsner

OCIS
Oncology Center Information System

OCL
Occupational Check List (psychologic test)
oral colonic lavage

OCLG
osteoclast-like giant cell *also* OLGC

OCM
oral contraceptive medication

OCN
oculomotor nucleus *also* OMN
Oncology Certified Nurse

OCP
octacalcium phosphate
ocular cicatricial pemphigoid
oral contraceptive pill
ova, cysts, and parasites (stool exam)

OCR
ocular counterrolling
ocular countertorsion reflex
oculocardiac reflex
oculocephalic reflux
oculocerebrorenal

OCRF
ovine corticotropin-releasing factor

OCRS
oculocerebrorenal syndrome

OCS
Ondine curse syndrome
open canalicular system (of platelets)
oral cancer screening
oral contraceptive steroid
outpatient clinic substation
oxycorticosteroid

OCT
Object Classification Test
optical coherence tomography
optimal cutting temperature (medium)
oral contraceptive therapy
ornithine carbamoyltransferase
ornithine carbamoyl-transferase
osseous coagulum trap
oxytocin challenge test

O₂CT
oxygen content

oct.
pint [L. *octarius*] *also* O, Ō, ō

OCTD
ornithine carbamoyltransferase deficiency

OCTT
orocecal transit time

octup.
eightfold [L. *octuplus*]

OCU
observation care unit

OCV
ordinary conversational voice

OCVM
occult vascular malformation
oculocerebrovasculometer

O-D
obstacle-dominance
original-derived

OD
Doctor of Optometry
(drug) overdosage
(drug) overdose
occipital dysplasia
occupational dermatitis
occupational disease
oculus dexter (right eye)
Ollier disease
on duty
open drop (anesthesia)
open duct
optical density
optic disk
optimal dose
organization development
originally derived
outdoor
outer diameter
out-of-date
outside diameter
overdose

O.D.
right eye [L. *oculus dexter*] *also* RE

o.d.
every day [L. *omni die*] *also* q.d., q.q.d.

O

NOTES

od
daily

ODA
osmotic driving agent
right occipitoanterior (fetal position)
[L. *occipitodextra anterior*]

ODAC
on-demand analgesia computer

ODAP
Oncovin (vincristine),
dianhydrogalactitol, Adriamycin
(doxorubicin), and Platinol (cisplatin)

ODAT
one day at a time

ODB
opiate-directed behavior

ODC
ornithine decarboxylase
orotidylate decarboxylase (deficiency)
outpatient diagnostic center
oxygen dissociation curve

ODCH
ordinary disease of childhood

ODD
oculodentodigital (dysplasia, syndrome)
once-daily dosing
opposition defiance disorder

OD'd
(drug) overdosed

ODE
o–desmethylencainide

ODM, ODm
ophthalmodyamometry
ophthalmodynamometer

ODOD
oculodentoosseous dysplasia

Odont
odontology

odont
odontogenic

ODP
offspring of diabetic parents
right occipitoposterior (fetal position)
[L. *occipitodextra posterior*]

ODQ
on direct questioning
opponens digiti quinti (muscle)

ODSG
ophthalmic Doppler sonogram

ODT
oculodynamic test
right occipitotransverse (fetal position)
[L. *occipitodextra transversa*]

ODTS
organic dust toxic syndrome

ODU
optical density unit

OE
on examination *also* O/E
orthopedic examination *also* OX
otitis externa

O&E
observation and examination

O/E
on examination *also* OE
(ratio of) observed to expected

Oe
oersted (centimeter-gram-second unit
of magnetic field strength)

OEC
outer ear canal

OEE
osmotic erythrocyte enrichment
outer enamel epithelium

OEF
oil emersion field
oxygen extraction fraction

OEIS
omphalocele, exstrophy (of the
bladder), imperforate (anus) and
spinal (abnormalities)

OEM
occupational and environmental
medicine
open-end marriage
opposite ear masked
original equipment manufacturer
(computers)

OER
osmotic erythrocyte (enrichment)
oxygen enhancement ratio

O₂ER
oxygen extraction ratio

OES
Olympus endoscopy system
optical emission spectroscopy
oral esophageal stethoscope

oesoph
esophagus (oesophagus) *also* E, ES, ESO, esoph

OESP
orthopedic examination, special

OET
open epicutaneous test
oral endotracheal tube *also* OETT
oral esophageal tube

OETT
oral endotracheal tube *also* OET

OF
occipitofrontal *also* occip F
optic fundi
orbitofrontal
osmotic fragility (test)
osteitis fibrosa
Ostrum-Furst (syndrome)
other (medical/surgical) facility
Ovenstone factor
oxidation-fermentation (medium) *also* O-F, O/F

O-F, O/F
oxidation-fermentation (medium) *also* OF

OFA
oncofetal antigen

OFBM
oxidation-fermentation basal medium

OFC
occipitofrontal circumference
orbitofacial cleft
osteitis fibrosa cystica

ofc
office *also* off.

OFCTAD
occipito-faciocervico-thoraco-abdomino-digital (dysplasia)

OFD
object-film distance (radiology) *also* ofd
occipitofrontal diameter
oral-facial-digital
orofaciodigital (dysostosis, syndrome)

ofd
object-film distance (radiology) *also* OFD

Off
official *also* off.

off.
office *also* ofc
official *also* Off

OF-HA
occipitofrontal headache *also* occip-F HA

OFM
open face mask
orofacial malformation

OFNE
oxygenated fluorocarbon nutrient emulsion

OFPF
optic fundi and peripheral fields

OF rad
occipitofrontal radiation

OFTT
organic failure to thrive

OG
obstetrics and gynecology *also* OBG, ObG, OB-GYN, OB/GYN, O&G
occlusogingival
oligodendrocyte
optic ganglion
orange green (stain)
orogastric (feeding)

O&G
obstetrics and gynecology *also* OBG, ObG, OB/GYN, OG

OGA
orogastric gonococcal aspirate

OGC
oculogyric crisis

OGCT
ovarian germ cell tumor

OGD
old granulomatous disease

O

NOTES

OGF
ovarian growth factor
oxygen gain factor

OGH
ovine growth hormone

OGM
outgrowth medium

OGS
oxygenic steroid

OGT
oral glucose tolerance
orogastric tube

OGTT
oral glucose tolerance test

OH
hydroxycorticosteroid *also* HCS, OHCS
hydroxyl group
hydroxyl radical
obstructive hypopnea
occipital horn
occupational health
occupational history
on hand
open-heart (surgery)
oral hygiene
orthostatic hypotension
osteopathic hospital
out of hospital
outpatient hospital

o.h.
every hour [L. *omni hora*] *also* omn. hor.

OHA
oral hypoglycemic agent

OHAHA
ophthalmoplegia-hypotonia-ataxia-hypacusis-athetosis (syndrome)

OHB$_{12}$
hydroxocobalamin (vitamin B$_{12}$) *also* OH-Cbl

O$_2$Hb
oxyhemoglobin

OHC
hydroxycholecalciferol *also* OHD
occupational health center
outer hair cell

OH-Cbl
hydroxocobalamin *also* OHB$_{12}$

OHCS
hydroxycorticosteroid *also* HCS, OH

OHD
hydroxycholecalciferol *also* OHC
organic heart disease

25-OH-D3
25-hydroxyvitamin D

1,25(OH)2 D3
1,25-dihydroxyvitamin D
1,25-dihydroxyvitamin D$_3$

OHDA
hydroxydopamine *also* HD, HDA
6-hydroxydopamine

OH-DOC
hydroxydeoxycorticosterone

OHF
old healed fracture
Omsk hemorrhagic fever
overhead frame

OHFA
hydroxy fatty acid

OHFT
overhead frame trapeze

OHG
oral hypoglycemic

OHI
ocular hypertension indicator
oral hygiene index
oral hygiene instructions

OHI-1
oral hygiene index

OH-IAA
hydroxyindoleacetic acid *also* HIAA

4-OHIPA
4-hydroxyifosfamide

OHI-S
Oral Hygiene Index-Simplified

OHL
oral hairy leukoplakia

ohm-cm
ohm-centimeter

OHN
Occupational Health Nurse

OHP
hydroxyproline
orthogonal-hole test pattern
oxygen under high pressure

17-OHP
17α-hydroxyprogesterone

OHRR
open heart recovery room

OHS
obesity hypoventilation syndrome
ocular hypoperfusion syndrome
open heart surgery
ovarian hyperstimulation syndrome
Overcontrolled Hostility Scale

OHSS
ovarian hyperstimulation syndrome

OHT
Occupational Health Technician
ocular hypertension
ocular hypertensive (glaucoma
  suspect)
orthotopic heart transplant

OHTA
Office of Health Technology
  Assessment

OHTx
orthotopic heart transplantation

OHU
hydroxyurea

OI
objective improvement
obturator internus
occipitoiliacus
opportunistic infection
opsonic index
orgasmic impairment
Orientation Inventory (psychologic
  test)
orthoiodohippurate *also* OIH
osteogenesis imperfecta
otitis interna
ouabain insensitive
oxygenation index
oxygen income
oxygen intake

O-I
outer-to-inner

OID
optimal immunomodulating dose
organism identification (number)

OIF
observed intrinsic frequency
oil immersion field

OIH
orthoiodohippurate *also* OI
ovulation-inducing hormone

OIHA
orthoidohippurate
orthoiodohippuric acid

oint
ointment

OIP
organizing interstitial pneumonia

OIT
ovarian immature teratoma
(Tien) organic integrity test
  (psychiatry)

OIU
optical internal urethrotomy

OJ, oj
orange juice *also* OrJ

OK, ok
all right
approved
correct

OKAN
optokinetic after nystagmus

OKC
Oklahoma City cable

OKN
optokinetic nystagmus

OKT
Ollier-Klippel-Trenaunay (syndrome)
ornithine-ketoacid transaminase
Ortho-Kung T (cell)

OL
other location

O.L.
left eye [L. *oculus laevus*] *also* LE,
  O.S.

Ol, ol.
oil [L. *oleum*]

O

NOTES

OLA
left occipitoanterior (fetal position)
[L. *occipitolaeva anterior*]

OLB
olfactory bulb *also* OB
open-liver biopsy

OLD
obstructive lung disease
orthochromatic leukodystrophy

OLGC
osteoclast-like giant cell *also* OCLG

OLH
ovine lactogenic hormone
ovine leuteinizing hormone *also* oLH

oLH
ovine leuteinizing hormone *also* OLH

OLIB
osmiophilic lamellar inclusion body

OLIDS
open-loop insulin delivery system

OLM
ophthalmic laser microendoscope

OLMAT
Otis-Lennon Mental Ability Test

OLNM
occult lymph node metastasis

ol. oliv.
olive oil [L. *oleum olivarium*]

OLP
left occipitoposterior (fetal position)
[L. *occipitolaeva posterior*]

OLR
otology, laryngology, and rhinology

ol res
oleoresin

OLSID
Oral Language Sentence Imitation
Diagnostic Inventory

OLSIST
Oral Language Sentence Imitation
Screening Test

OLT
left occipitotransverse (fetal position)
[L. *occipitolaeva posterior*]
orthotopic liver transplant *also* Olt

Olt
orthotopic liver transplant *also* OLT

OLV
one-lung ventilation

OM
obtuse marginal
obtuse marginal (coronary artery)
occipitomental
occupational medicine
oculomotor
Osborn-Mendel (rat)
osteomalacia
osteomyelitis *also* osteo
osteopathic manipulation
otitis media
outer membrane
ovulation method (birth control)

OM-1
first obtuse marginal artery

OM-2
second obtuse marginal artery

o.m.
every morning [L. *omni mane*] *also*
omn. man.

OMA
obtuse marginal artery

OMAC
otitis media, acute, catarrhal

OMAD
Oncovin (vincristine), methotrexate,
Adriamycin (doxorubicin), and
dactinomycin

OMAS
occupational maladjustment syndrome
otitis media, acute, suppurating

OMB
obtuse marginal branch

OMB$_1$
first obtuse marginal branch

OMB$_2$
second obtuse marginal branch

OMC
open mitral commissurotomy

OMCA
otitis media, catarrhal, acute

OMCC, OMCCH
otitis media, catarrhal, chronic

OMChS
otitis media, chronic, suppurating

OMD
ocular muscle dystrophy

oculomandibulodyscephaly
organic mental disorder
oromandibular dystonia

OME
Office of Medical Examiner
omeprazole
otitis media with effusion

Ω
ohm
omega (24th and last letter of Greek
alphabet), uppercase

ω
angular frequency
angular velocity
carbon atom farthest from principal
functioning group
omega (24th and last letter of Greek
alphabet), lowercase

OMF
oculomandibulofacial syndrome

OMFS
oral and maxillofacial surgery

OMG
ocular myasthenia gravis

om. 1/4 h.
every quarter hour [L. *omni
quadranta hora*] *also* omn. quad.
hor., om. quad. hor.

OMI
old myocardial infarction
oocyte maturation inhibitor

OML
orbitomeatal line

OMM
ophthalmomandibulomelic (dysplasia,
syndrome)
outermitochondrial membrane

om. mane vel noc.
every morning or night [L. *omni
mane vel nocte*]

OMN
oculomotor nerve
oculomotor nucleus *also* OCN

omn. bid.
every two days [L. *omni bidendis*]

omn. bih.
every two hours [L. *omni bihora*]

omn. hor.
every hour [L. *omni hora*]

omn. 2 hor.
every second hour [L. *omni secunda
hora*]

omn. man.
every morning [L. *omni mane*] *also*
o.m.

omn. noct.
every night [L. *omni nocte*] *also*
ON, o.n.

omn. quad. hor.
every quarter hour [L. *omni
quadrante hora*] *also* om. 1/4 h., om.
quad. hor.

omn. sec. hor.
every second hour [L. *omni secunda
hora*]

OMP
oculomotor palsy (third nerve)
olfactory marker protein
orotidine 5′-monophosphate
orotidylate
orotidylic acid
outer membrane protein

OMPA
octamethyl pyrophosphoramide
otitis media, purulent, acute

OMPC, OMPCh
otitis media, purulent, chronic

om. quad. hor.
every quarter hour [L. *omni
quadrante hora*] *also* om. 1/4 h.,
omn. quad. hor.

OMR
operative mortality rate

OMS
offshore medical school
organic mental syndrome
otomandibular syndrome

OM&S
osteopathic medicine and surgery

O

NOTES

OMSA
otitis media, suppurative, acute

OMSC, OMSCh
otitis media, secretory, chronic
otitis media, suppurative, chronic

OMT, OM/T
oral mucosal transudate
osteopathic manipulation treatment

OMU
ostiomeatal unit

OMVC
open mitral valve commissurotomy

OMVI
operating motor vehicle while
intoxicated

ON
every night [L. *omni nocte*] *also*
omn. noct., o.n.
occipitonuchal
office nurse
onlay
optic nerve
optic neuritis
optic neuropathy
oronasal
orthopedic nurse *also* ORN
osteonecrosis
overnight

o.n.
every night [L. *omni nocte*] *also*
omn. noct., ON

ONC
oncology *also* onco, oncol
Orthopedic Nursing Certificate
over-the-needle catheter

ONCG-A
oncogenic virus battery-acute

onco, oncol
oncology *also* ONC

ONCORNA
oncogene ribonucleic acid

OncoScint CR/OV
OncoScint colorectal/ovarian
(carcinoma localization scintigraphy)

OND
orbitonasal dislocation
other neurologic disease
other neurologic disorder

ONDS
Oriental nocturnal death syndrome

ONH
optic nerve head
optic nerve hypoplasia

ONP
operating nursing procedure

ONPG, ONP-GAL
o-nitrophenyl-β-galactosidase

ONS
Oncology Nursing Society

ONSD
optic nerve sheath decompression

ONSF
optic nerve sheath fenestration

ONTG
oral nitroglycerin

ONTR
orders not to resuscitate

O-O
outer-to-outer

OO
oophorectomy
oral order

O&O
off and on

o/o
on account of

OOA
outer optic anlage

OOB
out of bed
out-of-body (experience)

OOBBRP
out of bed (with) bathroom
privileges

OOC
onset of contractions
out of cast
out of control

OOH&NS
ophthalmology, otorhinolaryngology,
and head and neck surgery

OOL
onset of labor

OOLR
ophthalmology, otology, laryngology,
and rhinology

OOP
out on pass

out of pelvis
out of plaster (cast)

OOR
out of room

OOS
out of sequence
out of stock *also* OS

OOT
out of town

OOW
out of wedlock *also* OW

OP
oblique presentation
occipitoparietal
occipitoposterior
occiput posterior
old patient (previously seen)
olfactory penduncle
opening pressure
operation *also* op
operative
operative procedure
ophthalmology
opponens pollicis muscle
original package
oropharynx
orthostatic proteinuria
oscillatory potential
osmotic pressure
osteoporosis
other (than) psychotic
outpatient *also* O/P, OPT
overproof
ovine prolactin

OP-3
Orthopantomograph-3

OP-10
Orthopantomograph-10

O/P
outpatient *also* OP, OPT

O&P
ova and parasites (stool exam)

Op
opisthocranion

op
operation *also* OP

operational
operator
opposite
work [L. *opus*]

OPA
oral pharyngeal airway
outpatient anesthesia

OPAL
Oncovin (vincristine), prednisone, and
L-asparaginase

OPAT
outpatient parenteral antibiotic therapy

OPB
outpatient basis

OPC
oculopalatocerebral (syndrome)
operable pancreatic carcinoma
oropharyngeal candidiasis
outpatient care
outpatient catheterization
outpatient clinic
oxypneumocardiogram

OPCA
olivopontocerebellar atrophy *also*
OCA

op. cit.
in the work cited [L. *opere citato*]

OPCOS
oligomenorrheic polycystic ovary
syndrome

OPD
obstetric prediabetes
optical path difference
otopalatodigital (syndrome)
outpatient department
outpatient dispensary

OpDent
operative dentistry

OPDG
ocular plethysmodynamography

OPE
outpatient evaluation

OPG
ocular plethysmography
oculoplethysmograph

O

NOTES

OPG *(continued)*
oculoplethysmography
oculopneumoplethysmography *also*
  OPPG
ophthalmoplethysmograph
ophthalmoplethysmography
oxypolygelatin (plasma volume
  extender)

opg
opening *also* O, o

OPH, Oph
obliterative pulmonary hypotension
ophthalmia
ophthalmologist *also* Ophth
ophthalmology *also* Ophth
ophthalmoscope *also* Ophth
ophthalmoscopy *also* Ophth

oph
ophthalmic
ophthalmologic

OphD
Doctor of Ophthalmology

OphSeg
ophthalmic segment

Ophth
ophthalmologist *also* OPH, Oph
ophthalmology *also* OPH, Oph
ophthalmoscope *also* OPH, Oph
ophthalmoscopy *also* OPH, Oph

OPI
oculoparalytic illusion
Omnibus Personality Inventory

OPK
optokinetic

OPL
osmotic pressure (of proteins in)
  lymph
outer plexiform layer
ovine placental lactogen

OPLL
ossification of posterior longitudinal
  ligament

OPM
occult primary malignancy
ophthalmoplegic migraine
opponens digiti minimi

OPN
ophthalmic nurse
osteopontin

OPOC
oral pharynx, oral cavity

OPP
Oncovin (vincristine), procarbazine,
  and prednisone
osmotic pressure of plasma
ovine pancreatic polypeptide
oxygen partial pressure

opp
opposing
opposite

OPPES
oil-associated pneumoparalytic
  eosinophilic syndrome

OPPG
oculopneumoplethysmography *also*
  OPG

op reg
operative region

oprg
operating

OPRT
orotate phosphoribosyl transferase

OPS
operations
osteoporosis-pseudolipoma syndrome
outpatient service
outpatient surgery
output signal processor

OPSA
ovarian papillary serous
  adenocarcinoma

OpScan
optical scanning

OPSI
overwhelming postsplenectomy
  infection

OPSR
Office of Professional Standards
  Review

OPST-BQA
Office of Professional Standards
  Review—Bureau of Quality
  Assurance

OPT
outpatient *also* OP, O/P
outpatient treatment

Opt
optometrist

opt.
  best [L. *optimus*]
  optical
  optician
  optics
  optimal
  optimum
  optional

OPT c̄ CA
  Ohio pediatric tent with compressed
  air

OPT c̄ O₂
  Ohio pediatric tent with oxygen

OPTP
  Orthopaedic Physical Therapy
  Products

OPV
  oral (attenuated) poliovirus vaccine
  oral polio vaccine
  oral poliovirus vaccine
  outpatient visit

OPW, OPWL
  opiate withdrawal

OQSMAT
  Otis Quick Scoring Mental Abilities
  Test

OR
  oblique ridge
  odds ratio
  oil retention (enema)
  open reduction
  operating room
  optic radiation
  oral rehydration
  organ recovery
  orienting reflex
  orienting response
  orthopedic *also* O, Orth, ortho
  orthopedic research
  own recognizance
  oxidized-reduced

O-R
  oxidation-reduction (system)

Or
  outflow rate

ORA
  occiput right anterior (fetal position)
  opiate receptor agonist

ORAN
  orthopedic resident admit note

ORBC
  ox red blood cell

ORC
  order/results communication
  ox red cell

ORCH
  orchiectomy

orch
  orchitis

ORD
  optical rotary dispersion
  optical rotatory dispersion
  oral radiation death

Ord
  orotidine *also* O

ord
  orderly *also* O
  ordinate

OREF
  open reduction, external fixation

OR en
  oil-retention enema

OR&F
  open reduction and fixation

org
  organ
  organic
  organism

ORIF
  open reduction, internal fixation

orig
  origin
  original

OrJ
  orange juice *also* OJ, oj

ORL
  otorhinolaryngology

NOTES

O

ORMF
open reduction metallic fixation

ORN
operating room nurse
orthopedic nurse *also* ON
osteoradionecrosis

Orn
ornithine

ORNL
Oak Ridge National Laboratory

ORO
oil red O

Oro
orotate
orotic acid *also* OA

OROS
oral osmotic
ostomotic release oral system

ORP
occiput right posterior (fetal position)
oxidation-reduction potential *also* E_h,
eH, E_o+, $E°$

ORPM
orthorhythmic pacemaker

ORS
olfactory reference syndrome
oral rehydration salt
oral rehydration solution
oral surgeon
oral surgery *also* OS
orthopedic surgeon *also* OS
orthopedic surgery

ORSIST
Oral Language Sentence Imitation
Screening Test

ORT
ocular radiation therapy
operating room technician
oral rehydration therapy
orthodromic reciprocating tachycardia
Registered Occupational Therapist

OR tech
operating room technician

Orth, ortho
orthopedic *also* O, OR
orthopedics

orthot
orthotonus

ORx
oriented

ORx1
oriented to time

ORx2
oriented to time and place

ORx3
oriented to time, place, and person

OS
by mouth
occipitosacral (fetal position)
occupational safety
oculus sinister (left eye)
Omenn syndrome
opening snap (heart sound)
operating suite
oral surgery *also* ORS
orthopedic surgeon *also* ORS
orthopedic surgery
Osgood-Schlatter (disease)
osteogenic sarcoma
osteoid surface
osteosarcoma
osteosclerosis
ouabain sensitive
out of stock *also* OOS
overall survival
oxygen saturation *also* O_2 sat., SaO_2,
SO_2

O.S.
left eye [L. *oculus sinister*] *also* LE,
O.L.

Os
osmium

os
bone [L. pl. *ossa*]
mouth [L. pl. *ora*]

OSA
obstructive sleep apnea

OSAP
Office Sterilization and Asepsis
Procedures Research

OSAS
obstructive sleep apnea syndrome

O_2 sat.
oxygen saturation *also* OS, SaO_2,
SO_2

OSBCL
Ottawa School Behavior Check List

OSBT
ovarian serous borderline tumor

osc
oscillate

OSCE
objective structural clinical
examination

OSCJ
original squamocolumnar junction

OSD
outside doctor
overside drainage

OSESC
opening snap ejection systolic click

OSF
outer spiral fibers (of cochlea)
outlet strut fracture
overgrowth-stimulating factor

OSFT
outstretched fingertips

OSHA
Occupational Safety and Health Act
Occupational Safety and Health
Administration

OSIQ
Offer Self-Image Questionnaire (for
Adolescents)

OSL
Osgood-Schlatter lesion

OSM
osmolality
ovine submaxillary mucin
oxygen saturation meter

Osm
osmole *also* osmol

osM
osmolar

osm
osmosis
osmotic

OSMF
oral submucous fibrosis

Osm/kg
osmole per kilogram (osmolality)

Osm/L, Osm/l
osmole per liter (osmolarity)

osmo
osmolality

osmol
osmole *also* Osm

OSM S
osmolality serum

OSM U
osmolality urine

OSN
off-service note

OSS
Object Sorting Scales (psychologic
test)
occupational stress syndrome
osseous
over-shoulder strap

OS-SPT
osmolality urine spot (test)

OST
object-sorting test

Ost
osteotomy

Osteo
osteopathologist *also* osteopath
osteopathy

osteo
osteoarthritis *also* OA
osteomyelitis *also* OM
osteopathology

osteocart
osteocartilaginous

osteopath
osteopathologist *also* Osteo

OT
(Koch) old tuberculin
objective test
oblique talus
occipitotransverse
occiput transverse
occlusion time
occupational therapist *also* OccTh
occupational therapy
ocular tension

NOTES

O

OT *(continued)*
Oestreicher-Turner (syndrome)
office treatment
old term
old terminology (anatomy)
old tuberculin
olfactory threshold
olfactory tubercle *also* OTU
optic tract
orientation test
original tuberculin
orotracheal (tube)
orthopedic treatment
otolaryngology *also* Ot, OTO, Oto, Otolar
otology *also* OTO, Oto, Otol
oxytocin *also* OX, OXT, OXY, oxy

O/T
oral temperature

Ot
otolaryngology *also* OT, OTO, Oto, Otolar

OTA
open to air
Opinions toward Adolescents (psychologic test)
ornithine transaminase
orthotoluidine arsenite

OTAPS
Ohio Tests of Articulation and Perception of Sounds

OTC
ornithine transcarbamylase (deficiency)
oval target cell
over-the-counter
over-the-counter (nonprescription drug) *also* OTCD
oxytetracycline

OTc
heartrate-corrected OT interval

OTCD
over-the-counter drug (nonprescription) *also* OTC

OTC Rx
over-the-counter prescription

OTD
optimal therapeutic dose
oral temperature device
organ tolerance dose
out the door

OTE
optically transparent electrode

OTF
oral transfer factor

OTFC
oral transmucosal fentanyl citrate

OTH
other

OTI
ovomucoid trypsin inhibitor

OTM
orthotoluidine manganese (sulfate)

OTO, Oto
otolaryngology *also* OT, Ot, Otolar
otology *also* OT, Otol

OTOD
Organization of Teachers of Oral Diagnosis

Otol
otologist
otology *also* OT, OTO, Oto

Otolar
otolaryngology *also* OT, Ot, OTO, Oto

OTR
Occupational Therapist, Registered
Ovarian Tumor Registry

OT/RT
Occupational Therapy/Recreational Therapy

OTS
occipital temporal sulcus
orotracheal suction

OTSG
Office of the Surgeon General

OTT, OT(T)
orotracheal tube

OTU
olfactory tubercle *also* OT
operational taxonomic unit

OTW
over-the-wire

OU
Observation Unit
oculi unitas (both eyes)
Oppenheim-Urbach (syndrome)

O.U.
both eyes (together) [L. *oculi unitas*]
each eye [L. *oculi uterque*]

OULQ
outer upper left quadrant

OURQ
outer upper right quadrant

OUS
overuse syndrome

OV
oculovestibular
office visit
Osler-Vaquez (disease)
osteoid volume
outflow volume
ovalbumin *also* OA, OVA
overventilation
ovulating
ovulation

O₂V
oxygen ventilation equivalent

Oᵥ
outflow volume

Ov
ovary

ov
ovarian

ov.
egg [L. *ovum*]

OVA
ovalbumin *also* OA, OV

OVAL
ovalocyte

OVC
ovarian carcinoma

OVD
occlusal vertical dimension

OvDF
ovarian dysfunction

OVDQ
Organizational Value Dimensions
Questionnaire

OVIS
Ohio Vocational Interest Survey

OVIT
Oral Verbal Intelligence Test

OVLP
overlap myositis

OVLT
organum vasculosum of lamina
terminalis

OVS
obstructive voiding symptom

OVX
ovariectomized

OW
off work
once weekly
open wedge (osteotomy)
ordinary warfare
outer wall
out of wedlock *also* OOW
oval window

O/W
oil in water (emulsion)
oil-water (ratio)

o/w
otherwise

OWA
organics-in-water (analyzer)

OWNK
out of wedlock and not keeping
(child)

OWR
Osler-Weber-Rendu (syndrome)
ovarian wedge resection

OWS
overwear syndrome

OWVI
Ohio Work Values Inventory

OX
optic chiasm *also* OC
orthopedic examination *also* OE
oxacillin
oxymel (honey, water, and vinegar)
oxytocin *also* OT, OXT, OXY, oxy

Ox
oxygen *also* O, O2, O₂, OXY, oxy

O

NOTES

539

Oxi
oximeter
oximetry

OXLAT
oxalate

OXP
oxypressin

OXT
oxytocin *also* OT, OX, OXY, oxy

OXY, oxy
oxygen *also* O, O2, O_2, Ox
oxytocin *also* OT, OX, OXT

OYE
old yellow enzyme

oz, oz.
ounce

oz ap
apothecary's ounce

oz t
ounce troy

P

after [L. *post*] *also* p
by weight [L. *pondere*]
father [L. *pater*]
form perception (in General Aptitude
 Test Battery)
gas partial pressure
handful [L. *pugillus*]
near [L. *proximum*]
near point (of vision) [L. *punctum
 proximum*] *also* PP, pp
page
pain
para (parity)
parent
parenteral
parietal electrode placement in
 electroencephalography
parity
parous
part *also* pt
partial pressure *also* p, PP
passive
paternal
paternally contributing
patient *also* PNT, Pnt, PT, Pt, pt
pelvis
penicillin *also* PCN, PEN, Pen, pen.,
 PN, PNC
per
percent
percentile
perceptual speed
percussion
perforation *also* perf
peripheral
permeability
permeability constant
peta-
peyote
pharmacopoeia
phenacetin
phenolphthalein
phenylalanine *also* F, PA, PHA,
 PHE, Phe
phon (unit of loudness)
phosphate (group)
phosphorus
physiology *also* PHY, PHYS
pico-
pig
pilocarpine
pin

pink (indicator color)
pint *also* p, PT, pt
placebo *also* PBO, PL
plan
plasma
point
poise (unit of dynamic viscosity)
poison
poisoning
polarity
polarization
pole
polymyxin
pons
poor
popular response
population
porcelain
porcine
porphyrin
position *also* pos
positive *also* POS, pos
posterior *also* post, post.
postpartum
power
precipitin
prednisone *also* PDN, PRED
premolar
presbyopia *also* PR, Pr
press
pressure *also* p, PR, press.
pressure, (partial)
primary
primipara *also* I-para, primip, PRIMP
primitive (hemoglobin)
private (patient, room)
probability
probable error
product
progesterone
prolactin *also* P, PR, Pr, PRL, Prl
proline *also* Pro
properdin
propionate
protein *also* PR, Pr, PRO, pro, prot
Protestant
proximal
psoralen
psychiatry *also* PS, Psy, psychiat
psychosis
pulmonary *also* P, PUL, pul, pulm
pulse
pupil

P

P *(continued)*
    P wave (in electrocardiography)
    pyloroplasty
    radiant flux
    radiant power
    rho (17th letter of Greek alphabet), uppercase
    significance probability (value)
    sound power
    weight [L. *pondus*]

P-2 *(var. of* P_2*)*

P-50
    oxygen half-saturation pressure of hemoglobin

P-55
    hydroxypregnanedione

P-170
    P-glycoprotein *also* P-gp, Pgp

P-900
    900 mOsmolar amino acid-glucose solution

/P
    partial lower denture

P/
    partial upper denture

P/3
    proximal third (of bone)

^{32}P
    phosphorus-32
    radioisotope of phosphorus

^{33}P
    phosphorus-33

P_1
    first parental generation

P_2, P-2
    pulmonic second (heart) sound

P_3
    luminous flux
    proximal third (of bone) *also* P/3

P_4
    progesterone

P_{700}
    chloroplast pigment bleached by 700 nm

P_{870}
    bacterial chromatophore pigment bleached by 870 nm

p
    after *also* P

    atomic orbital with angular momentum quantum number 1
    (freeze) preservation
    frequency of the more common allele of a pair
    momentum
    page
    papilla (optic)
    para
    partial (pressure) *also* P, PP
    peripheral
    phosphate
    pico-
    pint *also* P, PT, pt
    pond
    pressure *also* P, PR, press.
    probability
    probable error
    proton
    pupil
    sample proportion (in statistics)
    short arm of chromosome
    sound pressure

$\bar{p}$
    after [L. *post*]
    mean pressure (gas)

p-
    para- (chemical prefix for two symmetrical substitutions in benzene ring)

P-A
    posteroanterior *also* PA

PA
    alveolar pressure
    panic attack
    pantothenic acid
    paralysis agitans
    paranoia
    parietal (cell) antibody
    partial pressure
    passive aggressive
    paternal aunt
    pathology *also* PATH, path.
    pentanoic acid
    periarteritis
    peridural artery
    periodic acid
    periodontal abscess
    permeability area
    pernicious anemia
    peroxidatic activity
    phakic-aphakic
    phenol alcohol

phenylalanine *also* F, P, PHA, PHE, Phe
phosphatidic acid
phosphoarginine
photo-allergy
phthalic anhydride
physical assistance
Physician Assistant
Picture Arrangement (psychology)
pineapple (test for butyric acid in stomach)
pituitary-adrenal
plasma aldosterone
plasminogen activator
platelet adhesiveness
platelet aggregation
platelet associated
polyacrylamide
polyarteritis
polyarthritis
postaural
posteroanterior
prealbumin
predictive accuracy
pregnancy-associated
presents again
primary aldosteronism
primary amenorrhea
primary anemia
prior to admission
proactivator
proanthocyanidin
procainamide
professional association
proinsulin antibody
prolonged action
prophylactic antibiotic
propionic acid
prostate antigen
proteolytic activity
prothrombin activity
protrusio acetabuli
Pseudomonas aeruginosa
psychiatric aide
psychoanalysis *also* PYA
psychogenic aspermia
pulmonary artery (banding)
pulmonary atresia
pulpoaxial
puromycin aminonucleoside

pyrophosphate arthropathy
pyrrolizidine alkaloid
yearly [L. *per annum*]

P/A
percussion (and) auscultation
position (and) alignment

P&A
percussion and auscultation
position and alignment
present and active (reflex)

P.A.
physician assistant

$P_2 = A_2$
pulmonic second heart sound equal to aortic second heart sounds

$P_2 > A_2$
pulmonic second heart sound greater than aortic second heart sound

$P_2 < A_2$
pulmonic heart sound less than aortic second heart sound

Pa
arterial partial pressure
arterial pressure
pascal (unit of pressure measurement)
protactinium
pulmonary arterial (pressure)
pulmonary artery (line)

pA
picoampere

pA_2
affinity constant (binding drug to drug receptor)

p.a.
after application [L. *post applicationem*]
for the year [L. *pro anno*]

PAA
partial agonist activity
phenylacetic acid
physical abilities analysis
plasma angiotensinase activity
polyacrylamide
polyacrylic acid

NOTES

543

PAA *(continued)*
polyamino acid
premarket approval application
pyridine acetic acid

p.a.a.
let it be applied to the affected area
[L. *parti affectase applicetur*]

P(A-aDO₂)
alveolar-arterial oxygen tension
difference

p(A-a)O₂
alveolar-arterial pressure difference

pAAT
plasma alpha 1-antitrypsin

PAB
p-aminobenzoic acid *also* PABA
para-aminobenzoate
pharmacologic autonomic block
polyacrylamide bead
Positive Attention Behavior
premature atrial beat
purple agarbase (medium)

PAb
protein antibody

PABA
p-aminobenzoic acid *also* PAB
para-aminobenzoic acid

PABP
pulmonary artery balloon pump

PAC
papular acrodermatitis of childhood
para-aminoclonidine
parent-adult-child (in transactional
analysis)
phenacetin (acetophenetidin), aspirin,
and caffeine
plasma aldosterone concentration
Platinol (cisplatin), Adriamycin
(doxorubicin), and cyclophosphamide
also PAC-V
preadmission certification
premature atrial contraction
premature auricular contraction
Progress Assessment Chart (of Social
and Personal Development)
prophylactic anticonvulsant
pulmonary artery catheter

PAC-1
Platinol, Adriamycin, and
cyclophosphamide

PACAP
pituitary adenylate cyclase activating
polypeptide

PACC
protein A (immobilized in) colodion
charcoal

PACE
Pacing and Clinical Electrophysiology
performance and cost efficiency
Personal Assessment for Continuing
Education
personalized aerobics for
cardiovascular enhancement
Platinol, Adriamycin,
cyclophosphamide, etopside
promoting aphasics communicative
effectiveness
pulmonary angiotensin I converting
enzyme

PA_{CO2}, Pa_{CO2}
partial pressure of carbon dioxide in
arterial gas

PACONA
periodic acid-concanavalin A

PACP
pulmonary artery counterpulsation

PACS
picture archival communication system
picture archiving and communications

PACT
papillary carcinoma of thyroid
precordial acceleration tracing

PACU
Postanesthesia Care Unit

PAC-V
Platinol (cisplatin), Adriamycin
(doxorubicin), and cyclophosphamide
also PAC

PAD
pelvic adhesive disease
per adjusted discharge
percutaneous abscess drainage
peripheral arterial disease
phenacetin, aspirin, and
desoxyephedrine
phonologic-acquisition device
photon absorption densitometry
pre-aid to the disabled
primary affective disorder
psychoaffective disorder

pulmonary artery diastolic *also* PAd
pulsatile assist device

PAd
pulmonary artery diastolic *also* PAD

PADDS
photon-activated drug delivery system

PADP
pulmonary artery diastolic pressure

PAE
paradoxical air embolism
postanoxic encephalopathy
postantibiotic effect
progressive assistive exercise

p. ae.
equal parts [L. *partes aequales*]

paed
paediatrics *also* PD, PED, ped, Peds

PAEDP
pulmonary artery end-diastolic
pressure

PAF
paroxysmal atrial fibrillation *also*
PAFIB
paroxysmal auricular fibrillation
phosphodiesterase-activating factor
platelet-activating factor
platelet-aggregating factor *also* PAgF
platelet aggregation factor
pollen adherence factor
premenstrual assessment form
pseudoamniotic fluid
pulmonary arteriovenous fistula

PA&F
percussion, auscultation, and fremitus

PAF-A
platelet-activating factor of
anaphylaxis

PAFD
pulmonary artery filling defect

PAFG
picric acid formaldehyde-
glutaraldehyde

PAFI
platelet-aggregation factor inhibitor

PAFIB
paroxysmal atrial fibrillation *also*
PAF

PAFP
pre-Achilles fat pad

PAG
periaqueductal gray (matter)
phenylacetylglutamine
polyacrylamide gel
pregnancy alpha-2 glycoprotein
pregnancy-associated globulin

pAg
protein A-gold (technique)

PAGE
polyacrylamide gel electrophoresis

PAgF
platelet-aggregating factor *also* PAF

PAGG
penta-acetylglucopyranosyl guanine

PAGIF
polyacrylamide gel isoelectric focusing

PAGMK
primary African green monkey
kidney

PAH
p-aminohippuric acid *also* PAHA
para-aminohippurate
phenylalanine hydroxylase
polycyclic aromatic hydrocarbon
postatrophic hyperplasia
pulmonary artery hypertension
pulmonary artery hypotension

PAHA
p-aminohippuric acid *also* PAH
para-aminohippuric acid

PAHVC
pulmonary alveolar hypoxic
vasoconstriction

PAI
Pair Attraction Inventory
plasminogen activator inhibitor
platelet accumulation index

PAI-1
type-1 plasminogen activator inhibitor

NOTES

P

PAI-2
type-2 plasminogen activator inhibitor

PAIC
procedures, alternatives, indications and complications

PAIDS
pediatric acquired immunodeficiency syndrome

PAIg
platelet-associated Ig

PAIgG
platelet-associated immunoglobulin G

PAIR
Personal Assessment of Intimacy in Relationships

PAIS
Psychosocial Adjustment to Illness Scale

PAIVS
pulmonary atresia with intact ventricular septum

PAJ
paralysis agitans juvenilis

PAK
maximal velocity *also* V_{max}
percutaneous access kit

PAL
pathology laboratory
phenylalanine ammonia lyase
posterior axillary line
powered air loss
product of activated lymphocyte
pyogenic abscess of liver

pal.
palate

PALA
N-phosphonoacetyl-*l*-aspartic acid

PA&Lat
posteroanterior and lateral

PALM
premature accelerated lung maturation

PALN
paraaortic lymph node

palp
palpable
palpate
palpation
palpitation *also* palpi

palpi
palpitation *also* palp

PALS
Paired Associate Learning Subtest
pediatric advanced life support
periarteriolar lymphocyte sheath
prison-acquired lymphoproliferative syndrome

PA-LS-ID
pernicious anemia-like syndrome and immunoglobulin deficiency

PALST
Picture Articulation and Language Screening Test

Palv
alveolar pressure

PAM
crystalline penicillin G in 2% aluminum monostearate
pancreatic acinor mass
penicillin aluminum monostearate
phenylalanine mustard
postauricular myogenic
potential acuity meter
pralidoxime
primary amebic meningoencephalitis
pulmonary alveolar macrophage
pulmonary alveolar microlithiasis
pyridine aldoxime methiodide

2-PAM
2-pralidoxime

PAMC
pterygoarthromyodysplasia congenital

PAMD
primary adrenocortical micronodular dysplasia

PAME
primary amebic meningoencephalitis

PAMI
Primary Angioplasty in Myocardial Infarction

PAMP
pulmonary artery mean pressure

PAN
periarteritis nodosa *also* PN
periodic alternating nystagmus
peroxyacetal nitrate
polyacrylonitrile
polyacrylonitryl
polyarteritis nodosa *also* PN
positional alcohol nystagmus

posterior ampullary nerve
puromycin aminonucleoside *also*
PANS
puromycin aminonucleoside
nephropathy

pan.
pancreas
pancreatectomy
pancreatic

p-ANC
perinuclear antineutrophil cytoplasmic

PAND
primary adrenocortical nodular
dysplasia

PANDO
primary acquired nasolacrimal duct
obstruction

PANESS
physical and neurologic examination
for soft signs

PANP
pelvic autonomic nerve preservation

PANS
puromycin aminonucleoside *also* PAN

PANSS
Positive and Negative Syndrome
Scale

PAO
peak acid output
peripheral airway obstruction
plasma amine oxidase
polyamine oxidase

PAO$_2$, PaO$_2$
partial pressure alveolar oxygen
partial pressure arterial oxygen

P$_{ao}$
airway opening pressure

PAo
pulmonary artery occlusion (pressure)

PaO$_2$ (*var. of* PAO$_2$)

Pao
ascending aortic pressure

PAOD
peripheral arterial occlusive disease

peripheral arteriosclerotic occlusive
disease
popliteal artery occlusive disease

PAOI
peak acid output insulin-induced

PAOP
pulmonary artery occlusion pressure

PAO$_2$–PaO$_2$
alveolar-arterial difference in partial
pressure of oxygen

PAOx
phenylacetone oxime

PAP
Papanicolaou (smear, test) *also* Pap
papaverine
para-aminophenol
passive-aggressive personality
Patient Assessment Program
peak airway pressure
peroxidase antibody to peroxidase
peroxidase-antiperoxidase (technique,
complex)
3'-phosphoadenosine 5'-phosphate
placental acid phosphatase
placental alkaline phosphatase
positive airway pressure
primary atypical pneumonia
prostatic acid phosphatase
pulmonary alveolar proteinosis
pulmonary artery pressure *also* PA
purified alternate pathway

Pap
Papanicolaou (smear, test) *also* PAP
papillary

pap.
papilla

PAPase
phosphatidic acid phosphohydrolase

PAPF
platelet adhesiveness plasma factor

Pap in. canthus
papilloma, inner canthus

papova
papilloma-polyoma-vacuolating agent
(virus)

NOTES

P

PAPP
p-aminopropiophenone
Pappenheimer bodies
pregnancy-associated plasma protein

PAPPA
pregnancy-associated plasma protein A

PAPPC
pregnancy-associated plasma protein C

PAPS
adenosine 3'-phosphate 5'-
phosphosulfate
3'-phosphoadenosine 5'-phosphosulfate
primary antiphospholipid (antibody)
syndrome

PA/PS
pulmonary atresia/pulmonary stenosis

Paps
papillomas

PAPUFA
physiologically active polyunsaturated
fatty acid

Pa-Pv
pulmonary arterial pressure-pulmonary
venous pressure

PAPVC
partial anomalous pulmonary venous
connection

PAPVD
partial anomalous pulmonary venous
drainage

PAPVR
partial anomalous pulmonary venous
return

PAPW
posterior aspect (of the) pharyngeal
wall

PAQ
Personal Attributes Questionnaire
Position Analysis Questionnaire (job
analysis)

PAR
paraffin
parallel *also* par.
passive avoidance reaction
perennial allergic rhinitis
photosynthetically active radiation
physiologic aging rate
plain abdominal radiography
platelet aggregate ratio
positive attention received
postanesthesia recovery (room) *also*
PARR
posterior apical radius
probable allergic rhinitis
problem-analysis report
Program for Alcohol Recovery
proximal alveolar region
pulmonary arteriolar resistance

PAr
polyarteritis

Par
paranoid

par.
paraffin
parallel *also* PAR
paralysis

Para
paraplegic
parous (having borne one or more
children) *also* para

para
number of pregnancies producing
viable offspring
paraparesis
paraplegia
paraplegic *also* Para
parathyroid *also* PT, PTH
parathyroidectomy
parous (having borne one or more
children) *also* Para
woman who has given birth

para 0
nullipara (no child borne)

para 1
unipara (having borne one child)

para 2
bipara (having borne two children)

para 3
tripara (having borne three children)

para 4
quadripara (having borne four
children)

I-para
primipara (first pregnancy) *also* P,
para 1, primip

II-para
secundipara (second pregnancy)

III-para
tertipara (third pregnancy)

para C, para c
paracervical

par. aff.
part affected
to the part affected [L. *pars affecta*]

para L
paralumbar

parapsych
parapsychology

parasit
parasite
parasitic
parasitology

parasym
parasympathetic (division of antonomic nervous system) *also* PS

para T
parathoracic

PARC
perennial allergic rhinoconjunctivitis

PARD
platelet aggregation as a risk of diabetes

parent.
parenteral
parenterally

PARH
plasminogen activator-releasing hormone

parox
paroxysm
paroxysmal

PAR-Q
Physical Activity Readiness Questionnaire

PARR
postanesthesia recovery room *also* PAR

PARS
Personal Adjustment and Role Skills (Scale)

PaRS
pararectal space

part.
of a part [L. *partis*]
partly [L. *partim*]
parturition

part. aeq.
equal parts [L. *partes aequales*]

part. dolent.
painful parts [L. *partes dolentes*]

part. vic.
in divided doses [L. *partitis vicibus*]

PARU
postanesthetic recovery unit

parv.
small [L. *parvus*]

PAS
p-aminosalicylic acid *also* PASA
para-aminosalicylate *also* PASA
Parent Attitude Scale
patient appointments and scheduling
periodic acid-Schiff (stain)
peripheral access system
peripheral anterior synechia
persistent atrial standstill
personality assessment system
phosphatase acid serum
photoacoustic spectroscopy
Physician's Activity Study
pneumatic antiembolic stocking
postanesthesia score
posterior airway space
preadmission screening
pregnancy advisory service
premature atrial stimulus
premature auricular systole
Professional Activities Study
progressive accumulated stress
pseudoachievement syndrome
pulmonary arterial stenosis
pulmonary artery stenosis
pulmonary artery systolic

Pas
pascal (unit of pressure)

Pa·s
pascal-second

PASA
p-aminosalicylic acid *also* PAS
para-aminosalicylic acid *also* PAS

NOTES

P

PASA *(continued)*
primary acquired sideroblastic anemia
proximal articular set angle

PAS-AB
periodic acid Schiff-Alcian blue combination stain

PASAT
Paced Auditory Serial Addiction Task

PaSat
saturation of oxygen in arterial blood

PAS-C
para-aminosalicylic acid crystallized (with ascorbic acid)

PASCC
pseudovascular adenoid squamous cell carcinoma

PASCCL
pseudovascular adenoid squamous cell carcinoma of the lung

PASD
after diastase digestion

P'ase
alkaline phosphatase *also* AKP, ALK-P, alk phos, alk p'tase, ALP, AlPase, AP, KA

PASES
Performance Assessment of Syntax Elicited and Spontaneous

Pas Ex
passive exercise

PASG
pneumatic antishock garment

PASH
periodic acid-Schiff hematoxylin
pseudoangiomatous stromal hyperplasia

PASI
psoriasis area sensitivity index

PASK
peripheral anterior stent keratopathy

PASM
periodic acid-silver methenamine

PAS/MAP
Professional Activities Study Medical Audit Program (medical records)

PASP
pulmonary artery systolic pressure

pass.
here and there [L. *passim*]
passive

PAST
periodic acid-Schiff technique

PASVR
pulmonary anomalous superior venous return

PAT
Pain Apperception Test
paroxysmal atrial tachycardia
paroxysmal auricular tachycardia
patella *also* pat.
patient
percentage of acceleration time
percutaneous aspiration thromboembolectomy
Photo Articulation Test (psychology)
physical abilities test
picric acid turbidity
platelet aggregation test
polyamineacetyltransferase
preadmission (screening and) assessment team
preadmission testing
Predictive Ability Test (psychology)
pregnancy at term
prism adaptation test
prophylactic antibiotic treatment
psychoacoustic testing
pulmonary artery trunk

pat.
patella *also* PAT
patent
paternal origin

PATCO
prednisone, ara-C, thioguanine, cyclophosphamide, and Oncovin (vincristine)

PATE
psychodynamic and therapeutic education
pulmonary artery thromboembolism
pulmonary artery thromboendarterectomy

PATENT
Prourokinase and t-PA Enhancement of Thrombolysis

PATH
Partnership Approach to Health
pathologic

pathology *also* PA, path.
pituitary adrenotropic hormone

path.
pathogen
pathogenesis
pathogenic
pathologic
pathologist
pathology *also* PA, PATH

path. fx
pathologic fracture

PATLC
Progressive Achievement Tests of
Listening Comprehension

pat. med.
patent medicine

PA-T-SP
periodic acid-thiocarbohydrazide-silver
proteinate

pat. T
patellar tenderness

PAT/TM
patient's time

p. aur.
behind the ear [L. *post aurem*]

PAV
partial atrioventricular
Pavulon (pancuronium bromide)
percutaneous aortic valvuloplasty
poikiloderma atrophicans vasculare
posterior arch vein
proportional assist ventilation

Pa Va Ex
passive vascular (or venoarterial)
exercise (a negative pressure)

PAVe
L-phenylalanine mustard and
vinblastine
procarbazine, Alkeran (melphalan),
and Velban (vinblastine sulfate)

PA-VF
pulmonary arteriovenous fistula

PAVM
pulmonary arteriovenous malformation

PAVN
paraventricular nucleus

PAVNRT
paroxysmal atrioventricular nodal
reciprocal tachycardia

PAW
peak airway pressure
peripheral airway
pulmonary artery wedge

Paw
mean airway pressure

Pawo
pressure at airway opening

PAWP
pulmonary artery wedge pressure

Pa x s
pascal per second

PB
barometric pressure
British Pharmacopeia [*Pharmacopoeia
Britannica*] *also* BP
pancreaticobiliary
paraffin bath
Paul-Bunnell (antibody, test)
pentobarbital
perineal body
periodic breathing
peripheral blood
peroneus brevis
phenobarbital
phonetically balanced (word lists)
pinch biopsy
pinealoblastoma
piperonyl butoxide
polymyxin B
posterior baffle
powder bed
powder board
power building
premature beat
pressure balanced
pressure breathing
protein binding
protein bound
pudendal block
punch biopsy

NOTES

P

PB%
  phonetically balanced percentage (of word lists)

P&B
  pain and burning
  phenobarbital and belladonna

P_B
  barometric pressure

Pb
  lead [L. *plumbum*]
  phenobarbital
  presbyopia
  probenecid

PBA
  percutaneous bladder aspiration
  polyclonal B-cell activity
  pressure breathing assister
  prolactin-binding assay
  prune belly anomaly
  pulpobuccoaxial

P_BA
  brachial arterial pressure

PBB
  polybromated biphenyl

Pb-B
  lead level in blood

PBC
  perfusion balloon catheter
  peripheral blood cell
  point of basal convergence
  prebed care
  pregnancy and birth complications
  primary biliary cirrhosis
  progestin-binding complement

PBCL
  parafollicular B-cell lymphoma

PBD
  percutaneous biliary drainage
  postburn day
  proliferative breast disease

PBE
  partial breech extraction

PBF
  peripheral blood flow
  phosphate-buffered formalin
  placental blood flow
  pulmonary blood flow *also* Qp

PB-Fe
  protein-bound iron

PBG
  Penassay broth plus glucose
  porphobilinogen

PBGM
  Penassay broth plus glucose plus menadione

PBG-S
  porphobilinogen synthase

PBH
  pulling boat hands

PBI
  parental bonding instrument
  partial bony impaction
  penile-brachial index
  phenformin
  protein-bound iodine

PbI
  lead intoxication

PBK
  phosphorylase *b* kinase
  pseudophakic bullous keratopathy

PBL
  peripheral blood leukocyte
  peripheral blood lymphocyte

PBLI
  premature birth, live infant

PBLT
  peripheral blood lymphocyte transformation

PBM
  peripheral basement membrane
  peripheral blood mononuclear (cell) *also* PBMC

PBMC
  peripheral blood mononuclear cell *also* PBM

PBMV
  pulmonary blood mixing volume

PBN
  paralytic brachial neuritis
  peripheral benign neoplasm
  polymyxin B sulfate, bacitracin, and neomycin

PBNA
  partial body neutron activation

PBNS
  percutaneous bladder neck stabilization

PBO
    penicillin in beeswax and oil
    placebo *also* P, PL

PbO
    lead monoxide

PBP
    peak blood pressure
    penicillin-binding protein
    percutaneous balloon pericardiotomy
    porphyrin biosynthetic pathway
    progressive bulbar palsy
    prostate-binding protein
    protein-bound polysaccharide
    pseudobulbar palsy
    purified *Brucella* protein

PBPC
    peripheral blood progenitor cell

PBPI
    penile-brachial pulse index

PBQ
    phenylbenzoquinone
    Preschool Behavior Questionnaire

PBRT
    phonetically balanced rhyme test

PBS
    peripheral-blood smear
    peroneus brevis split
    phenobarbital sodium
    phosphate-buffered saline
    phosphate-buffered sodium
    polybrominated salicylanilide
    prune belly syndrome
    pulmonary branch stenosis

PBSC
    penicillin, bacitracin, streptomycin, caprylate
    peripheral blood stem cell

PBSP
    prognostically bad signs during pregnancy

PBT
    Paul Bunnell test
    phenacetin breath test
    profile-based therapy

PBT$_4$
    protein-bound thyroxine

PBV
    percutaneous balloon valvuloplasty
    Platinol (cisplatin), bleomycin, and vinblastine
    predicted blood volume
    pulmonary blood volume

PBW
    posterior bite wing

PB word
    phonetically balanced word

PBZ
    phenoxybenzamine
    phenylbutazone
    Pyribenzamine (tripelennamine)

PC
    avoirdupois weight [L. *pondus civile*]
    packed cells
    palmitoyl carnitine
    pancreatic cancer
    paper chromatography
    parent cell
    parent to child
    particulate component
    partition coefficient
    pelvic cramp
    penicillin
    pentose cycle
    peritoneal cell
    pharmacology
    phosphate cycle
    phosphatidylcholine (lecithin)
    phosphocreatine
    phosphorylcholine
    photoconductive
    phrase construction
    Physicians' Corporation
    picryl chloride
    picture completion
    pill counter
    piriform cortex
    plasma concentration
    plasma cortisol
    plasma cytoma
    platelet concentrate
    platelet count
    pneumotaxic center
    polycentric
    polyposis coli
    poor condition

NOTES

P

PC *(continued)*
popliteal cyst
portacaval (shunt)
portal cirrhosis
postcoital
posterior cervical
posterior chamber
posterior circumflex artery
posterior column
posterior commissure
posterior cortex
precordial
prepiriform cortex
present complaint
primary cleavage
primary closure
principal cell
printed circuit
procollagen
producing cell
productive cough
professional corporation
proliferative capacity
prostatic carcinoma
provisional cortex
proximal colon
pseudocyst
Psychodevelopment Checklist
pubococcygeus (muscle) *also* PCG
pulmonary capillary
pulmonic closure
pulp canal
Purkinje cell
pyloric canal
pyruvate carboxylase

P-C
phlogistic corticoid

P&C
prism and (alternative) cover test (crossover test, screen and cover test in ophthalmology)

Pc
penicillin *also* PC

p.c.
after a meal [L. *post cibum*]

pc
parsec
percent
picocurie *also* pCi, PCi

pc1
platelet count pretransfusion

pc2
platelet count posttransfusion

PCA
pancreatic carcinoma
para-chloramphetamine
parietal cell antibody
passive cutaneous anaphylaxis
patient care aide
patient care assistant
patient-controlled analgesia
perchloric acid
percutaneous carotid arteriogram
percutaneous coronary angioplasty
personal care attendant
phenylcarboxylic acid
photocontact allergic
plasma catecholamine concentration
porous coated anatomic (prosthesis)
portacaval anastomosis
postciliary artery
postconceptional age
posterior cerebral artery
posterior communicating aneurysm
posterior communicating artery
posterior cricoarytenoid
precoronary care area
President's Council on Aging
principal components analysis
procainamide
procoagulant activity
prostatic carcinoma
pyrrolidone carboxylic acid

pCa
prostate cancer

PCAS
Psychotherapy Competence Assessment Schedule

PCAVC
persistent complete atrioventricular canal

PCB
pancuronium bromide
paracervical block
polychlorinated biphenyl
portacaval bypass
prepared childbirth
procarbazine *also* PCZ

PcB, Pcb
near point of convergence to intercentral baseline [L. *punctum convergens basalis*]

PC-BMP
phosphorylcholine-binding myeloma protein

PCBS
percutaneous cardiopulmonary bypass support

PCC
Pasteur Culture Collection
percutaneous cecostomy
peripheral cholangiocarcinoma
personal care clinic
pheochromocytoma
phosphate carrier compound
plasma catecholamine concentration
Poison Control Center
postcoital contraception
posterior central curve
precoronary care
premature chromosome condensation
primary care clinic
prothrombin-complex concentration

PCc
periscopic concave

PCCC
pediatric critical care center

PCCP
percutaneous cord cyst puncture

PCCS
parent-child communication schedule

PCCU
post-coronary care unit

PCD
pacer-cardioverter defibrillator
papillary collecting duct
paroxysmal cerebral dysrhythmia
phosphate-citrate-dextrose
plasma cell dyscrasia
polycystic disease
posterior corneal deposit
postmortem cesarean delivery
primary ciliary dyskinesia
programmable cardioverter-defibrillator
prolonged contractile duration
pulmonary clearance delay

PCDC
plasma clot diffusion chamber

PCDF
polychlorinated dibenzofuran

PCDUS
plasma cell dyscrasia of unknown significance

PCE
cis-platinum, cyclophosphamide, Eldesine
physical capacity evaluation
pseudocholinesterase *also* PCHE
pulmocutaneous exchange

PCEA
patient-controlled epidural analgesia *also* PEA

PCF
peripheral circulatory failure
pharyngoconjunctival fever
posterior cranial fossa
prothrombin conversion factor

pcf
pound per cubic foot

PCFT
platelet complement fixation test

PCG
paracervical ganglion
phonocardiogram
Planning Career Goals (psychologic test)
pneumocardiogram
primate chorionic gonadotropin
pubococcygeus (muscle) *also* PC

pcg
picogram *also* pg

PCGG
percutaneous coagulation of gasserian ganglion

PCH
paroxysmal cold hemoglobinuria
polycyclic hydrocarbon
pulp chamber

PCHE
pseudocholinesterase *also* PCE

PC&HS
after meals and at bedtime

PCI
pneumatosis cystoides intestinalis
posterior curve intermediate (cornea)

NOTES

P

PCI *(continued)*
Premarital Communication Inventory
prophylactic cranial irradiation
prothrombin consumption index

PCi, pCi
picocurie *also* pc

PCIC
Poison Control Information Center

PCINA
patient-controlled intranasal analgesia

PCIOL
posterior chamber intraocular lens

PCIRF
radiologic contrast-induced renal
failure

PCIRV, PC-IRV
pressure-controlled inverse ratio
ventilation

PCIS
Patient Care Information System
postcardiac injury syndrome

PCIVOT
Prostate Cancer Intervention Versus
Observation Trial

PCK
polycystic kidney

PCKD
polycystic kidney disease

PCL
pacing cycle length
persistent corpus luteum
plasma cell leukemia
posterior chamber lens
posterior cruciate ligament
proximal collateral ligament

PCLC
Paneth cell-like change

PCLD
polycystic liver disease *also* PLD

PCLI
posterior chamber lens implant

P closure
plastic closure

PCM
primary cutaneous melanoma
protein-calorie malnutrition
protein carboxymethylase
pulse code modulation

PCMB, p-CMB
p-chloromercuribenzoate

PCMBSA
para-chloromercuribenzine sulfonic
acid

PCMC
Primary Children's Medical Center

PCMF
perceptual cognitive motor function

PCMO
Principal Clinical Medical Officer

PCMT
pacemaker circus movement
tachycardia

PCMX
chloroxylenol
para–chloro-*m*-xylenol

PCN
penicillin *also* P, PEN, Pen, pen.,
PN, PNC
percutaneous nephrostomy
pregnenolone carbonitril
primary care network
primary care nursing

PCNA
proliferating cell nuclear antigen

PCNA-LI
PCNA-labeling index

PCNB
pentachloronitrobenzene

PCNL
percutaneous nephrolithotomy *also*
PNL
percutaneous nephrostolithotomy

PCNV
postchemotherapy nausea and
vomiting

PCO
patient complains of
polycystic ovary
posterior capsular opacification
predicted cardiac output
procytoxid

Pco, P$_{CO}$
carbon monoxide pressure or tension

P$_{CO2}$, PCO2, Pco$_2$
partial pressure of carbon dioxide

PCoA
posterior communicating artery *also* PCom

PCOD
polycystic ovarian disease

PCom
posterior communicating artery *also* PCoA

PCOS
polycystic ovary syndrome *also* POS

PCP
parachlorophenate
patient care plan
pentachlorophenol
peripheral coronary pressure
persistent cough and phlegm
phencyclidine
pneumocystic pneumonia
Pneumocystis carinii pneumonia
postoperative constrictive pericarditis
primary care physician
prochlorperazine
procollagen peptide
pulmonary capillary pressure
pulse cytophotometry

PCPA
para-chlorophenylalanine

PCPB
percutaneous cardiopulmonary bypass

PCPL
pulmonary capillary protein leakage

pcpn
precipitation *also* pcpt, precip

PCPS
percutaneous cardiopulmonary support
peroral cholangiopancreatoscopy
phosphatidylcholine-phosphatidylserine

pcpt
perception
precipitate
precipitation *also* pcpn, precip

PCR
pathologically confirmed complete
  remission
patient contact record
phosphocreatine

plasma clearance rate
polymerase chain reaction
probable causal relationship
protein catabolic rate

PCr
phosphocreatine

PCRA
percutaneous coronary rotational
  atherectomy

PCRC
primary colorectal cancer

PCS
palliative care service
Patient Care System
patterns of care study
pelvic congestion syndrome
peroral cholangioscopy
pharmacogenic confusional syndrome
portable cervical spine
portacaval shunt
postcardiac surgery
postcardiotomy syndrome
postcholecystectomy syndrome
postconcussion syndrome
precordial stethoscope
primary cancer site
primary cesarean section
Priority Counseling Survey
proportional counter spectrometry
proximal coronary sinus
pseudotumor cerebri syndrome

P c/s
primary cesarean section

Pcs, pcs
preconscious

PCSD
prone cranial support device

PCSM
percutaneous stone manipulation

PCT
Physiognomic Cue Test (psychology)
plasma clotting time
plasmacrit test (for syphilis)
plasmacytoma
platelet hematocrit
polychlorinated triphenyl
porcine calcitonin

NOTES

P

PCT *(continued)*
porphyria cutanea tarda
portacaval transportation
portacaval transposition
positron computed tomography
postcoital
postcoital test
posterior chest tube
progestin challenge test
prothrombin consumption time
proximal convoluted tubule
pulmonary care team

pct
percent

PCTA
percutaneous coronary transluminal angioplasty

PCU
pain control unit
palliative care unit
patient care unit
primary care unit
progressive care unit
protective care unit
protein-calorie undernutrition
pulmonary care unit

p cut
percutaneous

PCV
packed cell volume
parietal cell vagotomy
polycythemia vera *also* PV
postcapillary venule
premature ventricular contraction

PCVC
percutaneous central venous catheter

PCV-M
polycythemia vera (with myeloid) metaplasia

PCW
pulmonary capillary wedge (pressure) *also* PCWP
purified cell walls

PCWP
pulmonary capillary wedge pressure *also* PCW

PCX
paracervical

PCx
periscopic convex

PCXR
portable chest radiograph
portable chest x-ray

PCZ
procarbazine *also* PCB
prochlorperazine

PD
by the day [L. *per diem*] *also* p.d.
Doctor of Pharmacy
(inter)pupillary distance
Paget disease
pancreas divisum
pancreatic duct
papilla diameter
paralyzing dose
Parkinson disease
parkinsonian dementia
paroxysmal discharge
pars distalis (pituitary)
patent ductus
patient day
patient demonstration
pediatrics *also* paed, PED, ped, Peds
percutaneous diskectomy
percutaneous drain
peritoneal dialysis
personality disorder
pharmacodynamics
phenyldichlorarsine
phenyldichloroarsine
phosphate dehydrogenase
photosensitivity dermatitis
Pick disease
plasma defect
poorly differentiated
Porak-Durante (syndrome)
porphobilinogen deaminase
posterior division
postnasal drainage
postural drainage
potential difference
present disease
pressor dose
primary dendrite
prism diopter *also* p.d.
problem drinker
progression (of) disease
protein degradation
protein deprived
protein diet
provocation dose
psychopathic deviate
psychotic dementia
psychotic depression
pulmonary disease *also* PUD, PuD

pulpodistal
pulse duration
pupillary distance
pyloric dilator

P/D
packs per day (cigarettes) *also* p/d, PPD

P(D+)
probability of having disease

P(D−)
probability of not having disease

PD$_{50}$
median paralyzing dose

Pd
palladium
pediatrics *also* paed, PD, PED, ped, Peds

pd
papilla diameter
period

p/d
packs per day (cigarettes) *also* P/D, PPD

p.d.
by the day [L. *per diem*] *also* PD
for the day [L. *pro die*]
prism diopter *also* PD

PDA
parenteral drug abuser
patent ductus arteriosus
patient distress alarm
pediatric allergy *also* PdA
poorly differentiated adenocarcinoma
posterior descending (coronary) artery
predialyzed human albumin
pulmonary disease anemia

PdA
pediatric allergy *also* PDA

PDAB
para-dimethylaminobenzaldehyde

PDAF
platelet-derived angiogenesis factor

PDB
Paget disease of bone
para-dichlorobenzene *also* PDCB

phosphorus-dissolving bacteria
preperitoneal distention balloon
preventive dental (health) behavior

PDC
parkinsonism-dementia complex
pediatric cardiology
pentadecylcatechol
physical dependence capacity
plasma digoxin concentration
plasma disappearance curve
poorly differentiated carcinoma
postdecapitation convulsion
preliminary diagnostic clinic
private diagnostic clinic
pyrindinol carbamate

PD&C
postural drainage and clapping

PdC
pediatric cardiology

PDCB
para-dichlorobenzene *also* PDB

PDCD
primary degenerative cerebral disease

PD-CSE
pulsed Doppler cross-sectional echocardiography

PDD
pervasive developmental disorder
platinum diamminedichloride (cisplatin)
primary degenerative dementia
pyridoxine-deficient diet

PDDB
phenododecinium bromide

PDE
paroxysmal dyspnea on exertion
peritoneal dialysis effluent
phosphodiesterase (inhibitor)
progressive dialysis encephalopathy
pulsed Doppler echocardiography

PdE
pediatric endocrinology

PDF
peritoneal dialysis fluid
probability density function

NOTES

PDFC
premature dead female child

PDG
parkinsonism dementia (complex of) Guam
phosphate-dependent glutaminase
phosphogluconate dehydrogenase

PDGA
pteroyldiglutamic acid

PDGF
platelet-derived growth factor

PDGS
partial form of DiGeorge syndrome

PDGXT
predischarge graded exercise test

PDH
past dental history
phosphate dehydrogenase
pyruvate dehydrogenase

PDHC
pyruvate dehydrogenase complex

PdHO
pediatric hematology-oncology

PDI
Periodontal Disease Index
plan-do integration
Psychomotor Development Index

Pdi
transdiaphragmatic pressure

PDIE
phosphodiesterase

PDIg
platelet-directed Ig

P-diol
pregnanediol

PDL
periodontal ligament
polycystic disease of liver
poorly differentiated lymphocyte
population doubling level
primary dysfunctional labor
progressively diffused
leukoencephalopathy
pulsed dye laser

Pdl, pdl
poundal (force of acceleration)
pudendal

PDLC
poorly differentiated lung cancer

PDLD
poorly differentiated lymphocytic-diffuse

PDLL
poorly differentiated lymphocytic lymphoma

PDLN
poorly differentiated (lymphocytic) lymphoma-nodular

PDLP
predigested liquid protein

PDLS
physical daily living skills

PDM
polymyositis and dermatomyositis
predentin matrix

PDMC
premature dead male child

PDMEA
phosphoryldimethylethanolamine

PDMS
Patient Data Management Systems
pharmacokinetic drug-monitoring service

PDN
prednisone *also* P, PRED
private day nurse
private duty nurse

PdNEO
pediatric neonatology

PdNEP
pediatric nephrology

PDP
pancreatic duct pressure
pattern disruption point
peak diastolic pressure
piperidinopyrimidine
platelet-depleted plasma
primer-dependent deoxynucleic acid polymerase
Product Development Protocol

PD&P
postural drainage and percussion

PDPD
prolonged-dwell peritoneal dialysis

PDPH
postdural puncture headache

PDPI
> primer-dependent deoxynucleic acid polymerase index

PDQ
> parental development questionnaire
> Personality Diagnostic Questionnaire
> Premenstrual Distress Questionnaire
> Prescreening Development Questionnaire
> pretty damn quick (slang)
> protocol data query

PDR
> pandevelopmental retardation
> pediatric radiology
> peripheral diabetic retinopathy
> *Physician's Desk Reference*
> pleiotropic drug resistance
> postdelivery room
> primary drug resistance
> proliferative diabetic retinopathy

PdR
> pediatric radiology

pdr
> powder *also* powd, pwd

PDRB
> Permanent Disability Rating Board

PDRc̄VH
> proliferative diabetic retinopathy with vitreous hemorrhage

PDS
> pain-dysfunction syndrome
> paroxysmal depolarizing shift
> patient data system
> pediatric surgery *also* PdS, PS
> peritoneal dialysis system
> polydioxanone
> predialyzed (human) serum
> primary dependence study

PdS
> pediatric surgery *also* PDS, PS
> psychiatric deviate, subtle

PDT
> percutaneous dilational tracheostomy
> phenyldimethyltriazine
> photodynamic therapy
> population doubling time

PDTA
> propanoldiaminotetraacetic acid

PDU
> pulsed Doppler ultrasonography

PDUF
> pulsed Doppler ultrasonic flowmeter

PDUR
> Predischarge Utilization Review

PDV
> peak diastolic velocity

PDW
> platelet distribution width

PDWHF
> platelet-derived wound healing factor

PE
> expiratory pressure *also* P_E
> pancreatic extract
> paper electrophoresis
> parallel elastic (component of muscle)
> partial epilepsy
> Pel-Ebstein (disease)
> pelvic examination
> penile erection
> percutaneous endoscopic
> pericardial effusion
> peritoneal exudate
> phakoemulsification
> pharyngoesophageal
> phenylephrine
> phosphatidylethanolamine
> photographic effect
> phycoerythrin
> physical education *also* PED, PEd, Phys Ed
> physical evaluation
> physical examination *also* PEx, PX, Px
> physical exercise
> physiologic ecology
> pigmented epithelium
> pigment epithelium
> plasma exchange
> plating efficiency
> Platinol (cisplatin) and etoposide
> pleural effusion
> point of entry
> polyethylene

NOTES

P

PE *(continued)*
polynuclear eosinophil
potential energy
powdered extract
preeclampsia
preexcitation
present examination
pressure equalization
prior to exposure
probable error
probe excision
protein excretion
pulmonary edema
pulmonary embolism
pyramidal eminence
pyroelectric
pyrogenic exotoxin

PE2
secondary plating efficiency

P$_E$
expiratory pressure *also* PE

Pe
Peclet number
perylene
pregnenolone
pressure on expiration

pe
for example [L. *per exemplum*]

PEA
patient-controlled epidural analgesia
also PCEA
pelvic examination under anesthesia
phenylethyl alcohol (agar)
phenylethylamine
polysaccharide egg antigen
pulseless electrical activity

PE↓A
pelvic examination under anesthesia
also PEA

PEACH
Preschool Evaluation and Assessment
for Children with Handicaps

PEAO
phenylethylamine oxidase

PEAP
positive end-airway pressure

PEAQ
Personal Experience and Attitude
Questionnaire

PEARLA
pupils equal and react to light and
accommodation

PEB
Platinol (cisplatin), etoposide, and
bleomycin

PEBG
phenethylbiguanide

PEC
parallel elastic component
patient evaluation center
peduncle of cerebrum
peritoneal exudate cell
pulmonary ejection click
pyrogenic exotoxin C

PECCE
planned extracapsular cataract
extraction

PECHO, Pecho
prostatic echogram

PECHR
peripheral exudative choroidal
hemorrhagic retinopathy

PECO$_2$
mixed expired carbon dioxide tension

PECT
positron emission computed
tomography

PED
paroxysmal exertion-induced
dyskinesia
pediatrics *also* paed, PD, ped, Peds
peduncle (cerebral)
pharyngoesophageal diverticulum
pigment epithelial detachment
pollution and environmental
degradation
postentry day
postexertional dyspnea

PEd, P Ed
physical education *also* PE, Phys Ed

ped
pedangle
pedestrian
pediatrics *also* paed, PD, PED, Peds

ped ed
pedal edema

PEDG
phenylethyldiguanide

PED/MV
pedestrian hit by motor vehicle

PeDS
Pediatric Drug Surveillance

Peds
pediatrics *also* paed, PD, PED, ped

PEE
parallel elastic element

PEEP
peak end-expiratory pressure
positive end-expiratory pressure

PEEP/CPAP
positive end-expiratory
pressure/continuous positive airway
pressure

PEEPi
intrinsic positive end-expiratory
pressure

PEER
Pediatric Examination of Educational
Readiness
pronation-eversion-external rotation

PEEX
Pediatric Early Elemental Examination

PEF
peak expiratory flow (rate) *also*
PEFR
pharyngoepiglottic fold
Psychiatric Evaluation Form
pulmonary edema fluid

PEFR
peak expiratory flow rate *also* PEF

PEFSR
partial expiratory flow-static recoil
(curve)

PEFT
peak expiratory flow time

PEFV
partial expiratory flow volume

PEG
Patient Evaluation Grid
percutaneous endoscopic gastrostomy

pneumoencephalogram
pneumonencephalography
polyethylene glycol

PEG-ADA
pegademase bovine
polyethylene glycol-modified adenosine
deaminase

PEG-ELS
polyethylene glycol electrolyte lavage
solution

PEG-IL-2
polyethylene glycol-modified
interleukin-2

PEG-J
percutaneous endoscopic
gastrojejunostomy

PEG-L-ASP
polyethylene glycol-conjugated *l*-
asparaginase

PEI
percutaneous ethanol injection
phosphate excretion index
phosphorus excretion index
physical efficiency index
Platinol (cisplatin), etoposide, and
ifosfamide
polyethylenimine

PEIT
percutaneous ethanol injection therapy

PEJ
percutaneous endoscopic jejunostomy

PEK
punctate epithelial keratopathy

PEL
peritoneal exudate lymphocyte
permissible exposure limit

Pel
elastic recoil pressure of lung

PELISA
paper enzyme-linked immunosorbent
assay

PEM
peritoneal exudate macrophage
polymorphic epithelial mucin

NOTES

P

563

PEM (continued)
precordial electrocardiographic mapping
prescription event monitoring
primary enrichment medium
probable error of measurement
protein energy malnutrition
pulmonary endothelial membrane

PEMA
phenylethylmalonamide

PEMF
pulsating electromagnetic field
pulsed electromagnetic field

PEMS
physical, emotional, mental, and safety

PEN
pancreatic endocrine neoplasm
parenteral and enteral nutrition

Pen, pen.
penicillin also P, PCN, PEN, PN, PNC

pen.
penetrating

PENG
photoelectronystagmography

PENS
percutaneous epidural nerve stimulator

Pent
pentothal

PEO
progressive external ophthalmoplegia

PEP
peptidase
performance evaluation procedure
phosphoenolpyruvate
polyestradiol phosphate
positive expiratory pressure
postencephalitic parkinsonism
preejection period
progestogen-dependent endometrial protein
protein electrophoresis
Psychiatric Evaluation Profile

Pep
peptidase

PEPA
peptidase A
protected environment (units and) prophylactic antibiotics

PEPC
peptidase C

PEPc
corrected preejection period

PEPCK, PEPK
phosphoenolpyruvate carboxykinase

PEPD
peptidase D

PEPI
preejection period index

PEPK (var. of PEPCK)

PEP/LVET
preejection period/left ventricular ejection time

PEPP
positive expiratory pressure plateau

PEPR
precision encoder and pattern recognizer

PEPS
peptidase S

PER
peak ejection rate
pediatric emergency room
periodic evaluation record
protein efficiency ratio
pudendal evoked response

per
perineal
periodic
periodicity
person
through, by [L. per]

per bid.
for a period of two days [L. per bidum]

PERC
perceptual
percutaneous
potential erythropoietin-responsive cell

percus, PERCUSS
percussion

PERD
photoelectric registration device

PERF
peak expiratory flow rate

perf
perfect
perforation also P

PERG
pattern-evoked electroretinogram

PERI
peritoneal fluid
Psychiatric Epidemiology Research
Interview

peri
perineal

periap
periapical

perim
perimeter

Perio
periodontics

PERK
prospective evaluation of radial
keratotomy

PERL
pupils equal and react to light

PERLA
pupils equal, reactive to light and
accommodation

perm
permanent
permutation

per. op. emet.
when action of emetic is over [L.
peracta operatione emetici]

perp
perpendicular

Per pad
perineal pad

PERR
pattern evoked retinal response

PERRLA
pupils equal, round, reactive to light
and accommodation

PERS
patient evaluation rating scale

pers
personal

PERT
product-enhanced reverse transcriptase

program evaluation and review
technique

PES
pacing esophageal stethoscope
photoelectron spectroscopy
plastic endosurgical system
postextrasystolic
preepiglottic space
preexcitation syndrome
primary empty sella (syndrome)
programmed electrical stimulation
pseudoexfoliation syndrome *also* PXS

PESDA
perfluorocarbon-exposed sonicated
dextrose albumin

PESP
postextrasystolic potentiation

pe SPL
peak equivalent sound pressure level

Pess
pessary

PESST
Patterned Elicitation Syntax Screening
Test

PEST
point estimation by sequential testing

PET
paraffin-embedded tissue
parent effectiveness training
peak ejection time
pear-shaped extension tube
peritoneal equilibration test
polyethylene terephthalate
polyethylene tube
poor exercise tolerance
positron emission tomography
preeclamptic toxemia
pressure equalizing tube
progressive exercise test
Psychiatric Emergency Team

PETA
pentaerythritol triacrylate

PETCO₂
extrapolated end-tidal carbon dioxide
tension

NOTES

P

PET-FDG
positron emission tomography with [^{18}F]-labeled fluorodeoxyglucose

PETH
pink-eyed, tan-hooded (rat)

PETN
pentaerythritol tetranitrate

petr
petroleum

PETT
pendular eye-tracking test
positron emission transaxial tomography
positron emission transverse tomography

PEU
plasma equivalent unit
polyether urethane

PEV
pulmonary extravascular (fluid) volume

PeV
peripheral vein *also* PV

pev, peV
peak electron volt

PEVN
periventricular nucleus

PEWV
pulmonary extravascular water volume

PEx
physical examination *also* PE, PX, Px

PF
parafascicular (nucleus)
parallel fiber
parotid fluid
partially follicular
patellofemoral (joint)
peak flow
pericardial fluid
peripheral field
peritoneal fluid
permeability factor
personality factor
phenol formaldehyde
physicians' forum
picture-frustration (study, test) *also* P-F
plantar flexion
plasma factor
plasma fibronectin
platelet factor
pleural fluid
power factor
precursor fluid
preservative free
proflavin
prostatic fluid
protection factor
pterygoid fossa
pulmonary factor
pulmonary function
Purkinje fiber
purpura fulminans
push fluids

P-F
picture-frustration (study, test) *also* PF

P/F
pass/fail (system)

PF$_{1-4}$
platelet factors 1 through 4

pF
picofarad

PFA
phosphonoformatic acid
profunda femoris artery

PFAGH
penalty, frustration, anxiety, guilt, and hostility

PFAS
performic acid-Schiff (reaction)

PFB
properdin factor B
pseudofolliculitis barbae

PFC
pelvic flexion contracture
perfluorocarbon
perfluorochemical
pericardial fluid culture
permanent flexure contracture
persistent fetal circulation
plaque-forming cell
Press-Fit component

pFc
noncovalently bonded dimer of C-terminal immunoglobulin of Fc fragment

PFCPH
persistent fetal circulation with pulmonary hypertension

PFD
polyostotic fibrous dysplasia
primary flash distillate

PFE
pelvic floor exercise
Platinol (cisplatin), 5-FU, etoposide

PFEAAC
posterior fossa extra-axial arachnoid
cyst

PFFD
proximal femoral focal deficiency
proximal femur focal deficiency

PFFFP
Pall-filtered fresh-frozen plasma

PFG
peak-flow gauge

PFGE
pulsed field gel electrophoresis

PFIB
perfluoroisobutylene

PFJS
patellofemoral joint syndrome

PFK
phosphofructoaldolase
phosphofructokinase

PFKL
phosphofructokinase, liver (type)

PFKM
phosphofructokinase, muscle (type)

PFKP
phosphofructokinase, platelet (type)

PFL
Platinol, 5-fluorouracil, leucovorin
profibrinolysin

PFM
peak flow meter
porcelain fused to metal
primary fibromyalgia

PFN
partially functional neutrophil

PFNA
percutaneous fine-needle aspiration

PFNAB
percutaneous fine-needle aspiration
biopsy

PFO
patent foramen ovale

PFOB
perfluorooctyl bromide

PFP
pentafluoropropionyl
platelet-free plasma
preceding foreperiod

PFPC
Pall-filtered packed cells

PFQ
personality factor questionnaire

PFR
parotid flow rate
peak filling rate
peak flow rate
pericardial friction rub

PFRC
plasma-free red cell
predicted functional residual capacity

PFS
penile flow study
primary fibromyalgia syndrome
progression-free survival
protein-free supernatant
pulmonary function score

PFST
positional feedback stimulation trainer

PFT
pancreatic function test
posterior fossa tumor
prednisone, fluorouracil, and
tamoxifen
pulmonary function test

PFT$_4$
proportion free thyroxin

PFTBE
progressive form of tick-borne
encephalitis

PFU
plaque-forming unit
pock-forming unit

NOTES

P

PFUO
prolonged fever of unknown origin

PFV
physiologic full value

PFW
peak flow whistle

PFWB
Pall-filtered whole blood

PFWT
pain-free walking time

PG
parapsoriasis guttata
paregoric
parotid gland
pentagastrin
pepsinogen
peptidoglycan
pergolide
Pharmacopoeia Germanica also PhG
phosphate glutamate
phosphatidylglycerol
phosphatidyl glycine
phosphogluconate
phosphoglycerate
pigment granule
pituitary gonadotropin
plasma gastrin
plasmaglucose
plasma triglyceride
polygalacturonate
postgraduate
postgraft
pregnanediol glucuronide
pregnant
propylene glycol
prostaglandin
proteoglycan
pyoderma gangrenosum

P_G
plasma glucose

Pg
gastric pressure
nasopharyngeal electrode placement in electroencephalography
pogonion
pregnancy
pregnant
pregnenolone

pg
page
picogram *also* pcg

PGA
phosphoglyceric acid
polyglandular autoimmune (syndrome)
polyglycolic acid
prostaglandin A
pteroylglutamic acid

PGAC
phenylglycine acid chloride

PGAS
persisting galactorrhea-amenorrhea syndrome
polyglandular autoimmune syndrome

PGB
prostaglandin B

PGC
percentage of goblet cells
pontine gaze center
primordial germ cell
prostaglandin C

PGD
phosphogluconate dehydrogenase
phosphoglyceraldehyde dehydrogenase
prostaglandin D

PGD2
prostaglandin D_2

PGDH
phosphogluconate dehydrogenase

PGDR
plasma glucose disappearance rate

PGE
platelet granule extract
posterior gastroenterostomy
primary generalized epilepsy
prostaglandin E *also* PGE2

PGE2
prostaglandin E_2

PGE_1
prostaglandin E_1

PGEM
prostaglandin E metabolite

PGF
paternal grandfather *also* pgf
prostaglandin F

PGF2α
prostaglandin $F_{2\alpha}$

pgf
paternal grandfather *also* PGF

PGG
    polyclonal gamma globulin
    prostaglandin G

PGG-Q
    porphobilinogen—quantitative

PGH
    pituitary growth hormone
    plasma growth hormone
    porcine growth hormone
    prostaglandin H

PGH2
    prostaglandin H_2

PGI
    pepsinogen I
    phosphoglucose isomerase
    potassium, glucose, and insulin
    prostaglandin I *also* PGI_2

PGI₂
    prostacyclin
    prostaglandin I *also* PGI
    prostaglandin I_2

PGK
    phosphoglycerate kinase
    phosphoglycerokinase

PGL
    persistent generalized lymphadenopathy
    phosphoglycolipid
    primary gastric lymphoma

PGlyM
    phosphoglyceromutase

PGM
    paternal grandmother *also* pgm
    phosphoglucomutase

pgm
    paternal grandmother *also* PGM

PGMA
    polyglycerol methacrylate

PGN
    proliferative glomerulonephritis

PGO
    pontogeniculooccipital (spike)

PGP
    postgamma proteinuria
    prepaid group practice
    protein gene product

Pgp, P-gp
    P-glycoprotein *also* P-170

PGR
    percutaneous glycerol rhizolysis
    progesterone receptor *also* PgR
    psychogalvanic response

PgR
    progesterone receptor *also* PGR, PR

1,3-P₂Gri
    1,3-diphosphoglycerate

2,3-P₂Gri
    2,3-diphosphoglycerate

P-GRN
    progranulocyte

PGS
    persistent gross splenomegaly
    pineal gonadal syndrome
    plant growth substance
    postsurgical gastroparesis syndrome
    prostaglandin synthetase
    proteoglycan subunit

PGSE
    pulsed-gradient spin-echo

PGSI
    prostaglandin synthetase inhibitor

PGSR
    psychogalvanic skin response

PGSRA
    psychogalvanic skin response audiometry

PGT
    play group therapy

PGTR
    plasma glucose tolerance rate

PGTT
    prednisolone glucose tolerance test

PGU
    peripheral glucose uptake
    postgonococcal urethritis

PGUT
    phosphogalactose uridyl transferase

PGV
    proximal gastric vagotomy

NOTES

P

PGX
prostaglandin X

PGY
postgraduate year

PGYE
peptone, glucose, and yeast extract (medium)

PH
parathyroid hormone *also* PTH
partial hepatectomy
passive hemagglutination
past history *also* Px
peliosis hepatitis
perianal herpes
persistent hepatitis
personal history
pharmacopeia
phenethicillin
phenylalanine hydroxylase
pinhole
polycythemia hypertonica
poor health
porphyria hepatica
posterior hypothalamus
post history
previous history
primary hyperparathyroidism
prolylhydroxylase
prostatic hypertrophy
pseudohermaphroditism
pubic hair
public health
pulmonary hypertension
pulp horn
punctate hemorrhage

Ph
pharmacopeia
phenanthrene
phenyl *also* Φ
Philadelphia chromosome *also* Ph^1, Ph1
phosphate

Ph1, Ph^1
Philadelphia chromosome *also* Ph

pH
hydrogen ion concentration

pH$_1$
isoelectric point *also* IEP, IP, I.P., i.p., PI, pI, pIs

ph
phase

phial
phote (unit of surface illumination)

PHA
passive hemagglutination
peripheral hyperalimentation
phenylalanine *also* F, P, PA, PHE, Phe
phytohemagglutinin
phytohemagglutinin activation
phytohemagglutinin antigen
pseudohypoaldosteronism
pulse-height analyzer

pH$_A$
arterial blood hydrogen tension

pHa
arterial pH

PHA-E
Phaseolus vulgaris erythroglutinin

PHAL
peripheral hyperalimentation
phytohemagglutinin-stimulated lymphocyte

phal
phalanges
phalanx

PHAlb
polymerized human albumin

PHA-m
phytohemagglutinin-mucopolysaccharide (fraction)

PHA-p
phytohemagglutinin-protein (fraction)

PHAR, phar
pharmaceutical
pharmacopeia *also* pharm
pharmacy
pharynx

Phar G
Graduate in Pharmacy *also* Gph, PhG

PHARM
pharmacy *also* pharm

pharm
pharmacopeia *also* PHAR, phar
pharmacy *also* PHARM

Pharm D
Doctor of Pharmacy [L. *Pharmaciae Doctor*] *also* PhD

PHB
preventive health behavior

PHBB
propylhydroxybenzyl benzimidazole

PHC
personal health cost
posthospital care
premolar aplasia, hyperhidrosis, and
(premature) canities
premolar hypodontia, hyperhidrosis,
and canities prematura (Böök
syndrome)
primary health care
primary hepatic carcinoma
primary hepatocellular carcinoma
proliferative helper cell

PhC
pharmaceutical chemist

PHCA
profoundly hypothermic circulatory
arrest

PHCC
primary hepatocellular carcinoma

PHD
paroxysmal hypnogenic dyskinesia
pathological habit disorder
photoelectron diffraction
potentially harmful drug
pulmonary heart disease

PhD
Doctor of Pharmacy [L. *Pharmaciae
Doctor*] *also* Pharm D
Doctor of Philosophy [L.
Philosophiae Doctor]

PHDD
personal history of depressive
disorders

PHDPE
porous high-density polyethylene

PHE
periodic health examination
phenylalanine *also* F, P, PA, PHA,
Phe
postheparin esterase
proliferative hemorrhagic enteropathy

Phe
phenylalanine *also* F, P, PA, PHA,
F

PhEEM
photoemission electron microscopy

Phen
phenformin

Pheo, pheo
pheochromocytoma

PHF
paired helical filaments
personal hygiene facility

PHFG
primary human fetal glia

PHG
portal hypertensive gastropathy

PhG
Graduate in Pharmacy *also* Gph,
Phar G
Pharmacopoeia Germanica also PG

Phgly, phgly
phenylglycine

PHH
posthemorrhagic hydrocephalus

φ
ability continuum
magnetic flux
osmotic coefficient
phi coefficient (statistics)
phi (21st letter of Greek alphabet),
lowercase *also* Φ
quantum yield

Φ
phenyl *also* Ph
phi (21st letter of Greek alphabet),
uppercase *also* φ

PHI
passive hemagglutination inhibition
peptide histidine isoleucine
phosphohexose isomerase
physiologic hyaluronidase inhibitor
prehospital index

PhI
Pharmacopoeia Internationalis also PI

NOTES

P

philtrum
philtra

PHIM
posthypoxic intention myoclonus

PHIS
post-head injury syndrome

PHIV
portal hypertensive intestinal vasculopathy

PHK
platelet phosphohexokinase
postmortem human kidney

PHKC
postmortem human kidney cell

PHLA
postheparin lipolytic activity

PHLS
Public Health Laboratory Service

PHM
posterior hyaloid membrane
psyllium hydrophilic mucilloid

PhM
pharyngeal musculature

PHN
paroxysmal noctural hemoglobinuria
passive Heymann nephritis
postherpetic neuralgia
public health nurse
public health nursing

PhNCS
phenylisothiocyanate *also* PITC

PHNI
pinhole no improvement

PHO
public health official

PH$_2$O
partial pressure of water vapor

phos
phosphatase
phosphate
phosphorus *also* PHP

PHP
partial hospitalization program
passive hyperpolarizing potential
persistent hyperphenylalaninemia
phosphorus *also* phos
postheparin phospholipase
prehospital program
prepaid health plan

primary hyperparathyroidism
pseudohypoparathyroidism (PHPT)
pyridoxylated hemoglobin-polyoxyethylene

PHPP, *p*-HPPO
p-hydroxyphenyl pyruvate oxidase

PHPT
pseudohypoparathyroidism
pseudohypoparathyroidism

pHPT
primary hyperparathyroidism

PHPV
persistent hyperplastic primary vitreous

PHR
peak heart rate
photoreactivity

PHRT
procarbazine, hydroxyurea, and radiotherapy (protocol)

PHS
partial hospitalization program
patient-heated serum
phenylalanine hydroxylase stimulator
pooled human serum
posthypnotic suggestion
Public Health Service

PHSC
pluripotent hemopoietic stem cell

PHSL
primary hepatosplenic lymphoma

pH-stat
apparatus for maintaining pH of solution

PHT
peroxide hemolysis test
phentolamine
phenytoin
portal hypertension
primary hyperthyroidism
pulmonary hypertension

PhTD
Doctor of Physical Therapy

PHTN
portal hypertension

PHTS
Pediatric Home Treatment Service

PHV
persistent hypertrophic vitreous

PHx
  past history

Phx
  pharynx

PHY, phy
  pharyngitis
  physical
  physiology *also* P, PHYS
  phytohemagglutinin

PHYS
  physiology *also* P, PHY

PhyS
  physiologic saline (solution)

phys
  physical
  physician

phys dis
  physical disability

Phys Ed
  physical education *also* PE, PED,
  PEd

physio
  physiologic
  physiotherapy

Physiol
  physiology

Phys Med
  physical medicine

Phys Ther
  physical therapy *also* PT

π
  pi (16th letter of Greek alphabet)
  ratio of circumference to diameter
  (3.1415926536)

PI
  international protocol
  isoelectric point *also* IEP, IP, I.P.,
  i.p., pH_1, pI, pIs
  pacing impulse
  package insert
  pancreatic insufficiency
  parainfluenza (virus)
  pars intermedia
  paternity index
  patient's interest

percutaneous injury
performance index
performance intensity
perinatal injury
Periodontal Index
peripheral iridectomy
permanent incidence
permeability index
personal injury
personality inventory
phagocytic index
Pharmacopoeia Internationalis *also*
  PhI
phosphatidylinositol *also* PtdIns
physically impaired
pineal body
plaque index
pneumatosis intestinalis
poison ivy
ponderal index
posteroinferior
postictal immobility
postinfection
postinjury
postinoculation
preinduction (examination)
premature infant
prematurity index
preparatory interval
present illness
pressure on inspiration
primary infarction
primary infection
proactive inhibition
proactive interference
programmed instruction
proinsulin
prolactin inhibitor
proliferative index
protamine insulin
protease inhibitor
proximal intestine
pulmonary incompetence
pulmonary infarction
pulsatility index

Pi
  inorganic phosphate
  inorganic phosphorus
  parental generation

NOTES

P

Pi *(continued)*
pressure in inspiration
protease inhibitor

pI
isoelectric point *also* IEP, IP, I.P.,
i.p., pH_1, PI, pIs
platelet count increment

pi
platelet count increment *also* pI

PIA
peripheral interface adapter
phenylisopropyladenosine
photoelectronic intravenous
angiography
plasma insulin activity
porcine intestinal adenomatosis
preinfarction angina

PIAP
placental alkaline phosphatase *also*
PLAP

PIAT
Peabody Individual Achievement Test

PIAVA
polydactyly-imperforate anus-vertebral
anomalies (syndrome)

PIB
partial ileal bypass
psi-interactive biomolecules

PIBC
percutaneous intra-aortic balloon
counterpulsation

PIBIDS
photosensitivity, ichthyosis, brittle
hair, intellectual impairment,
decreased fertility, and short stature

PIC
peripherally inserted catheter
Personality Inventory for Children
posterior intermediate curve
postinflammatory corticoid
postintercourse

PICA
Porch Index of Communicative
Abilities
posterior-inferior cerebellar artery
posterior-inferior communicating artery

PICAC
Porch Index of Communicative
Abilities in Children

PICC
peripherally inserted central catheter

PICD
primary irritant contact dermatitis

PiCO$_2$
partial pressure of intramuscular
carbon dioxide

PICSO
pressure-controlled intermittent
coronary sinus occlusion

PICSYMS
picture symbols

PICT
pancreatic islet cell transplantation

PICU
pediatric intensive care unit
pulmonary intensive care unit

PICVC
peripherally inserted central venous
catheter

PID
pain intensity difference (score)
pelvic inflammatory disease
photoionization detector
plasma iron disappearance
position indicating device
prolapsed intervertebral disk
proportional-integral-derivative
protruded intervertebral disk

PIDDST
pediatric infectious disease
developmental screening test

PIDRA
portable insulin dosage-regulating
apparatus

PIDS
primary immunodeficiency syndrome
also PIS

PIDT
plasma iron disappearance time

PIE
postinfectious encephalomyelitis
preimplantation embryo
prosthetic infectious endocarditis
pulmonary infiltrate with eosinophilia
pulmonary infiltration and eosinophilia
pulmonary interstitial edema
pulmonary interstitial emphysema

PIEF
isoelectric focusing in polyacrylamide

PIEx
posteroinferior external

PIF
peak inspiratory flow
pigment inspiratory factor
point of identical flow
premorbid inferiority feeling
proinsulin-free
prolactin-inhibiting factor
proliferation-inhibiting factor
prostatic interstitial fluid

PIFG
poor intrauterine fetal growth

PIFR
peak inspiratory flow rate

PIFT
platelet immunofluorescence test

PIG
pertussis immune globulin

Pig
pigmentation

PIGI
pregnancy-induced glucose intolerance

pigm
pigment
pigmented

PIGN
postinfectious glomerulonephritis

PIGPA
pyruvate, inosine, glucose phosphate, and adenine

pIgR
polyimmunoglobulin receptor

PIH
pregnancy-induced hypertension
prolactin-inhibiting hormone

PIHH
postinfluenza-like hyposmia and hypogeusia

PII
plasma inorganic iodine
primary irritation index

PIIID
peripheral indwelling intermediate infusion device

PIIn
posteroinferior internal

PIIP
portable insulin infusion pump

PIIS
posterior inferior iliac spine

PIL
primary intestinal lymphangiectasia

pil.
pill [L. *pilula*] *also* bol.

PIM
penicillamine-induced myasthenia

PIMS
programmable implantable medication system

PIN
personal identification number
prostatic intraepithelial neoplasia

PINN
proposed international nonproprietary name

PINS
person in need of supervision

PINV
postimperative negative variation

PIO
progesterone in oil

PIO$_2$
inspired oxygen tension
intraalveolar oxygen tension
partial pressure of inspiratory oxygen

PIOK
poikilocytosis

PIOPED
Prospective Investigation of Pulmonary Embolus Diagnosis

PIP
paraffin immunoperoxidase
paralytic infantile paralysis
peak inflation pressure
peak inspiratory pressure

NOTES

P

PIP *(continued)*
   personal injury protection
   piperacillin
   positive inspiratory pressure
   postinflammatory polyposis
   postinfusion phlebitis
   postinspiratory pressure
   pressure inversion point
   proximal interphalangeal (joint) *also*
   PIPJ
   psychosis, intermittent hyponatremia,
   polydipsia (syndrome)
   Psychotic Inpatient Profile

PI4P
   phosphatidylinositol phosphate

PIP$_2$
   phosphatidylinositol 4,5-bisphosphate

PIPA
   platelet ^{125}I-labeled (staphylococcal)
   protein A

PI-PB
   performance versus intensity function
   for phonetically balanced words

PIPE
   persistent interstitial pulmonary
   emphysema

PIPES
   piperazine diethanesulfonic acid

PIPIDA
   paraisopropyliminodiacetic acid (scan)

PIPJ
   proximal interphalangeal joint *also*
   PIP

PIQ
   Performance Intelligence Quotient

PIR
   piriform
   postinhibition rebound
   pressure increment rate

P-IRI
   plasma immunoreactive insulin

PIRS
   plasma immunoreactive secretion

PIS
   primary immunodeficiency syndrome
   also PIDS
   Provisional International Standard

pIs
   isoelectric point *also* IEP, IP, I.P.,
   i.p., pH$_1$, PI, pI

PISA
   phase-invariant signature algorithm
   proximal isovelocity surface area

PISCES
   percutaneously inserted spinal cord
   electrical stimulation

PIT
   pacing-induced tachycardia
   perceived illness threat
   picture identification test
   plasma iron turnover

Pit
   patellar inhibition test

pit.
   pituitary

PITC
   phenylisothiocyanate *also* PhNCS

PITP
   pseudoidiopathic thrombocytopenic
   purpura

PITR
   plasma iron turnover rate

PITS
   parent-infant traumatic stress

PIU
   polymerase-inducing unit

PIV
   parainfluenza virus
   peripheral intravenous
   polydactyly-imperforate anus-vertebral
   anomalies (syndrome)

PIVD
   protruded intervertebral disk

PIVH
   peripheral intravenous
   hyperalimentation
   periventricular-intraventricular
   hemorrhage

PIVKA
   protein induced by vitamin K
   antagonism
   protein in vitamin K absence

PIVM
   passive intervertebral motion

PIWT
   partially impacted wisdom teeth

PIXE
   particle-induced x-ray emission

proton-induced x-ray emission *also*
PIXIE

pixel
picture element

PIXIE
proton-induced x-ray emission *also*
PIXE

PJ
pancreatic juice
patellar jerk
Peutz-Jeghers (syndrome)

PJB
premature junctional beat

PJC
premature junctional contraction

PJP
pancreatic juice protein

PJRT
permanent junctional reciprocating
tachycardia

PJS
peritoneojugular shunt
Peutz-Jeghers syndrome

PJT
paroxysmal junctional tachycardia

PJVT
paroxysmal junctional-ventricular
tachycardia

PK
pack (cigarette)
penetrating keratoplasty *also* PKP
pericardial knock
pharmacokinetic
pig kidney
Prausnitz-Küstner (reaction)
protein kinase
psychokinesis
pyruvate kinase

P_K
plasma potassium

pK
ionization constant of acid
negative logarithm of dissociation
constant *also* pK′

pK′, pK-
apparent value of pK
negative logarithm of dissociation
constant of acid *also* pk

pK$_a$
negative logarithm of acid ionization
constant

pk
peck

PKA
prekallikrein activator
prokininogenase

pKa
measure of acid strength

PKAR
protein kinase activation ratio

PKase
protein kinase

pkat
picokatal

PKB
prone knee bend

PKC
protein kinase C

PKD
polycystic kidney disease
proliferative kidney disease

PKF
phagocytosis and killing function

PKI
potato kallikrein inhibitor

PKK
plasma prekallikrein
prekallikrein

PKN
parkinsonism

PKP
penetrating keratoplasty *also* PK

PKR
phased knee rehabilitation

PKT
Prausnitz-Küstner test

NOTES

PKU
phenylketonuria

PKV
killed poliomyelitis vaccine

pkV
peak kilovoltage

PL
palmaris longus
pancreatic lipase
perception of light
phospholipase
phospholipid *also* PPL
photoluminescence
place
placebo *also* P, PBO
placental lactogen
plantar
plasma lemma
plastic surgery
platelet *also* PLT, Plt
platelet antigen
platelet lactogen
plural
polymer of lactic (acid)
posterior lip (of acetabulum)
preferential looking
preleukemia platelet *also* PLT, Plt
premature labor
problem list
procaine and lactic acid
psychosocial-labile
pulpolingual
pulpolinguoaxial
Purkinje layer
transpulmonary pressure

PL/1
programming language 1 (one)

P$_L$
pulmonary venous pressure *also* PVP
transpulmonary pressure

Pl
plasma
Poiseuille (law, space)

pL, pl
picoliter

pl
place
pleural
plural

PLA
peripheral laser angioplasty
peroxidase-labeled antibodies (test)

phospholipase A
platelet antigen
polylactic acid
potentially lethal arrhythmia
pulpolabial
pulpolinguoaxial

PLA2
phospholipase A$_2$

PLa
pulpolabial

Pla
left atrial pressure

PLAC
Pravastatin Limitation of
Atherosclerosis in Coronary Arteries
Pravastatin, Lipids, and
Atherosclerosis in the Carotids

PLAD
proximal left anterior descending
(artery)

PLAI
Preschool Language Assessment
Instrument

PLAP
placental alkaline phosphatase *also*
PIAP
polyclonal antiplacental alkaline
phosphatase

Plat
platelet

PLAX
parasternal long axis

PLB
parietal lobe battery
phospholipase B
porous layer bead
posterolateral branch

PLBO
placebo

PLC
personal locus of control
phospholipase C
primary liver cell
proinsulin-like component
protein-lipid complex
pseudolymphocytic choriomeningitis

PLCC
primary liver cell cancer

PLCL
polyclonal gammopathy identified

PL-CLP
platelet clump

PLCO
postoperative low cardiac output

PLD
partial lower denture
percutaneous laser diskectomy
peripheral light detection
phospholipase D
platelet defect
polycystic liver disease *also* PCLD
posterior latissimus dorsi (muscle)
postlaser day
potentially lethal damage
pregnancy, labor, and delivery

PLDD
percutaneous laser disk decompression
poorly differentiated lymphoma,
diffuse

PLDH
plasma lactic dehydrogenase

PLDR
potentially lethal damage repair

PLE
panlobular emphysema
paraneoplastic limbic encephalopoathy
pleura
polymorphous light eruption *also*
PMLE
protein-losing enteropathy
pseudolupus erythematosus (syndrome)

PLED
periodic lateralizing epileptiform
discharge

PLES
parallel-line equal spacing

PLET
polymyxin, lysozyme, EDTA, and
thallous acetate (in heart infusion
agar)

PLEU
pleural (fluid)

PLEVA
pityriasis lichenoides et varioliformis
acuta

PLF
perilymphatic fistula

PLFC
premature living female child

PLFS
perilymphatic fistula syndrome

PLG
plasminogen

PLGA
polymorphous low-grade
adenocarcinoma

P-LGV
psittacosis lymphogranuloma venereum

PLH
paroxysmal localized hyperhidrosis
placental lactogenic hormone
pulmonary lymphoid hyperplasia

PLHB
percutaneous left heart bypass

PLIF
posterior lumbar interbody fusion
posterolateral interbody fusion

PLISSIT
permission, limited information,
specific suggestions, and intensive
therapy

PLL
peripheral light loss
poly-L-lysine
posterior longitudinal ligament
pressure length loop
prolymphocytic leukemia

PLM
percentage of labeled mitoses
periodic leg movement
plasma level monitoring
polarized light microscopy
precise lesion measuring

PLMC
premature living male child

PLMT
plasmacytoid lymphocyte

PLMV
posterior leaf mitral valve

NOTES

P

PLN
pelvic lymph node
peripheral lymph node
popliteal lymph node
posterior lip nerve

PLND
pelvic lymph node dissection

PLO
polycystic lipomembranous
osteodysplasia

PLOP
partial laryngopharyngectomy

PLP
paraformaldehyde-lysine-periodate
parathyroid hormonelike protein
partial laryngopharyngectomy
phantom limb pain
plasma leukopheresis
polystyrene latex particle
pyridoxal phosphate
pyridoxal 5′-phosphate

PLPD
pseudoperiodic lateralized paroxysmal
discharge

PLPH
postlumbar puncture headache

PLR
pronation-lateral rotation (fracture)
pupillary light reflex

PLS
Papillon-Lefevre syndrome
plastic leafspring
plastic surgery
preleukemic syndrome
Preschool Language Scale
primary lateral sclerosis
prostaglandin-like substance

pls
please

PLSO
posterior leafspring orthosis

PLST
progressively lowered stress threshold

PLT
pancreatic lymphocytic infiltration
platelet *also* PL, Plt
primed lymphocyte test
primed lymphocyte typing
psittacosis-lymphogranuloma venereum-
trachoma (group)

Plt
platelet *also* PL, PLT

PLT EST
platelet estimate

PLT-G
giant platelet

plumb.
lead [L. *plumbum*]

PLUT
Plutchnik (geriatric rating scale)

PLV
panleukopenia virus
phenylalanine, lysine, and vasopressin
poliomyelitis live vaccine
posterior left ventricular

PLWS
Prader-Labhart-Willi syndrome

plx
plexus

PLYM
prolymphocyte

PM
after death [L. *post mortem*]
afternoon [L. *post meridiem*] *also*
p.m.
evening
pacemaker
pagetoid melanocytosis
papillae mammae
papillary muscle
papular mucinosis
paromycin
partially muscular
partial meniscectomy
perinatal mortality
periodontal membrane
peritoneal macrophage
petit mal (epilepsy)
photomultiplier
physical medicine
plasma membrane
platelet membrane
platelet microsome
pneumomediastinum
poliomyelitis
polymorph
polymorphonuclear
polymyositis
poormetabolizer
poor metabolizer
porokeratosis of Mibelli
posterior mitral

postmenopausal
postmortem *also* post, post.
prednimustine
premamillary nucleus
premarketing (approval)
premolar
presents mainly
presystolic murmur
pretibial myxedema
preventive medicine *also* PRM, PrM, PVMed
primary motivation
prostatic massage
protein methylesterase
pterygoid muscle
puberal macromastia
pulmonary macrophage
pulpomesial

P/M
parent-metabolite (ratio)

Pm
promethium

pM
picomolar

p.m.
afternoon [L. *post meridiem*] *also* PM

pm
picometer

PMA
papillary, marginal, attached (gingiva)
para-methoxyamphetamine
phenylmercuric acetate
phorbolmyristate acetate
phosphomolybdic acid
premenstrual asthma
primary mental abilities
Prinzmetal angina
progressive muscular atrophy
psychomotor agitation
pyridylmercuric acetate

PMAC
phenylmercuric acetate

PMB
papillomacular bundle
para-hydroxymercuribenzoate
polychrome methylene blue

polymorphonuclear basophil
polymyxin B
postmenopausal bleeding

PMBC
percutaneous mitral balloon commissurotomy

PMBV
percutaneous mitral balloon valvotomy
percutaneous mitral balloon valvuloplasty *also* PMV

PMC
percutaneous mitral commissurotomy
phenylmercuric chloride
pleural mesothelial cell
premature mitral closure
pseudomembranous colitis

PMCP
para-monochlorophenol

PMD
perceptual motor development
posterior mandibular depth
primary myocardial disease
private medical doctor
programmed multiple development
progressive muscular dystrophy

PMDD
premenstrual dysphoric disorder

PM/DM
polymyositis/dermatomyositis

PMDS
persistent müllerian duct syndrome
primary myelodysplastic syndrome

PME
phosphomonoester
polymorphonuclear eosinophil
postmenopausal estrogen
progressive myoclonus epilepsy

PMEC
pseudomembranous enterocolitis

PMF, pmf
progressive massive fibrosis
proton motive force
pterygomaxillary fossa

PMGCT
primary mediastinal germ-cell tumor

NOTES

P

PMH
past medical history *also* PMHx
posteromedial hypothalamus
programmed medical history

PMHR
predicted maximal heart rate

PMHx
past medical history *also* PMH

PMI
past medical illness
patient medical instructions
patient medication instruction
perioperative myocardial infarction
phosphomannose isomerase
plea of mental incompetence
point of maximal impulse
point of maximal intensity
posterior myocardial infarction
postmyocardial infarction
present medical illness
previous medical illness

PMIS
postmyocardial infarction syndrome
PSRO (Professional Standards Review
Organization) Management
Information System

PMK
pacemaker
primary monkey kidney

PML
polymorphonuclear leukocyte *also*
PMN, PMNL, POLY, poly
posterior mitral leaflet
progressive multifocal leukodystrophy
progressive multifocal
leukoencephalopathy
prolapsing mitral leaflet
promyelocytic leukemia
pulmonary microlithiasis

pML
posterior mitral valve leaflet

PMLE
polymorphous light eruption *also*
PLE

PMM
perilacunar mineral matrix
protoplast maintenance medium

PMMA
polymethylmethacrylate

PMMF
pectoralis major myocutaneous flap

PMN
polymorphonuclear (leukocyte) *also*
PML, PMNL, POLY, poly
polymorphonuclear neutrophil *also*
M_7, PMNN

PMNC
percentage of multinucleated cells
peripheral blood mononuclear cell

PMNG
polymorphonuclear granulocyte

PMNL
polymorphonuclear leukocyte *also*
PML, PMN, POLY, poly

PMNN
polymorphonuclear neutrophil *also*
M_7, PMN

PMNR
periadenitis mucosa necrotica
recurrens

PMO
postmenopausal osteoporosis
Principal Medical Officer

pmol
picomole

PMP
pain management program
past menstrual period
patient management problem
patient medication profile
persistent mentoposterior (fetal
position)
previous menstrual period
psychotropic medication plan

PMPO
postmenopausal palpable ovary

PMPS
postmastectomy pain syndrome

PMQ
phytylmenaquinone (vitamin K)

PMR
perinatal morbidity rate
perinatal mortality rate
periodic medical review
physical medicine and rehabilitation
polymorphic reticulosis
polymyalgia rheumatica
prior medical record
proportional morbidity ratio
proportional mortality ratio
proton magnetic resonance
psychomotor retardation

PM&R
    physical medicine and rehabilitation

PMRS
    physical medicine and rehabilitation service

PMS
    patient management system
    perimenstrual syndrome
    phenazine methosulfate
    postmarketing surveillance
    postmenopausal syndrome
    postmenstrual stress
    postmitochondrial supernatant
    pregnant mare serum
    premenstrual symptoms
    premenstrual syndrome
    pureed, mechanical, soft (diet)

PMSC
    pluripotent myeloid stem cell

PMSF
    phenylmethyl sulfonyl fluoride

PMSG
    pregnant mare's serum gonadotropin

PMT
    pacemaker-mediated tachycardia
    photoelectric multiplier tube
    photomultiplier tube
    point of maximum tenderness
    Porteus maze test
    premenstrual tension
    pseudosarcomatous myofibroblastic tumor

PMTS
    premenstrual tension syndrome

PMTT
    pulmonary mean transit time

PMV
    paralyzed and mechanically ventilated
    percutaneous mitral balloon valvuloplasty *also* PMBV
    percutaneous mitral valvuloplasty
    prolapse of mitral valve

PmvCO$_2$
    partial pressure of mesenteric venous carbon dioxide

PMVL, pMVL
    posterior mitral-valve leaflet

PMVP
    pulmonary microvascular permeability to protein

PMW
    pacemaker wire

PMZ
    pentamethylenetetrazol

PN
    nightmare [L. *pavor nocturnus*]
    papillary necrosis
    parenteral nutrition
    penicillin *also* P, PCN, PEN, Pen, pen., pen., PNC
    perceived noise
    percussion note
    percutaneous nephrostogram
    periarteritis nodosa *also* PAN
    peripheral nerve
    peripheral neuropathy *also* PNP
    peripheral node
    phrenic nerve
    plaque neutralization
    pneumonia *also* Pn, pneu, PNM
    polyarteritis nodosa *also* PAN
    polynephritis
    polyneuritis
    pontine nucleus
    poorly nourished
    positional nystagmus
    posterior nares
    postnasal
    postnatal
    Practical Nurse
    predicted normal
    premie nipple
    primary nurse
    progress note
    propoxyphene napsylate
    psychiatry and neurology
    psychoneurotic
    pulmonary disease
    pyelonephritis
    pyridine nucleotide
    pyrrolinitrin

P/N
    positive to negative (ratio)

NOTES

P

P&N
psychiatry and neurology

PN₂, P_{N2}, P_{n2}
nitrogen partial pressure

Pn
pneumonia *also* PN, pneu, PNM

PNA
Paris Nomina Anatomica
peanut agglutinin
pediatric nurse associate
pentose nucleic acid

P_{Na}
plasma sodium

PNAB
percutaneous needle aspiration biopsy

PNAH
polynuclear aromatic hydrocarbon

PNAS
prudent no-salt-added (diet)

PNAvQ
positive-negative ambivalent quotient

PNB
percutaneous needle biopsy
polymyxin, neomycin, bacitracin
premature newborn
premature nodal beat
prostatic needle biopsy

PNBT
para-nitroblue tetrozolium

PNC
paranasal cancer
penicillin *also* P, PCN, PEN, Pen,
pen., PN
peripheral nerve conduction
peripheral nucleated cell
pneumotaxic center
postnecrotic cirrhosis
premature nodal contraction
prenatal care
purine nucleotide cycle

PND
paroxysmal nocturnal dyspnea
partial neck dissection
pelvic node dissection
postnasal drainage
postnasal drip
postneonatal death
pregnancy, not delivered
purulent nasal drainage

pnd.
pound *also* L, lb., lib.

PNdB
perceived noise level

PNdb
perceived noise decibel

PNE
peripheral neuroepithelioma
plasma norepinephrine
pneumoencephalography
primary nocturnal enuresis
pseudomembranous necrotizing
enterocolitis

PNEC
pulmonary neuroendocrine cell

PNET
peripheral neuroectodermal tumor
permeative neuroectodermal tumor
primitive neuroectodermal tumor

PNET-MB
permeative neuroectodermal tumor-
medulloblastoma

pneu
pneumonia *also* PN, Pn, PNM

PNF
prenatal fluoride
proprioceptive neuromuscular
facilitation
proprioceptive neuromuscular
fasciculation (reaction)

PNG
penicillin G
pneumogram

PNH
paroxysmal nocturnal hemoglobinuria

PNI
peripheral nerve injury
postnatal infection
prognostic nutritional index
pseudoneointimal
psychoneuroimmunology

PNID
Peer Nomination Inventory for
Depression

PNK
polynucleotide kinase

PNKD
paroxysmal nonkinesigenic dyskinesia

PNL
    percutaneous nephrolithotomy *also* PCNL
    percutaneous nephrostolithotomy
    peripheral nerve lesion
    polymorphonuclear neutrophilic leukocyte

PNLA
    percutaneous needle lung aspiration

PNM
    perinatal mortality
    peripheral dysostosis, nasal hypoplasia, and mental retardation
    peripheral nerve myelin
    pneumonia *also* PN, Pn, pneu
    postneonatal mortality (syndrome)

PNMG
    persistent neonatal myasthenia gravis

PNMT
    phenylethylamine N-methyl transferase

PNO
    Principal Nursing Officer

P-NP
    para-nitrophenol *also* PNP

PNP
    para-nitrophenol *also* P-NP
    peak negative pressure
    Pediatric Nurse Practitioner
    peripheral neuropathy *also* PN
    platelet neutralization procedure
    polyneuropathy
    progressive nuclear palsy
    psychogenic nocturnal polydipsia
    purine nucleoside phosphorylase

PNPB
    positive-negative pressure breathing

PNPG
    para-nitrophenyl-β-galactoside

pNPP, *p*NPP
    para-nitrophenylphosphate

PNPR
    positive-negative pressure respiration

PNPS
    para-nitrophenylsulfate

PNRS
    premature nursery

PNS
    paraneoplastic syndrome
    parasympathetic nervous system
    partial nonprogressive stroke
    peripheral nervous stimulator
    peripheral nervous system
    posterior nasal spine

PNSS
    Pediatric Nutrition Surveillance System

PNT
    partial nodular transformation
    patient *also* P, Pnt, PT, Pt, pt
    percutaneous nephrostomy tube

Pnt
    patient *also* P, PNT, PT, Pt, pt

PNU
    protein nitrogen unit

PNV
    prenatal vitamin

Pnx
    pneumonectomy
    pneumothorax *also* PT, PTX, Px

PNZ
    posterior necrotic zone

P-O
    postoperative *also* PO, POP, POp, postop, post-op

PO
    by mouth [L. *per os*] *also* p.o.
    parapineal organ
    parietal operculum
    parietooccipital
    perceptual organization
    period of onset
    perioperative
    phone order *also* P/O
    physician only
    posterior
    postoperative *also* P-O, POP, POp, postop, post-op
    postoperatively *also* postop
    predominating organism

NOTES

P

P/O
oxidative phosphorylation ratio
phone order *also* PO
protein to osmolar (ratio)

P&O
parasites and ova

PO$_2$, P$_{O2}$, P$_{o2}$
partial pressure of oxygen

Po
polonium
porion
position response
progesterone

p.o.
by mouth, orally [L. *per os*] *also*
PO

POA
pancreatic oncofetal antigen
phalangeal osteoarthritis
point of application
preoptic area
primary optic atrophy

POACH
prednisone, Oncovin (vincristine), ara-
C (cytarabine), cyclophosphamide,

POAG
primary open-angle glaucoma

POA-HA
preoptic anterior hypothalamic area

POB
penicillin, oil, and beeswax
phenoxybenzamine
place of birth

POBE
Profile of Out-of-Body Experiences

POC
particulate organic carbon
polyolefin copolymer
postoperative care
procarbazine, Oncovin (vincristine),
and CCNU (lomustine)
products of conception

Po/C
ocular pressure

POCC
procarbazine, Oncovin (vincristine),
CCNU (lomustine), and Cytoxan
(cyclophosphamide)

pocill.
small cup [L. *pocillum*]

pocul.
cup [L. *poculum*]

POCY
postoperative chronologic year

POD
pacing on demand
peroxidase
place of death
podiatry *also* Pod
polycystic ovary disease
postoperative day
postovulatory day

Pod
podiatry *also* POD

Pod D
Doctor of Podiatry

PODx
preoperative diagnosis

POE
pediatric orthopedic examination
port of entry
position of ease
postoperative endophthalmitis
postoperative exercise
proof of eligibility

POEMS
polyneuropathy, organomegaly,
endocrinopathy, monoclonal
gammopathy, and skin changes
polyneuropathy, organomegaly,
endocrinopathy, M protein, and skin
changes (syndrome)

POET
pulse oximeter/end tidal (carbon
dioxide)

POEx
postoperative exercise

POF
position of function
premature ovarian failure
primary ovarian failure
pyruvate oxidation factor

PofE
portal of entry

POG
Pediatric Oncology Group
polymyositis ossificans generalisata
products of gestation

Pog
pogonion

pOH
hydroxide ion concentration in a concentration/solution
hydroxyl concentration

POHI
physically or otherwise health-impaired

POHS
presumed ocular histoplasmosis syndrome

POI
Personal Orientation Inventory

POIK
poikilocytosis

poik
poikilocyte
poikilocytosis

pois
poison
poisoned
poisoning

POL
posterior oblique ligament
premature onset of labor

pol
polish
polishing

polio
poliomyelitis

POLIP
polyneuropathy, ophthalmoplegia, leukoencephalopathy, and intestinal pseudoobstruction

poll.
pollicis

POLY
polymorphonuclear (leukocyte) *also* PML, PMN, PMNL, poly

poly
polydipsia
polymorphonuclear (leukocyte) *also* PML, PMN, PML, POLY
polymorphonuclear neutrophilic granulocyte

polyphagia
polyuria

poly-A
polyadenylic (acid)

poly-C, poly(C)
polycytidylic (acid)

POLY-CHR
polychromatophilia

poly-G, poly(G)
polyguanylic (acid)

poly-HEMA
poly-(2-hydroxyethyl methacrylate)

poly-I, poly(I)
polyinosinic (acid)

poly-LC, poly-L:C
copolymer of polyinosinic and polycytidylic acids
synthetic RNA polymer

% POLYS
percent of polymorphonuclear leukocytes

polys
polymorphonuclear leukocytes

polys(segs)
polymorphonuclear segmented neutrophils

poly-T, poly(T)
polythymidylic (acid)

poly-U, poly(U)
polyuridylic (acid)

POM
pain on motion
polyoximethylene
prescription only medicine
pulse oximetry monitoring

POMC
propiomelanocortin

POMP
phase-offset multiplanar
phase-ordered multiplanar
prednisone, Oncovin (vincristine), methotrexate, and Purinethol (mercaptopurine)
principal outer material protein

NOTES

P

POMR
problem-oriented medical record *also* POR

POMS
Profile of Mood States

PON
paraxonase
particulate organic nitrogen

pond.
by weight [L. *pondere*]

PONI
postoperative narcotic infusion

PONV
postoperative nausea and vomiting

POOH
postoperative open heart (surgery)

POOR
poor clot

POP
diphosphate group
pain on palpation
paroxypropione
PCL oriented placement
persistent occipitoposterior (fetal position)
pituitary opioid peptide
plasma oncotic pressure
plasma osmotic pressure
plaster of Paris *also* PP
polymyositis ossificans progressiva
popliteal *also* Pop., poplit
posterior oral pharynx
postoperative *also* PO, P-O, POp, postop, post-op

POp
postoperative *also* PO, P-O, POP, postop, post-op

Pop.
popliteal *also* POP, poplit
population

poplit
popliteal *also* POP, Pop.

POR
physician of record
postocclusive oscillatory response
problem-oriented (medical) record *also* POMR
problem-oriented record

PORH
postocclusive reactive hyperemia
postoperative reactive hyperemia

PORN
progressive outer retinal necrosis

PORP
partial ossicular replacement prosthesis

Porph
porphyrin

PORT
perioperative respiratory therapy
postoperative respiratory therapy

port
portable

POS
paraosteal osteosarcoma
polycystic ovary syndrome *also* PCOS
positive *also* P, pos
psychoorganic syndrome

pos
position *also* P
positive *also* P, POS

POSC
problem-oriented system (of) charting

POSCH
Program on the Surgical Control of Hyperlipidemias

POSM
patient-operated selector mechanism

Pos pr
positive pressure

POSS
percutaneous on-surface stimulation
proximal over-shoulder strap

poss
possible

post, post.
posterior *also* P
postmortem *also* PM

postgangl
postganglionic

postop, post-op
postoperative *also* PO, P-O, POP, POp
postoperatively *also* PO

post prand.
after dinner [L. *post prandium*]

POSTS
positive occipital sharp transients of sleep

post sag D
posterior sagittal diameter

post sing. sed. liq.
after very loose stool [L. *post singulas sedes liquidas*]

POT
periostitis ossificans toxica
postoperative treatment
purulent otitis media

pot.
a drink [L. *potus*]
potash
potassa
potassium *also* K, Kal, potass
potential *also* poten
potion

PotAGT
potential abnormality of glucose tolerance

potass
potassium *also* K, Kal, pot.

poten
potential *also* pot.

POU
placenta, ovary, and uterus

PoV
portal vein

POVT
puerperal ovarian vein thrombophlebitis

POW
Powassan (encephalitis)
prisoner of war

owd
powder *also* pdr, pwd

POZ
posterior optical zone

P
diphosphate group
near point of accommodation [L. *punctum proximum*] *also* P, pp
pacesetter potential *also* PCP

pancreatic polypeptide
paradoxical pulse
parietal pleura
partial pressure *also* P, p
pathology point
pedal pulse
pellagra preventive
pentose pathway
perfusion pressure
peripheral pulse
peritoneal pseudomyxoma
permanent partial
persisting proteinuria
Peyer patch
phosphorylase phosphatase
pink puffer (sign of emphysema)
pinpoint
pinprick
placental protein
plane polarization
planned parenthood
plasma pepsinogen
plasmapheresis
plasma protein
plaster of Paris *also* POP
polypeptide
polystyrene agglutination plate
poor person
population planning
porcine pancreatic
posterior papillary
posterior pituitary
postpartum *also* pp
postprandial *also* pp, PPD
preferred provider
presenting part
private patient
private practice
prothrombin-proconvertin
protoporphyria
protoporphyrin
proximal phalanx
pseudomyxoma peritonei
pterygoid process
pulse pressure
pulsus paradoxus
punctum proximum of convergence
purulent pericarditis
push pills
pyrophosphate *also* PYP, Pyro, PPi

NOTES

P

P&P
pins and plaster
policy and procedure
prothrombin and proconvertin (test)

PP$_1$
free pyrophosphate

PP$_i$ (*var. of* PPi)

p.p.
punctum proximum

pp
after meals [L. *post prandial*] *also*
p̄p̄, post prand.
near point of accommodation [L.
punctum proximum] *also* P, PP
polyphosphate
postpartum *also* PP
postpill (amenorrhea)
postprandial *also* PP, PPD
private patient

p̄p̄
after meals [L. *post prandial*] *also*
pp, post prand.

PP5
placental protein 5

PIIIP
procollagen type III aminoterminal
peptide

PPA
first shake well [L. *phiala prius
agitata*]
palpation, percussion, and auscultation
also PP&A, pp&a
pelvic phased-array coil
pepsin A
phenylpropanolamine
phenylpyruvic acid
Pittsburgh pneumonia agent
polyphosphoric acid
postpartum amenorrhea
postpill amenorrhea
pulmonary artery pressure *also* PAP
pure pulmonary atresia

PP&A, pp&a
palpation, percussion, and auscultation
also PPA

p.p.a.
shake well [L. *phiala prius agitata*]

PPACK
D-Phe-L-Pro-L-Arg-chloromethyl
ketone

PPAF
progressive perivenular alcoholic
fibrosis

PPAS
peripheral pulmonary artery stenosis
postpolio atrophy syndrome

Ppaw
pulmonary artery wedge pressure

PPB, ppb
parts per billion
platelet-poor blood
positive pressure breathing

PPBE
postpartum breast engorgement
proteose-peptone beef extract

PPBS
postprandial blood sugar

PPC
pentose phosphate cycle
peripheral posterior curve
plasma prothrombin conversion
plaster of Paris cast
pneumopericardium
pooled platelet concentrate
posterior peripheral curve
progressive patient care
prostatic pressure coefficient
proximal palmar crease

PPCA
plasma prothrombin conversion
accelerator
proserum prothrombin conversion
accelerator

PPCD
polymorphous posterior corneal
dystrophy
posterior polymorphous corneal
dystrophy

PPCF
peripartum cardiac failure
plasma prothrombin conversion factor
plasmin prothrombin conversion facto

PPCH
piperazinylmethyl cyclohexanone

PPCM
postpartum cardiomyopathy

PPD
packs per day (cigarettes) *also* P/D,
p/d
paraphenylenediamine

percussion and postural drainage *also*
P and PD, P&PD
permanent partial disability
phenyldiphenyloxadiazole
posterior polymorphous dystrophy
postpartum day
postprandial *also* PP, pp
primary physical dependence
progressive perceptive deafness
(Siebert) purified protein derivative
(of tuberculin)

P and PD, P&PD
percussion and postural drainage *also*
PPD

ppd
prepared *also* Ppt, ppt.

PPD-B
purified protein derivative–Battey

PPDR
preproliferative diabetic retinopathy

PPD-S
purified protein derivative–standard

PPDS
phonologic programming deficit
syndrome

PPE
palmoplantar erythrodysesthesia
partial plasma exchange
permeability pulmonary edema
polyphosphoric ester
porcine pancreatic elastase
programmed physical examination

PPEM
potentially pathogenic environmental
mycobacterial

PPES
palmar-plantar erythrodysesthesia
syndrome
pedal pulses equal and strong

PF
pellagra preventive factor
phagocytosis promoting factor
plasma protein fraction

PFA
Planned Parenthood Federation of
America

p-p factor
pellagra-preventing factor

PPG
pediatric pneumogram
phalloplethysmography
photoplethysmography *also* ppg
polymorphonuclear (cells)
perglomerulus
polypropylene glycol
polyurethane-polyvinyl graphite
postprandial glucose
pretragal parotid gland

ppg
photoplethysmography *also* PPG
picopicogram

PPGA
postpill galactorrhea/amenorrhea

PPG-AFO
polypropylene glycol-ankle-foot
orthosis

PPGF
polypeptide growth factor

PPGI
psychophysiologic gastrointestinal
(reaction)

PPGP
prepaid group practice

PPG-TLSO
polypropylene glycol-
thoracolumbosacral orthosis

PPH
past pertinent history
persistent pulmonary hypertension
postpartum hemorrhage
primary pulmonary hypertension
protocollagen proline hydroxylase

pphm
parts per hundred million

PPHN
persistent pulmonary hypertension of
newborn

PPHP
pseudopseudohypoparathyroidism

ppht
parts per hundred thousand

NOTES

P

PPHx
previous psychiatric history

PPI
partial permanent impairment
patient package insert
Plan-Position-Indication
preceding preparatory interval
present pain intensity
proton pump inhibitor
purified porcine insulin

PPi, PP$_i$
inorganic pyrophosphate *also* IPP
pyrophosphate *also* PYP, PP

PPID
peak pain intensity difference (score)

PPIE
prolonged postictal encephalopathy

PPIM
postperinatal infant mortality

PPJ
pure pancreatic juice

PPK
palmoplantar keratoderma
palmoplantar keratosis
partial penetrating keratoplasty

PPL
pars plana lensectomy
penicilloylpolylysine
phospholipid *also* PL
protein polysaccharide

Ppl
intrapleural pressure

PPLF
postperfusion low flow

PPLO
pleuropneumonia-like organism

PPLOV
painless progressive loss of vision

PPM
parts per million *also* ppm
permanent pacemaker
persistent pupillary membrane
phosphopentomutase
pigmented pupillary membrane
posterior papillary muscle

ppm
parts per million *also* PPM
pulses per minute

PPMA
postpoliomyelitis muscular atrophy
progressive postmyelitis muscular
atrophy

PPMD
posterior polymorphic dystrophy (of
cornea)

PPMM
postpolycythemia myeloid metaplasia

PPMS
psychophysiologic musculoskeletal
(reaction)

PPN
partial parenteral nutrition
pedunculopontine nucleus
peripheral parenteral nutrition

PPNA
peak phrenic nerve activity

PPNAD
primary pigmented nodular
adrenocortical disease

PPNG
penicillinase-producing *Neisseria
gonorrhoeae*

PPO
diphenyloxazole
2,5-diphenyloxazole
peak pepsin output
platelet peroxidase
pleuropneumonia organism
preferred provider organization
prepatient periods to oocyst

PPO-HSA
penicillin-penicilloyl human serum
albumin

PPP
palatopharyngoplasty
palmoplantar pustulosis
passage, power, and passenger
(progress of labor)
pedal pulse present
pentose phosphate pathway
peripheral pulse palpable
Pickford projective pictures
plasma protamine precipitating
platelet-poor plasma
polyphoretic phosphate
porcine pancreatic polypeptide
postpartum psychosis
protamine paracoagulation phenomenon

purified placental protein
pustulosis palmaris et plantaris

PP&P
posterior pole and periphery

PPPBL
peripheral pulses palpable both legs

PPPD
pylorus-preserving
pancreatoduodenectomy

PPPG
postprandial plasma glucose

PPPH
purified placental protein, human

PPPI
primary private practice insurance

PPPPP
pain, pallor, pulse loss, paresthesia,
and paralysis

PPPPPP
pain, pallor, paraesthesia,
pulselessness, paralysis, and
prostration

PPR
patient-physician relationship
patient progress record
photopalpebral reflex
physiologic pattern release
poor partial response
Price precipitation reaction

PPr
paraprosthetic

PPRF
paramedian pontine reticular formation
postpartum renal failure

PPRibp
5-phospho-α-d-ribosyl 1-pyrophosphate
also PPRP, PRPP

PPROM
preterm premature rupture of
membranes
prolonged premature rupture of
membranes

PPRP
5-phospho-α-d-ribosyl 1-pyrophosphate
also PPRibp, PRPP
phosphoribosyl pyrophosphate

PPRWP
poor precordial R-wave progression

PPS
pepsin
pepsin A
peripheral pulmonary stenosis
personal portable stimulator
Personal Preference Scale
phosphoribosylpyrophosphate synthetase
polyvalent pneumococcal
polysaccharide
postpartum sterilization
postperfusion syndrome
postpericardiotomy syndrome
postpolio syndrome
postpump syndrome
Prausnitz-Küstner sclerosis
primary acquired preleukemic
syndrome
prospective payment system
prospective pricing system
protein plasma substitute
pulse per second

PPSB
prothrombin, proconvertin, Stuart
factor, antihemophilic B factor

PPSH
pseudovaginal perineoscrotal
hypospadias

PPT
parietal pleural tissue
partial prothrombin time
peak-to-peak threshold
plant protease test
postpartum thyroiditis
potassium phosphotungstate
pressure pain threshold
pulmonary platelet trapping

Ppt
parts per trillion
precipitate *also* ppt
prepared

NOTES

ppt
  precipitate *also* Ppt
  precipitation *also* pptn

ppt.
  prepared [L. *praeparatus*] *also* ppd,
  Ppt

pptd
  precipitated

PPTL
  postpartum tubal ligation

pptn
  precipitation *also* ppt

PPTT
  postpartum painless thyroiditis (with
  transient) thyrotoxicosis
  prepubertal testicular tumor

PPU
  perforated peptic ulcer

PPV
  pars plana vitrectomy
  porcine parvovirus
  positive predictive value
  positive pressure ventilation
  progressive pneumonia virus

PPVT
  Peabody Picture Vocabulary Test

PPVT-R
  Peabody Picture Vocabulary Test,
  Revised

Ppw
  pulmonary wedge pressure *also* PWP

PPZ
  perphenazine

PPZSO
  perphenazine sulfoxide

PQ
  paraquat
  permeability quotient
  plastoquinone
  pronator quadratus
  pyrimethamine-quinine

PQ-9
  plastoquinone-9

PQD
  protocol data query

PQNS
  protein, quantity not sufficient

PR
  far point (of accommodation) [L.
  punctum remotum]
  palindromic rheumatism
  Panama red (variety of marijuana)
  parallax (and) refraction
  pars recta
  partial reinforcement
  partial remission
  partial response
  patient relations
  peer review
  pelvic rock
  percentile rank
  peripheral resistance
  phenol red
  photoreaction
  photoreactivation
  physical rehabilitation
  physician reviewer
  pityriasis rosea
  polymyalgia rheumatica
  posterior root
  postural reflex
  potency ratio
  potential relation
  preference record
  pregnancy *also* preg, pregn
  pregnancy rate
  premature *also* Pr, prem
  presbyopia *also* P, Pr
  pressoreceptor
  pressure *also* P, press.
  prevention
  Preyer reflex
  proctology
  production rate
  professional relations
  profile
  progesterone receptor *also* PgR
  progressive relaxation
  progressive resistance
  progressive resistive exercise *also*
  PRE
  prolactin *also* P, Pr, PRL, Prl
  prolonged remission
  propicillin
  propranolol
  prosthion
  prot
  protein *also* P, Pr, PRO, pro, prot
  psychotherapy responder
  public relations
  Puerto Rican
  pulmonary regurgitation

pulmonary rehabilitation
pulse rate
pulse repetition
pyramidal response
by way of rectum [L. *per rectum*]
also p.r., p rec

P–R
time between P wave and beginning
of QRS complex in
electrocardiography

P&R
pelvic and rectal (examination)
pulse and respiration

P/R
productivity to respiration (ratio)

Pr
pair
praseodymium
premature *also* PR, prem
presbyopia *also* P, PR
primary
prism
proctologist
production rate (of steroid hormones)
prolactin *also* P, PR, PRL, Prl
propyl
protein *also* P, PR, PRO, pro, prot

p.r.
far point of accommodation [L.
punctum remotum]
by way of rectum [L. *per rectum*]
also PR, p rec

PRA
panel-reactive antibody
phonation, respiration, articulation-
resonance
phosphoribosylamine
plasma renin activity
progesterone receptor assay

prac, pract
practice
practitioner

PrA-HPA
protein A hemolytic plaque assay

PRAMS
Pregnancy Risk Assessment
Monitoring System

prand.
dinner [L. *prandium*]

PRAS
prereduced anaerobically sterilized
(medium)
pseudo-renal-artery syndrome

PRAT
platelet radioactive antiglobulin test

p. rat. aetat.
in proportion to age [L. *pro ratione
aetatis*]

PRB
Prosthetics Research Board

PRBC
packed red blood cells *also* PRC

PRBV
placental residual blood volume

PRC
packed red blood cells *also* PRBC
packed red cells
peer review committee
phase response curve
plasma renin concentration

PRCA
pure red cell agenesis
pure red cell aplasia

PRD
partial reaction of degeneration
phosphate restricted diet
polycystic renal disease
postradiation dysplasia

PRDX
postradiation dysplasia

PRE
passive resistance exercise
photoreacting enzyme
physical reconditioning exercise
pigmented retina epithelial (cell)
progressive resistive exercise *also* PR

pre
preliminary

pre-AIDS
pre-acquired immune deficiency
syndrome

NOTES

P

p rec
by way of rectum [L. *per rectum*]
also PR, p.r.

precip
precipitate
precipitated
precipitation *also* pcpn

PRED, Pred
prednisone *also* P, PDN

pred
predicted

PREE
partial reinforcement extinction effect

prefd
preferred

PREG
pregnelone

preg, pregn
pregnancy *also* PR
pregnant *also* PR

prelim
preliminary

prem
premature *also* PR, Pr
prematurity

premie
premature (infant)

PR enzyme
phosphorylase-rupturing enzyme
photoreactivating enzyme

preop, pre-op
preoperative
preoperatively

prep
preparation
prepare (for surgery)
preposition

prepd
prepared (for surgery)

PRERLA
pupils round, equal, react to light
and accommodation

PREs
progressive resistive exercises
(ophthalmology)

preserv
preservation
preserve

press.
pressure *also* P, p, PR

prev
prevention
preventive
previous

PrevAGT
previous abnormality of glucose
tolerance

PREVMEDU
preventive medicine unit

PRF
partial reinforcement
patient report form
pontine reticular formation
progressive renal failure
prolactin-releasing factor
pyrogen-releasing factor

pRF
polyclonal rheumatoid factor

PRFA
plasma-recognition-factor activity

PRFM
premature rupture of fetal membranes
also PROM
prolonged rupture of fetal membranes
also PROM

PRFN
percutaneous radiofrequency

PRFR
pressure-retaining flow-relieving

PRG
phleborheogram
phleborheography
purge

PRGI
percutaneous retrogasserian glycerol
injection

PRH
past relevant history
preretinal hemorrhage
prolactin-releasing hormone

PRHBF
peak reactive hyperemia blood flow

PRI
Pain Rating Index
phosphate reabsorption index
phosphoribose isomerase
plexus rectales inferiores

PRIAS
Packard radioimmunoassay system

PRICES
protection, rest, ice, compression, elevation, support (first aid)

PRIH
prolactin release-inhibiting hormone

prim
primary

PRIME
Prematriculation Program in Medical Education
procarbazine, iglosamide, and methotrexate

primip
primipara *also* I-para, P, PRIMP

prim. luc.
early in morning [L. *prima luce* at first light]

prim. m.
first thing in morning [L. *primo mane*]

PRIMP
primipara *also* I-para, P, primip

PRIND
prolonged reversible ischemic neurologic deficit

PRISM
Pediatric Risk of Mortality Score

PRIST
paper radioimmunosorbent technique
paper radioimmunosorbent test

priv
private

PRK
photorefractive keratectomy
primary rabbit kidney

PRL, Prl
prolactin *also* P, PR, Pr

PRLA
pupils react to light and accommodation

PRM
partial rebreathing mask

phosphoribomutase
photoreceptor membrane
prematurely ruptured membrane
preventive medicine *also* PM, PrM, PVMed
Primary Reference Material
primidone

PrM
preventive medicine *also* PM, PRM, PVMed

PRM-SDX, PRM-SOX
pyrimethamine sulfadoxine

PRN, p.r.n., prn
as needed
as required [L. *pro re nata*]

PRNT
plaque reduction neutralization test

PRO
peer review organization
projection
prolapse
pronation *also* pron
protein *also* P, PR, Pr, pro, prot

Pro
proline *also* P
prophylactic *also* prop., proph, prophy
prothrombin

pro
protein *also* P, PR, Pr, PRO, prot

prob
probability
probable
problem

proc
procedure
proceeding
process

Procarb
procarbazine

Proct
proctology

procto
proctoscopy

NOTES

prod.
product
production

pro dos.
for a dose [L. *pro dose*]

Pro El
protein electrophoresis

PROG
progesterone
prognathism
program
progressive

prog, progn
prognosis *also* Prx, Px

progr
progress

prolong.
prolongation
prolonged

PROM
passive range of motion
premature rupture of (fetal)
 membranes *also* PRFM
programmable read-only memory
prolonged rupture of (fetal)
 membranes *also* PRFM

PROMIN
programmable multiple ion monitor

PROMIS
Problem-oriented Medical Information
System

Promy
promyelocyte

pron
pronation *also* PRO
pronator *also* PRO

PROP
propranolol

prop.
prophylactic *also* Pro, proph, prophy
prophylaxis *also* Pro, proph, prophy

ProPac
Prospective Payment Assessment
Commission

proph, prophy
prophylactic *also* Pro, prop.

PROPLA
prophospholipase A

pro rat. aet.
according to age [L. *pro ratione
aetatis*]

pros, prostat
prostate
prostatic

PROSO
protamine sulfate

prosth
prosthesis
prosthetic

prot
protein *also* P, PR, Pr, PRO, pro

proTime
prothrombin time *also* PT

PROTO
protoporphyrin

pro us. ext.
for external use [L. *pro usum
externum*]

prov
provisional (diagnosis)

PROVIMI
proteins, vitamins, and minerals

prox
proximal

prox. luc.
the day before [L. *proxima luce*]

PRP
panretinal photocoagulation
penicillinase-resistant penicillin
physiologic rest position
pityriasis rubra pilaris
platelet-rich plasma
polymer of ribose phosphate
polyribophosphate
polyribosyl ribitol phosphate
postreplication repair
postural rest position
pressure rate product
problem reporting program
progressive rubella panencephalitis
proliferative retinopathy
 photocoagulation
Psychotic Reaction Profile
pulse repetition frequency

PRP-D vaccine
polyribosylribitol phosphate conjugated
 with diphtheria toxoid

PRPP
5-phospho-α-d-ribosyl pyrophosphate

PRR
proton relaxation rate

PRRE
pupils round, regular, and equal

PR-RSV
Prague Rous sarcoma virus

PRS
parent's rating scale
Personality Rating Scale
Pierre Robin syndrome
plasma renin substrate
positive rolandic spike
pupil rating scale

PRSA
plasma renin substrate activity

PRSIS
Prospective Rate Setting Information
System

PRSM
peripheral smear

PRSP
penicillinase-resistant synthetic
penicillin

PRT
Penicillium roqueforti toxin
pharmaceutical research and testing
phosphoribosyltransferase *also* PRTase
photoradiation therapy
postoperative respiratory treatment

PRt
prospective randomized trial

PRTase
phosphoribosyltransferase *also* PRT

PRTH-C
prothrombin (time) control *also* PT-C

PRU
peripheral resistance unit

PRV
polycythemia rubra vera
pseudorabies virus

PRVA
peripheral vein renin activity

PRVEP
pattern reversal visual evoked
potential

PRVR
peak-to-resting-velocity ratio

PrVS
prevesicle space

PRW
polymerized ragweed

PRWP
poor R-wave progression
(electrocardiogram)

PRX
pseudoexfoliation

Prx
prognosis *also* prog, progn, Px

PRZ
prazepam

PRZF
pyrazofurin

PS
chloropicrin
pacemaker syndrome
paired stimulation
paradoxical sleep
paralaryngeal space
paranoid schizophrenia
paraseptal
parasternal
parasympathetic (division of
autonomic nervous system) *also*
parasym
partial shoulder
pathologic stage
patient's serum
pediatric surgery *also* PDS, PdS
performance status
performing scale (IQ)
periodic syndrome
peripheral smear
permeability surface
phosphate saline (buffer)
phosphatidylserine
photosynthesis
phrenic (nerve) stimulation
physical status
pigeon serum

NOTES

P

PS *(continued)*
plastic surgery *also* PSurg
point of symmetry
polysaccharide
polystyrene
population sample
Porter-Silber (chromogen) *also* P-S
postmaturity syndrome
pregnancy serum
prescription
pressure support
prestimulus
principal sulcus
programmed symbols
prostatic secretion
protamine sulfate
protective services
protein synthesis
psychiatric *also* psychiat
pulmonary stenosis
pulse sequence
pyloric stenosis

P-S
pancreozymin-secretin
Porter-Silber (chromogen) *also* PS
pyramid surface

P/S
polisher-stimulator
polyunsaturated/saturated (fatty acid ratio)

P&S
pain and suffering
paracentesis and suction
permanent and stationary
pharmacy and supply

Ps
prescription
pseudocyst

ps
per second
picosecond *also* psec

PSA
picryl sulfonic acid
polyethylene sulfonic acid
polysubstance abuse
product selection allowed
progressive spinal ataxia
prolonged sleep apnea
prostate-specific antigen
public service announcement

PsA
psoriatic arthritis

Psa
systemic blood pressure *also* SBP

PSAD
prostate specific antigen density
psychoactive substance abuse and dependence

PSAGN
poststreptococcal acute glomerulonephritis

PSAn
psychoanalysis
psychoanalytic

PSAP
prostate-specific acid phosphatase

PSAV
prostate specfic antigen velocity

PSAX
parasternal short axis

PSB
protected specimen brush

PSBO
partial small bowel obstruction

PSC
partial subligamentous calcification
patient services coordination
percutaneous suprapubic cystostomy
physiologic squamocolumnar
pluripotential stem cell
Porter-Silber chromogen
posterior semicircular canal
posterior subcapsular cataract *also* PSCC
primary sclerosing cholangitis
pulse-synchronized contractions

PSCC
posterior subcapsular cataract *also* PSC

PSCE
presurgical coagulation evaluation

PSCH
peripheral stem cell harvest

PsChE
pseudocholinesterase

Psci
pressure at slow component intercept

PSCM
pokeweed activated spleen conditioned medium

P/score
    pressure score

PSCP
    posterior subcapsular cataractous
    plaque

PSCT
    peripheral stem cell transplant

PSD
    particle size distribution
    peptone, starch, and dextrose
    periodic synchronous discharge
    phosphate supplemental diet
    photon-stimulated desorption
    posterior sagittal diameter
    poststenotic dilation
    postsynaptic density

PSDES
    primary symptomatic diffuse
    esophageal spasm

PSE
    paradoxical systolic expansion
    partial splenic embolization
    penicillin-sensitive enzyme
    point of subjective equality
    portal systemic encephalopathy
    postshunt encephalopathy
    purified spleen extract

PSEC
    poststress ethanol (alcohol)
    consumption

psec
    picosecond *also* ps

PSF
    peak scatter factor
    point spread function
    posterior spinal fusion
    prostacyclin production-stimulating
    factor
    pseudosarcomatous fasciitis

psf
    pound per square foot

PSG
    peak systolic gradient
    phosphate, saline, glucose
    polysomnogram
    presystolic gallop

PSGN
    poststreptococcal glomerulonephritis

PSH
    past surgical history
    postspinal (anesthetic) headache

PsHD
    pseudoheart disease

ψ
    psi (23rd letter of Greek alphabet),
    lowercase
    wave function

Ψ
    pseudouridine *also* Q
    psi (23rd letter of Greek alphabet),
    uppercase
    psychology

PSI
    personal security index
    physiologic stability index
    posterior sagittal index
    posterior superior iliac (spine) *also*
    PSIS
    pound per square inch *also* lb/in^2
    problem solving information
    prostaglandin synthetic inhibitor
    psychologic screening inventory
    psychosomatic inventory
    punctate subepithelial infiltrate

p.s.i.
    pounds per square inch

psia
    pounds per square inch absolute

pSIDS
    partially unexplained sudden infant
    death syndrome

PSIFT
    platelet suspension
    immunofluorescence test

psig
    pounds per square inch gauge

PSIL
    preferred frequency speech
    interference level

PSIS
    posterior sacroiliac spine

NOTES

P

PSIS *(continued)*
posterior superior iliac spine *also* PSI

PSL
parasternal line
percent stroke length
potassium, sodium chloride, and sodium lactate (solution)

PSLT
Picture-Story Language Test

PSM
presystolic murmur

PSMA
progressive spinal muscular atrophy
prostate specific membrane antigen
proximal spinal muscular atrophy

PSMed
psychosomatic medicine *also* PsychosMed

PSMF
protein-sparing modified fast

PSMT
psychiatric services management team

PSNS
parasympathetic nervous system

PSO
pelvic stabilization orthosis
physostigmine salicylate ophthalmic
proximal subungual onychomycosis

Psol
partly soluble

PSOR
psoralen

P/sore
pressure sore

PSP
pacesetter potential *also* PP
pancreatic spasmolytic peptide
paralytic shellfish poisoning
parathyroid secretory protein
periodic short pulse
phenolsulfonphthalein (phenol red)
positive spike pattern
postsynaptic potential
professional simulated patient
progressive supranuclear palsy
pseudopregnancy

psp
posterior subcapsular plague

PSPF
prostacyclin synthesis-stimulating plasma factor

PSQ
Parent Symptom Questionnaire
patient satisfaction questionnaire

PSR
(extrahepatic) portal-systemic resistance
pain sensitivity range
percutaneous stereotactic radiofrequency (rhizotomy)
problem status report
proliferative sickle retinopathy
pulmonary stretch receptor

PSRBOW
premature spontaneous rupture of bag of waters

PSRC
Plastic Surgery Research Council

PSRO
Professional Standards Review Organization

PSS
painful shoulder syndrome
physiologic saline solution
porcine stress syndrome
primary Sjögren syndrome
progressive systemic scleroderma
progressive systemic sclerosis
psoriasis severity scale
Psychiatric Status Schedule
pure sensory stroke
quantitative sacroiliac scintigraphy

PST
pancreatic suppression test
paroxysmal supraventricular tachycardia
Pascal-Suttle Test (psychiatry)
penicillin, streptomycin, tetracycline
perceptual span time
peristimulus time
phenolsulfotransferase
phonemic segmentation test
platelet survival time
poststenotic
poststimulus time
prefrontal sonic treatment
protein-sparing therapy
proximal straight tubule

PSTH
poststimulus time histogram
poststimulus time histograph

PSTI
pancreatic secretory trypsin inhibitor

PSTP
pentasodium triphosphate

PSTT
placental site trophoblastic tumor

PSTV
potato spindle tuber viroid

PSU
photosynthetic unit
postsurgical unit
primary sampling unit

PSurg, P-Surg
plastic surgery *also* PS

PSV
pressure supported ventilation
psychological, social, and vocational
(adjustment factors)

PSVER
pattern-shift visual-evoked response

PSVT
paroxysmal supraventricular
tachycardia

PSW
past sleepwalker
primary surgical ward
psychiatric social worker

PSX
pseudoexfoliation

PSY, Psy
psychiatry *also* P, PS, psychiat
psychology

Psych, psych
psychologic *also* psychol
psychology *also* psychol

psychiat
psychiatric *also* P, PS, Psy
psychiatry *also* P, PS, Psy

psychoan
psychoanalysis
psychoanalytical

psychol
psychologic *also* psych
psychology *also* psych

psychopath.
psychopathologic
psychopathology

PsychosMed
psychosomatic medicine *also* PSMed

psychother
psychotherapeutic
psychotherapy

psy-path
psychopathic *also* psychopath.

Ps-ZES
pseudo-Zollinger-Ellison syndrome

PT
parathormone *also* PTH
parathyroid *also* para, PTH
paroxysmal tachycardia
patient *also* P, PNT, Pnt, Pt, pt
pericardial tamponade
permanent and total
pharmacy and therapeutics
phenytoin
phonation time
photophobia
phototoxicity
physical therapist
physical therapy *also* PT
physical training
physiotherapy
pinetar
pint *also* P, p, pt
plasma thromboplastin
pneumothorax *also* Pnx, PTX, Px
polyvalent tolerance
posterior tibial (artery pulse)
posttransplantation
preterm
propylthiouracil
prothrombin time *also* proTime
protriptyline
pulmonary thrombosis
pulmonary toilet
pulmonary trunk
pulmonary tuberculosis *also* PTB
pure tone (audiometry)

NOTES

P

PT *(continued)*
pyramidal tract
temporal plane

P&T
paracentesis and tubing (of ears)
peak and trough
permanent and total
pharmacy and therapeutics

Pt
patient *also* P, PNT, Pnt, PT, pt
platinum
psychoasthenia

pt
part *also* P
patient *also* P, PNT, Pnt, PT, Pt
pint *also* P, p, PT
point

pt.
let it be continued [L. *perstetur*]

PTA
parathyroid adenoma
percutaneous transluminal angioplasty
persistent trigeminal artery
persistent truncus arteriosus
phosphotungstic acid
physical therapy assistant
plasma thromboplastin antecedent
platelet thromboplastin antecedent
posttraumatic amnesia
pretreatment anxiety
prior to admission
prior to arrival
prothrombin activity
pure tone acuity
pure tone average *also* PT(A)

PT(A)
pure tone average *also* PTA

PTAF
policy target adjustment factor

P-TAG
target-attaching globulin precursor

PTAH
phosphotungstic acid hematoxylin

PTAP
purified (diphtheria) toxoid
(precipitated by) aluminum phosphate

PTB
patellar tendon-bearing (cast
prosthesis)
prior to birth
pulmonary tuberculosis *also* PT

PTBA
percutaneous transluminal balloon
angioplasty

PTBD
percutaneous transhepatic biliary
drainage
percutaneous transluminal balloon
dilatation

PTBD-EF
percutaneous transhepatic biliary
drainage-enteric feeding

PTBE
pyretic tick-borne encephalitis

PTBNA
protected transbronchial needle
aspirate

PTBP
para-tertiary butylphenol

PTBS
posttraumatic brain syndrome

PTC
patient to call
percutaneous transhepatic
cholangiography
phase transfer catalyst
phenylthiocarbamide
phenylthiocarbamoyl
pheochromocytoma, thyroid carcinoma
(syndrome)
plasmathromboplastin component
premature tricuspid closure
prior to conception
prothrombin complex
pseudotumor cerebri

PT-C
prothrombin time control *also* PRTH-
C

PTCA
percutaneous transluminal coronary
angioplasty

PtcCO$_2$
transcutaneous carbon dioxide tension

PTCL
peripheral T-cell lymphoma

PTCP
pseudothrombocytopenia

PTCR
percutaneous transluminal coronary
recanalization

PTCRA
   percutaneous transluminal coronary
   rotational atherectomy

PT-CT
   prothrombin time control

PTD
   para-toluenediamine
   percutaneous transluminal dilatation
   period to discharge
   permanent total disability
   persistent trophoblastic disease
   personality trait disorder
   prior to delivery
   prior to discharge

Ptd
   phosphatidyl

PtdCho
   phosphatidylcholine

PtdEtn
   phosphatidylethanolamine

PtdIns
   phosphatidylinositol *also* PI

PTDP
   permanent transvenous demand
   pacemaker

PtdSer
   phosphatidylserine

PTE
   parathyroid extract
   peritumoral edema
   posttraumatic endophthalmitis
   posttraumatic epilepsy
   pretibial edema
   proximal tibial epiphysis
   pulmonary thromboembolism

PTED
   pulmonary thromboembolic disease

PteGlu
   pteroylglutamic (acid)

PTEN
   pentaerythritol tetranitrate

pter
   end of short arm of chromosome

PTF
   patient treatment file
   plasma thromboplastin factor

PTFA
   prothrombin time fixing agent

PTFE
   polytetrafluoroethylene

PTFS
   posttraumatic fibromyalgia syndrome

PTG
   parathyroid gland

PTGA
   pteroyltriglutamic acid

PTGBD
   percutaneous transhepatic gallbladder
   drainage

PTH
   parathormone *also* PT
   parathyroid *also* para, PT
   parathyroid hormone *also* PH
   phenylthiohydantoin
   plasma thromboplastin (component)
   posttransfusion hepatitis
   prior to hospitalization

PTh
   primary thrombocythemia

PTHBD
   percutaneous transhepatic biliary drain
   (age)

PTHC
   percutaneous transhepatic
   cholangiography

PTHS
   parathyroid hormone secretion (rate)

PTI
   pancreatic trypsin inhibitor
   persistent tolerant infection
   Pictorial Test of Intelligence
   pressure time index

PTJV
   percutaneous transtracheal jet
   ventilation

PTK
   phototherapeutic keratectomy

NOTES

P

PTL
perinatal telencephalic leukoencephalopathy
pharyngeotracheal lumen
posterior tricuspid (valve) leaflet *also* pTL
preterm labor
protriptyline
(Sodium) Pentothal

pTL
posterior tricuspid (valve) leaflet *also* PTL

PTLC
precipitation thin-layer chromatography

PTLD
posttransplantation lymphoproliferative disorder

PTM
posterior trabecular meshwork
posttransfusion mononucleosis
posttraumatic meningitis
pressure time per minute
preterm milk

Ptm
pterygomaxillary (fissure)
transmural pressure (airway, blood vessel)

PTMA
phenyltrimethylammonium

PTMC
percutaneous transvenous mitral commissurotomy

PTMDF
pupils, tension, media, disc, and fundus

PTN
pain transmission neuron

pTNM
pathological tumor, nodes, metastases (pathological staging of cancer)

PTO
Klemperer tuberculin [Ger. *Perlsucht Tuberculin Original*]
percutaneous transhepatic obliteration
personal time off
please turn over

PTP
percutaneous transhepatic portography
posterior tibial pulse
posttetanic potentiation
posttransfusion purpura

prior to program
prothrombin-proconvertin
proximal tubular pressure

Ptp
transpulmonary pressure

PTPI
posttraumatic pulmonary insufficiency

PTPM
posttraumatic progressive myelopathy

PTPN
peripheral (vein) total parenteral nutrition

PTPS
postthrombophlebitis syndrome

PTR
paratesticular rhabdomyosarcoma
patella tendon reflex
patient to return
patient termination record
peripheral total resistance
prothrombin time ratio
psychotic trigger reaction
tuberculin *Mycobacterium tuberculosis bovis* [Ger. *Perlsucht Tuberculin Rest*]

PTr
porcine trypsin

PTRA
percutaneous transluminal renal angioplasty

PTRIA
polystyrene-tube radioimmunoassay

Ptrx
pelvic traction

PTS
painful tonic seizure
para-toluenesulfonic (acid)
patellar tendon suspension
patella tendon socket
permanent threshold shift
phosphotransferase system
postthrombotic syndrome
posttraumatic syndrome
prior to surgery

6-PTS
6-pyruvoyltetrahydropterin synthase

Pts, pts
patients

PTSD
posttraumatic stress disorder

PTT
 partial thromboplastin time
 particle transport time
 platelet transfusion therapy
 posterior tibial transfer
 pulmonary transit time
 pulse transmission time

PTT-CT
 partial thromboplastin time control

PTU
 pain treatment unit
 propylthiouracil

PTUCA
 percutaneous transluminal ultrasonic
  coronary angioplasty

PTV
 posterior tibial vein

PTWTKG
 patient's weight in kilograms

PTX
 parathyroidectomy *also* PTx
 pelvic traction
 phototoxic reaction
 picrotoxinin
 pneumothorax *also* Pnx, PT, Px

PTx
 parathyroidectomy *also* PTX
 pelvic traction

PTXA
 parathyroidectomy and
  autotransplantation

PTZ
 pentamethylenetetrazole
 pentylenetetrazol
 phenothiazine

PU
 passed urine
 paternal uncle
 pelvic-ureteric
 pepsin unit
 peptic ulcer
 posterior urethra
 precursor uptake
 pregnancy urine
 prostatic urethra
 by way of urethra [L. *per urethra*]

Pu
 plutonium
 purple (indicator color) *also* Pur
 putrescine *also* PUT

pub, publ
 public

PUBS
 percutaneous umbilical blood sampling
 purple urine bag syndrome

PUC
 pediatric urine collector

PUD
 peptic ulcer disease
 pulmonary disease *also* PD, PuD

PuD
 pulmonary disease *also* PD, PUD

PUE
 pyrexia of unknown etiology

PUFA
 polyunsaturated fatty acid

PUFFA
 polyunsaturated free fatty acid

PUH
 pregnancy urine hormone

PUL, pul
 percutaneous ultrasonic lithotripsy
 pubourethral ligament
 pulmonary *also* P, pulm

pulm
 gruel [L. *pulmentum*]
 pulmonary *also* P, PUL, pul
 pulmonic

PULSES
 general physical, upper extremities,
  lower extremities, sensory, excretory,
  social support (physical profile)

pulv.
 powder [L. *pulvis*]

pulv. gros.
 coarse powder [L. *pulvis grossus*]

pulv. subtil.
 smooth powder [L. *pulvis subtilis*]

pulv. tenu.
 very fine powder [L. *pulvis tenuis*]

PUN
plasma urea nitrogen

PUND
pregnancy uterine, undelivered

PUNL
percutaneous ultrasonic
nephrolithotripsy

PUO
pyrexia of undetermined origin
pyrexia of unknown origin

PUP
percutaneous ultrasonic pyelolithotomy

PU-PC
polyunsaturated phosphatidylcholine

PUPPP
pruritic urticarial papules and plaques
of pregnancy

PUR
polyurethane

Pur
purple *also* Pu

purg
purgative

PUS
percutaneous ureteral stent

PUT
putamen
putrescine *also* Pu

PUVA
psoralen plus ultraviolet light of A
wave length
pulsed ultraviolet actinotherapy

PUVD
pulsed ultrasonic (blood) velocity
detector

PUW
pick-up walker

PV
pancreatic vein
papillomavirus
paraventricular
pemphigus vulgaris
peripheral vascular
peripheral vein *also* PeV
peripheral vessel
phonation volume
photovoltaic
pinocytotic vesicle
pityriasis versicolor
plasma viscosity
plasma volume
pneumococcus vaccine
polio vaccine
polycythemia vera *also* PCV
polyoma virus
polyvinyl
popliteal vein
portal vein
postvasectomy
postvoiding
predictive value
pressure-volume
pulmonary vein
pure vegetarian
by way of vagina [L. *per vaginam*]

P-V
Paton-Valentine (leukocidin)
pressure-volume (curve)

P/V
pressure to volume (ratio)

P&V
peak and valley
percuss and vibrate
pyloroplasty and vagotomy

Pv
venous pressure *also* VP

Pv$_{O2}$
partial oxygen pressure in mixed
venous blood

Pv$_{CO2}$
partial pressure of carbon dioxide in
mixed venous blood

PVA
partial villous atrophy
polyvinyl alcohol (fixative)
Prinzmetal variant angina

PVAc
polyvinyl acetate

PVARP
postventricular atrial refractory period

PVAS
postvasectomy (specimen)

PVB
Platinol (cisplatin), vinblastine, and
bleomycin
premature ventricular beat

PVBS
possible vertebral-basilar system

PVC
persistent vaginal cornification
polyvinyl chloride
postvoiding cystogram
predicted vital capacity
premature ventricular complex
premature ventricular contraction
primary visual cortex
pulmonary venous capillary
pulmonary venous congestion

PVCM
paradoxical vocal cord motion

PVD
patient very disturbed
percussion, vibration, and drainage
peripheral vascular disease
portal vein dilation
posterior vitreous detachment
postural vertical dimension
postvagotomy diarrhea
premature ventricular depolarization
pulmonary vascular disease

PVE
perivenous encephalomyelitis
periventricular echogenicity
premature ventricular extrasystole
prosthetic valve endocarditis

PVEP
pattern visual evoked potential

PVF
peripheral visual field
portal venous flow
primary ventricular fibrillation

PVFS
postviral fatigue syndrome

PVG
pulmonary valve gradient

PVH
periventricular hemorrhage
pulmonary vascular hypertension

PVI
peripheral vascular insufficiency
periventricular inhibitor

PVK
penicillin V potassium

PVL
perivalvular leakage
periventricular leukomalacia

P-VL
Panton-Valentine leukocidin

PVM
pneumonia virus of mice
proteins, vitamins, and minerals

PVMed
preventive medicine *also* PM, PRM, PrM

PVMS
paravertebral muscle spasm

PVN
paraventricular nucleus
peripheral venous nutrition
predictive value of a negative (test)

PVNPS
post-Vietnam psychiatric syndrome

PVNS
pigmented villonodular synovitis

PVO
peripheral vascular occlusion
pulmonary venous obstruction
pulmonary venous occlusion

PVOD
peripheral vascular occlusive disease
pulmonary vascular obstructive disease
pulmonary venoocclusive disease

PVP
penicillin V potassium
peripheral vein plasma
peripheral venous pressure
polyvinylpyrrolidone (povidone)
portal venous pressure
posteroventral pallidotomy
predictive value of a positive (test)
pulmonary venous pressure *also* P_L

PVP-I
polyvinylpyrrolidone (povidone)–iodine

PVR
paraventricular nuclear stratum
peripheral vascular resistance
postvoiding residual
proliferative vitreoretinopathy

NOTES

P

PVR *(continued)*
pulmonary vascular resistance
pulmonary venous redistribution
pulse-volume recording

PVRI
peripheral vascular resistance index

PVS
paravesical space
percussion, vibration, and suction
peripheral vascular surgery
peritoneovenous shunt
persistent vegetative state
persistent viral syndrome
pigmented villonodular synovitis
Plummer-Vinson syndrome
poliovirus sensitivity
polyvinyl sponge
premature ventricular systole
programmed ventricular stimulation
pulmonary vein stenosis
pulmonic valve stenosis

PVT
paroxysmal ventricular tachycardia
physical volume test
portal vein thrombosis
pressure, volume, temperature
private (patient) *also* pvt

pvt
private (patient) *also* PVT

PVW
posterior vaginal wall

PW
pacing wire
patient waiting
peristaltic wave
posterior wall (of heart)
Prader-Willi (syndrome) *also* P-W
pulmonary wedge (pressure)
pulsed wave
puncture wound

P-W
Prader-Willi (syndrome) *also* PW

P&W
pressures and waves

Pw
progesterone withdrawal

PWA
people with acquired
immunodeficiency syndrome

PWB
partial weightbearing
psychologic wellbeing

PWBC
peripheral white blood cell

PWBRT
prophylactic whole brain radiation
therapy

PWC
peak work capacity
physical work capacity

PWD
precipitated withdrawal diarrhea
pulsed-wave Doppler

pwd
powder *also* pdr, powd

PWE
posterior wall excursion

PWI
posterior wall infarct

PWLV
posterior wall of left ventricle

PWM
pokeweed mitogen

PWMI
posterior wall myocardial infarction

PWO
persistent withdrawal occlusion

PWP
pulmonary wedge pressure *also* Ppw

PWS
port wine stain
Prader-Willi syndrome
pulse-wave speed

pwt
pennyweight

PWV
peak weight velocity
polistes wasp venom
posterior wall velocity
pulse wave velocity

PX
pancreatectomized
peroxidase
physical examination *also* PE, PEx,
Px

Px
past history *also* PH

physical examination *also* PE, PEx, PX
pneumothorax *also* Pnx, PT, PTX
prognosis *also* prog, progn, Prx

PXA
pleomorphic xanthoastrocytoma

PXE
pseudoxanthoma elasticum

PXM
projection x-ray microscopy

PXS
pseudoexfoliation syndrome *also* PES

PY, P/Y
pack-year (cigarettes)
person-year

Py
phosphopyridoxal
polyoma (virus)
pyrene
pyridine

PYA
psychoanalysis *also* PA

PYC
proteose-yeast castione (medium)

PyC
pyogenic culture

PYE
peptone yeast extract

PYG
peptone-yeast(extract)-glucose (broth)

PYGM
peptone-yeast-glucose-maltose (broth)

PYLL
potential years of life lost

PYM
psychosomatic

PYP
pyrophosphate *also* PP, Pyro

PYR
person-year rad

Pyr
pyridine
pyruvate

Pyro
pyrophosphate *also* PP, PYP

PyrP
pyridoxal phosphate

PYS
pyriform sinus

PZ
pancreozymin
peripheral zone
prazosin
pregnancy zone
proliferative zone

Pz
parietal midline (zero) electrode
placement in electroencephalography

pz
pieze (unit of pressure)

PZA
pyrazinamide

PzB
parenzyme, buccal

PZ-CCK
pancreozymin-cholecystokinin

PZD
piperazinedione

PZE
piezoelectric

PZI
protamine zinc insulin

PZP
pregnancy zone protein

NOTES

P

Q

cardiac output *also* CO, QT
clerical perception (General Aptitude
  Test Battery)
coenzyme Q. (ubiquinone) *also* CoQ
coulomb *also* C
each, every [L. *quaque*] *also* q, q.q.
electrocardiographic wave
1,4-glucan branching enzyme
glutamine *also* Gln
glutaminyl *also* Gln
perfusion (flow)
pseudouridine
Quaalude
quantitative *also* qt, quant
quantity (of heat)
quart *also* q, qt
quarter *also* q, qr
quartile
quaternary
Queensland (fever)
query (fever)
question *also* quest.
quinacrine (fluorescent method)
quinidine
quinone
quotient *also* quot.
radiant energy
reaction energy
reactive power
volume of blood flow

Q-6, Q₆
ubiquinone-6
ubiquinone-Q₆

Q°, q°
every hour

Q̇
blood flow *also* B, Q$_B$

Q1°
every hour around the clock

Q2°
every two hours around the clock

Q₆ (*var. of* Q-6)

Q₉
ubichromanol-9
ubichromenol-9

Q₁₀
temperature coefficient
ubiquinone-50

-Q₆
ubiquinone-6

-Q₁₀
ubiquinone-10

q
each, every [L. *quaque*] *also* Q, q.q.
electric charge
four [L. *quattuor*] *also* Quat, quat.
frequency of rarer allele of a gene
  pair
long arm of chromosome
quantity *also* Q, qt, qty, quant
quart *also* Q, qt
quarter *also* Q, qr
quintal
quodque
volume *also* V, vol

q° (*var. of* Q°)

QA
quality assessment
quality assurance
quinaldic acid
quisqualic acid

QAC
quaternary ammonium compound

QALE
quality-adjusted life expectancy

QALY
quality-adjusted life years

QAM
quality assurance monitor

Qa m, qAM, q.a.m.
every morning [L. *quaque ante
  meridiem*] *also* q.m.

Q angle
Quatrefages angle (parietal angle)

Q-angle
quadriceps angle

QAP
quality assurance program
quinine, Atabrine (quinacrine
  hydrochloride), and pamaquine

QAR
quality assurance reagent
quantitative autoradiographic

QA/RM
quality assurance/risk management

QAS
quality assurance standards

QAT
quality assurance technical (material)

QAUR
quality assurance and utilization review

QB
Quantitative (Electrophysiological) Battery
whole blood *also* B, WB, W Bld

Q_B
blood flow *also* BF, $\dot{Q}$
total body clearance *also* TBC

QBC
quality buffy coat

QBCA
quantitative buffy-coat analysis

QBV
whole blood volume

QC
quality control
quick catheter
quinine and colchicine

Qc
pulmonary capillary blood flow (perfusion)

QCA
quantitative coronary angiography

QCD
quantum chromodynamics

Q_{CO2}
microliters of carbon dioxide given off per mg of dry weight of tissue per hour

QC-PCR
quantitative competitive polymerase chain reaction

Q_{CSF}
rate of bulk flow of cerebrospinal fluid from cerebrospinal space by arachnoid villi uptake

QCT
quantitative computed tomography

q.d.
every day [L. *quaque die*] *also* o.d., q.q.d.

QDR
quantitative digital radiography

qds
to be taken four times a day [L. *quater die sumendum*]

QED
quantum electrodynamics
that which is to be demonstrated [L. *quod erat demonstrandum*] *also* q.e.d.

q.e.d.
that which is to be demonstrated [L. *quod erat demonstrandum*] *also* QED

QEE
quadriceps extension exercise

QEEG
quantitative electroencephalography

QET
Quality Extinction Test

QEW
quick early warning

QF
quality factor
quality factor (relative biologic effectiveness)
query fever *also* Q fever
quick freeze

Qf
rate of fluid filtration

Q fever
(Australian) query fever *also* QF

Q fract
quick fraction

Q-H₂
ubiquinol *also* H_2Q

q.h.
every hour [L. *quaque hora*] *also* q.q. hor.

q.2h.
every two hours [L. *quaque secunda hora*]

q.3h.
every three hours [L. *quaque tertia hora*]

q.4h.
every four hours [L. *quaque quarta hora*] *also* q.q.h.

QHS
quantitative hepatobiliary scintigraphy

q.h.s.
each bedtime, every night [L. *quaque hora somni* every hour of sleep]

QI
quality improvement

QID
Quantum inflation device

q.i.d.
four times daily [L. *quater in die*]

QIE
quantitative immunoelectrophoresis

QIg
quantitative immunoglobulin

QJ
quadriceps jerk

q.l.
as much as desired [L. *quantum libet*]

QLQ-C30
Quality of Life Questionnaire-C30

QLS
Quality of Life Scale

qlty
quality

QM
Quénu-Muret (sign)
quinacrine mustard

q.m.
every morning [L. *quaque mane*] *also* Qa m, qAM, q.a.m.

QMI
Q-wave myocardial infarction

QMT
quantitative muscle testing

QMWS
quasimorphine withdrawal syndrome

q.n.
every night [L. *quaque nocte*]

QNB
quinuclidinyl benzilate

QNS, qns
quantity not sufficient
quantity not sufficient for evaluation

QO2
oxygen quotient

Qo
oxygen consumption *also* Q_{O2}

Q_{O2}
oxygen consumption *also* Qo
oxygen quotient
oxygen utilization

QOC
Quality of Contact

q.o.d.
every other day [L. *quaque altera die*]

q.o.h.
every other hour [L. *quaque altera hora*]

QOL
quality of life

q.o.n.
every other night [L. *quaque altera nocte*]

QP
quadrant pain
quanti-Pirquet (reaction)

Qp
pulmonary blood flow *also* PBF

q.p.
as much as desired [L. *quantum placeat*]

QPC
quadrigeminal plate cistern
quality of patient care

Qpc
pulmonary capillary blood flow

Q-PCR
quantitative polymerase chain reaction

QPEEG
quantitative pharmacoelectroencephalography

NOTES

Qpm, qPM, q.p.m.
each evening [L. *quaque post meridiem*]

QP/QS
ratio of pulmonary to systemic circulation

Qp/Qs
flow ratio
left-to-right shunt ratio (electrocardiography)

QPT
quick prothrombin time

QPVT
Quick Picture Vocabulary Test

q.q.
each or every [L. *quaque*] *also* Q, q

q.q.d.
every day [L. *quoque die*] *also* o.d., q.d.

q.q.h.
every four hours [L. *quaque quarta hora*] *also* q.4h.

q.q. hor.
every hour [L. *quaque hora*]

QR
quadriradial
quality review
quantity is correct [L. *quantum rectum*] *also* q.r.
Quick Recovery (Defibrillator)
quieting reflex
quieting response
quiet room
quinaldine red

q.r.
quantity is correct [L. *quantum rectum*] *also* QR

qr
quadriradial
quarter *also* Q, q

QRB
Quality Review Bulletin

Q-RB
electrocardiographic time-wave interval

QRN
quasiresonant nucleus

QRS
electrocardiographic wave (complex or interval)

QRS-ST
electrocardiographic junction between QRS complex and ST segment

QRS-T
electrocardiographic angle between QRS and T vectors

QRZ
wheal reaction time [Ger. *Quaddel Reaktion Zeit*]

QS
quantity sufficient
quiet sleep

QS2
total electromechanical systole

Qs
systemic blood flow

q.s.
as much as may suffice [L. *quantum sufficiat*]
sufficient quantity [L. *quantum satis*] *also* q. sat.

q.s. ad
to a sufficient quantity [L. *quantum satis ad*]
sufficient quantity to make [L. *quantum sufficiat ad*]

QSAR
quantitative structure-activity relationship

q. sat.
sufficient quantity [L. *quantum satis*] *also* q.s.

QSC
quasistatic compliance

QS$_2$I
shortened electrochemical systole

Q sign
Quant sign

Qsp
physiologic shunt flow

QSPV
quasistatic pressure volume

Qs/Qt
intrapulmonary shunt fraction
intrapulmonary shunt ratio
right-to-left shunt ratio

Qsrel
  relative shunt flow

QSS
  quantitative sacroiliac scintigraphy

Q-S test
  Queckenstedt-Stookey test

q. suff.
  as much as suffices [L. *quantum sufficit*]

Q-T
  electrocardiographic interval from the beginning of QRS complex to end of the T wave
  Quick Test (psychology, pregnancy, prothrombin) *also* QT

QT
  blood volume (quantity) per unit time
  cardiac output *also* CO, Q
  qualification test
  Queckenstedt test
  Quick Test (psychology, pregnancy, prothrombin) *also* Q-T

Qt
  quiet *also* qt

qt
  quantitative *also* Q, quant
  quantity *also* Q, q, qty, quant
  quart *also* Q, qt
  quiet *also* Qt

QTC
  quantitative tip culture

QTc, QT$_c$
  QT corrected for heart rate

qter
  end of long arm of chromosome

qty
  quantity *also* Q, q, qt, quant

quad
  quadrant
  quadriceps
  quadrilateral
  quadriplegia
  quadriplegic

quad ex
  quadriceps exercise

quadrupl.
  four times as much [L. *quadruplicato*]

qual
  qualitative
  quality

qual anal
  qualitative analysis

quant
  quantitative *also* Q, qt
  quantity *also* Q, q, qt, qty

quar
  quarantine

QUART
  quadrantectomy, axillary dissection, radiation therapy

quart.
  fourth [L. *quartus*]
  quadrantectomy, axillary dissection, and radiotherapy
  quarterly

Quat, quat.
  four [L. *quattuor*] *also* q

quats
  quaternary ammonium compounds

quer
  querulous

QUEST
  Quality, Utilization, Effectiveness, Statistically Tabulated

quest.
  question *also* Q
  questionable

QuF
  (Australian) Q (Queensland) fever

QUICHA
  quantitative inhalation challenge apparatus

quinq.
  five [L. *quinque*]

quint.
  fifth [L. *quintus*]

NOTES

quor.
of which [L. *quorum*]

quot.
as often as necessary [L. *quoties*]
daily [L. *quotidie*] *also* quotid.
quotient *also* Q

quotid.
daily [L. *quotidie*] *also* quot.

quot. op. sit, quot. o. s.
as often as necessary [L. *quoties
opus sit*]

q.v.
as much as you desire [L. *quantum
vis*]

which see (literature citation) [L.
quod vide]

QW
quality of working (life) *also* QWL

qwk
once a week

QWL
quality of working life *also* QW

QYD
Qi (and) Yin deficiency

R

arginine *also* ARG, Arg
Behnken unit (of roentgen-ray exposure)
Broadbent registration point
drug-resistant plasmid
electrocardiographic wave in QRS complex
far point [L. *remotum*] *also* r
gas constant (8.315 joules)
metabolic respiratory quotient
organic radical
race
racemic
rad
radioactive *also* RA
radiology
radius *also* r, Ra, rad
ramus
range
Rankine (scale)
rare
rate
ratio
rationale
raw
reaction
reading
Réaumur (scale)
recessive
rectal
rectified average
rectum *also* rect
red (indicator color) *also* rub.
reference *also* ref
regimen
registered (trademark) *also* Reg
regression coefficient
regular *also* reg
regulator (gene)
rejection (factor)
relapse
relaxation
release (factor)
remission
remote point of convergence
repressor
resazurin
resident
residuum
resistance determinant (plasmid)
resistance (electrical) *also* RES

resistance unit (in cardiovascular system) *also* RU
resistant
respiration *also* Resp, resp
respiratory exchange ratio *also* R_E, RER
response *also* resp
rest (cell cycle)
resting
restricted
reticulocyte *also* RET, RETIC
reverse (banding) *also* REV
review *also* REV
rhythm
rib
ribose *also* r, Rib
right *also* (R), RT, Rt, rt
Rinne (hearing test)
roentgen *also* r, ROE, roent
root
rough (bacterial colony)
routine
rub
side chain in amino acid formula
stimulus [G. *Reiz*] *also* S, ST
take [L. *recipe*]
total response *also* TR

R1
longitudinal relaxivity

R2
transverse relaxivity

°R
(degree) Rankine
(degree) Réaumur

+R
Rinne test positive

R#1
good risk (for anesthesia)

R#2
fairly good risk (for anesthesia)

R#3
poor risk (for anesthesia)

R#4
very poor risk (for anesthesia)

(R)
rectal
right *also* R, RT

-R
Rinne test negative

r

angle of refraction
correlation coefficient
product moment
racemic
radius *also* R, Ra, rad
reproductive potential
ribose *also* R, Rib
ring chromosome
roentgen *also* R, ROE, roent
round
sample correlation coefficient

r.

far point [L. *remotum*] *also* R

r²

coefficient of determination

RA

radioactive *also* R
radionuclide angiography *also* RNA
radium *also* Ra, Rad
ragocyte (cell)
ragweed antigen
rales
Raynaud (phenomenon)
reading age
reciprocal asymmetrical
refractory anemia
refractory ascites
regional anesthesia
remittance advice
renal artery
renin activity
renin-angiotensin
repeat action (drugs)
residual air
retinoic acid
rheumatic arthritis
rheumatoid agglutinin *also* Rh agglut
rheumatoid arthritis
rifampicin
right angle
right arm
right atrial (pressure)
right atrium
right auricle
Rokitansky-Aschoff (sinus)
room air

R$_A$

airway resistance *also* AR, RAW,
R$_{AW}$, R (AW)

Ra

radial *also* rad
radium *also* RA, Rad

radius *also* R, r, rad
Rayleigh number

²²⁶Ra

radium-226

rA

riboadenylate

RAA

renin-angiotensin-aldosterone (system)
right atrial abnormality
right atrial appendage

RAAGG

rheumatoid arthritis agglutinin

RAAS

renin-angiotensin-aldosterone system
also RAS

rAAT

recombinant alpha₁ antitrypsin

RAB

remote afterload brachytherapy
rice, applesauce, and banana (diet)

Rab

rabbit

RABA

rabbit antibladder antibody

RABBI

Rapid Access Blood Bank
Information

RABCa

rabbit antibladder cancer

RABG

room air blood gas

RAbody

right atrium body

RABP

retinoic acid-binding protein

RAC

radial artery catheter
right atrial contraction

rac

racemate
racemic

RACAT

rapid acquisition computed axial
tomography

RACCO

right anterior caudocranial oblique

R

RACT
  recalcified (whole-blood) activated clotting time

RAD
  radiation absorbed dose *also* rad
  radical *also* rad
  radiology *also* Rad, Radiol
  reactive airway disease
  right anterior descending
  right atrial diameter
  right axis deviation
  roentgen administered dose

Rad
  radiologist *also* Radiol
  radiology *also* RAD, Radiol
  radiotherapist
  radiotherapy *also* RADIO, RT, Rx
  radium *also* RA, Ra

rad
  radial *also* Ra
  radian
  radiation-absorbed dose *also* RAD
  radical *also* RAD
  radiculitis
  radius *also* R, r, Ra
  roentgen absorbed dose
  root [L. *radix*]

RADA
  right acromiodorsoanterior (fetal position)

RADCA
  right anterior descending coronary artery

RADIANCE
  Randomized Assessment of Digoxin on Inhibitors of Angiotensin-Converting Enzyme

rad imp
  radium implant

RADIO
  radiotherapy *also* Rad, Rad Ther, RT, Rx

Radiol
  radiologist *also* Rad
  radiology *also* RAD, Rad

RADISH
  rheumatoid arthritis, diffuse idiopathic skeletal hyperostosis

RAD ISO VENO BILAT
  radioactive isotopic venogram, bilateral

RadLV
  radiation leukemia virus

RADP
  right acromiodorsoposterior (fetal position)

RADS
  reactive airway disease syndrome
  reactive airway dysfunction syndrome
  retrospective assessment of drug safety

rad/s
  radian per second

Rad Ther
  radiotherapy *also* Rad, RADIO, RT, Rx

RADTS
  rabbit antidog-thymus serum

Rad Ul
  radius-ulna

RADWASTE
  radioactive waste

RAE
  right atrial enlargement

RaE
  rabbit erythrocyte

RAEB
  refractory anemia, erythroblastic
  refractory anemia with excess blasts

RAEB-T
  refractory anemia with excess of blasts in transformation

RAEM
  refractory anemia with excess myeloblasts

RAF
  rapid atrial fibrillation
  rheumatoid arthritis factor

NOTES

Ra-F
radium-F

RAFF
rectus abdominis free flap

RAG
ragweed
room air gas

Ragg
rheumatoid agglutinator

RAH
radioactive Hippuran (test)
regressing atypical histiocytosis
right anterior hemiblock *also* RAHB
right atrial hypertrophy

RAHB
right anterior hemiblock *also* RAH

RAHO
rabbit antibody to human ovary

RAHTG
rabbit antihuman-thymocyte globulin

RAI
radioactive iodide
radioactive iodine *also* ^{131}I
resting ankle index
right atrial involvement

RAID
radioimmunodetection *also* RID

RAIS
reflection-absorption infrared
spectroscopy

RAIU
radioactive iodine uptake *also* RIU

RAL
resorcylic acid lactone

RALPH
renal-anal-lung-polydactyly-
hamartoblastoma (syndrome)

RALT
Riley Articulation and Language Test
routine admission laboratory test

RAM
radar absorbent material
radioactive material
random-access memory
rapid alternating movements
rectus abdominis muscle
rectus abdominis myocutaneous (flap)
reduced-acquisition matrix

research aviation medicine
right anterior measurement

RAMI
Risk-Adjusted Mortality Index

RAMP
radioactive antigen microprecipitin
right atrial mean pressure

RAMT
rabbit antimouse-thymocyte

RAN
resident's admission notes

RANA
rheumatoid arthritis nuclear antigen

RAND
random (sample, specimen)

RANT
right anterior

RANTES
regulated upon activation, normal T
cell expressed and secreted

RAO
right anterior oblique
right anterior occipital

RaONC
radiation oncology

RAP
receptor-associated protein
recurrent abdominal pain
regression-associated protein
renal artery pressure
rheumatoid arthritis precipitin
right atrial pressure

RAPA
radial artery pseudoaneurysm

RAPC
resistance activated protein C

RAPD
relative afferent pupillary defect

RAPE
right atrial pressure elevation

RAPM
refractory anemia with partial
myeloblastosis

RAPO
rabbit antibody to pig ovary

RAQ
right anterior quadrant

RAR
rat insulin receptor
right arm reclining
right arm recumbent

RARLS
rabbit antirat-lymphocyte serum

RARTS
rabbit antirat-thymocyte serum

RAS
recurrent aphthous stomatitis
reflex-activating stimulus
renal artery stenosis
renin-angiotensin-aldosterone system
also RAAS
renin-angiotensin system
reticular activating system
rheumatoid arthritis serum (factor)
Rokitansky-Aschoff sinuses
rotational atherectomy system

ras.
scrapings, filings [L. *rasurae*]

RASP
rapidly alternating speech
Rapidly Alternating Speech Perception
Test

RASS
rheumatoid arthritis and Sjögren
syndrome

RAST
radioallergosorbent assay test
radioallergosorbent test

RASV
recovered avian sarcoma virus

RAT
rat aortic tissue
repeat action tablet
rheumatoid arthritis (factor) test
right anterior thigh
rotating aspiration
thromboembolectomy

RATA
radioimmunologic assay antithyroid
antibody

RATG
rabbit antithymocyte globulin

RATHAS
rat thymus antiserum

RATS
rabbit antithymocyte serum

RATx
radiation therapy

RAU
radioactive uptake
recurrent aphthous ulcer

RAUC
raw area under curve

RAV
Rous-associated virus

RAVES
Reduced Anticoagulation in Vein
Graft Stent

RAW, R(AW), R_{AW}
airway resistance *also* AR, R_A

RAZ
razoxane

RB
rating board
rebreathing
Renaut body
respiratory bronchiole
respiratory burst
reticulate body
retinoblastoma
retrobulbar
right bundle
right buttock
round body

R&B
right and below

Rb
rubidium

RBA
relative binding affinity
rescue breathing apparatus
right basilar artery
right brachial artery
rose bengal antigen

RBAF
rheumatoid biologically active factor

R

NOTES

RBAP
repetitive bursts of action potential

RBAS
rostral basilar artery syndrome

RBB
right breast biopsy
right bundle branch

RBBB
right bundle branch block

RBBsB
right bundle branch system block

RBBX
right breast biopsy examination

RBC
red blood cell *also* rbc
red blood (cell) count
red blood corpuscle

rbc
red blood cell *also* RBC
red blood count

RBC-ADA
red blood cell adenosine deaminase

RBCD
right border cardiac dullness

RBC FO
red blood cell fallout

RBC frag
red blood cell fragility

RBC/hpf
red blood cells per high power field

RBCM
red blood cell mass

RBC/P
red blood cell to plasma (ratio)

RBC s/f
red blood cell spun filtration

RBCV
red blood cell volume *also* VRBC

RBD
right border of dullness (percussion of heart)

RBE
radiobiologic equivalent
relative biologic effectiveness

RBF
regional blood flow
renal blood flow
riboflavin

RBG
random blood glucose

Rb Imp
rubber base impression

RBL
rat basophilic leukemia
Reid baseline
rubber band ligator

RBM
Raji (cell)-binding material
regional bone mass

RBME
regenerating bone marrow extract

RBN
retrobulbar neuritis

RBON
retrobulbar optic neuritis

RBOW
rupture of bag of waters

RBP
resting blood pressure
retinol-binding protein
riboflavin-binding protein

RBR
radiation bowel reaction

RBS
Randall-Baker Soucek
random blood sugar
rutherford backscattering

RbSA
rabbit serum albumin *also* RSA

RBU
Raji (cell)-binding unit

RBV
right brachial vein

RB-V
right bundle ventricular

RBW
relative body weight

RBZ
rubidazone (zorubicin)

RC
radiocarpal
reaction center
receptor-chemoeffector (complex) *also* RCC
recrystallized
red cell
red (cell) cast *also* RCC

R

red corpuscle
Red Cross
referred care
reflection coefficient
regenerated cellulose
resistance and capacitance
respiration cease
respiratory care
respiratory center
response, conditioned *also* Rc
rest cure
retention catheter *also* ret cath
retrograde cystogram
rib cage
right (ear), cold (stimulus)
Roman Catholic
root canal
rotator cuff
Roussy-Cornil (syndrome)
routine cholecystectomy

R/C
reclining chair

Rc
receptor
response, conditioned *also* RC

RCA
radionuclide cerebral angiogram
Raji cell assay
red cell adherence
red cell agglutination
relative chemotactic activity
renal cell carcinoma
right carotid artery
right coronary artery
rotational coronary atherectomy

RCAI
Restorative Care of America,
Incorporated

rCBF
regional cerebral blood flow

RCBV
regional cerebral blood volume

RCC
radiographic coronary calcification
radiologic control center
rape crisis center
ratio of cost to charges

receptor-chemoeffector complex *also*
RC
red cell cast *also* RC
red cell concentrate
red cell count
renal cell carcinoma
right common carotid
right coronary cusp

Rcc
radiochemical

RCCA
right common carotid artery

RCCT
randomized controlled clinical trial
results of clinical controlled trial

RCD
relative (area of) cardiac dullness

RCDA
recurrent chronic dissecting aneurysm

RCDP
rhizomelic chondrodysplasia punctata

RCDR
relative corrected death rate

RCE
reasonable compensation equivalent

RCF
red cell filter ability
red cell folate
Reiter complement fixation
relative centrifugal field
relative centrifugal force
ristocetin cofactor *also* RCoF
Ross carbohydrate free

RCFS
reticulocyte cell-free system

RCG
radioelectrocardiography *also* RECG

RCGP
Royal College of General
Practitioners

RCH
rectocolic hemorrhage

RCHF
right-sided congestive heart failure

NOTES

RCI
rate change induced
respiratory control index

RCIA
red cell immune adherence

RCIT
red cell iron turnover

RCITR
red cell iron turnover rate

RCL
radial collateral ligament
range of comfortable loudness
renal clearance

RCLAAR
red cell-linked antigen-antiglobulin
reaction

RCM
radiocontrast material
radiographic contrast medium
red cell mass
reinforced clostridial medium
replacement culture medium
retinal capillary microaneurysm
rheumatoid cervical myelopathy
right costal margin
Roux conditioned medium

RCMI
red cell morphology index

rCMRO$_2$
regional cerebral metabolic rate for
oxygen

RCN
right caudate nucleus

RCoF
ristocetin cofactor *also* RCF

RCP
random chemistry profile
retrocorneal pigmentation
riboflavin carrier protein

rcp
reciprocal (translocation)

RCPH
red cell peroxide hemolysis

RCPM
Raven Colored Progressive Matrix

RCQG
right caudal quarter ganglion

RCR
relative consumption rate
replication-competent retrovirus
respiratory control ratio

RCRC
recurrent colorectal cancer

RCRS
Rehabilitation Client Rating Scale

RCS
rabbit (aorta)-contracting substance
red cell suspension
red-color sign
repeat cesarean section *also* R/CS
reticulum cell sarcoma *also* RSA
right coronary sinus

R/CS
repeat cesarean section *also* RCS

RCT
randomized clinical trial
rectal carcinoid tumor
red colloidal test
retrograde conduction time
root canal therapy
Rorschach content test

RC TNTC
red cells too numerous to count

RCU
recurrent calcium urolithiasis
respiratory care unit

RCV
red cell volume

RD
radial deviation
rate difference
Raynaud disease
reaction of degeneration
reaction of denervation
reflex decay
Registered Dietician
Reiter disease
renal disease
Rénon-Delille (syndrome)
resistance determinant
respiratory disease
respiratory distress
retinal detachment
Reye disease
rhabdomyosarcoma *also* RMS
rheumatoid disease
right deltoid
right dorsoanterior
Riley-Day (syndrome)
Rolland-Desbuquois (syndrome)

rubber dam
ruptured disk

R&D
research and development

Rd, rd
reading
rutherford (unit of radioactivity)

RDA
recommended daily allowance
recommended dietary allowance
registered dental assistant
right dorsoanterior (fetal position)
rubidium dihydrogenarsenate

RdA
reading age

RDB
randomized double-blind (trial)
research and development board

RDC
research diagnostic criteria

RDD
renal dose dopamine

RDDA
recommended daily dietary allowance

RDDP
ribonucleic acid-dependent
deoxynucleic acid polymerase *also*
RDPase

RDE
receptor-destroying enzyme

RDEA
right deviation of electrical axis

RDEB
recessive dystrophic epidermolysis
bullosa

RDES
remote data entry system

RDF
rapid dissolution formula

RDFC
recurring digital fibroma of childhood

RDFS
ratio of decayed and filled surfaces

RDFT
ratio of decayed and filled teeth

RDG
Research Discussion Group
retrograde duodenogastroscopy
right dorsogluteal

RDH
Registered Dental Hygienist

RDHBF
regional distribution of hepatic blood
flow

RDI
recommended daily intake
recommended dietary intake
respiratory disturbance index
rupture-delivery interval

RDIH
right direct inguinal hernia

RDLBBB
rate-dependent left bundle branch
block

RDLS
Reynell Development Language Scales
(psychologic test)

RDM
readmission *also* Rdm
right deltoid muscle
rod disk membrane

Rdm
readmission *also* RDM

RDMS
Registered Diagnostic Medical
Sonographer

rDNA
recombinant deoxyribonucleic acid
ribosomal deoxyribonucleic acid

RDOD
retinal detachment, oculus dexter
(right eye)

RDOS
retinal detachment, oculus sinister
(left eye)

RDP
radiopharmaceutical drug product

R

NOTES

RDP *(continued)*
random-donor platelet
right dorsoposterior (fetal position)

RDPase
ribonucleic acid-dependent
deoxyribonucleic acid polymerase
also RDDP

RDPE
reticular degeneration of pigment
epithelium

RDQ
respiratory disease questionnaire

RdQ
reading quotient *also* RG

RDRC
radioactive drug research committee

RDRV
Rhesus diploid (cell strain) rabies
vaccine

RDS
research diagnostic (criteria)
respiratory distress syndrome (of
newborn)
reticuloendothelial depressing
substance

RDT
regular (hemo)dialysis treatment
retinal damage threshold
routine dialysis therapy

RDTD
referral, diagnosis, treatment, and
discharge

RDVT
recurrent deep vein thrombosis

RDW
red (blood cell) distribution width
(index)
red (cell) diameter width
reticulocyte distribution width

RE
concerning *also* re
racemic epinephrine
radium emanation
readmission
rectal examination
reflux esophagitis
regional enteritis
regular education
renal and electrolyte
renal excretion
resting energy

reticuloendothelial
retinol equivalent
right ear
right eye *also* O.D.
ring enhancement
rostral end

R&E
research and education
rest and exercise
round and equal

R↑E
right upper extremity

RE√
recheck

R$_E$
respiratory exchange ratio *also* R,
RER

R$_e$
Reynolds number

Re
rhenium

^{188}Re
rhenium-188

^{186}Re
rhenium-186

re
concerning *also* RE
regarding

REA
radiation emergency area
radioenzymatic assay
renal anastomosis
right ear advantage

REACH
Reassurance to Each (assistance to
family of mentally ill)

readm
readmission

REAS
reasonably expected as safe

REAT
radiologic emergency assistance team

REB
roentgen-equivalent biologic
rubber-reinforced bandage

R-EBD-HS
recessive epidermolysis bullosa
dystrophica-Hallopeau-Siemens
(syndrome)

R

REC
    radioelectrocomplexing
    rear end collision
    receptor
    recommend
    record *also* rec
    recovery
    recreation *also* rec
    recur
    right external carotid

rec
    reactive
    recent
    recombinant chromosome
    recommendation
    record *also* REC
    recreation *also* REC
    recurrence *also* recur, recur
    recurrent *also* recur, recur

rec.
    fresh [L. *recens*]

RECA
    right external carotid artery

recd, rec'd
    received

RE CEL
    reticulum cell

RECG
    radioelectrocardiography *also* RCG

recip
    recipient
    reciprocal

recom
    smallest unit of DNA capable of
    recombination

recond
    reconditioned
    reconditioning

reconstr
    reconstruction

recryst
    recrystallization

rect
    rectal *also* R

rectification
rectified
rectum *also* R
rectus (muscle)

recur
    recurrence *also* rec
    recurrent *also* rec

RED
    radiation experience data
    rapid erythrocyte degeneration

Re-D
    reevaluation deadline

red.
    reduce
    reducing
    reduction *also* redn

redig. in pulv.
    let it be reduced to powder [L.
    redigatur in pulverem]

redn
    reduction *also* red.

redox
    oxidation-reduction

red. in pulv.
    reduced to powder [L. *reductus in*
    pulverem]

REE
    rapid extinction effect
    rare earth element
    resting energy expenditure

re-ed
    reeducation

REEDS
    retention (of tears), ectrodactyly,
    ectodermal dysplasia, and strange
    (hair, skin, and teeth syndrome)

REEG
    radioelectroencephalography

R-EEG
    resting electroencephalogram

REEGT
    Registered Electroencephalographic
    Technician

NOTES

REEL
Receptive-Expressive Emergent Language (Scale)

ReEND
reproductive endocrinology

REEP
right end-expiratory pressure
role exchange/education-practice

REF
ejection fraction at rest
referred
refused
renal erythropoietic factor

ref
reference *also* R
reflex *also* Refl

Ref Doc
referring doctor

REFI
regional ejection fraction image

ref ind
refractive index *also* RI

Refl
reflect
reflection
reflex *also* ref

REFMS
Recreation and Education for Multiple Sclerosis (Victims)

Ref Phys
referring physician

REFRAD
released from active duty

REG
radiation exposure guide
radioencephalogram
radioencephalography
rheoencephalography

Reg
registered *also* R

reg
regarding
region
regular *also* R
regulation

regen
regenerate
regeneration

reg rhy
regular rhythm

reg R&R
regular rate and rhythm *also* RRR

reg. umb.
umbilical region [L. *regio umbilici*]

regurg
regurgitation

REH
renin essential hypertension

REHAB, rehab
rehabilitated
rehabilitation

REL
rate of energy loss
relative
religion
resting expiratory level

rel
related
relation
relative

RELE
resistive excrcises, lower extremities

reliq.
remainder [L. *reliquus*]

REM
radiation-equivalent-man
rapid eye movement (sleep)
recent event memory
reticular erythematous mucinosis
return electrode monitor
roentgen-equivalent-man *also* rem

Rem
removal *also* rem

rem
radiation equivalent in man
removal *also* Rem
roentgen-equivalent-man *also* REM

REMA
repetitive excess mixed anhydride (method)

REMAB
radiation-equivalent-manikin absorption

REMCAL
radiation-equivalent-manikin calibration

REMP
roentgen-equivalent-man period

REMS
rapid eye movement sleep *also* REM

REN, ren
renal *also* RN

ren. sem.
renew only once [L. *renovetum semel*]

REO
Receptive-Expressive Observation Scale
respiratory enteric orphan (virus)

REP
reactive eosinophilic pleuritis
repeat *also* rept
report *also* rep, rept
rest-exercise program
retrograde pyelogram *also* RP
roentgen equivalent-physical *also* rep
(surgical) repair

rep
replication
report *also* REP, rept
roentgen equivalent-physical *also* REP

rep.
let it be repeated [L. *repetatur*]

rep B&S
repetitive bending and stooping

REPC
reticuloendothelial phagocytic capacity

repet
to be repeated [L. *repetatur*]

repol
repolarization

Rep-PCR
repetitive PCR

reprep
repreparation

REPS
reactive extensor postural synergy
repetitions

rept
repeat *also* REP
report *also* REP, rep

req
requested
required

REQF
wrong test requested-floor error

RER
renal excretion rate
respiratory exchange ratio *also* R, R_E
rough endoplasmic reticulum

RES
(electrical) resistance *also* R
radionuclide esophageal scintigraphy
recurrent erosion syndrome
resection
resident
reticuloendothelial system

Res
research *also* res

res
research *also* Res
reserve
residence
resident
residue

RESC, resc
resuscitation *also* resus

RESCUE
Randomized Evaluation of Salvage Angioplasty with Combined Utilization of Endpoints

resist. ex.
resistive exercise

Resp
respectively *also* resp
respiration *also* R, resp
respiratory *also* R, resp

resp
respective *also* Resp
respectively *also* Resp
respiration *also* R, Resp
respiratory *also* R, Resp
response *also* R
responsible

RESP-A
respiratory battery, acute

NOTES

REST
Raynaud (phenomenon), esophageal (motor dysfunction), sclerodactyly, and telangiectasia (syndrome)
regressive electric shock therapy
restoration
reticulospinal tract

resus
resuscitation *also* RESC, resc

RET
rational-emotive therapy
retention
reticulocyte *also* R, RETIC
retina
retired *also* ret
return
right esotropia

ret
rad equivalent therapeutic
retired *also* RET

RETC
rat embryo tissue culture

ret cath
retention catheter *also* RC

RETIC
reticulocyte *also* R, RET

Retro Pyelo
retrograde pyelogram *also* REP, RP

RETUL
reticulum cell

REUE
resistive exercises to upper extremities

REUS
rectal endoscopic ultrasonography

REV, rev
reticuloendotheliosis virus
reversal
reverse *also* R
review *also* R
revolution *also* rev

REVL
to be reviewed by laboratory (pathologist)

rev/min
revolution per minute

Rev of Sym
review of symptoms

Rev of Sys
review of systems

re-x
reexamination

RF
radial fiber (of cochlea)
radiofrequency *also* rf
rate of flow (chromatography) *also* R_F
receptive field (of visual cortex)
recognition factor
reflecting (platelet)
regurgitant fraction
Reitland-Franklin (unit)
relative flow
relative fluorescence
release factor
releasing factor
renal failure
replicative form
resistance factor
resorcinol formaldehyde
respiratory failure
respiratory frequency *also* Rf
retardation factor *also* Rf
reticular formation
retroflexed
retroperitoneal fibromatosis
rheumatic fever
rheumatoid factor
riboflavin
Riga-Fede (syndrome)
risk factor
root (canal) filling
rosette formation
Rundles-Falls (syndrome)

R&F
radiographic and fluoroscopic

R_F
rate of flow *also* RF

Rf
respiratory frequency *also* RF
retardation factor *also* RF
rutherfordium

rf
radiofrequency *also* RF

RFA
radiofrequency ablation
right femoral artery
right forearm
right frontoanterior (fetal position)

RFB
retained foreign body
rheumatoid factor binding

RFb
respiratory feedback

RFC
radiofrequency current
retrograde femoral catheter
right frontal craniotomy
rosette-forming cell

RFCA
radiofrequency catheter ablation

RFE
relative fluorescence efficiency
return flow enema

RFFIT
rapid fluorescent focus inhibition test

RFI
recurrence-free interval
renal failure index

RFL
right frontolateral (fetal position)

RFLA
rheumatoid factor-like activity

RFLC
resistant Friend leukemia cell

RFLP
restriction fragment length
polymorphism *also* RLP

RFLS
rheumatoid factor-like substance

RFM, Rfm
rifampin

RFOL
results to follow

RFP
request for payment
request for proposal
right frontoposterior (fetal position)

RFR
rapid filling rate
refraction

RFS
rapid frozen section

relapse-free survival
renal function study

RFT
right fibrous trigone
right frontotransverse (fetal position)
rod-and-frame test
routine fever therapy

RFTB
riboflavin tetrabutyrate

RFTSW
right foot switch

RFV
right femoral vein

RFW
rapid filling wave

RG
retrograde
right gluteal

R/G
red/green

Rg
Rodgers antibody

RGAS
retained gastric antrum syndrome

RGBMT
renal glomerular basement membrane
thickness

RGC
radio-gas chromatography
remnant gastric cancer
retinal ganglion cell
right giant cell

RGD
range-gated Doppler

RGE
relative gas expansion
respiratory gas equation

RGH
rat growth hormone

RGM
right gluteus maximus

R

NOTES

rGM-CSF
recombinant human granulocyte-macrophage colony-stimulating factor *also* rhGM-CSF

RGMT
reciprocal geometric mean titer

RGN
Registered General Nurse

RGO
reciprocating gait orthosis

RGP
retrograde pyelogram
rigid gas-permeable (contact lens)
rural general practitioner

RGR
relative growth rate

RGT
reversed gastric tube

RH
radial hemolysis
radiant heat
radiologic health
reactive hyperemia
recurrent herpes
reduced haloperidol
regional heparinization
regulatory hormone
relative humidity
releasing hormone
rest home
retinal hemorrhage
rheumatoid
Richner-Hanhart (syndrome)
right hand
right hemisphere
right hyperphoria
room humidifier

Rh
Rhesus (blood factor)
rhinion (craniometric point)
rhodium
rhonchi *also* rh

Rh+
Rhesus positive

Rh−
Rhesus negative

rh
rheuma *also* rheum
rheumatic *also* rheum
rhonchi *also* Rh

r/h
roentgen per hour

RHA
right hepatic artery

RhA
rheumatoid arthritis

Rha.
l-rhamnose

Rh agglut
rheumatoid agglutinins *also* RA

RHAMM
receptor for hyaluronan-mediated motility

RHB
raise head of bed
right heart bypass

rHBcAg
recombinant HBcAg

RHBF
reactive hyperemia blood flow

RHBV
right heart blood volume

RHC
resin hemoperfusion column
respiration has ceased
right heart catheterization
right hemicolectomy
right hypochondrium

RHD
radial head dislocation
radiant heat device
radiologic health data
relative hepatic dullness
renal hypertensive disease
rheumatic heart disease *also* rheu ht dis
round heart disease

RhD
Rhesus (hemolytic) disease

RHE
respiratory heat exchange
retinohepatoendocrinologic (syndrome)

RHEED
reflection high-energy electron diffraction

rheo
rheostat

rh-EPO
recombinant human erythropoietin

R

rheu ht dis
rheumatic heart disease *also* RHD

rheum
rheuma *also* rh
rheumatic *also* rh

RHF
right heart failure

RHG
radial hemolysis in gel
relative hemoglobin
right hand grip

rhG-CSF
recombinant human granulocyte
colony-stimulating factor

rhGH
recombinant human growth hormone

rhGM-CSF
recombinant human granulocyte-
macrophage colony-stimulating factor
also rGM-CSF

RHH
right homonymous hemianopia

Rhi
rhinology *also* Rhin

RhIG
Rhesus immune globulin

RhIGIV
Rh immune globulin intravenous

rhIL
recombinant human interleukin

Rhin
rhinologist
rhinology *also* Rhi

rhin
rhinitis

rhino
rhinoplasty

r-hirudin
recombinant hirudin

RHL
recurrent herpes labialis
right hemisphere lesion
right hepatic lobe

RHLN
right hilar lymph node

rhm
roentgen per hour at one meter

rhMCAF
human macrophage-monocyte
chemotactic and activating factor

rHM-CSF
recombinant human macrophage
colony-stimulating factor

rHm EPO
recombinant human erythropoietin

RhMK, RhMk, RhMkK
Rhesus monkey kidney *also* RMK

RHMV
right heart mixing volume

RHN
Rockwell hardness number

Rh neg
Rhesus factor negative

Rh$_{null}$
Rhesus factor null (all Rh factors
are lacking)

ρ
electrical resistivity
electric charge density
mass density
population correlation coefficient
reactivity
rho (17th letter of Greek alphabet),
lowercase

RHO
right heeloff

RHOCS
right-handed orthogonal coordinate
system

rhom
rhomboid (muscle)

RHP
right hemiparesis
right hemiplegia

RHPA
reverse hemolytic plaque assay

NOTES

RHR
  resting heart rate

r/hr
  roentgens per hour

RHS
  Ramsay Hunt syndrome
  reciprocal hindlimb-scratching
    (syndrome)
  right hand side
  right heel strike
  rough hard sphere

RHT
  renal homotransplantation
  right hypertropia

RHU
  Registered Health Underwriter
  rheumatology

RHV
  right hepatic vein

RHW
  radiant heat warmer

RI
  input resistor
  radiation intensity
  radioimmunology
  radioisotope
  recession index
  recombinant inbred (strain)
  refractive index *also* ref ind, n
  regenerative index
  regional ileitis
  regular insulin
  relative intensity
  release inhibition
  remission induced
  remission induction
  renal insufficiency
  replicative intermediate
  resistance index
  respiratory illness
  respiratory index
  reticulocyte index
  retroactive inhibition
  retroactive interference
  rhythmic initiation
  ribosome
  right iliac (crest)
  rooming in
  rosette inhibition

R/I
  rule in

RIA
  radioimmunoassay
  reversible ischemic attack
  right iliac artery

RIA-DA
  radioimmunoassay double antibody
    (test)

RIAST
  Reitan Indiana Aphasic Screening
    Test

RIAT
  radioimmune antiglobulin test

Rib
  ribose *also* R, r

RIBA
  recombinant immunoblot assay

RIBS
  rutherford ion backscattering

RIC
  renomedullary interstitial cell
  right iliac crest
  right internal capsule
  right internal carotid

RICA
  reverse immune cytoadhesion
  right internal carotid artery

RICE
  rest, ice, compression, and elevation

RICM
  right intercostal margin

RICS
  right intercostal space

RICU
  respiratory intensive care unit

RID
  radial immunodiffusion
  radioimmunodetection *also* RAID
  radioimmunodiffusion
  remission-inducing drug
  remove intoxicated driver
  right (ventricular) internal diameter
  ruptured intervertebral disk

RIDCSF
  radial immunodiffusion cerebrospinal
    fluid

RIE, RIEP
  rocket immunoelectrophoresis

RIF
  release-inhibiting factor

resistance-inducing factor
rifampin
right iliac fossa
right index finger
rigid internal fixation
rosette inhibitory factor

RIFA
radioiodinated fatty acid

RIFC
rat intrinsic factor concentrate

rIFN-A, rIFN-a
recombinant interferon alpha

rIFN-gamma
recombinant interferon gamma

RIG
rabies immune globulin

RIGH
rabies immune globulin, human

RIGS
radioimmunoguided surgery

RIH
right inguinal hernia

RIHSA
radioactive iodinated human serum
albumin

RIJ
right internal jugular (vein or
catheter)

rIL-2
recombinant interleukin-2

RILT
rabbit ileal loop test

RIM
radioisotope medicine
recurrent induced malaria
relative-intensity measure

RIMA
right internal mammary anastomosis
right internal mammary artery

RIMS
resonance ionization mass
spectrometry

RIN
rat insulinoma

RINB
Reitan-Indiana Neuropsychological
Battery

RIND
resolving ischemic neurologic deficit
reversible ischemic neurologic deficit
reversible ischemic neurologic
disability

RINN
recommended international
nonproprietary name

RIO
right inferior oblique (muscle)

RIOJ
recurrent intrahepatic obstructive
jaundice

RIP
radioimmunoprecipitation (test)
rapid infusion pump
reflex-inhibiting pattern
respiratory inductance plethysmography
respiratory inversion point

RIPA
radioimmunoprecipitation assay

RIR
right iliac region
right inferior rectus

RIRB
radioiodinated rose bengal (dye)

RIS
radiographic imaging system
radioimmunoglobulin scintigraphy
rapid immunofluorescence staining
resonance ionization spectroscopy

RISA
radioactive iodinated serum albumin
radioimmunosorbent assay
radioiodinated serum albumin

RISE
rifampin-isoniazid-streptomycin-
ethambutol

RIST
radioimmunosorbent test

RIT
radioimmunoglobulin therapy

NOTES

RIT *(continued)*
radioiodinated triolein
Rorschach Inkblot Test *also* Ror
rosette inhibition titer

RITA
Randomized Intervention in the
Treatment of Angina
right internal thoracic artery

RITC
rhodamine isothiocyanate
rhodamine isothiocyanate conjugated

RIU
radioactive iodine uptake *also* RAIU

RIV
ramus interventricularis
right innominate vein

RIVC
radionuclide (imaging of) inferior
vena cava
right inferior vena cava

RIVD
ruptured intervertebral disk

RIVS
ruptured interventricular septum

RJ
radial jerk (reflex)

RJA
regurgitant jet area

RJI
radionuclide joint imaging

RJS
reduced joint survey

RK
rabbit kidney
radial keratotomy
right kidney

RKG
radio(electro)cardiogram

RKH
Rokitansky-Kuster-Hauser (syndrome)

RKID
right kidney (urine sample)

RKS
renal kidney stone
retrograde kidney study

RKV
rabbit kidney vacuolating (virus)

RKW
renal kalium (potassium) wasting

RKY
roentgen kymography

R L, R-L, R→L, R/L
right to left (shunt)

RL
coarse rales
radiation laboratory
reduction level
resistive load
reticular lamina
right lateral *also* R LAT, R Lat, RT
LAT, rt lat
right leg
right lower
right lung
Ringer lactate (solution) *also* RLS

RL$_3$
numerous coarse rales

R$_L$
pulmonary resistance *also* R$_L$R$_P$

Rl
medium rales

Rl$_2$
moderate number of medium rales

rl
fine rales

rl$_1$
few fine rales

RLA
radiographic lung area

R LAT, R Lat
right lateral *also* RL

RLBCD
right lower border of cardiac
dullness

RLC
rectus and longus capitus
residual lung capacity
rhodopsin-lipid complex

RLD
related living donor
resistive load detection
right lateral decubitus (position)
ruptured lumbar disk

RLE
recent life events
right lower extremity

RLF
    retained lung fluid
    retrolental fibroplasia
    right lateral femoral

RLL
    right liver lobe
    right lower limb
    right lower lobe

RLMD
    rat liver mitochondria (and
    submitochondrial particles derived
    by) digitonin (treatment)

RLN
    recurrent laryngeal nerve
    regional lymph node

RLNC
    regional lymph node cell

RLND
    regional lymph node dissection
    retroperitoneal lymph node dissection

RLO
    residual lymphocyte output

RLP
    radiation leukemia protection
    restriction fragment length
    polymorphism *also* RFLP
    ribosome-like particle

RLQ
    right lower quadrant

RLR
    right lateral rectus (muscle)

$R_L R_P$
    pulmonary resistance

RLS
    person who stammers having
    difficulty in enunciating R, L, and
    S
    rat lung strip
    Reaction Level Scale
    restless leg syndrome
    Ringer lactate solution *also* RL
    Roussy-Levy syndrome

RLSB
    right lower scapular border
    right lower sternal border

rl-sh
    right-left shunt

RLT
    reduced liver transplant
    right lateral thigh

RLTCS
    repeat low transverse cesarean section

RLV
    Rauscher leukemia virus

RLWD
    routine laboratory work done

RLX
    right lower extremity

RM
    radical mastectomy
    random migration
    range of movement
    red marrow
    reference material
    regional myocardial
    rehabilitation medicine
    repetition maximum
    resistive movement
    respiratory metabolism
    respiratory movement
    Riehl melanosis
    right median
    risk management
    room
    Rosenthal-Melkersson (syndrome)
    Rothmann-Makai (syndrome)
    ruptured membranes

1-RM
    one-repetition maximum

R&M
    routine and microscopic

Rm
    relative mobility
    remission

rm
    room

RMA
    Registered Medical Assistant
    relative medullary area (of kidney)
    right mentoanterior (fetal position)

R

NOTES

RMB
right main-stem bronchus

RMBF
regional myocardial blood flow

RMC
right middle cerebral (artery) *also* RMCA

RMCA
right main coronary artery
right middle cerebral artery *also* RMC

RMCAT
right middle cerebral artery thrombosis

RMCL
right midclavicular line

RMCP
rat mast cell protease

RMCT
rat mast cell technique

RMD
rapid movement disorder
ratio of midsagittal diameter
retromanubrial dullness
right manubrial dullness

RME
rapid maxillary expansion
resting metabolic expenditure
right mediolateral episiotomy *also* RMLE

RMEE
right middle ear exploration

RMF
right middle finger

RMI
Reading Miscue Inventory

RMK
Rhesus monkey kidney *also* RhMK, RhMk, RhMkK

RML
radiation myeloid leukemia
right mediolateral
right mentolateral
right middle lobe (of lung)

RMLB
right middle lobe bronchus

RMLE
right mediolateral episiotomy *also* RME

RMLS
right middle lobe syndrome

RMLV
Rauscher murine leukemia virus *also* RMuLV

RMM
rapid micromedia method

RMO
Resident Medical Officer

RMP
rapidly miscible pool
resting membrane potential
rifampin
right mentoposterior (fetal position)

RMR
resting metabolic rate
right medial rectus (muscle)

RMS
rectal morphine sulfate (suppository)
repetitive motion syndrome
respiratory muscle strength
rhabdomyosarcoma *also* RD
rheumatic mitral stenosis
rigid man syndrome
root-mean-square *also* rms

rms
root-mean-square *also* RMS

RMSD
root-mean-square deviation

RMSE
root-mean-square error

RMSF
Rocky Mountain spotted fever

RMT
Registered Music Therapist
relative medullary thickness
retromolar trigone
right mentotransverse (fetal position)

RMUI
relief medication unit index

rMu IL-6
murine interleukin-6

RMuLV
Rauscher murine leukemia virus *also* RMLV

RMV
respiratory minute volume

RN
radionucleotide (scanning)

radionuclide
red nucleus
reflex nephropathy
Registered Nurse
renal (disease) *also* REN, ren
reticular nucleus

Rn
radon

²²²Rn
radon-222

RNA
radionuclide angiography *also* RA
Registered Nurse Anesthetist
ribonucleic acid
rough, noncapsulated, avirulent
(bacterial culture)

RNAA
radiochemical neutron activation
analysis

RNASe, RNase
ribonuclease

RNase D
ribonuclease D

RNase P
ribonuclease P

RND
radical neck dissection
reactive neurotic depression

RNEF
resting (radio)nuclide ejection fraction

RNFL
retinal nerve fiber layer

RNG
radionuclide angiography

RNICU
regional neonatal intensive care unit

RNL
renal laboratory profile

RNMT
Registered Nuclear Medicine
Technologist

RNP
Registered Nurse Practitioner
ribonucleoprotein

RNR
ribonucleotide reductase

RNS
reference normal serum

RNSC
radionuclide superior cavography

RNST
reactive nonstress test

RNT
radioassayable neurotensin

Rnt
roentgenology *also* roent

RNTC
rat nephroma tissue culture

RNV
radionuclide venography
radionuclide ventriculography *also*
RNVG

RNVG
radionuclide ventriculography *also*
RNV

RO
reality orientation
relative odds
reverse osmosis
Ritter-Oleson (technique)
routine order
rule out *also* R/O

R/O
rule out *also* RO

R₀
resting radium

ROA
reversal of antagonist
right occipitoanterior (fetal position)

ROAC
repeated oral (doses of) activated
charcoal

ROAD
reversible obstructive airway disease

ROAM
roaming optical access multiscope

ROATS
rabbit ovarian antitumor serum

NOTES

rob.
robertsonian (translocation)

ROC
receiver operating characteristic
relative operating characteristic
resident on call
residual organic carbon

roc
reciprocal ohm centimeter

ROCFT
Rey-Estreich Complex Figure Test

Roch-Ochs
Rochester-Ochsner

ROCKET
Regionally Organized Cardiac Key
European Trial

RODAC
replicate organism detection and
counting

ROE
return on equity
roentgen *also* R, r, roent

roent
roentgen *also* R, r, ROE
roentgenologist
roentgenology *also* Rnt

ROH
rat ovarian hyperemia (test)

ROI
region of interest

ROIDS
hemorrhoids

ROIH
right oblique inguinal hernia

ROJM
range of joint motion

ROL
right occipitolateral (fetal position)

ROM
range of motion
range of movement
read-only memory
right otitis media
rupture of membranes

Rom, Romb
Romberg (sign)

rom
reciprocal ohm meter

ROM C P
range of motion complete and pain-
free

ROMI
rule out myocardial infarction

ROMSA
right otitis media, suppurative, acute

ROMSC
right otitis media, suppurative,
chronic

ROM WNL
range of motion within normal limits

ROP
retinopathy of prematurity
right occipitoposterior (fetal position)

ROPE
respiratory ordered phase encoding

Ror
Rorschach (Inkblot Test) *also* RIT

ROS
reactive oxygen species
review of symptoms *also* RS
review of systems *also* RS
rod outer segment

RoS
rostral sulcus

ROSC
restoration of spontaneous circulation

ROSS
review of signs and symptoms
review of subjective symptoms
review other subjective symptoms

ROT
real oxygen transport
remedial occupational therapy
right occipitotransverse (fetal position)
rotating *also* Rot, rot.
rotator
rule of thumb

Rot, rot.
rotating *also* Rot, rot.
rotation *also* ROT

rot. ny
rotatory nystagmus

ROU
recurrent oral ulcer

rout.
routine

ROW
rat ovarian weight
Rendu-Osler-Weber (syndrome)

ROWPVT
Receptive One-Word Picture
Vocabulary Test

RP
radial pulse
radiographic planimetry
radiopharmaceutical
rapid processing (of film)
Raynaud phenomenon
reaction product
reactive protein
readiness potential
rectal prolapse
reentrant pathway
refractory period
Registered Pharmacist
regulatory protein
relapsing polychondritis
relative potency
respiratory rate:pulse rate (index)
resting potential
resting pressure
restorative proctocolectomy
rest pain
retinitis pigmentosa
retinitis proliferans *also* R Pr
retrograde pyelogram *also* REP
retroperitoneal
reverse phase
rheumatoid polyarthritis
ribose phosphate

R_p
pulmonary resistance

RPA
radial photon absorptiometry
restenosis postangioplasty
resultant physiologic acceleration
reverse passive anaphylaxis
right pulmonary artery

RPAW
right pulmonary artery withdrawal

rPBF
regional pulmonary blood flow

RPC
recurrent pyogenic cholangiohepatitis
relapsing polychondritis
relative proliferative capacity

RPCF, RPCFT
Reiter protein complement-fixation
(test)

RPCGN
rapidly progressive crescenting
glomerulonephritis

RPCV
retropubic cytourethropexy

RPD
removable partial denture

RPE
rate of perceived exertion
recurrent pulmonary emboli
retinal pigment epithelium

RPF
relaxed pelvic floor
renal plasma flow
retroperitoneal fibrosis

rPF4
recombinant platelet factor-4

RPF^a
arterial renal plasma flow

RPF^v
venous renal plasma flow

RPG
radiation protection guide
retrograde percutaneous gastrostomy
retrograde pyelogram
rheoplethysmography

RPGG
retroplacental gamma globulin

RPGN
rapidly progressive glomerulonephritis

RPH
retroperitoneal hemorrhage

RPh
Registered Pharmacist

RPHA
reversed passive hemagglutination

NOTES

R

RPHAMCFA
reversed passive hemagglutination by miniature centrifugal fast analysis

RP-HPLC
reversed phase high-performance liquid chromatography

RPI
resting pressure index
reticulocyte production index

RPICA
right posterior internal carotid artery

RPICCE
round pupil intracapsular cataract extraction

RPIPP
reversed phase ion-pair partition

RPL, RPLAD
retroperitoneal lymphadenectomy

RPLC
reversed-phase liquid chromatography

RPLD
repair of potentially lethal damage

RPLND
retroperitoneal lymph node dissection
retroperitoneal pelvic lymph node dissection

RPM, rpm
radical pair mechanism
rapid processing mode
revolutions per minute

RPMD
rheumatic pain modulation disorder

RPN
renal papillary necrosis
resident's progress note

RPND
retroperitoneal (lymph) node dissection

RPO
right posterior oblique (radiologic view)

RPP
(heart)rate-(systolic blood) pressure product
radical perineal prostatectomy
retropubic prostatectomy

RPPC
regional pediatric pulmonary center

RPPI
role perception picture inventory

RPPR
red (cell) precursor production rate

RPR
rapid plasma reagent (test)
rapid plasma reagin
Reiter protein reagin

R Pr
retinitis proliferans *also* RP

RPRCF
rapid plasma reagin complement fixation

RPRCT
rapid plasma reagin card test

RPS, rps
renal pressor substance
revolutions per second

RPT
rapid pullthrough
refractory period of transmission
Registered Physical Therapist

rpt
repeat
report

RPTA
renal percutaneous transluminal angioplasty

Rptd
ruptured

RPU
retropubic urethropexy

RPV
right portal vein
right pulmonary vein

RPVP
right posterior ventricular pre-excitation

RQ
reading quotient *also* RdQ
recovery quotient
respiratory quotient

RQS
repeated quick stretch

RQS-E
repeated quick stretch from elongation

RQS-SEC
    repeated quick stretch superimposed upon an existing contraction

RR
    radial rate
    radiation reaction
    radiation response
    rapid radiometric
    rate ratio
    reading retarded
    recovery room
    red reflex
    regular rate
    regular respiration
    relative response
    relative risk
    renin release
    respiratory rate
    respiratory reserve
    response rate
    retinal reflex
    rheumatoid rosette
    right rotation
    risk ratio
    Riva-Rocci (sphygmomanometer) *also* RRS
    road rash
    roentgenographic pelvimetry
    ruthenium red

R/R
    rales/rhonchi

R&R
    rate and rhythm
    recent and remote
    recession and resection
    rest and recuperation

RRA
    radioreceptor activity
    radioreceptor assay
    Registered Record Administrator
    right radial artery
    right renal artery

RRAM
    rapid rhythmic alternating movements
    relative response attributable to the maneuver

RRC
    residency review committee

    risk reduction component
    routine respiratory care

RRCT no (m)
    regular rate, clear tones, no murmurs

RRD
    rhegmatogenous retinal detachment

RRE
    radiation-related eosinophilia
    regressive resistive exercise
    round, regular, and equal (pupils) *also* RR&E

RR&E
    round, regular, and equal (pupils) *also* RRE

RREF
    resting radionuclide ejection fraction

RREID
    rapid rabies enzyme immunodiagnosis

RRF
    residual renal function
    right rectus femoris

RR-HPO
    rapid recompression-high pressure oxygen

RRI
    reflex relaxation index
    relative response index
    renal resistive index

rRNA
    ribosomal ribonucleic acid

RRND
    right radical neck dissection

RROM
    resistive range of motion

RRP
    radical retropubic prostatectomy
    relative refractory period

RRpm
    respiratory rate per minute

RRQG
    right rostral quarter ganglion

RRR
    regular rate and rhythm *also* R&R
    renin-release rate

NOTES

RRR *(continued)*
renin-release ratio
risk rescue rating

RRRN
round, regular, react normally (pupils)

RRS
retrorectal space
Richards-Rundle syndrome
Riva-Rocci sphygmomanometer *also* RR

RRT
randomized response technique
Registered Respiratory Therapist
relative retention time
resazurin reduction time

RRU
respiratory resistance unit

RRV
Rhesus rotavirus
right renal vein

RRVN
retrolabyrinthine/retrosigmoid vestibular neurectomy

RRVO
repair relaxed vaginal outlet

RS
random sample
rapid smoking
rating schedule
Raynaud syndrome
reading of standard
recipient's serum
rectal sinus
rectosigmoid
Reed-Sternberg (cell) *also* R-S
rehydrating solution
reinforcing stimulus
Reiter syndrome
relative survival
remnant stomach
renal specialist
Repression-Sensitization (Scale)
reproductive success
resolved sarcoidosis
resorcinol-sulfur
respiratory syncytial (virus)
respiratory system
response to stimulus (ratio)
reticulated siderocyte *also* R-S
Rett syndrome
review of symptoms *also* ROS
review of systems *also* ROS

Reye syndrome
rhythm strip
right sacrum
right septum
right side
right stellate (ganglion)
right subclavian
Ringer solution
Ritchie sedimentation
Roberts syndrome

R-S
Reed-Sternberg (cell) *also* RS
reticulated siderocyte *also* RS
rough-smooth (variation)

R/S
rest stress
rupture spontaneous

R&S
restraint and seclusion

R/s
roentgen per second

Rs
respond
response
(total) systemic resistance

r_s
rank correlation coefficient

RSA
rabbit serum albumin *also* RbSA
rat serum albumin
recurrent spontaneous abortion
regular spiking activity
relative specific activity
relative standard accuracy
respiratory sinus arrhythmia
reticulum (cell) sarcoma *also* RCS
right sacroanterior (fetal position)
right sacrum anterior
right subclavian artery

Rsa
(total) systemic arterial resistance

RSB
reticulocyte standard buffer
right sternal border

RSBT
rhythmic sensory bombardment therapy

RSC
rat spleen cell
rested state contraction

reversible sickle cell
right side colon (cancer)

RScA
right scapuloanterior (fetal position)

RSCN
Registered Sick Children's Nurse

RScP
right scapuloposterior (fetal position)

RSCT
Rach Sentence Completion Test
Rotter Sentence Completion Test

rscu-PA
recombinant, single-chain, urokinase-
type plasminogen activator

RSD
reflex sympathetic dystrophy
relative sagittal depth
relative standard deviation

RSDS
reflex sympathetic dystrophy
syndrome

RSE
rat synaptic ending
reverse sutured eye
right sternal edge

RSEP
right somatosensory evoked potential

RSES
Rosenberg Self-Esteem Scale

RSF
raw soybean flour

RSG
Reitan Strength of Grip

RSG/IAC
retrosigmoid/internal auditory canal

RSI
rapid sequence induction
repetition strain injury

R-SICU
respiratory-surgical intensive care unit

RSIVP
rapid-sequence intravenous
pyelography

RSL
right sacrolateral (fetal position)

R SL brace
right short leg brace

RSLD
repair of sublethal damage

RSLR
reverse straight leg raise

RSM
risk-screening model

RSMR
relative standardized mortality ratio

RSN
right substantia nigra

RSO
Resident Surgical Officer
right salpingo-oophorectomy
right superior oblique (muscle)

RSP
rapid straight pacing
rat serum protein
recirculating single pass
removable silicone plug
rhinoseptoplasty
right sacroposterior (fetal position)

RSPK
recurrent spontaneous psychokinesis

RSR
rectosphincteric reflex
regular sinus rhythm
relative survival rate
response-stimulus ratio
right superior rectus (muscle)

RSS
rat stomach strip
rectosigmoidoscope
repetitive stress syndrome
Russell-Silver syndrome
Russian spring-summer (encephalitis)
also RSSE

RSSE
Russian spring-summer encephalitis
also RSS

RSSR
relatively slow sinus rate

R

NOTES

RST
radiosensitivity test
rapid surfactant test
reagin screen test
right sacrotransverse (fetal position)
rubrospinal tract

RSTL
relaxed skin tension line

RSTS
retropharyngeal soft tissue space

RSTs
Rodney Smith tubes

RSV
respiratory syncytial virus
right subclavian vein
Rous sarcoma virus

RSVC
right superior vena cava

RSV-IGIV
Rous sarcoma virus immunoglobulin
  intravenous

RSW
right-sided weakness

RT
rabbit trachea
radiation therapy *also* RXT, XRT
Radiologic Technologist
Radiologic technology
radiotelemetry
radiotherapy *also* Rad, RADIO, Rad
  Ther, Rx
radium therapy
random transfusion
raphe transection
reaction time
reading task
reading test
reading time
receptor transforming
reciprocating tachycardia
recreational therapy
rectal temperature *also* R/T
red tetrazolium
reduction time
Registered Technologist
relaxation time
renal transplant
repetition time
Reporter's Test
reptilase time
resistance transfer
respiratory technology

Respiratory Therapist
Respiratory therapy
rest tremor
retransformation
reverse transcriptase
right *also* R, (R), Rt, rt
right thigh
right triceps
room temperature *also* rt
Rubinstein-Taybi (syndrome)
running total

R/T
rectal temperature *also* RT
related to *also* R/t

RT$_3$
(serum) resin triiodothyronine (uptake)
  also RT$_3$U

RT$_4$
resin thyroxin

R$_T$
total pulmonary resistance

Rt
right *also* R, (R), RT, Rt

R/t
related to *also* R/T

rT
ribothymidine

rT$_3$
reverse triiodothyronine

rt
right *also* (R), RT, Rt, rt
room temperature *also* RT

RTA
renal tubular acidosis
renal tubular antigen
road traffic accident

RTA-I
renal tubular acidosis I

RT(ARRT)
Registered Technologist (certified by)
  American Registry of Radiologic
  Technologists

RTAS
radiology telephone access system

RTB
return to baseline

RTC
(a)round the clock
randomized trial, controlled

renal tubular cell
research and training center
residential treatment center
return to clinic

RTD
repetitive trauma disorder
resubmission turnaround document
routine test dilution

Rtd
retarded
retired

RTE
rabbit thymus extract

RTECS
Registry of Toxic Effects of
Chemical Substances

RTER
return to emergency room

RTF
replication and transfer
resistance transfer factor
respiratory tract fluid
return to flow

RTFNA
real-time fine-needle aspiration

RtH
right-handed

RTI
respiratory tract infection

Rti
tissue resistance

RTK
rhabdoid tumor of the kidney

RTKP
radiothermokeratoplasty

RTL
reactive to light (pupils)

rtl
rectal

RT LAT, rt lat
right lateral *also* RL, RT LAT, rt lat

RTLX
real-time, low-intensity x-ray

RTM
routine medical care

R$_{tmf}$
total matrix formation rate

rTMP
ribothymidylic acid *also* TMP

RTN
renal tubular necrosis
routine

RT(N)
Registered Technologist in Nuclear
Medicine

rtn
return

RT(N)(AART)
Registered Technologist in Nuclear
Medicine (certified by) American
Registry of Radiologic Technologists

rTNM
retreatment (staging of cancer)

RTO
return to office
right toe off

RTOG
Radiation Therapy Oncology Group

RTP
renal transplant patient
reverse transcriptase-producing (agent)

RTPA, rt PA, rtPA, rt-PA
recombinant tissue-type plasminogen
activator

RT-PCR
reverse transcriptase-polymerase chain
reaction

RTPS
radiation therapy planning system

RTR
Recreational Therapist, Registered
red (blood cell) turnover rate
retention time ratio
return to room

NOTES

RT(R)(ARRT)
Registered Technologist in Radiography (certified by) American Registry of Radiologic Technologists

RTRR
return to recovery room

RTS
real-time scan
relative tumor size
return to sender
right toe strike
Rubinstein-Taybi syndrome

rTSAB
rodent thyroid-stimulating antibody

rt scap bord
right scapular border

r$_{tt}$
obtained coefficient
reliability coefficient

RT(T)(AART)
Radiologic Technologist in Radiation Therapy (certified by) American Registry of Radiologic Technologists

RTU
ready to use
real-time ultrasonography *also* RTUS
relative time unit

RT$_3$U
resin triiodothyronine uptake *also* RT$_3$

rTU
ribosomal ribonucleic acid transcription unit

RTUS
real-time ultrasonography *also* RTU

RTV
room temperature vulcanization
room temperature vulcanizing

RTW
return to work *also* R/W

RTWD
return to work determination

RTx
radiation therapy

RU
radioactive uptake
radioulnar
rat unit
reading of unknown
rectourethral
recurrent ulcer
residual urine
resin uptake
resistance unit *also* R
retrograde urogram
retroverted uterus
right uninjured
right uninvolved
right upper
rodent ulcer
roentgen unit
routine urinalysis

RU-1
human embryonic lung fibroblast

RU 486
mifepristone

Ru
ruthenium

^{82}Ru
rubidium-82

RUA
routine urine analysis

rub.
red [L. *ruber*] *also* R

RuBP
ribulose bisphophate

RUE
right upper extremity

RUG
resource utilization group
retrograde urethrogram
retrograde urethrography

RUL
right upper (eye)lid
right upper lateral
right upper limb
right upper lobe
right upper lung

RUM
right upper medial

RUO
right ureteral orifice

RUOQ
right upper outer quadrant

RUP
rat urine protein
right upper pole

rupt
ruptured

RUQ
right upper quadrant

RUR
resin uptake ratio

RURTI
recurrent upper respiratory tract
infection

RUS
radioulnar synostosis
recurrent ulcerative stomatitis

RUSB
right upper sternal border

RUSS
recurrent ulcerative scarifying
stomatitis

RUV
residual urine volume

RUX
right upper extremity

RV
random variable
rat virus
Rauscher virus
rectal vault
rectovaginal
reinforcement value
renal venous
reovirus
reserve volume
residual volume
respiratory volume
retinal vasculitis
retrovaginal
retroversion
return visit
rheumatoid vasculitis
rhinovirus
right ventricle
right ventricular
rubella vaccine
rubella virus
Russell viper (time) *also* RVT,
RVVT

R$_v$
radius of view

RVA
rabies vaccine adsorbed
reentrant ventricular arrhythmia
right ventricular activation
right ventricular apex
right ventricular apical
right vertebral artery

RVAD
right ventricular assist device

RVAW
right ventricle anterior wall

RVB
red venous blood

RVC
radioactivity of vegetative cells
respond to verbal command

RVD
relative vertebral density
relative volume decrease
right ventricular dimension
right vertebral density

RVDO
right ventricular diastolic overload

RVDP
right ventricular diastolic pressure

RVDV
right ventricular diastolic volume

RVE
right ventricular enlargement

RVECP
right ventricular endocardial potential

RVEDD
right ventricular end-diastolic diameter

RVEDP
right ventricular end-diastolic pressure

RVEDV
right ventricular end-diastolic volume

RVEF
right ventricular ejection fraction
right ventricular end-flow

NOTES

RVESVI
right ventricular end-systolic volume index

RVET
right ventricular ejection time

RVF
renal vascular failure
Rift Valley fever
right ventricular failure
right ventricular function
right visual field

RVFP
right ventricular filling pressure

RVG
radionuclide ventriculogram
radionuclide ventriculography
relative value guide
right ventrogluteal
right visceral ganglion

RVH
renovascular hypertension
right ventricular hypertrophy

RVHD
rheumatic valvular heart disease

RVI
relative value index
right ventricle infarction

RVID
right ventricular internal dimension

RVIDd
right ventricle internal dimension diastole

RVIDP
right ventricular initial diastolic pressure

RVIT
right ventricular inflow tract (view)

RVL
right vastus lateralis

RVLG
right ventrolateral gluteal

RVN
retrolabyrinthine vestibular neurectomy

RVO
relaxed vaginal outlet
retinal vein occlusion
right ventricular outflow
right ventricular overactivity

RVOT
right ventricular outflow tract

RVP
red veterinary petrolatum
renovascular pressure
resting venous pressure
right ventricular pressure

RVPFR
right ventricular peak filling rate

RVPRA
renal vein plasma renin activity

RVR
rapid ventricular response
reduced vascular response
reduced vestibular response
renal vascular resistance
renal vein renin
repetitive ventricular response
resistance to venous return

RVRA
renal vein renin activity
renal venous renin assay

RV/RA
renal vein/renal activity (ratio)

RVRC
renal vein renin concentration

RV/RF
retroverted/retroflexed

RVRI
renal vascular resistance index

RVS
rabies vaccine, adsorbed
relative value scale
relative value schedule
relative value study
reported visual sensation
retrovaginal space
Rokeach Value Survey (psychologic test)

RVSO
right ventricle stroke output

RVSP
right ventricular systolic pressure

RVSW
right ventricular stroke work

RVSWI
right ventricular stroke work index

RVT
Registered Vascular Technologist

renal vein thrombosis
Russell viper (venom) time *also* RV,
RVVT

RVTE
recurring venous thromboembolism

RV/TLC
residual volume/total lung capacity
(ratio)

RVU
relative value unit

RVV
rubella vaccine-like virus
Russell viper venom

RVVT
Russell viper venom time *also* RV,
RVT

RVWD
right ventricular wall device

R-W
Rideal-Walker (coefficient)

RW
radiologic warfare
ragweed
respiratory work
right (ear), warm (stimulus)
Romano-Ward (syndrome)
round window

R/W
return to work *also* RTW

RWAGE
ragweed antigen E

RWG
rye whole-grain

RWIS
restraint and water immersion stress

RWM
regional wall motion

RWMA
regional wall motion abnormality

RWP
ragweed pollen

R-wave progression
(electrocardiography)

RWS
ragweed sensitivity

RWT
relative wall thickness
R-wave threshold (electrocardiography)

RX
rapid exchange

Rx
drug
medication
pharmacy
prescribe
prescription
prescription drug
radiotherapy *also* Rad, RADIO, Rad
Ther, RT
take [L. *recipe*]
therapy
treatment

r(X)
right X (chromosome)

Rxd
treated

Rx'd US, trx
treated with ultrasound, diathermy,
and traction

RXLI
recessive X-linked ichthyosis

RXN
reaction

Rx Phys
treating physician

RXT
radiation therapy *also* RT
right exotropia

R-Y
Roux-en-Y (anastomosis)

R

NOTES

S

apparent power
area *also* A, a
entropy (in thermodynamics)
exposure time (radiology)
half [L. *semis*] *also* HF, hf, s.,
  sem., semi, ss
label [L. *signa* mark, write on] *also*
  s, sig
left [L. *sinister*] *also* s
mean dose per unit cumulated
  activity
midpoint of sella turcica (point)
relative storage capacity
response to white space
sacral
saline *also* SA, Sa, SAL, sal
same
saturated
saturation (of hemoglobin)
schizophrenia
screen-containing cassette
second *also* s, sec
section *also* s, SEC, sec, sect
sedimentation coefficient
sella (turcica)
semilente (insulin)
senile
senility
sensation *also* s
sensitivity *also* sen, sens
sensory
septum
sequential (analysis)
series *also* s, ser
serine *also* Ser
serum
sick
siderocyte
siemens
sign *also* /S/, /s/, s
signature (prescription) *also* /s/
signed *also* /S/, /s/, s
silicate
single (marital status)
singular
sinus
sister
small *also* Sm, sm
smooth (bacterial colony)
soft
soil
solid

soluble
solute
son
sone (unit of loudness)
space *also* sp
spasm
spatial aptitude (in General Aptitude
  Test Battery)
specific activity *also* SA
spherical (lens) *also* Sph, sph
spleen
sporadic
standard normal deviation
stem (cell)
stimulus *also* R, ST
storage
streptomycin *also* SM, STM
subject
subjective (findings)
substrate
suction
sulcus
sulfur
sum of arithmetic series
supervision
supravergence
surface
surgery *also* SURG, surg
suture
Svedberg (unit of sedimentation
  coefficient)
swine
Swiss (mouse)
symmetrical
sympathetic
synthesis (phase in cell cycle)
systole
without *also* O, ō, s̄, WO, w/o, wo
write, let it be written [L. *signa*]

S/β
sickle cell beta

/S/
sign *also* S, /s/, s
signature (prescription) *also* S, /s/
signed *also* S, s, /s/

^{35}S
sulfur-35

S_1, S_2, S_3, S_4
first to fourth heart sound
suicide risk classification

S₇

summation gallop

/s/

signature (prescription) *also* S, /S/
signed *also* S, /S/

s

atomic orbital with angular
 momentum quantum number zero
distance
label [L. *signa*] *also* S, sig
left [L. *sinister*] *also* S
length of path
sample standard deviation
sample variance *also* s²
satellite (chromosome)
scruple
second *also* S
section *also* S, SEC, sec, sect
sedimentation coefficient
selection coefficient
sensation *also* S
series *also* S, ser
sign *also* S, /S/, /s/
signed *also* S
steady state *also* ss
suckling
without [L. *sine*, Fr. *sans*] *also* ō,
 S, s̄, WO, wo, w/o

s.

half [L. *semis*] *also* HF, hf, S,
 sem., semi, ss

s̄

conductivity *also* cond
cross-section
millisecond *also* msec, ms, σ
population standard deviation
reflection coefficient
standard deviation *also* SD
Stefan-Boltzmann constant
stress
surface tension *also* ST
type of molecular bond
wave number
wavenumber
without *also* O, ō, S, WO, w/o, wo
without spectacles

s²

sample variance *also* s

S1–S5

first to fifth sacral nerves
first to fifth sacral vertebrae

SA

according to art [L. *secundum artem*]

sacroanterior
salicylamide
salicylic acid
saline *also* S, Sa, SAL, sal
salt added
sarcoma *also* sarc
second antibody
secondary amenorrhea
secondary anemia
secondary arrest
self-agglutinating
self-analysis
semen analysis
sensitizing antibody
septal apical
serum albumin *also* SAB
serum aldolase
short acting
sialic acid
sialoadenectomy
siblings (raised) apart
simian adenovirus
sinoatrial (node) *also* SN
sinus arrest
sinus arrhythmia
skeletal age
sleep apnea
slightly active
social acquiescence
soluble in alkaline (medium)
Spanish-American
spatial average
specific activity *also* S
spectrum analysis
sperm abnormality
sperm agglutinin
spiking activity
spinal anesthesia
splenic artery
standard accuracy
Staphylococcus aureus
stimulus artifact
Stokes-Adams (attack, syndrome) *also*
 SAA
subarachnoid
suicide alert
suicide attempt
surface antigen
surface area
surgeon's assistant
surgical assistant
sustained action
sympathetic activity

systemic artery
systemic aspergillosis

S-A
sinoatrial (node) *also* SA, SN
sinoauricular

S/A
same as
sugar and acetone *also* S&A

S&A
sickness and accident (insurance)
sugar and acetone *also* S/A

Sa
most anterior point of anterior
  contour of the sella turcica (point)
saline *also* S, SA, SAL, sal
samarium

sA
statampere

s.a.
by skill [L. *secumdum artem*
  according to art] *also* sec. a.

SAA
same as above
serum amyloid-A
severe aplastic anemia
Stokes-Adams attack *also* SA

SAAG
serum-ascites albumin gradient

SAARD
slow-acting antirheumatic drug

SAAST
self-administered alcohol screening
  test

SAB
serum albumin *also* SA
significant asymptomatic bacteriuria
sinoatrial block
spontaneous abortion
subarachnoid bleed
subarachnoid block

SABP
spontaneous acute bacterial peritonitis

SAC
saccharin
screening and acute care

segmental antigen challenge
serum aminoglycoside concentration
short arm cast
Simpson Coronary AtheroCath *also*
  SCA
space available for the cord
splenic adherent cell
stable access cannula
subarea advisory council
substance abuse counselor

SACC
short arm cylinder cast

sacc
cogwheel respiration [Fr. *saccades* to
  jerk]

SACD
subacute combined degeneration *also*
  SCD

SACE
serum angiotensin-converting enzyme
  (activity)

SACH
small animal care hospital
soft ankle, cushioned heel
  (orthopaedic appliance)
solid ankle, cushion heel (orthopedic
  appliance)

SACHT
serum antichromotrypsin

sac-il
sacroiliac *also* SI

SACS
secondary anticoagulation system

SACSF
subarachnoid cerebrospinal fluid

SACT
sinoatrial conduction time

SAD
Scale of Anxiety and Depression
seasonal affective disorder
Self-Assessment Depression (Scale)
separation anxiety disorder
sinoaortic denervation
small airway dysfunction
social avoidance and distress
source-to-axis distance

NOTES

S

SAD *(continued)*
subacromial decompression
subacute dialysis
sugar and acetone determination
sugar, acetone, diacetic acid (test)
superior axis deviation
suppressor-activating determinant

SADBE
squaric acid dibutylester

SADD
Standardized Assessment of
Depressive Disorders
Students Against Drunk Driving

SADL
simulated activities of daily living

SADQ
Self-Administered Dependency
Questionnaire

SADR
suspected adverse drug reaction

SADS
Schedule for Affective Disorders and
Schizophrenia
Shipman Anxiety Depression Scale

SADS-C
Schedule for Affective Disorders and
Schizophrenia-Change

SADS-L
Schedule for Affective Disorders and
Schizophrenia-Lifetime (Version)

SADT
Stetson Auditory Discrimination Test

SAE
serious adverse event
short above-elbow (cast)
specific action exercise
subcortical atherosclerotic
encephalopathy
supported arm exercise

SAEB
sinoatrial entrance block

SAEKG
signaled average electrocardiogram

SAEP
Salmonella abortus equi pyrogen

SAF
self-articulating femoral (hip
prosthesis)
serum accelerator factor

simultaneous auditory feedback
Spanish-American female

SAFA
soluble antigen fluorescent antibody
(test)

SAFE
sexual assault forensic evidence
simulated aircraft fire and emergency
solid ankle flexible endoskeletal
stationary ankle flexible endoskeleton
stationary attachment flexible
endoskeletal

SAFHS
sonic-accelerated fracture healing
system

SAG
Swiss(-type) agammaglobulinemia

sag
sagittal

Sag D
sagittal diameter

SAGES
Society of American Gastrointestinal
Endoscoping Surgeons

SAGM
sodium chloride, adenine, glucose,
mannitol

SAH
S-adenosyl-L-homocysteine
subarachnoid hemorrhage
systemic arterial hypertension

SAHIOES
Staphylococcus aureus
hyperimmunoglobulinemia E
syndrome

SAHS
sleep apnea-hypersomnolence
syndrome

SAI
Schema Assessment instrument
Self-Analysis Inventory
Sexual Arousability Inventory
Social Adequacy Index
Sodium Amytal interview
systemic active immunotherapy
without other qualification [L. *sine
altera indicatione*]

SAICAR
succinoaminoimidazole carboxamide
(ribonucleotide)

SAID
　　sexually acquired immunodeficiency
　　(syndrome)

SAIDS
　　simian acquired immunodeficiency
　　syndrome

SAL
　　according to the rules of the art [L.
　　secundum artis legis] *also* s.a.l.
　　salbutamol
　　salicylate
　　saline *also* S, SA, Sa, sal
　　Salmonella
　　sensorineural acuity level
　　specified antilymphocytic
　　sterility assurance level
　　suction-assisted lipectomy

SAL 12
　　sequential analysis of twelve
　　chemistry constituents

Sal
　　salicylate *also* sal
　　salicylic *also* sal

s.a.l.
　　according to the rules of the art [L.
　　secundum artis legis] *also* SAL

sal
　　salicylate *also* Sal
　　salicylic *also* Sal
　　saline *also* S, SA, Sa, SAL
　　saliva
　　salt

SALT-P
　　Slosson Articulation Language Test
　　with Phonology

SAM
　　S-adenosyl-*l*-methionine
　　salicylamide
　　scanning acoustic microscope
　　self-administered medication
　　sex arousal mechanism
　　sleep apnea monitor
　　smart anesthesia multigas
　　Spanish-American male
　　structural aluminum malleable
　　subcutaneous augmentation material
　　sulfated acid mucopolysaccharide

　　surface-active material
　　synthetic, adhesive, moisture (vapor
　　permeable)
　　systolic anterior motion (of mitral
　　valve)

SAMF
　　single antibody millipore filtration

SAMI
　　socially acceptable monitoring
　　instrument

SAMO
　　Senior Administrative Medical Officer

sAMP
　　adenylosuccinic acid

S-AMY
　　serum amylase

SAN
　　side-arm nebulizer
　　sinoatrial node
　　sinoauricular node
　　slept all night
　　solitary autonomous nodule

SANA
　　sinoatrial node artery

Sanat
　　sanatorium

SANC
　　short arm navicular cast

SANDR
　　sinoatrial nodal reentry

sang.
　　sanguinous

sanit
　　sanitarium
　　sanitary
　　sanitation

SANS
　　Scale for the Assessment of
　　Negative Symptoms
　　sympathetic autonomic nervous system

SAO
　　small airway obstruction
　　splanchnic artery occlusion

S

NOTES

SaO₂, S$_{A0_2}$
arterial oxygen saturation
oxygen saturation *also* OS, O₂ sat.,
SO₂

SAP
sensory action potential
serum acid phosphatase
serum alkaline phosphatase
serum amyloid P (component)
situs ambiguus with polysplenia
Staphylococcus aureus protease
systemic arterial pressure

sap.
saponification
saponify

SAPA
spatial average-pulse average

SAPD
self-administration of psychotropic
drug

SAPH
saphenous

SAPHO
synovitis-acne-pustulosis-hyperostosis
osteomyelitis

SAPMS
short arm posterior-molded splint

sapon
saponification

SAPP
sodium acid pyrophosphate

SAPS
short arm plaster splint
Simplified Acute Physiology Score
single-action pumping system

SAQ
Seattle angina questionnaire
short-arc quadriceps (test)

SAQC
statistical analysis and quality control

SAR
scaffold-associated regions
seasonal allergic rhinitis
sexual attitude reassessment
sexual attitude restructuring
structure-activity relationship

Sar
sarcosine
sulfarsphenamine

SARA
sexually acquired reactive arthritis
system for anesthetic and respiratory
administration

SARC
seasonal allergic rhinoconjunctivitis

sarc
sarcoma *also* SA

SART
sinoatrial recovery time
Society for Assisted Reproductive
Technology
standard acid reflux test

SAS
saline, agent, and saline
scalenus anticus syndrome
self-rating anxiety scale
short arm splint
Sklar Aphasia Scale
sleep apnea syndrome
small animal surgery
small aorta syndrome
sodium amylosulfate
space-adaptation syndrome
statistical analysis system
sterile aqueous solution
sterile aqueous suspension
subaortic stenosis
subarachnoid space
sulfasalazine
supravalvular aortic stenosis *also*
SVAS
surface-active substance
synthetic absorbable suture

SASH
saline, agent, saline, and heparin

SASMAS
skin-adipose superficial
musculoaponeurotic system

SASP
salazosulfapyridine
salicylazosulfapyridine

SASPP
syndrome of absence of septum
pellucidum with perencephaly

SAT
satellite
saturated *also* Sat, sat., sat'd, std
saturation *also* Sat, sat.
Scholastic Aptitude Test
School Ability Test
School Attitude Test

Senior Apperception Technique
serum antitrypsin
Shapes Analysis Test
single-agent (chemo)therapy
slide agglutination test
specific antithymocytic
speech awareness threshold
spermatogenic activity test
spontaneous activity test
spontaneous autoimmune thyroiditis
Stanford Achievement Test
structural atypia
subacute thyroiditis
symptomless autoimmune thyroiditis
systematized assertive therapy
systemic assertive therapy

Sat
saturated *also* SAT
saturation *also* SAT, sat.

sat.
satisfactory
saturated *also* SAT, Sat, sat'd, std
saturation *also* SAT

s.a.t.
without thymonucleic acid [L. *sine acido thymonucleinico*]

SATA
spatial average/temporal average

SATB
Special Aptitude Test Battery

sat. cond
satisfactory condition

sat'd
saturated *also* std

SATL
surgical Achilles tendon lengthening

SATM
sodium aurothiomalate

satn
saturation

SATP
spatial average temporal peak

sat. sol., sat. soln.
saturated solution

SAU
statistical analysis unit

SAV
sequential atrioventricular (pacing)
streptavidin
supraannular valve

SAVD
spontaneous assisted vaginal delivery

SAVE
Survival and Ventricular Ectopy

SAX
short axis

SAZ
sulfasalazine

SB
safety belt
sandbag
Schwartz-Bartter (syndrome)
scleral buckle
Sengstaken-Blakemore (tube)
septal basal
serum bilirubin
shortness of breath
sick bay (Navy)
sideroblast
Silvestroni-Bianco (syndrome)
single blind
single breath
sinus bradycardia
small bowel
sodium balance
soybean
spina bifida
spontaneous blastogenesis
spontaneously breathing
stand by *also* ST BY
Stanford-Binet (Intelligence Scale) *also* SBIS
stereotyped behavior
sternal border
stillbirth
stillborn *also* Stb, stillb
stone basketing
suction biopsy
surface binding (protein)

S-B
Sengstaken-Blakemore (tube) *also* SB

S

NOTES

S-B *(continued)*
Stanford-Binet (Intelligence Scale)
also SB

+SB
wearing seat belt

S/B
seen by
side bending

SB-
not wearing seat belt

Sb
antimony
antimony [L. *stibium*]
strabismus *also* strab

sb
stilb (unit of luminous intensity)

SBA
serum bactericidal activity
serum bile acid
soybean agglutinin
spina bifida aperta
standby angioplasty
standby assistance

SBAC
small bowel adenocarcinoma

SBB
simultaneous binaural bithermal
small bowel biopsy
stereotactic breast biopsy
stimulation-bound behavior

SBBO
small bowel bacterial overgrowth

SBC
sensory binocular cooperation
serum bactericidal concentration
single base cane
standard bicarbonate
strict bed confinement
sunburn cell

SBD
straight bag drainage
suggested brain dysfunction

S-BD
seizure-brain damage

SbDH
sorbitol dehydrogenase

SBE
breast self-examination
saturated base excess
self-breast examination
short below-elbow (cast)
shortness of breath on exertion
small-bowel enteroscopy
subacute bacterial endocarditis

SBEP
somatosensory brainstem evoked
potential

SBF
serologic-blocking factor
serum blocking factor
specific blocking factor
splanchnic blood flow
splenic blood flow
systemic blood flow

SBFT
small bowel followthrough *also*
SMBFT

SBG
selenite brilliant green
standby guard

SBGM
self blood-glucose monitoring

SBH
sea-blue histiocyte

SBI
soybean trypsin inhibitor
systemic bacterial infection

SBIS
Stanford-Binet Intelligence Scale *also*
SB, S-B

SBJ
skin, bones, joints

SBL
serum bactericidal level
soybean lecithin
sponge blood loss

SBLLA
sarcoma, breast and brain tumors,
leukemia, laryngeal and lung cancer

SBMPL
simultaneous binaural midplace
localization

SBN$_2$, SB$_{N2}$
single-breath nitrogen (test)

SBNT
single-breath nitrogen test

SBNW
single-breath nitrogen washout

SBO
small bowel obstruction
spina bifida occulta

SBOD
scleral buckle, right eye (oculus dexter)

SBOM
soybean oil meal

SBOS
scleral buckle, left eye (oculus sinister)

SBP
school breakfast program
scleral buckling procedure
serotonin-binding protein
small bowel phytobezoar
spontaneous bacterial peritonitis
steroid-binding plasma (protein)
sulfobromophthalein
systemic blood pressure *also* Psa
systolic blood pressure *also* SYS BP

SBPC
sulfobenzyl penicillin

SBPN
simultaneous bilateral percutaneous nephrolithotomy

SBQ
Smoking Behavior Questionnaire

SBQC
small-based quad cane

SBR
sluggish blood return
spleen-to-body (weight) ratio
stillbirth rate
strict bedrest
styrene-butadiene rubber

SBS
shaken baby syndrome
short bowel syndrome
sick building syndrome
side to back to side
side by side
sinobronchial syndrome
small bowel series
social breakdown syndrome

staff burnout scale
straight back syndrome

SBSE
supine bicycle stress echocardiography

SBSM
self-blood sugar monitoring

SBSRT
Spreen-Benton Sentence Repetition Test

SBSS
Seligmann buffered salt solution

SBT
serum bactericidal test
serum bactericidal titer
serum bacteriologic titer
single-breath test
skin bleeding time
sulbactam

SBTB
sinus breakthrough beat

SBTI
soybean trypsin inhibitor *also* STI

SBTPE
State Boards Test Pool Examination

SBTT
small bowel transit time

SBV
single binocular vision

SBX
symphysis, buttocks, and xiphoid

SC
sacrococcygeal
Sanitary Corps
schedule change
schizophrenia
Schüller-Christian (disease)
Schwann cell
Sciana (blood group)
sciatic (nerve)
science
scruple *also* scr
secondary cleavage
secretory coil
secretory component
self-care

S

NOTES

SC *(continued)*
self-control
semicircular
semiclosed
semilunar-valve closure
serum complement
serum creatinine *also* SCr
service connected
sex chromatin
Sezary cell
shallow compartment
short circuit
sick call
sickle cell *also* S-C
silicone coated
single chemical
skin conduction
slow component
Smeloff-Cutter
Snellen chart
sodium citrate
soluble complex
special care
specific characteristic
spinal cord
spleen cell *also* SPC
squamous carcinoma
statistical control
stellate cell
stepped care
sternoclavicular
stimulus, conditioned
stratum corneum
stroke count
subcellular
subclavian
subcoastal (view)
subcorneal
subcortical
subcutaneous *also* sc, SQ, subcu,
  subcut, subq
subtotal colectomy
succinylcholine *also* SCH
sugar coated
sulfur colloid
sulfur containing
superior colliculus
superior constrictor (muscles of
  pharynx)
superior cornu
supplementary canal
supportive care
suppressor cell
supracondylar (suspension)
surface colony

surgical cone
systemic candidiasis
systolic click
without correction (without glasses)
  [L. *sine correctione*] *also* s̄ gl

S-C
sickle cell *also* SC

S&C
sclerae and conjunctivae
singly and consensually

^{99m}Tc-SC
technetium-99m sulfur colloid

Sc
scandium
scapula
science *also* Sci
scientific *also* Sci

^{47}Sc
scandium-47

sC
statcoulomb

sc
scant
sclera
subcutaneous *also* subcu, subq, SQ,
  SC
subcutaneously

sc.
one may know (certainly, evidently,
  of course) [L. *scilicet*]

s̄c
without correction (without glasses)

SCA
School and College Ability (tests)
selfcare agency
severe congenital anomaly
sickle cell anemia
Simpson Coronary AtheroCath *also*
  SAC
single-channel analyzer
sperm-coating antigen
spleen colony assay
steroidal-cell antibody
subclavian artery
subcutaneous abdominal (block)
superior cerebellar artery
suppressor cell activity

SCa, S$_{Ca}$
serum calcium

ScA
scapuloanterior

SCAA
sporadic cerebral amyloid angiopathy

SCAb
autoantibody to stratum corneum

SCABG
single coronary artery bypass graft

SCAD
short chain acylcoenzyme A
dehydrogenase
spontaneous coronary artery dissection

SCAG
single coronary artery graft

SCAN
Screening (Test for Identifying)
Central Auditory Disorder
suspected child abuse (and) neglect
systolic coronary artery narrowing

SCAP
stem cell apheresis

SCARF
skeletal abnormalities, cutis laxa,
craniostenosis, psychomotor

SCARMD
severe childhood autosomal recessive
muscular dystrophy

SCAS
semicontinuous activated sludge

SCAT
sheep cell agglutination test
sickle cell anemia test
Simvastatin/Enalapril Coronary
Atherosclerosis Regression Trial

scat.
box [L. *scatula*]

scat. orig.
original package [L. *scatula
originalis*]

SCB
sedative cabinet bath
stratum corneum basic
strictly confined to bed

SCBA
self-contained breathing apparatus

SCBC
small cell bronchogenic carcinoma

SCBE
single-contrast barium enema

SCBF
spinal cord blood flow

SCBG
symmetrical calcification of basal
(cerebral) ganglia

SCBH
systemic cutaneous basophil
hypersensitivity

SCBP
stratum corneum basic protein

SCBU
special care baby unit

ScBU
screening bacteriuria

SCC
sequential combination chemotherapy
Services for Crippled Children
short circuit current
short course chemotherapy
sickle cell crisis
small cell carcinoma
small cleaved cell
squamous carcinoma of cervix
squamous cell carcinoma *also* SCCA,
SqCCA, sq cell ca

SCCA
semiclosed circle absorber (system)
squamous cell carcinoma *also* SCC,
SqCCA, sq cell ca
squamous cell carcinoma antigen

SCCB
small cell carcinoma of bronchus

SCCE
squamous cell carcinoma of the
esophagus

SCCH
sternocostoclavicular hyperostosis

SCCHN
squamous cell carcinoma of head
and neck

S

NOTES

SCCHO
sternocostoclavicular hyperostosis

SCCI
subcutaneous continuous infusion

S-CCK-Pz
secretin-cholecystokinin-pancreatozymin

SCCL
small cell carcinoma of lung

SCCM
Sertoli cell culture medium

SCD
sequential compression device
service-connected disability
sickle cell disease
spinal cord disease
spinocerebellar degeneration
subacute combined degeneration *also*
 SACD
subacute combined degeneration (of
 spinal cord)
sudden cardiac death
sudden coronary death
sulfur-carbon drug
systemic carnitine deficiency

ScD
Doctor of Science

ScDA
right scapuloanterior (fetal position)
 [L. *scapulodextra anterior*]

S-C disease
sickle cell-hemoglobin C disease

ScDP
right scapuloposterior (fetal position)
 [L. *scapulodextra posterior*]

SCE
saturated calomel electrode
secretory carcinoma of the
 endometrium
sister chromatid exchange
specialized columnar epithelium
subcutaneous emphysema

SCEP
sandwich counterelectrophoresis
somatosensory cortical evoked
 potential

SCER
sister chromatid exchange rate

SCF
stem cell factor
supercritical fluid

SCFA
short-chain fatty acid

SCFE
slipped capital femoral epiphysis

SCFI
specific clotting factor and inhibitor

SCG
seismocardiography
serum chemistry graft
serum chemogram
sodium cromoglycate
superior cervical ganglion

SCH
Schirmer (test)
sole community hospital
succinylcholine *also* SC
suprachiasmatic

SCh
succinylcholine chloride

SChE
serum cholinesterase

sched
schedule

SCHISTO, SCHIZ
schizocyte

schiz
schizophrenia

SCHL
subcapsular hematoma of liver

SCHLP
supracricoid hemilaryngopharyngectomy

SCHNC
squamous cell head and neck cancer

SCI
Science Citation Index
short crus of incus
spinal cord injury
structured clinical interview
subcoma insulin

Sci
science *also* Sc
scientific *also* Sc

SCIBTA
stem cell indicated by transplantation
 assay

SCID
severe combined immunodeficiency
 disease

SCII
Strong-Campbell Interest Inventory

SCIPP
sacrococcygeal to inferior pubic point

SCIS
severe combined immunodeficiency syndrome
surface carcinoma in situ

SCIU
spinal cord injury unit

SCIV
subclavian intravenous
subcutaneous intravenous

SCIWORA
spinal cord injury without radiographic abnormality

SCJ
squamocolumnar junction
sternoclavicular joint

SCK
serum creatine kinase

SCL
scaphocapitolunate arthrodesis
scleroderma *also* SD
serum copper level
sinus cycle length
skin conductance level
soft contact lens
spinocervicolemniscal
symptom checklist
syndrome checklist

Scl, scl
sclerosis
sclerotic

ScLA
left scapuloposterior (fetal position)
[L. *scapulolaeva anterior*]

SCLAX
subcostal long axis

SCLC
small cell lung carcinoma

SCLD
sickle-cell chronic lung disease
sickle cell lung disease

SCLE
subacute cutaneous lupus erythematosus
subcutaneous lupus erythematosis

ScLP
left scapuloposterior (fetal position)
[L. *scapulolaeva posterior*]

SCL-90R
Symptoms Checklist 90 Revised

SCLS
systemic capillary leak syndrome

SCM
scalene muscle
Schwann cell membrane
sensation, circulation, and motion
soluble cytotoxic medium
spleen cell-conditioned medium
split-cord malformation
spondylotic caudal myelopathy
State Certified Midwife
steatocystoma multiplex
sternocleidomastoid
streptococcal cell membrane
structure of the cytoplasmic matrix
supraclavicular muscle
surface-connecting membrane

ScM
scalene muscle

SCMC
sodium carboxymethylcellulose
spontaneous cell-mediated cytotoxicity

SCMD
senile choroidal macular degeneration

SCMO
Senior Clerical Medical Officer

SCMV
serogroup C meningococcal vaccine

SCN
serum thiocyanate
sodium thiocyanate
special care nursery
suprachiasmatic nucleus

SC_{Na}
sieving coefficient for sodium

NOTES

S

SCNS
subcutaneous nerve stimulation

SCO
somatic crossing-over
subcommissural organ

SCOP, scop
scopolamine

SCP
single-celled protein
sodium cellulose phosphate
soluble cytoplasmic protein
squamous cell papilloma
Standardized Care Plan
submucous cleft palate
superior cerebellar peduncle

ScP
scapuloposterior

scp
spherical candle power

SCPK, S-CPK
serum creatine phosphokinase

SCPN
serum carboxypeptidase N

SCPNT
Southern California Postrotary
Nystagmus Test

SCPP
spinal cord perfusion pressure

SCR
silicon-controlled rectifier
skin conductance response
special care room
spondylotic caudal radiculopathy
stem cell rescue

SCr
serum creatinine *also* SC

sCR
soluble complement receptor

scr
scruple *also* SC

SCRAM
speech-controlled respirometer for
ambulation measurement

SCRAP
Simple-Complex Reaction-Time
Apparatus

SCRIP
Stanford Coronary Risk Intervention
Project

SC-RNV
subcutaneous radionuclide venography

SCRS
Short Clinical Rating Scale

SCS
Saethre-Chotzen syndrome
silicon-controlled switch
spinal canal stenosis
spinal cord stimulation
suspected catheter sepsis
systolic click syndrome

SCSAX
subcostal short axis

SCSP, SC-SP
supracondylar-suprapatellar

SCT
salmon calcitonin
Sentence Completion Test
Sertoli cell tumor
sex chromatin test
sickle cell trait
sperm cytotoxic
spinal computed tomography
spinocervicothalamic
staphylococcal clumping test
sugar-coated tablet

SCTAT
sex cord tumor with annular tubules

SCTX
static cervical traction

SCU
selfcare unit
special care unit

SCUBA
self-contained underwater breathing
apparatus

SCUCP
small cell undifferentiated carcinoma
of the prostate

SCUD
septicemic cutaneous ulcerative
disease

SCUF
slow continuous ultrafiltration

SCUM
secondary carcinoma of the upper
mediastinum

SCUT
schizophrenia, chronic undifferentiated
type

SCV

sensory conduction velocity
slow-component velocity
smooth, capsulated, virulent (bacteria)
squamous cell carcinoma (of) vulva
subclavian vein
subcutaneous vaginal (block)

SCV-CPR

simultaneous compression ventilation-
cardiopulmonary resuscitation

S-D

sickle cell (hemoglobin) D (disease)
strength-duration (curve)

SD

sagittal depth (of cornea)
Sandhoff disease
scleroderma *also* SCL
secretion droplet
senile dementia
septal defect
serologically defined
serologically detectable
serologically determined
serum defect
severely disabled
shoulder disarticulation
shoulder dislocation
Shy-Drager
single dose
skin destruction
skin dose
sleep deprived
socialized delinquency
somadendritic
somatic dysfunction
spasmodic dysphonia
speech discrimination
spontaneous delivery
sporadic depression
Sprague-Dawley (rat)
spreading depression
stable disease
standard deviation
standard diet
statistical documentation
Stensen duct
sterile dressing
Still disease
stimulus drive *also* Sd

stone disintegration
straight drainage
streptodornase
streptozocin and doxorubicin
succinate dehydrogenase *also* SDG
sudden death
sulfadiazine
superoxide dismutase
surgical drain
systolic discharge

S/D

sharp/dull
systolic/diastolic (ratio)

S&D

seen and discussed
stomach and duodenum

S^d

stimulus, discriminative

Sd

stimulus drive *also* SD

SDA

right sacroanterior (fetal position) [L.
sacrodextra anterior]
Sabouraud dextrose agar
salt-dependent agglutinin
serotonin/dopamine antagonist
Seventh Day Adventist
sialodacryoadenitis (virus)
specific dynamic action
steroid-dependent asthmatic
succinic dehydrogenase activity
superficial distal axillary (node)

SDAT

senile dementia, Alzheimer type

SDB

sleep-disordered breathing

SDBP

seated diastolic blood pressure
standing diastolic blood pressure
supine diastolic blood pressure

SDC

salivary duct carcinoma
sensitivity depth compensation (ramp)
serum digoxin concentration
serum drug concentration
size/date consistency
sodium deoxycholate

NOTES

SDC *(continued)*
subacute combined degeneration
subclavian hemodialysis catheter
succinyldicholine
sulfodeoxycholate

SD&C
suction, dilation, and curettage

SDCL
symptom distress check list

SDD
selective digestive (tract)
decontamination
sporadic depressive disease
sterile dry dressing

SDE
specific dynamic effect

SDEEG
stereotactic depth electroencephalogram

SDES
symptomatic diffuse esophageal spasm

SDF
slow death factor
stream dilution factor
stress distribution factor

SDFP
single-donor frozen plasma

SDG
short distance group
succinate dehydrogenase *also* SD
sucrose density gradient

SDGC
sucrose density gradient centrifugation

SDGU
sucrose density gradient
ultracentrifugation

SDH
serine dehydrase
sorbitol dehydrogenase
spinal dorsal horn
subdural hematoma
subjacent dorsal horn
succinate dehydrogenase (activity)

SDHD
sudden death heart disease

SDI
size/date inconsistency
standard deviation interval
Surtees Difficulties Index

SDIHD
sudden death ischemic heart disease

SDII
sudden death in infancy

SDL
self-directed learning
serum digoxin level
serum drug level
speech discrimination loss

SDLRS
self-directed-learning readiness scale

sdly
sidelying

SDM
sensory detection method
single, divorced, married
soft drusen maculopathy
standard deviation of mean
sulfadimidine

S/D/M
systolic, diastolic, mean

SDMT
Symbol Digit Modalities Test

SDN
sexually dimorphic nucleus

SD/N
signal-difference-to-noise ratio

SDNA
single-strand deoxyribonucleic acid

SDO
sudden-dosage onset

SDP
right sacroposterior (fetal position)
[L. *sacrodextra posterior*]
single-donor platelets
stomach, duodenum, and pancreas

SDPH
sodium diphenylhydantoin

SDR
selective dorsal rhizotomy
spontaneously diabetic rat
surgical dressing room

SDRT
Stanford Diagnostic Reading Test

SDS
same day surgery
school dental service
Self-Rating Depression Scale
sensory deprivation syndrome

sexual differentiation scale
Shy-Drager syndrome
simple descriptive scale
single dose suppression
sodium dodecyl sulfate *also*
NaDodSO$_4$
somatropin deficiency syndrome
specific diagnosis service
speech discrimination score
standard deviation score
sudden death syndrome
sulfadiazine silver
sustained depolarizing shift

Sds, sds
sounds

SD-SK
streptodornase-streptokinase

SDSO
same day surgery overnight

SDS-PAGE, SDS/PAGE
sodium dodecyl sulfate-polyacrylamide
gel electrophoresis

SDT
right sacrotransverse (fetal position)
[L. *sacrodextra transversa*]
sensory decision theory
single-donor transfusion
speech detection threshold

SDU
short double upright
Standard Deviation Unit
stepdown unit

SDW
separated, divorced, widowed

SE
saline enema
sanitary engineering
Seeing Eye
self-explanatory
sheep erythrocyte
side effect
smoke exposure
smoke extract
soft exudate
solid extract
sphenoethmoidal
spherical equivalent

spin-echo
spongiform encephalopathy
Spurway-Eddowes (syndrome)
squamous epithelium
standard error
starch equivalent
Starr-Edwards (prosthesis) *also* S-E
status epilepticus
sterol ester
subendocardial
subendothelial
supernormal excitability
sustained engraftment

S-E
Starr-Edwards (prosthesis) *also* SE

S&E
safety and efficiency

Se
selenium

^{75}Se
selenium-75

SEA
seronegativity, enthesopathy, and
arthropathy
sheep erythrocyte agglutination
shock-elicited aggression
side-entry access
soluble egg antigen
Southeast Asia
spontaneous electrical activity
staphylococcal enterotoxin A
synaptic electronic activation

SEAR
Southeast Asia refugee

SEAT
sheep erythrocyte agglutination test

SEB
Scale for Emotional Blunting
staphylococcal enterotoxin B

SEBA
staphylococcal enterotoxin B
antiserum

seb derm
seborrheic dermatitis

seb ker
seborrheic keratosis *also* SK

NOTES

S

SEBL
self-emptying blind loop

SEC
according to [L. *secundum*]
secondary *also* sec
secretin
secretion
section *also* S, s, sec, sect
series elastic component (of muscles)
Singapore epidemic conjunctivitis
size exclusion chromatography
soft elastic capsule
spontaneous echo contrast
squamous epithelial cell
strong exchange capacity (re: resin)
superficial esophageal carcinoma

Sec
Seconal

sec
second *also* S, s
secondary *also* SEC
secretary
section *also* S, s, SEC, sect

sec. a.
by skill [L. *secundum artem*
according to art] *also* s.a.

SECG
scalp electrocardiogram
stress electrocardiography

SECPR
standard external cardiopulmonary
resuscitation

SECSY
spin-echo correlated spectroscopy

sect
section *also* S, s, SEC, sec

SED
sedimentation (rate) *also* SED, sed rt
skin erythema dose
spondyloepiphyseal dysplasia
standard error of difference
staphylococcal enterotoxin D
strain energy density
suberythemal dose
surgeon, emergency department

sed.
sedate
sedative
sedimentation (rate) *also* SED, sed rt
stool [L. *sedes*]

SEDD
Szondi's Experimental Diagnostics of
Drives

sed rt
sedimentation rate *also* SED, sed rt

SEE
scopolamine-Eukodal-Ephetonin
series elastic element
standard error of estimate

SEE₁
Seeing Essential English

SEE₂
Signing Exact English

SEEP
small end-expiratory pressure

SEER
surveillance-epidemiology-end results
Surveillance, Epidemiology, and End
Results (network, program)

SEF
somatically evoked field
spectral edge frequency
staphylococcal enterotoxin F

SEG
segment
soft elastic gelatin (capsule)
sonoencephalogram

seg
segmented neutrophil

SEG-CES
segmental cement extraction system

sEGF
salivary epidermal growth factor

segm
segment
segmented

SEGS, segs
segmented neutrophils
(polymorphonuclear leukocytes)

SEH
spinal epidural hematoma
subependymal hemorrhage

SeHCAT
selenium-labeled homocholic acid
(conjugated with) taurine

SEI
Self-Esteem Inventory
subepithelial (corneal) infiltrate
Suretee Events Index

SELF
Self-Evaluation of Life Function scale

SELFVD
sterile elective low forceps vaginal delivery

SELU
seromuscular enterocystoplasty lined with urothelium

SEM
scanning electron micrograph
scanning electron microscope
scanning electron microscopic
scanning electron microscopy
secondary enrichment medium
semen *also* sem
serum methylguanidine
slow eye movement
smoke exposure machine
standard error of mean
systolic ejection murmur
(verbal) sample evaluation method

sem
semen *also* SEM
seminal

sem.
half [L. *semis*] *also* HF, hf, S, s., semi, ss

sem. in d.
once a day [L. *semil in die*]

SEMDJL
spondyloepimetaphyseal dysplasia (with) joint laxity

SEMI
subendocardial myocardial infarction
subendocardial myocardial injury

semi
half [L. *semis*] *also* HF, hf, S, s., sem., ss

semid
half a dram

semih.
half an hour [L. *semihora*]

SEMS
self-expanding metallic stent

SEN
State Enrolled Nurse

sen
sensitive
sensitivity *also* S, sens

SENA
sympathetic efferent nerve activity

sens
sensation
sensitivity *also* S, sen
sensorium
sensory

SEO
surgical emergency officer

SEP
sensory-evoked potential
separate
separation of ghosts
serum electrophoresis
somatosensory evoked potential *also* SSEP, S-SEP
sperm entry point
spinal evoked potential
surface epithelium
systolic ejection period

SEPA
superficial external pudendal artery

separ
separately
separation

sept
septum

sept.
seven [L. *septem*]

SEQ
side-effects questionnaire
simultaneous equation

seq
sequel
sequela
sequelae
sequence
sequestrum

seq dev ex
sequential developmental exercises

S

NOTES

seq. luce
the following day [L. *sequenti luce*]

SEQOL
Study of Economics and Quality of Life

SER
scanning equalization radiography
sebum excretion rate
sensory evoked response
service *also* serv
signal enhancement ratio
smooth endoplasmic reticulum *also* sER
somatosensory-evoked response *also* SSER
supination external rotation (type of fracture)
systolic ejection rate

SER-IV
supination-external rotation IV (fracture)

Ser
serine *also* S

sER
smooth endoplasmic reticulum *also* SER

ser
serial
series *also* S, s

SERHOLD
National Biomedical Serials Holding Database

SERI
Spondee Error Index

ser ind
serum index

SERLINE
Serials on Line

sero, serol
serologic
serology

ser sect
serial sections

SERT
sustained ethanol release tube

serv
service *also* SER

serv.
keep, preserve [L. *serva*]

SERVHEL
Service and Health (Records)

SES
socioeconomic status
spatial emotional stimuli
standard electrolyte solution
subendothelial space

SESAP
Surgical Education and Self-Assessment Program

sesquih.
an hour and a half [L. *sesquihora*]

sesquiunc.
an ounce and a half [L. *sesquiuncia*]

Sess
sessile

SET
signal extraction technology
skin endpoint titration
systolic ejection time

sev
sever
several
severe
severed

SEW
slice excitation wave

SEWHO
shoulder-elbow-wrist-hand orthosis

SEXAF
surface extended x-ray absorption fine (structure)

SeXO
serum xanthine oxidase

s. expr.
without pressing [L. *sine expressioe*]

SF
Sabin-Feldman (dye test)
safety factor
salt free
saturated fat
scarlet fever
Schilder-Foix (disease)
seizure frequency
seminal fluid
serosal fluid
serum factor
serum ferritin
serum fibrinogen
sham feeding

shell fragment
shrapnel fragment
shunt flow
sickle (cell-hemoglobin) F (disease)
simian foam-virus
skin fibroblast
skin fluorescence
slow function
slow (initial) function
snack food
sodiumazide, fecal (medium)
soft feces
spinal fluid *also* sp fl
spontaneous fibrillation
spontaneous fission (radioactive
 isotopes)
spontaneous fluctuation
spontaneous fracture
stable factor
sterile female
stimulating factor
stress formula
sucrose-free
sugar free
sulfation factor (of blood serum)
superior facet
suppressor factor
suprasternal fossa
survival fraction
Svedberg flotation (unit)
symptom free
synovial fluid *also* syn fl

S&F
soft and flat

SF%
shortening fraction percentage

S_f
flotation constant
negative sedimentation Svedberg unit

Sf
Svedberg flotation (unit)

SFA
saturated fatty acid
seminal fluid assay
serum folic acid
stimulated fibrinolytic activity
superficial femoral angioplasty
superficial femoral artery

SFB
Sanfilippo (syndrome type) B
saphenofemoral bypass
single frequency bioimpedance
surgical foreign body

SFBL
self-filling blind loop

SFC
serum fungicidal
soluble fibrin-fibrinogen complex
spinal fluid count
subaracyhnoid fluid collection

SFD
sheep factor delta
short foot drape
skin-film distance
small for dates (gestational age)
soy-free diet
spectral frequency distribution

SFEMG
single fiber electromyography

SFF
speaking fundamental frequency

SFFA
serum-free fatty acid

SFFF
sedimentation field flow fractionation

SFFV
spleen focus-forming virus
spleen focus Friend virus

SFG
spotted fever group

SFH
schizophrenia family history
serum-free hemoglobin
stroma-free hemoglobin

SFHb
pyridoxilated stroma-free hemoglobin

SFI
sciatic function index
Sexual Functioning Index
Social Function Index

SFL
synovial fluid lymphocyte

NOTES

SFLE
Stress From Life Experience

SFM
scanning force microscopy
soluble fibrin monomer

SFMC
soluble fibrin monomer complex

SFO
subfornical organ

SFP
screen filtration pressure
simulated fluorescence process
simultaneous foveal perception
spinal fluid pressure
stopped flow pressure

SFPT
standard fixation preference test

SFR
screen-filtration resistance
stroke with full recovery

SFS
serial focus seizures
serum fungistatic
skin and fascia stapler
split function study

SFT
sensory feedback therapy
serum-free thyroxin
skinfold thickness
solitary fibrous tumor

SFTR
sagittal, frontal, transverse, rotation

SFUP
surgical followup

SFV
Semliki Forest virus
shipping fever virus
Shope fibroma virus
squirrel fibroma virus
superficial femoral vein

SFW
sexual function of women
shell fragment wound
shrapnel fragment wound
slow filling wave

SG
Sachs-Georgi (test) *also* S-G
salivary gland
scrotography
secretory granule

serous granule
serum globulin
serum glucose
sign
skin graft
soluble gelatin
specific gravity *also* SPG, SpG, sp
gr, sp. gr.
substantia gelatinosa
supplemental groove
Surgeon General
Swan-Ganz (catheter) *also* S-G, SGC

S-G
Sachs-Georgi (test) *also* SG
Swan-Ganz (catheter) *also* SG, SGC

SGA
small for gestational age

SGAT
salivary gland anlage tumor

SGAW, SG$_{AW}$
specific airway conductance

SG-C
serum gentamicin concentration

SGC
spermicide-germicide compound
Swan-Ganz catheter *also* SG, S-G

SGc
specific conductance

SGD
straight gravity drainage

SGE
secondary generalized epilepsy
significant glandular enlargement

SGF
sarcoma growth factor
silica gel filtered
skeletal growth factor

SGFR
single-nephron glomerular filtration
rate *also* SNGFR

SGGT
serum γ-glutamyltransferase

SGH
subgaleal hematoma

SGL
salivary gland lymphocyte

s̄ gl
without correction/without glasses *also*
SC

SGM
serum glucose monitoring

SGO
Society of Gynecologic Oncology
Surgeon General's Office
surgery, gynecology, and obstetrics

SGOT
serum glutamic-oxaloacetic
transaminase (aspartate
aminotransferase)

SGP
serine glycerophosphatide
sialoglycoprotein
soluble glycoprotein

SGP-2
sulfated glycoprotein-2

SGPT
serum glutamic-pyruvic transaminase
(alanine aminotransferase)

SGR
Sachs-Georgi reaction
Shwartzman generalized reaction
submandibular gland renin

SGS
second generation sulfonylurea
subglottic stenosis

S-Gt
Sachs-Georgi test

SGTCS
secondarily generalized tonic-clonic
seizure

SGTT
standard glucose tolerance test

SGV
salivary gland virus
selective gastric vagotomy
small granular vesicle

SH
Salter-Harris (fracture)
Schönlein-Henoch (purpura) *also* SHP
serum hepatitis
service hours
sex hormone
sexual harassment
sham operated

shared haplotypes
Sherman (rat)
short
shoulder *also* Sh, sh, SHLD
shower
sick in hospital
sinus histiocytosis
social history
somatotropic hormone *also* STH
spontaneously hypertensive (rat)
sulfhydryl
surgical history
symptomatic hypoglycemia
systemic hyperthermia

S/H
sample and hold
suicidal/homicidal (ideation)

S&H
speech and hearing

SH2
src-homology 2

Sh
sheep
short *also* sh
shoulder *also* SH, sh, SHLD

sh
short *also* Sh
shoulder *also* SH, Sh, SHLD

SHA
soluble HLA antigen
staphylococcal
hemagglutinatingantibody
super-heated aerosol

SHAA
serum hepatitis-associated antigen

SHAA-Ab
serum hepatitis-associated antigen
antibody

SHAFT
sad, hostile, anxious, frustrated,
tenacious (patient)

SHAL
standard hyperalimentation

SHARP
School Health Additional Referral
Program

S

NOTES

SHAS
supravalvular hypertrophic aortic stenosis

SHAV
superior hemiazygos vein

SHB
sequential hemibody (irradiation)
subacute hepatitis with bridging
sulfhemoglobin *also* HbS, SHb, SULFHB

S Hb
sickle hemoglobin (screen)

SHb, S-Hb
sulfhemoglobin *also* HbS, SHB, SULFHB

SHBD
serum hydroxybutyric dehydrogenase

SHBG
sex hormone-binding globulin

SHC
sclerosing hepatic carcinoma

SHCO
sulfated hydrogenated caster oil

SHDI
supraoptical hypophysial diabetes insipidus

SHE
Syrian hamster embryo

SHEENT
skin, head, eyes, ears, nose, and throat

SHEP
Systolic Hypertension in the Elderly Program

SHF
simian hemorrhagic fever

shf
super high frequency

SHG
synthetic human gastrin

SHGT
somatic cell human gene therapy

SHH
syndrome of hyporeninemic hypoaldosteronism

SHHP
semihorizontal heart position

SHJR4
side-hole Judkins right, curve 4

SHJR4s
side-hole Judkins right, curve 4, short

SHL
sensorineural hearing loss *also* SNHL
sudden hearing loss
supraglottic horizontal laryngectomy

SHLD
shoulder *also* SH, Sh, sh

SHM
simple harmonic motion

SHML
sinus histiocytosis with massive lymphadenopathy

SHMO
Senior Hospital Medical Officer

SHMT
serine hydroxymethyltransferase

SHN
spontaneous hemorrhagic necrosis
subacute hepatic necrosis

SHO
secondary hypertrophic osteoarthropathy
Senior House Officer

SHORT, S-H-O-R-T
short (stature), hyperextensibility (of joints or) hernia (or both), ocular (depression), Rieger (anomaly), teething (delayed)

SHP
Schönlein-Henoch purpura *also* SH
secondary hyperparathyroidism
state health plan
surgical hypoparathyroidism

SHPDA
State Health Planning and Development Agency

SHPL
sacral horizontal plane line

sHPT
secondary hyperparathyroidism

SHR
scapulohumeral rhythm
spontaneously hypertensive rat

SHRC
shortened, held, resisted, contracted

SHS
Sayre head sling
sheep hemolysate supernatant
Shipley-Hartford Scale
student health service
super high speed

SHSP
spontaneously hypertensive stroke-
prone (rat)

SHSS
Stanford Hypnotic Susceptibility Scale

SHT
simple hypocalcemic tetany
subcutaneous histamine test

SHUR
System for Hospital Uniform
Reporting

SHV
simian herpes virus

SHx
social history

Shy
6-mercaptopurine *also* 6-MP

SI
International System of Units [Fr.
Système International d'Unites]
sacroiliac *also* sac-il
saline infusion
saline injection
saturation index
self-inflicted
sensitive index
serious illness
serum insulin
serum iron
service index
severity index
sex inventory
sexual intercourse
Singh Index
single injection
small intestine
social introversion
soluble insulin
special intervention
spirochetosis icterohaemorrhagica
stimulation index

streptozotocin induced
stress incontinence
strict isolation
stroke index
suicidal ideation
sulfated insulin
suppression index
syncytium-inhibiting
systolic index

S&I
suction and irrigation

S/I
sucrose to isomaltase (ratio)
superior/inferior

Si
most anterior point on lower contour
of sella turcica (point)
silicon
(venous) sinus

SIA
serum inhibitory activity
small intestinal atresia
stimulation-induced analgesia
stress-induced analgesia
stress-induced anesthesia
subacute infectious arthritis
synalbumin-insulin antagonism
syncytia induction assay

Sia
sialic acids

SIADH
syndrome of inappropriate secretion
of antidiuretic hormone

SIAT
supervised intermittent ambulatory
treatment

SIB
self-injurious behavior

sib
sibling

SIBC
serum iron-binding capacity
synchronous ipsilateral breast cancer

SIBIS
self-injurious-behavior inhibiting
system

NOTES

679

SIBO
small intestinal bacterial overgrowth

sibs
siblings

SIC
dry [L. *siccus*] *also* sic.
self-intermittent catheterization
serum inhibitory concentration
serum insulin concentration
squamous intraepithelial cell

SiC
silicon carbide

sic.
dry [L. *siccus*] *also* SIC

SICD
Sequenced Inventory of
Communication Development
serum isocitrate dehydrogenase
sudden infant crib death

SICSVA
sequential impaction cascade sieve
volumetric air (sampler)

SICT
selective intracoronary thrombolysis

SICU
spinal intensive care unit
surgical intensive care unit

SID
selective intestinal decontamination
source image distance
source-to-image(-receptor) distance
sucrase-isomaltase deficiency
sudden inexplicable death
sudden infant death
suggested indication of diagnosis
systemic inflammatory disease

s.i.d.
once a day [L. *semel in die*]

SIDD
syndrome of isolated diastolic
dysfunction

SIDER
siderocyte

SIDFF
superimposed dorsiflexion of foot

SIDS
sudden infant death syndrome

SIE
stroke in evolution

SIECUS
Sex Information and Educational
Council of the United States

SIEP
serum immunoelectrophoresis

SIESTA
snooze-induced excitation of
sympathetic triggered activity

SIF
serum inhibitory factor
small, intensely fluorescent (ganglia)
somatotropin release-inhibiting factor
also SRIF

Sif
segment inferior

SIFT
selected ion flow tube

SIG
sigmoidoscope
special interest group

SIg
serum immunoglobulin
surface immunoglobulin *also* sIg

Sig
signature *also* /S/, /s/
signed

sIg
surface immunoglobulin *also* SIg

sig
sigmoidoscopy
signal
significant

sig.
label, write [L. *signa*] *also* S, s
let it be written, labeled [L.
signetur]

S-IgA
secretory immunoglobulin A

SIgA
surface immunoglobulin A

sIgA
secretory IgA

σ
millisecond *also* msec, ms, s̄
sigma (18th letter of Greek
alphabet), lowercase

Σ
foaminess

sigma (18th letter of Greek alphabet), uppercase
sum
summation of all quantities following the symbol
syphilis

sig. n. pro.
label with proper name [L. *signa nomine proprio*]

SIH
somatotropin release-inhibiting hormone
stimulation-induced hypalgesia
stress-induced hyperthermia

SIHE
spontaneous intramural hematoma of the esophagus

SIhPTH
serum immunoreactive human parathyroid hormone

SI-I
shunt index via the inferior mesenteric vein

SIJ, SI jt
sacroiliac joint

SIL
seriously ill list
speech interference level
squamous intraepithelial lesion

SILD
Sequenced Inventory of Language Development

SILFVD
sterile indicated low forceps vaginal delivery

SILS
Shipley Institute of Living Scale

SILV
simultaneous independent lung ventilation

SIM
selected ion monitoring
Similac
small intestine mesentery

sucrose-isomaltose
sulfide, indole, motility (medium)

SIMA
single internal mammary artery

Simkin
simulation kinetics (analysis)

simp.
simple [L. *simplex*]

SIMS
secondary ion mass spectroscopy

simul
simultaneously

SIMV
spontaneous intermittent mandatory ventilation
synchronized intermittent mandatory ventilation

SIN
salpingitis isthmica nodosa

sin.
six times a night [L. *sex in nocte*]
without [L. *sine*]

SINES
short interspersed elements

sing.
of each [L. *singulorum*]
singular

sing. aur.
every morning [L. *singulis auroris*]

sing. hor. quad.
every quarter of an hour [L. *singulis horae quadrantibus*]

si non val.
if it is not enough [L. *si non valeat*]

SIO
sacroiliac orthosis

si op. sit
if it is necessary [L. *si opus sit*]

SIP
segment inertial properties
Sickness Impact Profile
slow inhibitory potential
surface inductive plethysmography

S

NOTES

sIPTH
serum immunoreactive parathyroid hormone

SIQ
sick in quarters (military)

SIR
single isomorphous replacement
specific immune release
standardized incidence ratio

SIREF
specific immune-response-enhancing factor

SIRF
severely impaired renal function

SIRS
soluble immune response suppressor
systemic inflammatory response syndrome

SIS
Second International Standard
sisomicin
sister
social information system
spontaneous interictal spike
sterile injectable solution
sterile injectable suspension

SI-S
shunt index via the superior mesenteric vein

SISI
short increment sensitivity index

SISS
serum inhibitor of streptolysin S
severe invasion streptococcal syndrome

SISV, SiSV
simian sarcoma virus *also* SSV

SIT
serum-inhibiting titer
Simultaneous Interview Technique
Slosson Intelligence Test
sperm immobilization test

SIT BAL
sitting balance

SIT-F
Sperm Immobilization Test-Fjabrant

SIT-I
Sperm Immobilization Test-Isojima

SIT TOL
sitting tolerance

SIV
simian immunodeficiency virus
Sprague-Dawley-Ivanovas (rat)

si vir. perm.
if strength will permit [L. *si vires permitant*]

SIVP
slow intravenous push

SIW
self-inflicted wound

SIWIP
self-induced water intoxication (and) psychosis

SJ, S-J
Stevens-Johnson (syndrome) *also* SJS

SJR
Shinowara-Jones-Reinhart (unit)

S-JRA
systemic juvenile rheumatoid arthritis

SJS
Stevens-Johnson syndrome *also* SJ, S-J
Swyer-James syndrome

SjS
Sjögren syndrome *also* SS

SjVO$_2$
jugular venous oxygen saturation

SK
seborrheic keratosis *also* seb ker
senile keratosis
skin *also* Sk, SKI
Sloan-Kettering (Institute) *also* SKI
solar keratosis
spontaneous killer (cell)
streptokinase *also* STK
striae keratopathy
swine kidney

Sk
skin *also* SK, SKI

sk
skeletal *also* skel
skimmed

SKA
supracondylar knee-ankle (orthosis) *also* SKAO

SKAB
skeletal antibody

SKAO
supracondylar knee-ankle orthosis *also* SKA

SKAT
Sex Knowledge and Attitude Test

SKC
single knee to chest

skel
skeletal *also* sk
skeleton

SK&F 104864
topotecan *also* TPT

SKI
skin *also* SK, Sk
Sloan-Kettering Institute *also* SK

SKL
serum-killing level

SKOLD
Screening Kit of Language Development

SKSD, SK-SD
streptokinase-streptodornase

sk tr
skeletal traction

SKW
Sturge-Kalischer-Weber (syndrome)

SL
according to rules [L. *secundum legem*] *also* sl
salt loser
sarcolemma
satellite-like
scapholunate
sclerosing leukoencephalopathy
sensation level (of hearing)
sensory latency
sentinel lymphadenectomy
serious list
short leg (cast) *also* SLC
Sibley-Lehninger (unit)
signal level
Sinding Larsen (disease)
Sjögren-Larsson (syndrome) *also* SLS
slight
slit lamp
small leukocyte

small lymphocyte
soda lime
sodium lactate
solidified liquid
sound level
spinal length
Stein-Leventhal (syndrome) *also* SLS
streptolysin
Strümpell-Lorrain (disease)
sublingual (ly)

S/L
slit lamp (examination) *also* SLE
sucrase to lactase (ratio) *also* S:L

S:L
sucrase to lactase (ratio) *also* S/L

Sl
slight
Steel (mouse)

s.l.
according to rules [L. *secundum legem*] *also* SL

sl
slice
slight
slow
slyke (unit of buffer value)
sublingual

SLA
left sacroanterior (fetal position) [L. *sacrolaeva anterior*]
single-cell liquid cytotoxic assay
slide latex agglutination
soluble liver antigen
superficial linear array
surfactant-like activity

SLAC
scaphoid-lunate advanced collapse

SLAM
scanning laser acoustic microscope

SLAP
serum leucine aminopeptidase
superior labral anteroposterior
superior labrum anterior position
superior labrum anterior and posterior (lesion)

S

NOTES

SLAS
salt-losing adrenogenital syndrome

SLB
short leg brace

SLC
short leg cast *also* SL
Sociopolitical Locus of Control
sodium lithium countertransport
sodium-lithium countertransporter
synovial lining cell

SLCC
short leg cylinder cast
sulfated lithocholic conjugate

SLCG
sulfolithocholylglycine

SLD, SLDH
second-line drug
serum lactate dehydrogenase

SLE
slit-lamp examination *also* S/L
St. Louis encephalitis
systemic lupus erythematosus

SLEA
sheep erythrocyte antibody
sheep erythrocyte antigen

SLEP
short latent-evoked potential

SLEV
St. Louis encephalitis virus (serology)

SLFIA
substrate-labeled fluorescent
immunoassay
substrate-linked fluorescent
immunoassay

SLFVD
sterile low forceps vaginal delivery

SLGXT
symptom-limited graded exercise test

SLHR
sex-linked hypophosphatemic rickets

SLI
secretin-like immunoreactivity
selective lymphoid irradiation
somatostatin-like immunoreactivity
also SLIR
speech and language impaired
splenic localization index
subdermal levonorgestrel implant

SLIP
Singer-Loomis Inventory of
Personality

SLIR
somatostatin-like immunoreactivity
also SLI

SLK, SLKC
superior limbic keratoconjunctivitis

SLL
second-look laparotomy
small lymphocytic lymphoma

SLM
sound level meter

SLMC
spontaneous lymphocyte-mediated
cytotoxicity

SLMFD
sterile low midforceps (vaginal)
delivery *also* SLMFVD

SLMFVD
sterile low midforceps vaginal
delivery *also* SLMFD

SLMP
since last menstrual period

SLN
sentinel lymph node
sublentiform nucleus
superior laryngeal nerve

SLNTG
sublingual nitroglycerin

SLNWBC
short leg nonweightbearing cast

SLNWC
short leg nonwalking cast

SLO
scanning laser ophthalmoscope
second-look operation
streptolysin O

SLOS
Smith-Lemli-Opitz syndrome

SLP
left sacroposterior (fetal position) [L.
sacrolaeva posterior]
segmental limb (systolic) pressure
sex-limited protein
short luteal phase
speech language pathologist
subluxation of patella

SLPI
secretory leukocyte protease inhibitor
SLPMS
short leg posterior-molded splint
SLPP
serum lipophosphoprotein
SLR
Shwartzman local reaction
single lens reflex
straight-leg raising
Streptococcus lactis R
SLRT
straight-leg raising tenderness
straight-leg raising test
SLS
second-look sonography
segment long-spacing (collagen)
short leg splint
single limb support
Sjögren-Larsson syndrome *also* SL
stagnate loop syndrome
Stein-Leventhal syndrome *also* SL
SLSQ
Speech and Language Screening
Questionnaire
SLT
left sacrotransverse (fetal position)
[L. *sacrolaeva transversa*]
scanning laser tomography
single lung transplant
swing light test
SLTEC
Shigella-like toxin-producing
Escherichia coli
SlTr
silent treatment
SLUD
salivation, lacrimation, urination, and
defecation
SLUDGE
salivation, lacrimation, urination,
defecation, gastrointestinal distress
and emesis
SLWC
short leg walking cast

SLZ
serum lysozyme
SM
Master of Science
sadomasochism
self-monitoring
semimembranous
Sexual Myths (Scale)
Shigella mutant
simple mastectomy
skim milk
small
smoker
smooth muscle
somatomedin
sonomicrometry
space medicine
sphingomyelin
splenic macrophage
sports medicine
stapedius muscle
staphylococcus medium
streptomycin *also* S, STM
Strümpell-Marie (disease)
submandibular
submucosal
submucous
substituted metabolite
substitute for morphine
suckling mouse *also* sM
sucrose medium
suction method
sulfamerazine
superior mesenteric
supramamillary (nucleus)
sustained medication
symptoms *also* Sx, S$_x$
synaptic membrane
synovial membrane
systolic mean (pressure)
systolic motion
systolic murmur
S/M
sadism/masochism
Sm
samarium
small *also* S, sm
Smith (antigen)
symptom *also* sx, sym, symp, sympt

NOTES

sM
suckling mouse *also* SM

sm
small *also* S, Sm

SMA
schedule of maximal allowance
sequential multichannel autoanalyzer
sequential multiple analysis
sequential multiple analyzer
serial multiple analysis
serum muramidase activity
shape memory alloy
simultaneous multichannel autoanalyzer
smooth muscle actin
smooth muscle antibody
smooth muscle autoantibody
spinal muscular atrophy
spontaneous motor activity
standard method agar
superior mesenteric artery
supplementary motor area

SM-A
somatomedin A

SMA-6
Sequential Multiple Analysis—six
different serum tests

SMA 6/60
Sequential Multiple Analysis—six
tests in sixty minutes

SMA-12
Sequential Multiple Analysis—twelve-
channel biochemical profile

SMA 12/60
Sequential Multiple Analysis—twelve
different serum tests in sixty
minutes

SMA-20
Sequential Multiple Analysis of
twenty chemical constituents

SMA-60
Sequential Multiple Analysis of sixty
chemical constituents

SMABF
superior mesenteric artery blood flow

SMABV
superior mesenteric artery blood
velocity

SMAC
Sequential Multiple Analyzer
Computer

SMAE
superior mesenteric artery embolus

SMAF
smooth muscle activating factor
specific macrophage-arming factor
superior mesenteric artery (blood)
flow

SMAL
serum methyl alcohol level

sm an
small animal

SMAO
superior mesenteric artery occlusion

SMAP
systemic mean arterial pressure

SMART
simultaneous multiple-angle
reconstruction technique
sperm microaspiration retrieval
technique

SMAS
submucosal aponeurotic system (flap)
superficial musculoaponeurotic system
superior mesenteric artery syndrome

SMAST
Short Michigan Alcoholism Screening
Test

SMAT
School Motivation Analysis Test

SMB
selected mucosal biopsy
standard mineral base

sMB
suckling mouse brain

SMBFT
small bowel followthrough *also*
SBFT

SMBG
self-monitored blood glucose

SMBP
serum myelin basic protein

SM-C, Sm-C
somatomedin C

SMC
smooth muscle cell
special monthly compensation
special mouth care
succinylmonocholine

SMCA
smooth muscle contracting agent

SMCD
senile macular chorioretinal degeneration

SM-C/IGF
somatomedin C/insulin-like growth factor

SMD
senile macular degeneration
sternocleidomastoid diameter
submanubrial dullness

SMDA
starch methylenedianiline

SMDS
secondary myelodysplastic syndrome

SME
severe myoclonic epilepsy
significant medial event

SMEDI
stillbirth, mummification, embryonic death, infertility (syndrome)

SMEM
supplemented (Eagle) minimal essential medium

SMEPP
subminiature end-plate potential

SMF
streptozotocin, mitomycin, 5-fluorouracil

sm-FeSV
McDonough feline sarcoma virus

SMFP
state medical facilities plan

SMFVD
sterile midforceps vaginal delivery

SMG
submandibular gland

SMH
state mental hospital
strongyloidiasis with massive hyperinfection

SMI
Self-Motivation Inventory

senior medical investigator
sensory motor integration
severely mentally impaired
silent myocardial infarction
stress myocardial image
Style of Mind Inventory
supplementary medical insurance
sustained maximal inspiration

SmIg
surface membrane immunoglobulin

SMILE
Survival of Myocardial Infarction Long-Term Evaluation
sustained maximal inspiratory lung exercise

SMIT
standard mycological identification technique

SML
single major locus

SMMD
specimen mass measurement device

SMN
second malignant neoplasm

SMNB
submaximal neuromuscular block

SMO
Sarns membrane oxygenator
Senior Medical Officer
serum monoamine oxidase
slip made out

SMo
stainless steel and molybdenum

SMOH
Senior Medical Officer of Health

SMON
subacute myeloopticoneuropathy

SMP
self-management program
simultaneous macular perception
slowest moving protease
slow-moving protease
special monthly pension
standard medical practice

S

NOTES

SMP *(continued)*
standard medical procedure
submitochondrial particle

SMPN
sensorimotor polyneuropathy

SMPS
sympathetic maintained pain syndrome

SMR
senior medical resident
sensorimotor rhythm
severe mental retardation
skeletal muscle relaxant
somnolent metabolic rate
standardized metabolic rate
standardized mortality ratio
standard mortality ratio
stroke with minimal residuum
submucous resection

SMRD
stress-related mucosal damage
(SRMD)

SMRR
submucous resection and rhinoplasty

SMRV
squirrel monkey retrovirus

SMS
scalded mouth syndrome
senior medical student
somatostatin *also* SOM, SS, SST
stiff-man syndrome
supplemental minimal sodium

SMSA
standard metropolitan statistical area

SMSV
San Miguel sea lion virus

SMT
Sertoli cell/mesenchyme tumor
Snider Match Test
spinal manipulative therapy
spindle microtubule
spontaneous mammary tumor
stereotactic mesencephalic tractotomy

SMuLV
Scripps murine leukemia virus

SMV
slow-moving vehicle
small volume
submental vertex (view)
submentovertical
superior mesenteric vein

SMVR
supraannular mitral valve replacement

SMVT
sustained monomorphic ventricular
tachycardia

SMX
sulfamethoxazole *also* SMZ

SMX/TMP
sulfamethoxazole and trimethoprim
also SMZ-TMP

SMZ
sulfamethazine

SMZL
splenic marginal zone lymphoma

SMZ-TMP
sulfamethoxazole-trimethoprim *also*
SMX/TMP, TMP-SMX

S-N
sella to nasion (cephalometrics)

SN
school of nursing
sciatic notch
sclerema neonatorum
scrub nurse
sensorineural
sensory neuron
seronegative
serum neutralization
serum neutralizing
single nephron
sinoatrial node *also* SA
sinus node
spinal needle
spontaneous nystagmus
staff nurse
standard nomenclature
streptonigrin
student nurse
subnormal
substantia nigra
superior nasal
supernatant
supernormal
suprasternal notch *also* SSN

S/N
sample to negative (control ratio)
signal to noise (ratio)
speech to noise (ratio)

Sn
subnasale
tin [L. *stannum*]

¹¹³Sn
tin-113

s.n.
according to nature [L. *secundum naturam*]

S-N-A
sella-nasion-subspinale (-point A, in cephalometrics)

SNA
specimen not available
superior nasal artery
sympathetic nerve activity
systems network architecture

SNa
serum sodium (concentration)

SNagg
serum normal agglutinator

SNAI
Standard Nomenclature of Athletic Injuries

SNAP
sensory nerve action potential

SNAT
suspected nonaccidental trauma

S-N-B
sella-nasion-supramentale (-point B, in cephalometrics)

SNB
scalene node biopsy
Silverman needle biopsy

SNC
central nervous system [L. *sistema nervosum centrale*]
skilled nursing care
spontaneous neonatal chylothorax

SNCC
small non-cleaved cell

SNCL
sinus node cycle length

SNCV
sensory nerve conduction velocity

SND
single needle device

sinus node dysfunction
striatonigral degeneration

SNDA
Student National Dental Association

SNDO
Standard Nomenclature of Diseases and Operations

SNE
sinus node electrogram
spatial non-emotional (stimuli)
subacute necrotizing encephalomyelopathy

SNEF
skilled nursing extended (care) facility

SNES
supracapsular nerve entrapment syndrome

SNF
sinus node formation
skilled nursing facility

SNFH
schizophrenia non-family history

SNGBF
single-nephron glomerular blood flow

SNGFR
single-nephron glomerular filtration rate *also* SGFR

SNGPF
single-nephron glomerular plasma flow

SNHHD
simplified nocturnal home hemodialysis

SNHL
sensorineural hearing loss *also* SHL

SNM
Society of Nuclear Medicine
sulfanilamide

SnO₂
tin oxide

SNOBOL
String-Oriented Symbolic Language

NOTES

SNODO
Standard Nomenclature of Diseases and Operations

SNOMED
Standardized Nomenclature of Medicine

SNOOP
Systematic Nursing Observation of Psychopathology

SNOP
Systematized Nomenclature of Pathology

SNP
School Nurse Practitioner
simple neonatal procedure
sinus node potential
sodium nitroprusside

SNQ
superior nasal quadrant

SNR, S/N ratio
signal-to-noise ratio
substantia nigra zona reticulata
supernumerary rib

SNRB
selective nerve root block

snRNA
small nuclear ribonucleic acid
small nuclear RNA

SNRP, snRNP
small nuclear ribonucleoprotein

SNRT
sinus node recovery time *also* SRT

SNRTd
sinus node recovery time, direct (measuring)

SNS
sterile normal saline
sympathetic nervous system

SNSA
seronegative spondyloarthropathy

SNT
sinuses, nose, throat
suppan nail technique

SNUC
sinonasal undifferentiated carcinoma

SNV
spleen necrosis virus
superior nasal vein

SO
salpingo-oophorectomy *also* S-O
Schlatter-Osgood (disease)
second opinion
sex offender
shoulder orthosis
significant other *also* S/O
slow oxidative
sphenooccipital (synchondrosis)
sphincter of Oddi
spinal orthosis
standing orders
suboccipital
superior oblique
supraoptic
supraorbital
sutures out
sympathetic ophthalmia

S-O
salpingo-oophorectomy *also* SO

S/O
significant other *also* SO

SO₂
oxygen saturation *also* OS, O₂ sat., SaO₂
sulfur dioxide

So
socialization *also* SOC

⁸²So
strontium-82

SOA
serum opsonic activity
spinal opioid analgesia
supraorbital artery
swelling of ankles

SOAA
signed out against (medical) advice *also* SOAMA

SOAM
stitches out in morning
sutures out in morning

SOAMA
signed out against medical advice *also* SOAA

SOA-MCA
superficial occipital artery to middle cerebral artery

SOAP
subjective (data), objective (data), assessment, and plan (problem-oriented record)

SOAPIE
subjective (data), objective (data), assessment, plan, implementation, and evaluation (problem-oriented record)

SOAPS
suction, oxygen, apparatus, pharmaceuticals, saline (anesthesia equipment)

SOB
see order blank
see order book
shortness of breath
side of bed
suboccipitobregmatic

SOBOE
shortness of breath on exertion

SOC
see old chart
sequential oral contraceptive
socialization *also* So
standard of care
state of consciousness *also* SoC
syphilitic steochondritis

S&OC
signed and on chart

SoC
state of consciousness *also* SOC

soc
social
society

SOCD
Separation of Circle-Diamond

SocSec
Social Security

S-OCT
serum ornithine carbamoyltransferase

SOD
sinovenous occlusive disease
sphincter of Oddi dysfunction
spike occurrence density
superoxide dismutase
surgical officer of the day

sod
sodium

sod bicarb
sodium bicarbonate

SOFS
spontaneous osteoporotic fracture of sacrum

SOFT
Sorting of Figures Test

SOG
suggestive of good

SOH
sexually oriented hallucination
sympathetic orthostatic hypotension

SOHN
supraoptic hypothalamic nucleus

SOI
surgical orthotopic implantation (implant)
syrup of ipecac

SOL
solution *also* sol, soln
space-occupying lesion

sol
soluble
solution *also* SOL, soln

SOLER
squarely (face person), open (posture), lean (toward person), eye (contact), relaxed

soln
solution *also* SOL, sol

SOLST
Stephens Oral Language Screening Test

solu
solute

solv
dissolve [L. *solve*]
solvent

SOLVD
Studies of Left Ventricular Dysfunction

SOM
secretory otitis media
sensitivity of method

NOTES

S

691

SOM *(continued)*
serous otitis media
somatization
somatostatin *also* SMS, SS
somatotropin
somnolent
sphincter of Oddi manometry
sulformethoxine

SOMA
System of Multicultural Assessment

somat
somatic

SOMI
sternooccipital-mandibular
immobilization (brace, orthosis)

SOMPA
System of Multicultural Pluralistic
Assessment

SON
supraoptic nucleus

SONK
spontaneous osteonecrosis of knee

sono
sonogram
sonography

SONP
soft organs not palpable
solid organs not palpable

SOOL
spontaneous onset of labor

SOP
sphincter of Oddi pressure
standard operating procedure

SOPA
syndrome of primary aldosteronism

SOPCA
sporadic olivopontocerebellar ataxia

SOPM
stitches out in afternoon

SOPP
splanchnic occluded portal pressure

s. op. s., s. op. sit.
if it is necessary [L. *si opus sit*]
also SOS

SOQ
Suicide Opinion Questionnaire

SOR
sign own release
stimulus-organism response

SOr
supraorbitale

Sorb, sorb
sorbitol

SOREMP
sleep-onset rapid eye movement
period

SOS
if it is necessary [L. *si opus sit*]
also s. op. s., s. op. sit., s.o.s.
self-obtained smear
stimulation of senses
supplemental oxygen system
Surgitek One-Step

s.o.s.
if it is necessary [L. *si opus sit*]
also s. op. s., s. op. sit., SOS

SOSOB
sit on side of bed

SOT
solid organ transplant
something other than
stream of thought
superficial ocular trauma
systemic oxygen transport

SOTT
synthetic (medium) old tuberculin
trichloroacetic (acid precipitated)

SP
sacral promontory
sacroposterior
sacrum posterior
sacrum to pubis
salivary progesterone
schizotypal personality
secretory piece
semiprivate *also* S/P
senile plaque
septal pore
septum pellucidum
sequential pulse
serine proteinase
seropositive
serum protein *also* S/P
shunt pressure
shunt procedure
silent period
skin potential
sleep deprivation
small protein
soft palate
solid phase

spatial peak
speech
speech pathology
spike potential
spinal *also* S/P
spine
spiramycin
spirometry
spleen
spouse
standard of performance
standard practice
standard procedure
stand and pivot *also* S/P
staphylococcal protease
status post *also* S/P
steady potential
stool preservative
subliminal perception
substance
substance P
subtilopeptidase
suicide precautions *also* S/P
sulfapyridine
summating potential
suprapatellar
suprapatellar pouch
suprapubic *also* S/P
suprapubic puncture
symphysis pubis
synthase phosphatase
systolic pressure *also* S/P

SP1
stimulatory protein 1

S&P
sharp and pink

S/P
semiprivate *also* SP
serum protein *also* SP
spinal *also* SP
stand and pivot *also* SP
status post *also* SP
suicide precautions *also* SP
suprapubic *also* SP
systolic pressure *also* SP

Sp
most posterior point on posterior
 contour of sella turcica
sacropubic

species *also* sp
speech
spine *also* sp, spin
summation potential

sP
senile parkinsonism

sp
space *also* S
spec
species *also* Sp
specific *also* spec
spinal
spine *also* Sp, spin

sp.
spirit, alcohol [L. *spiritus*] *also* spir.,
 Spt.

SPA
salt-poor albumin
schizophrenia with premorbid
 asociality
serum prothrombin activity
sheep pulmonary adenomatosis
sperm penetration assay
spinal progressive amyotrophy
spondyloarthropathy
spontaneous platelet aggregation
staphylococcal protein A *also* SpA
stimulation-produced analgesia
suprapatellar amputation
suprapubic aspiration

SpA
spondyloarthropathy
staphylococcal protein A *also* SPA

SPAC
satisfactory postanesthesia course
sectionally processed antibody coated

SPACE
single potential analysis cavernous
 electrical activity

SPAD
stenosing peripheral arterial disease
subcutaneous peritoneal administration
 device

SPAF
Stroke Prevention in Atrial
 Fibrillation

S

NOTES

SPAG
small particle aerosol generator

SPAI
steroid protein activity index

SPAM
scanning photoacoustic microscopy

SPAMM
spatial modulation of magnetization

span.
spansule

SPAR
sensitivity prediction by acoustic reflex
sensitivity prediction from the acoustic reflex

SPARS
spatially-resolved spectroscopy

SPAT
side platelet aggregation test
Silverstein permanent aeration tube
slow paroxysmal atrial tachycardia

SPBI
serum protein-bound iodine

S-PBIgG
serum-platelet bindable immunoglobulin G

SPBT
suprapubic bladder tap

SPC
salicylamide, phenacetin, caffeine
serum phenylalanine concentration
sickle-shaped particle cell
simultaneous prism cover test
single palmar crease
single photoelectron counting
single proton counting
small pyramidal cell
spike-processed contraction
spleen cell *also* SC
standard platelet count
statistical process control
synthesizing protein complex

sPC
sequential postremission chemotherapy

SPCA
serum prothrombin conversion accelerator (factor VII)

sp cd
spinal cord

SPCK
serum creatinine phosphokinase

SPCT
simultaneous prism and cover test

SPD
salmon-poisoning disease
schizotypal personality disorder
silicon photodiode
sociopathic personality disorder
specific paroxysmal discharge
spectral power distribution
spermidine
standard peak dilution
subcorneal pustular dermatosis
suprapubic drainage

Spd
spermidine

SPDC
striopallidodentate calcinosis

SPDP
N-succinamidylproprionate

SPDT
single-pole, double-throw (switch)

SPE
septic pulmonary edema
serum protein electrolyte
serum protein electrophoresis
streptococcal pyrogenic exotoxin
subjective paranormal experience
sucrose polyester
superficial punctate erosion

SPEB
streptococcal pyrogenic exotoxin B

SPEC
streptococcal pyrogenic exotoxin C

Spec
specialist
specialty

spec
special
specific *also* sp
specimen

Spec Ed
special education

SPECT
single-photon emission computed tomography
single-photon emission computerized tomography

SPEEP
   spontaneous positive end expiratory pressure

SPEG
   serum protein electrophoretogram

SPELT-P
   Structure Photographic Expressive Language Test-II

SPEM
   smooth pursuit eye movement

SPEP
   serum protein electrophoresis

SPET
   single photon emission tomography

SPF
   skin protection factor
   specific pathogen free
   spectrophotofluorometer
   split products of fibrin
   standard perfusion fluid
   streptococcal proliferative factor
   Stuart-Prower factor
   sun protection factor
   suntan photoprotection factor

sp fl
   spinal fluid *also* SF

SPFT
   Sixteen Personality Factors Test

SPG
   scrotopenogram
   serine phosphoglyceride
   specific gravity *also* SG, SpG, sp gr, sp. gr.
   sphenopalatine ganglion
   sucrose-phosphate-glutamate
   symmetrical peripheral gangrene

SpG
   specific gravity *also* SG, SPG, sp gr, sp. gr.

spg
   sponge

SPGR
   spoiled GRASS

sp gr, sp. gr.
   specific gravity *also* SG, SPG, SpG

SPH
   secondary pulmonary hemosiderosis
   severely and profoundly handicapped
   sighs per hour
   spherocyte
   sphingomyelin *also* Sph

Sph
   sphenoidale
   spherical
   spherical (lens) *also* S, sph
   spherocytosis
   sphingomyelin *also* SPH

sph
   sphere
   spherical (lens) *also* S, Sph, sph
   spheroid

SPHE, SPHER
   spherocytes

sp ht
   specific heat

SPI
   selective protein index
   serum precipitable iodine
   Shipley Personal Inventory
   somatotyping ponderal index
   speech processor interface
   Standards for Pediatric Immunization
   subclinical papillomavirus infection

SPIA
   solid-phase immunoabsorbent assay
   solid-phase immunoassay

SPICU
   surgical pulmonary intensive care unit

SPID
   summed pain intensity difference

SPIF
   solid-phase immunoassay fluorescence
   spontaneous peak inspiratory force

SPIH
   superimposed pregnancy-induced hypertension

S-PIN
   Steinmann pin

NOTES

S

spin
  spinal
  spine

spir
  spiral

spir.
  spirit, alcohol [L. *spiritus*] *also* sp.,
  Spt.

spiss.
  dried [L. *spissus*]
  inspissated, thickened by evaporation
  [L. *spissatus*]

SPK
  serum pyruvate kinase
  simultaneous pancreas and kidney
  spinnbarkeit
  superficial punctate keratitis

spkr
  speaker

SPL
  skin potential level
  sound pressure level
  spontaneous lesion
  staphylococcal phage lysate

SPLATT
  split anterior tibial tendon (transfer)
  also SPLATTT

SPLATTT
  split anterior tibial tendon transfer
  also SPLATT

SPLV
  serum parvo virus-like virus

SPM
  scaning probe microscopy
  self-phase modulation
  shocks per minute
  significance probability mapping
  spectinomycin
  spermine
  subhuman primate model
  suspended particulate matter
  syllables per minute
  synaptic plasma membrane

SpM
  spiriformis medialis (nucleus)

spm
  suppression and mutation

SPMA
  spinal progressive muscular atrophy

SPMB
  strong partial maternal behavior

SPMI
  status post myocardial infarction

SPMR
  standardized proportionate mortality

SPN
  solitary pulmonary nodule
  student practical nurse
  supplementary parenteral nutrition
  support parenteral nutrition
  sympathetic preganglionic neuron

sp. n.
  new species [L. *species novum*]

SPO
  status postoperative

SpO₂ SpO$_2$
  arterial oxyhemoglobin saturation
  oxygen saturation as measured using
  pulse oximetry

SPOD
  spouse's perception of disease

spon, spont
  spontaneous

SPOOL
  simultaneous peripheral operation on-
  line

SPORO
  sporatrichosis

Sport Px
  Sport Physical

SPP
  Sexuality Preference Profile
  skin perfusion pressure
  stannous pyrophosphate
  super packed platelets
  suprapubic prostatectomy

Spp, spp
  species (plural)

SPPS
  solid phase peptide synthesis
  stable plasma protein solution

SPPT
  superprecipitation (response)

SPR
  scan projection radiography
  selective posterior rhizotomy
  serial probe recognition
  skin potential reflex

solid phase radioimmunoassay *also* SPRIA

solid phase receptacle

superior peroneal retinaculum

SPRIA

solid phase radioimmunoassay *also* SPR

SPRINT

Secondary Prevention Reinfarction Israeli Nifedipine Trial

SPROM

spontaneous premature rupture of membranes

SPRT

sequential probability ratio test

SPS

shoulder pain and stiffness

simple partial seizure

single patient system

slow-progressive schizophrenia

sodium polyethylene sulfonate

sound production sample

special Pap smear

status post surgery

stimulated protein synthesis

sulfite polymyxin sulfadiazine (agar)

Symonds Picture-Story (Test) *also* SPST

systemic progressive sclerosis

SpS

sphenoid sinus

spSHR

stroke-prone spontaneous hypertensive

SPST

single-pole, single-throw (switch)

Symonds Picture-Story Test *also* SPS

SPT

skin prick test

slow pullthrough

sound production tasks

spectinomycin

spinal tap

Spondee Picture Test

standing pivotal transfer

station pullthrough

Supervisory Practices Test

Symbolic Play Test

Spt.

spirit, alcohol [L. *spiritus*] *also* sp., spir.

SPTA

spatial peak temporal average

Sp tap

spinal tap

SPTI

systolic pressure time index

SPTP

spatial peak temporal peak

SPTS

subjective posttraumatic syndrome

SPTURP

status post transurethral resection of prostate

SPTx

static pelvic traction

SPU

short procedure unit

SPUT

sputum

SPV

selective proximal vagotomy

Shope papillomavirus

slow-phase velocity

sulfophosphovanillin

SPVR

systemic peripheral vascular resistance

SPZ

secretin pancreozymin

sulfinpyrazone

SQ

social quotient

squalene

square *also* sq

status quo

subcutaneous *also* SC, sc, subcu, subcut, subq

survey question

symptom questionnaire

Sq, sq

squamous

S

NOTES

sq
square *also* SQ

SQC
semiquantitative culture

SqCCA, sq cell ca
squamous cell carcinoma *also* SCC, SCCA

sq cm
square centimeter

sq m
square meter

sq mm
square millimeter

SQMP
subcutaneous morphine pump

sqq.
and following [L. *sequentia*]

SQUID
superconducting quantum interference device

S-R
smooth-rough (bacterial colony) *also* SR

SR
sarcoplasmic reticulum
saturation recovery
scanning radiometer
screen
secretion rate
sedimentation rate
see report
seizure resistant
self-recording
senior
sensitivity response
sensitization response (cell)
sentence repetition
service record
sex ratio
short hair (guinea pig)
side rails
sigma reaction
silicone rubber
sinus rhythm
skin resistance
slow release
smooth-rough (bacterial colony)
soluble repository
specific release
specific resistance
specific response
speech reception
stabilizing reversal
stage of resistance
stimulus response
stress relaxation
stretch reflex
sulfonamide-resistant
superior rectus
supply room
sustained release
systemic reaction
systemic resistance
systems research
systems review

S&R
seclusion and restraint (s)

SR$_{AW}$
specific airway resistance

Sr
strontium

^{85}Sr
strontium-85

^{87m}Sr
strontium-87m

^{89}Sr
strontium-89 *also* ^{89}St

^{90}Sr
strontium-90

sr
steradian (unit of three-dimensional measure)

SRA
segmented renal artery
spleen repopulating activity
steroid resistant asthma

SRAM
static random access memory

SRBC
sheep red blood cell *also* SRC
sickle red blood cell

SRBOW
spontaneous rupture of bag of waters

SRC
sedimented red cell
sheep red cell *also* SRBC

SRCA
specific red cell adherence

SRCBC
serum reserve cholesterol binding capacity

SRCP
superficial renal cortical perfusion

SRD
service-related disability
sodium-restricted diet
specific reading disability

SRDT
single radial diffusion test

SRE
Schedule of Recent Experiences

SRF
severe renal failure
skin-reactive factor
slow-reacting factor
somatotropin-releasing factor
split renal function
subretinal fluid

SRF-A
slow-reacting factor of anaphylaxis *also* SRFOA

SRFC
sheep (red cell) rosette-forming cell

SRFOA
slow-reacting factor of anaphylaxis *also* SRF-A

SRFS
split renal function study

SRGVHD
steroid resistant graft-versus-host disease

SRH
signs of recent hemorrhage
single radial hemolysis
somatotropin-releasing hormone
spontaneously responding hyperthyroidism
stigmata of recent hemorrhage

SRI
serotonin reuptake inhibitor
severe renal insufficiency

SRID
single radial immunodiffusion

SRIF
somatotropin release-inhibiting factor *also* SIF

SRM
Standard Reference Material
subretinal membrane
superior rectus muscle

SRMD
stress-related mucosal damage
stress-related mucosal damage

SRN
subretinal neovascularization *also* SRNV

SRNA, sRNA
soluble ribonucleic acid

SR/NE
sinus rhythm, no ectopy

SRNG
sustained release nitroglycerin

SRNP
soluble ribonuclear protein

SRNS
steroid-responsive nephrotic syndrome

SRNV
subretinal neovascularization *also* SRN

SRNVM
senile retinal neovascular membrane
subretinal neovascular membrane

SRO
sagittal ramus osteotomy
single room occupancy

SROM
spontaneous rupture of membranes

SRP
septorhinoplasty
short rib-polydactyly (syndrome) *also* SRPS
signal recognition particle
signal recognition protein
simple response paradigm
stapes replacement prosthesis
State Registered Physiotherapist

SRP instrument
single reference point instrument

NOTES

SRPS
short rib-polydactyly syndrome *also* SRP

SRR
slow rotation room
stabilized relative response
standardized rate ratio
surgical recovery room

SRRS
Social Readjustment Rating Scale

SR-RSV
Schmidt-Ruppin (strain) Rous sarcoma virus

SRS
schizophrenic residual state
sex reassignment surgery
Silver-Russell syndrome
slow-reacting substance
Social and Rehabilitation Service
somatostatin receptor scintigraphy
Symptom Rating Scale

SRSA, SRS-A
slow-reacting substance of anaphylaxis

SRT
sedimentation rate test
sick role tendency
simple reaction time
sinus (node) recovery time *also* SNRT
smoke removal tube
speech reception test
speech reception threshold
spontaneously resolving thyrotoxicosis
Stroke Rehabilitation Technician
surfactant replacement therapy
sustained release theophylline
Symptom Rating Test

SRU
side rails up
solitary rectal ulcer
structural repeating unit

SRUS
solitary rectal ulcer syndrome

SRV
Schmidt-Ruppin virus
superior radicular vein

S-R variation
smooth-rough variation

SRVG
silicone elastomer ring vertical gastroplasty

SRVT
sustained reentrant ventricular tachyarrhythmia

SRW
short ragweed (test)

SRY
sex-determining region

SS
sacrosciatic
saline soak
saline solution
saliva sample
saliva substitute
Salmonella-Shigella (agar) *also* SSA
salt substitute
saturated solution *also* sat. soln.
schizophrenia spectrum
Schizophrenia Subscale
seizure sensitive
serotonin syndrome
serum sickness
Sézary syndrome
siblings
sickle cell (anemia) *also* SSA
side-to-side
signs and symptoms
single stranded *also* ss
Sjögren syndrome *also* SjS
sliding scale
slip sent
slow-wave sleep
soapsuds *also* ss
Social Security
social services
somatostatin *also* SMS, SOM
sparingly soluble
special service
stable sarcoidosis
staccato syndrome
standard score
statistically significant
steady state *also* s, ss
sterile solution
steroid sensitivity
steroid sulfurylation
Stickler syndrome
Strachan-Scott (syndrome)
subaortic stenosis
subscapularis
subsegmental
subsequent sibling
substernal
suction socket
sulfasalazine

sum (of) squares
supersaturated
support (and) stimulation
susceptible
Sweet syndrome
symmetrical strength
systemic sclerosis

S/S
signs and symptoms *also* S&S

S&S
shower and shampoo
signs and symptoms *also* S/S
sling and swathe
soft and smooth (prostate)
support and stimulation
swish and spit
swish and swallow

Ss
serum soluble (antigen)
subjects

ss
half [L. *semis*] *also* HF, hf, S, s.,
   sem., semi
single stranded *also* SS
soapsuds *also* SS
steady state *also* SS, s
subspinale

SS-A
Sjögren syndrome A (antibody)

SSA
sagittal split advancement
salicylsalicylic acid
Salmonella-Shigella agar *also* SS
sickle cell anemia
Sjögren syndrome antigen A
skin-sensitizing antibody
skin sympathetic activity
Smith surface antigen
Social Security Administration
special somatic afferent
sperm-specific antigen
sperm-specific antiserum
subsegmental airway
subsegmental atelectasis
sulfosalicylic acid

SSAER
steady-state auditory evoked response

SSAV
simian sarcoma-associated virus

SS-B
Sjögren syndrome B (antibody)

SSB
short spike burst
stereospecific binding

SSBG
sex steroid-binding globulin

SSBR
see separate bacteriology report

SSC
sign symptom complex
single-stripe colitis
somatosensory cortex
stainless steel crown
standard saline citrate
Stein Sentence Completion (test)
superior semicircular canal
suprascapular nerve compression
syngeneic spleen cell

SSc
systemic sclerosis

SSCA
sensitized sheep cell agglutination
single shoulder contrast arthrography
spontaneous suppressor cell activity

SSCCS
slow spinal cord compression
   syndrome

SSCF
sleep stage change frequency

SSCP
single-strand conformation
   polymorphism
substernal chest pain

SSCr
stainless steel crown

SSCT
Sacks Sentence Completion Test

SSCVD
sterile spontaneous controlled vaginal
   delivery

SSD
serosanguineous drainage

S

NOTES

SSD (*continued*)
shock(-induced) suppression of drinking
sickle cell disease
silver sulfadiazine
single saturating dose
Social Security Disability
source-skin distance
source-surface distance
speech-sound discrimination
succinate semialdehyde dehydrogenase
sudden sniffing death
sum of square deviations
syndrome of sudden death

SSDBS
symptom schedule for the diagnosis of borderline schizophrenia

SSDI
Social Security disability income

SS-DNA, ssDNA
single-stranded deoxyribonucleic acid

SSE
saline solution enema
skin self-examination
soapsuds enema
steady-state exercise
systemic side effects

SSEA
stage-specific embryonic antigen

SSEH
spontaneous spinal epidural hematoma

S-SEP
somatosensory-evoked potential *also* SEP, SSEP

SSEP
short-latency somatosensory-evoked potential
somatosensory evoked potential *also* SEP, S-SEP

SSER
somatosensory evoked response *also* SER

SSF
soluble suppressor factor
subscapular skinfold (thickness)
supplementary sensory feedback

SSFI
social stress and functionability inventory

SSG
sublabial salivary gland

SSHb
homozygous for sickle cell hemoglobin

SSHL
severe sensorineural hearing loss

SSI
segmental sequential irradiation
segmental spinal instrumentation
shoulder subluxation inhibitor
sliding scale insulin
small-scale integration
Social Security income
stuttering severity instrument
subshock insulin
superior sector iridectomy
Supplemental Security Income
symptom severity index
synthetic sentence identification
System Sign Inventory

SSIAM
Structured and Scaled Interview to Assess Maladjustment

SSIDS
sibling of sudden infant death syndrome (victim)

SSIE
Smithsonian Science Information Exchange

SSII
Safran Student's Interest Inventory

SSIT
subscapularis, supraspinatus, infraspinatus, and teres minor (muscles)

SSKI
saturated solution of potassium iodide

SSL
skin surface lipid
subtotal supraglottic laryngectomy
synthetic sentence list

S-sleep
synchronized sleep

SSM
skin surface microscopy
subsynaptic membrane
superficial spreading melanoma

SSN
severely subnormal
Social Security number
subacute sensory neuropathy
suprasternal notch *also* SN

SSNS
steroid-sensitive nephrotic syndrome

SSO
Society of Surgical Oncology
Spanish-speaking only
special sense organs

SSOP
Second Surgical Opinion Program

SSP
Sanarelli-Shwartzman phenomenon
small spherical particle
subacute sclerosing panencephalitis
also SSPE
supersensitivity perception

Ssp, ssp
subspecies *also* subsp

SSPE
subacute sclerosing panencephalitis
also SSP

SSPG
steady-state plasma glucose

SSPI
steady-state plasma insulin

SSPL
saturation sound pressure level

SSPP
subsynaptic plate perforation

SSPS
side-to-side portacaval shunt

SS-PSE
Schizophrenic Subscale of Present
State Examination

SSPU
surgical short procedure unit

SSQ
Social Support Questionnaire

SSR
somatosensory response
somatostatin receptor
steady-state rest
steroid-resistant rejection
substernal retraction
surgical supply room
sympathetic skin response

SSRFC
surrounding subretinal fluid cuff

SSRI
selective serotonin reuptake inhibitor

SSS
layer upon layer [L. *stratum super
stratum*] *also* s.s.s.
scalded skin syndrome
secondary Sjögren syndrome
sensation-seeking scale
sick sinus syndrome
soluble specific substance
specific soluble substance
Stanford Sleepiness Scale
sterile saline soak
strong soap solution
structured sensory stimulation
systemic sicca syndrome

s.s.s.
layer upon layer [L. *stratum super
stratum*] *also* SSS

SSSB
sagittal split setback

SSSC
Social Support Scale for Children
test

SSSS
Scandinavian Simvastatin Survival
Study
staphylococcal scalded skin syndrome

SSST
superior sagittal sinus thrombosis

SSSV
superior sagittal sinus velocity

SST
sagittal sinus thrombosis
sodium sulfite titration
somatosensory thalamus
somatostatin

SSTN
Sandostatin

s. str.
in the strict sense [L. *sensu stricto*]

NOTES

SSU
self-service unit
sterile supply unit

SSV
Schoolman-Schwartz virus
sheep seminal vesicle
simian sarcoma virus *also* SISV,
SiSV
under a poison label [L. *sub signo
veneni*]

SSVD
sterile, spontaneous vaginal delivery

SSW
staggered spondaic word (test)

SSX
sulfisoxazole

S/SX
signs/symptoms

ST
electrocardiographic wave segment
esotropia
(heat-)stable (entero)toxin
sacrotransverse
sacrum transverse
scala tympani
sclerotherapy
sedimentation time
semitendinosus
septal thickness
serum transferrin
shock therapy
siblings (raised) together
similarly tested
sinus tachycardia
sinus tympani
skin temperature
skin test
skin thickness
slight trace
slow twitch
speech therapist
sphincter tone
split thickness
standard test
starting time
sternothyroid
stimulus *also* R, S
stomach *also* St, st, stom
store *also* STO
straight
stress test
stretcher
striatum *also* Str

sublingual tablet
subtalar
subtotal
sulfathiozole
surface tension *also* σ
surgical therapy
survival time
systolic time

S-T
sickle cell thalassemia

ST37
hexylresorcinol

St, st
stage (of disease)
stere (measure of capacity)
stokes (unit of kinematic viscosity)
stomach *also* ST, stom
stomion (median point of oral slit
when lips are closed)
stone (unit)
straight
stroke
subtype

St.
stomion

⁸⁹St
strontium-89 *also* ⁸⁹Sr

st (*var. of* St)

st.
let it stand [L. *stet*]
let them stand [L. *stent*]

STA
second trimester abortion
serum thrombotic accelerator
serum tobramycin assay
superficial temporal artery
superior temporal artery

Sta
staphylion
station

stab
stabilization
"stabkernige" (staff or band
neutrophils)
stab nuclear neutrophil

STACL
Screening Test for Auditory
Comprehension of Language

St AE
standard above-elbow (cast)

S-TAG
slow-binding target-attaching globulin

STAG
split thickness autogenous graft
striped tag myocardial tagging system

STAI-I
State Trait Anxiety Index-I

STA-MCA
superficial temporal artery to middle
cerebral artery
superior temporal artery-middle
cerebral artery

STAMP
Solid Tumor Autologous Marrow
Transplant Program

StanPsych
standard psychiatric (nomenclature)

STA-PCA
superficial temporal artery to
posterior cerebral artery

staph
staphylococcus

STAR
staged abdominal repair

STARS
Short-Term Auditory Retrieval and
Storage Test

START
stereotactic-assisted radiation therapy

StaRT
stereotactic radiation therapy

STA-SCA
superficial temporal artery-superior
cerebellar artery

STAT
at once [L. *statim*] *also* stat.
Suprathreshold Adaptation Test

stat
radiation emanation unit (German)

stat.
at once [L. *statim*] *also* STAT

STB, Stb
stillborn *also* SB, stillb

STBAL
standing balance

ST BY
stand by *also* SB

STC
serum theophylline concentration
sexually transmitted condition
soft tissue calcification
stimulate to cry
Stroke Treatment Center
subtotal colectomy
sugar tong cast

STD
sexually transmitted disease
skin test done
skin test dose
skin-to-tumor distance
sodium tetradecyl (sulfate)
standard density (reference)
standard test dose

std
saturated *also* SAT, Sat, sat., sat'd
standardized

STDH
skin test for delayed-type
hypersensitivity

STDS
stone-tissue detection-system

STDT
standard tone-decay test

STD TF
standard tube feeding

STEAM
stimulated-echo acquisition mode

STEL
short-term exposure limit

STEM
scanning transmission electron
microscope

sten
stenosed
stenosis

STEPS
sequential treatment employing
pharmacologic support

NOTES

stereo
    stereogram
    stereophonic

STET
    single photon emission tomography
    submaximal treadmill exercise test

STETH
    stethoscope

STF
    serum thymus factor
    slow twitch fiber
    small third-trimester fetus
    specialized treatment facility
    special tube feeding
    standard tube feeding
    sudden transient freezing

ST-FeSv
    Synder-Thielen feline sarcoma virus

STG
    short-term goal
    split-thickness graft
    superior temporal gyrus

STGC
    syncytiotrophoblastic giant cell

STH
    soft tissue hemorrhage
    somatotropic hormone *also* SH
    subtotal hysterectomy
    supplemental thyroid hormone

STh, S-Thal
    sickle cell thalassemia

STHB
    said to have been

STI
    scientific and technical information
    serum trypsin inhibitor
    soft tissue injury
    soybean trypsin inhibitor *also* SBTI
    systolic time interval

STIC
    serum trypsin inhibition capacity
    solid-state transducer intracompartment

stillat.
    drop by drop [L. *stillatim*]

stillb
    stillborn *also* SB, Stb

stim, stimn, stm
    stimulation *also* stm, stmn

STIP
    (basophilic) stippling

STIR
    short inversion imaging recovery
    short tau inversion recovery
    short TI inversion recovery

STJ
    scapulothoracic joint
    subtalar joint

STK
    streptokinase *also* SK

STL
    serum theophylline level
    status thymicolymphaticus
    swelling, tenderness, limited (motion)

STLE
    St. Louis encephalitis

STLOM
    swelling, tenderness, limitation of motion

STLS
    subacute thyroiditis-like syndrome

STLV
    simian T-cell lymphotropic virus

STM
    scanning tunneling microscope
    short-term memory
    streptomycin *also* SM

stm, stmn (*var. of* stim)

StMPM
    syncytiotrophoblast microvillar plasma membrane

STN
    sialyl Tn antigen
    subthalamic nucleus
    supratrochlear nucleus

STNR
    symmetric tonic neck reflex

STNS
    sham transcutaneous nerve stimulation

STNV
    satellite tobacco necrosis virus

STO
    store *also* ST
    surgical treatment objective

stom
    stomach *also* ST, St, st

STOP
surgical termination of pregnancy

STORCH
syphilis, toxoplasmosis, rubella,
cytomegalovirus, and herpes (virus)

STP
scientifically treated petroleum
serenity, tranquility, peace user's term
for (dimethoxymethylamphetamine)
Sibling Training Program
sodium thiopental
standard temperature and pressure
standard temperature and pulse

S-TPA
serum tissue polypeptide antigen

STPD
standard temperature and pressure,
dry

STPI
State-Trait Personality Inventory

STPP
sodium tripolyphosphate

STPS
specific thalamic projection system

STQ
superior temporal quadrant

STR
soft-tissue rheumatism
special treatment room
stone-tissue recognition system

Str
striatum *also* ST

strab
strabismus *also* Sb

STRAN
surgical resident's admission note

Strep
streptomycin

strep
streptococcus

STRESS
subject's treatment-emergent symptom
scale

STRT
skin temperature recovery time

struct
sructural
structure

STS
serologic test for syphilis
sexual tubal sterilization
short-term storage
silicone thermoplastic splinting
sodium tetradecylsulfate
sodium thiosulfate
soft tissue sarcoma
soft tissue swelling
standard test for syphilis
sugar-tong splint

STSE
split-thickness skin excision

STSG
split-thickness skin graft

STSS
staphylococcal toxic shock syndrome

STSs
sequence-tagged sites

STT
scaphotrapeziotrapezoid (joint)
sensitization test
serial thrombin time
skin temperature test
soft tissue tumor
standard triple therapy

STTOL
standing tolerance

STU
shock trauma unit
skin test unit

STUMP
stromal tumors of unknown malignant
potential

STV
short-term variability
soft tissue view
superior temporal vein

STVA
subtotal villous atrophy *also* SVA

S

NOTES

STVS
short-term visual storage

STX
saxitoxin
stricture
structure

STYCAR
Screening Tests for Young Children
and Retardates

STZ
streptozocin *also* SZ, Sz, SZN
streptozotocin
streptozyme

SU
salicyluric (acid)
sensation unit
sensory urgency
solar urticaria
Somogyi unit
sorbent unit
spectrophotometric unit
strontium unit
subunit
sulfonamide *also* Su
sulfonylurea
supine

S/U
shoulder/umbilicus

S&U
supine and upright

Su
sulfonamide *also* SU

su.
let him take [L. *sumat*]

SUA
serum uric acid
single umbilical artery
single unit activity

SUB
Skene, urethral and Bartholin (glands)

subac
subacute

subconj
subconjunctival

subcu, subcut, subq
subcutaneous *also* SC, sc, SQ, subq

sub fin coct
toward the end of boiling [L. *sub
finem coctionis*]

subl, subling
sublingual

submand
submandibular

SubN
subthalamic nucleus

subq (*var. of* subcu)

subsp
subspecies *also* Ssp, ssp

substd
substandard

suc.
juice [L. *succus*]

SUCC
succinylcholine

Succ
succinate
succinic

SUD
skin unit dose
sudden unexpected death
sudden unexplained death

SUDI
sudden unexpected death in infants
sudden unexplained death in infants

SUDS
single-unit delivery system
single-use diagnostic system
Subjective Unit of Distress Scale
sudden unexplained death syndrome

SUE
single-use electrode

SUF
sequential ultrafiltration

Suff
sufficient

SUHT
subject's height (in inches)

SUI
stress urinary incontinence
suicide

SUID
sudden unexpected infant death
sudden unexplained infant death

sulf
sulfate

sulfa
sulfonamide

SULFHB
sulfhemoglobin *also* HbS, SHB, SHb

SULF-PRIM
sulfamethoxazole (and) trimethoprim

sum.
to be taken [L. *sumendum*]
let him take [L. *sumat*]
summation

SUMIT
streptokinase-urokinase myocardial
infarction trial

sum. tal.
let the person take one like this [L.
sumat talem]

SUN
serum urea nitrogen
Standard Units and Nomenclature

SUO
syncope of unknown origin

SUP
stress ulcer prophylaxis
superficial *also* sup
superior
supination *also* supin
supinator (muscle)
symptomatic uterine prolapse

sup
above [L. *supra*]
superficial *also* SUP, sup
superior *also* SUP, sup
supervision
supervisor
supinator (muscle) *also* SUP

SupHypArt
superior hypophyseal artery

supin
supination *also* SUP

supp, suppos
support
suppository

suppl
supplement
supplementary

SUR
suramin

SURG, surg
surgeon
surgery *also* S
surgical

SURS
solitary ulcer of rectum syndrome

SUS
solitary ulcer syndrome
stained urinary sediment
suppressor sensitive

susp
suspended
suspension

SUTI
symptomatic urinary tract infection

SUUD
sudden unexpected, unexplained death

SUX
succinylcholine
suction

SUZI
subzonal insemination

SV
saphenous vein
sarcoma virus
satellite virus
selective vagotomy
semilunar valve
seminal vesicle
Sendai virus
severe
sigmoid volvulus
simian virus
single ventricle
sinus venosus
snake venom
splenic vein
spoken voice
spontaneous ventilation
stroke volume
subclavian vein
subventricular
supravital

S/V
surface/volume (ratio)

S

NOTES

SV40
simian vacuolating virus 40

Sv
sievert (unit) *also* sv

s.v.
spirit of wine [L. *spiritus vini*]

sv
sievert (unit) *also* Sv
single vibration

SVA
selective vagotomy with antrectomy
selective visceral angiography
sequential ventriculoatrial (pacing)
spatial voltage (at maximal) anterior
(force)
special visceral afferent
subtotal villous atrophy *also* STVA

SVAS
subvalvular aortic stenosis
supravalvular aortic stenosis *also*
SAS

SVB
saphenous vein bypass

SVBG
saphenous vein bypass graft

SVC
segmental venous capacitance
slow vital capacity
subclavian vein catheterization
subclavian vein compression
superior vena cava
suprahepatic vena cava

SVCCS
superior vena cava compression
syndrome

SVCG
spatial vectorcardiogram

SVCO
superior vena cava obstruction

SVCP
Special Virus Cancer Program

SVC-PA
superior vena cava-pulmonary artery
(shunt)

SVCR
segmented venous capacitance ratio

SVC-RPA
superior vena cava-right pulmonary
artery (shunt)

SVCS
superior vena cava syndrome

SVD
single vessel disease
singular value decomposition
small vessel disease
spontaneous vaginal delivery
spontaneous vertex delivery
swine vesicular disease

SVE
slow volume encephalography
soluble viral extract
special visceral efferent
sterile vaginal examination
Streptococcus viridans endocarditis
supraventricular ectopy

SVG
saphenous vein graft

SVI
seminal vesicle invasion
stroke volume index
systolic velocity integral (Doppler)

S VISC
serum viscosity

SVL
severe visual loss
superficial vastus lateralis

SVM
seminal vesicle microsome
spatial voltage at maximal (posterior
force)
syncytiovascular membrane

SVN
small volume nebulizer

SVO
splenic vein obstruction

SvO$_2$, S$_{VO2}$
mixed venous oxygen saturation
venous oxygen saturation

SVOM
sequential volitional oral movement

SVP
selective vagotomy with pyloroplasty
small volume parenteral (infusion)
spatial voltage (at maximal) posterior
(force)
spontaneous venous pulse
standing venous pressure
static volume pressure
superficial vascular plexus

SVPB
supraventricular premature beat

SVPC
supraventricular premature contraction

SVR
sequential vascular response
supraventricular rhythm
systemic vascular resistance

s.v.r.
rectified spirit of wine (distilled) [L. *spiritus vini rectificatus*]

SVRI
systemic vascular resistance index

SVS
slit ventricle syndrome

SVSe
supravaginal septum

SVT
sinoventricular tachyarrhythmia
subclavian vein thrombosis
supraventricular tachyarrhythemia
supraventricular tachycardia

s.v.t.
thin spirit of wine (diluted) [L. *spiritus vini tenuis*]

SVVD
spontaneous vertex vaginal delivery

SW
Schwartz-Watson (test)
seriously wounded
short wave
slow wave
social worker
spherule wall
spike wave
spiral wound
stab wound
sterile water
stroke work
Sturge-Weber (syndrome) *also* SWS
Swiss Webster (mouse)

S&W
soap and water

Sw
swine

sw
switch

SWAMI
Speech with Alternating Masking Index

SWAMP
swine-associated mucoprotein

SWC
submaximal working capacity

SWD
short-wave diathermy

SWE
slow-wave encephalography

SWFI
sterile water for injection *also* SWI

SWG
standard wire gauge

SWI
skin and wound isolation
sterile water for injection *also* SWFI
stroke work index
surgical wound infection

SWIFT
Should We Intervene Following Thrombolysis

SWIM
sperm-washing insemination method

SWIORA
spinal cord injury without radiologic abnormality

SWM
segmental wall motion

SWO
superficial white onychomycosis

SWOG
Southwest Oncology Group

SWORD
Survival with Oral d-sotalol

SWP
small whirlpool

SWR
serum Wassermann reaction
surface wrinkling retinopathy

NOTES

SWS
slow-wave sleep
spike-wave stupor
Sturge-Weber syndrome *also* SW

SWT
sine-wave threshold
Speech Weber Test
stab wound of throat

SWU
septic workup

SX
sulfamethoxypyridazine

Sx, S$_x$
signs
surgery
symptoms

sx
symptom *also* Sm, sym, symp,
sympt

SXA
single energy x-ray absorptiometry

SXR
skull x-ray

SXT
sulfamethoxazole/trimethoprim *also*
SMX/TMP, SMZ-TMP, SULF-PRIM,
TMP-SMX

SY
syphilis *also* syph
syphilitic *also* syph

SYA
subacute yellow atrophy

SYC
small, yellow, constipated (stool)

sym
symmetrical
symptom *also* Sm, symp, sympt, sx

symb
symbol
symbolic

symp
symptom *also* Sm, sym

sympath
sympathetic

symph
symphysis

sympt
symptom *also* sx, sym

SYN
synaptophysin

syn, synd
syndrome
synonym
synovial

sync
synchronous

syndet
synthetic detergent

syn fl
synovial fluid *also* SF

synth
synthetic

syph
syphilis *also* SY
syphilitic *also* SY

SYR
Syrian (hamster)

Syr
syrup [L. *syrupus*] *also* syr

syr
syringe

syr.
syrup [L. *syrupus*] *also* Syr

SYS
stretching-yawning syndrome

sys
system *also* syst
systemic *also* syst

SYS BP
systolic blood pressure *also* SBP

syst
system *also* sys
systemic *also* sys
systole
systolic

SZ
schizophrenic
seizure *also* Sz
Skevas-Zerfus (disease)
streptozocin *also* STZ, Sz, SZN
suction
sulfamethizole

Sz
schizophrenia
seizure *also* SZ
skin impedance
streptozocin *also* STZ, SZ, SZN

SZD
 streptozocin diabetes

SZN
 streptozocin *also* STZ, SZ, Sz

NOTES

S

T

absolute temperature (Kelvin)
electrocardiographic wave
 corresponding to repolarization of
 ventricles
life (time) *also* t
obtained under test conditions
period (time)
ribosylthymine
ribothymidine *also* Thd
tablespoonful *also* tbsp
tamoxifen *also* TAM, TMX
tanycyte (ependymal cell)
tau (19th letter of Greek alphabet),
 uppercase
T bandage
T bar
telomere (banding of chromosomes)
temperature *also* temp
temporal electrode placement in
 electroencephalography
temporary *also* temp
tender
tension (intraocular) *also* TEM
tera-
terminal (banding of chromosomes)
tertiary *also* t, ter, tert
tesla
testicle
testosterone
tetra
tetracycline *also* TC, Tc, TCN,
 TCNE, TE, TET
T fiber
theophylline
thoracic *also* Th, th, thor
thoracoabdominal (stapler)
thorax *also* th, Th, thor
threatened (animal)
threonine *also* Thr
thrombus *also* throm, thromb
thymidine *also* TdR
thymine *also* Thy
thymus (cell) *also* thy.
thymus-derived (lymphocyte)
thyroid
tidal (gas)
time
timolol
tincture *also* TR, Tr, tr
tocopherol
tone

tonometer (reading)
topical *also* top.
torque
total
toxicity *also* Tox, tox
trace *also* TR, Tr, tr
tracheotomy (set)
training (group)
transition (point) *also* TP
transmittance
transverse *also* trans
tray
triangulation
triggered
tritium *also* t
tuberculin
tuberculosis *also* TB, Tb, tb, TBC,
 Tbc, tuberc
tuberculum
tuberosity
tumor (antigen)
turnkey (system)
type

T+

increased intraocular tension
increased tension (pressure)

T-

decreased tension (pressure)

T1

first twitch height
spin-lattice or longitudinal relaxation
 time (MRI scan)

T1–T12

first to twelfth thoracic nerves
first to twelfth thoracic vertebrae

T2

spin-spin or transverse relaxation time
 (MRI scan)

2,4,5–T

2,4,5-trichlorophenoxyacetic acid

T3

Tylenol with codeine (30 mg)

T-7

free thyroxin factor

T12

terminal half-life

T28

Trapezoidal-28

T-1824
Evans blue (dye)

T₁
monoiodotyrosine
tricuspid first heart sound

T₂
diiodothyronine
second stage of decreased intraocular tension
tricuspid second heart sound

T₃
triiodothyronine *also* TIT, TITh, TRIT
3,5,3′-triiodothyronine *also* TITh

T₄
levothyroxine
tetraiodothyronine (thyroxine)
thyroxine

t
duration
life (time) *also* T
student test variable
teaspoonful
temperature (Celsius, Fahrenheit)
temporal
terminal
tertiary *also* T, ter, tert
test (of significance)
time
ton (metric)
tonne
translocation
tritium *also* T

t.
three (times) [L. *ter*]

T½
(mitral) pressure half-time (Doppler)
terminal half-life (of isotopes)

t½
reaction half-time
time taken for half of initialconcentration of deoxyribonucleic acid to renature

t½elim
elimination half-life

T-A
toxin-antitoxin *also* TA

TA
alkaline tuberculin
tactile afferent
Takayasu arteritis

tantalum *also* Ta
technical assistance
teichoic acid
temperature, axillary *also* T(A)
temporal arteritis
temporal average
tendon of Achilles
tension by applanation *also* Ta
tension, arterial
terminal antrum
terminal arteriole
test age
therapeutic abortion *also* TAB
thermophilic *Actinomyces*
thymocytotoxic autoantibody
thyroglobulin autoprecipitation
thyroglobulin autoprecipitin
thyroid antibody
thyroid autoantibody
tibialis anterior
titratable acid
total alkaloids
toxic adenoma
toxin-antitoxin *also* T-A, TAT
tracheal aspirate
traffic accident *also* T/A
transactional analysis
transaldolase
transantral
transplantation antigen
trapped air
treatment assignment
triamcinolone acetonide *also* TAA
tricholomic acid
tricuspid annuloplasty
tricuspid atresia
trophoblast antigen
true anomaly
truncus arteriosus
tryptamine
tryptophan-acid (reaction)
tryptose agar
tube agglutination
tuberculin, alkaline
tumorantigen
tumor associated

TA-4
tumor-antigen 4

T of A
transposition of aorta

T&A
tonsillectomy and adenoidectomy
tonsils and adenoids

T/A
time and amount
traffic accident *also* TA, TAT

T(A)
temperature, axillary *also* TA

¹⁷⁸TA
tantalum-178 *also* ¹⁷⁸Ta

TA₄
tetraiodothyroacetic acid

Ta
T-amplifier
tantalum *also* TA
tension by applanation *also* TA
tonometry applanation

¹⁷⁸Ta
tantalum-178 *also* ¹⁷⁸TA

¹⁸²Ta
tantalum-182

TAA
thoracic aortic aneurysm
total ankle arthroplasty
transverse aortic arch
triamcinolone acetonide *also* TA
tumor-associated antigen

TAAA
thoracoabdominal aortic aneurysm

TAAF
thromblastic activity of amniotic fluid

TAB
tablet *also* tab.
therapeutic abortion *also* TA
triple antibiotic
typhoid, paratyphoid A, and
paratyphoid B (vaccine)

TAb
therapeutic abortion

ab.
tablet *also* TAB

TABC
total aerobic bacteria count
typhoid, paratyphoid A, paratyphoid
B, and paratyphoid C (vaccine)

TABTD
typhoid, paratyphoid A, paratyphoid
B, tetanus toxoid, and diphtheria
toxoid (vaccine)

TAC
terminal antrum contraction
tetracaine, Adrenalin (epinephrine),
and cocaine
time-activity curve
total abdominal colectomy
total aganglionosis coli
total allergen content
Toxicant Analysis Center
triamcinolone acetonide cream

TACC
thoracic aortic crossclamping

TACE
teichoic acid crude extract
transcatheter arterial
chemoembolization
trianisylchloroethylene

tach, tachy
tachycardia

TACL
Test for Auditory Comprehension of
Language

TACL-R
Tests for Auditory Comprehension of
Language-R

TAD
thoracic asphyxiant dystrophy
total administered dose
transient acantholytic dermatosis
transverse abdominal diameter
tricyclic antidepressant drug

TADAC
therapeutic abortion, dilation,
aspiration, and curettage

TAE
total abdominal evisceration
transcatheter arterial embolization

TAER
transient auditory-evoked response

TAF
albumose-free tuberculin [Ger.
Tuberculin Albumose frei]

NOTES

TAF *(continued)*
tissue angiogenesis factor
toxoid-antitoxin floccule
trypsin-aldehyde-fuchsin
tumor angiogenic factor

TAG
target-attaching globulin
thymine, adenine, and guanine
triacylglycerol
tumor-associated glycoprotein

TAG-72
tumor-associated glycoprotein-72

TAGH
triiodothyronine, amino acids,
glucagon, and heparin

TAGVHD, TA-GVHD
transfusion-associated graft-versus-host
disease

TAH
total abdominal hysterectomy
total artificial heart

TAHBSO
total abdominal hysterectomy and
bilateral salpingo-oophorectomy

TAI
tissue antagonist of interferon

TAIM
Trial of Antihypertensive Interventions
and Management

TAL
tendo Achillis lengthening
tendon Achilles lengthening
thick ascending limb
thymic alymphoplasia
total arm length
triamcinolone lotion

tal.
such a one [L. *talis*]

TALC
transairway laryngeal control

talc
talcum

tal dos
such doses

TALH
thick ascending limb of Henle (loop)

TALL, T-ALL
T-cell acute lymphoblastic leukemia

TALT
testicular adrenal-like tissue

TALTFR
tendo Achillis lengthening and toe
flexor release

TAM
tamoxifen *also* T, TMX
teenage mother
thermoacidurans agar modified
total active motion
toxoid-antitoxoid mixture
transient abnormal myelopoiesis
transtelephonic ambulatory monitoring
(system)
tumor-associated macrophages

TAMe
toxoid-antitoxoid mixture esterase

TAMI
Thrombolysis and Angioplasty in
Myocardial Infarction

TAMIS
Telemetric Automated Microbial
Identification System

TAML, t-AML
therapy related acute myelogenous
leukemia
therapy-related acute myeloid
leukemia

TAN
total adenine nucleotide
total ammonia nitrogen

tan.
tandem translocation
tangent

TANI
total axial (lymph) node irradiation

TAO
thromboangiitis obliterans
triacetyloleandomycin
triamcinolone ointment
turning against object

TAP
tension by applanation
tonometry by applanation
transabdominal preperitoneal
(laparoscopic hernia repair)
transesophageal atrial pacing *also*
TEAP

TAPET
tumor amplified protein expression
therapy

TAPP
transabdominal preperitoneal polypropylene (meshplasty)

TAPS
training and placement service
trial assessment procedure scale

TAP-S
Test of Articulation Performance-Screen

TAPVC
total anomalous pulmonary venous connection

TAPVD
total anomalous pulmonary venous drainage

TAPVR
total anomalous pulmonary venous return

TAQW
transient abnormal Q wave

TAR
thrombocytopenia-absent radius
tissue-air ratio
total abortion rate
total ankle replacement
Treatment Authorization Request

TARA
total articular replacement arthroplasty
total articular resurfacing arthroplasty
tumor-associated rejection antigen

TART
tumorectomy, axillary dissection, radiotherapy

TAS
test for ascendance-submission
tetanus antitoxic serum
Therapeutic Activities Specialist
thoracoabdominal syndrome
Thrombolytic Assessment system
turning against self
typical absence seizure

TASA
tumor-associated surface antigen

T'ase, Tase
tryptophan synthetase

TASS
thyroiditis, Addison disease, Sjögren syndrome, sarcoidosis (syndrome)

TAT
Tell a Tale (psychiatry)
tetanus antitoxin
thematic apperception test
thematic aptitude test
thrombin-antithrombin
thrombin-antithrombin III complex
thromboplastin activation test
till all taken
total antitryptic activity
toxin-antitoxin *also* TA, T-A
transaxial tomogram
transverse axial tomography
tray agglutination test
tumor activity test
turnaround time
tyrosine aminotransferase

TATA
tumor-associated transplantation antigen

TATBA
triamcinolone acetomide *tert*-butyl acetate

TATR
tyrosine aminotransferase regulator

TATST
tetanus antitoxin skin test

τ
life (of radioisotope)
relaxation time
shear stress
spectral transmittance
tau (19th letter of Greek alphabet), lowercase
transmission coefficient

TAUC
time-averaged urea concentration

TAUSA
Thrombolysis and Angioplasty in Unstable Angina

TAV
transvenous aortovelography
trapped air volume

NOTES

TAX
 cefotaxime *also* CTX

TB
 Tapes for the Blind
 Taussig-Bing (syndrome)
 terminal bronchiole
 thromboxane B
 thymol blue
 toluidine blue
 total base
 total bilirubin *also* TBIL, T Bili,
 TOT BILI
 total body
 tracheal bronchiolar (region)
 tracheobronchitis
 trapezoid body
 tub bath
 tubercle bacillus *also* Tb, TBA
 tuberculin
 tuberculosis *also* T, Tb, tb, TBC,
 Tbc, tuberc
 tumor bearing

T-B
 Thomas-Binetti (test)

T$_b$
 temperature, body

Tb
 terbium
 tubercle bacillus *also* TB, TBA
 tuberculosis *also* T, TB, tb, TBC,
 Tbc, tuberc

tb
 biologic half-life
 tuberculosis *also* T, TB, Tb, TBC,
 Tbc, tuberc

TBA
 to be absorbed
 to be added
 to be administered
 to be admitted
 tertiary butyl acetate
 testosterone-binding affinity
 thiobarbituric acid
 thyroxin-binding albumin
 total bile acid
 total body (surface) area
 traditional birth attendant
 trypsin-binding activity
 tubercle bacillus *also* TB, Tb
 tumor-bearing animal

TBAB
 tryptose/blood/agar base

TBARS
 thiobarbituric acid-reactive substance

TBB
 transbronchial biopsy

TBBC
 total (vitamin) B$_{12}$ binding capacity

TBBM
 total body bone mineral

TBC
 thyroxin-binding coagulin
 total body calcium
 total body clearance *also* Q$_B$
 total body counting
 tubercidin
 tuberculosis *also* T, TB, Tb, tb,
 Tbc, tuberc
 tuberculous

Tbc
 tuberculosis *also* T, TB, Tb, tb,
 TBC, tuberc

TBD
 total body density
 Toxicology Data Base

TBE
 tick-borne encephalitis
 tuberculin bacillary emulsion

TBF
 total body fat

TBFB
 tracheobronchial foreign body

TBFVL
 tidal breathing flow-volume loop

TBG
 testosterone-binding globulin
 thyroid-binding globulin
 thyroxin-binding globulin
 tracheobronchogram
 tris-buffered Grey (solution)

TBGE
 thyroxin-binding globulin, estimated

TBGI
 thyroid-binding globulin index
 thyroxin-binding globulin index

TBGP
 total blood granulocyte pool

TBH
 total body hematocrit

TBHT
 total body hyperthermia

TBI
thyroid-binding index
thyroxin-binding index
tooth-brushing instruction
total body irradiation *also* TBX
tracheobronchial injury
traumatic brain injury

TBII
thyroid-stimulating hormone
(TSH)-binding inhibitory
immunoglobulin

TBIL, T Bili
total bilirubin (assay)

TBK
total body kalium (potassium)

TBLB
transbronchial lung biopsy

TBLC
term birth, living child

TBLF
term birth, living female

TBLI
term birth, living infant

TBLM
term birth, living male

TBM
thin basement membrane
thyroxin-binding meningitis
total body mass
tracheobronchomalacia
tuberculous meningitis
tubular basement membrane

TBMD
thin basement membrane disease

TBN
bacillus emulsion
total body nitrogen

TBNA
total body neutron activation
total body sodium
transbronchial needle aspiration
treated but not admitted

TBNAA
total body neutron activation analysis

t-BOC
t-butoxycarbonyl *also* BOC, Boc

tBoc
tert-butyloxycarbonyl

TBP
testosterone-binding protein
thiobisdichlorophenol (bithionol)
thyroxin-binding protein
total body photograph
total bypass
tributyl phosphate
tuberculous peritonitis

TBPA
thyroxin-binding prealbumin

TBPT
total body protein turnover

TBR
total bed rest
tumor-bearing rabbit

TB-RD
tuberculosis-respiratory disease

TBRS
Timed Behavioral Rating Sheet

TBS
The Bethesda System
total body solids
total body solute
total body surface
total burn size
tracheobronchial submucosa
tracheobronchoscopy
tribromsalan (tribromosalicylanilide)
triethanolamine-buffered saline

tbs
tablespoon

TBSA
total body surface area
total burn surface area

tbsp
tablespoonful *also* T

TBTNR
Toronto Biculture Test of Nonverbal
Reasoning

TBTT
tuberculin tine test

T

NOTES

TBUT
tear breakup time

TBV
total blood volume
transluminal balloon valvuloplasty

TBV$_p$
total blood volume predicted (from body surface)

TBW
total body washout
total body water *also* TBWA
total body weight

TBWA
total body water *also* TBW

TBX
thromboxane *also* Thx, TX
total body irradiation *also* TBI

TBZ
tetrabenazine
thiabendazole

TC
to contain
tandem colonoscopy
target cell
taurocholate
taurocholic (acid)
telephone call *also* T/C
temperature compensation
teratocarcinoma
tertiary cleavage
tetracycline *also* T, Tc, TCN, TCNE, TE, TET
therapeutic community
therapeutic concentrate
thermal conductivity (detectir) *also* λ
thoracic cage
throat culture *also* TH-CULT
thyrocalcitonin *also* TCA, TCT
tissue culture
total calcium
total capacity
total cholesterol
total colectomy
total colonoscopy
total correction
transcobalamin
transcutaneous *also* tc
transhepatic cholangiography *also* THC
transplant center
transverse colon
trauma center
Treacher Collins (syndrome)

treatment completed
true conjugate
tuberculin, contagious
tuberculosis, contagious
tubocurarine
tumor cell
tungsten carbide
type (and) crossmatch *also* T&C, T&M

TC I
transcobalamin I

TC II
transcobalamin II

3TC
lamivudine, Epivir

TC7
Interceed

T/C
to consider
telephone call *also* TC

T:C
tumor:cerebellum (ratio)

T&C
test and crossmatch
turn and cough
type and crossmatch *also* TC, T&M

TC$_{50}$
median toxic concentration

T$_4$(C)
serum thyroxin measured by column chromatography

T$_c$
generation time of cell cycle

Tc
core temperature
T (cell) cytolytic
T (cell) cytotoxic
technetium
temporal complex
tetracycline *also* T, TC, TCN, TCNE, TE, TET
transcobalamin

^{99}Tc
technetium-99

^{99m}Tc
technetium-99m

tc
transcutaneous *also* TC
translational control

TCA
terminal cancer
terminal carcinoma
tetracyclic antidepressant
thioguanine and cytarabine
thyrocalcitonin *also* TC, TCT
total cholic acid
total circulating albumin
total circulatory arrest
transluminal coronary angioplasty
tricalcium aluminate
tricarboxylic acid
trichloroacetate
trichloroacetic acid
tricuspid atresia
tricyclic amine
tricyclic antidepressant *also* TCAD
trihydrocoprostanic acid

TCABG
triple coronary artery bypass graft
also TCAG

TCAD
transplant coronary artery disease
tricyclic antidepressant *also* TCA

TCAG
triple coronary artery (bypass) graft
also TCABG

TCB
to call back
tetrachlorobiphenyl
total cardiopulmonary bypass
transcatheter biopsy
tumor cell burden

TCBS
triosulfate-citrate-bile salts-sucrose
(agar)

TCC
thromboplastic cell component
toroidal coil chromatography
transitional cell carcinoma
trichlocarban *also* Tcc
trichlorocarbanilide

Tcc
trichlocarban *also* TCC

TCCA
transitional cell cancer-associated
(virus)

transitional cell cancer (of the
bladder)

TCCB
transitional cell carcinoma of bladder

TCCL
T-cell chronic lymphocytic (leukemia)

TC CO$_2$
transcutaneous carbon dioxide
(monitor)

TCCS
transcranial color-coded (real-time)
sonography

TCD
thermal conductivity detector *also* λ
tissue culture dose
transcerebellar diameter
transcranial Doppler (sonography,
ultrasound)
transcystic duct
transverse cardiac diameter

TCD$_{50}$
median tissue culture dose
tissue culture infectious dose *also*
TCID$_{50}$

TCDB
Traumatic Coma Data Bank

TC&DB
turn, cough, deep breath

TCDC
taurochenodeoxycholate

TcDISIDA
technetium diisopropyliminodiacetic
acid (scan)

TCE
T-cell enriched
tetrachlorodiphenyl ethane
trichloroethanol
trichloroethylene

TCES
transcutaneous cranial electrical
stimulation

TCESOM
trichloroethylene-extracted soybean-oil
meal

NOTES

T

TCET
transcerebral electrotherapy

TCF
tissue-coding factor *also* TSF
total coronary flow
Treacher-Collins-Franceschetti
syndrome

TCFU
tumor colony-forming unit

TCG
time compensation gain

TCGF
thymus cell growth factor

TCH
tanned cell hemagglutination
total circulating hemoglobin
turn, cough, and hyperventilate

TChE
total cholinesterase

TcHIDA
technetium hepatoiminodiacetic acid
(scan)

TCI
to come in (to hospital)
target-controlled infusion
total cerebral ischemia
Totman Change Index
transient cerebral ischemia
tricuspid insufficiency

TCi
teracurie

TCID
tissue culture infective dose
tissue culture inoculated dose

TCID$_{50}$
median tissue culture infective dose
tissue culture infectious dose *also*
TCD$_{50}$

TcIDA
technetium iminodiacetic acid

TCIE
transient cerebral ischemic episode

TCIFTT
transcervical intrafallopian tube
transfer

TCIPA
tumor-cell-induced platelet aggregation

TCL
thermochemiluminescence

tibial collateral ligament
total capacity of lung
triazine chlorguanide

T-CLL
T-cell chronic lymphatic leukemia

TCM
tissue culture medium
traditional Chinese medicine
transcutaneous monitor

TCMA
transcortical motor aphasia

tc-MER
motor-evoked response to transcranial
(stimulation)

TCMH
tumor-direct cell-mediated
hypersensitivity

TCMP
thematic content modification program

TCMS
transcranial cortical magnetic
stimulation

TCMZ
trichloromethiazide

TCN
talocalcaneonavicular (joint)
terminal capillary network
tetracycline *also* T, TC, Tc, TCNE,
TE, TET

TCNE
tetracycline *also* T, TC, Tc, TCN,
TE, TET

TcNM
tumor with lymph node metastases

TCNS
transcutaneous nerve stimulator *also*
TNS

TCNU
tauromustine

TCO
total contact orthosis

TCOM
transcutaneous oxygen monitor *also*
TOM

TCP
teacher-child-parent
therapeutic class profile
therapeutic continuous penicillin
total circulating protein

transcutaneous pacing
tranylcypromine
tricalcium phosphate
trichlorophenol
tricresyl phosphate
tumor control probability

TCPA
tetrachlorophthalic anhydride

TCPC
total cavopulmonary connection

TCPCO₂, tcPCO₂
transcutaneous carbon dioxide pressure

TCPE
trichlorophenoxyethanol

TCPO₂
transcutaneous (partial) pressure of
oxygen

tcPO₂
transcutaneous oxygen pressure
measurement
transcutaneous partial pressure of
oxygen

TCPS
total cavopulmonary shunt

TCR
T-cell reactivity
T-cell receptor
T-cell rosette
thalamocortical relay
total cytoplasmic ribosome

TCRBCL
T cell-rich, B-cell lymphoma

TCRE
transcervical resection of the
endometrium

tcRNA
translational control ribonucleic acid

TCRP
total cellular receptor pool

TCRV
total red cell volume

TCS
T-cell supernatant
tethered cord syndrome
total cellular score

total coronary score
transcranial stimulation
Tricomponent Coaxial System

Tcs
T-cell-mediating contact sensitivity

TCSA
tetrachlorosalicylanilide

TCT
taurine cotransporter
thrombin clotting time
thyrocalcitonin *also* TC, TCA
transcatheter therapy

tcu-PA
2-chain urokinase plasminogen
activator

TCV
thoracic cage volume
three concept view

TCVA
thromboembolic cerebral vascular
accident

TD
to deliver
Takayasu disease
tardive dyskinesia *also* TDK
T-cell dependent
temperature differential
temporary disability
teratoma differentiated
terminal device
tetanus-diphtheria (toxoid) *also* Td
tetrodotoxin
therapeutic dietitian
therapy discontinued
thermal dilution
thermodilution
thoracic duct
three (times per) day
threshold of detectability
threshold of discomfort
threshold dose
thymus-dependent
tidal volume *also* TV, VT, V_T
timed disintegration
tocopherol deficient
tolerance dose
tone decay

NOTES

TD *(continued)*
torsion dystonia
total disability
total dose
totally disabled
toxic dose
tracheal diameter
tracking dye
transdermal
transverse diameter *also* trans D
traveler's diarrhea
treatment discontinued
tuberoinfundibular dopaminergic
typhoid dysentery

TD$_{50}$
median toxic dose

T$_4$(D)
serum thyroxin measured by
  displacement analysis

T$_D$
time required to double number of
  cells in given population

T$_d$
diffusion time

Td
tetanus-diphtheria (toxoid; adult type)

t.d.
three times daily [L. *ter die*]

TDA
therapeutic drug assay
thyroid-stimulating hormone-displacing
  antibody
thyrotropin-displacing activity
tryptophan deaminase agar
TSH-displacing antibody

TDAC
tumor-derived activated cell

TDB
Toxicology Data Bank

TDC
taurodeoxycholate
taurodeoxycholic (acid)
thermal dilution catheter
total dietary calories

TDCO
thermodilution cardiac output

TDD
telecommunication device (for the)
  deaf
tetradecadiene

thoracic duct drainage
total digitalizing dose

t.d.d.
three times a day [L. *ter de die*]

TDDA
tetradecadiene acetate

TDE
tetrachlorodiphenylethane
time-delayed exponential
total daily energy (requirement)
total digestible energy
triethylene glycol diglycidyl ether

TDEC
test declined (no longer offered)

TDF
testis-determining factor
Thinking Disturbance Factor
thoracic duct fistula
thoracic duct flow
time-dose fractionation (factor)
tissue-damaging factor *also* TF
tumor dose fractionation

TDH
threonine dehydrogenase
total decreased histamine
toxic dose, high

TDI
temperature difference integrator
three-dimensional interlocking (hip)
toluene diisocyanate
total dose infusion

TDK
tardive dyskinesia *also* TD

TDL
temporal difference limen
thoracic duct lymphocyte
thymus-dependent lymphocyte
toxic dose, low

TDLU
terminal duct lobular unit

TDM
tartaric dimalonate
therapeutic drug monitoring
thermodeltameter
trehalose dimycolate

TDN
total digestible nutrients
transdermal nitroglycerin *also* TDNTG

tDNA
transfer deoxyribonucleic acid

TDNTG
transdermal nitroglycerin *also* TDN

TDNWB
touchdown nonweightbearing

TDO
trichodentoosseous (syndrome)

TDP
thermal death point
thoracic duct pressure
thymidine diphosphate

TdP
torsade des pointes

TdPVT
torsade de pointes ventricular
tachycardia

TDPWB
touchdown partial weightbearing

TdR
thymidine *also* T

TDS
temperature, depth, and salinity

t.d.s.
to be taken three times a day [L.
ter die sumendum]

TDSP
time domain signal processor

TDT
tentative discharge tomorrow
terminal deoxynucleotidyl transferase
also TdT
thermal death time
tone decay test
tumor doubling time

TdT
terminal deoxynucleotidyl transferase
also TDT

TDU
time domain ultrasound

TDWB
touchdown weightbearing

TDZ
thymus-dependent zone (of lymph
node)

TE
echo delay time
echo-time
tennis elbow
test ear
tetanus *also* Te, tet
tetracycline *also* T, TC, Tc, TCN,
TCNE, TET
threshold energy
thromboembolic
thromboembolism
thymus epithelium
thyrotoxic exophthalmos
time estimation
tissue equivalent
tooth extracted
total estrogen (excretion)
Toxoplasma encephalitis
trace element
tracheoesophageal
transepithelial elimination (terminated)
transesophageal echocardiography
treadmill exercise
trial (and) error *also* T&E

T&E
testing and evaluation
training and experience
trial and error *also* TE

T$_E$
duration of expiration

Te
tellurium
tetanic (contraction)
tetanus *also* TE, tet

te
effective half-life *also* teff

TEA
temporal external artery
tetraethylammonium
thermal energy analyzer
thromboendarterectomy
total elbow arthroplasty
transient emboligenic aortoarteritis
transluminal extraction atherectomy
transversely excited atmospheric
(pressure)
triethanolamine

T

NOTES

TEAB
tetraethylammonium bromide

TEAC
tetraethylammonium chloride

TEAE
triethylaminoethyl

TEAM
Thrombolytic Trial of Eminase in Acute Myocardial Infarction
Training in Expanded Auxiliary Management

TEAP
transesophageal atrial pacing *also* TAP

TEB
tris-ethylenediaminetetraacetate borate

TEBG, TeBG
testosterone-estradiol-binding globulin

TEBS
transurethral electrical bladder stimulation

TEC
total eosinophil count
total exchange capacity
toxic *Escherichia coli*
transient erythroblastopenia of childhood
transluminal endarterectomy catheter
transluminal extraction catheter
transluminal extraction-endarterectomy catheter
transpapillary endoscopic cholecystotomy

T&EC
trauma and emergency center

TECA
technetium albumin (study)

tech
technical
technique

TECV
traumatic epiphyseal coxa vara

TED
Tasks of Emotional Development
threshold erythema dose
thromboembolic disease
thromboembolic disease (hose, stockings)
thyroid eye disease
tracheoesophageal dysraphism

tris-ethylenediaminetetraacetate dithiothreitol

TEDD
total end-diastolic diameter

TEDP
tetraethyl dithionopyrophosphate

TEE
thermal effect of exercise
total energy expended
transesophageal echocardiography
transnasal endoscopic ethmoidectomy
tyrosine ethyl ester

TEEM
tanned erythrocyte electrophoretic mobility

TEEP
tetraethylpyrophosphate
transesophageal echocardiography with pacing

TEF
thermal effect of food
tracheoesophageal fistula
trunk extension-flexion (unit)

teff
effective half-life *also* te

TEFS
transmural electrical field stimulation

TEG
thromboelastogram
thromboelastograph
thromboelastography

TEGDMA
tetraethylene glycol dimethacrylate

TEH, T.E.H.
theophylline, ephedrine, and hydroxyzine

TEI
total episode of illness
transesophageal imaging

TEIB
triethyleneiminobenzoquinone

TEL
telemetry *also* tele
tetraethyl lead

TELD
Tests of Early Language Development

tele
telemetry *also* TEL

TEM
transanal endoscopic microsurgery
transmission electron microscope
transmission electron microscopy
transtelephonic exercise monitor
transverse electromagnetic
transverse electromagnetic mode
triethylenemelamine

temp
temperature *also* T
temple
temporal
temporary *also* T

temp. dext.
to the right temple [L. *tempori dextro*]

temp. sinist.
to the left temple [L. *tempori sinistro*]

TEN
tension (intraocular pressure) *also* T
total enteral nutrition
total epidermal necrolysis
total excretory nitrogen
toxic epidermal necrolysis
toxic epidermal necrosis

tenac
tenaculum

TENS
transcutaneous electrical nerve stimulation
transcutaneous electrical nerve stimulator
transcutaneous electrical neuromuscular stimulator
transcutaneous electrode nerve stimulation
transelectrical nerve stimulator

TENVAD
Tests of Nonverbal Auditory Discrimination

TEOAE
transient evoked otoacoustic emission

TEP
thromboendophlebectomy
total extraperitoneal (laparoscopic hernia repair)

tracheoesophageal puncture
tubal ectopic pregnancy

TeP
tender point

TEPA
triethylenethiophosphoramide *also* TESPA

TEPG
triethylphosphine gold

TEPP
tetraethylpyrophosphate

TEQU
test equivocal (possible low titer)

TER
total elbow replacement
total endoplasmic reticulum
total energy requirement
transcapillary escape rate
transurethral electroresection

ter
terminal or end *also* term., TRML, Trml
ternary
tertiary *also* T, t, tert
threefold
three times

ter.
rub [L. *tere*]

Terb
terbutaline

term.
full term (infant)
terminal *also* ter, TRML, Trml

ter sim
rub together [L. *tere simul*]

tert
tertiary *also* T, t, ter

TES
tetradecyl sulfate, ethanol, and saline
therapeutic error signal
thoracic endometriosis syndrome
thymic epithelial supernatant
toxic epidemic syndrome
transcutaneous electrical stimulation

T

NOTES

TES *(continued)*
transmural electrical stimulation
treatment of emergent symptom

TESD
total end-systolic diameter

TESI
thoracic epidural steroid injection

TESPA
triethylenethiophosphoramide (thiotepa)

TEST
tubal embryo stage transfer

testos
testosterone

TET
tetanus *also* TE, Te, tet
tetracycline *also* T, TC, Tc, TCN,
  TCNE, TE
tetralogy (of Fallot) *also* Tet, TF,
  TOF
tetroxiprim
total exchangeable thyroxin
transcranial electrostimulation therapy
treadmill exercise test
triethyltryptamine
tubal embryo transfer

Tet
tetralogy of Fallot *also* TET, TF,
  TOF

tet
tetanus *also* TE, Te, TET

TETA
test-estrin timed action
triethylenetetramine

TETCYC
tetracycline *also* T, TC, Tc, TCN,
  TCNE, TE, TET

TETD
tetraethylthiuram disulfide (disulfiram)

TETRAC
tetraiodothyroacetic acid

tet tox
tetanus toxoid *also* TT

TEV
talipes equinovarus

TEVP
transesophageal ventricular pacing

TEWL
transepidermal water loss *also* TWL

TEZ
transthoracic electric impedance
  respirogram

TF
to follow
tactile fremitus
tail flick (reflex)
temperature factor
testicular feminization
tetralogy of Fallot *also* TET, Tet,
  TOF
thymol flocculation
thymus factor
thymus (tolerance) factor
thymus (transfer) factor
tissue-damaging factor *also* TDF
tissue factor
total flow
transfer factor
transferrin *also* Tf, TFN
transformation frequency
transfrontal
tube feeding
tuberculin filtrate
tubular fluid
tuning fork

T$_f$
temperature, freezing

Tf
transferrin *also* TF, TFN

TFA
tibiofemoral angle
topical fluoride application
total fatty acids
transverse fascicular area
trifluoroacetic acid

TFB
trifascicular block

TFB-PS
tibial fracture brace proximal support

TFC
threaded fusion cage
triangular fibrocartilage complex

TFCC
transjugular fibrocartilage complex

TFD
thin film dressing
transdermal fentanyl device

TFd
transfer factor, dialyzable

TFE
polytetrafluoroethylene (Teflon)

TFEV
timed forced expiratory volume

TFF
tangential flow filtration
tube-fed food

Tf–Fe
transferrin-bound iron

TFL
tensor fascia lata

TFM
testicular feminization mutation
total fluid movement
transmission electron microscopy
transverse friction massage
trifluoromethylnitrophenol

Tfm
testicular feminization (syndrome) *also* TFS

TFN
total fecal nitrogen
totally functional neutrophil
transferrin *also* TF, Tf

TFP
treponemal false positive
trifluoperazine *also* TFZ

TF/P
tubule fluid to plasma (ratio)

TFPI
tissue factor pathway inhibitor

(TF/P) In
tubule fluid to plasma insulin (ratio)

TFR
total fertility rate
total flow resistance

TFS
testicular feminization syndrome *also* Tfm
tube-fed saline

TFT
thrombus formation time
thyroid function test
tight filum terminale

transfer factor test
trifluorothymidine

TFZ
trifluoperazine *also* TFP

TG
tendon graft
testosterone glucuronide
tetraglycine
theophylline-guaifenesin
thioglucose
thioglycolate (broth) *also* THIO
thioguanine
thyroglobulin *also* Thg
toxic goiter
transglutaminase
transmissible gastroenteritis *also* TGE
treated group
triacylglycerol
trigeminal (neuralgia)
triglyceride *also* TRIG, trig
tumor growth
type genus *also* tg

6-TG
6-thioguanine

T$_g$
glass transition temperature

Tg
generation time *also* GT
thyroglobulin

tG$_1$
time required to complete G$_1$ phase of cell cycle

tG$_2$
time required to complete G$_2$ phase of cell cycle

tg
type genus *also* TG

TGA
taurocholate gelatin agar
thyroglobulin antibody *also* TgAb
total glycoalkaloids
transient global amnesia
transposition of great arteries
tumor glycoprotein assay

TgAb
thyroglobulin antibody *also* TGA

NOTES

TGAR
  total graft area rejected

TGB
  thyroid-binding globulin

TGC
  time-gain compensation
  time-gain compensator
  time-gain control
  time-varied gain control *also* TVGC

TGD
  thermal green dye

TGE
  theoretical growth evaluation
  transgastrostomic enteroscopy
  transmissible gastroenteritis (virus)
    also TG
  tryptone glucose extract

TGF
  T-cell growth factor
  transforming growth factor
  tubuloglomerular feedback
  tumor growth factor

TGFα
  transforming growth factor α

TGFβ
  transforming growth factor β

TGF-β1
  transforming growth factor β1

TGF-β2
  transforming growth factor β2

TGF-β3
  transforming growth factor β3

TGFA
  triglyceride fatty acid

TGG
  turkey gamma globulin

TGGE
  temperature-gradient gel
    electrophoresis

TGHA
  thyroglobulin antibody

TGL
  triglyceride
  triglyceride lipase

TGOR
  transverse groove of oblique ridge

TGP
  tobacco glycoprotein

TGR
  tenderness, guarding, rigidity
    (abdominal exam)
  thioguanosine

TGS
  tincture of green soap
  triglycine sulfate

TGT
  thromboplastin generation test
  thromboplastin generation time
  tolbutamide-glucagon test

TGV
  thoracic gas volume
  transposition of great vessels
  trapped gas volume

TGXT
  thallium-graded exercise test

TGY
  tryptone glucose yeast (agar) *also*
    TGYA

TGYA
  tryptone glucose yeast agar *also*
    TGY

TH
  tetrahydrocortisol
  T helper (cell)
  theophylline
  thrill
  thyrohyoid
  thyroid hormone
  thyrotropic hormone *also* TTH
  topical hypothermia
  torcular Herophili
  total hysterectomy
  tube holder
  tyrosine hydroxylase

T&H
  type and hold

Th
  T helper cell *also* TH
  thenar
  thoracic *also* T, th, thor
  thorax *also* T, th, thor
  thorium
  throat

th
  thoracic *also* T, Th, thor

THA
  tetrahydroaminoacridine (tacrine)
  total hip arthroplasty
  total hydroxyapatite

transient hemispheric attack
Treponema hemagglutination

ThA
thoracic aorta

THAM
Tris(hydroxymethyl)-aminomethane *also*
TRIS
tromethamine

THAN
transient hyperammonemia of newborn

THARIES
total hip arthroplasty with internal
eccentric shells

THb
total hemoglobin

THBI
thyroid hormone binding index

THbO$_2$
total oxyhemoglobin

THBR
thyroid hormone binding ratio

THC
delta-9-tetrahydrocannabinol
tetrahydrocannabinol
9-tetrahydrocannabinol
δ-9-tetrahydrocannabinol
tetrahydrocortisol
thiocarbanidin
transhepatic cholangiogram
transhepatic cholangiography *also* TC
transplantable hepatocellular carcinoma

THCA
trihydroxycoprostanoic acid

THCCRC
tetrahydrocannabinol cross-reacting
cannabinoids

TH-CULT
throat culture *also* TC

THC:YAG
thulium-holmium-chromium:YAG
(laser)

THD
thioridazine
transverse heart diameter

Thd
ribothymidine *also* T

THDOC
tetrahydrodeoxycorticosterone

THE
tetrahydrocortisone
tetrahydrocortisone E
tonic hind (limb) extension
transhepatic embolization
transhiatal esophagectomy
tropical hypereosinophilia

theor
theoretical
theory

ther
therapeutic *also* therap
therapy *also* therap
thermometer *also* therm

therap
therapeutic *also* ther
therapy *also* ther

Ther Ex, ther ex
therapeutic exercise

therm
thermometer *also* ther

θ
angular coordinate variable
customary temperature
latent trait (statistics)
temperature interval
theta (eighth letter of Greek
alphabet), lowercase

Θ
thermodynamic temperature
theta (eighth letter of Greek
alphabet), uppercase

THF
tetrahydrocortisone F
tetrahydrofluorenone
tetrahydrofolate
tetrahydrofolic
tetrahydrofuran
thymic humoral factor

THFA
tetrahydrofolic acid
tetrahydrofurfuryl alcohol

T

NOTES

Thg
thyroglobulin *also* TG

THH
telangiectasia hereditaria haemorrhagica

THI
transient hypogammaglobulinemia of infancy
trihydroxyindole

THIO
thioglycolate *also* TG

Thio-T, Thio-TEPA
thiotriethylene phosphoramide

THIP
tetrahydroisoxazolopyridinol

THIQ
tetrahydraisoquinolon

THKAFO
trunk-hip-knee-ankle-foot orthosis

THL
true histiocytic lymphoma

THM
Tamm-Horsfall mucoprotein
total heme mass

THO, TH$_2$O
titrated water

THOR
thoracentesis (fluid)

thor
thoracic *also* T, Th, th
thorax *also* T, Th, th

THORP
titanium hollow-screw osseointegrating reconstruction plate

thou.
thousandth

THP
take home pack
tetrahydropapaveroline
tissue hydrostatic pressure
total hip prosthesis
total hip replacement
total hydroxyproline
transhepatic portography
trihexyphenidyl

THPA
tetrahydropteric acid

THPC
tetrabis (hydroxymethyl) phosphonium chloride

tHPT
tertiary hyperparathyroidism

THPV
transhepatic portal vein

THQ
tetroquinone

THR
target heart rate
total hip replacement
training heart rate
transhepatic resistance

Thr
threonine *also* T

thr
thyroid
thyroidectomy

THR-CT
thrombin control

THRF
thyrotropic hormone-releasing factor

throm, thromb
thrombosis
thrombus *also* T

THS
tetrahydro-compound S
tetrahydrodeoxycortisol

THSC
totipotent hematopoietic stem cell

THSP
titanium hollow screw plate (system)

THU
tetrahydrouridine

THUG
thyroid uptake gradient

THVO
terminal hepatic vein obliteration

Thx
thromboxane *also* TBX, TX

Thy
thymine *also* T

thy.
thymectomy
thymus *also* T

THz
terahertz

TI
inversion time
temporal integration
terminal ileum
thalassemia intermedia
therapeutic index
thoracic index
threshold of intelligibility
thymus independent
thyroxin iodine
time information
time interval
tonic immobility
total iron
transischial
translational inhibition
transverse (diameter between) ischia
transverse inlet
tricuspid incompetence
tricuspid insufficiency
trunk index
tubulointerstitial
tumor inducing
tumor induction

T$_I$
duration of inspiration

Ti
inspiratory time
titanium

TIA
Test Anxiety Inventory
transient ischemic attack
tumor-induced angiogenesis

TIAH
total implantation of artificial heart

TIA-IR
transient ischemic attack, incomplete
recovery

TIB
tumor immunology bank

Tib, tib
tibia

TIBBS
Total Ischemic Burden Bisoprolol
Study

TIBC
total iron-binding capacity

TIBET
Total Ischaemic Burden European
Trial

tib-fib
tibia and fibula

TIC
ticarcillin
Toxicology Information Center
trypsin-inhibitory capability
trypsin-inhibitory capacity
tumor-inducing complex

tic
(diver)tic(ulum)

TICCC
time interval between cessation of
contraception and conception

TICE BCG
TICE Bacillus Calmette-Guérin (Live)

TID
three times a day [L. *ter in die*]
also t.i.d.
time interval difference
titrated initial dose

t.i.d.
three times a day [L. *ter in die*]
also TID

TIDA
tuberoinfundibular dopamine (system)

TIE
transient ischemic episode

TIF
tumor-inducing factor
tumor-inhibiting factor

TIFB
thrombin-increasing fibrinopeptide B

TIG, TIg
tetanus immunoglobulin

TIH
time interval histogram
tumor-inducing hypercalcemia

TII
terminal ileum intubation

TIL
tumor-infiltrating lymphocyte

T

NOTES

TIM
transthoracic intracardiac monitoring
triose isomerase

TIMC
tumor-induced marrow cytotoxicity

TIMI
Thrombolysis in Myocardial Infarction

TIMP-1, TIMP-2, TIMP-3
tissue metalloproteinase

TIN
three times a night [L. *ter in nocte*] *also* t.i.n.
Tone in Noise
tubulointerstitial nephritis
tubulointerstitial nephropathy

t.i.n.
three times a night [L. *ter in nocte*] *also* TIN

tinc, tinct
tincture

TINEM
there is no evidence of malignancy

TIP
thermal inactivation point
Toxicology Information Program
translation-inhibiting protein
tumor-inhibiting principle

TIPPS
tetraiodophenolphthalein sodium

TIPS
transjugular intrahepatic portacaval shunt
transjugular intrahepatic portosystemic shunt *also* TIPSS

TIPSS
transjugular intrahepatic portosystemic shunt *also* TIPS
transjugular intrahepatic portosystemic stent shunt

TIQ
tetrahydroisoquinoline

TIR
terminal innervation ratio
total immunoreactive

TIS
tetracycline-induced stenosis
transdermal infusion system
trypsin-insoluble segment
tumor in situ

TISP
total immunoreactive serum pepsinogen

TISS
Therapeutic Intervention Scoring System

TIT
Treponema (pallidum) immobilization test
triiodothyronine *also* T_3, TITh, TRIT
triple intrathecal therapy

TITh
triiodothyronine *also* T_3, TIT, TRIT
3,5,3'-triiodothyronine *also* T_3

TIU
trypsin-inhibiting unit

TIUP
term intrauterine pregnancy

TIUV
total intrauterine volume

TIVA
total intravenous anesthesia

TIVC
thoracic inferior vena cava

TIW, tiw, tiwk
three times a week

TJ
tendon jerk
tetrajoule
tight junction
triceps jerk
Troell-Junet (syndrome)

TJA
total joint arthroplasty

TJN
tongue jaw neck (dissection)
twin jet nebulizer

TJR
total joint replacement

TK
through the knee
thymidine kinase
tourniquet *also* TQ
toxicokinetics
transketolase
triose-kinase

TKA
total knee arthroplasty

transketolase activity
trochanter-knee-ankle

TKD
thymidine kinase deficiency
tokodynamometer

TKE
terminal knee extension

TKG
tokodynagraph

TKIC
true knot in cord

TKLI
tachykinin-like immunoreactivity

TKM
thymidine kinase, mitochondrial

TKNO
to keep needle open

TKO
to keep open (vein for IV)

TKP
thermokeratoplasty
total knee prosthesis

TKR
total knee arthroscopy
total knee replacement

TKS
thymidine kinase, soluble

TKVO
to keep vein open

TL
taper-lock
team leader
temporal lobe
terminal limen
theophylline
thermolabile
thermoluminescence
Thorndike-Lorge
threat to life
thymic lymphocyte antigen
thymus(-dependent) lymphocyte *also*
T-L
thymus leukemia (antigen)
thymus lymphoma
time lapse

time limited
tolerance level
total lipids
transverse line
trial leave
tubal ligation

T-L
thymus(-dependent) lymphocyte *also*
TL

T/L
terminal latency (electromyography)

Tl
thallium

²⁰¹Tl
thallium-201

TLA
tissue lactase activity
translaryngeal aspiration
translumbar aortogram
translumbar aortography
transluminal angioplasty
transperitoneal laparoscopic
adrenalectomy
trypsin-like amidase

TLAA
T-lymphocyte-associated antigen

TLAC
triple lumen Arrow catheter

TLC
tender loving care
Test of Language Competence
thin-layer chromatography
total L-chain concentration
total lung capacity
total lung compliance
total lymphocyte count
triple-lumen catheter

TLC-C
Test of Language Competence for
Children

²⁰¹TlCl
thallium chloride (radioisotope)

TLD
thermoluminescent dosimeter
thoracic lymphatic duct

T

NOTES

TLD *(continued)*
transluminescent dosimeter
tumor lethal dose

T/LD$_{100}$
minimal dose causing 100% death or malformation

TLE
temporal lobe epilepsy
thin-layer electrophoresis
total lipid extract

TLI
thymidine labeling index
tonic labyrinthine inverted
total lymphoid irradiation
Totman Loss Index
translaryngeal intubation
tritiated thymidine labeling index
trypsin-like immunoactivity

TLK
thermal laser keratoplasty

TLN
transperitoneal laparoscopic nephrectomy

TLNB
term living newborn

TLP
total laryngopharyngectomy
transitional living program

TLQ
total living quotient

TLR
tonic labyrinthine reflex

TLS
tight lens syndrome
tumor lysis syndrome

TLSO
thoracolumbar spinal orthosis
thoracolumbar standing orthosis
thoracolumbosacral orthosis
thoracolumbosacral spinal orthosis
also TLSSO

TLSO-FELR
thoracolumbosacral orthoses - flexion, extension, lateral (bending, and transverse) rotation

TLSSO
thoracolumbosacral spinal orthosis
also TLSO

TLT
tryptophan load test

TLV
threshold limit value
total lung volume

TLW
total lung water

TLX
trophoblast-lymphocyte cross-reactivity

TM
tectorial membrane
temperature by mouth
temporalis muscle
temporomandibular (joint)
teres major (muscle)
term milk
thalassemia major
Thayer-Martin (medium) *also* T-M
time and modifying
time-motion
tobramycin *also* TOB
trabecular meshwork
Transcendental Meditation
transitional mucosa
transmediastinal
transmetatarsal
transport maximum
transport mechanism
transport medium
transverse myelitis
trimester *also* TRI
Tropical Medicine
tubular myelin
tumor
tympanic membrane *also* MT
tympanometric

T-M
Thayer-Martin (medium) *also* TM

T&M
type and crossmatch *also* TC, T&C

TM$_{PAH}$
maximal tubular (excretory capacity for) *para*-aminohippuric acid

T$_m$
temperature midpoint (Kelvin)
tubular maximal (excretory capacity of kidneys) *also* Tm

T_m
maximal tubular excretory capacity of kidneys
melting point *also* MP
temperature midpoint *also* t_m

Tm
temperature, muscle

thulium
transport maximum
tubular maximal (excretory capacity of kidneys) *also* T_m
tubular maximum
tumor-bearing mice

tM
time required to complete M phase of cell cycle

t_m, t_m
temperature midpoint (Celsius)

TMA
tetramethylammonium
thrombotic microangiopathy
thyroid microsomal antibody *also* TMAb
transmetatarsal amputation
trimethoxyamphetamine
trimethoxyphenyl aminopropane
trimethylamine
trimethylxanthine amphetamine

TMAb
thyroid microsomal antibody *also* TMA

TMAF
temporary master apical file

TMAH
trimethylphenylammonium (anilinium) hydroxide

TMAI
trimethylphenylammonium (anilinium) iodide

TMAO
trimethylamine oxide

TMAS
Taylor Manifest Anxiety Scale

T-MAX
time of maximal (concentration) *also* T_{max}

T_{max}
highest temperature
time of maximal concentration *also* T-MAX

T-max
maximum temperature

TMB
tetramethyl benzidine
transient monocular blindness
trimethoxybenzoate
tris-maleate buffer

TMBA
trimethoxybenzaldehyde
trimethylbenzanthracene

TMC
transmural colitis
triamcinolone (and terra) mycincapsule

TMCA
trimethylcolchicinic acid

TMD
temporomandibular (joint dysfunction) *also* TMJ
trimethadione *also* TMO

TMDS, t-MDS
therapy-related myelodysplasia

TME
thermolysin-like metalloendopeptidase
total mesorectal excision
total metabolizable energy
transmissible mink encephalopathy
transmural enteritis

TMEP
telangiectasia macularis eruptiva perstans

TMET
treadmill exercise test

TMF
transformed mink fibroblast

TmG, TM_G
maximal tubular reabsorption rate for glucose

TMH
tetramethylammonium hydroxide
trainable mentally handicapped

TMI
threatened myocardial infarction
transmandibular implant
transmural infarction

TMIC
Toxic Materials Information Center

T

NOTES

TMIF
tumor-cell migratory inhibition factor

TMIS
Technicon Medical Information
System

TMJ
temporomandibular joint (dysfunction)
also TMD

TMJD
temporomandibular joint dysfunction

TMJ-PDS
temporomandibular joint-pain
dysfunction syndrome

TMJS
temporomandibular joint syndrome

TML
terminal motor latency
tetramethyl lead

TMLR
transmyocardial laser revascularization

TMM
torn medial meniscus

Tmm
McKay-Marg tension

TMNG
toxic multinodular goiter

TMNST
tethered median nerve stress test

TMO
trimethadione *also* TMD

T-MOP
6-thioguanine, methotrexate, Oncovin
(vincristine), and prednisone

TMP
ribothymidylic acid *also* rTMP
thallium myocardial perfusion
thymidine monophosphate
thymolphthalein
transmembrane (hydrostatic) pressure
transmembrane potential
trimethoprim
trimethylpsoralen
trimethyl psoralen

TMPD
tetramethylparaphenylinediamine

TMPDS
temporomandibular pain (and)
dysfunction syndrome

TMP-SMX
trimethoprim-sulfamethoxazole *also*
SMZ-TMP

TMR
tetramethylrhodamine
tissue maximal ratio
topical magnetic resonance
trainable mentally retarded
transmyocardial revascularization

TMRI
tetramethylrhodamine isothiocyanate

TMS
tetramethylsilane
thallium myocardial scintigraphy
thread mate system
trimethylsilane
trimethylsilyl *also* TMSi

TMSI
trimethylsilylimidazole

TMSi
trimethylsilyl *also* TMS

TMST
treadmill stress test *also* TST

TMT
tarsometatarsal
teratoma with malignant
transformation
Trail-Making Test (psychiatry)
treadmill test
tympanic membrane thermometer

TMTC
too many to count

TMTD
tetramethylthiuram disulfide

TMTX
trimethexate
trimetrexate

TMU
tetramethylurea

TMV
tobacco mosaic virus
tracheal mucous velocity

TMX
tamoxifen *also* T, TAM
trimazosin

TMZ
temazepam
transformation zone

TN
(intraocular) tension, normal *also* Tn
talonavicular
team nursing
temperature normal
tension
tension, normal
tiodazosin
total negatives
trigeminal nucleus
trochlear nucleus
true negative

T&N
tension and nervousness

T/N
tar and nicotine

T₄N
normal serum thyroxin

Tn
(intraocular) tension, normal *also* TN
ocular tension
thoron
transposon

TNA
total nutrient admixture

TNB
term newborn
transrectal needle biopsy (of the prostate)
Tru-Cut needle biopsy

TNBP
transurethral needle biopsy of the prostate

TNC
turbid, no creamy (layer)

TNCB
trinitrochlorobenzene

TND
term normal delivery

TNDM
transient neonatal diabetes mellitus

TNEE
titrated norepinephrine excretion

TNF
trinitrofluorenone

true negative fraction
tumor necrosis factor

TNF-α
tumor necrosis factor-α (assay)

TNG
toxic nodular goiter
trinitroglycerol (nitroglycerin)

Tng
training

tng
tongue

TNH
transient neonatal hyperammonemia

TNI
total nodal irradiation

TNM
(primary) tumor, (regional lymph) node, (remote) metastases (classification, staging)
thyroid node metastasis

TNMR
tritium nuclear magnetic resonance

TNP
total net positive
trinitrophenyl

TNPM
transient neonatal pustular melanosis

TNR
tonic neck reflex
true negative rate

TNS
total nuclear score
transcutaneous nerve stimulator
Tullie-Niebörg syndrome
tumor necrosis serum

TNT
triamcinolone and nystatin
trinitrotoluene

TNTC
too numerous to count

TNV
tobacco necrosis virus

TO
no evidence of primary tumor

T

NOTES

TO *(continued)*
old tuberculin
original tuberculin
target organ
telephone order
temperature, oral *also* T(O)
Theiler original (strain of mouse
  encephalomyelitis virus)
thoracic orthosis
tincture of opium *also* t.o.
total obstruction
tracheoesophageal
transfer out
tuboovarian
turned on
turnover

T&O
tandem and ovoids
tubes and ovaries

T(O)
oral temperature *also* TO

TO₂
oxygen transport rate

t.o.
tincture of opium *also* TO

TOA
time of arrival
tuboovarian abscess

TOAP
thioguanine, Oncovin (vincristine),
  ara-C (cytarabine), and prednisone

TOB
tobramycin *also* TM

TOBP
tobramycin, peak

TobRV
tobacco ringspot virus *also* TRSV

TOC
test of cure
total organic carbon
tuboovarian complex

TOCE
transcatheter oily chemoembolization

TOCO
tocodynamometer

TOCP
triorthocresyl phosphate

TOD
tail on detector

tension oculus dextra (tension of
  right eye)
Time-oriented Data (Bank)

TOE
tracheo(o)esophageal

TOES
toxic oil epidemic syndrome

TOF
tetralogy of Fallot *also* TET, Tet,
  TF
total of four
tracheo(o)esophageal fistula
train-of-four

TOFMS
time-of-flight mass spectometry

TOGV
transposition of great vessels

TOH
throughout hospitalization
transient osteoporosis of hip

TOHP
Trials of Hypertension Prevention

TOL
trial of labor

tol
tolerance
tolerated

tolb
tolbutamide

TOLD-I
Test of Language Development-
  Intermediate

TOLD-P
Test of Language Development-
  Primary

TOM
tomorrow
transcutaneous oxygen monitor *also*
  TCOM

tomo
tomogram

TON
tonight [L. *nocte*] *also* tonoc.

TONAR
the oronasal acoustic ratio

TONI
Test of Nonverbal Intelligence

tonoc.
tonight [to - L. *nocte*] *also* TON

TOP
temporal, occipital, parietal
termination of pregnancy
tissue oncotic pressure
total ossicular prosthesis

top.
topical *also* T

TOPA
topical oropharyngeal anesthesia

Topo II
topoisomerase II

TOPS
Take Off Pounds Sensibly

TopSS/ICG
topographic scanning/indocyanine
green

TOPV
trivalent oral poliovirus vaccine

TOR
toremifene

TORCH
toxoplasmosis, other infections,
rubella, cytomegalovirus infection,
and herpes simplex
toxoplasmosis, rubella,
cytomegalovirus, and herpes simplex
(titer)

TORP
total ossicular (chain) replacement
prosthesis

TOS
tension oculus sinister (tension of
left eye)
thoracic outlet syndrome
toxic oil syndrome

TOT
tincture of time
total operating time

TOTAL-C
total cholesterol

TOT BILI
total bilirubin *also* TB, TBIL, T Bili

TOTP
triorthotolyl phosphate

TOTPAR
total pain relief

Tot prot
total protein *also* TP, T PROT

TOV
thrombosed oral varix
trial of void

TOWER
testing, orientation, work, evaluation,
rehabilitation

Tox
toxicity *also* T, tox

tox
toxic
toxicity *also* T, Tox
toxoid

TOXGR
toxic granulation (differential)

TOXICON
Toxicology Information Conversational
On-Line Network

TOXLINE
Toxicology Information On-Line

TOXO, Toxo
toxoplasmosis

TP
tail pinch
temperature and pressure
temporal peak
temporoparietal
terminal phalanx
testosterone propionate
tetanus-pertussis
therapeutic pass
thickly padded
threshold potential
thrombocytopenic purpura
thrombophlebitis
thymic polypeptide
thymidine phosphorylase
thymus protein
tissue pressure
Todd paralysis
toilet paper

T

NOTES

TP *(continued)*
total population
total positives
total protein *also* Tot prot, T PROT
trailing pole
transforming principle
transition point *also* T
transpyloric
transverse polarization
treating physician
treatment period
triamphenicol
triazolophthalazine
trigger point
triphosphate
true positive
tryptophan *also* Tp, Trp, Try, W
tryptophan pyrrolase
tube precipitin
tuberculin precipitate
tuberculin precipitation

TP5
thymopoietin pentapeptide

T&P, T+P
temperature and pulse
turn and position

Tp
tampon
tryptophan *also* TP, Trp, Try, W

tp
physical half-life

TPA
12-O-tetradecanoylphorbol 13-acetate
tannic acid, polyphosphomolybdic acid, and amido acid (staining technique)
tissue plasminogen activator *also* t-PA
tissue polypeptide antigen
total parenteral alimentation
total phobic anxiety
Treponema pallidum agglutination
tumor polypeptide antigen

t-PA
tissue plasminogen activator *also* TPA

TPAL
term (infants), premature (infants), abortions, living (children) (obstetric history)

TPB
transpalatal bar
tryptone phosphate broth

TPBA
thermal/perfusion balloon angioplasty

TPBF
total pulmonary blood flow

TPBS
three-phase (radionuclide) bone scanning

TPC
telescoping plugged catheter
telopeptide-poor collagen
thenar palmar crease
thromboplastic plasma component
time-to-pulse-height converter
total patient care
total plasma catecholamines
total plasma cholesterol
treatment planning conference
Treponema pallidum complement

TPCC
Treponema pallidum cryolysis complement

TPCF
Treponema pallidum complement fixation

TPCH
6-thioguanine, procarbazine, CCNU, hydroxyurea

TPCV
total packed cell volume

TPD
temporary partial disability
thiamine propyldisulfide
tropical pancreatic diabetes
tumor-producing dose

TPDCV
6-thioguanine, procarbazine, dibromodulcitol, CCNU (lomustine), and vincristine

TPE
therapeutic plasma exchange
tissue-protective, end-cutting
total protective environment

TPEY
tellurite polymyxin egg yolk (agar)

TPF
thymus permeability factor

trained participating father
true positive fraction

TPG
therapeutic play group
transmembrane potential gradient
transplacental gradient
tryptophan peptone glucose (broth)

TPGYT
trypticase-peptone-glucose-yeast extract-trypsin (medium)

TPH
thromboembolic pulmonary hypertension
trained participating husband
transplacental hemorrhage
transrectal prostatic hyperthermia
Treponema pallidum hemagglutination
tryptophan hydroxylase

TPHA
Treponema pallidum hemagglutination

TPHOS
triple phosphate (crystal)

TPI
Treatment Priority Index
Treponema pallidum immobilization (test)
triosephosphate isomerase

TPIA
Treponema pallidum immune adherence

TPL
triphosphate of lime
tyrosine phenol-lyase

T plasty
tympanoplasty

TPM
temporary pacemaker
thrombophlebitis migrans
total particulate matter
total passive motion
triphenylmethane

TPMT
thiopurine methyltransferase

TPN
thalamic projection neuron

total parenteral nutrition
triphosphopyridine nucleotide

TPNH
triphosphopyridine nucleotide, (reduced)

TPO
thrombopoietin
thyroid peroxidase
trial prescription order
tryptophan peroxidase

TPP
tetraphenylporphyrin
thiamine pyrophosphate
transpulmonary pressure

TP&P
time, place, and person

TPPase
thiamine pyrophosphatase

TPPN
total peripheral parenteral nutrition

TPPV
trans pars plana vitrectomy

TPR
temperature
temperature, pulse, and respiration
testosterone production rate
total peripheral resistance
total pulmonary resistance
transsphenoidal pituitary resection
true positive rate

TPRI
total peripheral resistance index

T PROT
total protein *also* Tot prot, TP

TPS
titanium plasma sprayed
trypsin
tumor polysaccharide substance

TPST
true positive stress test

TPT
tetraphenyl tetrazolium
time to peak tension
topotecan *also* SK&F 104864
total protein tuberculin

T

NOTES

TPT *(continued)*
  treadmill performance test
  typhoid-paratyphoid (vaccine)

TpT
  thrombus precursor protein

TPTHS
  total parathyroid hormone secretion

TPTX
  thyroid-parathyroidectomy

TPTZ
  tripyridyltriazine

TPUR
  transperineal urethral resection

TPV
  tetanus-pertussis vaccine

TPVR
  total peripheral vascular resistance
  total pulmonary vascular resistance

TQ
  time questionnaire
  tocopherolquinone
  tourniquet *also* TK

TR
  recovery time
  rectal temperature *also* T(R)
  repetition time
  residual tuberculin
  to return
  tetrazolium reduction
  therapeutic radiology
  therapeutic recreation
  timed release
  tincture *also* T, Tr, tr
  total repair
  total resistance
  total response *also* R
  trace *also* T, Tr, tr
  trachea
  transfusion reaction
  transplant recipient
  transverse relaxation
  treatment *also* Tr, tr, treat., TX, Tx,
    T_x
  tremor
  tricuspid regurgitation
  triradial
  tuberculin residue
  tuberculin Ruckland (new tuberculin)
  tubular reabsorption
  tumor registry
  turbidity reducing
  turnover rate

T&R
  tenderness and rebound

T(R)
  rectal temperature *also* TR

T(°R)
  absolute temperature on the Rankine
    scale

T_r
  radiologic half-life
  retention time

Tr
  tincture *also* T, TR, tr
  trace *also* T, TR, tr
  tragion
  treatment *also* TR, tr, treat., TX, Tx,
    T_x
  trypsin

tr
  tincture *also* T, TR, Tr
  trace *also* T, TR, Tr, tr
  traction
  treatment *also* TR, Tr, tr, treat., TX,
    Tx, T_x
  tremor

TRA
  to run at
  therapeutic recreation associate
  total renin activity
  transaldolase
  transretinoic acid
  tumor-resistant antigen

tra
  transfer

TRAb
  thyrotrophin receptor antibody

TRACE
  Trandolapril Cardiac Evaluation

trach
  trachea
  tracheal
  tracheostomy
  tracheotomy

TRAcP
  tartrate resistant acid phosphatase

TRAIDS
  transfusion-related AIDS

TRAJ
  timed repetitive ankle jerk

TRALI
  transfusion-related lung injury

TRAM
transverse rectus abdominis muscle
transverse rectus abdominis myocutaneous (breast reconstruction)
Treatment Rating Assessment Matrix
Treatment Response Assessment Method

TRAMP
transversus and rectus abdominis musculoperitoneal

TRAMPCOL
6-thioguanine, rubidomycin, ara-C, methotrexate, prednisolone, cyclophosphamide, and Oncovin,

TRAMPE
tricho-rhino-auriculo-phalangeal multiple exostoses

TRAN
transfusion

tran, traum
trauma
traumatic

trans
transference
transverse *also* T

trans D
transverse diameter *also* TD

transm
transmission
transmitted

transpl
transplantation *also* TX
transplanted

trans sect
transverse section *also* TS, T sect

transsex
transsexual

TRAP
tartrate-resistant (leukocyte) acid phosphatase
thioguanine, rubidomycin, ara-C, and prednisone
6-thioguanine, rubidomycin, ara-C, prednisone

total radical-trapping antioxidant parameter

TRAS
transesophageal atrial stimulation
transplant renal artery stenosis

traum (*var. of* tran)

TRB
return to baseline
terbutaline

TRBC
total red blood cells

TRBF
total renal blood flow

TRC
tanned red cell
total renin concentration
total respiratory conductance
total ridge count

TRCA
tanned red cell agglutination

TRCH
tanned red cell hemagglutination

TRCHI
tanned red cell hemagglutination inhibition

TRCV
total red cell volume

TRD
tongue-retaining device
traction retinal detachment
traumatic rupture of the diaphragm

TRDN
transient respiratory distress of the newborn

TRDS
transient respiratory distress syndrome

TRE
true radiation emission

TREA
thoroughness, reliability, efficiency, analytic (ability)
triethanolamine

NOTES

treat.
treatment *also* TR, Tr, tr, TX, Tx, T_x

Tren, TREND
Trendelenburg (position) *also* TRND

TRF
T-cell replacing factor
thyrotropin-releasing factor

trf
transfer

TRFC
total rosette-forming cell

trg, trng
training

TRGI
triglycerides incalculable

TRH
tension-reducing hypothesis
thyroid-releasing hormone
thyrotropin-releasing hormone

TRH-ST
thyrotropin-releasing hormone
stimulation test

TRI
intracytoplasmic tuboreticular inclusion
tetrazolium reduction inhibition
Thyroid Research Institute
total response index
transient response imaging
trifocal
trimester *also* TM
tubuloreticular inclusion

tri
tricentric

T₃RIA, T₃(RIA)
triiodothyronine radioimmunoassay

T₄RIA, T₄(RIA)
tetraiodothyronine (thyroxine)
radioimmunoassay

TRIAC, Triac
triiodothyroacetic acid

TRIADS
time-resolved imaging by automatic
data segmentation

TRIC
trachoma inclusion conjunctivitis
(organism)

TRICB
trichlorobiphenyl

TRICH, Trich
trichinosis
Trichomonas

Trid.
three days [L. *triduum*]

TRIG, trig
triglyceride *also* TG

TRIMIS
Tri-Service Medical Information
System

TRIS, tris
tris (hydroxymethyl) -aminomethane
also THAM

Tris
Tris(hydroxymethyl)aminomethane *also*
tris
Tris(hydroxymethyl)methylamine

TRISS
Trauma and Injury Severity Score

TRIT
triiodothyronine *also* T₃, TIT

Trit, trit
triturate

TRITC
tetrarhodamine isothiocyanate

TRK
transketolase

TRL
triglyceride-rich lipoproteins

TRML, Trml
terminal *also* ter, term.

tRNA
transfer ribonucleic acid

TRNBP
transrectal needle biopsy of the
prostate

TRND
Trendelenburg (position) *also* Tren,
TREND

TRNG
tetracycline-resistant *Neisseria
gonorrhoeae*

trng (*var. of* trg)

TRO
to return to office
tissue reflectance oximeter

TROCA
tangible reinforcement of operant
conditioned audiometry

TROCH, Troch
troche (lozenge)

troch
trochiscus

TROM
total range of motion

Trop
tropical

TRP
Tactical Reproduction Pegboard
total refractory period
trichorhinophalangeal (syndrome)
tubular reabsorption of phosphate

Trp
tryptophan *also* TP, Tp, Try, W

TRPA
tryptophan-rich prealbumin

TrPl
treatment plan

TRPM-2
testosterone repressed prostate
message-2

TRPS
trichorhinophalangeal syndrome

TrPs
trigger points

TRPT
theoretical renal phosphorus threshold

TRR
total respiratory resistance

TRS
Therapeutic Recreation Specialist
total reducing sugars
tubuloreticular structure

TrS
traumatic surgery

TRSV
tobacco ringspot virus *also* TobRV

TRT
thermoradiotherapy

thoracic radiation therapy
total reading time
treatment-related toxicity

trt
treatment

TRU
turbidity-reducing unit

T₃RU
triiodothyronine resin uptake

TRUS
transrectal ultrasonography
transrectal ultrasound (scanning)
transurethral ultrasound

TRUSP
transrectal ultrasound of prostate

TRV
tobacco rattle virus

trx (*var. of* Rx'd US)

Try, Tryp
tryptophan *also* TP, Tp, Trp, W

TRZ
tartrozine
triazolam

TS
Tay-Sachs (disease) *also* TSD
temperature sensitive
temperature sensitivity
temporal stem
terminal sensation
testosterone sulfate
test solution
thermostable
thiosporin
thoracic surgery
tissue space
tocopherol supplemented
toe sign
total solids (in urine)
Tourette syndrome
toxic substance
toxic syndrome
tracheal sound
tracheal spiral
transitional sleep
transsexual

T

NOTES

TS *(continued)*
transverse section *also* trans sect, T sect
transverse sinus
Trauma Score
treadmill score
trichostasis spinulosa
tricuspid stenosis
triple strength
tropical sprue
trypticase soy (plate)
T suppressor (cell)
tuberous sclerosis
tubular sound
tumor specific
Turner syndrome
type specific

T-S
type and screen

T/S
thyroid serum (iodide ratio)
thyroid to serum (ratio)

Ts
skin temperature
tension by Schiotz (tonometer)
tosylate
T suppressor

tS
time required to complete S phase of cell cycle

ts, tsp
teaspoon

t-s
temperature-sensitive

TSA
technical surgical assistance
Test of Syntactic Ability
tissue-specific antigens
toluene sulfonic acid
Total Severity Assessment
total shoulder arthroplasty
total solute absorption
toxic shock antigen
trypticase-soy agar
tumor-specific antigen
tumor-susceptible antigen
type-specific antibody

T₄SA
thyroxine-specific activity

TSAb
thyroid-stimulating antibody

TSAE
transcatheter splenic arterial embolization

TSAP
toxic shock-associated protein

Tsaph
temperature in saphenous (vein)

TSAS
total severity assessment score

TSAT
tube slide agglutination test

TSB
total serum bilirubin
trypticase soy broth
tryptone soy broth

TSBA
total serum bile acids

TSBB
transtracheal selective bronchial brushing

TSBC
Time-Sample Behavioral Checklist

TSC
technetium sulfur colloid
theophylline serum concentration
thiosemicarbazide
total static compliance
total symptom complex
transverse spinal sclerosis
tuberous sclerosis complex

TSCA
Toxic Substance Control Act

TSCS
Tennessee Self-Concept Scale

TSD
target-skin distance
Tay-Sachs disease *also* TS
theory of signal detectability
transfer summary dictated

TSDP
tapered steroid dosing package

TSE
targeted systemic exposure
testicular self-examination
total skin examination
transmissible spongiform encephalopathy
trisodium edetate

TSEB
total skin electron beam

T sect
transverse section *also* trans sect, TS

TSEM
transmission scanning electron microscopy

TSF
thrombopoiesis-stimulating factor
tissue-(coding) factor *also* TCF
total systemic flow
triceps skinfold
T-suppressor factor

TSG
tumor-specific glycoprotein

TSH
thyroid-stimulating hormone

TSH-RF
thyroid-stimulating hormone-releasing factor

TSH-RH
thyroid-stimulating hormone-releasing hormone

TSI
thyroid-stimulating immunoglobulin
triple sugar iron (agar) *also* TSIA

TSIA
total small intestinal allotransplantation
triple sugar iron agar *also* TSI

tSIDS
totally unexplained sudden infant death syndrome

TSL
terminal sensory latency

TSLS
toxic shock-like syndrome

TSM
type-specific M protein

TSN
tryptophan peptone sulfide neomycin (agar)

TSP
total serum protein

total suspended particulate
tribasic sodium phosphate
trisodium phosphate
tropical spastic paraparesis

tsp (*var. of* ts)

TSPA
thiophosphoramide (Thiotepa)
thiotepa

TSPAP
total serum prostatic acid phosphatase

T-spica
thumb spica (bandage)

T-spine, T/spine
thoracic spine

TSPP
technetium stannous pyrophosphate
tetrasodium pyrophosphate

TSR
testosterone-sterilized (female) rat
theophylline-sustained release
thyroid-serum ratio
total shoulder replacement
total systemic resistance
transfer
transient situational reaction

TSRBC
trypsinized sheep red blood cell

TSRH
Texas Scottish Rite Hospital

TS III ROP
threshold stage III of retinopathy of prematurity

TSRPC
totally stapled restorative proctocolectomy

TSS
toxic shock syndrome
transverse spinal sclerosis
tropical splenomegaly syndrome

TSSA
tumor-specific (cell) surface antigen

TSSE
toxic shock syndrome exoprotein
toxic shock syndrome exotoxin

NOTES

751

TSST
toxic shock syndrome toxin

TSSU
(operating) theater sterile supply unit

TST
thromboplastin screening test
total sleep time
transition state theory
transscrotal testosterone
treadmill stress test *also* TMST
tumor skin test

TSTA
toxoplasmin skin test antigen
tumor-specific tissue antigen
tumor-specific transplantation antigen

TSTI
tumor-specific transplantation
immunity

TSU
triple sugar urea (agar)

TSV
total stomach volume

TSY
trypticase soy yeast

TT
tablet triturate
tactile tension
talking task
terminal transferase
tetanus toxin
tetanus toxoid *also* tet tox
tetrathionate (broth)
tetrazol
thrombin time
thrombolytic therapy
thromboplastin time
thymol turbidity
tibial tubercle
tibial tuberosity
tilt table
tine test
token test
tonometry
tooth treatment
total thyroxine
total time
total transfer
transferred to
transient tachypnea
transit time
transthoracic
transtracheal

triple therapy
tritiated thymidine *also* TTH
tuberculin test
tube thoracostomy
tumor thrombus
turnover time
twitch tension
tyrosine transaminase

T/T
trace of/trace of (different substances
on tests)

T&T
time and temperature
tobramycin and ticarcillin
touch and tone
tympanotomy and tube (insertion)

TT$_4$
total thyroxine

TTA
tetanus toxoid antibody
timed therapeutic absence
tissue texture abnormality
total toe arthroplasty
transtracheal aspiration

TTAP
threaded titanium acetabular prosthesis

TTAT
toe touch as tolerated

TTBV
total trabecular bone volume

TTC
transtracheal catheter
triphenyltetrazolium chloride
triphenyl tetrazolium chloride
T-tube cholangiogram

TTD
tarsal tunnel decompression
temporary total disability
tetraethylthiuramdisulfide
tissue tolerance dose
total temporary disability
transient tic disorder
transverse thoracic diameter

TTE
transthoracic echocardiography

TTF
time-to-treatment failure

TTFD
thiamine tetrahydrofurfuryl disulfide

TTG
tellurite, taurocholate, and gelatin

TTGA
tellurite, taurocholate, and gelatin agar

TTH
thyrotropic hormone *also* TH
tritiated thymidine *also* TT

TTI
tension-time index
time-tension index
tissue thromboplastin inhibition (test)
total time to intubation
transtracheal insufflation

TTIB
tension-time index per beat

TTJV
transtracheal jet ventilation

TTL
total lymphocyte
training and test lung

TTLC
true total lung capacity

TTM
total tumor mass
transtelephonic (arrhythmia) monitoring
transtelephonic (electrocardiographic) monitoring

TTMAD
Testing-Teaching Module of Auditory Discrimination

TTN
transient tachypnea of newborn *also* TTNB

TTNA
transthoracic needle aspiration

TTNB
transient tachypnea of newborn *also* TTN
transthoracic needle (aspiration) biopsy

TTO
to take out
transtracheal oxygen

TTOD
tetanus toxoid outdated

TTOT
transtracheal oxygen therapy

Ttot
total respiratory time

TTP
Testicular Tumor Panel
thrombotic thrombocytopenic purpura
thymidine triphosphate
time to peak
time to tumor progression

TTPA
triethylene thiophosphoramide

TTPD
thoracic-pelvic-phalangeal dystrophy

TTP-HUS
thrombotic thrombocytopenic purpura and hemolytic uremic syndrome

TTR
transthoracic resistance
triceps tendon reflex
type to token ratio

TTS
tarsal tunnel syndrome
temporary threshold shift
through the skin
through-the-scope
tight-to-shaft
transdermal therapeutic system

TTT
thymol turbidity test
tilt-table test
tolbutamide tolerance test
total tourniquet time
total twitch time

TTTT
test tube turbidity test

T-TURP
total transurethral resection of prostate

TTUTD
tetanus toxoid up-to-date

NOTES

TTV
tracheal transport velocity
transfusion transmitted virus

TTVP
temporary transvenous pacemaker

TTWB
touch-toe weightbearing

TTX
tetrodotoxin

TU
thiouracil
thiourea
thyroidal uptake
Todd unit
toxic unit
transmission unit
transurethral
tuberculin unit
turbidity unit

T₃U
triiodothyronine uptake *also* T₃UP

TUB
tubouterine (junction)

tuberc
tuberculosis *also* T, TB, Tb, tb,
TBC, Tbc

TUD
total urethral discharge

TUDC
tauroursodeoxycholate

TUDCA
tauroursodeoxycholic acid

TUE
transurethral extraction

TUEP
transurethral evaporation of prostate

TUF
total ultrafiltration

TUG
total urinary gonadotropin

TUI
transurethral incision

TUIBN
transurethral incision of bladder neck

TUIP
transurethral incision of prostate

TULIP
transurethral ultrasound-guided laser-
induced prostatectomy (system)

TUMT
transurethral microwave thermotherapy

TUN
total urinary nitrogen

TUNA
transurethral needle ablation

TUNEL
in situ DNA nick end labeling

T₃UP
triiodothyronine uptake *also* T₃U

TUPR
transurethral prostatic resection

TUR
transurethral resection *also* TUR-Cue
photometer

T₃UR
triiodothyronine uptake ratio

TURB
transurethral resection of bladder
(tumor)

turb
turbid
turbidity

TURBN
transurethral resection of bladder
neck

TURBT
transurethral resection of bladder
tumor

TUR-Cue photometer
transurethral resection *also* TUR

TURP
transurethral prostatectomy
transurethral resection of prostate

TURS
transurethral resection syndrome

TURV
transurethral resection of valves

TURVN
transurethral resection of vesical neck

tus.
cough [L. *tussis*]

TUSSI
Temple University Short Syntax
Inventory

TUU
transureteroureterostomy

TUV
transurethral valve

TUVP
transurethral vaporization of prostate

TV
talipes varus
temporary visit
tetrazolium violet
thoracic vertebra
tick-borne virus
tidal volume *also* TD, VT, V_T
total volume
toxic vertigo
transfer vesicle
transvenous
trial visit
Trichomonas vaginalis
tricuspid valve
trivalent
true vertebra
truncal vagotomy
tuberculin volutin
tubulovesicular

T/V
touch/verbal

TVA
true visual acuity
truncal vagotomy plus antrectomy

TVC
third ventricle cyst
timed ventilatory capacity
timed vital capacity
total viable cells
total volume capacity
transvaginal cone
triple voiding cystogram
true vocal cord

TVD
transmissible virus dementia
triple vessel disease

TVDALV
triple vessel diisease with abnormal
left ventricle

TVF
tactile vocal fremitus
Thiry-Vella fistula

TVG
time-varied gain (control)

TVGC
time-varied gain control *also* TGC

TVH
total vaginal hysterectomy
turkey virus hepatitis

TVI
total vascular isolation

TVL
tenth value layer (radiation)

TVN
tonic vibration response

TVP
tensor veli palatini
textured vegetable protein
transvenous pacemaker
transvesical prostatectomy
tricuspid valve prolapse
truncal vagotomy plus)pyloroplasty

TVR
total vascular resistance
total vibration reflex
tricuspid valve replacement

TVS
transvaginal sonography

TVSC
transvaginal (sector) scan

TVT
transmissible venereal tumor
tunica vaginalis testis

TVU
total volume of urine

TVUS
transvaginal ultrasound

TW
tap water
terminal web
test weight
thymic weight
total (body) water

T

NOTES

TWA
time-weighted average
TWAR
Taiwan acute respiratory
Twb
wet bulb temperature
TWBC
total white blood cells
TWD
total white and differential (cell count)
TWE
tap water enema
tepid water enema
TWETC
tap water enema til clear
TWF
Test of Word Finding
TWG
total weight gain
TWHW
toe walking and heel walking
TWI
T-wave inversion
TWL
transepidermal water loss *also* TEWL
TWN
twin
TWR
total wrist replacement
TWWD
tap water wet dressing
TX
derivative of contagious tuberculin
thromboxane *also* TBX, Thx
thyroidectomized
transplantation *also* transpl
treatment *also* TR, Tr, tr, treat., Tx, T_x
T&X
type and crossmatch *also* TXM
Tx, T_x
therapy
traction
transfuse
transplant
treatment *also* TR, Tr, tr, treat., TX
tympanostomy

tx
traction
treatment
TXA, TxA
thromboxane A
TXA2, TXA_2
thromboxane A2
TXB2, TXB_2
thromboxane B2
TXM
T-cell crossmatch
type and crossmatch *also* T&X
Txn
transplant
Ty
thyroxine
type
typhoid
tyrosine *also* Tyr, Y
TYCO
Tylenol with codeine
Tyl
Tylenol
tyloma
TYMP
tympanogram
Tymp
tympanic
tympanicity (auscultation of chest)
tympanium
tympanostomy
typ
typical
TYR
tyramine
tyrode
ITyr
monoiodotryrosine
Tyr
tyrosine *also* Ty, Y
TyRIA
thyroid radioimmunoassay
TZ
transition zone
triazolam
tuberculin zymoplastiche
zymoplastic tuberculin [Ger. *Tuberculin zymoplastische*]

TZT
    triazinate

NOTES

T

U
internal energy
International Unit (of enzyme
 activity)
kilurane (radioactivity unit)
Mann-Whitney rank sum statistic
potential difference (in volts)
ulna
ultralente (insulin)
uncertain
unerupted
unit
unknown *also* UK
upper
uracil *also* URA, Ura
uranium
urethra *also* UA, ureth
uridine *also* Urd
uridylic acid *also* UA
urinary *also* Ur, ur
urine *also* UR, Ur, ur
urology *also* Urol
uvula
wave on electrocardiogram

1/U
one fingerbreadth above umbilicus

U100
100 units per milliliter

U/1
one fingerbreadth below umbilicus

U/3
upper third (of long bone)

u
unified atomic mass unit

u.
to be used [L. *utendus*]

UA
Ulex agglutinin
ultra-audible (sound)
ultrasonic arteriogram
umbilical arterial
umbilical artery
unaggregated
unauthorized absence
uncertain about
unit of analysis
unrelated (children raised) apart
unstable angina
upper airway
upper arm

urethra *also* U, ureth
uric acid *also* U/A
uridylic acid *also* U
urinalysis *also* U/A
urinary aldosterone
urine aliquot
urocanic acid
uterine aspiration

U/A
uric acid *also* UA
urinalysis *also* UA
uterine activity

u.a.
as far as [L. *usque ad*]

ua
up to

UAC
umbilical artery catheter
underactive
upper airway congestion

UA/C
uric acid-creatinine (ratio)

UAD
upper airway disease

UAE
unilateral absence of excretion

UAG
uracil-adenine-guanine

UAI
uterine activity integral

UAL
umbilical artery line
up (out of bed) as desired [up + L.
 ad libitum]

UA&M
urinalysis and microscopy

U-AMY
urinary amylase

UAN
uric acid nitrogen

UAO
upper airway obstruction

UAP
unstable angina pectoris *also* USAP

UAPF
upon arrival patient found

U

UAR
upper airway resistance

UAS
upper abdominal surgery
upstream activating sequence

UASA
upper airway sleep apnea

UAT
up (out of bed) as tolerated

UAU
uterine activity unit

UAVC
univentricular atrioventricular
connection

UB
ultimobranchial body
Unna boot
urinary bladder

UBA
undenatured bacterial antigen

UBBC
unsaturated (vitamin) B_{12}-binding
capacity

UBC
unsaturated binding capacity

UBE
upper body ergometer

UBF
unknown black female
uterine blood flow

UBG
ultimobranchial gland
urobilinogen

UBI
ultraviolet blood irradiation

UBL
undifferentiated B-cell lymphoma

UBM
unknown black male
urothelial basement membrane

UBO
unidentified bright object

UBP
Universal bone plate
ureteral back pressure

UBT
C-urea breath test

UBW
usual body weight

UC
ulcerative colitis
Uldall catheter
ultracentrifugal
umbilical cholesterol
umbilical cord
unchanged
unclassifiable
unconscious *also* UCS, Ucs
undifferentiated carcinoma
unfixed cryostat
unit clerk
unit coordinator
unsatisfactory condition
untreated cell
urea clearance *also* UCL
urethral catheterization
urinary catheter
urine concentrate
urine culture *also* U/C, UCX
usual care
uterine contraction

U/C
urine culture *also* UC, UCX

U&C
urethral and cervical (cultures)
usual and customary

$U_{Ca}V$
urinary calcium volume (excretion
rate)

UCB
umbilical cord blood
unconjugated bilirubin *also* UCBR
unilateral calcaneal brace

UCBC
umbilical cord blood culture

UCBR
unconjugated bilirubin *also* UCB

UCC
urgent care center

UCD
urine collection device
usual childhood diseases *also* UCHD,
UDC

UCE
urea cycle enzymopathy

UCG
ultrasonic cardiogram

ultrasonic cardiography
urinary chorionic gonadotropin

UCHD
usual childhood diseases *also* UCD, UDC

UCHI
usual childhood illnesses *also* UCI

UCHS
uncontrolled hemorrhagic shock

UCI
urethral catheter in
urinary catheter in
usual childhood illnesses *also* UCHI

UCL
ulnar collateral ligament
uncomfortable level
uncomfortable listening level
uncomfortable loudness level *also* ULL
upper confidence limit
urea clearance *also* UC

UCLP
unilateral cleft of lip and palate

UCO
urethral catheter out
urinary catheter out

UCP
urethral closure pressure
urinary coproporphyrin
urinary C-peptide

UCPP
urethral closure pressure profile

UCPT
urinary coproporphyrin test

UCR
unconditioned reflex *also* UR
unconditioned response *also* UR
usual, customary, and reasonable (fees)

UCRE
urine creatinine

UCRP
Universal Control Reference Plasma

UCS
unconditioned stimulus *also* UDS, US

unconscious *also* UC, Ucs
uterine compression syndrome

UC&S
urine culture and sensitivity

Ucs
unconscious *also* UC, UCS

UCT
unchanged conventional treatment

UCTD
unclassifiable connective tissue disease
undifferentiated connective tissue disease

UCU
urinary care unit

UCV
uncontrolled variable

UCX
urine culture *also* UC

UD
ulcerative dermatosis
ulnar deviation
underdeveloped
undesirable discharge
unipolar depression
unit dose
urethral discharge
uridine diphosphate
uroporphyrinogen decarboxylase
uterine distention
uterus delivery

u.d.
as directed [L. *ud dictum*] *also* e.m.p., m.d., m. dict., MP, ut dict.

UDA
under direct vision

UDC
uninhibited detrusor (muscle) capacity
ursodeoxycholate
usual diseases of childhood *also* UCD, UCHD

UDCA
ursodeoxycholic acid

UDE
undetermined etiology

U

NOTES

UDI
urinary diagnostic index

UDMA
urethane dimethacrylate

UDN
updraft nebulizer

UDO
undetermined origin

UDP
unassisted diastolic pressure
uridine diphosphate
uridine 5'-diphosphate

UDPG
uridine diphosphoglucose *also*
UDPGlc

UDPGA
uridine diphosphoglucuronic acid

UDPGal
uridine diphosphogalactose

UDPGlc
uridine diphosphoglucose *also* UDPG

UDP-GlcUA
uridine diphosphoglucronic acid *also*
UDPGA

UDPGT
uridine diphosphoglucuronyl
transferase

UdR
uracil deoxyriboside (deoxyuridine)

UDRP
urine diribose phosphate

UDS
ultra–Doppler sonography
unconditioned stimulus *also* UCS, US
unscheduled deoxynucleic acid
synthesis
unscheduled deoxyribonucleic acid
synthesis

UDT
undescended testicle

UE
uncertain etiology
under elbow
undetermined etiology
uninvolved epidermis
upper esophagus
upper extremity *also* U/E

U/E
upper extremity *also* UE

UEA
upper extremity arterial

UEA-1
Ulex europaeus agglutinin I

UEG
ultrasonic encephalography
unifocal eosinophilic granuloma

UEM
universal electron microscope

UEMC
unidentified endosteal marrow cell

UER
unaided equalization reference

UES
undifferentiated embryonal sarcoma
upper esophageal sphincter

UESP
upper esophageal sphincter pressure

UESR
upper esophageal sphincter relaxation

u/ext
upper extremity

UF
ultrafiltrable
ultrafiltrate
ultrafiltration
ultrafine
ultrasonic frequency
unflexed
universal feeder
unknown factor
until finished
urea formaldehyde

UFA
unesterified fatty acid
unesterified free fatty acid *also* FFA

UFC
urinary free cortisol

UFCT
ultrafast computed tomography

UFD
ultrasonic flow detector

UFE
uniform food encoding

UFF
unusual facial features

UFFI
urea formaldehyde foam insulation

UFH
unfractionated heparin

UFN
until further notice

UFO
unflagged order
unidentified foreign object

UFOV
useful field of view

UFR
ultrafiltration rate
urine filtration rate

uFSH
urinary follicle-stimulating hormone

UFV
ultrafiltration volume
unclassified fecal virus

UG
until gone
urinary glucose
urogastrone
urogenital
uteroglobulin

UGA
under general anesthesia
urogenital atrophy

UGCR
ultrasound-guided compression repair

UGD
urogenital diaphragm

UGDP
University Group Diabetes Project

UGF
unidentified growth factor
urinary gonadotropin fragment

UGH
uveitis-glaucoma-hyphema (syndrome)

UGH+
uveitis-glaucoma-hyphema plus
(vitreous hemorrhage, syndrome)

UGI
upper gastrointestinal (tract) *also*
UGIT

UGIB
upper gastrointestinal bleeding

UGIH
upper gastrointestinal (tract)
hemorrhage

UGIS
upper gastrointestinal series

UGIT
upper gastrointestinal tract *also* UGI

UGK
urine glucose ketone

UGP
urinary gonadotropin peptide

UGPP
uridyl diphosphate glucose
pyrophosphorylase

UGS
urogenital sinus

UH
umbilical hernia
upper half

UHBI
upper hemibody irradiation

UHC
ultrahigh carbon

UHD
unstable hemoglobin disease

UHDDS
Uniform Hospital Discharge Data Set

UHF
ultrahigh frequency

u-hFSH
urinary-derived human follicle-
stimulating hormone

UHFV
ultrahigh-frequency ventilation

UHL
universal hypertrichosis lanuginosa

UHMW
ultrahigh molecular weight

UHMWPE
ultrahigh molecular weight
polyethylene

U

NOTES

UHR
underlying heart rhythm

UHSC
university health services clinic

UHT
ultrahigh temperature

UHV
ultrahigh vacuum
ultrahigh voltage

UI
Ulcer Index
urinary incontinence
uroporphyrin isomerase

U/I
unidentified

UIBC
unbound iron-binding capacity
unsaturated iron-binding capacity

UICC
International Union Against Cancer
Union Internationale Contre Cancrum

u.i.d.
once daily [L. *uno in die*]

UID/S
unilateral interfacetal dislocation or
subluxation

UIEP
urine immunoelectrophoresis

UIF
undegraded insulin factor

UIP
unusual interstitial pneumonitis
usual interstitial pneumonia (of
Liebow)
usual interstitial pneumonitis

UIQ
upper inner quadrant

UIS
Utilization Information Service

UJ
universal joint (syndrome)

UJT
unijunction transistor

UK
unknown *also* U
urinary kallikrein *also* UKa
urine potassium
urokinase

UKA
unicompartmental knee arthroplasty

UKa
urinary kallikrein *also* UK

UK IC
urokinase intracoronary

U_kV
urinary potassium volume (excretion
rate)

UL
unauthorized leave
Underwriters' Laboratories
undifferentiated lymphoma
upper limb
upper limit
upper lobe
utterance length

U/L
unit per liter *also* U/l
upper and lower *also* U&L

U&L
upper and lower *also* U/L

U/l
unit per liter *also* U/L

ULA
undedicated logic array

ULBW
ultralow birth weight

ULL
uncomfortable loudness level *also*
UCL

ULLE
upper lid, left eye

ULN
upper limits of normal

uln
ulna
ulnar

ULO
upper limb orthosis

ULP
ultralow profile
upper limb prosthesis

ULPA
ultra-low particulate air

ULPE
upper lobe pulmonary edema

ULQ
upper left quadrant

ULR
guaifenesin, phenylpropanolamine, and phenylephrine

ULRE
upper lid, right eye

ULSB
upper left sternal border

ULT
ultralow temperature

ult
ultimate
ultimately

ult. praes.
last prescribed [L. *ultimum praescriptus*]

ULV
ultralow volume

ULYTES
urine electrolytes

UM
unmarried
upper motor (neuron)
uracil mustard
Utilization Management

UMA
urinary muramidase activity

Umax
maximal urinary osmolality

UMB, umb
umbilical
umbilicus

UMCD
uremic medullary cystic disease

UMCL
upper midclavicular line

$U_{Mg}V$
urinary magnesium volume (excretion rate)

UMI
uterine manipulator/injector

UMN
upper motor neuron

UMNB
upper motor neurogenic bladder

UMNL
upper motor neuron lesion

UMP
uridine 5'-monophosphate
uridine monophosphate (uridylic acid)

UMPK
uridine monophosphate kinase

UMS
urethral manipulation syndrome

UMT
unit of medical time

UN
ulnar nerve
undernourished
unilateral neglect
urea nitrogen
urinary nitrogen

UNA
urinary nitrogen appearance

U_{Na}
urinary concentration of sodium

UNa
urinary sodium

UNaV
urinary sodium excretion

uncomp
uncompensated

uncond
unconditioned

uncor
uncorrected

UnCS, unCS
unconditioned stimulus *also* UnS

unct.
smeared [L. *unctus*]

UNCV
ulnar nerve conduction velocity

undet
undetermined

NOTES

U

UNE
urinary norepinephrine

UNG
uracil-N-glycosylase

ung.
ointment [L. *unguentum*]

U$_{NH4}$-
urinary ammonium

UNID
unidentified

unilat
unilateral

univ
universal

unk, unkn
unknown

UNL
upper normal limit

UNOS
United Network of Organ Sharing

UNS, uns
unsatisfactory *also* unsat
unsymmetrical

UnS
unconditioned stimulus *also* UnCS,
unCS

unsat
unsatisfactory *also* UNS, uns
unsaturated

unsym
unsymmetrical

UNTS
unilateral nevoid telangiectasia
syndrome

UNX
uninephrectomy

UO
under observation *also* U/O, u/o
undetermined origin
ureteral orifice
urinary output *also* UOP

U/O, u/o
under observation *also* UO

UOA
United Ostomy Association

UOP
urinary output *also* UO

UOQ
upper outer quadrant

UOsm
urinary osmolality

Uosm
urine osmolarity

UOV
unit of variance

UOZ
upper outer zone (quadrant)

UP
ulcerative proctitis
ultrahigh purity
unipolar
Unna-Pappenheim (stain)
upright posture
ureteropelvic
uridine phosphorylase
uroporphyrin
uteroplacental

U/P
up (out of bed) as desired [up + L
ad libitum] *also* UAL
urine-plasma ratio

uPA, u-PA
urokinase-type plasminogen activator
also u-PA

UPC
uknown primary carcinoma
usual provider continuity

UPD
urinary production (rate)

UPEP
urine protein electrophoresis

UPF
universal proximal femur (prosthesis)

UPG
uroporphyrinogen

UPI
uteroplacental insufficiency
uteroplacental ischemia

UPJ
ureteropelvic junction

UPL
unusual position of limbs

UPLIF
unilateral posterior lumbar interbody fusion

UPN
unique patient number

UPOC
Ultramatic Project-O-Chart projector

UPOR
usual place of residence

UPP
urethral pressure profile
urethral pressure profilometry
uvulopalatoplasty

UPPP
uvulopalatopharyngoplasty

UPPRA
upright peripheral plasma renin activity

UPRBC
units of packed red blood cells

UPS
ultraviolet photoelectron spectroscopy
uninterruptible power supply
uroporphyrinogen synthase
uterine progesterone system

UPSC
uterine papillary serous carcinoma

Y
upsilon (20th letter of Greek alphabet), uppercase

υ
kinematic viscosity *also* ν
upsilon (20th letter of Greek alphabet), lowercase

UPSIT
University of Pennsylvania Smell Identification Test

UPT
uptake
urine pregnancy test

UQ
ubiquinone
upper quadrant

UR
unconditioned reflex *also* UCR
unconditioned response *also* UCR
unrelated
upper respiratory
upper right
urinal
urinary retention
urine *also* U, Ur, ur
urology
utilization review

Ur, ur
urinary *also* U
urine *also* U, UR

URA, Ura
uracil *also* U
urethral resistance factor

ur anal
urinalysis
urine analysis

URC
upper rib cage
utilization review committee

URC-A
uric acid

URC SP
uric acid (urine) spot (test)

URD
undifferentiated respiratory disease
unrelated donor
upper respiratory disease

Urd
uridine *also* U

UREA-S
urea nitrogen (urine) spot (test)

URED
unable to read (lab result)

ureth
urethra *also* U, UA

URF
unidentified reading frame
uterine relaxing factor

UR-FST
urine-fasting

U

NOTES

urg
urgent

UR HR
urine-number of hours glucose tolerance

URI
upper respiratory illness
upper respiratory (tract) infection *also* URTI

URIN
random urine

url
unrelated

UR&M
urinalysis, routine and microscopic

URO
urology
uroporphyrin
uroporphyrinogen

UROB, UROBIL
urobilinogen

UROD
uroporphyrinogen decarboxylase

URO-GEN
urogenital

URO-2H
urobilinogen—2 hours

Urol
urologist
urology *also* U

UROS
uroporphyrinogen synthetase

URQ
upper right quadrant (of abdomen)

URS
ultrasonic renal scanning

URSB
upper right sternal border

URSO
ursodeoxycholic acid

URT
upper respiratory tract
uterine resting tone

URTI
upper respiratory tract illness
upper respiratory tract infection *also* URI

UR-TIM
urine-time

URVD
unilateral renovascular disease

UR VOL
urine volume

US
ultrasonic
ultrasonography
ultrasound *also* U/S
unconditional stimulus
unconditioned stimulus *also* UCS, UDS
unit secretary
upper segment
Usher syndrome

U/S
ultrasound *also* US

USA
unit services assistant

USAFH
United States Air Force Hospital

USAFRHL
United States Air Force Radiological Health Laboratory

USAH
United States Army Hospital

USAHC
United States Army Health Clinic

USAIDR
United States Army Institute of Dental Research

USAMEDS
United States Army Medical Service

USAN
United States Adopted Names (Council)

USAP
unstable angina pectoris *also* UAP

USASI
United States of America Standards Institute

USB
upper sternal border

USBS
United States Bureau of Standards

USCI
United States Catheter & Instrument Company

USCVD
unsterile controlled vaginal delivery

USD
United States Dispensary

USDA
United States Department of Agriculture

USDHHS
United States Department of Health and Human Services

USE
ultrasonic echography (ultrasonography) *also* USG

USFMG
United States foreign medical graduates

USG
ultrasonogram
ultrasonography *also* USE

USH
usual state of health

USHL
United States Hygienic Laboratory

USI
urinary stress incontinence

USM
ultrasonic mist

USMG
United States medical graduate

USMH
United States Marine Hospital

USN
ultrasonic nebulizer

USNH
United States Naval Hospital

USO
unilateral salpingo-oophorectomy

USOGH
usual state of good health

USOH
usual state of health

USP
unassisted systolic pressure
United States Pharmacopeia
upper sternal border

USPDI
United States Pharmacopeia Drug Information

USPET
Urokinase-Streptokinase Pulmonary Embolism Trial

USPHS
United States Public Health Service

USR
unheated serum reagin

USRDS
United States Renal Data System

USS
ultrasound scanning

ust.
burnt [L. *ustus*]

USUCVD
unsterile uncontrolled vaginal delivery

USVH
United States Veterans Hospital

USVMD
urine specimen volume measuring device

USVMS
urine specimen volume measuring system

USW
ultrashort wave

UT
Ullrich-Turner (syndrome) *also* UTS
Unna-Thost (syndrome)
unrelated (children raised) together
untested
untreated
urinary tract
urticaria

uT
unbound testosterone

ut
uterus

U$_{TA}$
urinary titrable acidity

NOTES

UTBG
unbound thyroxine-binding globulin

UTD
unable to determine
up to date

ut dict.
as directed [L. *ut dictum*] *also*
e.m.p., m.d., m. dict., MP, u.d.

utend.
to be used [L. *utendus*]

utend. mor. sol.
to be used in the usual manner [L. *utendus more solitus*]

UTF
usual throat flora

UTI
urinary tract infection
urinary trypsin inhibitor

UTL
unable to locate

UTLD
Utah Test of Language Development

UTM
urinary tract malformation

UTO
unable to obtain
upper tibial osteotomy

UTP
unilateral tension pneumothorax
uridine triphosphate
uridine 5′-triphosphate

UTS
Ullrich-Turner syndrome *also* UT
ulnar tunnel syndrome
ultimate tensile strength
ultrasound *also* UTZ

ut supr.
as above [L. *ut supre*]

UTTS
ultrathin-walled two-stage

UTZ
ultrasound *also* UTS

UU
urinary urea
urine urobilinogen

UUD
uncontrolled unsterile delivery

UUN
urinary urea nitrogen excretion
urine urea nitrogen

UUO
unilateral ureteral obstruction
unilateral ureteral occlusion

UUP
urine uroporphyrin

U UREA
urinary (concentration of) urea

UV
ultraviolet
ultraviolet light
umbilical vein *also* uv
ureterovesical
urinary volume

U$_v$
Uppsala virus

uv
umbilical vein *also* UV

UVA
ultraviolet A
ultraviolet light, long wavelength
ureterovesical angle

UVAC
uterine vacuum aspirating curette

UVB
midrange spectrum
midrange-wavelength ultraviolet light
ultraviolet B
ultraviolet light

UVC
ultraviolet C
umbilical vein catheter
umbilical venous catheter
urgent visit center

UVEB
unifocal ventricular ectopic beat

UVER
ultraviolet-enhanced reactivation

UVH
univentricular heart

UVI
ultraviolet irradiation

UVJ
ureterovesical junction

UVL
ultraviolet light
umbilical venous line

UV/MV
umbilical vein to maternal vein

UVP
ultraviolet photometry

UVR
ultraviolet radiation

UW
unilateral weakness
University of Wisconsin

U/WB
unit of whole blood

UWD
Urbach-Wiethe disease

UWF
unknown white female

UWL
unstirred water layer

UWM
unknown white male
unwed mother

UX
uranium X (proactinium)

ux.
wife [L. *uxor*]

UYP
upper yield point

NOTES

U

V

coefficient of variation
electrical potential (in volts)
gas volume
logical binary relation that is true if any argument is true and false otherwise
luminous efficiency
minute volume (of air or blood)
potential energy (joules)
unipolar chest lead
vaccinated
vaccine
vagina *also* VAG, Vag, vag
valine *also* VAL, Val
valve
vanadium (element)
variable *also* Var, var, var
variation *also* Var, var
varnish
vector
vegetarian
vegetation
vein *also* v
velocity *also* v
venous
venous (blood)
ventilation
ventral
ventricle
ventricular (fibrillation)
ventricular (wave)
venule
verbal (comprehension factor)
vertebral
vertex sharp transient (electroencephalography)
violet
viral *also* Vir
viral (antigen)
virulence *also* VI, Vi
virus *also* v, Vir
vision
visual acuity *also* VA
visual capacity
voice
volt *also* v
voltage
volume (of gas) *also* q, vol
vomiting

V̊

gas volume per unit of time (gas flow)
ventilation

+V

positive vertical divergence *also* +VD

V₁-V₆

precordial chest leads

V$_{CO}$ (*var. of* VCO)

V̊$_A$

alveolar ventilation *also* alv vent

v

rate of reaction catalyzed by an enzyme
specific volume
vein *also* V
velocity *also* V
venous (blood) *also* VB
versus *also* vs
very
virus *also* V, Vir
vitamin
volt *also* V

v̄

mixed venous (blood)

+v

positive vertical divergence

v.

see [L. *vide*]

v-

vicinal isomer

VA

vacuum aspiration
valeric acid
valproic acid
vancomycin
variant angina
vasodilator agent
venoarterial
ventricular arrhythmia
ventriculoatrial *also* V-A
ventroanterior
vertebral artery
Veterans Administration
viral antigen
visual activity
visual acuity *also* V
visual aid
visual axis

VA *(continued)*
volcanic ash
volt ampere
volume, alveolar
volume averaging

V-A
ventriculoatrial *also* VA

V&A
vagotomy and antrectomy

V/A
variety
volt/ampere

V$_A$
alveolar ventilation per minute

Va
arterial gas volume
visual acuity
volt ampere *also* va

va
volt ampere *also* Va

VAB
Velban, actinomycin D, and
bleomycin
vincristine, actinomycin D, and
bleomycin

VAB-II
Velban, actinomycin D, bleomycin,
and platinum

VAB-VI
cyclophosphamide, Velban,
actinomycin D, bleomycin, and
platinum

VAB-6
vinblastine, actinomycin D,
bleomycin, cisplatin,
cyclophosphamide

VABES
vasoablative endothelial sarcoma

VABP
ventroarterial bypass pumping

VAC
ventriculoarterial connection
ventriculoatrial condition
ventriculoatrial conduction
vincristine, actinomycin D, and
cyclophosphamide
vincristine, Adriamycin, and cisplatin
vincristine, Adriamycin (doxorubicin),
and cyclophosphamide

vac
vaccine
vacuum

VACA
vincristine, actinomycin A
(dactinomycin), cyclophosphamide,
and Adriamycin

VA cc
distance visual acuity with correction
also VA ccl

vacc
vaccination

VA ccl
distance visual acuity with correction
also VA cc

VACTERL
vertebral, anal, cardiac, tracheal,
esophageal, renal, limb

VAD
vascular access device
vascular access dressing
venous access device
ventricular assist device
vincristine, Adriamycin (doxorubicin),
and dexamethasone
virus-adjusting diluent
vitamin A deficiency

VaD
vascular dementia

VADA
vincristine, Adriamycin (doxorubicin),
dexamethasone, and actinomycin D

VADCS
ventricular atrial distal coronary sinus

VADS
Visual Aural Digit Span Test

VAE
venous air embolism

V$_A$eff
effective alveolar ventilation

VAER
visual auditory evoked response

VAERS
Vaccine Adverse Events Reporting
System

VAFAC
vincristine, Adriamycin (doxorubicin),
5-fluorouracil, Amethopterine
(methotrexate), and cyclophosphamide

VAFD
Vasceze Vascular Access Flush Device

VAG, Vag, vag
vagina *also* V
vaginal *also* V

VAG HYST
vaginal hysterectomy *also* VH

VAGM
vein of Galen aneurysmal malformation

VAH
vertebral ankylosing hyperostosis
Veterans Administration Hospital
virilizing adrenal hyperplasia

VAHBE
ventricular atrial His bundle electrocardiogram

VAHRA
ventricular atrial height right atrium

VAHS
virus-associated hemophagocytic syndrome

VAIN
vaginal intraepithelial neoplasia
vaginal intraepithelial neoplasm

VAKT
visual, association, kinesthetic, tactile (reading)

VAL, Val
valine *also* V

val
valve

VALE
visual acuity, left eye

VAM
ventricular arrhythmia monitor
vinblastine, Adriamycin, mitomycin C
VP-16 (etoposide), Adriamycin (doxorubicin), and methotrexate

VAMC
Veterans Administration Medical Center

VAMP
venous/arterial management protection
vincristine, actinomycin, methotrexate, and prednisone
vincristine, Adriamycin, and methylprednisolone

VAMS
Visual Analogue Mood Scale

VAN
ventricular aneurysmectomy

VANCO/P
vancomycin-peak

VANCO/T
vancomycin-trough

VAOD
visual acuity, right eye

VAOS
visual acuity, left eye

VAP
variant angina pectoris
venous access port
ventilator associated pneumonia
vincristine, Adriamycin (doxorubicin), and prednisone (or procarbazine)

vap
vapor

VAPA
vincristine, Adriamycin (doxorubicin), prednisone, and ara-C

VAPCS
ventricular atrial proximal coronary sinus

VAPS
visual analog pain score
volume-assured pressure support

$\dot{V}A/\dot{Q}$, V_A/Q_C
ventilation-perfusion quotient ratio *also* $\dot{V}/\dot{Q}$

$\dot{V}a/\dot{Q}$
ventilation/perfusion ratio

VAR
visual auditory range

Var, var
variable *also* V

V

NOTES

Var *(continued)*
variant
variation *also* V
variety

var
variant

VARE
visual acuity, right eye

Varivax
varicella vaccine

VAS
vascular *also* vasc
vasectomy *also* vas
vesicle attachment site
viral analog scale
visual analog scale
Visual Analogue Scale (pain)

vas
vasectomy *also* VAS

VASC
Verbal Auditory Screen for Children

VA sc
distance visual acuity without
correction

vasc
vascular *also* VAS

VA scl
distance visal acuity without
correction

vasodil
vasodilation *also* VD
vasodilator *also* VD

VAS RAD
vascular radiology

vas vit., vas vitr.
glass vessel [L. *vas vitreum*]

VAT
variable antigen type
ventricular activation time
ventricular (pacing), atrial (sensing),
triggered (mode, pacemaker)
visual action time
visual apperception test
vocational apperception test

VATER
vertebral (defects), (imperforate) anus,
tracheoesophageal (fistula), radial and
renal (dysplasia)

VATH
vinblastine, Adriamycin (doxorubicin),
thiotepa, and Halotestin
(fluoxymesterone)

VATS
video-assisted thoracic surgery
video-assisted thoracoscopic surgery

VATs
variable antigen, surface

VAV
VP-16 (etopside), Adriamycin
(doxorubicin), and vincristine

VAX-D
vertebral axial decompression

VB
vagina bulbi
valence bond
Van Buren (catheter)
venous blood *also* v
ventrobasal
Veronal buffer
viable birth
vinblastine and bleomycin
voided bladder

VB$_1$
first voided bladder specimen

VB$_2$
second midstream bladder specimen

VB$_3$
third midstream bladder specimen

VBAC
vaginal birth after cesarean section

VBAI, VBAIN
vertebrobasilar artery insufficiency

VBAP
vincristine, BCNU (carmustine),
Adriamycin (doxorubicin), and
prednisone

VBC
vincristine, bleomycin, and cisplatin

VBD
Veronal-buffered diluent

VBG
vagotomy and Billroth
gastroenterostomy
venoaortocoronary (artery) bypass
graft
venous blood gas
Veronal-buffered (serum with) gelatin
vertical banded gastroplasty

VBI
vertebrobasilar insufficiency
vertebrobasilar ischemia

VBL
vinblastine

VBM
vinblastine, bleomycin, and
methotrexate

VBMCP
vincristine, BCNU (carmustine),
melphalan, cyclophosphamide, and
prednisone

VBOS
Veronal-buffered oxalated saline

VBP
venous blood pressure
ventricular premature beat
vinblastine, bleomycin, and Platinol
(cisplastin)

VBR
ventricular-brain ratio

VBS
venous blood sample
Veronal-buffered saline
vertebral-basilar (artery) system

VBS:FBS
Veronal-buffered saline-fetal bovine
serum

VBT
vertebral body tenderness

VC
vascular change
vasoconstriction
vena cava
venous capacitance
venous capillary
ventilatory capacity
ventral column
verbal comprehension
vertebral canal
Veterinary Corps
videocassette
vincristine *also* VCR
vinyl chloride
vision, color
visual capacity

visual cortex
vital capacity
vocal cord
volume, capillary
voluntary closing
vomiting center
vowel-consonant
VP-16 (etoposide) and carboplatin

V-C
vowel-consonant

V/C
ventilation-to-circulation (ratio)

V&C
vertical and centric (bite)

V_c
pulmonary capillary blood volume

Vc
pulmonary capillary gas volume

VCA
anti-viral capsid antigen
vancomycin, colistin, and anisomycin
vasoconstrictor assay
viral capsid antigen

VCA-EB
viral capsid antigen, Epstein-Barr

VCAM-1
vascular cell adhesion molecule-1

VCAP
vincristine, cyclophosphamide,
Adriamycin (doxorubicin), and
prednisone

VCC
vasoconstrictor center
ventral cell column

VCCA
velocity, common carotid artery

VCD
vacuum constriction device
vibrational circular dichroism
vocal cord dysfunction

VCDF
volume-cycled decelerating-flow
ventilation

V

NOTES

VCDQ
verbal comprehension deviation quotient

VCE
vagina, ectocervix, and endocervix

V$_{CE}$
velocity of contractile element

VCF
Vaginal Contraceptive Film
velocity of circumferential fiber shortening

V$_{CF}$
velocity of circumferential fiber (shortening)

VCG
vectorcardiogram
vectorcardiography
voiding cystogram

VCI
volatile corrosion inhibitor

V-Cillin
penicillin V

VCIU
voluntary control (of) involuntary utterances

VCM
vinyl chloride monomer

VCMP
vincristine, cyclophosphamide, melphalan, and prednisone

VCN
vancomycin (hydrochloride), colistimethate (sodium), and nystatin (medium)
vibrio cholerae neuraminidase

VCO, V$_{CO}$
carbon monoxide (endogenous production)

VCO$_2$, V$_{CO2}$
carbon dioxide output
venous carbon dioxide production
volume, carbon dioxide elimination

V̊$_{CO2}$
carbon dioxide output

V̊$_{CO2}$
carbon dioxide elimination *also* VECO$_2$

V$_{CO2}$ (*var. of* VCO$_2$)

VCP
vincristine, cyclophosphamide, and prednisone

VCR
vasoconstriction rate
vincristine *also* VC
volume clearance rate

VCS
vasoconstrictor substance
vesicocervical space
Vocabulary Comprehension Scale

VCSA
viral cell surface antigen

VCSF
ventricular cerebrospinal fluid

VCT
venous clotting time

VCTS
vitreal corneal touch syndrome

VCU
videocystourethrogram
videocystourethrography
voiding cystourethrogram *also* VCUG

VCUG
vesicoureterogram
voiding cystourethrogram *also* VCU

VCV
ventricular conduction velocity
vowel-consonant-vowel

VD
vapor density
vascular disease
vasodilation *also* vasodil
vasodilator *also* vasodil
venereal disease
ventricular dilator
vertical deviation
video disk
viral diarrhea
voided
volume of distribution

V&D
vomiting and diarrhea

+VD
positive vertical divergence

V$_D$
dead space
physiological dead space ventilation per minute
physiologic dead space

ventilation per minute of dead space
volume of dead space *also* VDS

V_d
apparent volume of distribution

Vd
volume of distribution

vd
double vibrations

VDA
venous digital angiogram
video dimensional analysis
visual discriminatory acuity

V_DA
ventilation of alveolar dead space
volume of alveolar dead space

VDAC
vaginal delivery after cesarean
voltage-dependent anion channel

V_Dan
ventilation of anatomic dead space
volume of anatomic dead space

VDBCC
vincristine, dactinomycin, bleomycin,
cisplatin, cyclophosphamide

VDBR
volume of distribution of bilirubin

VDC
vasodilator center

VDD
vincristine, doxorubicin,
dexamethasone

VDDR
vitamin D-dependent rickets

VDEL
Venereal Disease Experimental
Laboratory

VDEM
vasodepressor material

VDF
ventricular diastolic fragmentation

VDG, VD-G
venereal disease, gonorrhea

Vdg, vdg
voiding

VDH
valvular disease of heart
vascular disease of heart

VDJ
variable diversity joining

VDL
vasodepressor lipid
visual detection level

VDM
vasodepressor material

VD or M
venous distention or mass

V_{DM}
volume of mechanical dead space

VDO
varus derotational osteotomy

VDP
ventricular premature depolarization
vinblastine, dacarbazine, and Platinol
vincristine, daunorubicin, and
prednisone

VDPCA
variable-dose patient-controlled
anesthesia

VDR
venous diameter ratio

V_Drb
rebreathing ventilation

VDRF
ventilator dependent respiratory failure

VDRL
Venereal Disease Research Laboratory
(test)

VDRR
vitamin D-resistant rickets

VDRS
Verdun Depression Rating Scale

VDRT

VDS, VD-S
vasodilator substance
venereal disease-syphilis *also* VD-S

NOTES

VDS *(continued)*
ventral derotating spinal
ventral derotation spondylodesis
vindesine
volume of dead space *also* V_D

Vd shunt
dead space effect of Qs/Qt

VDT
visual display terminal
visual distortion test

VDU
visual display unit

VDV
ventricular (end-)diastolic volume

VD/VT, V_D/V_T
dead-space gas volume to tidal gas
volume (ratio)

VE
expired volume
vacuum extraction
vaginal examination
Venezuelan encephalitis (virus)
venous emptying
venous extension
ventilation
ventricular elasticity
ventricular escape
ventricular extrasystole
vertex
vesicular exanthema
viral encephalitis
visual efficiency
visual examination
vitamin E
vocational evaluation
volume ejection
volume of expired gas
voluntary effort

V&E
Vinethine and ether

V_E
environmental variance
minute ventilation
respiratory minute volume
(volume) airflow per unit of time
volume of expired gas

Ve
ventilation

VEA
ventricular ectopic activity
ventricular ectopic arrhythmia

viral envelope antigen
viscoelastic agent

VEB
ventricular ectopic beat
ventricular extra beat

VEC
vecuronium

VECG
vector electrocardiogram

VE-cMRI
velocity-encoded cine-magnetic
resonance imaging

$VECO_2$
carbon dioxide elimination *also* $\dot{V}_{CO2}$

VECP
visually evoked cortical potential

vect
vector

VED
vacuum erection device
vacuum extraction delivery
ventricular ectopic depolarization
vital exhaustion and depression

VEDP
ventricular end-diastolic pressure

VEE
Venezuelan equine encephalitis (virus)
Venezuelan equine encephalomyelitis
(virus)

V-EEG
vigilance-controlled
electroencephalogram

VEF
ventricular ejection fraction
visually evoked field

VEGF
vascular endothelial growth factor

V_{EH}
extrahepatic distribution

VeHF
Veterans Heart Failure

vehic
vehicle

vel, veloc
velocity

VEM
vasoexcitor material
vergence eye movements

$V_{E\ max}$
maximal flow per unit of time

VEMP
vincristine, Endoxan
(cyclophosphamide), mercaptopurine,
and prednisone

vent
ventilation
ventilator
ventral
ventricular

vent fib
ventricular fibrillation *also* VF, V fib

ventric
ventricle

VEP
visual-evoked potential

VEPA
vinblastine, etoposide, prednisone,
Adriamycin

VEPA-B
vinblastine, etoposide, prednisone,
Adriamycin, and bleomycin

VER
ventricular escape rhythm
veratridine
visual evoked response

VERP
ventricular effective refractory period

vert
vertebra
vertebral
vertical

VES
ventricular extrasystole

ves.
bladder [L. *vesica*]
vesicular
vessel

vesic.
blister [L. *vesicula*]

vesp.
evening [L. *vesper*]

ves. ur.
urinary bladder [L. *vesica urinaria*]

VESV
vesicular exanthema of swine virus

VET
vestigial testis

Vet
veteran
veterinarian
veterinary

v.et.
see also [L. *vide etiam*]

Vet Med
veterinary medicine

VETS
Veterans (Adjustment) Scale

Vet Sci
veterinary science

VEWA
Vocational Evaluation and Work
Adjustment

VF
left leg electrode for
electrocardiogram
ventricular fibrillation *also* vent fib,
V fib
ventricular fluid
ventricular flutter
ventricular fusion
video frequency
vigil, fatiguing
visual field *also* F, Vf
vitreous fluorophotometry
vocal fremitus

V_f
variant frequency

Vf, vf
visual field *also* F, VF

VFA
volatile fatty acid

Vfactor
verbal (comprehension) factor

VFAM
vincristine, 5-fluorouracil, Adriamycin
(doxorubicin), and mitomycin C

NOTES

VFC
ventricular function curve

VFD
visual feedback display

VFDF
very fast death factor

VFFC
visual fields full to confrontation

VFI
visual field intact *also* VFIT

V fib
ventricular fibrillation *also* vent fib, VF

VFIT
visual field intact *also* VFI

VFL
ventricular flutter

VFP
ventricular filling pressure
ventricular fluid pressure
vitreous fluorophotometry

VFPN
Volu-feed premie nipple

VFR
voiding flow rate

VFRN
Volu-feed regular nipple

VFS
vascular fragility syndrome

VFT
venous filling time
ventricular fibrillation threshold
Verbal Fluency Test

VFW
velocity waveform

VG
vein graft
ventilated group
ventricular gallop
ventrogluteal
very good

V&G
vagotomy and gastroenterotomy

V$_G$
genetic variance

VGAD
vein of Galen aneurysmal dilatation

VGH
very good health
veterinary general hospital

VGP
viral glycoprotein

VH
vaginal hysterectomy *also* VAG HYST
venous hematocrit
ventricular hypertrophy
veteran's hospital
viral hepatitis
vitreous hemorrhage
von Herrick (grading system)

VH
hepatic distribution volume
variable domain of heavy chain immunoglobulin

VHD
valvular heart disease
vascular hemostatic device
ventricular heart disease
viral hematodepressive disease

VHDL
very-high-density lipoprotein

VHF
very high frequency
viral hemorrhagic fever
visual half-field

VHL
von Hippel-Lindau disease

VHN
Vickers hardness number

VI
inspired ventilation
untouched girl (virgin) [L. *virgo intacta*]
vaginal irrigation
variable interval
vastus intermedius
ventilation index
virulence *also* V, Vi
virulent *also* Vi, vir
viscosity index
Visual Imagery
visual impairment
visual inspection
visually impaired
vitality index
volume index

V$_I$
  volume of inspired gas (per minute)

Vi
  virulence *also* V, VI
  virulent *also* VI, vir

VIA
  virus-inactivating agent
  virus infection-associated antigen

vib
  vibration

VIBS
  vocabulary, information, block
  (design), and similarities
  (psychology)

VIC
  vasoinhibitory center
  vehicle for initial crawling
  visual communication (therapy)
  voice intensity controller

vic.
  times [L. *vices*]

VICA
  velocity internal carotid artery

VID
  vaginal intraepithelial dysplasia
  videodensitometry
  visible iris diameter

vid
  see [L. *vide*]

VIF
  virus-induced interferon

VIG
  vaccinia immunoglobulin
  vinblastine, ifosfamide, and gallium
  (nitrate)

VIg
  vaccinia immunoglobulin *also* VIg

vig
  vigorous

VIH
  violence-induced handicap

VIM
  ventralis intermedius
  video-intensification microscopy

VIN
  vaginal intraepithelial neoplasia
  vinbarbital
  vulvar intraepithelial neoplasia

VIN III
  vulvar carcinoma in situ

vin.
  wine [L. *vinum*]

VIP
  vasoactive intestinal peptide
  vasoactive intestinal polypeptide
  vasoactive intracorpeal
  pharmacotherapy
  vasoinhibitory peptide
  venous impedance plethysmography
  very important patient
  very important person
  vinblastine, ifosfamide, and Platinol
  voluntary interruption of pregnancy
  VP-16, ifosfamide, and Platinol

VIP-IR
  vasoactive intestinal polypeptide
  immunoreactivity

VIPoma
  vasoactive intestinal polypeptide tumor

VIQ
  Verbal Intelligence Quotient

VIR
  virology

Vir
  viral *also* V
  virus *also* V, v

vir
  green [L. *viridis*]
  virulent *also* VI, Vi

VIR AC
  viral antibody, acute

VIS
  vaginal irrigation smear
  venous insufficiency syndrome

V

NOTES

VIS *(continued)*
vertebral irritation syndrome
video imaging system
visible
visual information storage

vis
vision
visiting
visitor
visual

VISC
vitreous infusion suction cutter

visc
viscera
visceral
viscosity
viscous

VISI
volar-flexed intercalated segment
instability
volar intercalcated segment instability

VIT
venom immunotherapy
vital *also* vit
vitamin *also* Vit

Vit
vitamin *also* VIT

vit
vital *also* VIT
vitrectomy
vitreous

vit.
yolk [L. *vitellus*] *also* vitel.

VIT CAP
vital capacity *also* vit cap

vit cap
vital capacity *also* VIT CAP
vitamin capsule

vitel.
yolk [L. *vitellus*] *also* vit.

vit. ov. sol.
dissolved in egg yolk [L. *vitello ovis solutus*] *also* v.o.s.

vitr
vitreous

vitr.
glass [L. *vitrum*]

vits
vitamins

VIU
visual internal urethrotomy

viz
visualized

viz.
that is, namely [L. *videlicet*]

VJ
ventriculojugular (shunt)
Vogel-Johnson (agar)

VK
vervet (African green monkey)
kidney (cell)

VKC
vernal keratoconjunctivitis

VKDB
vitamin K deficiency bleeding

VKH
Vogt-Koyanagi-Harada (syndrome)

VL
left arm electrode for
electrocardiogram
vastus lateralis
ventralis lateralis
ventrolateral
visceral leishmaniasis
vision, left (eye)

V_L
(actual) volume of lung
variable domain of light chain
immunoglobulin

VLA
vanillacetic acid
vanillactic acid
very late activation
virus-like action
virus-like agent

VLAP
visual laser ablation of prostate
visual laser-assisted prostatectomy

VLB
vincaleukoblastine (vinblastine)

VLBR
very low birth rate

VLBW
very low birth weight

VLCD
very-low-calorie diet

VLCFA
very-long-chain fatty acid

VLD
very low density

VLDL, VLDLP
very-low-density lipoprotein

VLDL-TG
very-low-density lipoprotein
triglyceride

VLDS
Verbal Language Development Scale

VLE
vision left eye

VLF
very low frequency

VLG
ventral (nucleus of) lateral geniculate
(body)

VLH
ventrolateral (nucleus of)
hypothalamus

VLM
visceral larval migrans

VLP
ventriculolumbar perfusion
vincristine, L-asparaginase, and
prednisone
virus-like particle

VLR
vastus lateralis release

VLSI
very-large-scale integration

VM
vasomotor
vastus medialis
ventilated mask
ventricular mass
ventromedial
vestibular membrane
viomycin
viral myocarditis
voltmeter

VM-26
teniposide

V/m
volt per meter

VMA
vanillylmandelic acid
vastus medialis advancement

V-Mask
Venturi mask

V$_{max}$
maximal velocity *also* PAK
maximum velocity
peak flow velocity (Doppler)

VMC
vasomotor center
village malaria communicator
vinyl chloride monomer
void metal composite
von Meyenburg complex

VMCG
vector magnetocardiogram

VMCP
vincristine, melphalan,
cyclophosphamide, and prednisone

VMD
Doctor of Veterinary Medicine [L.
Veterinariae Medicinne Doctor]
vertical maxillary deficiency

vMDV
virulent Marek disease virus

VME
vertical maxillary excess

VMF
vasomotor flushing

VMH
ventromedial hypothalamic (neuron,
nuclei)

VMI
visual motor integration

V-MI
Volpe-Manhold Index

VMIT
visual-motor integration test

VMN
ventromedial nucleus

VMO
vaccinia melanoma oncolysate

V

NOTES

VMO *(continued)*
vastus medialis oblique (muscle)
vastus medialis obliquus

VMO:VL EMG
vastus medialis obliquus:vastus
lateralis electromyographic (ratio)

VMR
vasomotor rhinitis

VMS
visual memory span

VMSC
Vineland Measurement of Social
Competence

VMST
Visual-Motor Sequencing Test

VMT
vasomotor tone
ventilatory muscle training
ventromedial tegmentum

VMU
vertebral motion unit

VN
vesical neck
vestibular neurectomy
vestibular nucleus
virus neutralization
virus-neutralizing
visceral nucleus
Visiting Nurse
visual naming
Vocational Nurse
vomeronasal

VNA
Visiting Nurse Association

VNB
vinorelbine

VNC
vesical neck contracture

VNDPT
Visual Numerical Discrimination
Pretest

VNE
verbal nonemotional stimuli

VNO
vomeronasal organ

VNR
ventral nerve root

VNS
villonodular synovitis
Visiting Nursing Service

VNTR
variable numbers of tandem repeat

VO
verbal order
volume overload
voluntary opening

VO$_2$, $\dot{V}_{O_2}$
oxygen consumption per minute
peak exercise oxygen consumption
volume of oxygen consumption per
unit of time

voc
vocational

vocab
vocabulary

VOCTOR
void on call to operating room

VOD
venoocclusive disease
vision, right eye [L. *visio, oculus
dexter*]
visio oculus dextra (vision of right
eye)

VOE
vascular occlusive episode

vol
volar
volatile
volume *also* q, V
volumetric
voluntary
volunteer

vol%
volume percent

vol adm
voluntary admission

vol/vol
volume per volume (ratio)

VOM
vinyl chloride monomer
volt-ohm-millimeter
vomited *also* vom

vom
vomited *also* VOM

VO₂max
  maximum oxygen consumption
  maximum oxygen uptake

VOP
  venous occlusion plethysmography

VOR
  vestibuloocular reflex
  vestibuloocular response

VOS
  vision, left eye [L. *visio, oculus sinister*]
  visio oculus sinister (vision of left eye)

v.o.s.
  dissolved in egg yolk [L. *vitello ovi solutus*] *also* vit. ov. sol.

VOT
  Visual Organization Test
  voice onset time

VOU
  vision, each eye [L. *visio oculus uterque*]

voxel
  volume element

V-P, V/P
  ventilation and perfusion *also* V&P

VP
  etoposide *also* EP, EPEG, VP, VP-16
  vapor pressure
  variegate porphyria
  vascular permeability
  vasopressin
  velopharyngeal
  venipuncture
  venous pressure *also* Pv
  venous (volume) plethysmograph
  ventricular pacing
  ventricular premature (beat)
  ventriculoperitoneal
  ventriculoperitoneal (shunt)
  ventroposterior
  vertex potential
  vincristine and prednisone
  viral protein
  virus protein
  Voges-Proskauer (medium, test)

volume-pressure
vulnerable period

VP-16
  etoposide *also* EP, EPEG, VP

V&P
  vagotomy and pyloroplasty
  ventilation and perfusion *also* V-P, V/P

Vp
  plasma volume
  voltage peak

vp
  vapor pressure

VPA
  valproic acid
  ventricular premature activation

v-PA
  vascular plasminogen activator

VPAP
  variable positive airway pressure

VPB
  ventricular premature beat

VPC
  vapor-phase chromatography
  ventricular premature complex
  ventricular premature contraction
  volume-packed cells
  volume percentage

VPCA
  vincristine, prednisone, cyclophosphamide, and ara-C

VPCMF
  vincristine, prednisone, cyclophosphamide, methotrexate, and 5-fluorouracil

VPCT
  ventricular premature contraction threshold

VPD
  ventricular premature depolarization

VPDF
  vegetable protein diet (plus) fiber

VPF
  vascular permeability factor

NOTES

VPG
velopharyngeal gap
venting percutaneous gastrostomy

VPGSS
venous pressure gradient support stockings

VPI
velopharyngeal insufficiency
ventral posterior inferior

VPL
ventroposterolateral

VPLS
ventilation perfusion lung scan

VPM
Vantage Performance monitor
venous pressure module
ventilator pressure manometer
ventroposteromedial

vpm
vibration per minute

VPO
velopharyngeal opening

VPP
viral porcine pneumonia

VPR
volume-pressure response

VPRBC
volume of packed red blood cells

VPRC
volume of packed red (blood) cells

VPS
valvular pulmonic stenosis
visual pleural space

vps
vibration per second

VPT
vascularized patellar tendon

VQ
voice quality

V/Q
ventilation/perfusion (lung scan)

V̇/Q̇
ventilation-perfusion(-quotient) ratio
also V̇A/Q̇, V̇a/Q̇

VQR
ventilation-perfusion(-quotient) ratio

VR
right arm electrode for electrocardiogram
valve replacement
variable rate
variable ratio
vascular resistance
venous reflux
venous return
ventilation rate
ventilation ratio
ventral root
ventricular rate
ventricular response
ventricular rhythm
verbal reprimand
vesicular rosette
vision, right (eye)
visual reproduction
vital record
vitreoretinal
vocal resonance
vocational rehabilitation

Vr
ventral root *also* vr
volume of relaxation

vr
ventral root *also* Vr

VRA
visual reinforcement audiometry

VRBC
volume of red blood cells

VRC
venous renin concentration

VR CON
viral antibody, convalescent

VRCP
vitreoretinochoroidopathy

VRD
ventricular radial dysplasia
von Recklinghausen disease

VRE
vancomycin-resistant enterococcus

VR&E
vocational rehabilitation and education

VRG
vertical ring gastroplasty

VRI
viral respiratory infection

VRL
ventral root, lumbar
Virus Reference Laboratory

VRNA
viral ribonucleic acid

VRO
varus rotational osteotomy

VROM
voluntary range of motion

VRP
very reliable product

VRR
ventral root reflex

VRSA
vancomycin-resistant *Staphylococcus aureus*

VRT
variance of resident time
ventral root, thoracic
vertical radiation topography
Visual Retention Test

VRV
ventricular residual volume

VS
vaccination scar
vaccine serotype
vagal stimulation
valve system
vasospasm
venesection
ventral subiculum
ventricular sense
ventricular septum
verbal scale
versus
vertical shear
very sensitive
vesicular sound
vesicular stomatitis
veterinary surgeon
villonodular synovitis
visual storage
vital signs *also* vs, V/S
volumetric solution
voluntary sterilization

V/S
vital signs *also* VS, vs

V·s
vibration-second
volt-second

vs
single vibration
versus *also* v
vibration-second
vital sign *also* VS, V/S
voids

vs.
against [L. *versus*]

v.s.
to draw blood [L. *venae sectio* cutting of vein]
see above [L. *vide supra*]
vibration second

VSA
variant-specific surface antigen

V.s.B., v.s.b.
drawing blood from a vessel in arm [L. *venae sectio brachii*]

VSBE
very short below elbow (cast)

VSC
vertebral subluxation complex
voluntary surgical contraception

VSCS
ventricular specialized conduction system

VSD
ventriculoseptal defect
vesical external sphincter dyssynergia
virtually safe dose

VSFP
venous stop flow pressure

VSG
variant surface glycoprotein

VSHD
ventricular septal heart defect

VSI
visual motor integration

V

NOTES

VSMC
vascular smooth muscle cell

VSMS
Vineland Social Maturity Scale

VSN
vital signs normal

vsn
vision

VSO
vertical subcondylar oblique

VSOK
vital signs okay (normal)

VSP
variable screw placement
variable spinal plating

VSR
venereal spirochetosis of rabbits
venous stasis retinopathy

VSS
vital signs stable

VSSAF
vital signs stable, afebrile

VSULA
vaccination scar upper left arm

VSV
vesicular stomatitis virus

VSW
ventricular stroke work

VT
tetrazolium violet (stain)
tidal volume *also* TD, TV, V_T
total ventilation
vacuum tube
vacuum tuberculin
vasotocin
vasotonin
venous thrombosis
ventricular tachyarrhythmia
ventricular tachycardia
verocytotoxin

V&T
volume and tension

V_T
tidal volume *also* TD, TV, VT

V_t
pulmonary parenchymal tissue volume

VTA
ventral tegmental area

V_TA
alveolar tidal volume

V-TACH, V tach
ventricular tachycardia

VTCL
ventricular tachycardia cycle length

VTE
venous thromboembolism
ventricular tachycardia event
vicarious trial and error

VTEC
verotoxin-producing *Escherichia coli*

V-test
Voluter test (radiology)

VTG
volume thoracic gas

VTI
volume thickness index

VTM
mechanical tidal volume
variegated translocation mosaicism
virus transport medium

VT-NS
ventricular tachycardia nonsustained

VTO
visualized treatment objective

VTP
voluntary termination of pregnancy

VTS
vesicular transport system

VT-S
ventricular tachycardia sustained

VTSRS
Verdun Target Symptom Rating Scale

VTT
voice termination time

VT/VF
ventricular tachycardia/ventricular
fibrillation

VTVM
vacuum tube voltmeter

VTX, Vtx
vertex

VU
varicose ulcer
very urgent
volume unit (meter)

VUC
vacuum uterine cannula

VUJ
vesicoureteral junction

VUPP
voiding urethral pressure
measurements

VUR
vesicoureteral reflex
vesicoureteral reflux
vesicoureteral regurgitation

VUV
vacuum ultraviolet

V-V
vesicovaginal (fistula) *also* VV

VV
varicose vein
venovenous
vesicovaginal (fistula) *also* V-V
viper venom
vulva and vagina *also* V&V

V/V
volume to volume (ratio)

V&V
vulva and vagina *also* VV

vv
veins

v/v
vice versa
volume (of solute) per volume (of
solvent)

VVA
venous-to-venous anastomosis

VVB
venovenous bypass

VVC
village voluntary collaborator
vulvovaginal candidiasis

VVD
vaginal vertex delivery
vascular volume of distribution

VVFR
vesicovaginal fistula repair

V/VI
grade 5 on a 6-grade basis (cardiac
murmur)

vvi
vocal velocity index

vvMDV
very virulent Marek disease virus

VVOR
visual vestibuloocular reflex

VVQ
verbalizer-visualization questionnaire

VVS
vesicovaginal space
vulvar vestibulitis syndrome

VW
vascular wall
vessel wall
von Willebrand (disease) *also* vW

vW
von Willebrand (disease, syndrome)
also VW

v/w
volume per weight

VWD
ventral wall defect

vWD, vWd
von Willebrand disease

VWF
velocity waveform
vibration-induced white finger
von Willebrand factor *also* factor
VIIIR, vWF, vWf

vWF, vWf
von Willebrand factor *also* factor
VIIIR, VWF

VWFT
variable-width forms tractor

VWM
ventricular wall motion

vWS, vWs
von Willebrand syndrome

Vx
vertex
vitrectomy

V

NOTES

V x s
volts by seconds

V-XT
V-pattern exotropia

VY
veal yeast

V-Y
shape of incisions in V-Y procedure (plasty)

VZ, V-Z
varicella-zoster (virus) *also* VZV

VZIG, VZIg
varicella-zoster immunoglobulin

VZL
vinzolidine

VZV
varicella-zoster virus *also* VZ, V-Z

W

dominant spotting (mouse)
energy (work)
section modulus
shape of surgical incisions (plasty)
tryptophan *also* TP, Tp, Trp, Try
tungsten
tungsten [Ger. *wolfram*]
water
watt *also* w
Weber (test)
week *also* w, WK, wk
wehnelt (x-ray hardness)
weight *also* w
west
wetting
white *also* w, Wh, wh, wt
white cell
whole (response) *also* WR
widowed
width
wife
Wilcoxon rank sum statistic
Wistar (rat)
with *also* w
wolframium (tungsten)
word fluency
work

W+

weakly positive

^{188}W

tungsten-188

w

velocity (m/s)
watt *also* W
week *also* W, WK, wk
weight *also* W
white *also* W, Wh, wh, wt
widowed
wife
with *also* W

w/, w̄

with

WA

Wellness Associates
when awake
while awake *also* wa
wide awake *also* W/A
Wiskott-Aldrich (syndrome)

W/A

watt/ampere
wide awake *also* WA

W or A

weakness or atrophy

wa

while awake *also* WA

WAADA

Women's Auxiliary of the American Dental Association

WAB, WABT

Western Aphasia Battery (Test)

WACH

wedge adjustable cushioned heel (shoe)

WADAO

weak and dizzy all over

WAF

weakness, atrophy, and fasciculation
white adult female

WAGR

Wilms (tumor), aniridia, genitourinary (abnormalities), and (mental) retardation

WAIS

Wechsler Adult Intelligence Scale

WAIS-R

Wechsler Adult Intelligence Scale, Revised

WAK

wearable artificial kidney

WALK

Walking with Angina-Learning is Key
weight activated locking knee

WAM

white adult male

WAP

wandering atrial pacemaker
whole abdominopelvic irradiation

WAPT

Weidel Auditory Processing Test

WARDS

Welfare of Animals Used for Research in Drugs and Therapy

W

WARF
warfarin

WARI
wheezing associated respiratory infection

WAS
Ward Atmosphere Scale (psychology)
weekly activity summary
whiplash associated disorder
Wiskott-Aldrich syndrome

WASO
wakefulness after sleep onset

WASP
Weber Advanced Spatial Perception (test)
World Association of Societies of Pathology

Wass
Wasserman (reaction, test)

WAT
Word Association Test

WB
waist belt
washable base
washed bladder
water bottle
Wechsler-Bellevue (Scale)
weightbearing *also* Wb
well baby
Western blot
wet bulb
whole blood *also* B, QB, W Bld
whole body
Willowbrook (virus)

Wb
weber
weightbearing *also* WB

WBA
wax bean agglutinin
whole-body activity

Wb/A
weber per ampere

WBACT
whole blood activated clotting time

WBAPTT
whole-blood activated partial thromboplastin time

WBAT
weightbearing as tolerated

WBC
weightbearing with crutches
well baby clinic
white blood cell (count)
white blood corpuscle

WBC/hpf
white blood cells per high power field

WBCT
whole-blood clotting time

WBDS
whole-body digital scanner

WBE
whole-body extract

WBF
whole-blood folate

WBH
whole-blood hematocrit
whole-body hyperthermia

WBI
will be in

W Bld
whole blood *also* B, QB, WB

WBM
whole boiled milk

Wb/m²
weber per square meter

WBN
well born nursery
wide band noise

WBOS
wide base of support

WBPTT
whole-blood partial thromboplastin time

WBQC
wide-base quad cane

WBR
whole-body radiation
whole-body retention

WBRS
Ward Behavior Rating Scale

WBRT
whole-blood recalcification time
whole-brain radiation therapy

WBS
Wechsler-Bellevue Scale
whole-body scan

whole body shower
Wiedemann-Beckwith syndrome
withdrawal body shakes
wound-breaking strength

WBT
wet bulb temperature

WBTF
Waring Blender tube feeding

WBTT
weightbearing to tolerance

WBUS
weeks by ultrasound

WBV
whole blood volume

WC
ward clerk
ward confinement
water closet
Weber-Christian (syndrome)
wet compress
wheelchair *also* W/C, wh ch
white cell
white (cell) cast
white (cell) count
whole complement
whooping cough
will call
work capacity
writer's cramp

WC′
whole complement

W/C
wheelchair *also* WC, wh ch

WCB
will call back

WCC
Walker carcinoma cell
well-child care
white cell count

WCD
Weber-Christian disease

WCE
white coat effect
work capacity evaluation

WCH
white coat hypertension

WCL
Wenckebach cycle length
whole-cell lysate

WCOT
wall coated open tubular

WCR
Walthard cell rest

WCS
Wisconsin Compression System

WCST
Wisconsin Card Sorting Test

WD
wallerian degeneration
ward
warm and dry *also* W/D
well-developed (agar) *also* wd, w/d
well differentiated
wet dressing
Whipple disease
Whitney Damon (dextrose)
Wilson disease
with disease
withdrawal dyskinesia
without dyskinesia
Wolman disease
word *also* Wd
wound *also* WND, wnd
wrist disarticulation

W4D
Worth Four-Dot (test)

W/D
warm (and) dry *also* WD
withdrawal
withdrawn

W→D
wet-to-dry *also* W-T-D

Wd
ward
word *also* WD

wd
well-developed *also* WD, w/d
wound
wounded

W

NOTES

795

w/d
well-developed *also* WD, wd

WDCA
well-differentiated carcinoma

WDCC
well-developed collateral circulation

WDF
white divorced female

WDHA
watery diarrhea, hypokalemia, and achlorhydria (syndrome)

WDHH
watery diarrhea, hypokalemia, (and) hypochlorhydria

WDHHA
watery diarrhea, hypochlorhydria, hypokalemia, and alkalosis

WDI
warfarin dose index

WDLL
well-differentiated lymphatic lymphoma
well-differentiated lymphocytic lymphoma

WDM
white divorced male

WDPM
well-differentiated papillary mesothelioma

WDS
watery diarrhea syndrome
wet dog shakes (syndrome)
wounds *also* wds

wds
wounds *also* WDS

WDWN, WD,WN
well developed, well nourished

WE
wage earner
wax ester
weekend *also* W/E
western encephalitis
western encephalomyelitis
whiskey equivalent
wound of entry

W/E
weekend *also* WE

WEE
western equine encephalitis (virus)

western equine encephalomyelitis (virus)

WEG
water-ethyleneglycol

WEP
weekend pass

WES
wall-echo shadow

WESR
Westergren erythrocyte sedimentation rate
Wintrobe erythgrocyte sedimentation rate

WEST
work evaluation systems technology

WEUP
willful exposure to unwanted pregnancy

WF
Weil-Felix (reaction, test)
white female *also* W/F, wf
Wistar-Furth (rat)
word fluency

W/F, wf
white female *also* WF

WFE
Williams flexion exercise

WFI
water for injection

WFL
within functional limits

WF-O
will follow in office

WFR
Weil-Felix reaction
wheal-and-flare reaction

WFSS
Wolpe Fear Survey Schedule

WG
water gauge
Wegener granulomatosis
Wright-Giemsa (stain)

WGA
wheat germ agglutinin

WH
walking heel (cast)
well-healed
well-hydrated
Werdnig-Hoffmann (disease)

whole homogenate
wound healing

Wh
white *also* W, w, wh, wt

wh
whisper
whispered
white *also* W, w, Wh, wt

w·h
watt-hour

WHA
warmed, humidified air

wh ch
wheelchair *also* WC, W/C
white child

WHD
Werdnig-Hoffmann disease

WHML
Wellcome Historical Medical Library

WHMS
well-healed midline scar

WHNR
well-healed, no residuals

WHNS
well-healed, nonsymptomatic
well-healed, no sequelae

WHO
World Health Organization
wrist-hand orthosis

WHP, Whp, whp
whirlpool *also* WP, W/P

WHPB
whirlpool bath *also* WPB

whr
watt hour

WHS
Werdnig-Hoffman syndrome

WHV
woodchuck hepatic virus

WHVP
wedged hepatic venous pressure

WHYMPI
Westhaven Yale Multidimensional
Pain Inventory

WI
walk-in (patient)
wash-in
water ingestion
waviness index
Wistar (rat)

W/I
within

W&I
work and interest

WIA
walking imagined analgesia
wounded in action

WIC
women, infants, (and) children

wid
widow
widowed
widower

WIPI
Word Intelligibility by Picture
Identification

WIQ
Waring Intimacy Questionnaire

WIS
Ward Initiation Scale
Wechsler Intelligence Scale

WISC
Wechsler Intelligence Scale for
Children

WISC-R
Wechsler Intelligence Scale for
Children-Revised

WIST
Whitaker Index of Schizophrenic
Thinking

WIT
water-induced thermotherapy

WITT
Wittenborn (Psychiatric Rating Scale)

W

NOTES

W-J
Woodcock-Johnson (Psychoeducational Battery)

WJPB
Woodcock-Johnson Psychoeducational Battery

WK
week *also* W, w, wk
Wernicke-Korsakoff (syndrome)
work *also* wk

wk
weak
week *also* W, w, WK
work *also* WK

WKD
Wilson-Kimmelstiel disease

WKF
well-known fact

W/kg
watt per kilogram

WKS
Wernicke-Korsakoff syndrome

WKY
Wistar-Kyoto (rat)

WL
waiting list
waterload (test)
wavelength *also* λ
weight loss
workload

WLE
wide local excision

WLF
whole lymphocyte fraction

WLI
weight-length index

WLM
work-level month

WLR
within-list recognition

WLS
wet lung syndrome

WLT
waterload test
whole-lung tomography

WM
Waldenström macroglobulinemia
wall motion
ward manager

warm, moist
Wernicke-Mann (hemiplegia)
wet mount
white male *also* W/M, wm
whole milk *also* wm
whole mount (microscopy) *also* wm
Wilson-Mikity (syndrome)
woman milk

W/M
white male *also* WM, wm

w/m₂
watt per square meter

wm
white male *also* WM, W/M
whole milk *also* WM
whole mount (microscopy) *also* WM

WMA
wall-motion abnormality

WMC
weight-matched control

WMD
warm moist dressing (sterile)

WME
Williams medium E

WMF
white married female
white middle-aged female

WML
white matter lesion (cerebral)

WMM
white married male
white middle-aged male

WMP
warm moist pack (unsterile)
weight management program

WMR
work metabolic rate
World Medical Relief

WMS
wall-motion study
Wechsler Memory Scale

WMSI
wall motion score index

WMX
whirlpool, massage, exercise

WN, W/N, w/n, wn
well-nourished

WND, wnd
wound *also* WD

WNE
West Nile encephalitis

WNF
well-nourished female

WNL
within normal limits

WNLS
weighted nonlinear least squares

WNM
well-nourished male

WNV
West Nile virus

WO
wash-out
weeks old *also* wo
without *also* O, ō, S, s̄, w/o, wo
written order

W/O
water (in) oil (emulsion)
water in oil

w/o
without *also* O, ō, S, s̄, WO, wo

wo
weeks old *also* WO
without *also* O, ō, S, s̄, WO, w/o

WOB
work of breathing

WOE
wound of entry

WOFL
wound fluid

WOP
without pain

WOR
Weber-Osler-Rondu (syndrome)

WORM
write once, read many

WOSCOPS
West of Scotland Coronary
Prevention Study

WOU
women's outpatient unit

W/O/W
water in oil in water

WOWS
Weak Opiate Withdrawal Scale

WOX
wound of exit

WP
water packed
weakly positive
wet pack *also* WPk
wettable powder
whirlpool *also* WHP, Whp, whp,
W/P
white pulp
word processor
working point

W/P
water/powder (ratio)
whirlpool *also* WHP, Whp, whp, WP

WPB
whirlpool bath *also* WHPB

WPCU
weighted patient care unit

WPFM
Wright peak flowmeter

WPk
Ward pack
wet pack *also* WP

WPN
white (mucosa with) punctation

WPPSI
Wechsler Preschool and Primary
Scale of Intelligence

WPPSI-R
Wechsler Preschool and Primary
Scale of Intelligence-Revised

WPRS
Wittenborn Psychiatric Rating Scale

WPSI
Wittenborn Psychiatric Symptoms
Inventory

WPT
marbled pure tone

NOTES

WPW
Wolff-Parkinson-White (syndrome)

WR
washroom
Wassermann reaction *also* Wr
water retention
weakly reactive *also* Wr
whole response *also* W
wide range
wiping reaction
work rate
wrist

W/R
with respect to

WR-2721
ethiofos

Wr, wr
Wassermann reaction *also* WR
weakly reactive *also* WR
wrist

Wr^a
Wright antigen

WRAMC
Walter Reed Army Medical Center

WRAML
Wide Range Assessment of Memory and Learning

WRAT
Wide Range Achievement Test

WRBC
washed red blood cell

WRC
washed red (blood) cell
water-retention coefficient

WRE
whole ragweed extract

WRK
Woodward reagent K

WRMT
Woodcock Reading Mastery Test

WRS
Wiedemann-Rauten-Strauch syndrome

WRST
Wilcoxon rank sum test

WRVP
wedged renal vein pressure

WS
Wardenburg syndrome
ward secretory
Warthin-Starry (stain)
watermelon stomach
water soluble
water swallow
watt-second *also* ws, W·s
Werner syndrome
West syndrome
wet swallow
whole (response plus white) space
Wilder silver (stain)
Williams syndrome
work simplification

W&S
wound and skin

W·s
watt-second *also* WS, ws

ws
watt-second *also* WS, W·s

WSA
water-soluble antibiotic

WSB
wheat soy blend

WSD
water seal drainage

WSepF
white separated female

WSepM
white separated male

WSF
white single female

WSL
Wesselsbron (virus)

WSM
white single male

WSP
wearable speech processor

WSR
Westergren sedimentation rate

W/sr
watt per steradian

WT
walking tank
wall thickness
water temperature
wild type (strain)
Wilms tumor
wisdom teeth
work therapy

wt
  weight
  white *also* W, w, Wh, wh

WTD
  wet tail disease

W-T-D
  wet-to-dry *also* W→D

WTE
  whole time equivalent

WTF
  weight transferral frequency

W/U, w/u
  workup

WV
  walking ventilation
  whispered voice

W/V, w/v
  weight (of solute) per volume (of solution)

W$_v$
  variable dominant spotting (mouse)

WV-MBC
  walking ventilation to maximal breathing capacity (ratio)

WW
  Weight Watchers
  wet weight

W/W, w/w
  weight (of solute) per weight (of solvent)

W→W
  wet-to-wet

WWAC
  walk with aid of cane

WWidF
  white widowed female

WWidM
  white widowed male

WWTP
  wastewater treatment plant

WX
  wound of exit

WxB
  wax bite

WxP
  wax pattern

WY
  women years

WY/NRT
  Weidel Yes/No Reliability Test

WZa
  wide zone alpha (hemolysis)

NOTES

W

X
androgenic (zone)
break
chi (22nd letter of Greek alphabet),
 uppercase
cross
cross-bite
crossed with
crossmatch *also* XM
cross-section
decimal scale of potency or dilution
except
exophoria
exophoria distance *also* x
exposure
extra
female sex chromosome
homeopathic symbol for decimal
 scale of potencies
ionization exposure rate
Kienböck unit (of x-ray exposure)
magnification
multiplication sign
reactance (electric current)
removal of
respirations (anesthesia chart)
start of anesthesia
translocation between two X.
 chromosomes
transverse
unknown quantity
xanthine
xanthosine *also* Xao
xerophthalmia
X unit

X′
exophoria, near viewing *also* x′

X+
xyphoid plus (number of
 fingerbreadths)

X̄
except
sample mean

x
axis of cylindrical lens
except
exophoria distance *also* X
horizontal axis of rectangular
 coordinate system
mole fraction
multiplied by

roentgen (rays)
sample mean

x′
exophoria, near viewing *also* X′

X-A
xylene-alcohol (mixture)

XA
xanthurenic acid

Xa
chiasma

Xaa
unknown amino acid

X:Ag
factor X antigen

Xan
xanthine

XANT
xanthochromic

Xanth
xanthomatosis

Xao
xanthosine *also* X

XBT
xylose breath test

XC
excretory cystogram
excretory cystography

Xc
reactance *also* X

XCCE
extracapsular cataract extraction *also*
 ECCE

Xc/R
reactance and resistance

XD
times daily
xanthoma disseminatum
X-linked dominant

X&D
examination and diagnosis

XDFHom
Diploma of the Faculty of
 Homeopathy

XDH
xanthine dehydrogenase

X

XDP
xanthine diphosphate
xeroderma pigmentosum *also* XP

XDR
transducer

XDT
defibrillation threshold *also* DFT
diversional therapy

Xe
xenon

^{127}Xe
xenon-127

^{133}Xe
xenon-133

XeCl
xenon chloride

XECT, XeCT, Xe-CT
xenon-enhanced computed tomography
also Xe-CT

X-ed
crossed

XEF
excess ejection fraction

Xero
xeromammography
xeromammography

XES
x-ray energy spectrometry

XF
xerophthalmic fundus

Xfmr
transformer

XGP
xanthogranulomatous pyelonephritis
also XPN

XH
extra high

Ξ
xi (14th letter of Greek alphabet),
uppercase

ξ
xi (14th letter of Greek alphabet),
lowercase

XIC
X inactivation center

XIH
idiopathic hypercalcuria

XIP
x-ray in plaster

XIST
X inactive, specific transcript

XKDS
King-Denborough syndrome

XKO
not knocked out

XL
excess lactate
extra large
xylose-lysine (agar base)

X-LA
X-linked agammaglobulinemia

XLD
xylose-lysine-deoxycholate (agar)

X-leg
crossleg

XLFDP
crosslinked fibrin degradation product

XLH
X-linked hypophosphatemia

XLI
X-linked ichthyosis

XLJR
X-linked juvenile retinoschisis

XLMR
X-linked mental retardation

XLP
X-linked (lympho)proliferative
(syndrome)

XLR
X-linked recessive

XLS
X-linked recessive lymphoproliferative
syndrome

XM, X-mat., X-match
crossmatch *also* X

X_m
magnetic susceptibility

XMM
xeromammography (Xero)

XMP
xanthine monophosphate
xanthosine 5′-monophosphate

XN
night blindness

Xn
Christian

XNA
xenoreactive natural antibody

XO
gonadal dysgenesis of Turner type
presence of only one sex
 chromosome
xanthine oxidase

XOM
extraocular movement

XOP
x-ray out of plaster

XOR
exclusive operating room

XP
xeroderma pigmentosum *also* XDP

Xp
short arm of chromosome X

Xp-
deletion of short arm of chromosome
 X

XPA
xeroderma pigmentosum (group) A

XPC
xeroderma pigmentosum (group) C

XPN
xanthogranulomatous pyelonephritis
 also XGP

X-Prep
bowel evacuation prior to radiography

XPS
x-ray photoemission spectroscopy

Xq
long arm of chromosome X

Xq-
deletion of long arm of chromosome
 X

XR
x-linked recessive
x-ray

XRD
x-ray diffraction

XRF
x-ray fluorescence

XRN
X-linked recessive nephrolithiasis

XRT
radiation therapy *also* RT
x-ray technician
x-ray therapy (radiotherapy)

XS
corneal scar
cross-section
excess
excessive
xiphisternum

XSA
cross-sectional area
xenograph surface area

XS-LIM
exceeds limits (of procedure)

XSLR
crossed straight leg raising (sign)

XSP
xanthoma striatum palmare

XT, xT
exotropia

X(T), x(T)
intermittent exotropia

Xta
chiasmata

Xtab
crosstabulating

XTE
xeroderma, talipes, and enamel
 (defect)

XTM
xanthoma tuberosum multiplex

XTP
xanthosine triphosphate

XU
excretory urogram
excretory urogram/urography
X-unit *also* Xu

NOTES

X

Xu
X-unit *also* XU
x-unit

XULN
times upper limit of normal

XUV
extreme ultraviolet

xvse
transverse

XX
double strength
normal female sex chromosome type

46, XX
46 chromosomes, 2 X chromosomes
(normal female)

49, XXXXY
49 chromosomes, 4 X and 1 Y
chromosomes (XXXXY syndrome)

XX/XY
sex karyotypes

47, XXY
47 chromosomes, 2 X and 1 Y
chromosomes (Klinefelter syndrome)

XY
normal male sex chromosome type

46, XY
46 chromosomes, 1 X and 1 Y
chromosome (normal male)

47, XY +21
47 chromosomes, male, additional
chromosome 21 (Down syndrome,
chromosome 21 trisomy)

Xy
xylose *also* Xyl

XYL, XYLO
Xylocaine

Xyl
xylose *also* Xy

47, XYY
47 chromosomes, 1 X and 2 Y
chromosomes (XYY syndrome)

Y
coordinate axis in plane
male sex chromosome
ordinate
tyrosine *also* Ty, Tyr
year *also* y
yellow
young
yttrium

^{50}Y
yttrium-50

^{90}Y
yttrium-90

y
vertical axis of rectangular coordinate system
wave on phlebogram
year *also* Y
yield

YA
Yersinia arthritis

YAC
yeast artificial chromosomes

YACP
young adult chronic patient

YADH
yeast alcohol dehydrogenase

YAG
yttrium-aluminum-garnet (laser)

Y/B
yellow/blue

Yb
ytterbium

YBT
Yerkes-Bridges Test (psychology)

YCB
yeast carbon base

YCT
Yvon coefficient test

yd
yard

YDES
yin deficiency-yang excess syndrome

YE
yeast extract
yellow enzyme

YEH$_2$
reduced yellow enzyme

YEI
Yersinia enterocolitica infection

Yel, yel
yellow

YET
youth effectiveness training

YF
yellow fever

YFI
yellow fever immunization

YHMD
yellow hyaline membrane disease

YHT
Young-Helmholtz theory

YJV
yellow jacket venom

Yk
York (antibody)

YLC
youngest living child

YLF
yttrium lithium fluoride

YM
yeast and mannitol

YMA
yeast morphology agar

Y/N
yes/no

YNB
yeast nitrogen base

YNS
yellow nail syndrome

Y/O, y/o
years old

YOB
year of birth

YORA
younger-onset rheumatoid arthritis

YP
yeast phase
yield point
yield pressure

Y

YPA
yeast, peptone, and adenine (sulfate)

YPLL
years of potential life lost (before age 65)

yr
year

YRD
Yangtze River disease

YS
yellow spot
yolk sac *also* ys
Yoshida sarcoma

ys
yellow spot (on retina)
yolk sac *also* YS

YSC
yolk sac carcinoma

YST
yeast (cells)
yolk sac tumor

YT, yt
yttrium

YTD
year to date

YVS
yellow vernix syndrome

Z

atomic number symbol
carbobenzoxy *also* Cbz
contraction [Ger. *Zuckung*]
disk (band, line) that separates
 sacromeres [Ger. *Zwischenscheibe*
 intermediate disk]
glutamine
impedance
ionic charge number
no effect
point formed by line perpendicular
 to nasion-menton line through
 anterior nasalspine
proton number
section modulus
shape of surgical incision (-plasty)
standardized deviate
standard score
zero
zeta (sixth letter of Greek alphabet),
 uppercase
zone
zusammen

Z′, Z″

increasing degrees of contraction
 [Ger. *Zuckung*]

z

algebraic unknown or space
 coordinate
axis of three-dimensional rectangular
 coordinate system
catalytic amount
standardized device
standard normal deviate

ZAP

zymosan-activated plasma (rabbit)

ZAPF

zinc adequate pair-fed

ZAS

zymosan-activated autologous serum

ZB

zebra body

ZC

zona compacta

ZCP

zinc chloride poisoning

ZD

zero defect *also* Z/D

zero discharge
zinc deficient

Z/D

zero defect *also* ZD
zero defects

ZDDP

zinc dialkyldithiophosphate

ZDO

zero differential overlap

ZDS

zinc depletion syndrome

ZDV

zidovudine

ZE, Z-E

Zollinger-Ellison (syndrome) *also* ZES

ZEEP

zero end-expiratory pressure

ZES

Zollinger-Ellison syndrome *also* ZE

Z-ESR

zeta erythrocyte sedimentation rate

ζ

zeta (sixth letter of Greek alphabet),
 lowercase

ZF

zero frequency
zona fasciculata
zygomaticofrontal

ZG

zona glomerulosa

Z/G

zoster (serum) immunoglobulin *also*
 ZIG, ZIg

ZGM

zinc glycinate marker

ZI

zona incerta

ZI[a]

isotope with atomic number Z and
 atomic weight A

ZIFT

zygote intrafallopian transfer

ZIG, ZIg

zoster (serum) immunoglobulin *also*
 Z/G

Z

ZIM
zimelidine

ZIP
zoster immune plasma

ZLS
Zimmerman-Laband syndrome

Zm
zygomaxillare

ZMA
zinc meta-arsenite

ZMC
zygomatic
zygomatic maxillary complex
zygomaxillary complex

ZN
Ziehl-Neelsen (method, stain)

Zn
zinc

^{65}Zn
zinc-65

Zn fl
zinc flocculation (test)

ZnO
zinc oxide

ZnOE
zinc oxide-eugenol (white zinc) *also*
ZOE

ZNS
Ziehl-Neelsen stain
zonisamide

ZO
Zichen-Oppenheim (syndrome)
Zuelzer-Ogden (syndrome)

ZOE
zinc oxide-eugenol (white zinc) *also*
ZnOE

Zool
zoology

ZP
zona pellucida

ZPA
zone of polarizing activity

ZPC
zero point of charge
zopiclone

ZPG
zero population growth

ZPLS
Zimmerman Preschool Language Scale

ZPO
zinc peroxide

ZPP
zinc protoporphyrin

Z″ (*var. of* Z′)

ZPT
zinc pyrithione

ZR
zona reticularis

Zr
zircon
zirconium

ZrSiO$_4$
zirconium silicate

ZS
Zellweger syndrome

ZSB
zero stool (since) birth

ZSO
zinc suboptimal

ZSR
ζ sedimentation rate
zeta sedimentation ratio

ZT
Ziehen test

ZTN
zinc tannate (of) naloxone

ZTS
zymosan-treated serum

Z-TSP
zephiran-trisodium phosphate

ZTT
zinc turbidity test

ZVD
zydoridine

Zy
zygion

Zylo
Zyloprim

zz.
ginger [L. *zingiber*]

S Y M B O L S

Angles, Triangles, and Circles

∧ above
diastolic blood pressure
  (anesthesia records)
elevated
enlarged
improved
increased
superior (position)
upper

∨ below
decreased
deficiency
deficit
depressed
deteriorated
diminished
down
inferior (position)
lower
systolic blood pressure
  (anesthesia records)

> causes
demonstrates
distal
followed by
derived from
greater than
indicates
leads to
more severe than
produces
radiates to
radiating to
results in
reveals
shows
to
toward
worse than
yields

< caused by
derived from
less severe than
less than
produced by
proximal

∠ angle
flexion
flexor

∠̲ angle of entry

∠̸ angle of exit

∟ factorial product
right lower quadrant

⌐ right upper quadrant

¬ left upper quadrant

⌟ left lower quadrant

Δ anion gap
centrad prism
change
delta gap
heat
increment
occipital triangle
prism diopter
temperature (anesthesia
  records)

Δ+ time interval

Δ A change in absorbance

Δ dB difference in decibels

Δ P change in (intraocular)
  pressure

Δ pH change in pH

Δ t time interval

Δ H, H Δ Hesselbach triangle

○	respiration (anesthesia records)	Ⓜ	murmur
♀	female female sex	ⓜ	by mouth mouth (temperature) murmur
♂	male male sex	√ⓜ	factitial murmur
Ⓐ , ⓐx	axilla (temperature)	Ⓞ	by mouth oral orally
Ⓗ , ⓗ	hypodermic hypodermically	Ⓡ	rectal rectally rectum (temperature) right
Ⓜ	intramuscular intramuscularly		
Ⓘⓥ	intravenous intravenously	Ⓧ	end of anesthesia (anesthesia records) end of operation
Ⓛ	left		

Arrows

↑	above elevated elevation enlarged gas greater than improved increase increased increases more than rising superior (position) up upper	↓	below decrease decreased deficiency deficit depressed depression deteriorated deteriorating diminished diminution down falling inferior (position) less than low slower normal plantar reflex precipitate precipitates
↑g	increasing rising		
↑V	increase due to in vivo effect (lab)		

↓g	decreasing	←	caused by
	diminishing		derived from
	falling		direction of flow or reaction
	lowering		due to
↓V	decrease due to in vivo effect		produced by
	(lab)		proximal
∕	deviated		resulting from
	displaced		secondary to
	increasing		to left
＼	decreasing	⇈	extensor response (Babinski
→	approaches limit of		sign)
	causes demonstrates		positive Babinski
	direction of flow or reaction		testes undescended
	distal	⇊	down bilaterally
	due to		plantar response (Babinski
	followed by		sign)
	indicates		testes descended
	leads to	⥮	reversible reaction
	produces		up and down
	radiating to	⇄ , ⇌	reversible (chemical)
	results in		reaction
	reveals		
	shows		
	to		
	to right		
	toward		
	yields		

Genetic Symbols

□   male

○   female

◇   sex unspecified

□ ○   normal individuals

■ ● ◆   affected individual (with ≥ 2 conditions, the symbol is partioned and shaded with a different fill defined in a key or legend)

⑤ ⑤ ⟨5⟩   multiple individuals, number known (number of siblings written inside symbol)

ⓝ ⓝ ⟨n⟩   multiple individuals, number unknown ("n" used in place of specific number)

□─○   mating

□═○   consaguinity

(+)   uncommon or uncertain mode of inheritance

I   II   parents and offspring, in generations

△○   dizygotic twins

△○   monozygotic twins

④ ③   number of children of sex indicated

⊟⊙   adopted individuals

♀ ♀   individual died without leaving offspring

□┴○   no issue

■ ●   affected individuals

■ ●   proband or propositus (first affected family member coming to medical attention)

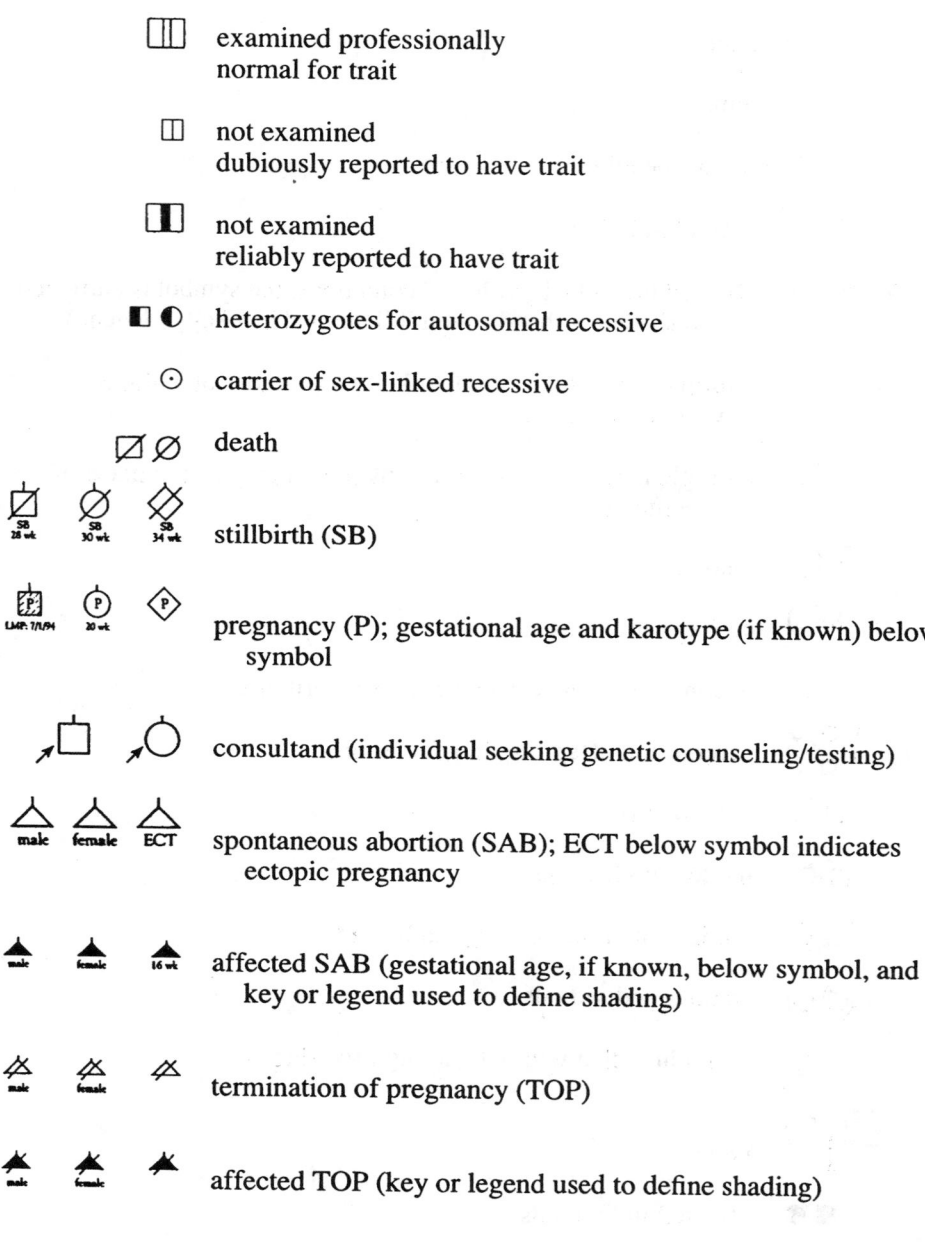

examined professionally
normal for trait

not examined
dubiously reported to have trait

not examined
reliably reported to have trait

heterozygotes for autosomal recessive

carrier of sex-linked recessive

death

stillbirth (SB)

pregnancy (P); gestational age and karotype (if known) below
symbol

consultand (individual seeking genetic counseling/testing)

spontaneous abortion (SAB); ECT below symbol indicates
ectopic pregnancy

affected SAB (gestational age, if known, below symbol, and
key or legend used to define shading)

termination of pregnancy (TOP)

affected TOP (key or legend used to define shading)

Source: Genetic symbols are public domain; we credit and gratefully acknowledge the *American Journal of Human Genetics* (56:746–747, 1995) as our source for these symbols.

Numbers

0	completely absent (pulse) no response (reflexes)		**3+**	moderate reaction (lab tests) more brisk than average (reflexes)
+1, 1+	markedly impaired (pulse)		**+4, 4+**	normal (pulse)
1+	low normal or somewhat diminished (reflexes) slight reaction or trace (lab tests)		**4+**	hyperactive (reflexes) large amount (lab tests) pronounced reaction (lab tests) very brisk (reflexes)
+2, 2+	moderately impaired (pulse)		$\dfrac{\bullet}{1}$	bowel movement (numeral indicates number of stools in a given period)
2+	average or normal (reflexes) noticeable reaction or trace (lab tests)		**1×**	once one time
+3, 3+	slightly impaired (pulse)		**2×, ×2**	twice two times
			3×, ×3	three times, etc.

Arabic	Roman		Arabic	Roman
0			17	XVII
1	I,		18	XVIII
2	II, ii		19	XIX
3	III, iii		20	XX
4	IV, iv		30	XXX
5	V, v		40	XL
6	VI, vi		50	L
7	VII, vii		60	LX
8	VIII, viii		70	LXX
9	IX, ix		80	LXXX
10	X, x		90	XC
11	XI, xi		100	C
12	XII, xii		1,000	M
13	XIII, xiii		5,000	$\overline{V}$
14	XIV, xiv		10,000	$\overline{X}$
15	XV		100,000	$\overline{C}$
16	XVI		1,000,000	$\overline{M}$

Pluses, Minuses, and Equivalencies

+   acid (reaction)
added to
convex lens
decreased or diminished
   (reflexes)
excess
less than 50%
inhibition of
hemolysis (Wassermann)
low normal (reflexes)
markedly impaired
   (pulse)
mild (severity)
plus
positive (lab tests)
present
slight reaction or trace
   (lab tests)
sluggish (reflexes)
somewhat diminished
   (reflexes)

(+)   significant

(+)ive   positive

+ to ++   slight pain

++   average (reflexes)
50% inhibition of
   hemolysis
   (Wassermann)
moderate (pain,
   severity)
moderately impaired
   (pulse)
normally active
   (reflexes)
noticeable reaction or
   trace (lab tests)

+++   increased reflexes
75% inhibition of
hemolysis (Wassermann)
moderate amount

moderate reaction (lab
   tests)
moderately, hyperative
   (reflexes)
moderately severe (pain,
   severity)
more brisk than average
   (reflexes)
slightly impaired (pulse)

++++   Complete inhibition of
   hemolysis
   (Wassermann)
large amount (lab tests)
markedly hyperactive
   (reflexes)
markedly severe (pain,
   severity)
normal (pulse)
pronounced reaction
   (lab tests)
very brisk (reflexes)

−   absent
alkaline (reaction)
concave lens
deficiency
deficient
minus
negative (lab test)
none
subtract
without

(−)   insignificant

±   doubtful
either positive or
   negative
equivocal (reflexes,
   qualitative tests)
flicker (reflexes)
indefinite
more or less
plus or minus

	possibly significant	◡	combined with
	questionable	≎	equivalent
	suggestive	≁	not equivalent to
	variable	≡	identical
	very slight (reaction, severity, trace)		identical with
	with or without	≢	not identical
(±)	possibly significant		not identical with
± to +	minimal pain	≒	nearly equal to
∓	minus or plus	≓	approximately equal
‡	moderate (severity)	≅	approximately
	normally active (reflexes)		approximately equals
#	fracture		congruent to
	gauge	≐	approaches
	number	⟂	equilateral
	pound(s)	△	equiangular
	weight	>	greater than
~	about	≯	not greater than
	approximate	<	less than
	approximately	≮	not less than
	proportionate to	≥, ⩾	greater than or equal to
≈	approximately equal to	≤, ⩽	less than or equal to
=	equal to		
≠	not equal to		

Primes, Checks, Dots, Roots, and Other Symbols

?	doubtful equivocal (reflexes) flicker (reflexes) not tested (severity) possible questionable question of suggested suggestive (severity) unknown	**√c̄**	check with
		√d	checked observed
		√g, √ing	checking
		√qs	voided sufficient quantity
		√	radical root
!	factorial product	**²√⎺**	square root
†	death deceased	**³√⎺**	cube root
/	divided by either meaning extension extensors fraction of per to	*****	birth multiplication sign (genetics) not verified presumed supposed
'	foot hour univalent	**°**	degree measurement (1/360 of circle) severity (burns, wounds) temperature time (hour)
"	bivalent ditto inch minute second (1/60 degree)	**:**	is to ratio
‴	line (1/12 inch) trivalent	**...**	no data (in given category)
√	check observe for urine voided (urine)	**∴**	therefore
		∵	because since
√.	urine and defecation voided and bowels moved	**::**	as equality between ratios proportion proportionate to

Statistical Symbols

α probability of Type I error significance level

β probability of Type II error

$1-\beta$ power of statistical test

$_nC_k; \left(\dfrac{n}{k}\right)$ binomial coefficient number of combination of n things taken k at a time

χ^2 chi-squared statistic

E expected frequency in cell of contingency table

$E(X)$ expected value of random variable X

F F statistic (variance ratio)

f frequency

H_0 null hypothesis

H_1 alternative hypothesis

μ population mean

N population size

n sample size

$n!$ n factorial

O observed frequency in a contingency table

ϕ ability continuum phi coefficient

P probability

p probability of success in independent trials

$P(A)$ probability that event A occurs

$P(A\backslash B)$ conditional probability that A occurs given that B has occurred

r sample correlation coefficient, usually the Pearson product-moment correlation

r^2 coefficient of determination

r_s Spearman rank correlation coefficient

ρ population correlation coefficient

s sample standard deviation

s^2 sample variance

SE standard error of estimate

σ population standard deviation

σ^2 population variance

$\sigma\text{diff.}$ standard error of difference between scores

$\sigma\text{est.}$ standard error of estimate

$\sigma\text{meas.}$ standard error of measurement

$\sum\limits_{i=1}^{n} x_1, \ \Sigma_i \overset{n}{=} x_i$ $x_1+x_2+ \ldots +x_n$

t Student t statistic Student test variable

θ	latent trait	$\neq$	not equal
U	Mann-Whitney rank sum statistic	$\approx$	approximately equal
		$>$	greater than
W	Wilcoxon rank sum statistic	$\not>$	not greater than
		$<$	less than
$\overline{X}$	sample mean	$\not<$	not less than
$|x|$	absolute value of x	$\geq, \geqslant$	greater than or equal to
$\sqrt{x}$	square root of x		
z	standard score	$\leq, \leqslant$	less than or equal to
$=$	equal	∞	infinity